A

Philip E. Lilienthal

BOOK

The Philip E. Lilienthal imprint
honors special books
in commemoration of a man whose work
at University of California Press from 1954 to 1979
was marked by dedication to young authors
and to high standards in the field of Asian Studies.
Friends, family, authors, and foundations have together
endowed the Lilienthal Fund, which enables UC Press
to publish under this imprint selected books
in a way that reflects the taste and judgment
of a great and beloved editor.

The publisher gratefully acknowledges the generous support of the
Philip E. Lilienthal Asian Studies Endowment Fund of the
University of California Press Foundation, which was established
by a major gift from Sally Lilienthal.

Hanoi's Road to the Vietnam War, 1954–1965

FROM INDOCHINA TO VIETNAM: REVOLUTION AND
WAR IN A GLOBAL PERSPECTIVE
Edited by Fredrik Logevall and Christopher E. Goscha

1. *Assuming the Burden: Europe and the American Commitment to War in Vietnam,* by Mark Atwood Lawrence
2. *Indochina: An Ambiguous Colonization, 1858–1954,* by Pierre Brocheux and Daniel Hémery
3. *Vietnam 1946: How the War Began,* by Stein Tønnesson
4. *Imperial Heights: Dalat and the Making and Undoing of French Indochina,* by Eric T. Jennings
5. *Catholic Vietnam: A Church from Empire to Nation,* by Charles Keith
6. *Vietnam: State, War, and Revolution, 1945–1946,* by David G, Marr
7. *Hanoi's Road to the Vietnam War, 1954–1965,* by Pierre Asselin

Hanoi's Road to the Vietnam War, 1954–1965

Pierre Asselin

UNIVERSITY OF CALIFORNIA PRESS
Berkeley   Los Angeles   London

University of California Press, one of the most distinguished university presses in the United States, enriches lives around the world by advancing scholarship in the humanities, social sciences, and natural sciences. Its activities are supported by the UC Press Foundation and by philanthropic contributions from individuals and institutions. For more information, visit www.ucpress.edu.

University of California Press
Berkeley and Los Angeles, California

University of California Press, Ltd.
London, England

© 2013 by The Regents of the University of California

FIRST PAPERBACK PRINTING 2015

Library of Congress Cataloging-in-Publication Data

Asselin, Pierre, author.
   Hanoi's road to the Vietnam War, 1954–1965 / Pierre Asselin.
      p.   cm.—(From Indochina to Vietnam : revolution and war in a global perspective ; 7)
   Includes bibliographical references and index.
   ISBN 978-0-520-28749-5 (pbk : alk. paper)
   ISBN 978-0-520-95655-1 (ebook)
      1. Vietnam (Democratic Republic)—History.   2. Vietnam (Democratic Republic)—Foreign relations.   3. Vietnam War, 1961–1975—Causes.   I. Title.
   DS560.68.A87   2013
   959.704′31—dc23   2013015154

Manufactured in the United States of America

21   20   19   18   17   16   15
10   9   8   7   6   5   4   3   2   1

For my father

CONTENTS

List of Maps	ix
Foreword by the Series Editors	xi
Acknowledgments	xiii
Glossary of Terms and Acronyms	xvii
Introduction	1
1. Choosing Peace, 1954–1956	11
2. Changing Course, 1957–1959	44
3. Treading Cautiously, 1960	72
4. Buying Time, 1961	91
5. Exploring Neutralization, 1962	118
6. Choosing War, 1963	145
7. Waging War, 1964	174
Epilogue	206
Notes	213
Bibliography	291
Index	309

Images follow page 117.

MAPS

1. Indochina, 1954–1975   *xx*
2. North Vietnam, 1954–1975   *xxi*
3. South Vietnam, 1954–1975   *xxii*

FOREWORD BY THE SERIES EDITORS

The literature on the Second Indochina War is large and growing larger. Until recently, however, the literature suffered from a U.S.-centric focus and a tendency to look solely at decision-making in Washington. To paraphrase historian Gaddis Smith's classic description of Cold War historiography, it was the history of "one hand clapping." Too few studies placed U.S. policymaking into its wider international context; fewer still gave a voice to the "other side," the Vietnamese who fought so long and hard to defeat first the French and then the South Vietnamese government and its American allies.

But the picture is changing, as scholars with the requisite linguistic skills begin to work in depth in Vietnamese archival and other materials, as well as in voluminous French- and English-language sources. Pierre Asselin knows these materials as well as anyone, having mined them for several pathbreaking studies over the past decade. Now Asselin gives us *Hanoi's Road to the Vietnam War, 1954–1965*, the first detailed scholarly assessment of the subject ever published in English. It is a penetrating, lucid, and compelling study of the period between the end of the First Indochina War and the large-scale escalation of the Second.

Other authors writing in English have examined North Vietnamese decision-making in this vital period. Few, however, have done so in the kind of detail—and using the wide array of primary sources—that Asselin does here. This book shows how Hanoi leaders viewed the evolving situation in the late 1950s and early 1960s, not merely in South Vietnam but also in the Cold War power centers of Washington, Moscow, and Beijing. In Asselin's telling, the North Vietnamese were never puppets of the Soviet Union and China; for the most part, they were able to make autonomous decisions during the period in question. More than that, North Vietnamese planners at times "exercised more leverage over their allies than the allies exercised over them." Gradually, and despite sharp internal differences of opinion, policy-makers in Hanoi shifted from a cautious strategy focused on non-violent political struggle to what Asselin sees as a "risky, even reckless" approach centered on resumption of military action. They never wanted war with the United States, he maintains, but they were determined to have what war would bring them: the reunification of the country under their control.

In telling this story the author adds much to the understanding of one of the most important conflicts of the twentieth century. It is with pleasure that we include his study in our series.

Christopher Goscha, Université du Québec à Montréal
Fredrik Logevall, Cornell University

ACKNOWLEDGMENTS

I wish to thank the manuscript's reviewers for their thoughtful comments. The anonymous reviewer provided useful suggestions for improvement. The other reviewer, Lien-Hang Nguyen, offered equally constructive advice. Hang is arguably the most capable among the latest generation of Vietnam War scholars. She has always been generous with her time, expertise, and source material. It is a blessing to have her as an academic nemesis, and a joy to be her friend.

Fredrik Logevall and Christopher Goscha, the editors of the "From Indochina to Vietnam" series at the University of California Press, also offered valuable guidance. Fred urged me to address the international context more diligently and shared the proofs of his latest manuscript (now published as *Embers of War*) to help me refine core arguments. Chris, for his part, scrupulously examined the manuscript. His consummate knowledge of Vietnamese history improved its quality in ways I cannot describe. Pierre Journoud, "Pierre 1," presented me with opportunities to share my research with colleagues and solicit feedback. I thank him for that, as well as for his hospitality in Paris and his friendship.

I am fortunate to be part of a coterie of scholars who not only have contributed in meaningful ways to our understanding of the Cold War and Vietnam's place in it but also became dear friends over the years. In addition to those already mentioned, I wish to acknowledge Ben Kerkvliet, Jim Hershberg, Pierre Grosser, John Prados, Larry Berman, Marc Gilbert, Lorenz Lüthi, Ed Miller, Jessica Chapman, Pete Zinoman, Balazs Szalontai, Jason Picard, Jay Veith, Mark Moyar, Marilyn Young, and Harish Mehta. They are a big part of the reason I enjoy what I do; they have also made professional conferences interesting on so many levels.

I have benefited from the wisdom of other colleagues in putting this project together, including William Duiker, Carl Thayer, Odd Arne Westad, Bill Turley, Ed Moïse, Mark Lawrence, Jeff Kimball, George Herring, Bob Brigham, Hue-Tam Tai, Merle Pribbenow, Jacques Portes, Shawn McHale, Tuong Vu, Nu-Anh Tran, Alec Holcombe, David Anderson, Piero Gleijeses, Kyle Horst, Calvin Thai, Liam Kelley, Sergei Radchenko, Matthew Connelly, Ang Cheng Guan, David Elliott, Sophie Quinn-Judge, Martin Grossheim, Qiang Zhai, Chen Jian, Patrick Bratton, and Ilya Gaiduk, whose untimely death hurt us all in more ways than one. My graduate students at Hawaii Pacific University have also helped me immeasurably. Special thanks to Gintare Janulaityte, Ed Zelczak, Nate Chase, Paul Carlock, Mark Snakenberg, Kevin O'Reilly, Jenya Jawad, and Joshua Taylor. Emily McIlroy provided thoughtful input on the title.

I am indebted to several people in Vietnam for their assistance over the years. Professor Phan Huy Le has sponsored my work there for nearly two decades. Nguyen Van Kim, Hoang Anh Tuan, and Nguyen Quang Ngoc have been extraordinary colleagues. Along with my friends Nhung and Phu and the late Nguyen Dinh Phuong, these individuals have made me look forward to each trip to their amazing country. "Chu Dinh," "em Thanh," and the rest of the staff at Vietnam National Archives Center 3 in Hanoi have always been accommodating and patient with me. Only Christian Lentz and I know how truly helpful they can be, and how well they can dance.

Several organizations and their staff were indispensable. I owe a special debt of gratitude to the Cold War International History Project and its director, Christian Ostermann; to the Vietnam Center and Archive at Texas Tech University and its director, Steve Maxner; to the Vietnam Studies Group and its contributors; to the Institut Pierre Mendès France in Paris, its president Eric Roussell, and his assistants Murielle Blondeau and Vincent Laniol; and to the staff at the French Diplomatic Archives at La Courneuve, the National Archives of the United Kingdom in Kew, and Library and Archives Canada in Ottawa. For generous financial support, I am indebted to the National Endowment for the Humanities, the Hawaii Council for the Humanities, and, above all, to Dr. Alan Zeccha and the Trustees' Scholarly Endeavors Program at Hawaii Pacific University.

At the University of California Press, my appreciation goes to Niels Hooper for betting on this project and to his assistant, Kim Hogeland. Profuse thanks to my conscientious editor, Suzanne Knott. Elizabeth Berg did a superb copyediting job, and promptly answered all my queries as I revised the final draft. Susan Ferber recommended that I send the manuscript to Niels, and Chuck Grench of the University of North Carolina Press provided useful guidance early on.

For allowing me to retain my sanity as I put this book together, I thank my friend, Eric Denton. His insights on the meaning of life have been invaluable, as have his humor and high tolerance for alcohol. My gratitude extends to the crew from stand-up paddling, as well as to Mitch Gray and the "boys" from the Hawaiian Ice Hockey League in Honolulu. Luckily for me, the latter are much better friends than they are hockey players. Pierre-Marie, I never forget that you look out for me.

My former professors continue to help and inspire me. Yves Frennette from Glendon College made me want to become a university professor. John Keyes and Tom Tynan formed me in my younger years. Tim Naftali, Gary Hess, Truong Buu Lam, Ronald Pruessen, Hy Van Luong, and the late Huynh Kim Khanh opened my eyes to important realities of Vietnamese and Cold War history. Stephen O'Harrow of the University of Hawaii has been a surrogate father. Idus Newby, now retired from "UH," has meticulously read and commented on all my major publications. I know of no academic more generous with their time and expertise. His astonishing editing skills substantially improved the readability and overall quality of the narrative that follows. "Dr. Newby" has also been unwavering in his support for my scholarly endeavors. I hope that through my research and teaching I have done justice to all that he and other educators have imparted to me.

My parents and my little sister have been an outstanding support system. I thank my mother and my father for their infectious passion for life; words cannot describe the love, respect, and admiration I have for them. My sister, the kindest human being I know, is always there when I need her (unless she has fainted). I hope this book makes her proud of her big brother; it is the least I can offer, considering how proud I am of the person she has become.

Lastly, I wish to thank my family, Selma and Grace. Selma, you understand me like few people do. You took good care of Grace when I was away researching for this book, and you were at my side, literally, as I put the finishing touches on it. It should not have been that way; I should have done a better job taking care of you, providing for you. You are, after all, a cat. I look forward to spending time at your side, when we reunite over the rainbow bridge. My wife Grace has for years nurtured my passion for Vietnam and tolerated my obsession with this project. Her virtues are without parallel. Grace, you scintillate as brilliantly as ever, and my love for you has only grown stronger over the years. Much of what I have become, the good part, and what I have achieved, the best things, I owe to you. You are exceptional in every way; I am so glad you are you. I am in your debt, eternally.

I dedicate this book to my father, for his unconditional love and support throughout the years. He is the best man I know.

GLOSSARY OF TERMS AND ACRONYMS

ARVN   Army of the Republic of Vietnam; formerly the Vietnamese National Army; armed forces of the RVN
CCP   Chinese Communist Party
COSVN   Central Office (Directorate) for Southern Vietnam; Politburo-run organ in charge of coordinating communist activity in the southern third of Vietnam (former Cochinchina), 1951–54 (including all of Cambodia) and 1961–75; "upgraded" incarnation of the Nam Bo Executive Committee
CPSU   Communist Party of the Soviet Union
DRV/DRVN   Democratic Republic of Vietnam; government of northern Vietnam, controlled by the VWP and based in Hanoi from October 1954; claimed sole jurisdiction over all of Vietnam
GPD   General Political Department; organ in charge of ideological conformity within the PAVN
ICP   Indochinese Communist Party; previous incarnation of the VWP; founded in 1930
ICSC   International Commission for Supervision and Control in Vietnam; organ consisting of representatives from India, Canada, and Poland set up after July 1954 to supervise implementation of the Geneva accords
Interzone IV   Northern central Vietnam, including a portion below the seventeenth parallel

Interzone V	Southern central Vietnam, including the Central Highlands
MAAG	Military Assistance Advisory Group, Indochina (1950–55), Vietnam (1955–62); created to promote military partnership between the United States and France and the SOVN/RVN; incorporated into MACV and renamed Field Advisory Element, Vietnam, in 1962
MACV	Military Assistance Command, Vietnam; U.S. military command in South Vietnam, 1962–73
Nam Bo Executive Committee	Politburo-run organ coordinating communist activity in the southern third of Vietnam (former Cochinchina), 1954–61; "downgraded" incarnation of COSVN
NATO	North Atlantic Treaty Organization; United States–led organization for collective defense in Europe and North America, 1949–present
NLF	National Front for the Liberation of South Vietnam; southern Vietnamese broad-based umbrella organization created in 1960 and controlled by Hanoi to oppose the RVN
PAVN	People's Army of Vietnam; armed forces of the DRVN controlled by the VWP
PCSVN	Party Committee of South Vietnam; southern branch of the VWP to 1962
PLAF	People's Liberation Armed Forces; armed wing of the NLF
PRC	People's Republic of China
PRP	People's Revolutionary Party, formerly the PCSVN; ostensibly an independent southern Vietnamese communist party established in 1962, in actuality part of the VWP
RVN	Republic of Vietnam, formerly the SOVN; proclaimed in October 1955 by President Ngo Dinh Diem from its capital at Saigon; claimed sole jurisdiction over all of Vietnam
SEATO	Southeast Asia Treaty Organization; United States–led organization for collective defense in Southeast Asia, 1955–77
SOVN	State of Vietnam; purportedly independent Vietnamese government organized by France in 1949 under Emperor Bao Dai as head of state; became the RVN in 1955
VFF	Vietnam Fatherland Front; mass organization promoting national unity, loyalty to the DRVN and VWP, and resistance to foreign aggression and internal subversion in the DRVN

Viet Cong/VC	Pejorative term used in reference to southern communists and their sympathizers, including, after 1960, members of the NLF; abbreviated form of either *Viet Nam Cong san* (Vietnamese Communist) or *Viet minh Cong san* (Viet Minh Communist)
Viet Minh	United front organized in 1941 by the ICP to fight the Japanese occupation of Indochina; served as the main nationalist front in the war against the French between 1946 and 1951, when it was officially dissolved and became part of the Lien Viet Front; blanket term used in reference to those who fought against the French during the Indochina War (1946–54)
VWP	Vietnamese Workers' Party, also known as Lao Dong Party; replaced the ICP in 1951 and controlled the DRVN government after 1954; renamed the Vietnamese Communist Party in 1976

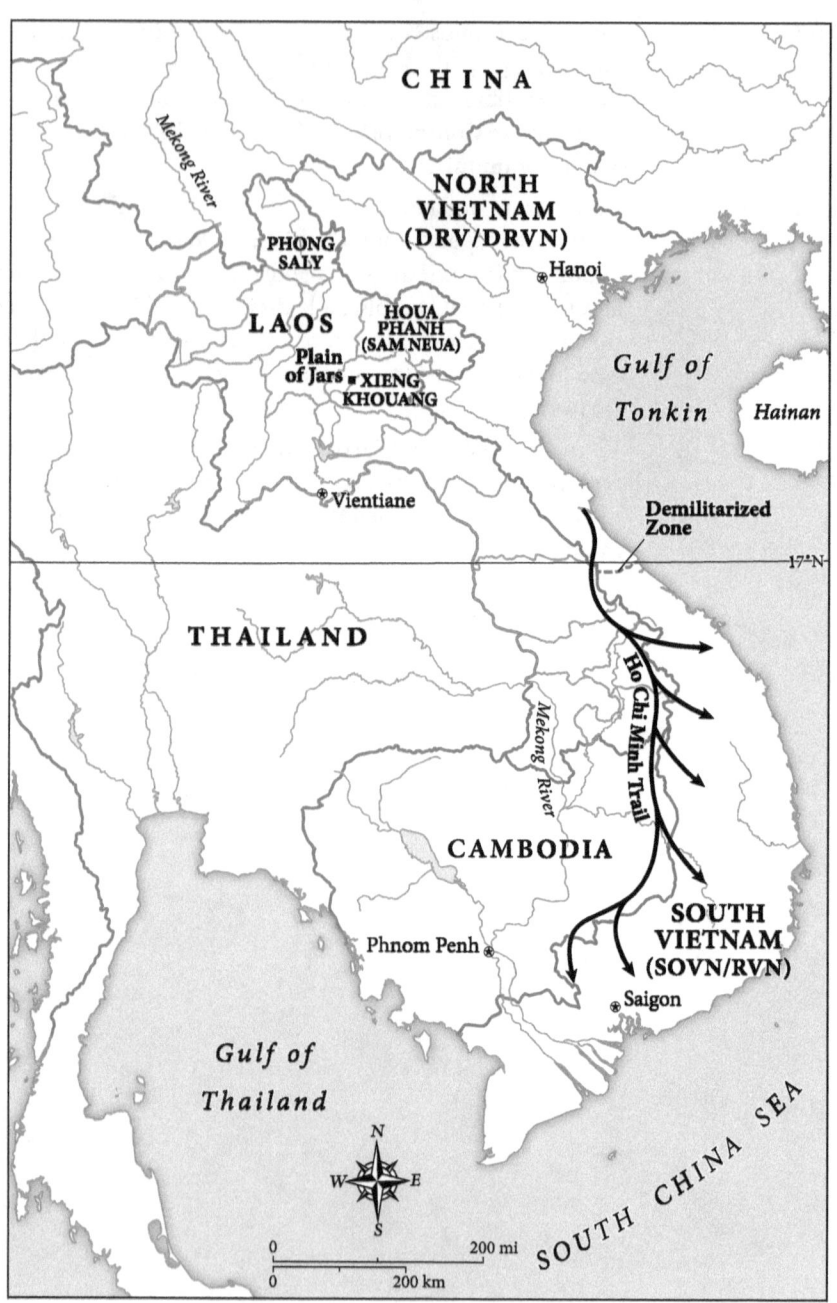

MAP 1. Indochina, 1954–1975

MAP 2. North Vietnam, 1954–1975

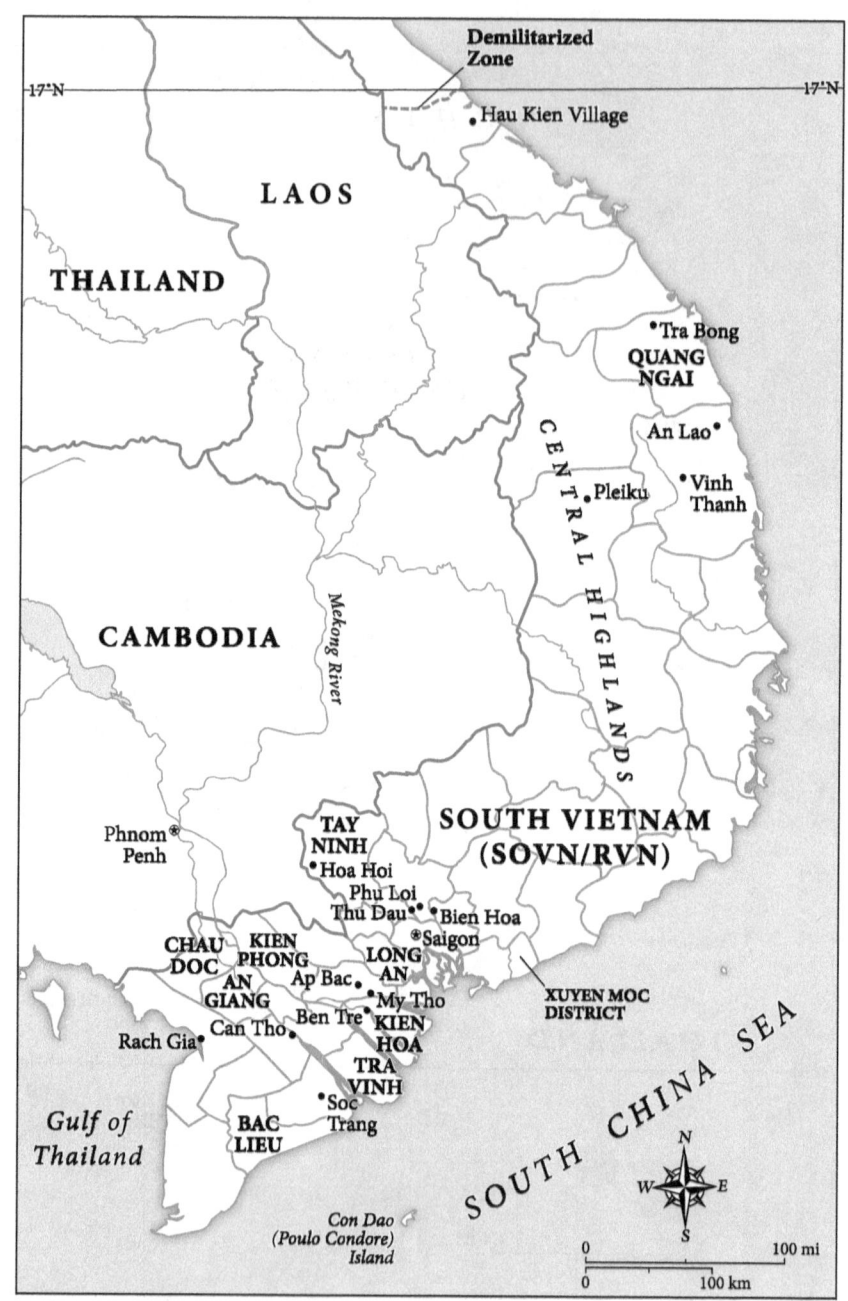

MAP 3. South Vietnam, 1954–1975

Introduction

This study relates the evolution of the strategic thinking on national liberation and reunification of the communist leadership of the Democratic Republic of Vietnam (DRVN) from the signing of the 1954 Geneva accords on Indochina to the onset of American military intervention in Vietnam in March 1965. It addresses that leadership's gradual shift from a cautious approach centered on nonviolent political struggle to a risky, even reckless strategy predicated on major combat operations and decisive victory over enemy forces. In doing so, the study elucidates the origins of the conflict DRVN authorities called the "Anti-American Resistance for National Salvation," which Vietnamese today refer to as the American War and Americans have always known as the Vietnam War. Specifically, it sheds light on the elements informing the Vietnamese communist revolutionary strategy and the domestic and foreign policies that strategy produced. It tells the story of how North Vietnamese decision-makers negotiated the Cold War during one of its "hot" phases and exposes—to the extent available sources permit—the mindset of those decision-makers and the worldview that conditioned it. In short, this is a history of the origins of the Vietnam War from the perspective of leaders on "the other side."

DRVN leaders accepted the Geneva accords in July 1954 because they hoped their implementation would preclude American military intervention and deliver what an eight-year war against France could not: the reunification of Vietnam under their governance. Because the latter prospect never materialized, they spent the better part of the next decade debating whether to fulfill their core objective by resuming hostilities, and otherwise searching for ways to "liberate" the South without provoking a military showdown with the United States or compromising other vital interests of Vietnam's revolutionary struggle.

Western accounts of the origins of the Vietnam War have tended to present DRVN leaders as relatively passive agents, emphasizing instead the pressures exerted upon them by key allies in Beijing and Moscow and the active roles assumed by rivals in Saigon and Washington. As it turns out, those leaders played a central role in shaping the events of 1954–65 in their country. To be sure, they were always mindful of the circumstances and imperatives they confronted, the Cold War context in which they operated, and the needs and desires of the Soviet Union and China, upon whom they depended heavily for political and material support. But despite these constraints, they implacably pursued what they saw as the best interests of the Vietnamese revolution and the so-called world revolution. Those interests included accommodating, or at least appearing to accommodate, the sometimes conflicting demands made on the DRVN by its socialist allies, who were more deeply invested in the global Cold War and, as time went by, increasingly at odds with one another over relations with the West and strategies to advance the global revolutionary process. That DRVN leaders managed their allies with such finesse is one of their impressive achievements. They were never puppets of those allies, and their ability to make autonomous decisions was never seriously compromised. In fact, owing to the Sino-Soviet dispute, whose ramifications in Vietnam are explored in some depth in this study, there were times when the Vietnamese exercised more leverage over their allies than the allies exercised over them. Informed alternately by nationalist, internationalist, and other considerations, the DRVN leadership's decisions were always its own, and the tragic events that unfolded in Indochina in the decade beginning in 1965 owe as much—if not more—to those decisions as to decisions made in Washington and Saigon.[1]

Vietnamese communists involved in the national liberation and reunification struggle did not always agree on strategic and other important matters. As historian Patricia Pelley writes of those who fought against the French, they were "internally divided" and sometimes "struggled violently among themselves."[2] After 1954 as before, sharp differences of opinion over strategy and tactics existed among members and leaders of the Vietnamese Workers' Party (VWP), the communist organ that controlled DRVN decision-making, though these rarely manifested themselves openly. Most notable was the tug-of-war between, on the one hand, those who supported suspension of hostilities in July 1954 and peaceful reunification under the Geneva accords thereafter and, on the other hand, those who believed that those accords unnecessarily abrogated revolutionary gains below the seventeenth parallel and who wanted to continue fighting until complete victory. Whereas the former feared the reaction of Washington and, to a lesser extent, that of their own allies to prolongation and then resumption of hostilities, the latter accepted the risks inherent in choosing war to expeditiously achieve the "liberation" of the South and national reunification under the communist aegis. On the basis of their attitudes and the reasoning behind them, the detractors of armed struggle formed the party's risk-averse, temporizing "moderate" wing, and its advocates constituted the risk-acceptant, impetuous "militant" wing.[3]

As prospects for peaceful reunification faded after 1956—the deadline set by the Geneva accords to hold countrywide elections on the issue—moderates at the helm of the VWP remained wary of American intervention and sought to postpone resumption of war at least long enough to complete the rehabilitation and socialist transformation of the northern economy as well as the reorganization and modernization of the armed forces undertaken following the signing of the accords. Militants, for their part, were at that point keener than ever to resort to war to finish the job in the South, even as the North and its armed forces underwent their makeover.[4] The onset of the Sino-Soviet dispute shortly thereafter exacerbated tensions within the VWP, as Moscow's new revolutionary prescriptions calling for peaceful settlement of disputes between the capitalist and socialist camps validated moderate injunctions against resumption of military struggle in Vietnam, and Beijing's radical theses on violent national liberation and the inevitability of war between the two camps emboldened militants. Ensconced in Hanoi after October 1954, the party leadership attempted to palliate the resulting discord between the two factions and shaped revolutionary strategy on the basis of majority consensus in the Politburo and Central Committee.

Whether of moderate or militant inclination, DRVN leaders never wanted military confrontation with the United States. It is therefore paradoxical that the eventual conflict between Hanoi and Washington—the Vietnam War—was precipitated by the outcome of a Central Committee meeting that convened in late 1963. Until then, Hanoi's cautiousness had precluded the introduction of American combat forces and a wider war, which seemed avertable for the immediate future. However, the final resolution adopted at the conclusion of the meeting, which called for unrestricted military struggle in the South and comprehensive commitment of the North to that struggle, proved to be a seminal development in the coming of the Vietnam War, producing as it did a drastic escalation of the ongoing insurgency below the seventeenth parallel in 1964. In light of that development, it is not unreasonable to consider the deployment of American combat forces to South Vietnam in massive numbers the following year as a response to—and not the source of—the onset of "big war" on the Indochinese peninsula. It was, of course, the Lyndon Johnson administration that decided to Americanize hostilities that year. But that decision was not made in a vacuum, and the prior decision of the VWP Central Committee hastened it and warranted, in Washington's view, mass deployments of American ground and other forces to Vietnam.[5]

Obviously, the United States cannot be exonerated for its role in creating the circumstances that produced the Vietnam War. However, it is important to understand that those who led the Vietnamese communist campaign against it and the regime in Saigon were neither passive nor innocent in that process. It is equally important to dispel the myth that those leaders were actually mere nationalists forced by circumstances to jump on the communist bandwagon and resort to war to protect their country against yet another foreign aggressor.[6] That is the narrative DRVN authorities at the time propagated in the West with great success, and which far too many Americans who write and teach about the Vietnam War have helped to perpetuate. The essence of that narrative is false, and this study exposes the deficiencies in its central tenets.

Why does the story of Hanoi in the 1954–65 period matter? Because during that time North Vietnam became a crucible of the global Cold War, of the postwar international environment shaped by the intersection of the Soviet-American rivalry, the Sino-Soviet dispute, and ardent political activism in the Third World. The DRVN was a proud member of the socialist camp, but it was also a newly decolonized polity engaged in a national liberation struggle below the seventeenth parallel. After signing the Geneva accords, its leaders contended with not just the United States and the regime it abetted in Saigon, but also socialist allies, whose support was desperately needed to build socialism in the North. The DRVN played a—if not the—leading role in the socialist camp's attempts to mediate Sino-Soviet discord, which was remarkable, considering that it was among that camp's youngest members. It also concerned itself with nonaligned and Third World states, considered ideological kith and kin to whom the DRVN hoped to be an example of the possibilities of national liberation.

In hindsight, North Vietnam after 1954 may well have been, as its leaders insisted at the time, "the center of big contradictions in the world." Thus, studying Hanoi, attempting to see the world through its eyes, enables us to better understand the currents and tendencies that conditioned politics globally and locally in the socialist camp and the Third World during an important phase of the Cold War. Despite the unique and singular aspects of its story—and they are many—Hanoi proposed to act as a standard-bearer for national liberation or, alternatively, a promoter of nonalignment, while fashioning itself as a vanguard for Marxism-Leninism and proletarian internationalism. "The most powerful states dominate international politics," historian Jeremy Suri writes, "but the small places in between define the fate of the world."[7] The DRVN certainly left an indelible mark on the world after 1954.

. . .

The best-known English-language study of Hanoi's decision-making during the period covered of this study is William Duiker's *The Communist Road to Power in Vietnam*, published more than three decades ago.[8] While still useful, Duiker's work, even in its second edition, is now dated because it rests on a narrower array of sources than is currently available. It is also largely descriptive; that is, it narrates a story of party and government policies without probing deeply into the motives and circumstances behind them. The same may be said of Carl Thayer's *War by Other Means*, a richly detailed story focusing on the period 1954–60.⁹ More recent and also useful are works by Ang Cheng Guan, including *The Vietnam War from the Other Side* and *Vietnamese Communists' Relations with China and the Second Indochina Conflict, 1956–1962*. The former is a concise, well-researched account of the origins and early stages of the Vietnam War with a focus on military strategy and operations; the latter is the only in-depth study of Hanoi's relationship with China prior to the onset of war.¹⁰ Lien-Hang Nguyen's *Hanoi's War* focuses on the 1965–73 period but provides excellent information about DRVN leaders' personalities and attitudes on war and diplomacy prior to the war against the United States.¹¹ Few scholars today understand the thinking of the Vietnamese communist leadership before and during the war better than Ang and Nguyen, and their contributions to our understanding of that thinking are the most valuable since Duiker's and Thayer's. The second edition of William Turley's *The Second Indochina War* covers both the Vietnamese communist and American perspectives, and it is the best book on the war.¹² Turley draws heavily from Vietnamese sources and offers revealing insights into DRVN decision-making. And there are several other works useful for making sense of Hanoi's policies and relations with its allies and enemies alike.¹³

This study is intended not to supersede these earlier works but to supplement and update them on the basis of new documentary evidence and interpretations. It builds on the contributions of Duiker, Thayer, Ang, Nguyen, and Turley especially, and cites their findings and assessments often—and gratefully. In tracing the evolution of the communist road to the Vietnam War, this study demonstrates how ideology informed the view that the leadership in Hanoi had of itself and its purposes and tasks in governing the country, furthering the Vietnamese revolution, navigating the Cold War, and meeting international obligations.¹⁴ More than previous works, this study addresses the diplomatic dimensions of Hanoi's revolutionary strategy.

In doing so, this study relies on Vietnamese as well as western primary sources to document Vietnamese policy and decision-making and will hopefully encourage students of these subjects to reassess long-standing assumptions about and understandings of Hanoi's strategic thinking, as well as its relationship with other important actors during the period leading to the war. Hopefully, too, this study will infuse new meaning into many details of a story now generally familiar, at least in its overall contours.

Chapter 1 examines DRVN policymaking between the signing of the Geneva accords in 1954 and the end of 1956. Despite opposition from within, the VWP resolved to abide by the accords because Ho Chi Minh and other key leaders thought they would likely eventuate in peaceful national reunification under their governance. To those ends, in September 1954 they instructed operatives and supporters in both halves of Vietnam to respect the accords, undertaking no activity that might undermine them or provoke or justify noncompliance by the enemy. Meanwhile, they committed themselves to economic recovery and consolidation in the area above the seventeenth parallel, to a "North-first" policy. These decisions, including the mandatory regroupment to the North of the bulk of southern Viet Minh forces, particularly frustrated Le Duan and other militant southern communists who considered suspension of armed struggle and the accords generally detrimental to the long-range goals of the communist revolution. After the deadline for national elections passed in mid-1956, Hanoi continued to adhere to peaceful political struggle in the South because it was by then consumed with the task of transforming the economy and the society in the North along socialist lines. In the meantime, the Ngo Dinh Diem regime in Saigon established itself as the sole vector of power in the South and nearly annihilated the remnants of the communist movement there. In late 1956, the VWP Central Committee authorized southern communists to conduct acts of terrorism against the regime and its supporters but would not sanction an actual military struggle despite pleas from southern militants, including the fiery and indignant Le Duan.

Chapter 2 considers the period from 1957 to 1959, when Hanoi authorized the resort to revolutionary violence in the South and permitted, albeit reluctantly, armed struggle on a limited scale and with only minimal support from the North. Resolution 15, as the authorizing document was called, and the guidelines for implementing it represented the first important revision of the party's revolutionary strategy in nearly five years. They spawned an insurgency in the South that enabled communists there to better protect themselves from Diem's regime but achieved little else. Chapters 3 to 5 relate the ups and downs of the southern insurgency as well as other pertinent developments between 1960 and the collapse of the Geneva accords on Laos in late 1962, including the implications of the Sino-Soviet dispute in Vietnam. Despite having revised its revolutionary strategy in 1959, the DRVN leadership for much of this period treaded cautiously both domestically and internationally as it sought to offset seemingly irreconcilable pressures. While southern militants took liberties in using violence and clamored for unrestricted military struggle and greater DRVN involvement below the seventeenth parallel, the Soviet Union—and China too for a period—exhorted Hanoi to avoid provoking the Americans in the South and concentrate instead on building socialism in the North. As these pressures mounted, Washington extended its interference in the South, as well as in Laos and Cambodia, both of which Hanoi had hoped would remain neutral.

By 1963, DRVN decision-makers faced a pressing dilemma: whether to respond favorably to the pleas of party militants and risk provoking the Americans or indulge Moscow's call for the peaceful settlement of Cold War disputes, thus maintaining the current course in the South and the "North-first" policy to the likely detriment of the reunification struggle. That dilemma produced a critical development in the coming of the Vietnam War—the VWP's internal debate on revolutionary strategy of late 1963. Until that point, moderates had for all intents and purposes dictated party policymaking. But the coup that overthrew Diem that year brought to a head the conflict between them and their militant detractors. A Central Committee meeting held immediately after the coup in Saigon produced a resolution sanctioning war in the South with full DRVN backing and shifted control of party decision-making to militants. Led by Le Duan, who was first secretary of the VWP by this time, the militants actually staged a coup of their own in Hanoi, overhauling the party leadership and changing the balance of power there through a purge of leading moderates and others opposed to war as a policy for liberating the South. The following year, communist-led forces began major combat operations below the seventeenth parallel. After the so-called Tonkin Gulf incident in August, the Politburo authorized the deployment of the first units of the People's Army of Vietnam (PAVN) to the South, effectively instigating the Vietnam War. These and related developments are the subject of chapter 7.

The epilogue explores the effects in Hanoi of Washington's decisions in the spring of 1965 to deploy American combat forces to South Vietnam and initiate sustained aerial and naval bombardments of the North. It also considers communist plans for defeating American forces in the South and neutralizing the impact of the bombings, and reflects on the relevance of the subject matter of this study for understanding the course and outcome of the Vietnam War.

NOTE ON DOCUMENTARY AND OTHER SOURCES

Vietnamese authorities closely guard their archives. The most revealing records—those of the party and of the Foreign and Defense Ministries—are essentially inaccessible. The end of the Cold War more than two decades ago has changed little in terms of how Vietnamese authorities treat documentary materials on the Vietnam War and the scholars who want access to them. Owing to the absence of the complete documentary record and the lack of transparency in Vietnamese communist policymaking in Vietnam today, as in the past, it is difficult to know precisely what went on behind closed doors when leaders met and what specific factors and circumstances informed their decisions. The resulting dearth of sources on party decision-making, and the proceedings of the Secretariat, Politburo, and Central Committee in particular, in the period of this study is a major impediment to understanding just what happened. For the period 1954–65, that impediment can be neutralized, to a degree at least.

In attempting to capture Hanoi's perspective on domestic and international issues, I used an assortment of Vietnamese primary and secondary materials. I found valuable sources of information in the holdings of Vietnam National Archives Center 3 (Trung tam Luu tru Quoc gia 3) in Hanoi, a governmental archive, especially in the files *(phong)* of the Prime Minister's Office (Phu Thu tuong) and the National Assembly (Quoc hoi). Though it had little power or influence, the National Assembly was a venue for debating domestic and foreign policies, and its records offer useful insights. Most relevant for my purposes were the party documents reproduced in *Van kien Dang—Toan tap* (Party Documents—Complete Series). Published by National Political Publishers (Nha xuat ban Chinh tri quoc gia), the series is organized chronologically, each volume typically encompassing a single year and including a wide array of documents on domestic and foreign affairs generated by the general/first secretary, the Secretariat, the Politburo, the Central Committee, and other prominent party leaders and organs. Especially useful are Central Committee resolutions, Politburo reports, various guidelines and directives, and Secretariat instructions. The documentary record in these volumes is incomplete, and the materials included have been vetted by party officials and the editors. Nonetheless, the series has much merit, providing as it does a sense of the evolving concerns of policymakers, like the *Foreign Relations of the United States* series does for our understanding of American decision-making. The Vietnam Center and Archive at Texas Tech University has an abundance of excellent Vietnamese communist documents in translation, many of which have been digitized and made available online through its Virtual Vietnam Archive. Other Vietnamese sources useful for my purposes include articles published at the time in *Hoc tap*, the party's theoretical journal, as well as official histories, scholarly works, and personal memoirs.

To fill gaps in the story I pieced together from Vietnamese sources, I consulted British, French, and Canadian governmental archives. London maintained a consulate general in Hanoi after 1954 and played a role in Vietnamese affairs as cochair of the Geneva Conference on Indochina. France had a high commission in Indochina headquartered in Hanoi, which became a general delegation following the partition of Vietnam. DRVN leaders welcomed the French presence because they needed the collaboration of Paris to implement the Geneva accords. By the time the collapse of the accords became obvious, the French had proven their usefulness to Hanoi by advocating peaceful resolution of the crisis in the South and opposing or otherwise manifesting only lukewarm support for the regime in Saigon and American intervention in the region. Canada, for its part, kept a permanent mission in Hanoi to fulfill its obligations as a member of the International Commission for Supervision and Control in Vietnam, the organ set up after July 1954 to supervise implementation of the Geneva accords. The British, French, and Canadian missions were in a unique position to observe and analyze situations in the DRVN, and they produced illuminating reports on political and economic developments there, which are now available for scrutiny in London, Paris, and Ottawa, respectively. The diplomats assigned to the missions also learned revealing details about goings-on in Hanoi through regular contacts with North

Vietnamese officials as well as with counterparts from socialist bloc countries, which they reported to their home governments. London's Foreign Office, the Quai d'Orsay (France's Ministry of Foreign Affairs), and Ottawa's Department of External Affairs similarly generated insightful reports on DRVN domestic and diplomatic developments, as did the British, French, and Canadian Embassies in Moscow and Beijing. To the extent possible, I have tried to let these and the Vietnamese documents tell the story of Hanoi's struggle for national reunification in the decade after July 1954. Because the United States tended to rely on the British and the Canadians for information about Hanoi, my use of American documents is limited.

NOTE ON THE VWP'S POWER STRUCTURE

The head of the VWP (Dang Lao dong Viet Nam) was known as the general secretary (Tong Bi thu) until the September 1960 National Party Congress, and the first secretary (Bi thu Thu nhat) thereafter. He presided over the Secretariat (Ban Bi thu), which managed the day-to-day business of the party and monitored implementation of party policies. The Politburo (Bo Chinh tri), comprising approximately a dozen members, including the secretary who also ran it, decided "in the spirit of collective leadership" both party and state policies. The Central Executive Committee (Ban Chap hanh Trung uong), or Central Committee in this study, consisted of sixteen full and sixteen alternate, or "candidate" (nonvoting), members before the 1960 Congress, and forty-seven to forty-nine full and thirty-one alternate members thereafter, including all members of the Politburo. It debated issues and policies, made recommendations to the Politburo, and on occasion sanctioned policies.

The policies formulated and approved by these organs were disseminated downward to the rest of the party membership, usually by the Secretariat, or relayed to the government for implementation. Publicly opposing or even questioning the so-called party line was forbidden; "unity of thought" was essential to achieving revolutionary objectives. Party regulations required that "members should be obedient to the organization, lower echelons should be obedient to higher echelons, and the entire party should be obedient to the central committee" and to the Politburo in particular.[15] Besides, the purported perfectionism and infallibility of Marxism-Leninism required that the VWP always appear confident in its decisions and abilities.[16]

Typically in a communist country, delegates representing the party membership convene every five years in a national congress, such as that of September 1960. The meetings of the congress are typically occasions for outlining plans for the next five years, formalizing policies, confirming a new Politburo and Central Committee (usually as nominated by the party's Organization Committee), and announcing the reappointment or selection of a new party secretary. Due to circumstances, the various incarnations of the Communist Party in Vietnam held only three congresses before 1976, in 1935, 1951, and 1960. After each National Congress, the numbering of Central Committee meetings, or "plenums," reverts to one. Thus, the famous Fifteenth Plenum of the Central Committee in 1959 was the fifteenth meeting of that organ since the 1951 Congress, and the seminal Ninth Plenum of 1963 was the ninth meeting of the Central Committee that was confirmed at the Third Party Congress of 1960.

NOTE ON TRANSLATIONS AND VIETNAMESE WORDS AND NAMES

Translations from French and Vietnamese are my own. Due to publishing constraints, Vietnamese diacritical marks have been omitted in the text and notes. As is standard in Vietnam, Vietnamese personal names are used where the entire name is not. In Vietnamese, the personal name comes last. For example, Pham Van Dong (surname "Pham") is known as "Dong." Exceptions to the rule include Ho Chi Minh, commonly called "Ho," and Le Duan and Truong Chinh, who are typically referred to by their full names.

1

Choosing Peace, 1954–1956

By the summer of 1954, the world seemed slightly safer than it had been just a few months before, as a "hot" phase in the Cold War came to an end. The Korean and Indochina Wars had done much to increase tensions between the United States and the Soviet Union while marking the emergence of the People's Republic of China (PRC) as an ardent opponent of American "neo-imperialism" and a dynamic player in global politics. But the death of Stalin, the cease-fire in Korea, and the Geneva accords on Indochina offered some reprieve. Specifically, they presented Washington and Moscow with an opportunity to ease tensions between them, for rapprochement.

As Moscow grappled with matters relating to Stalin's succession, Beijing attended to domestic problems, and Washington warily watched events. There was much cause for concern in Washington, including the antics of Senator Joseph McCarthy at home, the French humiliation at Dien Bien Phu followed by the onset of the Algerian war of independence, the advent of the fiercely nationalist and purportedly neutralist regime of Gamal Abdel Nasser in Cairo, and starting in September, Beijing's sustained bombardment of islands controlled by the pro-American regime of Jiang Jieshi (Chiang Kai-shek) in the first Taiwan Strait crisis. Alarmed by developments in Guatemala that year, the administration of U.S. president Dwight Eisenhower resorted to methods employed the previous year in Iran—in removing prime minister Mohammad Mosaddegh from power—to get rid of Jacobo Árbenz Guzmán's leftist and "touchy" government. Shortly thereafter, the administration affirmed its commitment to the containment of communist influence in Southeast Asia by signing the Manila Pact, which provided for the creation of the Southeast Asia Treaty Organization (SEATO). Fatefully, it also began a comprehensive aid program, jointly with the French at first, to prop up the regime of Ngo Dinh Diem in Saigon as a bulwark against communist expansion in Vietnam. Soon Americans were training Diem's fledgling armed forces and becoming otherwise more directly involved in Indochina.

After signing the Geneva accords, the communist leaders of the Democratic Republic of Vietnam (DRVN) did their best to abide by their letter and spirit. The accords, they hoped, would allow them to achieve national reunification under their authority without further bloodshed following countrywide elections to take place within two years. In a September 1954 directive formalizing their intentions, the leaders ordered most of their troops in the South to repatriate to the North and explicitly prohibited those who stayed from resuming hostilities. Owing largely to Diem, the elections never took place. Although that dimmed the prospect for peaceful reunification, DRVN leaders refused to amend their stance on military struggle in the South. Instead, they rehabilitated and developed the economy in the North, to the dismay of communists who remained in the South and became targets of the Diem regime.

BEGINNINGS

On 2 September 1945, in the immediate aftermath of Japan's surrender in World War II, Ho Chi Minh, a longtime communist and anticolonialist leader, proclaimed the independence of the DRVN from Ba Dinh Square in Hanoi. The proclamation culminated the relatively peaceful process known to Vietnamese as the August Revolution. In that revolution, communist and nationalist forces, who had been amalgamated into the Viet Minh united front in 1941 to resist the Japanese occupation of Indochina (that is, Vietnam, Cambodia, and Laos), wrested the reins of power from the defeated occupiers and forced the abdication of the last Nguyen emperor, a figurehead named Bao Dai, thus ending ten centuries of dynastic rule in Vietnam.[1] During the war, the Japanese had effectively ended French colonial control on the peninsula, though France never forswore its *mission civilisatrice* there and was in fact working to reassert it even as Ho made his proclamation. Unwilling to accept the reimposition of colonial rule, Ho and the DRVN leadership remobilized the Viet Minh to resist it.

Following the gradual reoccupation of most of Indochina by French forces over the next year and a half, full-scale war broke out in December 1946. The conflict became an integral part of the Cold War after the newly formed PRC extended diplomatic recognition to the DRVN government in January 1950, followed by the Soviet Union and the rest of the socialist camp. Having consented to a revolutionary division of labor with Moscow, Beijing thereafter provided massive assistance to the Viet Minh, including hundreds of military advisers. Reeling from the "loss" of China and suddenly alarmed at the possibility of communist domination of Southeast Asia, Washington, until then largely uninvolved in Indochinese affairs, responded in kind, supplying ever increasing aid to the French and to the ostensibly autonomous regime France had established in Saigon and named the State of Vietnam (SOVN), under none other than Bao Dai.[2] The outbreak of the Korean War in June solidified American resolve to prevent a Viet Minh victory.

The internationalization of the Indochina War markedly raised the stakes and intensified the hostilities in Vietnam but failed to tip the scale in favor of either side. Even the Viet Minh's spectacular victory over French forces at Dien Bien Phu did not meaningfully change the balance of forces in the country. In the end, pervasive war weariness among the Vietnamese masses and Viet Minh, as well as the nagging concerns of their Soviet and Chinese allies about prolonging the war and, most importantly, the chilling prospect of American intervention, convinced DRVN decision-makers to suspend their military struggle and try to settle their differences with France diplomatically.

On 21 July 1954, after long and contentious negotiations, French and DRVN authorities agreed to a cease-fire, division of the country into two regroupment zones separated at the seventeenth parallel, mandatory regroupment of all French and SOVN military forces south of that line and all Viet Minh forces north of it, and voluntary migration of civilians between the two zones.[3] Ho Chi Minh and the DRVN government received sanction to administer the northern regroupment zone while France—and by extension the SOVN—remained sovereign in the southern zone. As the division of the country was to be temporary, the "Final Declaration of the Geneva Conference" called for consultations between representatives of the two zonal governments to set terms for national elections to reunify the country under a single government.[4] Ominously, Washington refused to endorse the declaration.[5] Despite reservations of their own, DRVN leaders accepted the Geneva accords because they hoped their implementation would preclude American military intervention while delivering what war could not: reunification of Vietnam under their governance.

HOPING FOR THE BEST

After accepting the Geneva accords, DRVN leaders set out to convince their followers on both sides of the seventeenth parallel that suspending hostilities short of complete victory was strategically correct. To that end, they impressed upon their military forces and political operatives the need to respect the cease-fire and trust that national reunification would come in no more than two years, following general elections that their side would surely win. Unless otherwise instructed by the leadership, all troops in the South had to regroup to the North, and communists who stayed behind were to do nothing to undermine the new accords or precipitate hostilities. Violating the accords, DRVN authorities warned, would give the Americans and their allies an excuse to derail the reunification process and sabotage the promised elections. For the time being, the struggle for unification had to be carried out "according to a peaceful approach." "Our people must continue their protracted and arduous struggle by peaceful methods in order to consolidate peace and achieve reunification."[6] It was not just that the leadership wished to preclude American intervention and thought everyone, including its troops, needed a respite from war; it was also that much of the area which fell under its jurisdiction after July 1954 was in ruins, and improving conditions there was imperative.[7] A "North-first" policy was therefore in order.

To keep the reunification process on track in the South, DRVN leaders directed cadres—indoctrinated, "professional" communist revolutionaries responsible for mobilizing public support for DRVN policies—there to court groups friendly to western interests, including Catholics and those who had served in the colonial administration.[8] The purpose of this "political struggle" was to win hearts and minds, to convince such groups and the civilian population generally that DRVN authorities respected ideological, social, and political diversity as well as Vietnamese nationalism in all its guises, and to promote peaceful reunification of the country.[9] Treating the sizeable minority of Catholics, former civil servants, and other civilians solicitously could have a "very big influence" on the result of the upcoming elections, the communist leadership remarked.[10]

Admittedly, DRVN leaders shared "a genuine apprehension" that Paris, Washington, and the SOVN regime in Saigon would not respect the terms of the accords. Early on, defense minister Vo Nguyen Giap warned the Canadian commissioner on the International Commission for Supervision and Control in Vietnam (ICSC) that Ngo Dinh Diem, who had become SOVN premier during the Geneva Conference and had no real hand in forging the accords, "had no intention" of "carrying out the agreement" and "it would be difficult for anyone to force him to do so."[11] Nonetheless, the man hailed as the architect of the victory over the French at Dien Bien Phu and other key DRVN leaders thought it in their best interests, for now, to honor the main provisions of the accords. If the accords were successfully implemented, they would secure the withdrawal of foreign forces and national reunification under their own aegis without further bloodshed and material destruction. DRVN leaders "accepted the Geneva compromise," in the words of a French diplomat, "only because we made them realize that it presented them with a serious chance to achieve, by peaceful means, [their] wartime objectives."[12] For Vietnamese communist authorities, the Canadian commissioner told Ottawa, the outcome of the 1956 national elections on reunification mandated by the Geneva accords was "a foregone conclusion." The only major obstacle to reunification under their auspices was "foreign support of the competing government in the South" and Diem himself.[13] Under the circumstances, it seemed sensible to temporize. DRVN leaders, the Canadian commissioner believed, "expect the worst" but "hope for the best."[14]

MODERATES AND MILITANTS

Such were the calculations of the Politburo of the Vietnamese Workers' Party (VWP), the main decision-making body in the DRVN. Specifically, they were those of Giap, president Ho Chi Minh, VWP general secretary Truong Chinh, Party Organization Committee chairman and vice minister of the interior Le Van Luong, president of the Federation of Trade Unions Hoang Quoc Viet, and, possibly, prime minister Pham Van Dong, who then doubled as foreign minister. Wary—and weary—of war, these men pinned their hopes on the Geneva accords and political struggle in the South to peacefully bring about national reunification under communist rule. Among the heavyweights, Ho wished to prevent further bloodshed, preempt American intervention, and reconcile with France; Giap wanted to give the forces under his command a chance to rest, reorganize, and modernize; and Truong Chinh, a leading doctrinaire, was eager to complete the party's ambitious land reform program, launched the previous year, and get on with the North's economic modernization and socialist transformation.

The desire of key allies—namely, the Soviet Union and China—to avoid further conflict in Asia with the West reinforced these attitudes. In the aftermath of Stalin's death, a power struggle had ensued in Moscow that kept Soviet leaders largely focused on domestic issues for nearly two years. Meanwhile, in Beijing, chairman Mao Zedong and the rest of the leadership of the Chinese Communist Party (CCP) were working on a new constitution and envisioning the country's first five-year plan for socialist industrialization and transformation of agriculture. As they awaited Vietnam's peaceful reunification, Ho, Giap, Truong Chinh, and their likeminded comrades in the Politburo agreed that rehabilitating and developing the northern economy while upgrading the armed forces could and should take precedence. On account of their strategic priorities, including caution over adventurism in the South, and the elements that informed them, namely, fear of a war with the United States, these men—with the exclusion of Truong Chinh, who would be demoted in 1956 and would thereafter change his views on reunification—formed the core of the risk-averse and temporizing "moderate" wing of the party that steered DRVN decision-making until 1963.

The other two members of the Politburo, secretary of the Central Office (Directorate) for Southern Vietnam (COSVN) Le Duan and chairman of the General Political Department (GPD) of the People's Army of Vietnam (PAVN) General Nguyen Chi Thanh, dissented. Both had strong ties to the South, having fought there during the Indochina War, and thought that suspending hostilities on current terms wasted communist gains there. Regrouping communist forces to the

North was most galling to them. According to historian Stein Tønnesson, Le Duan, who was still in the South when the other members of the Politburo accepted the Geneva accords and ordered the troops to regroup to the North, felt betrayed by the acceptance.[15] The only way to achieve the party's objectives below the seventeenth parallel, he believed, was through military struggle, irrespective of the dangers entailed.[16] While Le Duan and Thanh might have reconciled themselves to a strategic pause in the war, they opposed an extended lull and especially the withdrawal of Viet Minh forces from the South. Also, they did not think the party should prioritize economic recovery and development in the North while waiting on events in the South; Paris, Washington, or Saigon, if not all three, would never allow Vietnam to be reunified under VWP authority without putting up a fight.

On the basis of their convictions, the two men formed the nucleus of the party's hard-line, risk-taking "militant" wing, a minority faction committed to expeditious violent liberation of the South after July 1954, whose influence over decision-making increased slowly but surely over time. That nucleus eventually expanded to include Le Duc Tho, Le Duan's deputy during the Indochina War and his closest ideological ally, and Pham Hung, COSVN's third-in-command. Though unhappy about the strategic line set by the Politburo majority, the militants did their best to conform to it. As every party member knew, once the Politburo reached consensus and ruled on a matter, publicly questioning or opposing its ruling was strictly forbidden. But the militants, and Le Duan in particular, were not about to give up on their ambition to resume military struggle in the South sooner rather than later.

Though he would play a central role in the coming and waging of the Vietnam War, Le Duan remains an obscure, enigmatic figure.[17] He was born Le Van Nhuan on 7 April 1907 in the village of Hau Kien in Quang Tri (now Binh Tri Thien) Province, and as a railway official traveled throughout the country sometime in the 1920s learning what he could about French colonialism and its impact on Vietnam. He joined the radical Revolutionary Youth League in 1928, changed his name to Le Duan, and became a founding member of the Indochinese Communist Party (ICP, the precursor to the VWP) in 1930. A year later he joined the ICP's Bac Ky (Tonkin, the northern third of Vietnam) Committee for Education and Training, which was in charge of ideological indoctrination. He was soon arrested in Haiphong on charges of subversion, for which he was sentenced to twenty years in solitary confinement. His sentence was commuted in late 1936, and shortly thereafter he became secretary of the Trung Ky (Annam, central Vietnam) branch of the ICP. He was arrested again in Saigon in 1940 and sentenced to ten years at the infamous prison on Con Dao (Poulo Condore) Island.

Le Duan's years of incarceration were formative, shaping him into a stern, dogmatic, and stoic revolutionary.[18] Freed in 1945, he then traveled to Hanoi to join the Party Central Committee in the newly proclaimed DRVN under Ho Chi Minh.[19] By the time war with the French broke out in December 1946, Le Duan was back in the South as head of the Nam Bo Executive Committee (Xu uy Nam Bo), tasked with coordinating party and Viet Minh political activities in the southern third of Vietnam, the strategically important area formerly known as Cochinchina. In 1951 he was appointed in absentia to the VWP Politburo, and his Nam Bo Executive Committee was renamed COSVN and granted authority over political as well as military activities.[20] After the partition of Vietnam in 1954, while most of his comrades regrouped to the North, Le Duan stayed in the South.[21] Variously described as "violent," "authoritarian," "tough," and "ruthless," he was fully determined to achieve prompt reunification of Vietnam, whatever the cost.[22]

THE NEW STRATEGIC LINE

In September 1954, the Politburo issued an important statement concerning the situation created by the Geneva accords that confirmed and actually formalized the policy line espoused by the party in the days after the signing of the Geneva accords. Entitled "Politburo Resolution: On the New Situation, New Tasks, and New Policy of the Party," the lengthy document detailed official views and listed pressing tasks and fundamental requirements to sustain peace and achieve reunification.[23] According to it, the party and state faced a series of simultaneous transitions in the postwar era: from war to peace, from national unity to political partition, from a rural to an urban base, and from dispersal to centralization. While the North was now "liberated," the struggle in the South was not yet over and would in fact continue as long as the Vietnamese there remained under the "yoke" of Diem and his foreign allies. However, the Geneva accords and the pressing need for peace dictated that the "mode of struggle" to complete the liberation of Vietnam must change. The party and its cadres and other loyalists in the South had to renounce violence and replace military struggle with political struggle to achieve reunification without risking the resumption of war.[24] Henceforth, propaganda would constitute "the main thrust" of communist activities below the seventeenth parallel.[25]

Above the seventeenth parallel, the party and the people had entirely different tasks. There, the need was to work together to rebuild an economy ravaged by years of war and foreign occupation, increase agricultural production as land redistribution continued, and develop industry. It was, in short, imperative to improve standards of living and overall quality of life. This stance would not just satisfy popular demands but also enhance the VWP's and the DRVN's legitimacy during the campaign for national unification.[26] As they sought to rehabilitate the North, DRVN leaders would collaborate closely with friendly political and military elements in Laos and Cambodia for greater regional security and improvement of conditions in those countries. For those leaders, the fate of Vietnam was inextricably linked to that of the peoples of Laos and Cambodia. They "considered

Indochina as one geographical entity and a single battlefield," a former party official later noted.[27] In fact, no sooner had the Geneva accords been signed than the VWP set out to support, politically and materially, the creation of a "puppet" state-within-a-state in the area of Laos amenable to its control.[28] Regarding other international matters, the Politburo urged its supporters to work with progressive elements in France and elsewhere to ensure implementation of the accords, and with that the reunification of Vietnam. Mobilizing world opinion on behalf of peaceful unification, the Politburo surmised, was fundamental for its achievement.

The document just summarized remained the basis for the DRVN's domestic and international policy, the foundation of its revolutionary strategy, until 1959. It was thus its most consequential policy statement in the immediate aftermath of the Geneva accords concerning matters related to the coming of the Vietnam War. In its tone and substance, the document reflected the moderate tendencies of the Politburo and Central Committee majority, and quickly became an object of scorn among party militants.

THE WAY FORWARD

Within the parameters of the policies enunciated in the Politburo document of September, the VWP insisted that Viet Minh military forces below the seventeenth parallel regroup to the North. In violation of the accords, the party instructed some troops, approximately ten thousand of them by one account, to remain in the South. Their assignment, however, was not to fight; it was instead to serve as a "hedge against failure of the unification of Vietnam" and support the work of communist "agents," that is, cadres and regional party leaders, similarly ordered to stay there.[29] The continued presence of political operatives in the South to "look after the population" and implement the Geneva settlement was authorized under the accords. But under no circumstances, the party maintained, could they and the remaining troops engage in activities flagrantly violating the accords, especially fighting.[30] French sources suggest that many Viet Minh troops whom the DRVN leadership ordered to regroup to the North actually remained in the South. In late August, for example, DRVN authorities contacted the French navy for assistance in transporting some seventeen thousand troops and their relatives from Xuyen Moc District on the coast just east of Saigon to the North. To the authorities' evident dismay and embarrassment, less than eleven thousand people showed up for regroupment.[31] Possibly these and other southerners refused to regroup because they disapproved of the terms of the Geneva accords or the decision to suspend hostilities, or simply because they could not bring themselves to leave the places they called home.[32]

The Canadian delegation to the ICSC estimated that 173,900 troops and 86,000 "additional persons," consisting of "military families, administrative cadres, and liberated prisoners of war," regrouped to the North in 1954–55.[33] The number of civilians who relocated there voluntarily is difficult to ascertain but appears to have been negligible. Following their regroupment, southern males of age were integrated into the PAVN, the DRVN's standing army, while their families were granted privileged access to educational, economic, and social services. Many eventually regretted relocating to the North, and some even asked to return to the South.[34] In agreeing to regroup, they had severed ties with friends and relatives and in time developed feelings of homesickness, remorse, or alienation as parochialism made it difficult for them to integrate into northern society. Even within the armed forces, some found it difficult to bond with northern comrades. "The Northerners stayed with Northerners, the Southerners with Southerners," one regroupee later commented; "they didn't mingle easily."[35] To ensure that southern regroupees remained where the government put them and did not return to the South (in violation of the Geneva accords), one or more of their children were sometimes sent to China or other socialist countries for education.[36] Given these constraints, it is remarkable that DRVN authorities succeeded in regrouping as many troops from the South as they did, and in keeping them in the North.

The voluntary migration of northern civilians to the South, permitted under the terms of the accords, proved a thorny issue for the authorities. To their consternation, significant numbers of people sought to join that exodus, so many in fact that the authorities came to believe that French and SOVN officials and supporters were "enticing" or "pressuring" the northern masses, especially Catholics, to emigrate. Petitions to the ICSC from about one hundred persons from the town of Thanh Hoa in March 1955 indicated that indeed "hooligans are spreading panicky rumours which influenced some of their relatives to move to the other zone." According to the petitions, priests from a local church had even told people that "if they did not go South atomic bombs will be dropped in North Vietnam and that God will leave for the South." Other priests allegedly promised people that they would be given land and buffaloes and money for travel if they went south.[37] While the imminence of a nuclear attack on the North was a recurrent theme used by DRVN detractors to incite northerners to move South, other themes, according to ICSC investigators, included assertions that "the souls of Catholics will be lost if they stay in North Vietnam"; "famine and flood will be in North Vietnam"; the "Holy Virgin appeared and ordered all the Catholics to go to the other zone"; and the "pope ordered all Catholics to go to the other zone; otherwise they will lose their souls."[38] "Propaganda in regards to atomic bomb [and] Christ moving South," an ICSC team concluded after visiting Nghe An Province, "appears to be causing an increasing amount of confusion in the population's minds."[39] In and around Hanoi, which became the capital of the DRVN following the French withdrawal in September and October, more than thirty thousand people had signed up for emigration to the South within days after the Geneva accords became effective.[40]

Enticing northerners to the South, DRVN leaders presumed, was part of a strategy devised by their enemies to influence the political situation and gather more votes for the 1956 elections. Thwarting that strategy thus became a "pressing struggle" for the party. To curtail the migration of people to the South, leaders urged cadres to work closely with Catholics and other groups with influence among would-be migrants in the North. The cadres were to publicize party and state policies regarding the protection of religious freedom, particularly among the sizeable Catholic communities of Bui Chu and Phat Diem. Those communities included many loyalists of the old French regime, whom cadres sought to co-opt by rallying sympathetic Catholics to spread among them information favorable to the DRVN. To placate Catholic landowners in areas of high Catholic concentration, the authorities suspended reductions in land rents and land redistribution, central features of the ongoing agrarian reform program. The authorities also allowed the circulation of foreign currencies, including SOVN currency, which was prohibited elsewhere in the DRVN. More significantly, they ordered the return of property earlier seized from Catholic organizations and the release of clergy previously placed under house arrest.[41] These efforts suffered a major setback on 11 November 1954, when DRVN security forces opened fire on a group of three hundred Catholics seeking to emigrate, killing four and wounding several more.[42] On other occasions Catholics provoked incidents, as in December in Tinh Gia District, where a group of approximately one thousand armed Catholics assaulted security and civilian officials while carrying banners reading "Down with Communism."[43]

In the end, Hanoi's efforts to keep Catholics and others from abandoning the North failed dismally, despite the use of both carrot and stick tactics.[44] A majority of Catholics, including almost the entire communities of Bui Chu and Phat Diem, opted to "follow the Virgin Mary" and go south.[45] Historian Seth Jacobs has surmised that the Catholic population in the North declined from 1,133,000 to 457,000 as a result of the migration.[46] Overall, some 930,000 northern civilians left for the South in 1954–55.[47] That outcome dealt a huge blow to Hanoi. Not only were those who resettled below the seventeenth parallel likely to vote against reunification under DRVN governance in 1956, but they—Catholics in particular—became in time dedicated supporters of the Diem regime who were eager to exact revenge on communists, whom they held responsible for their exile from the North.

To offset that blow, Hanoi set out to exploit "contradictions" among the French, the Americans, and their allies in the South, as well as between those parties and the perceived needs and interests of the Vietnamese people. DRVN decision-makers correctly estimated that despite their common goal of maintaining a pro-western, noncommunist state below the seventeenth parallel, Paris and Washington disagreed on important matters of governance.[48] To illustrate, Paris disapproved of Washington's decision to support Diem, who despised France and made no secret of it, as SOVN premier.⁴⁹ Indeed, the French were soon urging Washington to reconsider its decision and replace Diem, to "put together . . . another team" to preside in Saigon.⁵⁰ Having also learned that the chief of staff of the SOVN army, General Nguyen Van Hinh, a "stooge of the French colonial reactionaries," disapproved of the elevation of Diem, a "stooge of the Americans," to the SOVN premiership, Hanoi directed cadres in the South to exploit that enmity and, by extension, the policy differences between the Americans and the French and between Diem and his domestic critics.⁵¹ Specifically, it proposed spreading disinformation about the SOVN regime in Saigon and its armed forces while infiltrating both. Cadres were to "closely coordinate legal and illegal political activities, but make the illegal work principal," and above all to keep everything they did secret.⁵²

This was not an unpromising approach. The South was admittedly "deeply splintered" at the time, so much so that the Diem regime teetered on the brink of collapse.⁵³ The SOVN premier did not control the army, lacked a competent administration, and had little or no authority over sizeable portions of the South, including areas controlled by the powerful Hoa Hao and Cao Dai religious sects. His regime also had to deal with the logistical nightmare of welcoming, housing, feeding, and finding land or jobs for hundreds of thousands of refugees from the North.⁵⁴ With sufficient political pressure, Hanoi thought, Diem might be ousted and replaced by someone who "cared relatively little about the Americans."⁵⁵ "M. Diem has many of the qualities required by a Nationalist revolutionary leader dedicated to saving his country—courage, integrity, persistence, faith and an implacable hostility to communism," a western assessment noted about this time. He was, however, "incapable of compromise" and had "little administrative capacity."⁵⁶

SOUTHERN SKEPTICISM

Southern party leaders—those instructed to stay—did their best to follow Hanoi's prescriptions, repeatedly praising them in pamphlets and public meetings, and ordering cadres under their command to abide by the letter of those prescriptions. Privately, however, meaningful numbers of them and their subordinates shared Le Duan and Nguyen Chi Thanh's sentiments and disapproved of the prescriptions as well as the reasoning behind them. They questioned the leadership's acceptance of the Geneva accords; they could not reconcile themselves to the suspension of military struggle and the turn to political struggle only. Considering the duplicitous history of French colonialism and the mindset of American cold warriors in the mid-1950s, to say nothing of the grim determination of Diem himself, they thought it naive to assume that the other side would permit peaceful reunification under any circumstances.⁵⁷ Most upsetting to them was Hanoi's insistence that troops regroup to the North and that those who stayed forswear violence despite the vulnerability of the Diem regime. Vo Chi Cong, a prominent southern communist leader, admitted in a later memoir that he and many other southern party members always felt that regrouping troops and renouncing violence effectively nullified the gains revolutionary forces had theretofore made below the seventeenth parallel, that it crippled the communist movement there and proved detrimental to the long-term prospects for reunification.[58]

Following discussion of the Politburo policy pronouncement of September, the party's Executive Committee of Interzone IV, which straddled the seventeenth parallel, told Hanoi that the new policy violated the best interests of the revolution since it left southern communists unprotected, at the complete mercy of enemy violence. Suddenly sustaining a purely political struggle, the committee explained, was "extremely difficult and complex." While pledging to do the will of the party, the committee made certain that superiors in Hanoi understood the depth of its concern.[59] A month later, the Executive Committee of Interzone V, which encompassed northern South Vietnam and the Central Highlands, voiced similar concerns in even more explicit language. Following a three-day discussion in October, this committee sent Hanoi a lengthy critique detailing the negative effects the party's new strategy had already had.[60] Most notably, the regroupment of Viet Minh troops to the North was decimating southern communist ranks. As a result, reactionary and foreign forces suddenly "enjoy military and political supremacy" in the South, which was sure to create "many difficulties in the task to lead the reunification effort."

In language intimating a sense of betrayal, the committee's report captured the widespread pessimism enveloping southern revolutionaries, who were convinced that the "imperialists" and their local clients would never give up southern Vietnam without a fight. The Americans were a particularly significant threat, the committee warned, as they clearly intended to "carry out the destruction of peace in Indochina." With Washington's help, Paris and Saigon "will not allow us to achieve peace and national reunification through free general elections." As a result of such circumstances, the committee told Hanoi to prepare for "the subversion of the general elections" and "the resumption of war."

Hanoi ignored these warnings. On the contrary, it directed that the regroupment of forces from the South to the North continue, and that southern communist outfits restructure themselves with local recruits and otherwise adhere to Hanoi's policies and the terms of the Geneva accords.[61] "We must overcome subjective [and] remorseful" as well as "pessimistic" and "faltering" thoughts, the VWP Central Committee decreed. Supporters of the revolution in the South in particular had to overcome their "lack of belief in the triumph of the political struggle." Concerned about the consequences of a possible resort to violence by disgruntled southern elements, the committee repeated its earlier admonitions about the necessity of respecting the cease-fire. "We must give all our attention to protecting the foundation [laid by the accords], avoiding provocations, [and] avoiding manifestations of force," it intoned. Cadres in the South must promote peace actively through the use of such slogans as "Vietnamese Do Not Kill Vietnamese."[62]

But Hanoi had a difficult time persuading southern communists and particularly the militants among them of the merits of its strategy. By its own admission, "the campaign to carry out the [Geneva] agreement" experienced "many shortcomings," most occasioned by organizational problems. Its effort to implement the accords was poorly coordinated, it thought, because local party branches in the South were ineffectively connected to it. As a result, policies and directives were slow to reach lower levels and, when they did, were imperfectly understood. Implementation was thus "oftentimes belated and passive."[63] Such problems were indeed real, symptomatic of the party's chronic weakness in southern Vietnam. Throughout the Indochina War, the party had struggled to develop a solid base there. The number of members and cadres was persistently low, and their training poor. The pitiful state of the party in the South may have been another reason Le Duan and other militants rejected peace and pressed for immediate resumption of hostilities; war would compel Hanoi to suspend the repatriation of troops to the North and allocate more resources to the South, bringing the southern communist movement back from the brink of imminent extinction.[64]

To appease militants whose ideas on reunification imperiled party unity, Hanoi eventually professed that war in the South would resume, if necessary, as soon as the North had been consolidated. The DRVN was a brand-new polity created in fact by the Geneva accords, it maintained, and as such it had to be built economically and otherwise before it could guarantee victory in the coming elections, to say nothing of victory in an extended armed struggle in the South. "Our strength resides in the entire nation," Truong Chinh said in March, but the need for investing resources in the North was "most essential" for the time being.[65] "However much the South might demand the attention of the [DRVN] Government, consolidation of the North was not to take second place," the British Consulate General in Hanoi wrote of this stance.[66] In a public address, Ho Chi Minh maintained that the principal tasks of the party just then included not only implementing the Geneva accords and developing stronger leadership at all levels, but consolidating the North while intensifying political struggle in the South.[67] The militants were unmoved.

THE DRVN AND THE UNITED STATES

Progress in jump-starting the war-ravaged northern economy was slow. Basic transportation facilities—roads, bridges, and rail lines—had been damaged or destroyed during the war with France, and the production and distribution of food severely disrupted. "In many areas," historian Fredrik Logevall has written of this situation, Hanoi was "starting essentially from scratch," not least because in abandoning the North the French had cannibalized factories, post offices, and even hospitals.[68] In April 1955 rice rations had to be cut from 15 to 13½ kilos (from approximately 33.1 to 29.7 pounds) per household per month. This decline was due partly to domestic problems in the DRVN, but also to the fact that Saigon suspended all economic exchanges with the North, which had traditionally relied on the South's surplus production for a significant portion of its rice.[69] As a result of this suspension, many people in the DRVN now lived a precarious hand-to-mouth existence.[70] Foreign observers reported that the economic situation there deteriorated so much after July 1954 that "the population were not giving the regime full support."[71] Government spokesmen acknowledged that unspecified regions in the North actually experienced famine that year.[72]

The land reform program contributed in no insignificant degree to this situation, meeting as it did with considerable opposition from the rural masses and hindering production. Meanwhile, cadres were "constantly chided" by Hanoi for failing to "unmask the landlords' plots" that encouraged the rice shortages, and for not proceeding "ruthlessly enough" with tax collection. Some cadres had even been charged with "right-wing deviationism"—essentially, weakness and hesitation in enforcing party policies.[73] *Nhan dan,* the party daily, editorially exhorted those responsible for carrying out land reform to "banish selfish and pacifist doctrines," to be "careful but determined in action," and to "firmly believe in our own forces and resolutely lead the peasantry to crush the whole landlord class."[74] On the basis of these initiatives and priorities, the Indian commissioner on the ICSC wrote of the "indisputably communist character" of Hanoi leaders, whose methods, he suggested, conformed to communist, not nationalist, tradition.[75] In the more cynical view of French cabinet chief Claude Cheysson, the DRVN was clearly "committing itself to the infernal circle of the communist world."[76]

An important factor influencing Hanoi's choice of priorities was fear that the Eisenhower administration might exploit the vulnerability of the DRVN and attempt to "roll back" socialism there. "If our northern region is not consolidated, then not only will unification be impossible," Truong Chinh told the VWP Central Committee, but Washington and its allies "might use the South as a springboard to encroach upon the North."[77] Hanoi was sufficiently concerned about the American threat to fear an attack on the DRVN itself, a potentially devastating scenario that solidified its resolve to abide by the Geneva accords. It was perhaps the feeling that they were dealing with this danger that led party leaders to decide that only after they made the DRVN a viable economic entity would they reconsider their revolutionary strategy, and then only if circumstances dictated. For the time being, the North's need for peace was as absolute as the perils facing it were daunting. As a precautionary measure, in April 1955 Hanoi ordered the creation of local militias throughout the DRVN.[78]

By this time, DRVN leaders unanimously agreed that Washington represented the chief obstacle to Vietnamese reunification. In March the Central Committee determined that the United States was now "the primary and most dangerous enemy" of the Vietnamese people.[79] American "imperialists" were "the number one enemy of the people of the world" as well as the "number one and immediate enemy of the Indochinese people," Ho Chi Minh iterated in a public pronouncement.[80] Washington was compelling Paris to betray the Geneva accords, the Central Committee claimed, and was also determined to "rely on feudalists and the most reactionary bourgeois collaborators headed by Ngo Dinh Diem" to preclude peaceful national reunification.[81] American aid to the French and the Saigon regime, the DRVN National Assembly lamented, was "proof of the deliberate desire of the U.S. ruling circles to deepen their intervention in the internal affairs of Vietnam, prevent the implementation of the Geneva Agreement, and prepare for a definite partition of Vietnam."[82]

The American commitment to Diem's regime was indeed rapidly expanding. The previous October, Washington had instructed its Military Assistance Advisory Group (MAAG) in Vietnam, created in 1950 to marshal U.S. aid to French and allied forces there, to develop a training program for SOVN troops. Immediately thereafter, Eisenhower had informed Diem that he intended to assist the SOVN "in developing and maintaining a strong, viable state, capable of resisting attempted subversion or aggression through military means," and to that end would provide "an intelligent program of American aid given directly to your Government."[83] According to Fredrik Logevall, that pledge marked the actual beginning of the American commitment to South Vietnam.[84] In January 1955 the Americans had begun channeling aid directly to Saigon, bypassing the French, and a month later the U.S. Senate approved the creation of the Southeast Asia Treaty Organization (SEATO). That approval, in Hanoi's eyes, formalized America's commitment to preserving a noncommunist South Vietnam and constituted proof of Washington's intent to replace the French in Indochina and ignore the Geneva accords.[85] Ominously in Hanoi's view, by the end of spring, the United States had taken over the training of SOVN troops from France. American strategic concerns were turning Vietnam into a crucible of the Cold War.

In May, acting chairman of the DRVN National Assembly's Standing Committee Ton Duc Thang publicly stated that "our main task now is to oppose the U.S. imperialists' preparations for the resumption of hostilities in Indo-China and to attain free general elections in order to bring about national unification."[86] Meanwhile, the Politburo referred in the same vein to the Americans as "neo-fascists," and concluded that the United States hoped to keep Vietnam permanently divided, like Korea and Germany. Washington's decision to allow West Germany to join the North Atlantic Treaty Organization (NATO) and begin to rearm that year, which Moscow answered by creating the Warsaw Pact, informed such thinking.

Vietnamese communist policymakers, we now know, were keen observers of international affairs, and the so-called world situation as they saw it conditioned their ruminations on strategic matters to no insignificant degree. They understood that Cold War developments in Europe and elsewhere invariably ratcheted up the international stakes on the Indochinese peninsula. While there is no doubt that Hanoi was genuinely worried about Washington's intentions, its demonization of the United States also created a "useful adversary" that facilitated "gaining and maintaining public support for the core grand strategy," and thus for advancing the Vietnamese revolution.[87]

THE DIPLOMATIC STRUGGLE

In line with the substance of the September 1954 policy statement, DRVN authorities devised a plan to contain American ambitions in Vietnam by rallying world opinion against Washington. Diplomatically isolated, the Eisenhower administration would be hard-pressed to increase U.S. involvement in the country, they thought, or to interfere in the reunification process. To that end, the authorities instructed diplomats abroad to publicize Hanoi's commitment to peaceful reunification and the obstacles the Americans were raising to the achievement of that goal. The Foreign Ministry generally had to "make ... the people of the world understand clearly that we have always strongly advocated peace," that "the opponents of the [Geneva] agreement are the American imperialists and their puppets."[88] This "diplomatic struggle" essentially amounted to an internationalization of the political struggle for hearts and minds in the South.[89] Like the masses there, the rest of the world had to recognize the "noble" aspirations of Hanoi and the "wicked intentions" of Washington and be made to "feel resentment" toward the latter, the Politburo insisted.[90] Everyone had to accept the slogan "Oppose the Americans, Oppose Diem, for Peace, for Unification."[91]

To meet the aims of that effort, Hanoi intensified its public denunciations of the United States as an "imperialist aggressor." It even introduced and publicized a kind of "domino theory" of its own according to which the Americans, if unchecked, would "oust the French from Indo-China and turn Indo-China into an American colony, seize the economy and resources of Indo-China, suppress the national and democratic movement of the people of Indo-China, turn Indo-China into a springboard for the conquest of the [other] countries of South East Asia, [and] make out of Indo-China an American military base."[92] A few weeks later, DRVN authorities ordered the American Consulate in Hanoi to close down its diplomatic wireless, a move intended to pressure the United States into abandoning its official presence there and to signal Hanoi's conviction that its differences with Washington were irreconcilable.[93] The move had the desired effect, and by the end of the year Washington had closed the consulate.[94]

Meanwhile, Hanoi solicited political, moral, and other forms of support from the international community. This "line of conduct" was geared toward increasing cooperation with communist countries and strengthening "friendship ties" with neutralist states in Southeast Asia and elsewhere.[95] In the context of the Cold War, the Vietnamese crisis had global ramifications that its leaders clearly understood and exploited to their advantage. This involved them in a systematic effort to use diplomacy to get others to see their situation as they saw it themselves. Besides generating pressure on the Americans to limit their involvement in the South, favorable world opinion would help Hanoi garner material as well as political support. The opposition may have been better equipped, DRVN leaders reasoned, but it had no inherent advantage diplomatically. In fact, Cold War Washington had many enemies and even more critics, and Hanoi's chances of winning the battle for world opinion were far better than those of winning an actual war against American forces in the South.

As the leader of the moderate wing of the party, Ho Chi Minh assumed a central role in the diplomatic struggle. Most notably, he used his worldwide notoriety to cultivate an image of the Vietnamese revolution as a necessity prompted by tragic circumstances over which the Vietnamese had little or no control, and of himself as "Ho the conciliator," who sought merely to satiate the desire for peace of the people of Indochina and elsewhere.[96] The stratagem would pay valuable short- and long-term dividends. After a meeting with him in October, the Indian commissioner on the ICSC reported that Ho was a "patient and tolerant man" bent upon respecting the Geneva accords and "resist[ing] all attempts by Western Powers to draw him into their global conflicts."[97] Over time, Ho's travails helped promote the idea—the myth, it turned out—that all Vietnamese revolutionaries were in fact peace-loving nationalists compelled by "dark forces" to pick up a gun and fight. British diplomats in Hanoi immediately saw through the stratagem and attendant endeavors. DRVN authorities "attribute to their adversaries—the government of Monsieur Diem and his American backers—a desire to avoid elections and to perpetuate the present *de facto* partition of the country" with all that entailed, they reported of these endeavors. "They know that they must appeal to world opinion, and especially to the Geneva powers, if they are to succeed in getting their point of view accepted in Saigon" and elsewhere. They were thus "careful to phrase their official pronouncements in moderate and restrained language and to hang their desiderata upon the pegs provided in the Geneva agreement and Final Declaration."[98]

With these ends in mind, in April 1955 DRVN representatives attended the conference of Afro-Asian nations in Bandung, Indonesia, where the Cold War–era nonaligned movement originated. There, prime minister Pham Van Dong spoke with "studied moderation" of his government's commitment to the Geneva accords and to the peaceful reunification of his country promised by those accords.[99] A few weeks later, Ho himself led a DRVN delegation to the Soviet Union and China. There, he recycled some of the rhetoric Dong had used in Bandung to obtain pledges for not just moral backing but also "valuable" material advances toward the realization of the DRVN's political and economic objectives.[100] It was the success of such initiatives that the party leadership would assiduously seek to replicate thereafter, on a global scale.

CONFRONTING DIEM

As Hanoi concentrated on convincing southern communists to embrace the Geneva accords, on developing the northern economy, and on containing the United States, Diem slowly but effectively consolidated his authority in the SOVN. Having solved his most critical problems with his armed forces, he immediately targeted the rebel armies of the Hoa Hao, an eccentric Buddhist sect, and the Cao Dai, a more eclectic religious denomination, and the forces of the Binh Xuyen criminal syndicate. Collectively, these factions, not communists, represented the most serious internal challenge to Saigon after the DRVN entered into the Geneva accords and started regrouping the bulk of its forces to the North.

In the spring of 1955, SOVN military and security forces began moving systematically against the factions and their armies. Diem "embarked on a campaign of repression and widespread propaganda for the establishment of a hard authoritarian regime, employing ruthless... methods to root out rebels and establish authority," western observers noted.[101] The campaign was a resounding success. According to historian Jessica Chapman, the outcome of the "sect crisis" was a "key turning point" for Diem. His regime had begun the conflict with the factions "on the brink of collapse," but emerged "with what seemed uncontested control over South Vietnam" and "full support from Washington."[102] If that was not ominous enough for the VWP, in April the deadline for beginning consultations between representative authorities of northern and southern Vietnam to set the terms for the 1956 elections passed with no indication that Saigon or even France intended to respect that crucial provision of the Geneva accords. The French Foreign Ministry itself admitted later that it was a "spectacular violation" of the accords.[103] Suspending military struggle and banking on political struggle and the scheduled elections to prevail in the South now looked more and more like a mistake by DRVN leaders.

Despite these alarming developments and to the consternation of southern militants, the "principal aspirations" of leaders in Hanoi nonetheless remained to fulfill the terms of the Geneva accords and await the promised elections. According to *Nhan dan*, the effort to implement the Geneva accords entered in the summer of 1955 a new phase, in which the party and the people had to struggle even harder "against the reappearance of new hostilities and realize the 1956 elections."[104]

In secret dispatches to its agents in the South, the Party Secretariat reiterated that the plan of action for the South remained political, not armed, struggle. In light of Saigon's growing belligerence and disregard for the terms of the Geneva accords, however, the Secretariat authorized limited indirect support to noncommunist factions fighting Diem's forces.[105] That summer, Hanoi instructed Le Duan to seek a pact on behalf of the VWP with other organizations opposed to Diem in Nam Bo. As previously noted, the Politburo member doubled as head of COSVN, renamed the Nam Bo Executive Committee (Xu uy Nam Bo) in September, and in that capacity directed the activities of three interzonal subcommittees, each responsible for guarding the interests of the revolution in five to seven provinces.[106] In October, Le Duan met with noncommunist rebel leaders, including Nam Lua and Ba Cut of the Hoa Hao. Despite doctrinal differences, the three men agreed to form the Southern Committee of the Patriotic Front, which eventually encompassed surviving members of not just the Hoa Hao but the Cao Dai and Binh Xuyen rebel armies as well. Given its professed commitment to peace and to the Geneva accords, the VWP's ties to the new front remained secret.[107]

While acquiescing in such collaborations, Hanoi publicly followed an accommodationist course vis-à-vis Saigon. It had laid the foundation for this earlier in the year, when it openly called for normalizing relations between the two zones, a process it proposed should begin with talks on restoring postal communications.[108] The approach was sensible and not altogether unpromising. Constructive engagement of the southern regime might improve bilateral relations, save the Geneva accords, and improve the chances for peaceful reunification. At this time, Hanoi considered France, the other signatory to the Geneva agreement on Vietnam, officially responsible for implementing the accords, and therefore for arranging the general elections in the southern half of the country. However, it also understood that its "real interlocutor" in this matter must be the "competent *representative* authorities" in the South, that is, appropriate officials of the Diem regime, with whom it still hoped soon to begin pre-election consultations.[109] In January Pham Van Dong had confided to a western journalist that Hanoi was "prepared to make large concessions for the sake of reaching agreement" on such talks.[110] Toward that end, DRVN authorities refrained from using the familiar labels of "criminal" and "traitor" in public references to the SOVN regime.[111]

"There is no doubt in my mind," the British consul commented in a revealing cable to London in June, "that [DRVN leaders] are sincere in saying, as they have all along, that they really desire nation-wide elections; I consider that the achievement of this aim has first priority among their political objectives." National reunification "has always been one of their basic slogans," the consul continued, "and the fact that they are ready to work for this through the medium of elections reflects their confidence in the result of the polls." The leaders were "sufficiently sure of their own position in the North, and confident of a sizeable number of votes from the South," the consul believed, "to feel that they can afford to be flexible in their approach to the question and possibly to make certain concessions to democratic practice in electoral procedure." The consul thought it "likely" that DRVN leaders were preparing to come to the conference table for talks on elections "in an apparently conciliatory spirit and to make every effort to avoid a breakdown of the talks."[112] The Canadian ICSC commissioner concurred with that assessment. "Given the dominant role which they exert throughout the whole of the Democratic Republic territory [i.e., North Vietnam], and the strong position which their sympathies occupy in various areas in the South," he felt, "there is little doubt that the mood of [DRVN leaders] is one of confidence." "For this reason, the North is likely to be prepared, at least on paper, and possibly also in fact, to accept electoral arrangements which may surprise the world in their apparent liberality." The DRVN leaders' "most likely tactic," the commissioner concluded, "will be either to prepare or to agree to arrangements for all Vietnam elections, which will incorporate what they hope will be conditions acceptable to and defensible before free world opinion."[113]

During the summer of 1955, the DRVN Foreign Ministry developed "several alternative plans" for holding elections in Vietnam. Pham Van Dong told a Canadian diplomat that Hanoi thought it "inconceivable" that it should not be able to find some common ground, "some basis of agreement," with the South. It became especially important to placate Diem after he announced on 16 July that as a nonsignatory to the Geneva accords, the SOVN was "not bound in any way by those Agreements signed [between military representatives of France and the DRVN] against the will of the Vietnamese people," and his government would in fact refuse to participate in any political process designed to reunify Vietnam "if proof is not given us that [Hanoi] put the superior interests of the National Community above those of communism."[114]

Another calculation behind Hanoi's pursuit of rapprochement with Saigon despite Diem's intractableness was that any such endeavor might antagonize Washington or render it uneasy over the prospect of elections or any other cooperative process between the two Vietnamese governments. Aid from Washington sustained the Saigon regime, and anything that might pry the two apart was worth trying.[115] Admittedly, any effort to divorce Saigon from Washington by now had little chance of success, as DRVN leaders understood. But that they made the effort anyway attested to their eagerness to save the Geneva accords and keep alive their flickering hope for peaceful reunification.

Having for all intents and purposes eradicated the main threats to his authority —namely, the rebel armies of the Hoa Hao, Cao Dai, and Binh Xuyen—Diem was completely unresponsive to Hanoi's overtures and in fact moved to annihilate what remained of the communist presence in the South starting that summer. On 20 July, one day before the first anniversary of the Geneva accords, he launched a vigorous, violent campaign called "Denounce the Communists" *(To Cong)* to root out communists and "pro-Communist attitudes" among the population in the South.[116] Soon thereafter his government gave carte blanche to SOVN military and security forces to incarcerate or exterminate all known or suspected communists below the seventeenth parallel. The resulting campaign dealt a crushing blow to the southern communist movement, already enfeebled by repatriations to the North. It severely damaged most remaining party organizations and "succeeded in inducing a considerable proportion of the population to view that the authority of the [SOVN] Government had come to stay."[117] Diem's security initiatives in 1955, historian Mark Moyar writes, "created far more problems for the stay-behind Communists than Hanoi had anticipated."[118] Yet the sheer ruthlessness of the campaign may have had some collateral benefits for the revolutionary movement, as political scientist David Elliott maintains, for it alienated many nationalists from Diem's government and produced a pool of new recruits.[119]

In a desperate effort to encourage rapprochement with the SOVN, DRVN authorities developed a plan calling for a modus vivendi between Saigon and Hanoi, leading to a normalization of relations between the two governments as a prelude to reunification. According to the plan, following consultative talks between the two sides, a weak central government would be established, making Vietnam a confederation of two "zonal" governments. From there, each zone would organize its own "amalgamation" into a unitary central government.[120] "The problem of unification should be solved by electing two separate chambers of an all-Viet Nam National Assembly, one each for the North and the South," a revised draft of the plan urged. All political parties and organizations would be free to present candidates. After the elections, the two chambers would work together to elect a "joint Government." Although formally united under that government, "North and South would [each] retain a large measure of autonomy." The armed forces of the two zones would remain separate and independent until fused into one army by negotiation.[121] The Vietnam Fatherland Front (VFF), a broad-based organization formed in September 1955 in the North, circulated and publicized the first complete draft of the plan. The new organization's mandate was to promote national reconciliation according to popular shibboleths of independence, unity, and democracy, and to demonstrate the DRVN's repudiation of violence as a means of unifying the country.[122] Western observers cynically saw the VFF as essentially "a step designed to provide a policy to meet M. Diem's refusal to accept the Geneva Settlement."[123]

Unsurprisingly, Saigon promptly rejected the plan. In fact, none of Hanoi's efforts to mollify Diem bore fruit in the end, as he obdurately refused to cooperate with any of them and insisted that South Vietnam would have nothing to do with the 1956 elections. In October, Diem actually held a referendum of his own asking the southern population to elect him head of state as well as chief of government in a new, democratic, and fully sovereign Vietnamese state.[124] Officially, 98.2 percent of the resulting vote favored him.¹²⁵ Despite claims that the result was rigged, the referendum enhanced Diem's legitimacy as well as that of his regime, as it in effect abolished the French-sponsored SOVN and paved the way for creation of the Republic of Vietnam (RVN). Unlike its previous incarnation, the new state had no colonial past, no ties to France, and therefore even less reason to honor the terms of the Geneva accords.¹²⁶ The "obvious purpose" of the referendum, thought Pham Van Dong, was "creating a separate state in the Southern part of Vietnam, in stark contradiction with both the letter and spirit of the Geneva Agreements."¹²⁷ On the other hand, a western observer believed, "the success of the plebiscite was a measure of the success of the policies pursued by the [Saigon] Government and the extent to which the people had been successfully conditioned not merely to reject [Bao Dai, the ousted head of the SOVN,] but to accept M. Diem as leader." To be sure, "the methods employed undoubtedly increased the opposition and particularly intellectual opposition to M. Diem in South Vietnam," this observer noted, "but they also secured for the time being at least that that opposition was ineffective."¹²⁸

DRVN leaders had grossly underestimated Diem, it seemed, and overplayed their hand by opting to pursue their revolutionary objectives politically and diplomatically while suspending military operations. To Le Duan and other VWP militants, developments in the South since the Geneva accords reinforced the conviction that the moderates in the Politburo had erred in assuming that they could meet the main goals of the Vietnamese revolution without armed struggle. "As they had done in 1946, during the negotiations that preceded the outbreak of [the Indochina War]," Fredrik Logevall writes, Ho and like-minded leaders had "overestimated the power of what they like[d] to call 'democratic elements'" in enemy circles.¹²⁹ For all its heavy-handedness, Diem's rule in the South had quelled dissidence and established him as the sole vector of power there. As Diem's success continued unabated, many in the VWP came to see that the revolutionary movement in the South was in dire straits, as the "old-style French colonial society" there was transformed into "a new-style American colonial society," with Diem at its helm.¹³⁰

SUSTAINING PEACEFUL STRUGGLE

In 1956 Hanoi openly acknowledged for the first time that the prospects for peaceful national reunification were dim and the struggle for reunification would probably be longer and more difficult than anticipated.¹³¹ But because the moderate consensus prevailed in the Politburo and the Central Committee, the communist revolutionary strategy remained unchanged. Instead of arming and fighting, Hanoi advised its followers in the South to continue infiltrating the Saigon regime and subverting it from within. It also urged them to broaden their popular support by earning the trust and sympathy of "neutral" or indifferent southerners, to infiltrate labor unions, women's and youth organizations, and other such groups, and to try to integrate large numbers of rural and urban youths into mass-based revolutionary organizations similar to the VFF in the North. The party also initiated a major effort in both halves of the country to silence detractors of its revolutionary line inside and outside the VWP, and to "make cadres and the masses believe in the line of political struggle of the party at present," to convince them that that was "the most effective means" of achieving national reunification.[132]

DRVN decision-makers stuck to the current line for various reasons. Ideologically, Ho, Giap, and other leaders still strongly objected to a military solution; realistically, the success of Diem's "Denounce the Communists" campaign had "render[ed] very doubtful the issue of a recourse to force, at least in the short term."[133] Owing to the decimation of communist forces and their sympathizers in the South, Hanoi could not at that time launch an effective guerrilla struggle, even if it wanted to.[134] The PAVN, for its part, was unprepared for war. In 1955 Hanoi had initiated, at Giap's urging, a five-year plan to modernize the northern armed forces. But since then the government had reduced defense spending in the interests of the North's socialist transformation.[135] To that end, thousands of experienced soldiers had been demobilized and assigned to nonmilitary units and duties.[136] In June 1956 the government began demobilizing no less than eighty thousand additional soldiers to "strengthen the labor potential."[137] Also, the PAVN still had no armored units and no air force, indispensable assets in the event of a resumption of hostilities with possible American involvement.[138]

Satisfying allies' aspirations for peace was another incentive to wage only political struggle in the South. Both Beijing and Moscow opposed resumption of hostilities in Vietnam after the signing of the Geneva accords. Instead of fighting in the South, they advised, Hanoi should concentrate on rehabilitating the economy in the North and wait on events below the seventeenth parallel. Each had been emphatic about its desire to not see war start anew in Indochina; acting against their wishes therefore might jeopardize the aid they provided, a risk Hanoi simply could not afford to take at the time. More than 13 million people lived in the North in 1956. Yet among them were only thirty engineers and technical experts with the kind of training and expertise needed to improve the industrial base, the centerpiece of the economic development the party wanted to achieve.[139] Early in the year, the government launched a program of economic modernization centering around consolidation and expansion of the industrial base and production of manufactured goods for export. "Healthy [foreign] trade will stimulate the development of industry and agriculture," the program's originators promised, "contribute to raising the standard of living of the people, stabilize commodity prices, stabilize currency, consolidate state finances, [and] make the national economy thrive."[140] Without the support of its two biggest allies, Hanoi would never achieve the goals of the program. In fact, to help its neighbor meet their economic objectives, China dispatched the first of what eventually became thousands of technical and other advisers to North Vietnam.¹⁴¹ To sustain this flow of support, it was necessary for Hanoi to exercise caution in the South and at least pretend to heed the desires of its Soviet and Chinese allies "counseling moderation."¹⁴²

The insistence on respecting the Geneva accords and the continuing effort to influence domestic and world opinion encouraged the same conclusion. As part of the effort to win hearts and minds abroad, Hanoi dispatched urgent pleas to the British and Soviet governments, cochairs of the 1954 Geneva Conference, to convene "a new Geneva Conference on the Question of Indochina." A new conference, it affirmed, was "necessary and urgent" to put an end to the accruing military commitment of the Americans to Saigon.¹⁴³ It might also lead to better relations between the two halves of Vietnam, a necessary prelude to peaceful unification.¹⁴⁴ "It is clearly on the diplomatic front that DRVN political leaders have chosen for the time being to deal with their differences with the South," French diplomats in Hanoi reported in March in light of recent DRVN endeavors. Above all, Hanoi sought to "present itself before the eyes of world opinion as embracing pacifism at all costs," and to that end had "gotten into gear" its entire propaganda machine.¹⁴⁵ It was also pressing the French government to accept a permanent DRVN representation in Paris, which it planned to use to rally the Franco-Vietnamese community against Saigon and foreign interference in Indochina.¹⁴⁶

PEACEFUL COEXISTENCE

In late February 1956 Soviet premier Nikita Khrushchev stunned the socialist camp during the Twentieth Congress of the Communist Party of the Soviet Union (CPSU) by denouncing Stalin, condemning his "crimes," and detailing the errors of the personality cult he had cultivated. Without previously consulting or even informing allies, Khrushchev also proffered on behalf of the CPSU, the Soviet Union, and the rest of the socialist camp a commitment to "peaceful coexistence" with the West. This concept had first been voiced at the Soviet-sponsored World Peace Council in 1949, then codified in a treaty between China and India in 1954, and eventually adopted by the movement of nonaligned states. In the future, Khrushchev announced, Moscow and other members of the socialist camp would forswear violent struggle against capitalism and its proponents in favor of constructive diplomatic engagement and economic competition, all with the aim of reducing Cold War tensions.

Khrushchev's pronouncements had serious implications for Vietnam. According to historian Galia Golan, from that moment Moscow operated "under Khrushchev's doctrinal tenet that local wars would inevitably escalate to global, nuclear proportions"; as a result, it opposed even more determinedly the resumption of hostilities in Indochina.¹⁴⁷ "As one of the nuclear superpowers," a western assessment noted, the Soviet Union "had the same interest as the United States in avoiding any disturbance of the lines which have been gradually built up between the Communist and Western powers" since 1954, especially in Vietnam.[148] To impress upon DRVN leaders the seriousness of its commitment to peaceful coexistence and the attenuation of Cold War tensions, Moscow sent deputy premier Anastas Mikoyan to Hanoi in early April.[149] Mikoyan informed his hosts that "they were always assured of the support of his government and of communist bloc countries," but they had to "demonstrate patience and prudence in the pursuit of their final objective" of national reunification under communist authority.[150]

The VWP Central Committee convened shortly after Mikoyan's visit to discuss the meaning for Vietnam of Moscow's turn to peaceful coexistence. Though Khrushchev's position validated Hanoi's current strategy, including the "North-first" policy, many who spoke at the plenum voiced dismay at the apparent meaning of peaceful coexistence both for the socialist world generally and for Vietnam and its reunification struggle specifically. These speakers interpreted Khrushchev's move as a unilateral concession to the United States that constrained the freedom of action of communist parties, threatened the unity of the socialist camp, and set back the prospects for world revolution and for their own effort to reunify Vietnam should peaceful reunification on their terms fail to materialize. As much as socialist countries loved peace, they reasoned, it was not always a viable option because of the implacable nature of capitalism and imperialism and of the structural forces that determined American Cold War policy. The enemies of socialism "have aggressive designs," the committee reported in summarizing the discussions. Thus revolutionary forces in Vietnam and elsewhere must always be prepared to meet any challenge by any means.[151] Unfortunately, henceforth the VWP and other communist parties would be unable to resort to military struggle to meet their revolutionary goals without running the risk of alienating Khrushchev and losing Soviet political and material support.[152]

According to Ho Chi Minh, Hanoi's current strategy did satisfy the tenets of peaceful coexistence. However, even he, a force behind the decision to suspend military struggle in favor of political struggle in the South after July 1954, recognized that disavowing war altogether was unsound and potentially dangerous. "We must always remember that the enemies of our people are the American imperialists and their puppets," and "they are preparing for war."[153] The refusal of Saigon and Washington to comply with the Geneva accords proved that blind faith in peaceful coexistence was problematic concerning the future of the Vietnamese revolution.[154] Ho acknowledged that military action in the South might be warranted if the Americans and their lackeys continued their campaign of oppression, but he pointedly failed to specify at what point that warrant should be implemented.[155] Other speakers at the plenum objected to Khrushchev's attack on Stalin, whom Vietnamese communists generally held in high regard despite his flaws and errors. The denunciation of Stalin's personality cult was especially galling, since it could be read as a criticism of the VWP's cult of Ho Chi Minh, whose image was practically everywhere in Hanoi and whose every major public utterance was treated as an article of revolutionary faith. Equally offending was the fact that Khrushchev had presented Hanoi with a fait accompli, scoffing at the congeniality supposed to govern relations among "fraternal" world communist parties.

Despite these criticisms and reservations, the plenum's final resolution endorsed the outcome of the CPSU's Twentieth Congress. To do otherwise would have been an unthinkable breach of socialist etiquette and could have compromised Soviet–DRVN relations as well as the unity of the socialist camp more broadly. For the same reasons, after the plenum, DRVN leaders publicly praised the correctness of the views espoused by Khrushchev. "The collapse of the Stalin myth," a western assessment of this plenum and its aftermath noted, "has not, on the surface at least, embarrassed the leaders nor given rise to any [public] criticism of the Kremlin's leadership." Interestingly, within days of the plenum's conclusion, a large portrait of Ho was removed from the façade of the municipal theater in Hanoi, where the National Assembly convened. DRVN authorities also ceased to make official pronouncements in the name of the VWP and the DRVN government in addition to "President Ho Chi Minh." Given the dependence on Moscow's political and material backing, French diplomats believed, Hanoi "cannot hesitate in conforming in all circumstances its attitude" to "Soviet theses," or in expressing its ideological loyalty to the Kremlin.[156] At a minimum, it had to pretend to be loyal.

In an address to the nation shortly after the plenum, Ho Chi Minh reiterated that "resolutely implementing the Geneva accords by peaceful means on the basis of the unification of the North and the South . . . of the fatherland" was the "sacred mission" of the Vietnamese people.[157] But there were limits as to how far Hanoi would go to mollify Moscow. Most notably, the party continued to give precedence to its own concerns in decision-making and to exploit the personal prestige of Ho Chi Minh, of his personality cult. This exaltation of the DRVN president was a part of North Vietnamese cultural reality, not just an act of propaganda. Ho's prestige was "far too great an asset" to dispense with for the VWP posing as "champio[n] of a united and independent Vietnam."[158] Ho remained "a benign hero and father figure to the masses," another assessment of this phenomenon noted. "He is an exemplar of the Vietnamese virtues—'*l'homme vietnamien réussi*' [the accomplished Vietnamese man]—in the fullest sense, and not merely a material one."[159]

THE DEATH OF THE GENEVA ACCORDS AND DEMOCRATIZATION IN THE NORTH

In July 1956, the deadline for the promised elections on Vietnamese reunification passed. That outcome satisfied the United States. Fearful of a communist victory in those elections and thus of "losing" Vietnam, even while insisting publicly that free elections were impossible in a totalitarian state such as the DRVN, Washington had never supported elections or even reunification, just as it had never failed to impress those views upon Diem and his government. "Neither the United States nor Free Vietnam," Senator John F. Kennedy, a prominent Democrat, had argued, "is ever going to be a party to an election obviously stacked and subverted in advance."[160] Reassuringly for Hanoi in light of their recent endorsement of peaceful coexistence, the Soviets were quick to excoriate Washington for this lapse of the Geneva accords.[161] The Eisenhower administration's expressed opposition to the elections and other aspects of the Geneva accords and its perceived leverage over Saigon have convinced many scholars that Washington was indeed responsible for the collapse of the accords. The decision, it is now clear, was made by Ngo Dinh Diem, who needed no American pressure or even advice to prevent the elections by refusing to arrange for them in the South.[162] Diem was certain the DRVN would never permit free choice or an honest count in elections so vital to its interests.[163] More significantly, he felt that he had worked too hard to consolidate his authority in the South to risk everything in elections in which his opponent would be Ho Chi Minh.[164] Indeed, considering Diem's personal characteristics, "the hope of unifying the nation by peaceful methods may never have been capable of achievement."[165]

This outcome was a "grave disappointment" for DRVN leaders, but it was hardly shocking in light of developments in the South. Only recently, Diem had further solidified his position by successfully staging another election, this one for a constituent assembly mandated to draft a constitution for the newly established RVN. He had also ordered the withdrawal of all remaining French forces from the South and the closure of the French High Command, the organ charged with carrying out France's obligations under the Geneva accords. Western observers took the latter action, effective on 28 April, to signal the "death" of the Geneva accords.[166] Still, Hanoi reacted to these events with surprising passiveness, suggesting that key leaders, such as Ho and Giap, still thought peaceful reunification was ideologically sound and realistically achievable, or else that armed struggle remained an impossible choice.

Instead of going to war in the South, in late July 1956 the North actually "entered a period of calm" during which its leaders concerned themselves almost exclusively with domestic, northern matters. There were new initiatives of political and social liberalization, a domestic "détente" characterized by relaxation of personal controls and travel restrictions, reduction of mandatory political meetings, release of political prisoners and others arbitrarily arrested, and "remarkable" extensions of free speech.[167] By November, the Council of Ministers and the National Assembly were jointly working on legislation to "guarantee democratic liberties and the individual rights of the population," return the northern population to a "freer" life, end much of the arbitrary authority exercised by party cadres, and "reject all errors committed owing to 'stalinism.'"[168]

Why did Hanoi respond so passively to the "killing" of the Geneva accords? Why did it not resume military struggle at that point, choosing instead to loosen its control in the DRVN? Beyond the litany of reasons previously discussed that militated against resumption of war, including the state of the armed forces, the wishes of allies, and the fear of American intervention, a main reason for those decisions was the general state of affairs in the North. Even if other circumstances had been more favorable, by mid-1956 DRVN authorities had too much on their plate at home to effectively support and sustain hostilities in the South. During Hanoi's Municipal Party Congress in July and August, "grumbles" about party policies on such issues as security restrictions and tax collection were widely and aggressively pressed. These episodes, combined with similar ones a month later during the Eighth National Congress of the CCP, which concluded with a call for greater measures of conciliation on the part of the party with the people of China, played a meaningful role in precluding Hanoi from resuming hostilities in the South and spurred détente in the DRVN.[169]

Most consequential, however, was the fallout from the bungled handling of land reform. The party had so poorly managed that program that it caused both widespread hardship and resentment throughout the North. It distributed land to some eight million previously landless or poor peasants but created almost universal discontent due to the arbitrary methods used by cadres to classify households and reallocate land.[170] Following party condemnation of the lack of zeal and forcefulness among cadres tasked with implementing the redistribution, many cadres had overreacted, manifesting "too much of the ruthlessness that was necessary and successful during the war" but which alienated people when applied indiscriminately in peacetime.[171] At Quynh Luu in crisis-prone Nghe An Province, the political alienation and economic dislocation occasioned by the land reform campaign precipitated a rebellion. The denouement of that episode was bloody enough to compound the more general problems facing DRVN leaders trying to accomplish other basic social changes. Many of the rebels at Quynh Luu were Catholics, and many of the PAVN troops sent to suppress them were embittered southern regroupees.[172] So serious were the problems caused by this and other, less serious crises provoked by the land redistribution program that Hanoi suspended it that summer, and Ho Chi Minh publicly apologized for its shortcomings.[173]

At its Tenth Plenum, which exceptionally lasted for forty days, in September and October, the VWP Central Committee confirmed the party's commitment to the "democratization" these aforementioned actions represented, to the "North-first" policy that they amounted to, and to the current strategy in the South.[174] "In our struggle to reunify the country, the consolidation of the North is the fundamental task," the committee decreed. A subsequent official communiqué repeated the line that the struggle for national reunification would be "long, difficult, complex." A British assessment noted that after the July 1956 deadline for elections passed, the party had not only failed to react but actually had "relegated the struggle for peaceful reunification to third place behind democratization and improving the conditions of workers, soldiers, cadres and functionaries" in the North.[175]

The Tenth Plenum convened specifically to address and find remedies to the disastrous consequences of land reform and their debilitating effects on party morale. Among the policy innovations included in what foreign observers variously called détente, democratization, or "de-Stalinization" were a special review of land reform, new limits on police powers, suspension of special courts for arbitrary trials, reinstatement of party members who had been punished for lack of enthusiasm in enforcing land reform, and disciplining of members guilty of committing grave errors as a result of too much enthusiasm for enforcing party reforms.[176] The massiveness of the land reform program's excesses is hinted at by the stature of the leading men who became casualties of this disciplining process. Chief among them was Truong Chinh, who had to resign his post as general secretary of the party. His closest associates, who, like him, had been zealous supporters of modeling Vietnam's land reform program after China's, were also demoted. They included Le Van Luong, who stepped down as both head of the powerful Party Organization Committee and vice minister of the interior; Hoang Quoc Viet, who lost his seat in the Politburo; and Ho Viet Thang, who was expelled from the Central Committee and compelled to give up his posts as vice minister of agriculture and vice chairman of the Land Reform Committee.[177]

Possibly, the four men were scapegoats sacrificed for the serious errors of the leadership and its agents during the land reform campaign, and possibly, too, for the decision to suspend military struggle and accept the Geneva accords.[178] Also, it is not improbable that the sacking of Truong Chinh, Luong, Viet, and Thang had to do with a tug-of-war among DRVN leaders pitting those who thought the party should move as slowly and cautiously in the North as it was in the South on the one hand, against their more doctrinaire comrades committed to the rapid socialist transformation of the North in accordance with orthodox Marxist-Leninist principles on the other. In May the British Consulate had speculated about the possible emergence of a cleavage dividing "ideologists" headed by Truong Chinh and unnamed "responsible ministers and administrators" led by Ho and Giap. "The former group might wish to press ahead with the 'revolution' [in the North] too fast for the taste of the latter, and, in the name of communist solidarity, might be willing to yield greater influence to China than nationalist sentiment would welcome," the consulate hypothesized.[179] During the Tenth Plenum, the Central Committee in fact condemned "leftist deviations"—that is, dogmatism, a perversion typically associated with Chinese radical communism.[180]

In the wake of the purges, Nguyen Duy Trinh, Le Thanh Nghi, Pham Hung, and Hoang Van Hoan were promoted to the Politburo, and Le Duc Tho replaced Le Van Luong as head of the Organization Committee.[181] Until a suitable candidate for the position could be found and vetted, Ho Chi Minh took over as acting general secretary. Overall, these outcomes boded well for VWP militants. Trinh, Hung, and Hoan were no fans of the current strategic line. Tho, Le Duan's former deputy in the South and most trusted ally in the party, had joined the Politburo after his repatriation to the North in 1955. As Organization Committee head, he would become instrumental in facilitating the appointment of like-minded individuals to the Central Committee and the Politburo, setting the stage for the hijacking of party decision-making by militants in 1963–64.[182] For the time being, however, Ho, Giap, and other supporters of strategic peace continued to hold sway over VWP policymaking.

In assessing the latest Central Committee plenum, French diplomats concluded quite correctly that the tendency toward détente in the North and caution in the South had not ceased.[183] Immediately following the reshuffling in the Politburo, northern society actually experienced its most "democratic" period. The new, more liberal atmosphere encouraged freedom of thought and expression in all realms, a consequential result of which was the appearance of two new periodicals, *Nhan van* (Humanities) and *Tham hoa* (Hundred Flowers, a title borrowed from the Chinese movement of the same name, which encouraged criticism of leftist deviations by CCP leaders and cadres). Both periodicals featured items critical of the DRVN leadership and calling for reformist change. To illustrate, in *Nhan van*, Tran Duc Thao, a university professor, denounced bureaucratism, cliques, and the personality cult in the North. Until the state withered away, Thao suggested, only individual liberty and the freedoms of press, speech, and association could ensure popular democracy.[184] "Following in the footsteps of Soviet and Eastern European revisionist thinkers," historian Peter Zinoman has written of this episode, Thao and other writers "contrasted the virtues of Leninism with the evils of Stalinism and advocated a fundamentalist return to the humanistic origins of Communist thought." This criticism of the VWP actually represented a "relatively mild manifestation of [a] global phenomenon."[185]

As in China, it was not long before the criticism proved too much for party leaders. Under the supervision of To Huu, a dogmatic, rising member of the Central Committee who oversaw ideological conformity in cultural affairs, DRVN authorities suppressed the offending periodicals and jailed their contributors.[186] Eventually, the Politburo reversed the entire democratization project. Possibly, the anticommunist revolt in Hungary in October and November influenced the about-face.[187] Whatever its origins, the reversal underscored the pitfalls of flexible and conciliatory—essentially, moderate—policymaking, and put all its adherents, including Ho and Giap, on notice.

LE DUAN AND SOUTHERNERS AGITATE

That Hanoi refused to modify its revolutionary strategy after the July 1956 deadline passed validated the rather cynical belief of many below the seventeenth parallel that the primary function of the war against the French had been to further the hidden agenda of northern-based revolutionaries. That is, its real purpose all along had been to bring about the liberation of northern Vietnam only, and the fighting in the South was never more than "diversionary mischief for the French."[188] Whether this was ever in fact the view of southern revolutionary leaders, many of them were "less than happy with the strategy thrust upon them by the Hanoi leadership" after 1954.[189] Few in the South were more disappointed and frustrated with Hanoi at this point than Le Duan.[190] Since joining the revolution, he had committed himself to national—not zonal, sectional, or partial—liberation. He also believed not only that violence constituted the most effective tool for combatting imperialism and its lackeys, but that the bloodshed it caused sanctified the revolutionary process. Thus the Politburo majority's decision to eschew armed struggle starting in July 1954 remained "inconceivable" to Le Duan, who had "made of the unity of the country" one of his reasons "to fight and to live."[191] He, in fact, drafted his own fourteen-point "action plan" outlining a forward strategy of revolutionary militancy to support political struggle in the South and produce national reunification without further delay. Other southern party leaders with whom he conferred and shared his plan endorsed it, but Hanoi rejected it.[192]

Undeterred, Le Duan privately challenged Hanoi's stance, telling other southern party leaders and members that "the enemy will not implement the Geneva Agreement," and that they should all prepare to "wrest back power through violence."[193] According to historian Lien-Hang Nguyen, this member of the Politburo actually flouted the party's strategic line by mobilizing troops in preparation for a resumption of hostilities. Though he never publicly denounced the party line, Le Duan "fanned the revolutionary flames" in the South to "force his reluctant comrades in the North to go to war" against Saigon, she writes.[194] Unless Hanoi acted decisively and soon, Le Duan thought, the communist movement in the South would vanish. Southerners had taken the struggle as far as they could under Hanoi's constraints. VWP membership in the South was now down to perhaps fifteen thousand and dwindling.[195]

A few weeks before the next Central Committee plenum, scheduled for December, Le Duan sent a missive to Hanoi entitled *De cuong cach mang mien Nam* (Directions of the Southern Revolution).[196] A revised version of his fourteen-point plan, the document proposed a reassessment of VWP strategy and a bold new course of action in the conduct of the revolution in the South. Its conclusions rested on Le Duan's analysis as well as the substance of recent discussions with other southern revolutionaries. His proposals had been vetted and revised at a conference of Nam Bo communist leaders in Phnom Penh before he submitted them to the party leadership.[197] Le Duan's main hope was to "nudg[e] his comrades [in the North] to do more to support the revolution below the seventeenth parallel."[198]

In his missive, Le Duan made the case for abandoning the party's current line and at once resuming armed struggle in the South, with comprehensive northern backing. Since he understood that key leaders in the North opposed this course of action, he worded his proposals carefully. He refrained from explicit denunciation of the passive response to Diem's violent assault on communists and noncommunist former members of the Viet Minh. Similarly, he did not attack Khrushchev's doctrine of peaceful coexistence, though he thought it deeply misguided and altogether unsuitable for Vietnam. Instead, Le Duan shared his thinking on revolutionary policy and the urgency of the situation in the South. "As long as the [global] capitalist economy survives, it will always scheme to provoke war, and there will still remain the danger of war," he wrote. In Vietnam, the Americans had schemed to partition the nation politically and were now prepared to maintain the status quo with violence. The "fundamental" problem facing the party was "how to smash the U.S.–Diem scheme of division and war-provocation." Economic competition, coexistence, and even negotiations were all well and good in certain settings, but none was viable in a situation in which the imperatives that drove the United States and Saigon defied the will of the South Vietnamese people. Those imperatives could not be accommodated without sacrificing the South and surrendering the aims of the revolution.

In view of those circumstances, Le Duan affirmed his position that there was "no other path" but armed struggle for the party and the people of the South. The "line of the revolutionary movement must be in accord with the inclinations and aspirations of the people. Only in that way can a revolutionary movement be mobilized and succeed." According to Le Duan, now was an "opportune moment" to unleash a wave of revolutionary violence because the Americans and their Saigon allies faced a window of vulnerability before the rising tide of U.S. military assistance became overwhelming. The "vile and brutal" character of the imperialists and their lackeys alienated southerners and isolated Washington internationally. Given the demonstrated willingness of the Vietnamese people properly led and inspired to fight, victory would not take long and the human and material costs would be tolerable. "Any revolutionary movement has times when it falls and times when it rises," he told Hanoi; "any revolutionary movement has times that are favorable for development and times that are unfavorable." The French had tried for years to eradicate the communist movement in Vietnam, he claimed, and failed. "It was not the Communists but the French imperialists themselves and their feudal lackeys who were destroyed on our soil." Now, the United States and its lackeys were trying to annihilate what was left of the revolutionary movement in the South. But communists could prevail again with a new strategy that incorporated a military component.

Le Duan's appeal struck a somewhat positive note in Hanoi. After lengthy deliberation, the Central Committee authorized southern communists to conduct targeted assassinations of "reactionary traitors" as well as terror bombings of institutions and locations associated with the Diem regime and the American presence.[199] That fell far short of what Le Duan wanted, leading Ang Cheng Guan to conclude that after December 1956 Hanoi's revolutionary strategy remained "essentially unchanged."[200] Still, the authorization to use violence, even on a very limited scale, represented a victory for Le Duan and other militants, as it constituted a tacit acknowledgment by Hanoi, the first of its kind, that political struggle alone was not working and armed struggle might be the answer to the party's challenges in the South.

2

Changing Course, 1957–1959

It did not take long for Soviet-American relations to improve after Premier Khrushchev professed his commitment to peaceful coexistence in early 1956. Within months, Moscow and Washington began cultural exchanges. The concomitant growing militarization of the Cold War and lingering differences over the fate of Germany challenged superpower détente but did not derail it. In fact, in 1959 U.S. vice president Richard Nixon visited Moscow, and shortly thereafter, Khrushchev himself reciprocated with a goodwill tour of the United States during which he engaged in constructive dialogue with Eisenhower.

Moscow's overtures to Washington contributed to the precipitous decline of Sino-Soviet relations in the late 1950s. Committed to the eradication of capitalism and to "continuous revolution" in China, Mao and other CCP leaders could not reconcile themselves to peaceful coexistence, which they viewed as a form of revisionism, a heresy that threatened to undermine the unity of the socialist camp. Beijing leaders also objected to Soviet proposals for joint military and other ventures, intended, they thought, to humiliate China and undermine its sovereignty. Moscow's decision of 1959 to withhold from Beijing prototypes and data for producing a nuclear bomb, thus reneging on an agreement signed two years earlier, plus a tense summit between Mao and Khrushchev in October, only widened the gap between the two countries.

Sino-Soviet contentions and peaceful coexistence expanded Washington's margin for action in Indochina. Impressed by Diem's ability to defeat his enemies and consolidate his authority in the RVN, the Eisenhower administration increased the level of its aid to the Saigon regime even as it pursued détente with Moscow.

In light of these circumstances, Hanoi began to contemplate revising its revolutionary strategy. Its reluctance to act more decisively in the South, in conjunction with emergent Sino-Soviet differences, exacerbated tensions between southern and northern supporters of the DRVN as well as between militants and moderates within the VWP. To alleviate these and other pressing problems, the Central Committee adopted Resolution 15 in January 1959. Calling for the beginning of a communist-led insurgency in the South, the resolution represented the first meaningful revision of the party's revolutionary strategy in nearly five years. Fearful of American direct intervention and concerned about the reaction of Moscow and Beijing, both of which continued to oppose resumption of war in Vietnam, the Politburo mandated that the insurgency be restrained, and to that end provided only limited northern support.

NEW AND OLD CHALLENGES

In January 1957, during a meeting of the United Nations (UN) Special Political Committee, the United States introduced a draft resolution calling for the admission of "Vietnam"—not worded as the RVN, though that was implied—to the UN. Without consulting Hanoi, Moscow countered with a proposal recommending simultaneous admission of "the Democratic Republic of Vietnam" and "South Vietnam" as sovereign states in their respective territories. The proposal infuriated and alarmed DRVN leaders. They had unsuccessfully applied for DRVN membership in the UN in November 1948 and again in December 1951 to enhance their government's legitimacy during the Indochina War. By now, however, they had no such aspiration, unless of course the DRVN was admitted as the sole legitimate government of all of Vietnam. This, they understood, the United States would never allow. Gaining admission along with the RVN, as the Soviets were now proposing, was also inconceivable, since the DRVN, like the RVN, claimed de jure sovereignty over all of Vietnam.[1]

The Soviet proposal caused consternation in Hanoi not only because it contravened a core principle—that the DRVN was the only legitimate government in Vietnam—but also because it suggested that Moscow, the leader of the socialist camp and its most important ally, was willing to accept the permanent division of the country. Concerned about that prospect and fearful that others, including nonaligned and socialist states, might endorse the call for UN membership for both Vietnams, DRVN leaders suddenly became nervous, no longer certain that time was on their side.

Thereafter, Hanoi's foreign policy focused more self-consciously on reaffirming its loyalty to the socialist camp, the Third World, and national liberation movements, seeking thereby to enhance the legitimacy and prestige of the DRVN internationally, including among the nonaligned states, and continuing to advocate the reunification of Vietnam under the terms of the Geneva accords.² At the time, the DRVN had formal diplomatic relations only with members or close friends of the socialist camp, some of which had no representation in Hanoi. Britain and India each had a consulate general in Hanoi and France a general delegation, but none of them officially recognized the DRVN government.³ Starting in 1957, Hanoi sought to establish ties with other countries, including newly decolonized states in Asia and Africa.

DRVN leaders faced other serious challenges that year. Domestically, they confronted recurring waves of social and economic problems: food and housing shortages, rising inflation, and industrial unrest resulting from constant pressure on the part of government authorities for increased production.⁴ "There is little optimism that the economy of North Vietnam can be expected to develop quickly in the foreseeable future," a Canadian diplomat reported, following a visit to the DRVN, since "the [economic] plans formulated by the North Vietnamese, in collaboration with the foreign advisers, have neglected the present in favour of the future." The good news for Hanoi was that "there is little point in speaking of the possibilities of an economic collapse of North Vietnam," the diplomat derisively concluded, "since there is no economic structure to collapse in the first place."⁵

Then, too, there were lingering problems from the botched land reform program. The party reclassified more than half the households it had recently labeled "landlord" and punished accordingly, relabeling them "peasant" and withdrawing the punishment, when possible.⁶ It also re-educated cadres responsible for these and other "errors."⁷ According to a series of articles in *Hoc tap*, the party's theoretical journal, the re-education program was necessary to deal with doubts, confusion, and lack of solidarity among cadres.⁸ At the same time, in the newly formed northwestern Thai-Meo Autonomous Zone, disaffected local cadres joined disgruntled members of the Hmong, Dao, and Khu Mu minority groups to instigate an "armed loyalist movement" against what they saw as an "unjust" local regime. This only compounded the challenges facing Hanoi.⁹

Meanwhile, Diem continued to strengthen his rule in the South. In May he made a triumphant visit to the United States, where he was hailed as the "Miracle Man" of Asia and received assurances of continued American economic and military aid.¹⁰ As a result of the visit, in the words of Fredrik Logevall, the American commitment to South Vietnam was "personalized in a way it never was before," partly because of the "fawning" press coverage Diem received.¹¹ These developments coincided with the "darkest days" of the revolution in the South, as Diem's military and security forces successfully intensified their efforts to kill or capture communists.¹²

SUSTAINED CAUTION

Confronted with these challenges, Hanoi maintained a cautious stance vis-à-vis the South. Key leaders seemed "reconciled for the time being to the de facto division of the country."[13] In the name of peaceful struggle, Hanoi continued to press Saigon for improving relations, to call on Diem to agree to consultative talks on national elections, and to play the role of irritant when Diem refused. Recognizing that the DRVN might have to eventually intervene directly below the seventeenth parallel, Hanoi introduced compulsory military service, experimentally in one province in August and nationally by the end of the year.[14] In what would prove to be a fateful decision, DRVN leaders also called Le Duan to Hanoi and appointed him acting general secretary of the party.[15] Portending a possible revision of the VWP's revolutionary strategy, the move may have been engineered by moderates to appease disgruntled southern revolutionaries, including Le Duan himself, or to undermine southern militancy by relocating its loudest voice to the North.

As Hanoi began to prepare for a war it did not want, southern revolutionary leaders braced for the more active struggle they craved. The Interzone V Executive Committee instructed cadres under its command to "develop the ability to wage war" even as they sustained the political struggle for the time being. In response to continued attacks by forces of the Diem regime, revolutionaries in central and southwestern South Vietnam began to form armed units starting in October 1957.[16] By the end of the year, there were thirty-seven such units, and by mid-1958 they had engaged in a number of limited "actions" against RVN forces, with some success. Whether Hanoi authorized any of this is unknown. More likely than not, it did, though Lien-Hang Nguyen has suggested otherwise.[17]

Having recently obtained sanction from the Central Committee to eliminate "traitors," over the course of 1957, southern revolutionaries murdered, kidnapped, or enticed into their ranks 452 RVN officials, most of them village chiefs.[18] Meanwhile, encouraging news came from the Soviet Union: at a meeting of world communist parties in Moscow in November, the CPSU acknowledged under pressure from the Chinese that under certain circumstances episodes of world revolution— that is, transitions from nonsocialist to socialist polities and societies—might not always be peaceful. However, in the final declaration of the meeting in which that acknowledgment was made, the language on permissible forms of "nonpeaceful" struggle was vague to the point of opaqueness. And even that came at the cost of "acute conflict" between Beijing and Moscow over just what kinds of transition to socialism were and were not possible.[19]

As 1957 gave way to 1958, Hanoi continued its diplomatic advances toward Diem's regime, hoping to salvage what it could of the Geneva accords. During a visit to Burma in February, Ho Chi Minh repeated the DRVN's willingness to participate in talks with Saigon to discuss reunification elections.[20] Subsequently, via various cultural organs, DRVN authorities invited southern painters to exhibit their works in Hanoi, asked southern intellectuals to speak out publicly in support of reunification, proposed that an "all-Vietnamese" national education curriculum be adopted in both halves of the country, and suggested again that the postal services of the two Vietnams cooperate to permit the circulation of personal mail throughout the divided country.[21] Most notably, on 7 March Pham Van Dong wrote to Ngo Dinh Diem proposing a meeting of "the competent authorities of the two zones" to discuss bilateral reductions of armed forces and resumption of commercial exchanges.[22] Predictably, Dong's proposal elicited no response, but even that served the purposes of the political struggle, which may well have been the intent all along. According to the French Embassy in Saigon, southerners "closely followed" the affair of Dong's proposal, and "seem[ed] disappointed by the negativity manifest in the intransigence of the response of their Government."[23]

Consistent with the "North-first" policy, the National Assembly focused almost entirely on domestic matters during its spring 1958 session.[24] Meeting later that year, the Central Committee paid no heed to the situation in the South, addressing instead economic conditions in the North. The land reform campaign, it affirmed, had been an overall success "despite some errors."[25] Most importantly, it adopted a three-year plan (1958–60) for economic nationalization and modernization, including collectivization in agriculture. A year earlier, the committee had announced that for the first time overall production levels had exceeded those for 1939, the last year of peace, and the country was ready to move toward socialist transformation. The new three-year plan was intended to do just that.[26] This initiative coincided, not unintentionally, with China's Great Leap Forward.[27] "The China of today is the Vietnam of tomorrow," Hanoi officials proclaimed.[28] Collectivization was to be the final stage in the socialist transformation of the North Vietnamese countryside.[29] The three-year plan reaffirmed—and extended—Hanoi's commitment to the "North-first" policy and to moderation in the South.

As they collectivized the countryside, DRVN authorities sought to revamp the urban and industrial sectors of the economy along similar lines. The industrial sector was still notably underdeveloped, a result not only of French calculations during the colonial era but of the subsequent wars against Japan and France. Factories had been damaged, destroyed, or gutted, and those still operating were largely privately owned. Handicraft production still accounted for 59 percent of total nonagricultural production, much too large a share for a would-be modern economy in a self-professed socialist state.[30] That began to change as the DRVN expropriated private enterprises and began to build new ones of its own. In 1958, state-owned and -operated enterprises accounted for nearly half of all manufacturing, and the government was in the process of acquiring substantial control of retail trade and transportation.[31] Because of a shortage of investment capital and technical and managerial expertise, Hanoi allowed some bourgeois capitalists to retain control of their enterprises and encouraged others to develop new ones. Such actions were consistent with Lenin's endorsement of collaboration with capitalists where necessary to facilitate development and modernization of the industrial sector. Later that year, chairman of the State Planning Commission Nguyen

Duy Trinh told the National Assembly that the socialist transformation of the economy, to be completed by the end of 1960, must be assiduously pursued because it would solve the food problem and improve "the people's life" in the North.[32]

THE ONSET OF THE SINO-SOVIET DISPUTE

In October 1957, the Soviet Union successfully launched the *Sputnik* satellite into space. That plus Soviet claims of missile superiority over the United States a month later validated the very real concerns of the Eisenhower administration about a growing missile gap between the two superpowers. The second Berlin crisis of 1958 further hampered bilateral relations. Yet, in spite of these developments, Moscow remained committed to peaceful coexistence, and Soviet-American relations improved over time. The Soviet Union manifested its commitment to peaceful coexistence by offering to host the American National Exhibition in Moscow and Vice President Nixon in 1959, and even agreed to a visit to the United States by Premier Khrushchev.

Meanwhile, Beijing's domestic and foreign policy underwent a process of radicalization, largely the product of Mao's commitment to "continuous revolution," to pushing the Chinese revolution forward through successive mass mobilization campaigns. In 1958, Mao and the CCP launched the Great Leap Forward, an ambitious program of accelerated industrialization and communization. In August, they provoked the second Taiwan Strait crisis by resuming sustained bombardment of islands controlled by the Nationalist Chinese regime of Jiang Jieshi in Taipei.

China's "left" turn as the Soviet Union continued steering "right" strained relations between the two countries. Increasingly by this time, Mao openly objected to the Soviet foreign policy course set by Khrushchev. In April 1958, Moscow approached Beijing with a proposal to construct a long-wave radio transmission center and receiving station on Hainan Island to facilitate Soviet naval communications. Shortly thereafter it made another proposal, this one for setting up a joint submarine flotilla. Both proposals offended Mao, who thought they were part of a larger Soviet plan to gain more influence in the PRC, even to control it. According to historian Chen Jian, Mao's reaction was likely conditioned by "China's humiliating modern experiences," which encouraged Chinese leaders to "suspect the behavior of any foreign country as being driven by ulterior, or even evil, intentions."[33] Beijing soon accused Moscow of practicing "big-power chauvinism" and began taking its distance. The rift between the two became public for the first time shortly thereafter. When the PRC and India began to clash over their border, a conflict that intensified after Delhi granted asylum to the Dalai Lama, Moscow refused to side with Beijing in the dispute. For Mao and the CCP, the refusal was tantamount to supporting Delhi and betraying an ally.

The Sino-Soviet dispute was potentially devastating for the future of the Vietnamese revolution. Over the years, Hanoi had established proven, intimate ties with both countries. Each had supported its revolution politically and materially, helping to deter Washington from intervening militarily in Vietnam. The dispute between Moscow and Beijing was thus dismaying and dangerous. It was dismaying because Hanoi could find no obvious way to deal with the problem to its entire advantage, and because it threatened to compromise the world revolution and the special role DRVN leaders already envisioned for themselves in that revolution. It was dangerous because there might come a time when Hanoi would have to choose between its ideological and material benefactors—to pick a side in their dispute and thus risk vital losses.

As VWP members lamented the deterioration of Sino-Soviet relations, they also developed an affinity with either Moscow or Beijing. Party leaders did their best to preclude this taking of sides, since it risked undermining the unity of their organization, but even they succumbed. Militants, including Le Duan, who had been deeply disturbed by Khrushchev's call for peaceful coexistence, were quick to side with China, whose boldness they respected and even came to admire. After all, boldness was what they thought the leadership in Hanoi needed to show more of if Vietnam was ever going to be reunified. Moreover, militants considered China's recent historical experience more relevant than the Soviet Union's to Vietnam's present circumstances and their own purposes. They felt an "automatic identification" with China because it remained engaged in some of the same tasks confronting the Vietnamese, including completion of national liberation and reunification. Indeed, American support of rival governments on Chinese and Vietnamese soil drew together Vietnamese militants and Chinese hard-liners, and made both implacably hostile to the United States.[34] Vietnamese militants also remembered that during the recent war with France the DRVN had received far less assistance from the Soviet Union than from the PRC.[35]

Ho, Giap, and other moderates, on the other hand, tended to be more supportive of the Soviet Union. Despite their reservations, the policy of peaceful coexistence vindicated the current revolutionary line in both halves of Vietnam for which they were responsible. Like Moscow, they embraced moderation and flexibility in decision-making, had no desire to be involved in a major confrontation with the United States, and preferred to concentrate instead on strengthening the domestic economy. Moreover, leading moderates had a fondness for the Soviet Union, having studied or spent time there or otherwise admiring the accomplishments of the country, its leaders, and its people since the October Revolution. To them, the Soviets were the undisputed champions of the socialist cause. "At least sentimentally," moderates were "apt to be partial to the Soviet Union."[36] Conversely, the "Chinese element" appeared to most of them to "essentially be an element of instability, turmoil, even adventure."[37]

The Sino-Soviet dispute thus amplified cleavages within the VWP between militants and moderates, between advocates of armed struggle in the South and exponents of peaceful reunification and the "North-first" policy. Over time militants identified more closely with "radicals" in Beijing, as moderates did with "pacifists" in Moscow. As these tendencies continued and polarized the party, its militant wing became identified as "pro-Chinese" and the moderate wing as "pro-Soviet," although neither actually answered to foreign patrons.

THE CENTRAL COMMITTEE'S FIFTEENTH PLENUM

In January 1959, the VWP Central Committee met to "discuss the situation inside the country since the signing of the Geneva accords of 1954 and bring forward the revolutionary line for the entire country and the southern revolution."[38] To get a clear picture of the state of affairs in the South, the committee invited leading southern revolutionaries to describe the situation there and recommend policies for dealing with it. Those invited included Phan Van Dang, Hai Xo, Tran Luong, and Vo Chi Cong, all regional party heads. Le Duan, who had been shuttling between North and South since his appointment as acting general secretary of the party, also addressed the committee on what he called the "real situation and the struggle experiences of the southern compatriots over the last several years." Predictably, he presented a bleak picture. In addition to reiterating the substance of what he had reported to the Central Committee in December 1956, he now more urgently pressed the case for complementing political struggle with military struggle in the South. He movingly described the growing despair among revolutionaries there over the losses they had endured and the deteriorating conditions they faced. There was an urgent necessity, he insisted, to respond in kind to the mounting aggressiveness of Saigon's military and security forces, emboldened by increasing American aid and their successes over a virtually impotent communist resistance. It was time for communist and allied forces to fight back, or the cause of the revolution in the South would be lost.[39] Already, rogue, unsanctioned cadres were joining other dissidents in retaliatory violence, while other disaffected cadres had abandoned the party to protest its pusillanimity in responding to Diem's outrages. The widening credibility gap between Hanoi and the southern militants was threatening to compromise the party's integrity and the revolution itself. Hanoi had to respond radically, Le Duan insisted, and to do so before it was too late.[40]

The effectiveness of Le Duan's testimony and that of the other southern leaders, who echoed his sentiments, was electric. Politburo spokesmen acknowledged that organ's similar concerns over the growing successes of the Diem regime in the wake of increasing American assistance.[41] The regime's success was now much greater than Hanoi had anticipated it ever would be. "In the provinces and the districts," the Politburo reported to the Central Committee, Diem's regime had "increased the reactionary quality of the [political and security] organs" at its disposal. At every level in these organs, "the majority of old bureaucrats [are being] replaced by new people, some chosen from among local Catholic reactionaries, among [recent] immigrants [from the North], some from the armed forces, the police, and some were old government employees who had submitted to Diem." Even at the village level, Diem was "consolidating organs . . . more than before." The "U.S.-Diem clique" was thus now on the verge of "achieving a dictatorial fascist regime," the "most fundamental policy" of which was annihilation of all resistance, including the communist movement, in the South in the furtherance of American "imperialist" objectives.

The growing capabilities of Diem's military, the Army of the Republic of Vietnam (ARVN), were an alarming and immediate threat. His armed forces were significantly better trained, led, and equipped than before. The resulting effectiveness enabled them to "terrorize" revolutionaries and civilians alike. According to Politburo calculations, Washington had provided Saigon with more than $965 million in assistance between 1955 and 1958, two-thirds of it military. That assistance financed the significant increases in the strength of Diem's forces, which the Politburo estimated in 1959 at 150,000 regular and more than 50,000 irregular troops. All indications were that Washington intended to maintain or increase its present level of support, which meant that Saigon's armed forces would continue improving in quality and growing in size.

Economically, revolutionary prospects in the South were similarly parlous. By now the Americans had entirely supplanted the French there, the Politburo felt, because of their greater economic might: "The American imperialists have more money than the French, can pay more" and thus "buy" more allegiance. Those thus "bought" in turn became "the hand puppets of the Americans." This sustained an increasingly large "reactionary" class that would surely hinder the transition to socialism in the South following reunification, as would the growing "commercialization" of the southern economy. Only "a small part of [American] foreign aid has been in the form of foreign currency, while the large part . . . has taken the form of goods." That ratio would likely change, the Politburo believed, for Washington's goal was to make the South Vietnamese people not only militarily but also economically dependent on the United States. As this transformation progressed, the South would become an outpost of American capitalism as well as American imperialism. The more the economy integrated into global capitalism, the wider the divide between northern and southern societies would become, and the more difficult reunification would be. The American project in the South amounted to "nation-building" and would have to be confronted as such.

In view of this gloomy assessment, the Politburo candidly acknowledged that the results of its policy of favoring political struggle almost exclusively had indeed been misguided: "We used the political strength of the masses; the enemy used force." Unfortunately, "our political strength has not yet been able to translate into material strength [sufficient even] to fight back," much less to "topple" the Saigon regime. As a result, the "U.S.-Diem clique" had not only endured but now occupied a "dominant position" in the South. The Americans were "richer," "more ruthless," "more fascist," "more expansionist," and "stronger" than the French had ever been. The contradictions between "our people" and the "imperialists and feudalists" could only be "solved by revolution." To that end, the nation had to "increase its unity" and "elevate even more its revolutionary will" for the sake of "socialist revolution" in the North and consolidation of the "people's democratic revolution" in the South.

RESOLUTION 15

In response to these assessments and recommendations, the Central Committee adopted what came to be known as "Resolution 15."[42] This was one of the pivotal policy statements in the course of events that propelled Hanoi into the Vietnam War, the most meaningful revision of strategic policy since September 1954. The new resolution reiterated the priority of socialist transformation in the DRVN, remarking that "if we do not strive to consolidate the North and actively guide the North to socialism, then we will not have a firm base" to bring about Vietnamese reunification. But more significant for the eventual outbreak of hostilities was the acknowledgment in the same document that the conduct of the struggle in the South had been too restrained. "Resolving the problem of 'who defeats whom' between socialism and capitalism," it read, "is the objective requirement of northern society in its phase of development; at the same time, it is also the objective reality of the revolution in the entire country."

In its tone and substance, Resolution 15 called for more aggressive action against capitalism and feudalism below the seventeenth parallel. "Only the victory of the revolution can fully end the plight of the poor and miserable people in the South, thoroughly defeat each wicked policy of the American imperialists and their puppets to divide and provoke war," it noted. Conduct of the revolution below the seventeenth parallel "cannot deviate from the general revolutionary law" guiding liberation struggles everywhere. "The basic road to development" of the revolution there must be "insurrection," the Central Committee asserted. While the revolution would continue to use the "strength" and "political force" of the masses, henceforth it would also rely on "armed force" to protect itself and create favorable conditions to "topple the dominant regime of the imperialists and feudalists" and "bring about a revolutionary regime of the people." However, the wording of the resolution was careful enough to give cover to the concerns of Ho, Giap, and other leading moderates in the party, as well as to those of Moscow and Beijing: political struggle in the South would remain "primordial."

In authorizing armed insurrection, the Central Committee promised the formation of a "truly broad" "people's front for reunification and opposition to Diem and the Americans." The new front would include workers and peasants, of course, but also "representatives of all classes and segments" of the southern population, even including bourgeois "nationalist forces," in order to form "a wide democratic people's alliance" of everyone opposing Diem and the Americans: "We must unite all people who can be united." To facilitate recruitment, the new front would be an organization of southerners only, "only for the southern region." Only after a bourgeois revolution in the South—that is, after destruction of the Saigon regime, creation of a provisional coalition government, and expulsion of the Americans—would the party launch class struggle there as part of a socialist revolution. Until these intermediate goals were achieved, it was important to downplay divisions among the people. The united front would facilitate this by, among other things, making the party and its southern supporters appear to be nationalist patriots rather than communist ideologues. In effect, the Central Committee proposed to resurrect the Viet Minh under a different, southern guise.

By party reckoning, there were in the South no less than eleven socioeconomic classes that had significance for the prospects of the new front and thus for the eventual success of the revolution. Such a class division of society defied Marxist-Leninist orthodoxy but was consistent with Chinese revolutionary understandings of class divisions as reflecting political attitudes rather than relations of production.[43] The most important class by this criterion was the urban proletariat, which must be the "guiding force of the Revolution in the South" despite its minuscule size. Only by infiltrating and then dominating workers' groups in the cities could the front achieve its political objectives, especially in Saigon. Peasants, the rural proletariat, constituted the second most important class in party calculation because of their sheer numbers. The front aimed to organize and then co-opt a peasant protest movement by joining it to existing anti-Diem movements in the countryside protesting high taxes, high rents, and other oppressive practices. Yet, however numerous the peasants were and however significant their role in the southern economy, it was essential for revolutionary purposes that they be under the leadership of workers and worker representatives committed to Marxist-Leninist principles. "Without a stable alliance between the peasants and the workers under the leadership of the working class," the Central Committee pointed out, "the southern revolution cannot succeed."[44]

Other classes in South Vietnam would likely provide less support for the new front, but their members would be encouraged to join it nonetheless. These included the petty bourgeoisie (small capitalists who received no benefit from imperialism), intellectuals, and most religious and ethnic minorities. Catholics, many of them co-opted by the enemy as "support rear troops," would likely provide little support, but members of Hoa Hao, Cao Dai, and Buddhist groups disaffected in varying degrees from the Diem regime by concerns of their own were promising.[45] Among the remaining classes, the "national bourgeoisie," so called because of its opposition to the American presence, might support front appeals for peace and expulsion of the Americans. The same might be true of privates in the ARVN, who bore the brunt of the fighting burden on behalf of the Americans. They were almost invariably the sons of peasants (sometimes of workers), and rarely received the least reward or recognition for their sacrifice. Recent migrants with lingering loyalties to their northern homeland might also support reunification. The "compradore," or high bourgeoisie, and the landlords were the least likely to participate in the front since they benefited from the American presence and thus actively opposed the revolution. While the party could not know with absolute certainty who would or would not support the front, the Central Committee thought the "motive force" of the southern revolution would come from workers, peasants, and the petty bourgeoisie.[46] A "general uprising" of these groups was impending, party leaders thought, not so much because of their nationalist resentment of the American presence but because the logic of Marxism-Leninism dictated that once their consciousness was raised concerning the exploitive nature of their "objective" circumstances, workers and peasants in particular would naturally rise against those responsible for their exploitation.

THE LOGIC BEHIND RESOLUTION 15

The Central Committee endorsed Resolution 15 because the majority of its members concluded that the "balance of forces"—the barometer by which DRVN authorities measured progress in their revolution, consisting of the number and condition of military effectives under their command relative to those of the enemy—in the South had reached a crisis point. In some areas, revolutionary forces faced imminent eradication, allowing the Diem regime to assert its authority unopposed and claim legitimacy. In observing the shift in party policy resulting from these conclusions, western diplomats in Hanoi reported "increasing sensitiveness on the part of the DRV leadership to the international status of South Vietnam and the stability of the regime there" during the first half of 1959.[47] Unless Hanoi acted, and soon, the communist movement in the South risked disappearing, as militants there had been warning.

Militants had by 1959 long clamored for a more assertive and aggressive strategy, and their aggregate pressures on Hanoi had much to do with the Central Committee's decision to endorse Resolution 15. By now, they were joined by noncommunist veterans of the Indochina War and other nationalists and xenophobes. "Faced with the fact that the enemy was using guns, assassinations and imprisonment to oppose the people in their political struggle," an official history of the southern revolutionary movement remarks of this factor, "many voices among the masses appealed to the party to establish a program of armed resistance against the enemy."[48] A group of peasants from Hoa Hoi, in Tay Ninh Province outside Saigon, signed their names to a letter imploring Ho Chi Minh to help them. "The people are terrorized," "cadres get killed," they lamented. They implored Hanoi at the least to send back the troops who had regrouped to the North after 1954, so they could "fight the enemy and save the people."[49] Elsewhere, a meeting of village elders adopted this compelling plea: "Uncle Ho! The Americans and Diem have been wicked too much already—we ask your permission to cut off their heads."

In Thu Dau, a group of thirty peasants asked local party officials, "Has the [Nam Bo] Executive Committee reported on [our] situation to the Center [i.e., Hanoi], to Uncle Ho?" The officials forwarded this plea with one of their own urging a renewal of military struggle. Without that, they insisted, it was "impossible to win." Besides, they wrote, fighting was the "birthright of the South Vietnamese people."[50] Similarly, villagers from Ben Tre importuned: "We must arm ourselves in order to survive; otherwise we'll die." "The Americans and Diem tore up the Geneva accords long ago. . . . If we go on like this, they'll burn down our houses and will kill us one of these days. We won't have anything with which to fight back and it will be unbearable."[51] Implicit in some of these pleas was the belief, noted earlier, that Hanoi cared more about building socialism in the North than confronting Diem in the South and protecting the people from him, that narrow northern interests trumped pressing southern needs among DRVN leaders.[52] The Central Committee indirectly acknowledged its awareness of such implications in Resolution 15, a stated objective of which was to eliminate the perception among some people that the party believed "the socialist revolution in northern Vietnam is exclusively for northern Vietnamese" without regard to the well-being of southerners.[53]

According to one analyst of these developments, pressure from militant and other discontented southerners gave Hanoi no choice but to "go along" with their pleas to do something about the deteriorating situation.[54] That is also the judgment of historian Philippe Devillers, who wrote of the adoption of Resolution 15 that the "initiative of action came, not from Hanoi, but from the base, literally compelled by Diem to legitimate defense and to armed resistance."[55] In a memoir, Nguyen Thi Dinh, a party cadre in the South in 1959, stated that she and her fellow revolutionaries took the passage of Resolution 15 to mean that "the higher level [in Hanoi] had followed exactly the aspirations of the lower level [in the South] in an extraordinary manner."[56] "Insurrectionary activity against the Saigon government," according to a less nuanced view, "began in the South under southern leadership not as a consequence of any dictate from Hanoi, but contrary to Hanoi's injunctions."[57] At a minimum, Resolution 15 was a concession by DRVN leaders to appease party militants and their sympathizers below the seventeenth parallel.

While southern pressure was instrumental in prompting the Central Committee to approve Resolution 15, calls for revision of southern strategy from party members in the North were also likely weighty influences. Circumstantial evidence suggests that by 1959 there existed within the party in the North a growing number of individuals who frowned upon the privileging of political struggle and believed in "the transforming power of violent revolution."[58] Le Duan's presence in Hanoi undoubtedly played a part in this, as did the presence of Nguyen Chi Thanh, Le Duc Tho, and other hard-liners recently returned from the South. The Central Committee recognized the existence of this minority and was evidently sensitive to its charges that Hanoi refused to sanction armed struggle in the South because it was afraid of the reaction of the Americans and their Saigon "puppets." In the lexicon of the day, the militants believed the party leadership was subordinating itself to "revisionist" Soviet thinking at the expense of Marxist-Leninist orthodoxies concerning wars of national liberation and world revolution.[59] An official history of the party indirectly acknowledges this belief and insinuates that the adoption of Resolution 15 was a response to critics with "deviationist inclinations" within the VWP in the North.[60] The British Consulate thought it was not "unreasonable" to attribute the Central Committee's approval of Resolution 15 to pressure from northern militants who were "tiring" of the moderate strategy the party had pursued even after "it became plain (in 1956) that the South would not fall to them through elections."[61]

The alleged mass murder by food poisoning of perhaps a thousand political dissidents, including communists, at a detention camp at Phu Loi, on the outskirts of Saigon, added to the pressure on Hanoi for increased militancy in the South.[62] This event, which occurred on 1 December 1958 but was not announced in the DRVN until 18 January 1959, provoked "the most violent anti-Diemist, anti-American campaign ever mounted" in the North. For a week, "the streets of Hanoi resounded to cries of 'Down with the American-Diemists' and 'Americans Go Home'" while "well-organized companies of citizens were paraded up and down." The mass protest ended on 25 January in "a day of mourning and mass meetings," for which more than half the people of Hanoi were mobilized. State organs exploited the occasion and the protests for various purposes. After news of the murders broke, for example, the secretary of the Government Workers' Trade Union urged unionists to "avenge the murdered by outstanding achievements, by overfulfilling the Three-Year Plan, by taking the North toward socialism and by building it into an unshakable base of the struggle for national reunification."[63] The "Phu Loi massacre" and its aftermath may well have been decisive in prompting the Central Committee to authorize armed struggle below the seventeenth parallel.[64] The massacre not only galvanized northern opinion concerning the need to do more for southerners, but it also emboldened militants in both halves of Vietnam to press DRVN leaders to take a bold step to placate their critics. Whatever actually happened at the detention camp, according to an official history of the southern revolution, after the Phu Loi massacre "the situation truly ripened for an armed movement against the enemy."[65]

Deterioration of the situation in the Central Highlands, an area of strategic importance to the southern revolution, may also have been a factor behind the Central Committee's decision to sanction armed struggle. In March 1959, two months after the passage of Resolution 15, the Politburo expressed concern that the "crisis" in the Central Highlands could spread. Accordingly, the Politburo directed southern revolutionaries to reverse the recent gains of ARVN forces in the region and hold their position until they secured revolutionary bases there.[66] The document relating this information reveals that the enemy's gains in the Central Highlands alarmed Hanoi, and it suggests that another immediate concern behind the adoption of Resolution 15 was this portentous demonstration of Diem's ability to project his power into an area of critical importance to the revolution and to the DRVN specifically.

Another incentive for adopting a more forward strategy in the South was, possibly, the second Taiwan Strait crisis. In August of the previous year, Beijing had resumed sustained bombardment of the Jinmen (Quemoy) Islands, controlled by the rival Nationalist regime in Taiwan, raising Cold War tensions in the region. Truong Chinh, partially rehabilitated by then and serving as vice premier, promptly condemned "provocative acts" by the United States that he said caused the crisis, and expressed his government's support for the "resolute action" undertaken by Beijing. Pham Van Dong also announced that the leaders and people of the DRVN would "stand at the side" of the Chinese in the event the situation escalated, while Ho Chi Minh and other DRVN leaders expressed their support for the "liberation" of Taiwan from the clutches of American "imperialists" and Chinese "reactionaries."[67] In Hanoi, this episode plus the concurrent second Berlin crisis, resulting from Khrushchev's demand that western powers withdraw from that city, underscored the perils of prolonged national partition. It thus may have impressed upon the Central Committee the merits of, if not the necessity for, more "resolute action" in dealing with counterrevolutionary forces in southern Vietnam.

Finally, the Central Committee may have feared that the party would suffer a crisis of legitimacy if it failed to recommend more forceful action below the seventeenth parallel. By 1959, new mass-based fronts and organizations independent of the VWP were emerging across the South, some of them aspiring to organize and lead the "national" opposition to Diem and the Americans. Among these were the religious sects, which attracted to their militias party sympathizers and members, even cadres, as well as workers, students, and others from "progressive" classes.[68] Unless Hanoi acted, such organizations might hijack the anti-Diem resistance the VWP aspired to lead. In the estimate of one historian, by 1959 "various parareligious sects" and nationalist organizations were also vying to lead the resistance movement in the South. "Exasperated by the dictatorship of the ruling [Ngo] family," some people "began to see that only the nationalists were willing to take a stand, while Communists and leftists, who had formerly been leaders in the struggle against colonization, were now temporizing."[69] According to historian Ang Cheng Guan, Hanoi adopted Resolution 15 because it "understood that it could no longer continue to advocate restraint without losing the control and allegiance of the Southern communists as well as the reunification struggle to Diem."[70]

POLITBURO RESERVATIONS ABOUT RESOLUTION 15

Unsure of the impact implementation of Resolution 15 would have domestically and internationally, the Politburo delayed spelling out the tactical details for its execution. As an official source put it, Resolution 15 considered the "responsibilities and strategic aims of the South Vietnam revolution," but it failed to explain how to achieve these responsibilities and aims. Though it outlined some of these elements, the details were "not sufficient" to "formulate a precise program."[71] While the Politburo and the Secretariat worked out those details, the latter instructed regional party heads to reveal news of the adoption of Resolution 15 to no one except cadres with executive responsibilities.[72]

The operational guidelines to implement the resolution took no less than four months to finalize and were communicated to southern communist leaders by the Secretariat only on 7 May 1959. As it turned out, the guidelines were significantly more subdued than what Resolution 15 itself called for. They stipulated that southerners could now "use a quick-minded method of armed propaganda" to "help the political struggle." In practice, that tortured language authorized escalation of the campaign to assassinate "the most dishonest and cruel part of the enemy" that was already under way and to conduct intermittent, small-scale guerrilla operations against ARVN forces.[73] Thus news of the "historic resolution" adopted in January 1959 reached revolutionaries in the Central Highlands in early summer as directives giving them "the green light for switching from political struggle alone to political struggle combined" not with armed struggle but with "armed self-defense and support activity."[74] This ironic statement had the virtue of highlighting the top leaders' reserve. It was inconsistent with the letter if not the intent of Resolution 15, calling as it did for insurgent activity but under highly restrictive conditions.

Essentially, the Politburo's guidelines called for the expansion of terrorist activity and the beginning of small raids on enemy forces below the seventeenth parallel, thus a low-intensity conflict. They sanctioned revolutionary violence in the South for the express purpose of allowing southern revolutionary organs to defend themselves against the draconian measures instituted by Saigon but not to instigate an actual "war of liberation" to militarily defeat and overthrow the Diem regime. The Politburo's ambivalence toward revolutionary violence was reflected in the guidelines' characterizations of the new tactic as "armed propaganda activity" *(hoat dong vu trang tuyen truyen)* and of the units responsible for implementing it as "armed self-defense forces" *(luc luong vu trang tu ve)* and "armed propaganda units" *(luc luong vu trang tuyen truyen).*[75] These circumlocutions underscored the determination of the Politburo majority to keep political struggle as the cornerstone of the party's southern strategy while responding to pressures to resume armed struggle. A "people's war" in the South abetted by the DRVN, which party militants looked forward to, remained out of the question for key leaders. According to David Elliott's history of the revolution in the Mekong Delta, "building up larger units would have required heavy weapons for combat support units." However, such weapons "did not start arriving in quantity in the Mekong Delta from North Vietnam until 1963."[76] Implicit in all the party's formulations was an understanding that war was too risky or simply impossible at that juncture, and it would commence when conditions were ripe for it and not a day sooner. According to Carl Thayer, those formulations meant that force could be used to "protect the party and its bases" and create the conditions for a wider armed struggle later, if necessary.[77]

In disseminating the guidelines, the Secretariat told southern revolutionary leaders that the fascist policies and recent successes of Diem and the Americans warranted adjustments to, not yet major revisions of, party strategy. Thus, the guidelines for implementing Resolution 15 permitted southern revolutionaries to accomplish only what was minimally necessary and realistically achievable under current circumstances: to "mobilize a political struggle movement that is broad among the masses" and "at the same time" to "isolate [Diem] politically." This, southerners were told, would create "favorable opportunities" for preserving, consolidating, and eventually expanding the revolutionary movement below the seventeenth parallel. The guidelines also stressed political mobilization and agitation work among enemy soldiers *(binh van)* in conjunction with the defense and expansion of revolutionary bases, especially in remote regions such as the Central Highlands.

For the time being, then, political struggle would remain the central task.[78] "What is the lesson of our victories over the previous years?" the guidelines asked, responding that only "the political forces of the broad masses can cause defeat of the reactionary policies of the enemy." Toward that goal, "we must mobilize a broad political struggle movement with a stronger revolutionary spirit, not only among the working masses but among all the classes." Once that was accomplished, the southern masses would no longer "fret before the terror policies of the enemy" but, on the contrary, would become "revolutionized." Until then, the Politburo insisted, military adventurism had to be avoided.

The guidelines also instructed southern party leaders and cadres to organize small, localized uprisings in remote or critical areas, such as the Central Highlands. An official history of the VWP presents these instructions as authorizing "piecemeal uprising" to create local revolutionary regimes "on behalf of the people" and in the interests of the southern communist cause.[79] But the use of force in these uprisings had to remain subordinate to "the strategy of the political struggle of the masses." Any resort to excessively violent struggle would have "incorrect strategic implications." Southerners had to use political struggle backed by violence to establish new "revolutionary rear bases" manned by "revolutionary armed forces" with a view to enabling the southern communist movement to regroup, reorganize, and grow. Eventually, these bases would serve as loci from which to stage a "complete triumph over the enemy."

The guidelines stipulated that self-defense and armed propaganda units participating in the effort should be small, ideally no more than three to six people, never more than twelve or fifteen. The aim was to prepare for a subsequent larger struggle, not to pursue victory itself just yet. According to an official history, armed propaganda and self-defense units in the South in mid-1959 were so small, poorly trained, and ill equipped that they "would never be able to engage the enemy in warfare and would never be able to become an actual revolutionary army."[80] In view of such a reality, a Vietnamese scholar has explained, Hanoi hoped through the guidelines to create preconditions favorable to the growth of the revolutionary movement below the seventeenth parallel but "not completely" to challenge the Saigon regime and its American allies.[81] In the somewhat different formulation of another source, the guidelines for implementing Resolution 15 "permitted the active use of armed forces *only* in combination with the political struggle as local circumstances required and not for the purpose of militarily defeating the Diem regime by commencing a large-scale guerrilla war or 'people's war.'"[82] To take armed struggle to the point of striving for total victory was to risk total defeat under the present circumstances. "Tendencies to take adventurous violent actions," the guidelines warned, risked causing a major war that the party and southern revolutionaries could not handle and the DRVN could not sustain at this time. Instructions to southerners remained basically consistent with these views until 1963–64, when the next major—and most consequential—revision of the party's revolutionary strategy took effect.

The delay in drafting the guidelines, as well as the differences between their convolutions and the belligerent language of Resolution 15, is probably best explained by the lingering concerns of Ho and Giap, and doubts among the rest of the policymaking elite about the wisdom of instigating armed struggle in the South on any scale in the spring and summer of 1959. These concerns and doubts would also explain the injunction against immediately revealing news of the adoption of Resolution 15. To be fair, the Politburo had ample reason to reject a bolder strategy of armed struggle in the South that year. To have an impact, such a strategy would have required a substantial and immediate commitment of the DRVN's scarce human and material resources. Above the seventeenth parallel, many important tasks remained to be completed before a military push for southern liberation and national reunification could be successful. "The most important thing for us now," Ho Chi Minh repeated during an interview, "is to work and to improve the people's living conditions."[83] "A socialist country needs peace to achieve national construction in all fields, to make the country powerful," to "improve the people's living standards," and to ensure "the victory of the revolution," a writer in *Hoc tap* later explained. "Therefore, a socialist country, immediately after coming into existence, advocates the implementation of a peaceful foreign policy."[84] In April, the secretary of the Hanoi branch of the party listed the major tasks facing the people as completing the socialist transformation of private industry and commerce, accelerating economic and cultural development, and improving daily life.[85] Shortly thereafter, the National Assembly decreed that there could be no compromise or relaxation in the task for completing the socialist project in the North, for until it was completed the DRVN would never be a "firm socialist base for [national] reunification."[86] To expedite the transformation, Hanoi undertook currency reform, as well as campaigns against illiteracy and counterrevolutionary activity.[87]

Another source of concern at the time remained the state of the armed forces at Hanoi's disposal. Those in the South numbered less than ten thousand. Their weapons were archaic or nonexistent, their organization poor, and their training deficient. To have any chance of success in an actual war, they would need support from the North's armed forces. But those forces were also in no position to challenge the enemy successfully in a war. The modernization of the PAVN was ongoing, as previously noted, but had thus far "led many officers to stress discipline at the expense of persuasion and education."[88] Moreover, the recent introduction of mandatory three-year conscription for all men between the ages of eighteen and twenty-five had lowered the age of inductees, "straining the party's capacity to indoctrinate them" and increasing the time needed to train them adequately.[89] Until the armed forces in both halves of Vietnam overcame such challenges, political struggle had to remain the major form of struggle. That is, winning the allegiance of the southern people must be the chief objective in the contest against Saigon.

An additional obstacle to instigating a war in the South in 1959 was, in the eyes of the Politburo, the state of the party in the South. Both organization and leadership remained poor, and membership was still extremely low, a result of the pressure brought to bear upon southern communists by the Diem regime.[90] Many villages were without a party cell, and cells in many other villages amounted to only a few members. An official party history estimates that in 1957–59 more than ten thousand communists had been killed or captured in the provinces of Can Tho and Soc Trang alone. In Ben Tre, another seventeen thousand people with ties to the revolutionary movement were killed, captured, or tortured by Diem's forces, and one hundred party cadres had been exposed.[91] In all of Nam Bo, the party now counted less than five thousand members. In parts of the Central Highlands, the situation was even worse. There, 70 percent of party cell executives, 60 percent of district executives, and 40 percent of provincial executives had been killed or captured, and in twelve districts there was no party presence at all.[92] As for the surviving leaders and cadres, Hanoi suspected that many of them failed to understand or to agree with Politburo thinking on revolutionary tactics and strategy. The cadres especially were deficient in their understanding of the nature and centrality of political struggle—of propaganda activity—in the communist revolutionary effort.[93]

International circumstances were no more propitious than those in Vietnam for a turn to war in the South. Open engagement of PAVN forces below the seventeenth parallel would validate enemy claims that Hanoi was the driving force behind the instability in the South and thus in violation of the Geneva accords. That would, as historian Douglas Pike has observed, "undercut the DRV's legal position and its basic contention that only in the [Geneva] Agreements lay hope for a satisfactory settlement" of the Vietnam problem.[94] DRVN leaders still wanted to avoid being "liable to be arraigned as violators of the Geneva Agreement," to which they still attached importance.[95] Besides, openly violating the accords by deploying PAVN units would invalidate Hanoi's long-standing contention that the southern liberation movement was indigenous and sustained from within the South. It would also make it more difficult to retain international support for the revolutionary cause, especially in the Afro-Asian and western worlds, and thus would adversely affect the ongoing diplomatic struggle. "The current [international] propaganda campaign [of DRVN authorities] is organized according to a well-known formula," French diplomats surmised. "The southern regime is a fascist and antipopular regime"; "favorable to war, it wants to eliminate by all means possible the patriots who love peace." As the purported champion of those "patriots," Hanoi had to remain cautious.[96]

More important than this concern with appearances was the impact a turn to war in the South might have on relations with allies, Moscow in particular. Hanoi was at the time facing mounting pressure from the CPSU to "prevent the Vietnamese Communist revolution from becoming a major issue in East-West relations."[97] Though Chinese influence and material aid were increasing in 1959, while Soviet aid had been comparatively reduced, North Vietnamese leaders were "at pains" to not "lose touch" with Moscow despite the latter's lukewarm support for the Vietnamese revolution and its sustained commitment to peaceful coexistence.[98] Although the CPSU had endorsed the 1957 Moscow Declaration acknowledging the possibility of nonpeaceful transition to socialism, Khrushchev remained opposed to anything that might increase Cold War tensions and derail peaceful coexistence, which dramatically escalating hostilities in the South would surely do. The VWP Politburo knew that, which is why it did not share the substance of Resolution 15 with the Soviet Embassy in Hanoi until the middle of May.[99]

Finally, Hanoi resisted a more forward strategy in the South because it still feared the prospect of American intervention and wanted to give Washington no pretext to deploy its forces in Vietnam. "In adopting the 15th Resolution on political and military struggle," Nguyen Vu Tung of the Vietnamese foreign ministry has written, "a hope was pinned on a peaceful course" because the party "had in mind the danger of U.S. direct military intervention."[100]

RESOLUTION 15 IN CONTEXT

In view of all of these factors, what was the significance of Resolution 15 in the coming of the Vietnam War? What was its meaning? Most historians in Vietnam who have written on the subject maintain that the resolution marked a turning point in the course of the Vietnamese revolution, the beginning of the comprehensive effort to liberate the South from the ever tightening grip of Diem and the Americans. They have interpreted it as signaling that the time had come for Hanoi to "push the armed struggle against the enemy" in the South, to "coordinate the political strength of the masses with armed force in order to overthrow the yoke of the American imperialists and the feudals, [and] to elevate the revolutionary regime of the people."[101] In doing so, the resolution followed "historical logic."[102] Some western historians have accepted this assessment. K. C. Chen, for example, has contended that Resolution 15 "set the general policy of the 'liberation' of the South—i.e., the overthrow of the Diem regime, and the establishment of a coalition government favorably disposed toward reunification with communist North Vietnam."[103]

Admittedly, Resolution 15 meaningfully amended Hanoi's revolutionary strategy, sanctioning as it did the onset of insurgent activity in the South backed, to a limited degree, by the North.[104] Most notably, it augured the incremental deployment of thousands of "volunteer troops" *(quan tinh nguyen)* to the South. By one estimate, the DRVN dispatched approximately 4,600 cadres, technicians, and military advisers trained and equipped to organize guerilla squads, as well as armed propaganda brigades, to the South in 1959–60 alone.[105] It also sent supplies and other personnel, including nurses and physicians.[106] To facilitate the movement of these human and material resources, engineering units of the PAVN established a maritime infiltration route between North and South Vietnam, and also built or upgraded a network of roads running from the DRVN into the South via Laos and Cambodia—the so-called Ho Chi Minh Trail.[107]

That response gave southern revolutionary organs greater tactical freedom and support for their activities. It also forestalled further deterioration of the situation in the South and in fact may have saved the revolutionary movement there from impending annihilation. Arguably the most important long-term consequence of Resolution 15 was that it ended Hanoi's policy since 1954 of benign neglect of the

South and the revolutionary situation there. Beginning with the adoption of Resolution 15, party strategy below the seventeenth parallel became, by official account, to contain reactionary forces long enough to complete the socialist project in the North while consolidating and expanding the revolutionary movement, after which a full-fledged armed struggle could be undertaken with better, surer prospects for victory.

For the time being, however, the Politburo obdurately refused to comprehensively engage the North in the liberation of the South, or even to privilege violent struggle over political struggle there. More tellingly, it committed no PAVN units to the revolutionary surge sanctioned by the Central Committee. In fact, DRVN decision-makers had for the time being "no intention of employing PAVN regular units" in a war with Saigon's armed forces or "sanctioning a policy of all-out attack" on Diem's regime.[108] Therefore, as historian William Turley has noted, Resolution 15 encapsulated a party decision to extend "limited" northern support to the southern revolutionary movement, which it authorized to use violence "under restrictive conditions" mainly to protect itself.[109] These limitations are important in light of subsequent party decisions concerning the South. After January 1959, Hanoi's strategic priorities—pursuing socialist development in the DRVN, precluding American intervention in Indochina, accommodating the Cold War concerns of key allies, and encouraging international support for its revolutionary cause—remained unchanged. Resolution 15 was indeed a "relatively muted" response to the situation in the South.[110] "The constant if waning hope of top [DRVN] leaders was still that the party could attain its objectives by inducing the Saigon government to crumble without having to mount a major military effort backed by the North," Turley has written.[111]

In retrospect, Resolution 15 set no "general policy" for liberating the South, nor did it symbolize Hanoi's "opening shot" in the Vietnam War.[112] Similarly, the deployment thereafter of hundreds, eventually thousands, of troops did not mean that Hanoi's "war machinery" had been set into motion.[113] These were mostly PAVN troops, to be sure, but they were not actual northerners; they were almost exclusively southerners who had regrouped to the North in 1954–55, and had then been integrated into the DRVN's regular armed forces.[114] Some of them even asked to be sent back to the South, as noted in the previous chapter. And since these troops infiltrated—returned to, in actuality—the South as volunteers, they did not wear PAVN uniforms. If captured, it would be impossible for the enemy to ascertain that they indeed came from the North, unlike northerners, whose accents would betray their provenance. In that sense, their deployment posed minimal risk for Hanoi as it was entirely deniable. Sending ethnic Korean troops from Beijing's armed forces to North Korea "did not necessarily indicate that in late 1949 and early 1950 Mao supported Kim Il-sung's plan for reunifying Korea by means of war."[115] Similarly, dispatching southern regroupees to the South did not mean Hanoi had committed to bringing about Vietnamese reunification by force a decade later.

Resolution 15 represented an important revision of party strategy concerning the South as that strategy had existed since the signing of the Geneva accords. But its support of armed struggle was in qualified, deniable terms, particularly regarding the troop support it provided. These qualifications, that reserve, made clear Hanoi's continued unwillingness to achieve southern liberation at once, by force. The general policy of southern liberation—that is, Hanoi's commitment to war to meet revolutionary goals below the seventeenth parallel—was articulated not in 1959 but in 1963–64, as will be demonstrated later. Similarly, comprehensive engagement of DRVN resources in the South "with the expressed goal of attacking and annihilating the enemy's forces" occurred only after the latter date.[116] The importance of Resolution 15 has thus been overstated by historians, especially those in Vietnam. It marked the onset of an insurgency below the seventeenth parallel, of a "new politico-military struggle," to be sure, but not of an actual, truly national "war of liberation."[117] As Ang Cheng Guan surmises, the armed struggle that began as a result of Resolution 15 was intended merely to support, and not replace, the ongoing political struggle below the seventeenth parallel.[118]

REFOCUSING ON THE NORTH

At the next plenum of the Central Committee, in June, the situation in the South received almost no attention. Instead, the focus was on efforts to improve agricultural production in the North. In the aftermath of land reform and with the onset of collectivization mandated by the three-year plan, Truong Chinh reported that "there exists in the countryside a struggle between two ways, the socialist way and the capitalist way," and that resolving the contradiction was necessary to strengthen and complete the socialist transformation of the DRVN. To that end, the party must press on with rural collectivization, the most effective means of accomplishing urgent revolutionary objectives. These objectives were, in Truong Chinh's reckoning, to "contribute to the final eradication of the foundation of the regime of exploitation of man by man in the North of our country, consolidate the development of the rural economy on every front, effect complete renovation of agriculture, contribute in a big way to socialist industrialization of the state," and "bring about for the peasants as well as for the [rest of the] people of the North of our country a truly peaceful, free, and happy life." By official count there were 6,830 "agricultural production cooperatives" in the North at the end of March 1959, averaging thirty households each and encompassing most but not all peasant households above the seventeenth parallel.[119] The final resolution of the June plenum declared the completion of agricultural collectivization to be the "central revolutionary task of our party and people."[120]

The British consul's assessment of conditions in and around Hanoi at the time of the June plenum confirmed the economic challenges still confronting the North, despite recent improvements. "So far as Hanoi town is concerned, we can see with our own eyes that the standard of living is sinking steadily into ever shabbier and drabber uniformity. Even the poor are poorer," he noted. "We feel we are not exaggerating in saying that the number of people who have benefited from Communism in Hanoi (and I think the same can probably be said of the other towns) does not exceed 5 percent of the population." "No member of the Western community here has ever met a Vietnamese who was in favour of the regime, except the members of the regime itself and those few, mostly young men, who are attracted and convinced by the Communist ideology. The bourgeois, whether large or small, are in despair as the screw of cooperativisation [i.e., nationalization] is turned." The situation was slightly better in the countryside, where rice production had recently increased. Unfortunately for the peasants, "any increased revenue for [them] resulting from greater production has been more than taken care of by increased taxation." In parts of the countryside, peasants were demanding to leave the cooperatives into which they had just been organized.[121] Despite the increased rice harvests, total production was a million tons short of the planned target. Similarly, though "a considerable amount of new industrial construction is visible throughout the country," progress in that area was not "as rapid as planned."[122] Northerners generally, the consul concluded, were "worse off under Communism than they were before," and peasants remained "extremely reluctant" to join rural cooperatives.[123]

As long as such problems persisted, the North would be unable to sustain a war below the seventeenth parallel. To make sure that the membership understood their positions on these and other matters, DRVN leaders mandated a series of special "political re-education" sessions. The ten-day program studied the resolutions adopted at the last three plenary sessions of the Central Committee.[124] The sessions were also used to address persistent deviationist tendencies among party members and "serious" deficiencies in the performance of government officials, especially those responsible for such rural tasks as tax collection, dike repair, and consolidation of agricultural and other cooperatives.[125] A communiqué from the Council of Ministers in July boasted that the socialist revolution in the North had entered a "high tide," and admonished all workers in the state sector to improve their political and ideological standards to meet the requirements of that revolution.[126] A *Nhan dan* editorial emphasized the major aims of the re-education campaign: to "teach cadres and members of the party to understand seriously the basic problems of the revolution in the North," and in doing so enable them "to distinguish clearly the dividing line between socialism and capitalism, to recognize friends and enemies," and "to press forward with energy the policy of socialist reform."[127]

RESOLUTION 15 IN THE SOUTH

When southern revolutionaries finally learned of Resolution 15, they were relieved to hear that Hanoi at last supported armed struggle in the South, if only on measured terms so they could defend themselves against the punishing force of the Diem regime. In the Central Highlands, revolutionaries and their sympathizers were reportedly "elated," especially by the resolution's declaration that "the people are one, the party is one, our country is one." Hanoi, they thought, had not forgotten them after all.[128] A meeting of southern cadres "burst out in stormy applause" when told of the passage and provisions of the resolution.[129] The number of such reports in the Vietnamese archives indicates that the notion that Hanoi had abandoned the South after the Geneva accords was indeed widespread there. In this sense, Resolution 15 "solved" the "deep longing of the people" and "kindled the smoldering, once blazing, revolutionary flame, creating a fire spreading all over the countryside, the mountains, and the cities."[130]

Southern revolutionaries wasted no time in acting upon the resolution once they were apprised of it. They intensified their attacks on individuals with known or suspected ties to the Diem regime. Almost at once, armed propaganda units started assassinating bureaucrats, schoolteachers, hospital employees, village chiefs, and other civil servants at the rate of fifteen per week.[131] In 1959–60, they assassinated about 1,700 South Vietnamese officials and government employees, and kidnapped and detained or otherwise dealt with perhaps 2,000 others.[132] "Our purpose" in these activities, one revolutionary later stated, "was not only to eliminate those who could be harmful to the [communist] movement"; it was also to act "with a view toward making the people afraid and to prevent them from cooperating with the [RVN] government."[133] The "generalization of organized terrorism" in the South, which is really what implementation of Resolution 15 amounted to at first, was reportedly "effective" and paid immediate dividends for revolutionary forces.[134]

Southern communists were also quick to organize "popular uprisings" against the Diem regime, particularly in remote, minority-dominated areas of the Central Highlands. The first of these occurred not in the highlands but in Tra Bong, in Quang Ngai Province. The uprising had been planned for months and in fact broke out before Hanoi distributed the guidelines for implementing Resolution 15. This timing and sequence confirm that local party leaders and cadres frustrated by Hanoi's lack of response to worsening conditions sometimes "initiated combat without the knowledge" and in defiance of their superiors.[135] Vietnamese sources now acknowledge that long before adoption of Resolution 15 some of these leaders and cadres were planning an uprising at Vinh Thanh to take place in February of that year and had in fact begun implementing the plan before learning of the passage of the resolution.[136] In light of Saigon's aggressiveness and Hanoi's passivity, the plight of people sympathetic to the revolution was compelling enough to prompt some party operatives to "dare to lead the masses to look for weapons" and "take the initiative to rise up," even though "that was not the position" of the party leadership.[137] According to David Elliott, the first uprisings were precipitated not by party operatives at all but by disgruntled peasants and minority groups who took matters into their own hands. Several other uprisings soon followed the one in Tra Bong, most of them in the Central Highlands. The first uprising in the Mekong Delta occurred in September 1959 in Kien Phong Province. Resolution 15 reached communist leaders in the delta only in October 1959, Elliott claims, which meant that they too proceeded without authorization from Hanoi.[138]

Generally speaking, the results of these early initiatives were limited. According to a subsequent assessment by southern party leaders, the lasting achievements in this period were minor and largely limited to an ability to "restrict the enemy's sphere of control, force the enemy to recognize the just rights of the masses, and force [the enemy] to admit that their village and township administration was in a sorry state." "The South Vietnam people's forces did not yet have the capability of swiftly overthrowing the entire American-Diemist regime," this assessment explained, "because the revolutionary armed forces were still weak."[139]

In urban centers, the impact of this flurry of revolutionary activity was even more limited, and revolutionaries in Long An Province actually suffered major setbacks in this period.[140] Under Resolution 15, as one official account put it, the revolutionary movement only gradually expanded, "advanc[ing] close to the cities and close to the strategic communication routes" but making no inroads into those areas. This absence of a communist presence in the cities made it especially important that the political struggle be pressed forward: "When the South Vietnam cities, particularly Saigon-Cholon [i.e., Saigon's "Chinatown"], are able to rise up in coordination with the rural areas, the South Vietnam revolution will have the capability of overthrowing the enemy through the means of a general uprising."[141] Unfortunately, the movement did not have that capability. One reason for this was the lack of cadres effectively trained to accomplish the task. "There has been a failure to thoroughly understand the city proselytizing targets," namely, "the workers, the poor, and the elementary, high school, and college students," an item in *Hoc tap* soon explained. As a result, "the proper attention was not devoted to the matter of intensifying the propaganda, education, organization and training of cadres and masses in the cities" and "around the cities."[142] William Turley concluded that though "sizeable areas" of the South "quickly fell under the revolution's sway" following implementation of Resolution 15, Hanoi "judged the balance of forces, particularly on the military side of the equation, still to be decisively in Saigon's favor."[143]

SAIGON ANSWERS RESOLUTION 15

Saigon's response to the upsurge in insurgent activity during the second half of 1959 was effective and constituted a primary reason that communist initiatives had very limited success. Ferocious ARVN counterattacks led directly to the recapture of most villages lost to insurgents and to the Diem regime's consequent resumption of administrative control. Law 10/59, promulgated by Saigon in May as the revolutionary surge began, decreed a "sentence of death, and confiscation of the whole of or part of his property, with loss of rank in the case of army men" upon anyone who "commits or attempts to commit . . . crimes with the aim of sabotage, or of infringing upon the security of the state." Under that law, the RVN government rounded up thousands more dissidents and suspected dissidents, including student activists, leaders of religious sects, and anyone suspected of cooperation with or even sympathy for the communists.[144]

These actions soon had devastating consequences for southern revolutionaries. Carried out with "drive and energy" by Saigon, they raised the morale of southerners loyal to the regime or opposed to the revolutionary movement, while having a visibly "depressing" effect on communist forces.[145] Under the new law, Diem's security forces had within months rounded up half a million people with ties to the communist revolution, and killed more than 68,000.[146] According to a subsequent DRVN National Assembly report, Saigon had been particularly successful in Ben Tre Province, where "the party base suffered heavy losses" and "only 18 cells in 115 villages and 162 party members" survived at the end of 1959. The survivors developed one or the other of two "tendencies," the report noted. The first was to question their "belie[f] in political struggle" as defined by the party and either "demand of their superiors permission to fight" without restraint or to "cease working until ordered to [carry out unrestricted] armed struggle." Some "comrades" stopped "believ[ing] in [continuing the] political struggle," another report noted, and "demanded to stop working until orders for [a full escalation of] armed struggle were issued." The second tendency was to not want or not dare to do further work for the revolution because survivors "blamed the North for forgetting the South."[147]

The Nam Bo Executive Committee convened in late 1959 to review these developments and assess the state of the revolutionary situation within its jurisdiction. It concluded that the revolutionary movement in recent months had exposed the weakness of the Diem regime but had caused the regime no permanent damage.[148] In fact, the committee feared that the regime would soon seek to "drown the [revolutionary] movement in blood and fire even more savagely [and] devastatingly" than it had recently been doing. It was confident the movement would survive but expressed concern over Hanoi's failure to provide greater support to ensure its survival. Because of that failure, "we . . . have not yet used at the right level and also not yet brought into play" the "potential" of revolutionary forces to "attack" the enemy and secure long-term success. The use of violence was too restrained to "bring about realistic support to execute the political struggle of the masses." The struggle had to be "strengthened" to constrain enemy influence, especially in the cities but also in the countryside, if the appeal of revolutionary sentiment was to spread. The movement especially needed the wherewithal to combat "the policy of cruel terrorism, the policy of exploitation and confiscation, the policy of plundering the country and selling the country [and] enslaving the people and provoking war" of the Diem regime.

The committee had still other concerns. Rank-and-file revolutionaries and even cadres disobeyed orders, questioned party policies, or otherwise disregarded party discipline. Others supposedly under party discipline were "too timid" to use force even to carry out orders, as noted above. Such displays of "rightist deviationist inclinations," the committee warned, risked "guiding the [revolutionary] movement to passivity and creating more complex difficulties" by making it easy for the enemy to "bully" the masses and attack revolutionary bases. Other revolutionaries showed disdain for Hanoi's existing emphasis on political struggle. Admittedly, the committee told Hanoi, that emphasis "can only produce defeat or a draw." But "seeking the sympathy of the masses" without a willingness to use appropriate levels of violence against the enemy, it concluded bluntly in defense of the latter attitude among southern communists, did amount to a policy of gradual "surrender."

Despite such bluntness, the committee professed its endorsement of Resolution 15 and loyalty to Hanoi. It cautioned, however, that to be successful the movement in the South must have a more fully "revolutionary" thrust, one that would enable it to "seize [the] favorable opportunity to defeat completely the enemy and bring about final victory." Hanoi's cautious approach was sound policy, but failure to recognize when circumstances dictated major changes in tactics if not strategy could imperil the entire revolutionary project.

Throughout 1959, DRVN leaders faced challenge after challenge that forced them to make difficult choices balancing the imperatives of the three-year plan and the socialist project more broadly in the North with the vital necessity to sustain the revolution in the South. In endorsing Resolution 15, the Central Committee seemed to suggest that the latter trumped the former. In the guidelines to implement the resolution, however, Hanoi revealed that its greater commitment was still to the North. Clearly, those guidelines were an enterprise of the moderates who still controlled party decision-making. They seem to have been inspired less by a genuine commitment to the merits of revolutionary violence than by a perceived need to placate militants in both the North and the South. This cautious pragmatism, embodying as it did an acknowledgment of the revolution's weaknesses and dependencies without compromising the party's purposes, may have been the policy's most distinctive characteristic. It avoided for the time being risks Hanoi thought it could not afford to confront unsuccessfully.

There is no doubt that DRVN leaders averted a number of potential disasters by adopting a strongly worded resolution and then implementing it with tempered guidelines. Less immediately certain was whether that result would serve the long-term interests of the reunification struggle or only temporarily silence those inside and outside the party who favored a genuinely militant strategy.

3

Treading Cautiously, 1960

East-West détente suffered a major setback in May 1960 after a U.S. spy plane was shot down over the Soviet Union. The so-called U-2 incident affronted Moscow, embarrassed Washington, and derailed a summit between Khrushchev and Eisenhower. But that did not end Sino-Soviet contention, as Khrushchev refused to give up on peaceful coexistence. In fact, relations between Moscow and Beijing took a turn for the worse after the Soviets recalled all their experts from China and drastically cut military and other aid to the PRC in an apparent attempt to sow discord in CCP ranks and pressure Mao into adopting more moderate attitudes on domestic and international issues. Angered by Soviet actions and, specifically, the attempted meddling in their affairs, Chinese leaders decided they would no longer play second fiddle to the Soviets and began to vie for leadership of the world communist movement. By the end of the year, Mao and Khrushchev were openly attacking each other, amplifying tensions in the socialist camp.

Mounting concerns about the situation in Vietnam and the potential pitfalls of a failure to contain the nascent insurgency in the South informed Washington's decision that year to commit more resources, including military personnel, to improve Saigon's armed forces. Diem, for his part, continued to consolidate his authority in the RVN and proved successful in stemming the tide of insurgent activity during this period.

Judging conditions internationally and domestically unfavorable to escalating the insurgency spawned by Resolution 15, Hanoi continued to exercise caution in the South. Its refusal to involve the DRVN more deeply below the seventeenth parallel was a particularly tough pill to swallow for VWP militants, and it amplified intraparty tensions that year. The VWP's Third National Congress in the fall not only reaffirmed Hanoi's commitment to the socialist transformation of the northern economy, to the "North-first" policy, but also decreed a division of revolutionary labor between northerners and southerners that left no doubt as to where DRVN decision-makers stood on reunification of the country by force. Militants did, however, get some reprieve in December, when Hanoi announced the formation of a new united front in the South to contest Diem's rule and bring about his overthrow.

UPS AND DOWNS OF THE SOUTHERN INSURGENCY

In January 1960, Nam Bo leaders forwarded a new assessment of their situation to Hanoi, and in doing so pleaded, again, for increased militancy. "Political struggle supported by armed propaganda is not enough to protect revolutionary bases," they insisted. The party had to "elevate" violent struggle to the level of political struggle, to allow offensive in addition to defensive armed activity in order to grow the revolutionary movement. Otherwise, they could do no more than preserve their movement. "We must coordinate closely between the work to protect and strengthen the movement, look upon both fronts, 'strengthening' and 'preserving,'" and "not consider 'preserving' as central as before." They also repeated their wish for more support from the North.[1]

As Hanoi considered these recommendations, an uprising broke out in Ben Tre Province southwest of Saigon.[2] Communists there were reportedly so eager to take the offensive that their leaders were concerned that "once Ben Tre turns to military action we won't be able to restrain them."[3] The uprising began on the night of 17 January and resulted in the destruction of "large sections of the enemy's administrative and coercive apparatus in villages and hamlets," the formation of "people's committees" to replace that apparatus, and the confiscation and redistribution of land. Though ARVN forces quickly recaptured the area, the action generated revolutionary élan. "From there on," according to one account, "the tide of concerted uprisings swept over the provinces of Nam Bo, the Central Highlands and several places in Trung Bo [northern and central South Vietnam]."[4] The southern provinces of My Tho, Tra Vinh, Can Tho, Bac Lieu, Rach Gia, Tay Ninh, and Chau Doc were especially affected by this burst of action. In Tay Ninh, revolutionary forces joined Cao Dai rebels to overthrow local authorities, an action that demonstrated the party's willingness to continue working closely with other anti-Diem groups.[5]

Over the next several months, communists participated in hundreds of such actions across the South. "The uprising of the South Vietnamese peasants did not occur at one time throughout the land," an official account observes, "but occurred in various places at various times when the conditions were present."[6] Meanwhile, the effort to eliminate "traitors" intensified, averaging more than 130 assassinations per month that year.[7] As revolutionary forces thus chipped away at the sway of the

Diem regime, violent confrontation increased dramatically in the South, as southern revolutionaries took liberties in implementing the guidelines for Resolution 15 and ARVN forces responded in kind. Wherever uprisings were successful, cadres reconstituted party hierarchies and controls dissipated or destroyed by years of neglect and repression, and formed people's committees, as occurred in Ben Tre. The committees in turn undertook land reform and other measures to win the loyalty of the people. According to one official source, in 1960 such regimes existed in half the villages in the South (1,383 out of 2,627), and the number of people living in liberated areas exceeded 5,600,000, approximately a third of the South Vietnamese population.[8] These accomplishments enhanced the prestige of communism, enabled party operatives to exert greater influence over the anti-Diem cause, facilitated recruitment of fighters and other activists, and began to change the balance of forces below the seventeenth parallel. The new "offensive stance" ended the period of "temporary stability of the U.S.-Diem clique" and augured "a period of continuous crisis."[9]

Not to be outdone, Saigon responded as aggressively to this upsurge of revolutionary activity as it had the previous year. It unleashed its military and security forces on the insurgents and their supporters, and continued the Rural Community Development Program, begun the year before, which consisted of forced relocations of peasants to fortified "agroville" communities.[10] While the agrovilles produced mixed results at best, the use of force paid dividends; many of the latest gains by insurgents proved ephemeral. Alarmed by the growing tensions below the seventeenth parallel and fearful of the global implications of the "loss" of South Vietnam, the Eisenhower administration committed more military advisers and other resources to train ARVN forces, improve their efficiency, and contain the insurgency. The reluctance of DRVN decision-makers to provide more support for insurgent activity at this critical juncture severely undermined the cause of southern revolutionaries.

Paradoxically, the setbacks in the South reinforced Hanoi's predilection for caution there. Ton Duc Thang, now chairman of the Standing Committee of the National Assembly, told his colleagues in April that the timing remained inopportune for shifting to war below the seventeenth parallel. Even with DRVN support, the communist movement there remained too disorganized to prevail in such an undertaking. Besides, Thang declared, "the will and keen wish of our people are: work and peace."[11] Clearly, "our people" here meant northerners rather than southerners, for whom peace if not work remained elusive. "We want to preserve peace in order for our people to use their strength to build socialism," another official stated at the time, similarly ignoring the different circumstances and priorities of many people on both sides of the seventeenth parallel. "Real developments in the North of our country over the past years have been consistent with that wish," this official continued. The "clearest proof" was that "in recent years our state has demobilized tens of thousands of soldiers" to "increase the workforce" for building socialism. After 1954, "our defense budget has never stopped shrinking, from 27 percent of the national budget in 1955, to 19.2 percent in 1958, and approximately 16 percent this year [1960]."[12] International conditions also discouraged escalation, Thang told the National Assembly. "The international political climate has become peaceful, and upcoming summit meetings between leaders of big countries [i.e., the Four-Power Paris summit scheduled for May, at which the United States, the Soviet Union, Great Britain, and France would address the status of Berlin] promise new victories for the cause of peace."[13] On the basis of these considerations, in April the Politburo answered the Nam Bo leaders' plea for increased militancy by reiterating its policy of caution. Unless the party heeded domestic and international constraints, it wrote in a cable to them, it would "meet difficulties and possibly lose ground."[14]

None of this assuaged the concerns of southern militants, who kept generating pressure for intensifying the insurgency below the seventeenth parallel and for increased DRVN aid. In March 1960 a group calling itself "Former Resistance Fighters of the Nam Bo Region" and consisting largely of veterans of the war against the French, appealed to Hanoi for more military aid to escalate the armed struggle below the seventeenth parallel.[15] Albeit helpful, the group advised, the measures undertaken since the previous year had only marginally improved the position of revolutionary forces, and then only in parts of the South. Similarly, the representative from Ben Tre Province told the DRVN National Assembly that while Saigon continued to "rabidly increase war preparations" and "increase the repression of the people by violent methods," Washington "stubbornly" executed its "plan of invasion of the South" to "destroy peace" and prevent national reunification. In blunt criticism of Hanoi's southern policy, the Ben Tre representative added that while northerners strove to build socialism, improve their living standards, and "protect [their own] peace by any method," southerners faced "an extremely unsafe situation" caused by the ability of Washington and Saigon to impose their will on "the heads of our people" as they "hectically strengthen" their military capability and "prepare for war in accordance with the plans of the Americans." "The forced conscription of soldiers, the forced recruitment of laborers, home expulsions, land seizures, the construction of military roads and bases, plundering, [and] pauperization of the people," he continued, were causing "our compatriots in the South to endure untold misery and distress."[16]

Two separate measures adopted at two different meetings of southern party leaders that summer reiterated the desire of southern communists to escalate the insurgency, with corresponding support from the North. In the first of these, the Interzone V Executive Committee told Hanoi that recent increases in the number and intensity of attacks by South Vietnamese forces against revolutionary bases had caused significant "human and material losses for us." As a result, "the correlation of forces between the enemy and us [in Interzone V] at present is still essentially unchanged." Contrary to what DRVN leaders were saying, the committee insisted, the root of the problem lay not in the shortcomings of political struggle but in the weaknesses of armed struggle. The only viable strategy in the South was simultaneous use of military struggle and political struggle in mutual support.[17]

In July, the Nam Bo Executive Committee again made a plea to Hanoi for much the same purposes. Recent results of the political struggle, it told Hanoi, had been positive but disappointing. Propaganda efforts among South Vietnamese soldiers and civil servants *(chinh quyen van)* had been ineffective. At the same time, the armed struggle continued to be weak, plagued by its own inadequacies. Southern fighting forces waited anxiously for modern weapons from the North and "thought little" of "the merits of various types of rudimentary weapons" at their disposal. Most of their small arms were from stocks buried at the conclusion of the war with France by Viet Minh fighters anticipating a resumption of hostilities. These weapons were now "archaic" and in short supply.[18] "Our armed forces," the Nam Bo Executive Committee concluded, did not "meet the requirements of their responsibilities."[19] The meaning was clear and the solution simple: Hanoi had to endorse and support a more forward strategy in the South.

TENSIONS WITHIN THE PARTY

Through the summer of 1960, DRVN leaders studied their options. It was obvious Resolution 15 and the level of support they provided to southern revolutionaries had failed to satisfy the aspirations of many on both sides of the seventeenth parallel. That, in turn, amplified intraparty conflict over revolutionary strategy. The collapse of Syngman Rhee's "reactionary" regime in South Korea on 26 April and the shooting down of an American U-2 spy plane over the Soviet Union on 1 May, which compromised Soviet-American détente for a time, aggravated that conflict.[20] Rhee's regime and leadership style had had much in common with Diem's. Its fall did not just demonstrate to militants that "puppet regimes that faithfully obeyed every order by imperialists against the wishes of their people could not last long, even if supported by the bayonets of their foreign masters"; it also convinced them that war in the South would expedite the collapse of the Diem regime.[21] The U-2 incident, for its part, derailed the Four-Power Paris summit, which moderates in Hanoi had hoped would "consolidate peace in the world" and, by extension, in Vietnam. Militants, however, felt vindicated by the derailment. As adherents of Chinese revolutionary theses, they, like the Chinese, "had always maintained that this détente was nothing but an 'American ploy'" intended to deceive Third World revolutionaries as well as world opinion.[22]

In the aftermath of these events, western diplomats in Hanoi reported increasing tensions between moderates and militants within party and government organs. "We are witnessing" a "dangerous evolution," one of their reports surmised.[23] Indeed, by this time the affinity of views between radicals in Beijing and militants in the VWP was growing, producing a "sinization" of sorts within the party.[24] The party itself acknowledged the lack of ideological unity in its ranks at this time, confessing that "dogmatism," essentially hard-line thinking, colored the attitudes of members at all echelons.[25] According to *Nhan dan*, some cadres and members refused to "correctly conform to the discipline of the party" and were instead "obstinately creat[ing] factions and acting on their own impulses."[26] While it is impossible to gauge just how widespread "leftist deviationism" was in party ranks, the lack of unity was significant enough to prompt Hanoi in the spring of 1960 to mandate another round of political re-education for all members.[27]

The Vietnamese masses themselves were becoming polarized into moderate "pro-Soviet" and militant "pro-Chinese" camps at this time, a result of both conditions in Vietnam and the state of Sino-Soviet relations.[28] In rural areas, anti-Chinese sentiment inspired by historical memory was strong, a western assessment noted. Such sentiment also existed in the cities, among intellectuals and others who estimated that since the end of the war against France, the Vietnamese "have only changed masters: yesterday the French, today the Chinese.'" Conversely, low-level bureaucrats and other state employees boasted of their admiration for China, as did young adults who "have the conviction of sharing a greater affinity" with the Chinese. "The evolution of young Vietnamese generations in support of China," the assessment observed, "forces us to recognize that elements relatively favorable to Europe... will disappear little by little." Many Vietnamese workers had also become alienated from Moscow because of the behavior of Soviet and other East Europeans who had recently come to the DRVN in growing numbers as technical experts and economic advisers. It seemed to many workers that these people "incessantly complained about living conditions" and openly counted the days they had to remain in Vietnam before their contracts expired and they could go home. Some Vietnamese concluded on the basis of interactions with these and other Eastern Europeans that "'Whites' are always the same, Communist or non-Communist."[29]

By the summer of 1960, Le Duan and other party militants were exerting unprecedented influence in Hanoi and seemed poised to take over policymaking.[30] Signs of this were unmistakable: creation by the government of a "Union of Chinese Residents" in Hanoi; growing numbers of Vietnamese of Chinese descent working as civil servants and political commissars in Hanoi and Haiphong; "extreme hardening" of security concerns manifested in "mass arrests" of Vietnamese who had once served in pro-French armies; and renewed harassment of Catholic clergy and community leaders.[31] Though no evidence exists to substantiate the claim, foreign observers at the time even speculated about the possibility of a coup by "extremists" within the party and the armed forces to overthrow the "temporizers" who still dominated decision-making.[32]

Although their authority and acumen were being challenged, Ho, Giap, and other moderates in the Politburo and the Central Committee retained the upper hand for the time being. They "held their ground," the British Consulate surmised, after undergoing "a certain amount of criticism from some who complain that the policies of the past six years have brought reunification no nearer and who would therefore prefer a tougher line." Party militants, the consulate thought, "are at present most unlikely to succeed in modifying the Northern régime's reunification policy so far as to make open military intervention in the South at all probable."[33] Indeed, for the next three years that policy remained essentially unchanged.

That summer Hanoi mulled over a new plan to bring about reunification peacefully. The first step was the most daunting: replacing the Diem regime in Saigon with one that was "more independent toward the United States." Far-fetched as it seemed, Hanoi thought that might be achieved through skillful manipulation of public opinion and coordination of mass demonstrations in Saigon and elsewhere. Once Diem was gone, DRVN authorities would negotiate with his successor the amalgamation of the governments of the two Vietnams. Under any such plan, which recycled many ideas that had circulated in Hanoi since 1955, the Ministry of Foreign Affairs would fall under Hanoi's jurisdiction, and the Ministries of Defense and of Finance under Saigon's control. Control of other ministries would be decided through consultation and by mutual agreement. Eventually, the leadership itself would be amalgamated, presumably under communist control, but that was not spelled out. French diplomats believed in the summer of 1960 that Hanoi possibly had already established contacts with "'liberal' elements" in the South.[34] After a discussion of these subjects with Pham Van Dong in the early fall, a Canadian diplomat reported that Hanoi might even be open to the possibility of mediation by the UN, an organization DRVN leaders distrusted in the extreme by this time.[35]

CONFRONTING THE SINO-SOVIET DISPUTE

The insurgency in the South did not sit well with Hanoi's main allies. The Soviets, who had barely tolerated the passage of Resolution 15 and were still irate that Hanoi had waited weeks before sharing its contents with them, were deeply concerned over the violence and instability it was producing. "The present situation in South Vietnam does not furnish a basis to talk about a favorable internal revolutionary situation, about a possibility to overthrow the Diem regime and to establish the people's regime," Asia specialists in the Soviet Ministry of Foreign Affairs concluded in a 1960 report; carrying out an insurgency under such conditions was misguided and even dangerous.[36] Hanoi tried to assure Moscow that "the general line" of VWP policy in the South remained to preserve peace "at any price," but to no avail.[37] Soviet leaders worried that any escalation of communist-sponsored violence in Vietnam could lead to American intervention and therefore to an "international conflict" that would undermine or destroy East-West détente.³⁸ Socialist countries must "avoid everything that might be used by reactionaries in order to push the world into the 'Cold War' again," Khrushchev warned.³⁹

The Chinese saw things only somewhat differently. By now Beijing openly preached the inevitability of war between the socialist and capitalist camps. Yet during private meetings in Hanoi in May 1960, Zhou Enlai urged DRVN leaders to maintain the status quo in the South, avoid escalation, and concentrate on the socialist transformation of the North in order to create the "rear base" necessary for an actual war of national liberation.⁴⁰ Specifically, Zhou advised his hosts to complete agricultural collectivization and build up light industry. On account of domestic concerns of its own, Beijing was both unprepared and unwilling at this point to deal with a war in Vietnam, despite its public advocacy of violent national liberation in the Third World. "Chinese leaders did not encourage a rapid escalation of the fighting," historian Qiang Zhai wrote, because they "did not want to provoke a U.S. retaliation closer to home."⁴¹ Accordingly, when members of the PAVN General Staff traveled to Beijing shortly thereafter to request more and better weaponry for southern insurgents, their Chinese counterparts answered by "saying nothing."⁴² Instead, they warned that war in the South would involve Hanoi in costly struggles on both sides of the seventeenth parallel and possibly bring the United States into direct confrontation with China.⁴³ "There is no longer mention of the inevitability of wars [between socialist and capitalist states] or of the necessity of destroying American imperialism" in Chinese discussions with the North Vietnamese, the French General Delegation in Hanoi noted after the General Staff returned from Beijing. It was as if a "word of order" on "bleating peace" had been issued. By discouraging the escalation of hostilities in Vietnam, Beijing may also have been seeking to disarm the distrust of Asian states fearful of Chinese expansionism, thereby improving the PRC's prospects for admission to the UN, and perhaps even for reconciling with Moscow.⁴⁴ Whatever the reasoning, Beijing's "cautious but 'principled'" policy toward Vietnam contrasted meaningfully with its positions on other world issues.⁴⁵

The attitudes of Beijing and Moscow toward the southern insurgency perturbed Hanoi. At a time when the two socialist giants seemed incapable of agreeing on anything, they basically shared the same reservations about Vietnamese communist strategy below the seventeenth parallel. As DRVN leaders tried to reconcile themselves to these reservations, they confronted the nagging and important problem of how to deal with the escalation of Sino-Soviet tensions. In Beijing, articles openly critical of Khrushchev and the Soviet leadership were appearing in the press; heated exchanges took place between Soviet and Chinese delegates at the Third National Congress of the Romanian Communist Party in June; a month later the Soviets withdrew their experts, capital, and technology from the PRC.⁴⁶ In light of these circumstances, China decided to challenge the Soviet

Union for leadership of the socialist camp, dramatically increasing the stakes in their dispute.

The further deterioration of Sino-Soviet relations and the ruptures it caused amplified the significance of every decision Hanoi now faced concerning the revolution in the South.[47] Until then it had succeeded in maintaining an even balance in its relations with the two allies. Now its situation was more delicate, "more uncomfortable."[48] As the Sino-Soviet dispute intensified, it became increasingly difficult for DRVN leaders to separate Soviet-Vietnamese relations from Sino-Vietnamese relations and, more problematically, to make decisions without considering their short- as well as long-term implications for relations with each of the communist giants.

What to do? With a clear-headedness that seems surprisingly astute in hindsight, Hanoi acted not only to safeguard its special relations with each but to mend the breach itself. It understood only too well that to gain advantage from being a member of the socialist camp, that camp had to continue to exist.[49] Economically, that camp's support was "indispensable," the VWP acknowledged, especially since "our country is a backward agricultural country advancing toward socialism, bypassing the stage of capitalist development."[50] "Thanks to the help of our socialist brothers," Ho Chi Minh told the National Assembly, "we not only succeeded in healing the wounds of fifteen years of war, but we also developed the economy and culture to a level never achieved before in the history of our county."[51] The pursuit of these and related objectives required financial resources that Hanoi did not have, and which only socialist allies could provide.[52] Psychologically, socialist unity and "proletarian internationalism" boosted Hanoi's confidence in its ability to meet the economic as well as political goals of its revolution, and acted as a deterrent against American attacks on the DRVN. Hanoi thus refused to take sides in the dispute, choosing instead to lavish praise fulsomely on both Beijing and Moscow. It commended each for its generous and vital support for the Vietnamese revolution specifically and the world revolution generally. It pressed upon both the necessity of socialist unity for the well-being of all that international socialism stood for and which their own individual histories exemplified.

In August, Hanoi boldly offered to mediate the dispute between the two.[53] Three months later, at the second Moscow meeting of world communist parties organized to address the dispute, Ho Chi Minh "worked tirelessly to bring the Russian and Chinese leaders together."[54] In his address to the meeting, Ho praised both the Soviet Union and the PRC for their contributions to world socialism and national liberation movements. His aim was to impress upon delegates representing eighty-one parties, and those from the CCP and CPSU in particular, the importance of socialist unity and its preservation. "One extremely important international issue presently is preserving and increasing the unity among the socialist countries and among the communist parties and workers' parties of those countries," Ho urged. Only "increased unity" could guarantee the future of the socialist camp and the triumph of the world revolution. In Vietnam, Soviet and Chinese support "allowed us to secure many important achievements over the past years, and ensures that we will secure even bigger achievements in future years." Unity was "our invincible force" as communists. "We must continue to unite closely," he entreated.[55]

Ho's pleas failed; the modus vivendi between the two powers that he and others hoped to achieve did not materialize. But his initiatives were instrumental in convincing a reluctant Chinese delegation to sign the final declaration of the meeting, a feat of symbolic if not substantive significance given the etiquette that then governed the conclusions of international socialist confabulations. The tone of the declaration was neutralist on matters touching on the dispute, owing in part to Vietnamese input, though the language was more consistent with Moscow's positions on East-West relations and world revolution than with Beijing's. In one estimation, the declaration "leaned strongly" toward the Soviet position on these matters but remained "sufficiently ambiguous so that the Chinese could (and did) interpret it in their favor."[56] That was a major achievement for which Ho and the Vietnamese deserved some credit. Had the Chinese not signed the declaration, Hanoi would have had to decide whether to do as the Chinese or as the Soviets did. Had China not signed, the signature of the Vietnamese in the reckoning of one scholar "would have incurred the gravest displeasure on the part of China, and the consequences of this can only be guessed at, while a refusal to sign would have produced the same effect upon Russia."[57] At the banquet concluding the meeting, Khrushchev toasted the solidarity of socialist countries. According to a Yugoslav diplomat, before PRC premier Zhou Enlai could contest that statement, Ho Chi Minh "rushed round the table to speak to [Zhou], and it seems that this resulted in a conciliatory Chinese speech and the exchange of embraces at the end between Khrushchev and Chou En-lai."[58] Ho's role at the meeting may also have been instrumental in prompting Khrushchev to announce shortly afterward, in January 1961, that the CPSU intended to increase its assistance to national liberation movements in the Third World in order to "use postcolonialist momentum [to] break into the 'soft underbelly of imperialism' and win sympathies of the millions of people" in decolonizing and decolonized states.[59]

After the Moscow meeting, Hanoi continued to work assiduously to mend the Beijing-Moscow breach while studiously avoiding any public profession of support for one side over the other. This policy aimed not only to "avoid confrontation as long as possible" but "always [to look] for the common ground." In walking so tight a rope, it was vital that no North Vietnamese official be "caught" siding with one or the other major powers. The VWP Secretariat ordered members to take "advantage of any opportunity" to increase socialist unity, avoid "tension," and cause "*no hatred to anyone*" in acting in accordance with party directives. The pressing necessity was to "form [a] reasonable relationship" with each of the socialist giants "without turning the relations with one power against another and with full consideration to future developments and their implications within the overall regional and global framework."[60] Hanoi had to "balance its ideological position with the necessity of maintaining close relations with whichever disputing faction was capable of supplying the quantity and quality of assistance needed," one western assessment has noted. In doing so, it is possible that Hanoi "found it necessary to subordinate ideological questions to practical logistical considerations."[61] It is also possible, however, that Ho and Hanoi sought to mend Sino-Soviet differences for ideological reasons: to protect socialist unity, to follow Marxist-Leninist orthodoxies, and to prevent the socialist camp from splitting into western and eastern sections, European and Asian. A historical account of Vietnamese diplomacy is circumspect on this point. After 1960, it concludes, the main task of Vietnamese diplomacy was "contributing to and preserving" socialist unity "in the interests of Vietnam, of the socialist camp," and of "the world revolution."[62]

These developments undercut claims that Ho Chi Minh was first and foremost a nationalist who joined the socialist camp and paid lip service to Moscow and Beijing only because he needed their material and political support to achieve Vietnamese reunification and independence. They also dispel claims that Ho was an actual or potential "Asian Tito," a communist nationalist.[63] Ho, like the majority of his peers—whether moderate or militant—in the upper echelon of the party, genuinely believed in the world revolutionary process and in the imperative to eradicate capitalism domestically and at least contain it internationally. Unlike Tito, a nonmember of the Soviet-led socialist camp who disrupted its unity, Ho and his colleagues embraced that camp and endeavored to preserve its unity while appearing to accommodate themselves to Moscow and Beijing. "The fact that neither the Russians nor the Chinese showed any resentment towards these activities by Ho Chi Minh was partly due to his personal standing as a successful practical exponent of Communist theories," a Yugoslav diplomat noted. "It was also partly because they did not wish to offend him." Hanoi was "walking on a tightrope," this diplomat continued, "but her position at the center of the struggle between the two big Bloc powers gave her disproportionate influence."[64] Besides, Ho and the movement he led were too skeptical of American designs in Indochina to contemplate breaking with the eastern bloc and pursuing rapprochement with the western bloc, as Tito and Yugoslavia had done. Ho's sidelining from active leadership of the party shortly thereafter by militants vehemently opposed to "Tito revisionism," or national communism, nullified any prospect of transforming the DRVN into another Yugoslavia, if that prospect ever existed.

THE THIRD NATIONAL PARTY CONGRESS

As it navigated the dangerous waters of the Sino-Soviet dispute, the VWP confronted myriad continuing problems at home. Besides the lack of ideological conformity in its ranks addressed earlier, there was also the economic situation and popular opposition to the regime to deal with. Hanoi understood that these continuing problems had some relationship to the lack of popular understanding of its strategic priorities. Was the socialist transformation of the DRVN still its first priority? If so, how important was improving the revolutionary situation in the South, and what means were permissible to accomplish the latter? How was the balance between these goals to be explained not only to cadres but to the people?

At the Third National Party Congress in September, the first such gathering in nine years, 576 delegates representing more than half a million members approved a five-year plan (1961–65) emphasizing increased agricultural collectivization and the development of heavy industry in the North.[65] The goal of the plan, prepared by the Politburo, was to transform the DRVN economy into a "socialist economy" by 1965 through reorganizing the peasantry into cooperatives of more than a hundred households each, replacing private trade and industry with "state capitalism," and promoting industrialization.[66] This would constitute a major step toward the realization of "true" communism in Vietnam.

The plan was ambitious, to say the least. The economic situation in the North remained dire everywhere, despite advances in some fields. The Czechoslovak ambassador reported that some peasants refused to sell their surplus crops to the state and hoarded food because they feared the consequences of currency reform, launched the previous year.[67] As a result of that and other problems, during the second half of 1960 the government had had again to reduce rice rations, already dangerously low.[68] In the cities, many of the new factories functioned poorly, in part because the technicians who ran them had insufficient training or failed to follow the directions of foreign advisers. Elimination of that situation was unlikely, at least in the near future, because the standards of the technical training Vietnamese nationals received, most of it in Eastern Europe, were "deplorably low." Furthermore, in selecting individuals to study abroad, the government favored combat veterans over persons with appropriate skills or talent. Hanoi, the Czechoslovak ambassador felt, was squandering much of the assistance it received from its socialist allies.[69] According to other foreign observers, economic and other shortcomings of the regime were causing "considerable discontent" in cities, especially among intellectuals, shopkeepers, and Catholics.[70] This situation was also widespread in the countryside, where disenchantment with Hanoi and its policies was "rampant" and "90 percent of the population" was "ready for an uprising if it had the means."[71]

Party leaders were cognizant of the challenges they faced.[72] Because of the economic backwardness that was at once the cause and result of their circumstances, and in defiance of Chinese advice, the five-year plan included ambitious goals for development of heavy industry, which were to be achieved "at all costs."[73] But given the progress already made, the leaders were optimistic. By official account,

55 percent of peasants, 70 percent of handicraftsmen, and 49 percent of merchants were now members of cooperatives, and industrial production, which accounted for 17 percent of the gross economic product in 1955, had increased to 40 percent in 1960.[74] These improvements were the results of party guidance, support from the masses, and aid from China and the Soviet Union.[75] "The entire revolutionary project of the people of the North is firmly directed," Ho Chi Minh told the congress of this progress, "on the basis of a solid alliance between workers and peasants, by the [VWP], an authentic Marxist-Leninist party."[76]

To accomplish the five-year plan, the party pledged to complete a series of "sub-revolutions" to reduce private ownership of property, eliminate small-scale production for local use, centralize production, increase industrial production and productivity, and encourage national unity and party popularity through "moderate" approaches to economic change and social reform.[77] In thus prioritizing economic development and party popularity over class struggle, the party leadership promised the people a "new democracy," a concept introduced by Chinese communists to signify the combination of economic development and political consolidation that was requisite for successful transition to socialism.[78] To facilitate the promised changes, the party would streamline its oversight of the economy by bringing all economic assets into organizations managed by state employees, who would in turn be responsible to national economic planners for setting and meeting production targets, fixing prices, and performing other managerial tasks. The party even agreed to further reductions in the size of the regular army. "At present, economic construction in the North has become the initial [i.e., foremost] task of the party," Vo Nguyen Giap told the congress in explaining the reduction. "That is why our defense budget must be reduced and military effectives cut appropriately, so that both our manpower and material resources can be concentrated on economic construction." "This is a very correct policy," Giap said in an endorsement of the current line.[79] Party leaders hoped these measures would enable the DRVN to achieve autarky, as Marxist-Leninist orthodoxy prescribed.[80]

The congress also addressed the lingering general weakness of the party, another major problem. In the North, that weakness had much to do with the rapid expansion of the VWP, whose membership had grown from five thousand to more than half a million since 1945. According to Le Duc Tho, head of the VWP Organization Committee, this expansion had brought into the party "undesirables," mostly members from incorrect classes. In rural areas, to illustrate, a large percentage of the new members came from upper-middle and rich peasant backgrounds; some were even former landlords! Though all party members were expected to act as models for the masses, some of those from these classes failed to pay the mandatory rice tax or sell their surplus rice to the state. Similarly, of the approximately 110,000 national government cadres in the DRVN, many had never actually joined the party. These included holdovers from the French colonial era retained by the DRVN government after 1954, most of whom came from bourgeois backgrounds. By official account, only 34 percent of cadres were of poor peasant or working class origins, and overall, workers and poor peasants accounted for only 54 percent of party members. According to Tho, the membership generally did not understand core tenets of communism, and the practice of criticism and self-criticism was poorly developed and largely ineffective.[81] Moreover, cadres in urban areas wasted too much time in holding meetings and disseminating political propaganda, and offered too little "effective assistance" to the masses.[82]

To solidify the party's position in the DRVN and improve the quality and effectiveness of cadres and rank-and-file members who would be responsible for mobilizing the masses in support of the five-year plan, the congress adopted a new party statute. Among other provisions, the statute mandated a purge of members who "exploit" others, recruitment of new members only from "revolutionary elements" of the peasantry, shortening of the probationary period for new working class recruits from a year to nine months, and courses on theoretical communism for mid-rank and senior members of the party.[83] According to historian Lien-Hang Nguyen, the statute did much more than that, expanding as it did the powers of security agencies and transforming the DRVN into a police state. Working closely with other agencies, including the PAVN's own security forces *(Bao ve)*, in the immediate aftermath of the congress the Ministry of Public Security under Tran Quoc Hoan created "a web of security and intelligence personnel who served as watchdogs."[84] Hoan became the "Beria of Vietnam," and the DRVN thereafter took on the airs of a quintessential authoritarian and, at times, totalitarian state.[85]

The congress announced no substantive changes in policy regarding the struggle in the South. Given its commitment to reform the northern economy, the party could ill afford increased support for the insurgency there. "Without an adequate stock of necessary materials," one VWP leader said of the plan to build socialism in the North, "we cannot meet the demands for development of production in good time."[86] The congress maintained that for the time being the party had to give highest priority to strengthening the North "on Communist lines" with a view to transforming the area above the seventeenth parallel into a "strong base" for the reunification of the country.[87]

Not only did the congress reaffirm Hanoi's "North-first" policy, but it also decreed that building socialism in the North and carrying out the insurgency in the South would henceforth be pursued separately. That is, the one goal would be the responsibility of northerners and the other of southerners, under guidance from the party leadership in Hanoi. Fundamentally, this meant that the Vietnamese revolution would no longer be a unitary movement, but would consist of two parallel endeavors, which in turn suggested that southerners would in the future get even less material support from the North and have to learn to fend for themselves. "The two revolutionary tasks of the North and the South belong to two different strategies," the congress announced, "each task aiming at satisfying the concrete requirements of each zone under the specific conditions of our divided country."[88] The people in each zone had to assume responsibility for accomplishing the tasks assigned to them and do so largely with their own resources. From now on, this division of revolutionary tasks would be "the compass for all our actions and thoughts," at least until the DRVN completed its socialist transformation.[89]

The congress probably sanctioned the division of revolutionary tasks to impress upon southerners, and party militants specifically, that Hanoi had no intention of committing itself further to the insurgency below the seventeenth parallel, as well as to encourage southern self-sufficiency. The less Hanoi involved itself in the South, the easier it was to deny any involvement, and thus to rally world opinion, retain the constancy of allies, and keep Washington from attacking the North. The sanction was clearly the work of moderates within the VWP and indicated that their control over decision-making remained, for the time being at least, almost absolute. For militants, this was a major setback and a bigger disappointment.

During the congress, VWP leaders again confronted the "unwelcome and awkward problem" of the Sino-Soviet split. In their respective addresses to the assembled local and foreign delegates, Soviet and Chinese representatives attacked each other's national leaders for pursuing misguided foreign policies and sowing discord in the socialist camp. First, the Soviet delegate denounced Chinese "dogmatists" and "sectarians" who sought to "discover isolated formulas in Marxist-Leninist classics to justify purely subjective conceptualizations." Then, his Chinese counterpart criticized Soviet "revisionists" for misusing the works of communist luminaries to "distort and negate the living content of Marxist-Leninist theory." Delegates from other communist states were supportive of the Soviets, though the North Korean delegate expressed no opinion on the split and the Albanian delegate sided with the Chinese. The North Vietnamese themselves "went a considerable way to satisfy the Soviet Union" on matters relating to the split, but ultimately "tried to be middle-men and reserved some points in regard to which they favored China's views."[90] In his address, Pham Van Dong stuck to the party line on the Sino-Soviet dispute and praised both Moscow and Beijing for their contributions to world socialism, reiterated Hanoi's support for peaceful coexistence, and pledged that the VWP would continue to "contribute to solidifying the friendship between socialist states and the unity of views among communist parties on the basis of Marxism-Leninism and proletarian internationalism."[91]

To lead the party through the five-year plan and deal with the situation in the South, the congress named Le Duan first (no longer "general") secretary of the party and thus head of the Politburo. In retrospect, this was arguably the congress's most consequential act, for Le Duan's imprint on party policy, especially on the conduct of the struggle in the South, would become increasingly evident in the coming months and years. Le Duan was selected as first secretary over Vo Nguyen

Giap, a leading moderate and the victorious general at Dien Bien Phu, mainly because of his ties to the South. He had spent most of his adult life promoting the party agenda in central and southern Vietnam, and in fact led the party in Nam Bo more or less continuously between 1945 and 1957. He thus possessed the knowledge and experience necessary to preside over the effort to liberate the South if and when it came to that, and perhaps most importantly, the credibility among southern communists to reconcile them to the policies adopted at the congress, which Hanoi knew would dishearten them. His selection may thus have been part of an adroit effort by the moderates who still controlled the party to finesse the growing division that threatened to split the VWP over revolutionary strategy in the South. Whatever the validity of this line of reasoning, Le Duan's qualifications to lead the party included his background as a committed revolutionary, a proven organizer and mobilizer, and an experienced tactician.

The 1960 congress also selected a new Politburo whose membership reflected the party's growing internal divide for and against war. Its members included Ho Chi Minh and Le Duan, as well as Truong Chinh, Pham Van Dong, Pham Hung, Vo Nguyen Giap, Le Duc Tho, Nguyen Chi Thanh, Nguyen Duy Trinh, Le Thanh Nghi, and Hoang Van Hoan, as well as Tran Quoc Hoan and Van Tien Dung as alternate members. These thirteen men were also among the forty-seven members of the new Central Committee.[92] Besides Le Duan, three others, namely, Le Duc Tho, Pham Hung, and Nguyen Chi Thanh, were from the South or closely tied to it, and harbored strong militant sympathies, as previously noted. Their reappointment, as historian William Duiker has surmised, attested to "the growing importance of the Southern revolution" in party concerns.[93] Interestingly, though Le Duan, Hung, Tho, and Thanh were also appointed to the Secretariat, Ho and Giap were not. The rising fortunes of Nguyen Chi Thanh were especially telling. Until now, Vo Nguyen Giap had been the most notable military figure in the upper ranks of the VWP. Thanh's reappointment to the Politburo had been preceded the year before by his promotion to full general *(dai tuong)* in the PAVN—a rank previously held only by Giap. The promotion, a French assessment noted, presaged the "fading of [Giap's] star" and the rise of hard-line influence in Hanoi.[94] Certainly Le Duan, Thanh, and other militants were increasing their numbers and influence at the top levels of party leadership, but their views remained for now those of a minority in Hanoi.

THE FOUNDING OF THE NLF

In the aftermath of the National Congress, in December 1960, Hanoi announced the formation of the National Front for the Liberation of South Vietnam (NLF) and, soon thereafter, of the People's Liberation Armed Forces (PLAF). The latter was the military arm of the former, but it was also in fact "part of the [PAVN], created, constructed, trained, and led by the party."[95] The NLF was to be a broad-based alliance of "all the patriots from all social strata, political parties, religions and nationalities" in the South, much like the Viet Minh had been. In its own words, the NLF called on the South Vietnamese people to "form a bloc to rise up as one man and struggle heroically in order to fulfill the plan aimed at overthrowing the camouflaged colonial regime of the U.S. imperialists and puppet administration" in Saigon.[96] In Le Duan's words, the NLF was a "broad united front" to fight imperialists and their reactionary allies.[97] To Saigon, however, it was "nothing more than an extension of the machine of North Viet Nam, controlled by the [VWP]," its mission "to unify and reinforce VC [Viet Cong, i.e., indigenous communist] activities in the South."[98]

According to its own manifesto, the NLF "undertakes to unite all sections of the people [in the South], all social classes, nationalities, political parties, organizations, religious communities and patriotic personalities, without distinction of their political tendencies, in order to struggle and overthrow the rule of the U.S. imperialists and their stooge—the Ngo Dinh Diem clique—and realize independence, democracy, peace and neutrality and advance toward peaceful reunification of the Fatherland."[99] Its program, officially adopted in February 1961, included ten points: to overthrow the colonial regime of U.S. "imperialists" disguised as the "dictatorial" administration of Ngo Dinh Diem and to form in place of that regime a coalition government of all "democratic" forces; to establish a democratic state in the South; to build an independent economy there to improve living standards; to carry out rent reduction and land reform for peasants; to build a national education system and a democratic culture; to build an army to defend the Fatherland and the people; to guarantee equal rights for all nationalities and both genders and to protect the rights of foreign residents in Vietnam and of Vietnamese living abroad; to implement a foreign policy of peace and neutrality; to establish normal relations between northern and southern Vietnam and then peacefully reunify the country; and to oppose aggressive war and actively defend world peace.[100]

The NLF's establishment fulfilled the provision of Resolution 15 calling for a "people's front for reunification and opposition to Diem and the Americans." By late 1960, when Hanoi proclaimed the Front, southern communists needed an umbrella organization with wide appeal among southerners, especially in the cities, and the NLF, they hoped, would do that as well as facilitate the recruitment of partisans and fighters.[101] It would draw to its ranks people of all classes and political persuasions opposed to the Diem regime and the American presence. If successful, it would enhance party control of the southern insurgency by bringing large segments of the southern population into a single organization under a leadership secretly beholden to Hanoi. Control over the anti-Diem, anti-American movement in the South had always been tenuous for Hanoi. As previously shown, it had even had trouble reining in its own subordinates there. Since 1954, the

Nam Bo and Interzone V leaderships had continuously questioned its strategic priorities, albeit never openly. Southern communists' dissatisfaction with Hanoi's handling of the situation in the South had been increasingly problematic during 1959 and 1960. Though the NLF's rank-and-file was always more nationalist and anti-Saigon or anti-American than communist, its leaders were for the most part committed communist revolutionaries selected by and answering to Hanoi. These circumstances and considerations may have been decisive in the party's decision to shift to a united front strategy in the South.

According to a study based on classified files from Vietnam's Ministry of Foreign Affairs, there may have been another significant consideration underlying the creation of the NLF, stemming from the way foreign powers and international groups were beginning to perceive the situation in the South. The author of that study, Tran Minh Truong of the Institute of International Relations in Hanoi, claims that VWP leaders created the NLF in late 1960 expressly to enhance the legitimacy of the southern revolutionary movement in the eyes of the international community generally, and of Beijing and Moscow specifically. "In reality, the creation of the [NLF]" as a "representative organization for all classes of nationalists in the South," Truong writes, constituted "a flexible diplomatic tactic of the party and of Ho Chi Minh" to "win over wider consent and support from the world's people for the cause of southern liberation."

Specifically, Truong writes, Hanoi intended the tactic to serve two purposes, essentially the same as those behind the recent decree to divide revolutionary labor between northerners and southerners. The first purpose was to "give the USSR and China no reason to [continue to] oppose the armed struggle in the South" by showing that the revolutionary movement there was broad, inclusive, and indigenously southern. This would demonstrate to the socialist giants and the rest of the world that in endorsing Resolution 15 Hanoi had merely responded to the wishes of the people, and of southerners in particular. The second purpose was to "counterattack and defeat the propaganda theme" of Washington and Saigon that the insurgency below the seventeenth parallel was all Hanoi's doing, a case of external "communist aggression" against freedom-loving people who supported their established government and wanted to be left alone.[102] According to another Vietnamese source, with the formation of the NLF, "an important diplomatic offensive began with people's diplomacy at its core." The "banner of peace and neutrality proposed in the Front's political programme achieved widespread approval from the freedom and justice loving people in the world, including Americans and those who disagree with communism."[103]

After the Third National Congress came and went, Hanoi had to worry about the reaction of its partisans, especially in the South, to decisions to continue prioritizing the socialist project in the North and to separate northern and southern revolutionary tasks. In selecting Le Duan as first secretary and, specifically, forming the NLF, Hanoi may have been acting to pre-empt dissidence, which sometimes bordered on mutiny, over its strategic priorities. Though focused on transforming the North and, now, keeping a distance from the South, Hanoi still sought to control events—to the extent that it could—below the seventeenth parallel.

4

Buying Time, 1961

The year 1961 witnessed a dramatic escalation of Cold War tensions. After severing relations with Havana following the Cuban revolution of 1959, the administration of U.S. president John F. Kennedy sanctioned a failed invasion of that country, prompting Fidel Castro to declare himself a Marxist-Leninist and align with Moscow. Stern warnings from Washington against Soviet interference in Congo preceded an abortive Kennedy-Khrushchev summit in Vienna and the placement of U.S. nuclear-tipped missiles in Turkey, within striking distance of Moscow. Another crisis erupted over Berlin after Moscow issued a new ultimatum calling for the withdrawal of U.S. and allied armed forces from the western half of the city. This crisis led to the construction of the Berlin Wall, a telling symbol of the state of East-West relations at that point. It also produced a tense standoff between American and Soviet forces in the city, which Moscow followed up by resuming atmospheric nuclear testing, previously suspended.

As Beijing approached the Soviets to end their bitter feud, new cleavages within the socialist camp became manifest when Moscow severed diplomatic relations with Albania over Tirana's refusal to end its tirades against Khrushchev and peaceful coexistence. Kennedy's decision to send additional military personnel as well as helicopters to South Vietnam evinced the new president's desire to thwart communist ambitions there and portended the onset of yet another major Cold War crisis.

The perilous international situation and Kennedy himself deterred DRVN leaders from meaningfully revising their revolutionary strategy that year. On the one hand, they did not want to disrupt Sino-Soviet rapprochement; on the other, they feared that Kennedy, whom they considered a staunch cold warrior, might respond aggressively to the launching of an actual war of national liberation in the

South. They did, however, authorize a moderate escalation of insurgent activity there and undertook a series of other endeavors to improve the coordination and effectiveness of communist-led military and political activity. As Hanoi remained committed to the "North-first" policy, by the end of the year the Vietnamese revolution had developed the dual character sanctioned during the VWP's Third National Congress of 1960. As northerners transformed the DRVN, southerners resisted Saigon and Washington as best they could.

RECALIBRATING THE SOUTHERN STRATEGY

In January the new Politburo convened for the first time to assess the situation in the South, deemed uneven. In the Central Highlands conditions seemed to be improving. Support from ethnic minorities and peasants was strong and the presence of the Saigon regime diminishing, both of which facilitated the creation of active revolutionary bases. In the rural lowlands and the Mekong Delta, however, the picture was less rosy due to the ease of access by enemy forces and Saigon's consequent ability to exert its power and influence there. The "political strength of the masses" in those areas was considered high, but the revolutionary presence was "not strong enough." Specifically, there were too few cadres there, and the revolutionary tactics they employed were ineffectual. The situation in the cities was still more problematic. Though the "struggle movement of the [urban] masses" was developing, it was "not yet like [that] in the rural areas." As a result of this unevenness across the whole of the South, the Politburo concluded rather understandably that the "united front for reunification" remained "narrow and weak," having not yet "assemble[d] really widely" the forces and tendencies opposing Diem and the Americans.[1]

The Politburo determined that southern revolutionaries placed too much emphasis on violent struggle and committed too little of their efforts and resources to political struggle, to winning hearts and minds, especially in cities. The appeals of southern cadres elicited little or no response among students, petty capitalists, certain religious denominations, and even workers. The Politburo attributed this to the failure to get across the "united front" message—that the revolutionary movement was an expression of Vietnamese nationalism and anti-imperialism, an effort to force the Americans to leave Vietnam and to destroy their puppet regime, rather than a conspiracy to foment social revolution. The Politburo recognized that many southerners, especially in the urban classes, were variously indifferent to, apprehensive about, or hostile to anything that smacked of social revolution or communism.[2] Such sentiments were, in reality, probably increased by a sense of the lack of candor in the communists' message. Though cadres preached unity among exploited classes, many of them distrusted urban dwellers and only reluctantly recruited them into the NLF or worked with them after they joined. Cadres from rural and poor backgrounds, for example, often considered students to be privileged and self-indulgent, and thus unpromising recruits to the revolutionary cause. The same tended to be true of their attitude toward intellectuals, whom they almost invariably considered unfit and unwilling to struggle physically, and therefore untrustworthy "comrades." As for the petty bourgeoisie, what cadres knew of Marxist-Leninist orthodoxy taught them that such people were "objectively" unreliable.

After its deliberations on the state of the revolution in the South, the Politburo adopted what it called "a very important new strategic directive" concerning "the development of the theoretical position [of the party] on insurrection" below the seventeenth parallel. "The process of attacking the enemy [and] vanquishing the regime in the South," the directive stated, was not about to go from "relative calmness" to an "explosion" of revolutionary activity in a short period. However, the Politburo now recognized that resort to war would likely be necessary in the future to achieve the liberation of the South, that political struggle and self-defense would probably prove insufficient. Accordingly, it ordered operatives below the seventeenth parallel to work diligently to improve the strength of southern forces and raise the level of their combat readiness. Once that objective was met, the southern revolution would be better positioned to take on and destroy enemy troops in a protracted conflict and gradually bring about favorable changes to the balance of forces below the seventeenth parallel. As they carried out these orders, the Politburo cautioned, revolutionaries in the South had to continue concentrating on political struggle and avoid military adventurism.[3] The directive was not for waging war, but for making further preparations for war.

At long last, DRVN decision-makers unequivocally acknowledged the potential necessity of war to accomplish revolutionary objectives in the South. The acknowledgment portended a recalibration of the struggle in the South but not the overhaul of the party's revolutionary strategy there. For the time being, the Politburo stressed again, political struggle remained central to revolutionary purposes.[4] According to historian William Turley, this latest directive "laid down basic strategy for a long struggle." In that strategy, military struggle might "conceivably" become dominant, Turley observed, though for the time being "it was more important [to Hanoi] to develop the capacity for coordinated armed and political struggle."[5] Uncertainties about the reaction of the new Kennedy administration, which the Politburo considered more anticommunist and hot-tempered than its predecessor, and of close allies, whose position on war in Vietnam had not changed, made that caveat sensible in the party leadership's eyes.

These assessments rest less on the banal passage from the Politburo directive quoted above than on the language in which the directive was communicated to southern party leaders. The language was that of a fellow southerner who was now the party's highest official, the militant Le Duan, who, for the time being, quietly went along with the moderate consensus still dominant in Hanoi. In one of a series of "letters to the South," this one dated 7 February 1961, Le Duan told his southern compatriots that Vietnam must not repeat the Chinese revolutionary model of protracted military struggle, which called for liberation of the countryside and only then an assault on cities. That model had forced the CCP to endure a revolutionary struggle that lasted more than a quarter century, from the 1920s until 1949. Instead, Vietnam should follow its own model: simultaneous struggle in both urban and rural areas. In doing so, it should work to consolidate and increase its armed forces, expand its revolutionary bases perhaps only in isolated regions at first, but then wherever possible, and eventually coordinate local episodes of violent activity, culminating in a "general uprising." In that course of events, military struggle would at some point become important, but political struggle would remain dominant until that point arrived. "We must strengthen the building of our political forces while building our armed forces" for a general offensive, Le Duan told southerners, accentuating the aggressive potential while repeating the essence of the current line. "The correlation of forces is deterministic"; appraising it correctly was crucial for revolutionary success.

Presciently, Le Duan acknowledged an important reality that accounted for many of the shortcomings and failures of the communist movement in the South: its overall weakness. "We are weaker than the enemy," he pointedly admitted. The party below the seventeenth parallel did not yet have the human or material resources necessary to mount a successful comprehensive military campaign against Saigon and its armed forces. Resorting to war under such conditions would only imperil the southern revolution. It might even give the United States the pretext it sought to send its own armed forces to southern Vietnam, which would surely doom the communist effort there. Besides, the Russians, Chinese, Cubans, and Laotians, Le Duan wrote, had all demonstrated that successful revolutions draw their strength from the masses. However, due to the misapplication of party directives and a shortage of competent cadres, communists in the South had not yet won over the people. Addressing these fundamental problems was the most pressing task. "We must know to exploit time," Le Duan concluded.[6]

PREPARING FOR WAR IN THE SOUTH

As part of its preparations for war in the South, the Politburo ordered the unification of southern guerilla forces. Insurgent activity had theretofore largely been locally planned and executed. The uprisings in the Central Highlands and elsewhere in 1959–60, for example, had essentially been spontaneous and uncoordinated, sometimes with little purpose larger than the action itself. Some of them had been staged without Hanoi's knowledge or approval and even in defiance of its directives, as previously noted. To eliminate this problem and help set the stage for a new level of coordinated armed struggle, Hanoi mandated the creation of the Liberation Army of South Vietnam, soon renamed the People's Liberation Armed Forces (PLAF). Organized into regular as well as guerrilla or militia units within the PAVN, the PLAF was under direct command of party leaders in Hanoi.[7] To improve its organization and effectiveness, in 1961–62 Hanoi secretly dispatched to the South an additional 19,150 personnel from the North, mostly regroupees.[8] The PLAF became the chief engine of revolutionary violence in the South until the introduction of PAVN units three years later.

Pursuant to its January directive, the Politburo also changed the name of the Nam Bo Executive Committee back to Central Office for Southern Vietnam (COSVN). The change was revealing. COSVN had coordinated political as well as military activity in Nam Bo during the Indochina War. Following the Geneva accords and the September 1954 Politburo resolution formalizing the commitment to peaceful reunification, COSVN lost its license to direct military activity and became the Nam Bo Executive Committee. The decision to change the organization's name back to COSVN meant that its responsibilities had been enlarged and its license to direct military activity reinstated. More fundamentally, it affirmed the Politburo's commitment to military preparations in the South.

Nguyen Van Linh, who had replaced Le Duan after the latter was recalled to Hanoi in 1957, remained as COSVN's leader, assisted by PAVN major general Tran Luong.[9] Their chief aides were Vo Chi Cong and Vo Van Kiet, as well as Tran Van Tra, the acting military commander.[10] All of them had been involved in the party's organizational work in the South since the Indochina War and were protégés or loyal disciples of Le Duan. COSVN's mandate from this point was to oversee "all affairs of the party," political as well as military, in Nam Bo. Specifically, it was tasked with "executing the guidelines, policies, lines, [and] working plans" adopted by Hanoi and "guiding their implementation."[11] Whenever problems arose, COSVN had to ask for instruction from Hanoi. When that was impossible because of circumstances, COSVN was to take no action inconsistent with party guidelines. Otherwise, COSVN must at all times "execute the platform and the concrete determinations of the rule of the party in South Vietnam." The "line of party control" thus ran thereafter from the Politburo and Central Committee in Hanoi to COSVN, and then to party committees at provincial, district, and village levels.[12]

The actualities of COSVN's duties included selecting, training, supervising, and assigning party cadres in the area of its jurisdiction, administering party finances there, and running the insurgency.[13] American intelligence reported that COSVN not only had some "policy-making powers," but its responsibilities included the duty to "study the situation [in the South] and suggest policy to [VWP] Headquarters." "The direction given by the [VWP] to COSVN consists for the most part of suggestions rather than orders," the Americans estimated. Hanoi's "suggestions" became "directives" only after "long consultations with COSVN." In this way,

COSVN "tailors the policy directives of the [VWP] to the specific situation in the South and incorporates them in COSVN's own resolutions and policies." It also handled most military matters by itself, "though following the broad military policy laid down" by Hanoi. COSVN thus enjoyed a measure of autonomy, though less in policymaking than in policy implementation.[14] To avoid American and international outrage and perpetuate the notion that the southern insurgency, which COSVN actually directed in parts of the South, was purely indigenous and largely nationalist in character, the organization's existence was kept secret, and its ties to Hanoi were "top secret."[15]

To ensure compliance with its strategic directives, the VWP ordered a purge of all southern cadres of questionable loyalty and reliability and, when possible, replaced them with more dedicated operatives. It also placed "unprecedented emphasis" on training and indoctrinating cadres throughout the South, and dispatched there increasing numbers of agents specializing in "secret and important work" and warfare, as well as more physicians and nurses.[16] An average of 150 such agents infiltrated the South each month in 1961, each of them having assumed a new identity to conceal his or her northern origins in the event of capture (even though their accents would almost surely betray where they came from).[17]

Later that year, the VWP leadership instructed its southern branch, the Party Committee of South Vietnam (PCSVN), to rename itself the People's Revolutionary Party (PRP). This was another initiative designed to prepare the southern communist movement for a protracted struggle while concealing Hanoi's involvement in revolutionary activities in the South.[18] Retaining the old name, a COSVN directive explained, would reveal that the PCSVN was a branch of the VWP and thus "subjected to the leadership of the Party Center in the North." The enemy could exploit such a revelation to "slander" southern communists, "distort" the truth about their purposes, claim that "the North's intervention in the South is subversive," and otherwise "creat[e] difficulties." More positively, the new name would create "favorable conditions for the North in its effort of diplomatic struggle to serve the liberation of the South," as well as "favorable conditions for the PCSVN to call upon the people of the South to use every method of struggle to combat the enemy."[19]

Interestingly, a French assessment noted of the name change that "Hanoi's agents [in the South], who had until now opted to use the NLF to act in South Vietnam, may have estimated that it was preferable to present themselves henceforth with unconcealed faces to influence in an authentic Marxist way the all too independent orientation of the Front." The PRP was created, in other words, to leave no doubt as to the commitment of southern revolutionaries to the "triumph of Marxism," to the establishment in the South of "not a neutral government but a communist regime."[20] According to American intelligence, the founding of the PRP, which officially took place in 1962, was merely "a restructuring of the [VWP] in South Vietnam," a "tactical maneuver to disguise northern direction of the insurgency."²¹ Indeed, the maneuver enabled Hanoi to continue its control of a southern revolutionary movement that increasingly comprised "persons who are not party members and who do not realize the extent or degree of party control" over "their" movement.²² In the words of the VWP Central Committee, the creation of the PRP, like the earlier formation of the NLF, "allowed the southern revolution to win over more supporters and isolate the enemy to a high degree domestically and internationally."²³

In thus reconstituting and relabeling its organizational apparatus in the South, Hanoi was acting to not only conceal the central role it played in directing the insurgency there, but also to put the southern revolutionary movement in position, to borrow the formulation of historian Nguyen Vu Tung, to overthrow the Saigon regime and establish "a coalition government that would adopt a policy of neutrality, ask the U.S. to withdraw its military forces from Vietnam, and realize national reunification."²⁴ It still sought, in other words, to bring about a set of circumstances that would achieve victory through political struggle without resort to war. Hanoi hoped through policies of stealth, indirection, and subversion to generate a mass protest movement and a presence so evidently popular and so insistent in its demands as to collapse the Saigon regime. If successful, the effort would avoid DRVN entanglement in the South, preclude American military intervention, enable the socialist transformation of the North to continue apace, and satisfy foreign allies.

COPING WITH CHALLENGES IN THE DRVN

It was in light of these hopeful dreams about the South that in June 1961 Politburo member Nguyen Chi Thanh reaffirmed in *Hoc tap* Hanoi's prioritizing of socialist construction in the North over escalating and increasing its contribution to armed struggle in the South. Thanh, a leading militant, had recently been assigned to direct reform in agriculture. His appointment testified to Hanoi's determination to "put more drive" behind that important sector, and may also have been arranged by moderates to mollify Thanh by making him a stakeholder in the socialist transformation of the northern economy.²⁵ The VWP, Thanh stated, regarded socialist construction as its "central task." Although class struggle was ongoing "in a certain sphere" in the North, he wrote in a passage that reveals the emphasis Hanoi was giving to reform, "the struggle between laboring people and nature to eliminate poverty and economic and cultural backwardness has become extremely important." By highlighting the primacy of socioeconomic problems over other issues, Thanh was signaling just how important those problems remained in party thinking.²⁶

Despite satisfactory progress on some fronts, the DRVN's economic challenges in 1961 did remain daunting. According to the party's own statistics, between 1958 and 1960 foreign imports into the North increased by an average of 26.7 percent annually while exports grew by only 15.6 percent.[27] Unable to generate sufficient capital internally, Hanoi still depended heavily on foreign aid to finance its ambitious programs of socialist development and industrialization.[28] Prime minister Pham Van Dong revealed to the National Assembly in April that per capita production of grain in 1960 had fallen to 304 kilograms from 367 in 1959. This drop was partly due to the fact that the North's population was increasing by nearly half a million a year, and the implications for the people's quality of life were obvious. People's lives were "deficient and hard," Dong reported, and in a year of poor harvest such as 1960, "the consequences that everybody can see" were "unavoidable."[29]

Peasants unhappy about collectivization, heavy taxes, and squalid conditions in parts of the countryside migrated to the cities in large numbers, adding to the challenges authorities there faced. By one estimate, Hanoi's population grew by an astonishing 300,000 people in 1960–61, the year of the poor harvest.[30] Bad weather was largely responsible for the very low yield of paddy and other crops in 1960. Rice rations were often diluted with corn, and the state applied rationing to meat and sugar, among other commodities, as food prices generally rose. The agricultural shortfall severely impacted the industrial sector. During the first half of the year, many factories failed to meet production quotas due to shortages of raw materials, hurting exports and creating a slew of new financial difficulties.[31] "The standard of living of the population is very low," foreign observers reported. "The rice ration will be reduced again, and that for meat," including cat and dog, "will be only, starting in May, fifty grams for three days."[32]

These harsh conditions appear to have been the cause for mass protests and other incidents that threatened the DRVN's internal stability in mid-1961. "Disenchantment is, indeed, real among the masses," the French Delegation reported in June. Widespread social unrest occurred in Haiphong, where 1,500 PAVN troops had to be deployed to restore order. During ensuing clashes between the troops and protesters, the latter set fire to rice stocks and harassed policemen and firemen trying to put out the flames. In August, saboteurs set ablaze a bicycle factory, two state stores, and enough dwellings in Vinh to leave a reported twenty thousand people homeless. They also set fire to a state store in Hanoi; exploded a bomb that badly damaged an electrical plant in Dong Anh; targeted a rubber factory in Haiphong, cutting phone lines and neutralizing its guards before setting it on fire; and cut underground electric cables to a chemical products factory in Viet Tri, disrupting production.[33]

According to foreign observers, these episodes were caused by "the persistence of economic hardships and food shortages" above the seventeenth parallel.[34] Cadres and troops newly returned from service in the southern insurgency noted that overall material conditions were "much harsher" in the North than in the South.[35] The DRVN indeed remained a poor country, so poor in fact that it barely met its own needs. To develop, it desperately needed foreign aid. Unfortunately, a portion of the aid received from abroad, particularly from the socialist camp, had to be paid in kind, mainly by rice. According to political scientist Céline Marangé, China absorbed half of the DRVN's rice production, even during "lean" years, as well as three-quarters of its coal production.[36] That reality was not lost on the average peasant, who "understands that a large share of his paddy [i.e., rice] harvest will invariably be subjected to these rules" and therefore "suffers such exasperation" that "he starts to neglect, even sabotage, his own crops."[37] Disenchantment in the North became so widespread that even "the spouses of the highest ranking personalities in the Regime" complained about "the inadequacy of food rations allocated to their families and deplor[ed] the austerity measures imposed on the [people in the] capital"![38]

These problems were compounded by RVN commando units sent into the North to destabilize the DRVN government through economic sabotage and political subversion.[39] These units exploited popular disenchantment with central or local authorities, particularly in minority-dominated areas, to incite unrest and create "centers of resistance" within the DRVN. In June, French diplomats in Hanoi reported that men, weapons, and supplies had recently been air-dropped "in certain mountainous areas" in support of antigovernment forces, and that RVN commandos specializing in sabotage operations and psychological warfare had landed in certain coastal regions.[40] In July, the DRVN Foreign Ministry confirmed these reports, including the existence of resistance centers in the Thai-Meo Autonomous Zone, where disgruntled members of ethnic minorities had joined forces with newly infiltrated commandos and disillusioned southern regroupees to stir up trouble.[41] That same month, a group of regroupees aided by minority tribesmen attacked a PAVN convoy. Soon thereafter a "small revolt" broke out among PAVN units near Lao Cai.[42] Fearing the onset of an insurgency, Hanoi deployed several PAVN units to the northwest.[43] Despite this response, the troubles spread. In early August, Hmong tribesmen in Lao Cai attacked military convoys on two occasions.[44] Shortly thereafter, subversives derailed a train carrying supplies from China near Viet Tri and distributed anti-DRVN leaflets in Hoa Binh.[45] By September, new resistance centers existed in Son La, Lai Chau, and Sapa—all minority areas, prompting Hanoi to intensify its efforts against them.[46]

Cumulatively, these developments had important repercussions throughout the DRVN. Curfews, arbitrary arrests, and incarceration of anyone suspected of involvement in the disturbances became widespread. The suppression of resistance centers by PAVN forces was particularly ferocious and involved forced relocation of rebellious tribes.[47] Ultimately, the draconian measures proved effective. By October, the disturbances and rebelliousness had been contained; in November, PAVN forces were "methodically pursu[ing] the asphyxiation of resistance centers"; a month later, "the danger seem[ed] remote"; and in January 1962, dissident forces were "if not completely destroyed, at least neutralized."[48] Challenges to public order thereafter became rare in the North, particularly in cities, and people generally were in a mood of "passive resignation."[49]

As DRVN authorities repressed dissidence, they tried to appease the people by undertaking liberal economic measures, allowing soup vendors and tailors to exit cooperatives and increasing meat rations when possible.[50] Ho Chi Minh addressed economic and related problems in a "rectification" address to the Central Committee in July.[51] Reminding his listeners of the enthusiasm and fervor with which the party had launched economic reforms in January, he insisted that it was imperative to continue those reforms now. The party leadership remained entranced by the prospect of realizing its dream of socialist modernity. "We must strive to make fast, significant, and steady advances in the effort to develop agriculture," he said, and to "provide enough grains and raw materials to develop industry and bring about socialist industrialization." Summarizing the thinking of the leadership at this time, he stated that with "good agriculture" and "good industry" the socialist transformation of the North "can proceed well," eventually enabling the DRVN to "serve as a strong base" for the southern liberation struggle.[52] A North Vietnamese delegation had recently traveled to China, the Soviet Union, and much of Eastern Europe asking for economic assistance, and had received pledges totaling 295 million rubles to help finance the new five-year plan, the money to be spent on building some eighty new enterprises.[53] For its part, the party had recently "subjected itself to a process of self-examination" and resolved to give "higher priority" to agriculture by committing itself anew to the improvement of agricultural techniques.[54]

Since transforming the North into a strong rear base for the southern revolution required improvements in national defense, the leadership established air and antiaircraft forces, beefed up reserve and self-defense forces, upgraded airfields and ports, and expanded strategic transport routes throughout the DRVN. Finally, in a bid to increase discipline and quality in the armed forces, all PAVN political officers had to undergo a new round of ideological training.

ESCALATING POLITICAL AND DIPLOMATIC STRUGGLE

The year 1961 saw a dramatic escalation of Cold War tensions in flashpoints around the world: mounting tensions in Laos, another crisis in Berlin, accelerating decolonization in sub-Saharan Africa, the politically motivated assassination of Congolese prime minister Patrice Lumumba, the continuing war in Algeria, and the failed effort at the Bay of Pigs to overturn the Cuban revolution. Hanoi held capitalism and Washington in particular responsible for these developments.[55] "Consistent with traditional [American] policy," the Kennedy administration was "increasing weapons production, following a policy of 'limited war'" in the Third

World, and "creating tense situations and expanding [its] military ventures throughout the world," a DRVN report noted. As evidence of this, the report pointed to plans by Washington to "invade Cuba [and] to expand the war in Laos," to its role in the "coup d'état" in South Korea that brought the reactionary Park Chung-hee to power in Seoul, and to unspecified other government overthrows in South America.[56]

Such developments, actual or only apprehended, alarmed Hanoi and fueled its sense of siege. The significant activity related to national defense and security in the DRVN just noted, much like the substance of the Politburo's January resolution, reflected Hanoi's increasing concern about Washington's confrontational stance in the Cold War, and in Vietnam and the rest of Indochina in particular. In view of its continuing efforts to achieve southern liberation and national reunification without a major war, Hanoi's response to this stance in the middle months of 1961 was more political than military. Domestically, the DRVN's "subversive propaganda" concentrated on mobilizing the people in both halves of the country against the Americans and the legal authority of Diem's regime in Saigon, with a view to bringing to power there a new administration. That administration, Hanoi hoped, would be more amenable to the peaceful "fusion" of the two Vietnams.[57]

Internationally, Hanoi sought to mobilize and manipulate world opinion against the American presence in the South, and to enhance the prestige of the DRVN and the Vietnamese revolution as emblems of national liberation and anti-imperialism, thus isolating Washington. This amounted to "supplanting" Saigon and Washington "on the international chessboard."[58] The "diplomatic struggle," a report to the National Assembly noted in October, "is of major significance" in the DRVN's effort to "create conditions to elevate the spirit of self-reliance of our people for the cause of building socialism in the North." It was equally important in the effort to build momentum internationally for peaceful national reunification as well as "the consolidation of socialist unity."[59] "The spirit of unity and mutual cooperation between our country and all socialist countries," a national assemblyman said of Hanoi's diplomatic strategy, "is extremely important," "a firm guarantee for each of our revolutionary victories," "the foundation of our diplomatic policy."[60]

At this time, the DRVN Foreign Ministry was desperately trying to "win over" foreign governments to the nation's cause, not just those in the socialist camp but others in Africa and the rest of the postcolonial and decolonizing world. This was done chiefly by establishing diplomatic relations and extending political aid and whatever material support Hanoi could provide.[61] "The basic direction of our diplomatic policy," newly appointed foreign minister Ung Van Khiem, a staunch moderate, noted in October, consisted of "striving to tighten friendly, collaborative relations with fraternal socialist countries," "contributing to the effort to increase unity between the countries of the socialist camp," and developing ties with newly independent states.⁶² Through diplomacy, Hanoi also sought to obtain political and material support for its socialist project in the North while generating criticism of American activities in Indochina and increasing pressure on Washington to keep its military forces out of Vietnam. To those ends, in 1961 the Foreign Ministry again aggressively denounced recent American initiatives in the South on the grounds that they violated the Geneva accords.⁶³ Shortly thereafter, the government circulated a letter affirming its commitment to peace and to implementing the accords to "the governments of the entire world, whether they have diplomatic relations with us or not," with the exception of the United States and "a number of colonial countries of the United States." The letter denounced the perfidy of Washington and its friends in Saigon and warned of the disastrous consequences of leaving American ambitions unchecked. Hanoi also sent a letter to the governments whose representatives had endorsed the Geneva accords, urging them to pressure the ICSC to demand that the "U.S.-Diem clique" honor the accords.⁶⁴

CO-OPTING THE ICSC

As this last initiative suggests, Hanoi hoped that the ICSC could be used for its purposes, unlike Diem, who by now sought its abolition. "The North in the past manipulated the International Control Commission to their own advantage rather more successfully than the South did," the Foreign Office reported in early 1962. "No doubt" DRVN leaders "consider that, given the difficulty of establishing the facts about infiltration, they stand to gain a great deal in the near future by sticking to the [Geneva] Agreement" or maintaining the pretense thereof.⁶⁵ The ICSC "has had little effect on the preservation of peace in Indochina," a DRVN national assemblyman observed in October. However, "if it is determined to maintain a fair attitude then it might still contribute to the implementation of the Geneva accords in an equitable way."⁶⁶ Unfortunately, the ICSC could do little about anyone's violations of the accords and had in fact grown increasingly critical of Hanoi in the last year or two.⁶⁷ Whenever the commission voted to investigate an alleged violation by either side, Hanoi condemned the vote, "fearing that a step had been taken toward its being cited by the commission for violation of the Geneva Agreements." Such a citation might alienate some of Hanoi's foreign supporters and thus undermine the diplomatic struggle.⁶⁸

More to the point, Hanoi had always accused the Canadian representative on the ICSC of partiality toward Washington and Saigon, and by 1959–60 began accusing India, the "neutral" member of the commission, of the same thing. In commission deliberations, unaligned India was indeed increasingly siding with capitalist Canada against socialist Poland, a consequence of the deterioration of Sino-Indian relations that culminated in war in 1962. The "dramatic realignments in India's external relations" that accompanied these developments, in the words of one study of the subject, were "paralleled in [the ICSC] delegation's behaviour." India in fact joined Canada on the commission to vote against Hanoi on the legality of three "extremely critical issues": the presence of DRVN military forces in the South, the presence of American military advisers in the South, and Saigon's draconian Law 10/59 against dissidence in the South.[69] Not surprisingly and with some justification, Hanoi surmised from these votes that the ICSC was a deck stacked against its legitimate interests, a body acting in bad faith and thus itself "violating the accords of July 1954."[70] In 1961 a Polish diplomat concluded that "whatever happened at the Commission was interpreted by the Indians through the prism of their hostility toward China," and thus to the detriment of Hanoi.[71]

This partiality of the ICSC, in the estimation of historian Douglas Ross, reflected the conclusion of its Canadian and Indian members that the commission should function as a "shield" for the RVN, which was "too weak to defend itself" and thus "required a measure of external buttressing if American intervention and possible Sino-American confrontation were to be precluded." By June 1960, in Ross's judgment, the Canadians were using the ICSC "to the fullest possible extent" to "combat the DRVN campaign of 'indirect aggression' against the southern regime," and the Indians were "in effect working with Ottawa ... to strengthen the [Saigon] regime and thus forestall a return to open warfare between the two sides of the Indochina conflict." Thus "all of the truly important decisions and 'non-decisions' in this period were taken by Indo-Canadian majority vote" and, "without exception," favored Saigon to the detriment of Hanoi.[72]

The commission thus not only validated Washington's "magnified" claim that Hanoi was sending soldiers into the South but legitimated American efforts to protect the South.[73] In early July 1961, the VWP Secretariat took note of the fact that the ICSC majority had "illegally" assumed the right to investigate all subversive activities taking place below the seventeenth parallel, whether or not they had anything to do with the Geneva accords. That was, the Secretariat insisted, "entirely contrary to the responsibilities and mandate" of the commission. It was also "dangerous," inasmuch as it created a circumstance that would encourage the Americans to believe that they could introduce their own military forces into the South without reprimand for violating the Geneva accords.[74]

This change of direction by the ICSC dealt a major blow to Hanoi's diplomatic struggle. Nonetheless, DRVN leaders continued to regard the commission as "more useful than not." In a pointed effort to encourage the Indian commissioner to take a more "objective" stance on the introduction of more and more American military hardware and advisers into the South, Hanoi openly supported Delhi in its dispute with Portugal over Goa.[75] Also, to shore up diplomatic support for the DRVN generally, and in its treatment by the ICSC specifically, foreign minister Ung Van Khiem traveled to Guinea, Mali, Niger, Morocco, Tunisia, and the United

Arab Republic (that is, Egypt and Syria) in the spring.[76] Then, in June and July, Pham Van Dong visited China, North Korea, Mongolia, the Soviet Union, Poland, and Czechoslovakia for the same purpose, as well as to secure increased material and financial aid. Dong's visits were also meant to "remind the United States and her allies that North Vietnam had powerful friends, who could be expected to back North Vietnam if hostilities broke out."[77] The visits marked "a new phase in the relationship between our country and [host] countries," Khiem reported, and were "a positive contribution" to "the effort to increase the great spirit of friendship and the unity that cannot be broken between our people" and socialist as well as Third World countries.[78] In a nod to the Soviet leadership, Hanoi announced that Dong's visits had served to "increase the unity of the socialist camp, with the Soviet Union at its core."[79] Continuing this flurry of diplomatic activity, Nguyen Van Hien of the NLF soon also visited the Soviet Union, Czechoslovakia, Hungary, Cuba, China, Indonesia, North Korea, and, presumably, war-torn Algeria. Wherever they went, the Vietnamese travelers urged their hosts to do all they could to pressure Washington to exercise restraint in Indochina.

VIETNAMESE COMMUNIST INTERNATIONALISM

On a more general level, this series of diplomatic initiatives reflected Hanoi's views of its stake in the shifting currents of international relations in the early 1960s. The Cold War had created two implacable blocs and made the situation in South Vietnam a major expression of that implacability. Recognizing that fact, DRVN leaders convinced themselves that success in their revolution could tip the worldwide balance of power in favor of the socialist bloc. This conviction, combined with the fact that they had to conduct their diplomacy from a position of military weakness, made those leaders accomplished practitioners of international politics. So, too, did the totality of their commitment to Marxism-Leninism—however they interpreted it—and thus to anti-imperialism and anti-Americanism. Whatever side of the ideological divide they stood on, whether they were committed moderates or ardent militants, DRVN leaders never, even during the crisis years of the early 1960s, thought strictly in terms of their own interests narrowly defined. "No, no, and no, we are not isolationists," Pham Van Dong emphatically stated in an interview with a reporter who suggested Hanoi was not attuned to the attitudes of the international community because of its preoccupation with domestic affairs.[80]

Over the years DRVN leaders had repeatedly iterated this commitment to socialist internationalism and world revolution, and just as often emphasized the central role they assigned to their own revolution in the latter. To be sure, the Cold War, to say nothing of the Sino-Soviet dispute, created myriad challenges for Hanoi, but the contemporaneous process of decolonization in the Third World also created countless opportunities. Specifically, the Vietnamese, who had gained international notoriety for their contributions to decolonization through their war against France, and specifically their dramatic triumph at Dien Bien Phu, were now well positioned to lead the charge against American imperialism and its "reactionary" allies and to inspire others to do the same. Back in 1958, Truong Chinh had spoken to the VFF Central Committee about the DRVN's international obligations as a socialist state, even as it endeavored to liberate the South. In Truong Chinh's formulation, that meant contributing to world peace by "opposing all war-kindling schemes of the imperialist aggressors and their agents," strengthening "friendly solidarity and the fraternal cooperation with the USSR, China, and [other] people's democracies," and "support[ing] national liberation movements in the world." A year later, the VWP Central Committee expressed confidence that "the victory of the Vietnamese Revolution" would have "an enthusiastic effect on the movement of popular liberation in Asia, Africa, [and] Latin America" and precipitate "the disintegration of colonialism throughout the world."[81]

The peoples of Africa and Latin America "clearly grasp that the people of Vietnam are loyal friends and reliable friends in their struggle against colonialism and imperialism," a member of the DRVN National Assembly said, echoing these positions. They "turn to us not only to understand the experiences of revolutionary struggle, but also to understand the experiences of building the economy [and] culture of our country."[82] As Vietnam fought for its own national liberation, other assessments noted, it "vigorously supported national liberation movements in Africa," particularly in French North Africa, and it "quickly recognized newly independent countries."[83] That support sometimes took concrete forms, reportedly including sending "several North Vietnamese military instructors" based in the United Arab Republic to train insurgents to fight in the Algerian war of independence.[84] "The element that we must grasp is that our struggle against the U.S.-Diem clique is not solitary," another member of the National Assembly stated; it was in fact "part of a worldwide struggle" against "American lackeys, especially in Asia, Africa, and Latin America."[85]

In Hanoi's thinking, then, the prospects for the future of Vietnam and its revolution were linked to the prospects of the rest of the noncapitalist world. "The struggle to maintain peace" and "achieve national reunification of our homeland not only suits the vital interests of the people, our nation," as the VWP Central Committee put it, "but also suits the general interests of the movement for democratic peace in the world." The success of revolutionary efforts in both the North and the South hinged on defeating capitalist and reactionary enemies to create "a solid outpost of the socialist camp in Southeast Asia."[86] The liberation of South Vietnam, Pham Van Dong repeated in September 1960, was an integral part of "the national independence movements that agitated the entire world."[87] As "the banner of the movement for popular liberation, the center of big contradictions in the world," Vietnam had become in Washington's eyes the "ideal area" for implementing its "counterrevolutionary strategy."[88] In Hanoi's eyes, that made Vietnam the ideal place to explode that strategy. "Our struggle for national reunification has reached a new plateau: the international political plateau," a member of the National Assembly affirmed.[89] To foreign observers, by 1961 Hanoi was clearly acting as if it had a "unique calling" in the world.[90]

LINGERING EFFECTS OF THE SINO-SOVIET DISPUTE

The world revolution clearly mattered to DRVN leaders, but even they understood that it would never triumph as long as Beijing and Moscow bickered. Interestingly, by the middle of the year DRVN authorities were acting in public as if the Sino-Soviet dispute "hardly existed" at all and dismissed questions about its possibly complicating consequences by insisting on Hanoi's neutrality.[91] The French Foreign Ministry believed at this time that Hanoi's primary consideration was maintaining "a certain degree of independence" vis-à-vis the disputing parties, as well as a balance between them to avoid aggravating the situation.[92] An exasperated Soviet diplomat told a western counterpart in April that North Vietnamese leaders were just "too nationalistically minded for us to try to put pressure on them."[93] "While consulting their allies at every step, and being influenced by the advice they may receive," British diplomats observed, "they will reserve the right to make the final assessment themselves, and keep the final decisions in their own hands."[94]

Despite this practice of sitting "fairly firmly on the fence, trying always to play off one side against the other, and where possible to mediate between them," Hanoi's revolutionary strategy in 1961 remained generally consonant with Soviet aspirations.[95] It continued to adhere to "the great lines of Soviet foreign policy," the French Embassy in Moscow reckoned, "whether it be peaceful coexistence, general and complete [nuclear] disarmament, or the [unilateral] signing of a peace treaty with the two German states."[96] That was the result of Soviet influence in Hanoi, as well as the ideological and personal inclinations of key Politburo members, Ho and Giap specifically, who held the Soviet Union in high esteem and drew inspiration from its example and historic achievements as leader of the socialist bloc. The appointment of Ung Van Khiem, a man known for "his moderate sentiments and his desire to maintain and develop close contacts with the West and with France in particular," as foreign minister attested to the continued prevalence of moderate views in Hanoi. In the estimate of French diplomats, Khiem's appointment had represented "a sparkling victory for the moderate tendency in the DRVN."[97] The same tendency was visible in the promotions of two new Vietnamese generals, Song Hao and Hoang Van Thai, who were friends and close collaborators of Vo Nguyen Giap and, like Giap, harbored moderate, pro-Soviet and anti-Chinese sentiments.[98]

That Hanoi still held the Soviet Union in the highest esteem and valued Soviet aid more than that of the Chinese was evidenced by the growing number of Soviet technicians then in the DRVN, as well as the wider availability of Russian-language books and the higher opinions Vietnamese technicians had of Soviet over Chinese machinery.[99] The Soviet Union was the model and inspiration for the DRVN's socialist modernization; many of the hopes and dreams of Vietnamese communist leaders rested on continued moral and material support from Moscow. Without Soviet aid, Hanoi would never be able to execute its five-year plan of economic and industrial development.[100] It was as true for the DRVN as it was for North Korea and other socialist states at this time that only Soviet technology could help them develop heavy industry, since the PRC remained deficient in that field.[101] Hanoi "could hardly afford to get far out of line with the Soviet Union" at that time, the British Consulate reckoned; in 1961 the economic aid it received from the Soviet Union and other Eastern European countries remained greater than that received from China and more necessary to meet certain pressing goals. Besides, Hanoi may have sensed that Soviet influence could be "a useful counterweight to their uncomfortably large neighbor," the consulate added.[102]

Though the Soviet Union made massive contributions to the DRVN's development, growing numbers of VWP members were disenchanted with Moscow. Its continued insistence on peaceful coexistence and the fact that it did not respect the right of "fraternal" parties to deviate from that line irked dogmatic militants and others who were nationalistically inclined. Equally vexing to these groups was the fact that Khrushchev never delivered on his January pledge to provide greater assistance to national liberation movements. There was no change in Moscow's endeavors to restrain the use of violence in liberation movements, just as there was no assistance to advance Vietnam's liberation struggle.[103] That was a big disappointment for party militants, whose affinity for China and apathy toward moderate views only grew as a result.

Despite their vociferous public rhetoric in support of violent national liberation, Chinese leaders continued to privately counsel caution in South Vietnam because it suited their own practical interests at this time. Still reeling from the disastrous Great Leap Forward, Beijing wanted to avoid an actual war in Indochina, which was likely to produce American occupation of South Vietnam and perhaps even invasion of the DRVN.[104] In the former case maybe and in the latter case surely, China would have to intervene militarily, as it had to do in Korea, if not to rescue an ally or honor a commitment to wars of national liberation, then to protect its own national security.[105] Lacking nuclear weapons and estranged from Moscow, Beijing's capacity to deter American aggression in Indochina was limited.[106] "An apparent division of opinion within the Chinese Party on how far it would be wise to flout Moscow" under these circumstances may have accounted for Beijing's reticence to support a widening military struggle in South Vietnam.[107]

Beijing in fact sought rapprochement with Moscow during 1961 and the first half of 1962.[108]

Just as it appeared that unity of the socialist camp might be restored, new cleavages emerged, to Hanoi's great dismay. Having had enough of Albania's Enver Hoxha's diatribes against him and against peaceful coexistence, Khrushchev openly attacked the leadership of the small communist state during the CPSU's Twenty-Second Congress in late October. Moscow in fact broke diplomatic relations with Tirana, forcing other communist parties to decide whether to follow its lead.[109] After the congress, which they attended, Ho Chi Minh and Le Duan discussed the matter with Mao, who refused to break off relations with Albania and actually praised its boldness.[110] Citing its unbreakable commitment to socialist unity, and perhaps with the encouragement of Beijing, Hanoi too refused to sever diplomatic relations with Albania.[111] According to Hungarian diplomats, the VWP was genuinely disheartened by Khrushchev's attacks on the Albanians, but ordered members to be silent on the issue and not to discuss the recent CPSU congress until the leadership had formed an official opinion on the matter.[112] A month later, Ho returned to Moscow and then visited Beijing to defuse this latest crisis, evidently with no positive results in either place.[113] Shortly thereafter, the VWP on its own initiative contacted "fraternal parties" around the world to express its concerns and propose still another meeting to resolve the dispute.[114] These initiatives came to nothing, but the effort earned the Vietnamese more acclaim in the socialist world and attenuated Moscow's vexation at Hanoi's decision to not break ties with Albania.[115]

NEW CHALLENGES IN THE SOUTH

While such distractions diverted northern attention from the South, southerners came increasingly to rely on their own resources and resourcefulness to combat the Diem regime, as decreed during the recent VWP congress. According to a western intelligence estimate, by the end of 1961 the Ho Chi Minh Trail and the sea infiltration routes that had been opened earlier to supply the southern insurgency were no longer "vital" because the southern insurgency was learning to "feed itself."[116] Such resourcefulness reflected the growing efficiency and discipline of certain segments of southern revolutionary forces, as did a series of small military victories over Diem's army in 1961.[117] In fact, for a brief period the insurgents turned the Mekong Delta into "the most insecure part of the country," with "many of the provincial seats [of the Saigon government] resembling islands in a sea of hostile territory."[118] During the first half of the year alone, insurgents killed approximately 1,500 enemy troops and assassinated or kidnapped more than two thousand officials and other civilian supporters of the Saigon regime.[119] Meanwhile, in official reckoning, the NLF was enjoying increased popular support, and the PLAF, "though not yet strong," was gaining strength.[120]

These successes, while heartening, were variously ephemeral, limited, or overshadowed by concomitant setbacks. The NLF and the revolutionary movement in general developed hardly at all in the cities and in parts of the countryside.[121] A NLF assessment of this period noted that Hanoi's continued emphasis on "long-range revolutionary warfare," that is, on political struggle and preparation for war, turned "the weaknesses of the enemy" into "his strengths" while creating "severe difficulties for us."[122] By Hanoi's own admission, progress in the South had stalled after mid-1960 because Saigon and its allies still used "every method" and "every reactionary force" to "destroy the revolutionary movement very criminally."[123] Between 1956 and 1961, DRVN authorities estimated, American assistance to Saigon had grown tenfold, from $41 million to $400 million a year.[124] In November, U.S. military assistance to the South began to exceed the level allowed in the Geneva accords, a fact recognized by the ICSC.[125] If this were not alarming enough, during a public appearance with Diem in Saigon in May, U.S. vice president Lyndon Johnson not only referred to the South Vietnamese president as the "Winston Churchill of Asia" but pledged Washington's help in increasing the size and effectiveness of Diem's armed forces. Hanoi considered Johnson's public pledges to signal the onset of a "new aggression" against the people of Vietnam.[126]

The growth, modernization, and increasing effectiveness of Diem's forces were indeed a problem. According to historian Mark Moyar, even before the assistance Johnson proffered began arriving, ARVN forces were demonstrating "modest improvements in aggressiveness and military competence," which enabled them to score several "major victories" over insurgents.[127] In addition to his regular forces, Diem's Republican Youth Movement enlisted thousands of rural youths and trained them to "assist in community development projects, provide a fresh infusion of rural leadership," and "help protect villages" against enemies. In conjunction with a land reform program financed by the United States, this "community-based approach to security" enabled Saigon to extend its influence in rural districts while eroding popular support for the communist-led revolution.[128]

Equally troublesome for revolutionary forces was the strategic hamlet program Saigon initiated in mid-1961. By the end of the year, the program had established more than five hundred such hamlets, and a year later four thousand.[129] Unlike the previous effort to create fortified, autarkic agrovilles—which had proved a clear failure by this time—this latest program involved no forced relocation of peasants. Most importantly for its success, it assigned protective duties to trained and motivated self-defense forces, including members of the Republican Youth Movement, and governing duties to officials loyal to Diem's brother, Ngo Dinh Nhu, rather than often corrupt regional administrations or government ministries.[130]

The success of the program gave the Diem regime unprecedented access to and influence over rural communities. It also isolated a large segment of the rural population from the NLF, hindering the latter's access to new recruits and supplies.

"The scale of the regime's effort," historian Philip Catton has written of this program, served to "beef up Saigon's physical presence in rural areas and so threaten the guerrillas' access to the peasantry." In the Central Highlands, where the fortunes of the southern revolutionary movement had been improving, the creation of strategic hamlets and of militias loyal to Saigon soon resulted in shortages of food and medicine among insurgents, which in turn precluded expansion of the PLAF and demoralized NLF members. Strategic hamlets, in other words, erected "physical and psychological barriers" between southern revolutionaries and peasants, which the former for the time being could not breach.[131] A survey based on captured NLF documents concluded that in parts of the South the program hurt the Front "badly in many ways": "Young men were defecting to their native villages, intelligence agents were being arrested, tax collections were falling off," and "travel from base area to base area was becoming more difficult and dangerous." In Kien Hoa Province, this survey reported, the strategic hamlet program "came close to meeting the requirements for defeating a Communist war of national liberation and achieving the political stabilization which would allow economic and social development to proceed in a well-ordered manner." There and in other areas where the "basic problems" of land, justice, and "truly responsive government" were effectively handled by local RVN officials, the people readily submitted to the authority of the Saigon regime.[132]

Initial efforts by revolutionaries to destroy strategic hamlets and otherwise undermine the program produced mixed results. "The insurgents did not usually launch frontal assaults against strategic hamlets," Philip Catton has written. Instead, they tried to obstruct the construction of new hamlets by recruiting peasants to destroy their fortifications.[133] "It was not just a question of rising up one time and destroying a strategic hamlet," a southern revolutionary leader stated later in an assessment of the effort to destroy the program. "There were times when the masses had to rise up dozens of times and had very strong forces within the hamlet, as in Ben Tre, but the strategic hamlet continued to exist."[134] The program thus "threw the revolution off balance," as David Elliott has written.[135] For a period at least, it caused "considerable problems."[136]

COSVN CALLS FOR ESCALATION

In response to the successes of the strategic hamlet program, COSVN met in October 1961 to address deteriorating conditions in the lower South and ponder what to do about the program. The program was so effective, it acknowledged, that it had "definite potential" to threaten the future of the revolution below the seventeenth parallel. "The enemy is actively enforcing the [military] draft, developing his intelligence [capabilities], conducting sweep and encroachment operations [among the population], and relocating the population [wherever necessary] in order to restore his oppressive control," COSVN noted in detailing its understanding of the program and other enemy endeavors. It also noted, alarmingly, that "the enemy has switched from his policy of active preparation for an attack on the North while carrying out pacification in the South to a policy of concentration of pacification forces in the South while increasing destruction tactics against the North," the latter a reference to the aforementioned infiltration of RVN commandos above the seventeenth parallel to foment subversion.[137]

Though COSVN believed that most people in the South recognized "the just cause of the revolution," fear of Diem's regime made many of them hesitant to join and fight for the resistance. Besides, the southern revolution had more urgent problems. Its armed forces remained weak; the political struggle lacked uniformity; the NLF had no Central Committee and thus lacked direction; and cadres and party members still manifested "hesitancy and passiveness."[138] The party in the South remained undermanned due to Saigon's repressiveness and the "fairly major losses" suffered recently. For all these reasons, "committees and auxiliary agencies at all levels are still weak" and "we still have too many weaknesses to be up to the task of defeating all the enemy's schemes and changing the balance of forces between us and the enemy."[139]

Under these circumstances, COSVN surmised that it was best to intensify both political *and* armed struggle, calling for a "continuous offensive" to culminate in a "general uprising" in the South. It insisted that "our" forces must "attack the enemy in both the political and military fields" despite their weakness. To "speed up the process of the enemy's disorganization and the development of our own strength," to "change the balance of forces between us and the enemy," and to "yield ripe conditions for a general offensive and general uprising," there must be at least "limited offensives and uprisings."[140] In other words, to gain strength and momentum, the southern revolutionary movement must be proactive, more aggressive. The general uprising that COSVN envisaged as climaxing revolutionary success in the South would unfold gradually, in stages. Unlike the sporadic and ultimately unsuccessful rural uprisings of 1959–60, the final revolutionary upsurge was to be centrally planned and coordinated to ensure across-the-board success. It would begin "with an uprising of the rural population to eliminate the oppressive control of the enemy's administration in the hamlets and villages." Once consolidated in the countryside, it would "merge" with a coordinated surge in the cities to "overthrow the upper levels of the [Saigon] administration." That overthrow would signal the triumph of the southern revolution but "will take a relatively long period to achieve."

These recommendations echoed previous pleas by southern party leaders as well as the language of Resolution 15 and the Politburo's January resolution, but in stronger, more alarmist terms. COSVN was in fact asking for "a complete stepping up of the revolutionary potential of the people and our party"; it was recommending a return to the methods of the Indochina War, the resumption of combat operations. COSVN made this plea for now evident reasons. Revolutionary progress in the South was unsatisfactory despite the continuing vulnerability of the Diem regime. The regime's supporters "possess an outlook of defeat and desperation regarding the future," which COSVN thought the party could exploit by intensifying armed struggle. Granted, the armed forces were weak, but bold action on their part represented, in COSVN's view, the best way to draw people to join them. As to the possibility of large-scale U.S. troop deployments in the South, it concluded that that prospect was limited since American and world opinion would never approve of such wanton violation of the Geneva accords.

According to Gareth Porter, the COSVN declaration spelling out these scenarios marked the first time since the end of the Indochina War that a Vietnamese communist body "adopted the line that the revolutionary forces in the world were already on the offensive and that imperialism was on the defensive."[141] The declaration did indeed point out that now was a propitious time to escalate armed struggle because the global balance of forces between revolutionaries and imperialists had shifted in favor of the former. That passage was consonant with the rationale behind Beijing's denunciation of peaceful coexistence, which pointed to the inevitability of war between the capitalist and socialist camps and to the present as the time to risk that war (just not in Vietnam).[142] The substance of the COSVN policy statement underscored the growing disconnect between southern party leaders and Hanoi. The statement's language was unmistakably militant, endorsing as it did Beijing's professed views on revolutionary change and national liberation. As such it challenged Hanoi's moderate line, its "North-first" policy, and its apparent neutrality in the Sino-Soviet dispute. It also underscored the ripple effect of that dispute within the VWP. Hanoi's recent initiatives to increase "unity of thought" within the party were obviously falling short.

The potential appeal of COSVN's policy statement in Hanoi rested on the fact that DRVN leaders now generally recognized that not only was the revolutionary struggle in the South going badly, but the successes of the Diem regime were mounting.[143] Nonetheless, they resisted COSVN's plea. In William Duiker's estimate, key decision-makers in Hanoi "vigorously rejected COSVN's contention that there was a rigid dividing line between a strategy leading to a general uprising and a protracted military struggle resembling the war against the French." They agreed that the revolution in the South might "triumph by means of a general uprising" but insisted that talk of such an uprising was premature. Equally objectionable to them, Duiker notes, was COSVN's "apparent conviction" that "victory in the South could be achieved in a relatively short time" despite its own statements to the contrary.[144] To be sure, it was naïve to assume, as COSVN seemed to do, that victory was sure and not too distant, just as it was naïve to assume, as it certainly did, that Washington would not react aggressively to an escalation that threatened the Saigon regime simply because the American public opposed violating the Geneva accords.

In the final analysis, Hanoi rejected COSVN's recommendations because it wanted to focus on completing the socialist transformation of the North, and it continued to fear the likelihood of American intervention and the response of its allies to escalation. "As everyone knows, ever since he came to power, U.S. president Kennedy has aggressively prepared for war," warned foreign minister Ung Van Khiem; and since Hanoi had given him no legitimate cause for war, Kennedy was anxious for a pretext.[145] With such weighty considerations in mind, the National Assembly cautioned southerners to engage only in "just actions" that were "completely consistent with the UN Charter and the 1954 Geneva Agreements on Indochina."[146] Hanoi's strategy thus remained cautious, as William Turley has noted, because it aimed to "reconcile conflicting requirements." "On the one hand," to use Turley's formulation, "Hanoi needed to maintain good relations with a great power ally bent on 'peaceful coexistence' and therefore to avoid provoking the United States." "On the other hand, the party had to save its Southern branch from extinction if it were to make progress toward reunification under party rule." "The risk-minimizing path between these conflicting demands," Turley continued, "was to increase the North's involvement in gradual, deniable ways while encouraging Southern self-reliance." Thus Hanoi prepared for military struggle but relied "so far as possible on Southern resources to achieve its objectives."[147] According to a French assessment, Hanoi not only opposed escalation of the insurgency at this point but in fact did not even envisage attempting Vietnamese reunification in the near future. The reasons for this were allegedly that the "implantation" of communist forces in the South "remained insufficient to wage a decisive campaign," and because of its own economic problems the DRVN leadership "had no desire" to "burden itself further [*à s'attacher un nouveau boulet*] by assuming responsibility for a South Vietnam that survived only because of American assistance."[148]

"We must guard against a clash with the U.S. imperialists and their henchmen, who are armed with modern weapons," PAVN general Le Quang Dao wrote in *Hoc tap* in defending Hanoi's rejection of the COSVN proposal. Despite progress in modernizing and improving the PAVN, Dao remarked, "we are not satisfied with the achievements obtained," and therefore they were unprepared to cope with the American threat in the South. Highlighting the dangers of southern adventurism, Dao explained that "if a new aggressive war should break out, the anti-aggression war—which we will be compelled to carry out—will be a modern war involving the use of modern weapons and combat techniques." Such a war "will extend throughout the country and be at a much higher level than the guerilla warfare carried out during the former resistance" against France. It "will require of our army and people a very strong spirit of sacrifice and a sense of combat discipline."

It would also require "a revolutionary army having a high degree of standardization and modernization, an elevated political enlightenment and sense of discipline, and truly modern tactical and technical standards." Finally, it would necessitate "a powerful reserve, a great militia, and a guerilla force having better equipment and higher combat standards than it had during the resistance," as well as "a solid rear capable of supplying the front with manpower, foods, medicines, equipment, weapons, ammunition, vehicles, and so forth." The "quantitative and qualitative" attributes of each of these requirements must necessarily be "much greater and higher" than anything ever attempted in Vietnam. "Failure to fully realize the foregoing new demands," Dao warned, "will lead to dangerous mistakes and lack of appropriate preparation." Until "adequate material and moral preparations have been made in peacetime," the Vietnamese people would remain unable to "give the invaders more bitter lessons than that of Dien Bien Phu."[149] On the basis of such reasoning, both French and Canadian representatives in Hanoi concluded that DRVN leaders would not undertake "risky initiatives" in the foreseeable future.[150]

RAISING THE STAKES

In the fall, Maxwell Taylor, a senior U.S. general, and Walt Rostow, a senior adviser to President Kennedy, visited South Vietnam. In the days preceding their visit, which lasted from 18 to 24 October, a flotilla of forty American helicopters and four hundred U.S. military personnel to operate and maintain them arrived in Saigon. Hanoi complained loudly that this introduction of foreign combat troops into the South grievously violated the Geneva accords, but no one, including the ICSC, heeded the complaint.[151] The introduction of this equipment and the forces to man it, plus the Taylor-Rostow mission, notably heightened the stakes in the Washington-Hanoi confrontation, and moved the two governments closer to war.[152] As that reality sank in, Hanoi saw ever more clearly the perils of rash action by revolutionary forces in the South. At the same time, it understood that it must prepare for war with the United States, and it must do so sooner rather than later. American imperialism was becoming "uncontainable."[153]

In December, Hanoi welcomed a delegation of senior Chinese military officials led by Marshal Ye Jiangying. A Polish diplomat thought, no doubt correctly, that the mission was a "counter-demonstration" to the Taylor-Rostow mission to Saigon, and that Ye "might well be engaged in contingency planning with the North Vietnamese."[154] Similarly, the British Consulate believed that the "prime purpose" of Ye's mission "seems to have been to make clear for all to see China's strong military interest in Vietnam, and to warn the United States in particular that if she further enlarged her intervention in South Vietnam, and a clash between North and South resulted, China would go in on North Vietnam's side."[155]

As suggestive as these speculations may have seemed at the time, a former ranking member of the VWP later said the Chinese mission actually came to urge Hanoi to continue exercising caution in the South and to impress upon its followers there the importance of limiting the scale of their activities to reduce the risk of American military intervention. Beijing's "main worry," this ex-ranking member has written, was that "if we provoked the Americans into counterattacks close to the Chinese border, they [the Chinese] would have to intervene as had happened in Korea."[156] This interpretation is supported by historian Qiang Zhai, who writes that economic problems in China, including mass starvation, constrained Beijing to still favor caution in South Vietnam. Not only did escalating hostilities in the South require resources the PRC did not have or could not spare, but it might draw the country into a war with the United States that it was unfit to fight.[157]

During his visit, Ye publicly praised the DRVN as an "outpost" of the socialist camp in Southeast Asia, endorsed Vietnamese claims that the United States was violating the Geneva accords, and accused Washington of aggression in deploying combat forces in the South. Washington was trying to "drag the armies of subservient countries in the [SEATO] military bloc into interfering more deeply in South Vietnam," Ye claimed, and by such "criminal acts" was making the situation in Indochina "extremely tense and dangerous."[158]

Beijing's renewed interest in Vietnamese affairs, which Ye's mission signaled, was both welcome and worrisome for Hanoi. On the one hand, it made Chinese assistance likely in the event of an expansion of hostilities below the seventeenth parallel, a reassuring prospect. On the other, however, it risked compromising Hanoi's neutrality in the Sino-Soviet dispute. During his stay in the capital, Ye made no public tribute to or even mention of the Soviet Union, something that would have been standard before the dispute. In fact, he publicly alluded to China's divergence from the Soviet Union over Albania, to the consternation of his hosts. To limit the damage and perhaps also to make clear his personal disapproval of this and other Chinese positions on international affairs, Vo Nguyen Giap stressed in a public address of his own during Ye's visit that the "key to victory" in Vietnam was the "ever firmer solidarity of the countries of the socialist camp with the great Soviet Union as the nucleus." Giap also referred to the Soviet army and Soviet aid ahead of the Chinese army and Chinese aid, and praised Soviet achievements in building communism.[159] After reading the speeches of Giap and others on this subject, a Canadian diplomat noted that "the North Vietnamese have intended to make abundantly clear that they take a firm stand in the [Sino-Soviet] dispute—on the fence."[160] "One point that we can be certain of," historian Ang Cheng Guan has observed more substantively, "is that the visit [by Marshal Ye] did not lead to any Sino-Vietnamese military alliance to the exclusion of the Soviet Union."[161]

Yet even that plus the flatteries of Giap and others were not enough to assuage Moscow's pique over Hanoi's apparent flirtation with Beijing. That at least is one way to read the fact that shortly after Ye's visit the Soviet Defense Ministry failed to send a congratulatory message to its DRVN counterpart on the occasion of the latter's Army Day. Since the sending of such messages was routine courtesy in the socialist world, some in the diplomatic corps in Hanoi interpreted the failure as "a mark of Soviet disapproval of North Vietnam for not dropping completely into line over Albania, or perhaps a sign of Soviet disapproval of North Vietnam developing closer military contacts with China."[162]

TWO STRUGGLES

By the end of 1961, the Vietnamese revolution had developed the dual character envisioned in the final resolution of the Third Party Congress a year earlier. Northerners were building socialism and transforming their military capabilities; southerners were resisting Saigon and the Americans, more or less within parameters dictated by Hanoi and with limited support from the North. The two populations were waging separate but parallel struggles.

Behind this overly neat formulation, Hanoi's persistent refusal to engage the DRVN more fully in the southern insurgency disheartened increasingly large numbers of Vietnamese. "Since the day Kennedy became president of the United States," a southern representative in the National Assembly stated in late 1961, he had "made preparations for war, created tense situations, advanced the policy of provoking war in all places in Europe, Asia, Africa, and Latin America, organized adventurist aggression in Cuba, staged coups d'état in South Korea [and] Brazil, subverted the peace treaty with Germany, waged psychological warfare in the Berlin problem [and] widened the war in Laos." Because Kennedy had also increased American aid to Saigon, its armed forces could now "fight with modern weapons" and "kill people massively." The result was a growing "militarization" of southern Vietnamese society, including youth and women, who were now compelled to join military and other organizations of the enemy, such as the Republican Youth Movement. With so much help from the Americans, the Saigon regime would soon be able to inflict irrevocable damage on the southern revolution, perhaps as soon as the end of 1962.[163]

Evidence for this pessimistic assessment was revealing. According to incomplete statistics compiled by the NLF and submitted by the assemblyman, by early 1961 Saigon had conducted 2,185 "small and big sweep operations," built 874 political prisons, and incarcerated 270,000 political dissidents. An additional 200,000 dissidents lived as virtual prisoners in some 250 "forced" or "secret" settlements resembling concentration camps. Between 1954 and 1960, the same statistics showed, Diem's military and security forces killed 77,500 people and detained or tortured 725,000 others. "The life of the people of the South in the past seven years has been a life full of misery," the assemblyman said, summarizing this evidence.

In the South, "the life of one person has no value" and "the United Nations Charter is still worthless."[164]

The assemblyman concluded by implicitly deploring Hanoi's apparent indifference to the suffering he described. "The people of the North sympathize deeply with the compatriots of the South," he added with more than a touch of irony. They have supported them by "training millions of people through thousands of meetings" and produced "thousands of petitions submitted to the [ICSC]." Meanwhile, they "resolutely build socialism in the North to create stable conditions for the unification struggle of the southern compatriots," as the latter struggle against a ruthless enemy under the "brilliant leadership" of the NLF.[165] This aroused speaker was not the only assemblyman to praise southerners for resisting Saigon and the Americans and to deride northern contributions to the fight against the common enemy below the seventeenth parallel. Following a "tradition of heroic struggle," another assemblyman noted, southerners "struggled heroically against" Diem and the Americans without feeling "intimidated" by them. "The southern compatriots surely will secure victory."[166]

To avoid continued and possibly growing criticism, veiled or otherwise, of its revolutionary line, Hanoi would have to revisit its approach to the South and do so sooner rather than later—unless it could find, via the diplomatic struggle, peaceful ways of defusing the crisis. As it turned out, it would spend much of the next year trying to do just that.

FIGURE 1. Soviet ambassador to the DRVN Alexander Lavrishchev visiting Lang Son, November 1954 (courtesy of the Revolution Museum, Hanoi).

FIGURE 2. DRVN president Ho Chi Minh meeting with members of the Indian ICSC delegation, 1954 (courtesy of the Revolution Museum, Hanoi).

FIGURE 3. Vietnamese dockworkers posing with Soviet sailors following delivery of Chinese rice, Haiphong, undated (courtesy of the Revolution Museum, Hanoi).

FIGURE 4. Vietnamese demonstrators holding banners calling for U.S. withdrawal from the South (on left) and support for the independence struggle of the Algerian people, undated (courtesy of the Revolution Museum, Hanoi).

FIGURE 5. DRVN delegation led by prime minister Pham Van Dong during a visit to India, April 1955 (courtesy of the Revolution Museum, Hanoi).

FIGURE 6. PRC president Liu Shaoqi (on left), accompanied by Ho Chi Minh, greeted by Hanoians, May 1963 (courtesy of the Revolution Museum, Hanoi).

FIGURE 7. Crowd gathered at Ba Dinh Square in Hanoi to hear a speech by Liu Shaoqi, May 1963 (courtesy of the Revolution Museum, Hanoi).

FIGURE 8. Vietnamese of Chinese descent conducting a military training exercise, Haiphong, undated (courtesy of the Revolution Museum, Hanoi).

5

Exploring Neutralization, 1962

During the first half of 1962, the cessation of hostilities in Algeria, the recognition of its independence by France, and the signing of a multilateral agreement neutralizing Laos suggested that a less troublesome era in global politics was about to begin. However, the brief but fierce Sino-Indian War soon highlighted the limits of Asian and Third World solidarity, while the Cuban missile crisis brought the United States and the Soviet Union to the brink of nuclear war and dealt a near-fatal blow to the prospect for East-West détente. By year's end, the accords on Laos were unravelling. After a short-lived "ambiguous truce," Beijing's enmity toward Moscow resumed and reached new heights as a result of Khrushchev's refusal to forgive Albania even as he attempted rapprochement with Yugoslavia, maintained close contacts with Delhi during and after the Sino-Indian War, and "capitulated" during the Cuban crisis.

In this tense international context, the United States sustained its commitment to preservation of a noncommunist government in South Vietnam. The Cuban crisis underscored the dangers of unchecked communist expansion and validated presidential calls for increasing aid to Saigon to "save" the RVN.

Hanoi closely followed these events. During the first half of the year, it supported negotiations to neutralize Laos and, upon their successful culmination, envisaged a similar solution for South Vietnam. However, mounting American support for the regime in Saigon, the collapse of the accords on Laos within weeks after their signing, and the outcome of the Cuban crisis convinced many party members that neutralization of the South and any diplomatic solution to the situation there would not work. That conviction marked the passing of what may have been the last good chance for peace in Vietnam before the onset of war.

HANOI AND ITS NEIGHBORS

The deteriorating situation in the South, the growing credibility gap between Hanoi and southern revolutionaries, mounting intraparty tensions, and fissures in the socialist camp perturbed DRVN leaders in early 1962. Now they faced another, arguably more pressing danger: growing American interference in Laos and Cambodia. The machinations of the Americans and their agents in the two countries were not only "worrisome" to Hanoi but confirmed its "worst suspicions" about Washington's ambitions in Indochina.[1]

In 1958, Laotian prime minister Souvanna Phouma, a neutralist in Cold War terms, had sought to form a coalition government including members of the communist Pathet Lao revolutionary front led by Souphanouvong, the "Red Prince." Washington responded by suspending assistance to Vientiane, precipitating the fall of Souvanna's government. The new government under Phoui Sananikone was manifestly "reactionary," that is, pro-American and anticommunist. In July 1959, Phoui's government arrested and detained Souphanouvong and other leaders of the Pathet Lao.[2] As a result, the political situation in Laos began to draw "maximum attention" from Hanoi, which suspected that the United States intended to spark a civil war in its small, landlocked neighbor, in part to destabilize the DRVN.[3] But in mid-1960 units of the Royal Lao Army under Captain Kong Le captured Vientiane and reinstated the country's foreign policy of neutrality in the Cold War. Souvanna returned as prime minister and created a new, broadly based coalition government, again including representatives of the Pathet Lao. In December of that year, General Phoumi Nosavan, a staunch anticommunist, and troops loyal to him stormed the capital, ousted Souvanna's government, and installed the pliable Boun Oum as prime minister. Souvanna fled to the Plain of Jars, controlled by the Pathet Lao, where he proclaimed his the "legitimate" government of Laos, soon recognized by communist and nonaligned states but not the United States and its allies. Despite objections to his heavy-handed tactics by American diplomats in Vientiane, Phoumi secured Washington's patronage and assistance.[4] In fact, he capitalized on American support, even largesse, to consolidate his authority and hound his communist opponents.

The situation in Cambodia was less alarming to Hanoi, but troubling nonetheless. There, Norodom Sihanouk's government was under increasing pressure from Washington to abandon its neutrality in foreign policy, which Hanoi considered "compatible" with its own interests, and to align itself with the United States.[5] To defuse regional tensions and preserve his autonomy, Sihanouk responded to these pressures by calling for restraint on all sides. Sensing that the civil war between Phoumi's forces and those of the Pathet Lao might "explode into an international conflict" engulfing all of Indochina, a prospect Hanoi seriously feared, Sihanouk proposed an international conference on the future of Laos to involve essentially the same parties that had produced the 1954 Geneva accords on Indochina.[6]

NATION-BUILDING IN LAOS

After the fall of Souvanna's government in July 1958, Hanoi had redoubled its effort to strengthen the Pathet Lao. The need to prevent conditions in Laos from deteriorating may in fact have contributed to its unwillingness to commit more of its scarce resources to the insurgency in southern Vietnam. Also, as historian Christopher Goscha has noted, the Ho Chi Minh Trail, opened in 1959, "made all of eastern Laos vital to the northern supplying of southern Vietnam," limited as that supplying was at the time.[7] By this time, too, the Vietnamese and Laotian struggles for national liberation had been intertwined for years, ever since the war with France, if not earlier. The presence of nearly ten thousand PAVN troops and more than four thousand militiamen and support personnel from the DRVN in Laos in mid-1962, while DRVN leaders still refused to commit PAVN units to the insurgency in South Vietnam, attested to the importance Hanoi attached to Laos.[8] The military personnel, all officially "volunteer troops," not only advised and trained Pathet Lao forces but, beginning in the fall of 1960, joined them in combat operations against enemy forces.[9] The "economic crisis" in the DRVN, a June 1961 French assessment noted, "does not appear to bother the North Vietnamese Government" in Laos, where it continued to "provide aid to the troops of the Pathet Lao." Clearly, the assessment concluded, the Laotian problem was "at the forefront" of Hanoi's concerns.[10]

Over time the DRVN mission in Laos extended well beyond strengthening and protecting the Pathet Lao. It became a veritable nation-building effort aimed at containing American influence, stabilizing socioeconomic conditions in parts of the country, and laying the foundation for communist domination.[11] "The capitalist-imperialist camp will use every method of persuasion" to pull Laos into its orbit, a Vietnamese report stated in 1961. To preclude that eventuality, to help Laos "become a truly independent and positively neutral country, the countries of the socialist camp must have a comprehensive, long-term, and sustainable supply plan."[12] A special committee whose purpose was to achieve those goals coordinated the effort from Hanoi under the supervision of Politburo member Hoang Van Hoan.[13] Hoan's group concluded in 1961 that Souvanna Phouma's rump state represented Hanoi's best hope for an alternative to the current regime in Vientiane. A communist government in Vientiane would have been ideal for Hanoi, but the Pathet Lao was too weak to bid for national power. Unfortunately for Hanoi, Souvanna's government had as yet no "functional bureaucracy" and no "plan to develop the economy." It therefore required Hanoi's assistance to survive as a bulwark against American encroachment.[14] The "apparatus" of Souvanna's government had just begun to build itself, a Vietnamese assessment concluded.[15] Possibly, Hanoi armed the Pathet Lao and supported Souvanna's government with a view not only to frustrating Washington's ambitions in Laos but also to drawing its attention away from Vietnam.

In 1961 Hanoi signed a series of agreements with various Laotian factions, including Souvanna's government, demonstrating the seriousness of its intent to contain American influence and bring Laos into the Vietnamese orbit. In honoring those agreements, Hanoi dispatched political, economic, and other specialists to Laos, funded their endeavors, and funneled other aid to the Laotians from the DRVN and also from the rest of the socialist camp.[16] Hanoi welcomed the latter show of support for its efforts in Laos, despite the logistical difficulties it often encountered in delivering aid goods and materiel. "There are some misunderstandings between a number of [donor] countries and our party and government," DRVN authorities noted.[17] Despite those difficulties, between December 1960 and the end of June 1961, the Vietnamese delivered to Souvanna's government 4,229 arms of various kinds from the Soviet Union, five tons of medical supplies and fifteen tons of dry provisions from China, and significant assortments of foodstuffs, medications, and sugar from Czechoslovakia, East Germany, Mongolia, and Poland.

Abetted by Beijing and Pyongyang, Hanoi also secretly provided military aid to the Pathet Lao, despite pledges to the contrary to Souvanna Phouma and Moscow. During the six months ending in June 1961, the DRVN supplied Laotian communists with 6,447 arms of various kinds with ammunition from China, as well as 699 weapons plus ammunition from its own stocks. North Korea provided American weapons captured during the Korean War as well as antiaircraft artillery and 80-mm mortars.[18] This weaponry was in sharp contrast to the cameras, film projectors, and other such trivia sent to the Pathet Lao by Moscow via the DRVN in these years of peaceful coexistence.[19] In view of these disparities, DRVN representatives in Moscow were soon bragging, in defiance of Hanoi's instructions to keep such matters secret, that "the Vietnamese have played the leading role in the revolutionary struggle of the Indochinese people." In Laos, the braggarts boasted, the Pathet Lao armed forces, "which grew and became stronger, had many Vietnamese members who helped in the organization of political work and the preparation of cadres."[20] One Vietnamese source even called the DRVN "the supply rear base" of the Laotian revolution.[21] Indeed a French report noted that by July Hanoi's military contributions had been "more important for Laos" than the contributions in nonmilitary goods made by the Soviets and other allies.[22] While he appreciated Vietnamese contributions to the Laotian cause—those he was aware of—Soviet premier Khrushchev thought the Laotian situation should be resolved through diplomacy, not violent revolution.[23]

Moscow's limited support for these activities was only one of the challenges Hanoi faced in Laos. The roads connecting Vietnam to that country were in such disrepair that aid deliveries were often delayed and always difficult, sometimes simply impossible. Only a single road connected DRVN supply depots to the "liberated" Laotian province of Xieng Khouang, and that road was variously described as "destroyed, usable for only six months of the year, difficult [to use] during the rainy season, [and] impossible to use some months." After December 1960, the Vietnamese had at least ten Soviet transport aircraft at their disposal in the effort to supply Laos, but the small planes could transport only two tons of goods per sortie and were limited to two flights daily, and poor weather often forced cancellation of flights.[24] "Although the requirements of Laos are not very many," a DRVN report noted, "foreign aid is still not enough."[25] Part of the problem stemmed from the refusal of socialist states to coordinate their aid efforts because of the Sino-Soviet dispute. "It is at least possible that the USSR has undertaken the support" of Laos "as a gesture of good faith," a western analyst wrote at the time, "while the Chinese prefer to let the Russians get themselves involved in an area where China will inevitably have the ultimate profit."[26] Historian Ilya Gaiduk remarks that Moscow wanted to contain "reactionary" influence in Laos, but without running the risk of widening the conflict.[27] Keeping the Laotian situation "in hand" would deny Beijing a pretext to enter into it and thus to stir up trouble there that could threaten peaceful coexistence. According to historian Mari Olsen, Moscow came to the aid of Laos at the urging of Hanoi but limited its assistance because it feared further destabilization in Indochina.[28] Soviet suspicion that supplies earmarked for Laos were redirected to South Vietnam prompted Moscow to suspend aid deliveries to Hanoi temporarily in November 1961, further impeding the Vietnamese mission in that country.[29]

THE GENEVA CONFERENCE ON LAOS

As Hanoi endeavored to defend its interests in Laos, the International Conference on the Settlement of the Laotian Question convened in Geneva on 16 May 1961. The brainchild of Cambodian leader Norodom Sihanouk, as noted earlier, the conference aimed to avert internationalization and intensification of the civil war in Laos by creating a neutral government of national concord sanctioned by international accords. Hanoi had reservations about such a conference and also about the prospect of a neutral Laos. A genuinely neutral Laos would hamper its ability to support the insurgency in southern Vietnam and might cramp the freedom of movement of the Pathet Lao. Also, Washington might use the conference to sabotage Laotian sovereignty and create new obstacles for the Vietnamese revolution. The British Consulate thought DRVN leaders were "very hesitant" in "deciding whether a communist or a neutralist Laos would be best for them." A communist takeover in Vientiane would give Hanoi "an assured corridor of approach to supply the rebellion in South Vietnam" as well as a "guarantee" of security along part of the DRVN's western border. On the other hand, a premature or unsuccessful power grab by the Pathet Lao would likely cause the United States to "react sharply in defence of their position in South East Asia." If that reaction resulted in destruction of the Pathet Lao and consolidation of an anticommunist regime in Vientiane backed by western military force, Hanoi would certainly be less able to influence events in South Vietnam, and it might provoke the Chinese to intervene militarily in Laos. "I think," British consul general J. F. Ford wrote London, "that the North Vietnamese would not like to see a situation arise in Laos in which the Chinese would feel impelled to enter in strength." Their "main interest," he surmised, "is in having Laos friendly to them, and free of American influence."[30]

In the end, Hanoi attended the Geneva Conference on Laos and committed itself to neutrality. Hanoi recognized that the Pathet Lao movement was incapable of making a successful bid for control of the country, even with the help available from the socialist bloc. The movement, in their judgment, was too weak and disorganized to govern a state. By official account, Laotian communist forces had liberated three provinces—Houa Phanh (Sam Neua), Phong Saly, and Xieng Khouang—and parts of four others, which together constituted about three-fifths of the country's area and perhaps a million of its people.[31] On the basis of these successes, Hanoi believed the Pathet Lao had "a wide party base in the provinces." However, it also thought that the Pathet Lao leadership "from the center to the localities" was "not yet unified."[32] Moreover, the movement had no secure revolutionary bases outside the three liberated provinces. Given these realities, neutralization was a way to buy time for Laotian revolutionary forces, time they could use to consolidate and expand existing bases. Even if the proposed neutralization ultimately failed and hostilities resumed, Laotian communists would by then be better prepared.

A neutralist regime in Vientiane recognized by the international community might also preclude further American encroachment in Laos and possibly elsewhere in Indochina, a development that would isolate the Saigon regime. "Every day," a member of the National Assembly told his colleagues, "American forces and [allied] Thai forces maneuver across the Mekong River" and "collude with reactionaries in South Vietnam" to "intimidate liberated areas" in Laos. Such activities created a "very big threat to the security of our country and a threat to peace in Southeast Asia and the world." "We cannot not care about conditions in Laos," the assemblyman concluded.[33] According to this reasoning, Laotian neutrality would deny Washington a base for intervention in Vietnam. Also, a neutral Laos under Souvanna Phouma would have friendly political and economic ties to the DRVN, as Souvanna himself had made clear. Souvanna had also declared his support for the peaceful reunification of Vietnam under the terms of the Geneva accords. Together with the existing neutralist governments in Cambodia and Burma, a neutral Laos would form part of a purportedly neutral bloc that would "undercut the anticommunism of the South

Vietnamese Government," which would find itself "the odd man out" in a Southeast Asia tilted toward nonalignment in the Cold War.[34]

Finally, Laotian neutrality on terms Hanoi envisaged would facilitate northern support of the southern insurgency. Though largely self-sufficient at the current level of hostilities, that insurgency still depended on supplies and personnel from the North, and when hostilities intensified—an eventuality Hanoi was already preparing for—infiltration routes through Laos would become indispensable. That the movement of North Vietnamese troops and supplies via Laos would constitute a violation of Laotian sovereignty as well as the terms of its neutrality, even then being negotiated, did not trouble Hanoi. In fact, long before the end of this Geneva conference, the VWP Central Military Commission had issued orders to "develop capacity for mechanized transport over new routes still deeper in Laos."[35] In addition, sites in Laos had long served as sanctuaries for NLF leaders and PLAF units, and nothing in the available record suggests that Hanoi ever considered the possibility of ending that practice. In fact, should the Americans widen the war in South Vietnam, revolutionary forces would benefit from safe havens across the border in "neutral" Laos.

Hanoi thus wanted not actual or permanent neutrality of Laos, but neutrality on its terms and for as long as those terms served the purposes of the Vietnamese revolution and its desire to have a friendly, pliable government across the border. That meant until American interest in Laos subsided, until Pathet Lao forces seized power in Vientiane, and until Hanoi had contained the American threat in its own country. Accordingly, Hanoi pushed for a diplomatic solution in Laos in the interests not of peace in that country but of its own anti-American struggle. "I see the danger," one foreign diplomat wrote, that Hanoi "may profess to favour a neutralist Laos" and even work to that end, but then look on the achievement of that end "as a preliminary step towards a communist take-over."[36] "While it may be that the DRV will hesitate to push the Communization of Laos too hard for their own safety," another observer remarked, "it is difficult to accept the thesis that they will not push it at all."[37]

The Geneva agreement making Laos neutral was signed in July 1962, after prolonged, difficult negotiations.[38] It mandated the creation of a coalition government of representatives from the three largest political factions—"reactionaries," communists, and neutralists. Such a mandate hardly guaranteed peace or stability, but it was "the best which the circumstances allowed."[39] For Hanoi, the arrangement was acceptable: Washington would no longer have a pretext to interfere in Laos if the new government carried out its responsibilities, and with that government's legitimacy validated by the agreement it would be difficult for Washington to subvert and replace it.

The agreement on Laos was "a big victory" for its people, foreign minister Ung Van Khiem told the DRVN National Assembly. It "restores peace in Laos after many years of war on the basis of recognition and respect for the independence, sovereignty, unity, territorial integrity, and neutrality" of the country. It was also "a big victory for national liberation movements and other forces seeking to preserve peace worldwide." Perhaps more significantly, Khiem stated, the new agreement "not only reaffirmed the basic clauses of the old [1954] Geneva accords but also reinforced and developed them further," and in so doing "eliminated a threat of war" by precluding Washington from "intensifying the civil war in Laos and threatening peace in this region."[40] In Nguyen Vu Tung's later judgment, the outcome pleased Hanoi because it created favorable conditions for the expansion of revolutionary forces and eliminated for the time being the possibility of direct American intervention. Those were essentially the same goals Hanoi pursued in South Vietnam.[41]

Hanoi welcomed the agreement on Laos as evidence of the VWP's "policy of co-existence and the peaceful settlement of disputes by negotiation."[42] That sense of success may have prompted the repatriation of PAVN forces from Laos, which reduced the North Vietnamese presence there to less than 250 political and technical specialists by year's end.[43] That at least is the claim made in a PAVN internal history. "After the 1962 Geneva Agreement on Laos was signed," this unpublished history notes, "to implement our promises, our Central Committee and Central Military Party Commission ordered the withdrawal of all volunteer forces and the bulk of our military specialists back to Vietnam."[44] To first secretary Le Duan, the agreement represented "a big achievement not only for our dear friends of the Laotian revolution but for our entire side."[45] That assessment reflected Hanoi's conviction that the fate of Vietnam was inextricably linked to that of Laos.[46] Important as it was to defeat imperialism worldwide, it was more important for the moment to defeat it in Indochina. Imperialism and socialism could not coexist in a peaceful Indochina. Vietnamese independence and revolutionary success were pipe dreams as long as any part of Indochina remained under the rule of imperialists or their lackeys. Because Cambodian communists were problematic allies, a neutral Laos was all the more important. It would prevent the Americans from interfering in South Vietnam via Laotian territory.[47] It also lessened the potential for an immediate conflagration in Indochina.

CONTEMPLATING NEUTRALITY FOR SOUTH VIETNAM

This initial wave of enthusiasm for the idea that neutrality could prove an effective device for getting the Americans out of Laos and precluding a wider war raised Hanoi's interest in using the same device to the same ends in South Vietnam. Why not, DRVN leaders reasoned, have another round of multilateral negotiations on the neutralization of South Vietnam? In his report to the National Assembly in praise of the Laos agreement, Ung Van Khiem used language clearly suggesting that such a solution might be suitable for southern Vietnam. Neutralization of Laos had "expanded and strengthened the peaceful zone" and thus proven to be "a constructive factor for peace and security in Southeast Asia while weakening the network of military bases of the American imperialists in the region." Those results vindicated "the method of solving pressing international problems peacefully, which the socialist camp promulgates," Khiem said in a clear endorsement of peaceful coexistence. They also vindicated the views of Ho, Giap, and other leading moderates in the VWP, as suggested above. "To solve the Laotian issue, socialist countries advocated a policy of using a method of peaceful negotiations. The results have shown that the fundamentals of the 1954 Geneva Conference not only cannot be destroyed but [can be] reinforced, [even] supplemented to be made more comprehensive. That demonstrates," Khiem insisted, "that the method of peaceful negotiations is the best method to solve pressing international problems." Laotian neutrality thus had "a very important international significance."[48] For Vietnam, it represented a "first step."[49]

It might even have been the case that after initially hesitating, Hanoi supported negotiating Laotian neutrality to gauge the prospects for a similar solution to its own crisis in the South. In the judgment of historian Ken Post, it is "evident" that for DRVN leaders in the negotiations on Laos, that country "was acting as a surrogate for South Vietnam, where the struggle now being led by the NLF might also result in such a solution."[50] On many levels, the spirit and letter of the Laos agreement were consistent with the aspirations of the moderate wing of the VWP concerning the South at that juncture. "It is now clear," Nguyen Vu Tung has noted, "that Hanoi was considering a neutrality model for South Vietnam and therefore thought that the Laotian experience would be applied to South Vietnam."[51]

The NLF had broached the issue of neutrality for South Vietnam in February 1961 and actually made it part of its political platform.[52] During the first week of the Geneva Conference on Laos in May, DRVN representatives circulated a memorandum, presumably on behalf of the NLF, proposing "the convening of a conference to end foreign intervention in south Vietnam and to consider proposals . . . for [its] neutralization."[53] There seems to have been no substantive response to these proposals. It may have been to test international opinion on the subject of neutralization that in October Hanoi launched a propaganda offensive, a "broad and fierce political struggle," aimed at precluding further American encroachment in South Vietnam by increasing pressure on Washington to accept such a diplomatic solution to the intensifying crisis there. It did this by denouncing alleged "preparations by the U.S.-Diem clique to bring American forces into southern Vietnam" and stressing the "seriousness" of the threat to peace these preparations posed.[54] It was perhaps in the interests of the campaign to promote neutralization that Hanoi in late October called on France to "use its rights and its influence" to make a "precious contribution" to the reduction of tensions in Indochina.⁵⁵ It might have been part of the same effort that in December Hanoi went to special lengths to impress a visiting Indian diplomat with the idea that DRVN leaders "attached great importance" to maintaining the 1954 Geneva accords on Vietnam "in force." Tellingly, this diplomat was "struck" by the desire among North Vietnamese leaders for renewed contacts with the Saigon government and thus for negotiations between the two.⁵⁶ A month later the Foreign Office in London similarly concluded on the basis of information from Vietnam and elsewhere that Hanoi's desire for negotiations with Saigon and other governments over the status of the South was sincere. The Vietnamese demonstrated a "reasonable attitude" toward "renewed contacts" with RVN leaders, London believed.⁵⁷

On 18 February 1962, ten days after Washington and Saigon announced the creation of a new American organ with expanded responsibilities to replace MAAG and oversee their military partnership in the South—the Military Assistance Command, Vietnam (MACV)—DRVN authorities approached Soviet and British diplomats demanding that their governments, as cochairs of the 1954 Geneva Conference, "urgently study effective measures to end U.S. aggression in South Vietnam" and preserve the integrity of the accords that conference had produced. Later in February and then again in March and April, Hanoi repeated the request that the two governments "proceed to consultations with the interested countries to seek effective means of preserving the Geneva settlement of 1954 and safeguarding peace."⁵⁸ All these initiatives were indirect pleas for actual negotiations, and thus implicitly for the possibility of settling the status of the South by neutralizing it at least long enough to secure American disengagement.

In early March, during this flurry of diplomatic activity, Beijing publicly called for an international conference on the status of southern Vietnam.⁵⁹ Later that month, Cambodian leader Norodom Sihanouk, a neutralist with international credibility, published an editorial in the Cambodian newspaper *Nationaliste* seconding Beijing's proposal. Moscow also endorsed the initiative, and in April the DRVN National Assembly debated the "necessity to convene a new Geneva Conference to find a solution to problems lingering since July 1954."⁶⁰

By June, then, there were clear signs that Hanoi was seriously considering reconvening the 1954 Geneva Conference or participating in some other international forum to address the crisis below the seventeenth parallel.⁶¹ Shortly thereafter, North Vietnamese diplomats in Geneva suggested to Souvanna Phouma and Norodom Sihanouk that the matter of negotiations on neutrality for South Vietnam should be discussed in Geneva immediately after concluding the talks on Laos. One report on these contacts suggests that Vietnamese diplomats had actually tried to blackmail the two men by advancing that the agreement on Laos would never work "so long as there is still a dangerous situation in [South] Vietnam."⁶² On 1 July, the NLF dispatched a memorandum to the cochairs of the 1954 conference endorsing Sihanouk's March proposal, and shortly thereafter declared its willingness to accept a coalition government in Saigon inclusive of representatives of all political, socioeconomic, religious, and ethnic groups in the South.[63]

Little is known of Hanoi's internal deliberations on neutrality for South Vietnam as these events unfolded. Circumstantial evidence suggests that some in the Central Committee, and possibly the Politburo as well, were hostile to the idea of holding another Geneva Conference to neutralize the South.[64] But in the end, either key leaders or a clear majority in those organs supported neutrality and kept the idea alive. According to Nguyen Vu Tung, Le Duan—surprisingly—was instrumental in that process.[65] Support for negotiations that would have ended in neutrality for South Vietnam was indeed uncharacteristic of Le Duan, who almost invariably took militant positions on issues relating to the South. The reasons for this, if he did support the idea, are unclear. Possibly, Le Duan was acting on behalf of the Politburo, which was controlled by moderates. Most likely, Le Duan himself supported neutralization at that juncture as a way to buy time for revolutionary forces and for the party in the South. Whatever the reasoning, Le Duan and the rest of the Politburo agreed to explore the neutrality option in February 1962.[66]

Thereafter, historian Robert Brigham believes, "neutralism emerged as the centerpiece of the [VWP's] diplomatic strategy."[67] With that prospect in mind, the Politburo imposed a moratorium on combat operations in parts of the South and "put forth the policy of not allowing military units to resist sweep operations in order to preserve forces" and to encourage peace talks.[68] In a cable around this time to COSVN, Hanoi reiterated that "underestimating the importance of political struggle" was "very dangerous." More interestingly in the context of the evolving debate over neutralizing the South, Hanoi told COSVN that political struggle not only represented "a very efficient weapon and an extremely important force" in the struggle against Diem and the Americans but could also prove "transcendent" in the event of negotiations.[69]

THE CASE FOR NEUTRALITY

Hanoi's growing disposition toward neutralizing the South was sensible given current domestic and international circumstances. Foremost among these were the mounting problems below the seventeenth parallel and the pressing need to mitigate them. The Kennedy administration's Project Beefup produced a "massive influx" there of U.S. military and technical personnel as well as military hardware, including more helicopters, fixed-wing aircraft, armored personnel carriers, and river patrol boats.[70] This hardware, especially the helicopters, "caused considerable difficulty for the revolution," and "proved" Hanoi's contention that the Americans were building a striking force of overwhelming potential in the South.[71] It was to oversee this massive buildup that Kennedy's administration had sanctioned the creation of MACV, which would play an ever expanding role in the southern counterrevolutionary effort as the primary American authority in Vietnam.[72] In Hanoi's view, this amounted to "war without a declaration of war."[73] Equally alarming were developing ties between Saigon and the reactionary Nationalist Chinese regime in Taiwan. During the first half of 1962, that regime posted a number of its officers to Saigon to train ARVN officers in political affairs while even larger numbers of RVN military and political officials traveled to Taipei for training.[74] All this was of "genuine concern" in Hanoi since Nationalist Chinese involvement of any kind in the struggle in South Vietnam may have been intended to provoke Beijing "in a way which no other action could."[75]

The cumulative effect of the mounting American involvement in South Vietnam was a marked increase in the combat effectiveness of the ARVN. The battlefield fortunes of Saigon's armed forces "improved significantly" in 1962, historian Edward Miller has written, "as commanders used their improved mobility to strike more effectively at the enemy." Saigon was so pleased with the performance of its armed forces that its pessimism of previous months suddenly "gave way to new dreams of victory."[76] According to Mark Moyar, in that year ARVN performance "entered into a steady ascent that was to continue for the remainder of Diem's term in office."[77] A Vietnamese military history supports these assessments, observing that the enemy's new "methods of engagement" created "many difficulties for our armed forces" and produced "the loss of a number of [PLAF] units."[78] One insurgent noted that "a number of our cadres and fighters became demoralized when they faced the enemy's new tactics and schemes," and some of them were "frightened" by the mere sight of "the enemy's weapons and heliborne tactics."[79] As David Elliott has observed of these developments, the balance of forces in the South became "unfavorable to the revolutionary side" in 1962.[80] The Foreign Office concluded much the same thing when it reported that the North Vietnamese leadership was "clearly bothered by the 10,000 American troops in South Vietnam" and sought "the easiest way to get rid of them."[81] Meanwhile, the strategic hamlet program was growing "by leaps and bounds" and continuing to create logistical and recruitment problems for both the NLF and PLAF.[82] COSVN itself admitted at this point that the program was "enlarg[ing] the areas under Saigon's control and interfer[ing] with cadres' access to the people."[83]

It is easy to see how these mounting difficulties could have encouraged Hanoi to conclude that neutralizing the South under correct conditions was not an unreasonable option. "The difficulties facing Viet Cong subversion on the military front," a French assessment noted, had brought DRVN leaders to "a more realist conception of the solution to the South Vietnamese problem." The leaders knew they "must now make the diplomatic formula prevail," a position "hardly conceivable a year ago."[84] "Convinced that Viet Cong subversion would suffice to achieve reunification," another report explained, Hanoi initially "did not accept the formula providing for a South Vietnam transformed into a neutral state." However, "the obvious results achieved by the Diemist army with material and technical assistance from the Americans now inclines [the leadership] to soften its position [on this issue]." The idea of South Vietnam forming a neutral zone with Cambodia and Laos "is now taking an official character," this report continued. "The DRVN, doubting the possibility of conquering the South by force, now endeavors to promote the principle that the South Vietnamese problem should be resolved by diplomatic means."[85]

But was neutrality ideologically correct, or at least permissible? Decision-makers in Hanoi seemed to think so. Despite supporting Beijing on certain issues, including Albania, Cuba, and the Sino-Indian border conflict, Hanoi at this time still firmly endorsed peaceful coexistence and thus the settling of disputes through negotiations. At this time also, as noted earlier, Beijing preferred that Hanoi act cautiously in the South. Besides, DRVN leaders remained "sufficiently confident of the popularity of their regime and especially of their leader Ho Chi Minh" in the South "to be convinced that given a genuinely independent and popularly elected [neutral] government in South Vietnam it would only be a matter of time before reunification would be freely achieved" under Hanoi's aegis.[86] Why precipitate a military movement for liberation of the South when time was working in Hanoi's favor? observers asked.[87] "Considering themselves as they do, the vanguard of the resistance movement against the French, the victors of Dien Bien Phu and the liberation of Vietnam," a western assessment affirmed, DRVN leaders "are convinced that only the machinations of the Americans prevented them from taking over the whole of Vietnam by means of free nationwide elections."[88]

The need to satisfy Moscow, whose material and political support remained vital, was another reason neutralizing the South was an option worth exploring. Moscow still had no interest in becoming involved in a war over Vietnam. Besides, such a war might increase Chinese influence in Vietnam at the expense of the Soviets. In addition, Moscow was keen on demonstrating that peaceful coexistence was both "desirable and possible." Therefore, if things came "to a crunch" and war broke out between the DRVN and the United States, Moscow would surely "act to protect the peace," that is, work toward a prompt diplomatic resolution of the conflict. Khrushchev, for his part, was by now under "powerful pressure" from the "new 'technical class'" in the Soviet Union, which had "forced him to condemn antiparty activities and Albania" and also "stood for the furtherance of Soviet national interests and consequently for peaceful co-existence."[89] Those were among the factors that had, by Vietnamese account, prompted the Soviets to contribute so "greatly to the success of the conference on Laos."[90] They also made Moscow "perfectly ready" to continue supporting Hanoi "so long as the risk of an internationalization of the war is not immediately apparent."[91]

It should be said at this point that Moscow applied no discernible pressure on Hanoi to pursue neutralization.[92] Soviet leaders "retained the utmost respect for the Vietnamese leadership."[93] In their eyes, Ho Chi Minh was the architect of Vietnamese independence from France, and he and Pham Van Dong were regarded with "special cordiality" in Moscow.[94] At the same time, Soviet leaders had no reason to restrain DRVN leaders, who were seemingly convinced for the time being that neutralizing the South was the best way to keep the reunification process under Vietnamese control. To do so might have encouraged the latter to turn to China for support, something the Soviets were intent on avoiding.[95] Hanoi was thus in a position to act independently on matters related to neutralization and reunification, since Moscow and Beijing were jockeying for influence in the DRVN.[96] The Vietnamese enjoyed the advantage of being "wooed" by two suitors who just then wanted the same thing they wanted: to avoid widening the war in the South by provoking U.S. intervention while saving the revolutionary movement from annihilation and possibly advancing the cause of peaceful reunification.[97]

Hanoi's decision to pursue the neutrality option was thus its own, but it endeared Hanoi to Moscow even as it helped steer a middle course in the Sino-Soviet dispute.[98] "More than ever," the French Delegation reported, "the policy of balancing between Peking and Moscow seems to correspond to the interests of [the DRVN]."[99] "Basically, the Vietnamese need both their benefactors—it does not matter which provides more, as the contribution of each is essential—and they cannot afford to alienate one by favoring the other," a Canadian diplomat noted of Hanoi's dependence on the Chinese and the Soviets.[100] Beijing began supplying large quantities of small arms and munitions to the Vietnamese that year but insisted that Hanoi remain cautious in the South to avoid "open war" with the United States.[101] Chinese leaders remained wary of escalation in Indochina, and in fact were still in an "ambiguous truce" and trying to mend fences with Moscow during the spring and summer of 1962.[102] To satisfy its concerns about escalation, Beijing, as Ung Van Khiem put it, had assumed "a role that cannot be underestimated" during the conference on Laos.[103]

The need to temporize in order to mitigate lingering and even widening ideological and other divisions within party ranks appears to have been another reason DRVN leaders seriously considered neutrality for South Vietnam. The diplomacy that entailed took time, and that time could be used to deal with party militants, who were becoming more numerous and vocal, due chiefly to the unfavorable military situation in the South.[104] Asia experts in the French Foreign Ministry had surmised in late 1961 that "there has been a considerable swing" toward support for revolutionary militancy in the South among VWP members, but noted that the ruling majority was still "very reluctant to provoke the Russians to the point where the latter [might] cut off economic aid."[105] The Politburo in fact took advantage of the visit to Hanoi of Soviet cosmonaut Herman Titov to "correct any impression that coolness has sprung up" between the two governments. During the visit, Pham Van Dong again hailed the communist camp with "the powerful Soviet Union as its center."[106]

It was just about this time that DRVN authorities had to deal with yet another domestic challenge: the resurgence of dissident groups, now consisting largely of members of the "old plundering classes who have not been re-educated, feel profound hatred toward the socialist system, and have exploited every weakness [and] difficulty of ours to act against the revolution."[107] Such "counterrevolutionaries" threatened the "unity among the people" in the same way as corruption, waste, and red tape within the civil service.[108] Help from the Soviet Union in dealing with this challenge may have furthered Hanoi's commitment to dealing with the situation in the South through diplomacy and neutralization.

Manifest willingness to negotiate a settlement of the increasingly dangerous situation in the South might also enhance the possibilities of the political and diplomatic struggles by improving the image of the DRVN domestically and internationally. That image suffered an embarrassing blow in June 1962, when the Canadian-Indian ICSC majority found the DRVN guilty of violating the 1954 Geneva accords by sending military personnel into the South. "There is evidence to show," read the report, "that armed and unarmed personnel, arms, munitions and other supplies have been sent from the Zone in the North to the Zone in the South with the object of supporting, organizing and carrying out hostile activities, including armed attacks, directed against the Armed Forces and Administration of the Zone in the South." There was also evidence that "the PAVN has allowed the Zone in the North to be used for inciting, encouraging and supporting hostile activities in the Zone in the South, aimed at the overthrow of the Administration in the South."[109] As it wrote that, the ICSC majority merely chastised Saigon for violating the arms import and no-alliances clauses of those accords by receiving American military assistance.

According to Douglas Ross, these tortured findings by the ICSC amounted to convicting the North of aggression against the South.[110] For Paris at the time, the June report insinuated that "the actions perpetrated by the North against the South preceded the American intervention" in the form of a substantial increase in the number of advisers in 1961, hence that Hanoi had essentially provoked the Kennedy administration. It thus symbolized "the victory of American and South Vietnamese theses" regarding the party responsible for collapsing the Geneva accords.[111] Predictably and futilely, Hanoi raised "a storm of protest," declaring the findings "in complete contradiction with the truth" as well as "dangerous violation[s] of the Geneva Accords."[112] It also publicly denounced the partiality of the commission, and of the Indian commissioner specifically. Because of the frustrating findings, according to Robert Brigham, neutralization had even more appeal thereafter in DRVN ruling circles. "In [thus] promoting an all-Vietnamese solution to the political and military crisis in South Viet Nam" Hanoi hoped to improve its appeal abroad as well as in both halves of the country, even to "gain converts from Diem's base of support."[113]

The rapid deterioration of Sino-Indian relations during the first half of 1962 was another consequent influence on Hanoi's favorable attitude toward neutrality for the South. While China was a longtime supporter of the Vietnamese revolution, not only did India sit on the ICSC but Prime Minister Nehru was the most important leader of the nonaligned movement, which sought to influence international affairs through moral and pacifist means and whose blessing Hanoi deeply craved in its struggle against American imperialism. War between India and China would thus complicate things for Hanoi. It would almost certainly compel Hanoi to side with Beijing, thereby compromising its relationship with Delhi, which was already shaky, and perhaps with other nonaligned states as well. "The Sino-Indian border situation [is] very serious," Ung Van Khiem observed in the autumn of 1962. "The people of Vietnam and the government of the DRVN are very worried about this serious situation." Both "support the correct position of China" but also "wholeheartedly hope that the Sino-Indian border problem will be solved through negotiations between the two countries." (Later, in an attempt to co-opt India without alienating China, Hanoi urged reconciliation between the two in accordance not with "the correct position of China" but with "the spirit of Bandung.")[114] "This problem," Khiem continued, "has special importance" not only for Hanoi's diplomatic struggle but "for the unity among people of Afro-Asian countries and for the cause of preserving peace in Southeast Asia and the world."[115] While thus pressing for a diplomatic solution to the Sino-Indian dispute, Hanoi could hardly renounce diplomacy in dealing with its own problems below the seventeenth parallel.

For the moment, then, the bargaining table seemed to Hanoi a suitable venue from which to continue the revolution. In that sense, its call for neutralizing the South through negotiations was more than "a clever trick invented by the DRV to deceive the world." It was instead "a fact of life" forced upon Hanoi by circumstances. "It has become increasingly evident that neither the [NLF] rebels nor the South Vietnamese government (even with large-scale U.S. assistance) are likely to achieve a decisive victory in the foreseeable future," a western assessment noted at the time. As a result, Hanoi "has shown greater and greater readiness to accept a negotiated settlement even to the extent of agreeing to the neutralization of the South, and the temporary shelving of what has hitherto been the chief aim of her foreign policy, namely the reunification of North and South Vietnam." Reunification "still has of course great emotional appeal for the North Vietnamese, whether communist or not, and for economic reasons North Vietnam can never have a stable economy until she rejoins the agricultural South." Nevertheless, the assessment concluded, "it seems to be felt [in Hanoi] that the first step must be to get Diem and the Americans out of South Vietnam and to restore peace, even if this means postponing indefinitely any hope of reunification."[116] The French Delegation echoed these assessments. Hanoi hoped "at all costs," it reported, to "avoid all pretext for an American military intervention in the North."[117] "Even if it culminated in victory for the communist bloc," the delegation continued elsewhere, "a conflagration [in Vietnam] would bring about catastrophic destructions in Tonkin [i.e., North Vietnam]. The effort pursued for seventeen years to 'build up' the country, which the current Five-Year Plan will—in principle—conclude, would be reduced to nothing."[118] In the same vein, in July Pham Van Dong confided in Bernard Fall, a sympathetic and influential reporter, "We do not want to give pretexts that could lead to an American military intervention in the North."[119]

In William Duiker's judgment, Hanoi was by mid-1962 ready to settle the future of South Vietnam through negotiation, even if that meant accepting a coalition government in Saigon that would defer reunification. Specifically, it was prepared to accept an interim government of individuals of all political persuasions, including those in the Diem administration, but not Diem himself.[120] This government would be constituted through negotiations not unlike those that produced the neutralist government in Laos—that is, among the largest political factions in the South under auspices of an international conference involving the great powers. Once constituted, the government would be encouraged by communists within it to begin talks with Hanoi on the political future of the nation. Should that process eventuate in peace and then peaceful unification on anything like terms suitable to the DRVN, it would pay a large dividend on a small investment. Following a meeting with Ho and Dong in late July in which these eventualities were discussed, Bernard Fall surmised that Hanoi would accede to a neutralist regime in Saigon and postponement of reunification for one reason: to preclude further American involvement in Vietnam.[121] What Hanoi might do if and when the American presence in the South ended was presumably not discussed by the three men.

LE DUAN PUSHES FOR NEUTRALITY

In an especially revealing statement of just how seriously Hanoi was considering neutrality, Le Duan wrote to COSVN in July 1962 discussing the uncertain future of the revolution in the South and pointing out the "lessons" revolutionaries might learn from the recent neutralization of Laos.[122] In words clearly directed at those who saw no merit in neutrality, even as subterfuge, Le Duan praised the reasonableness Pathet Lao leaders had displayed in resolving their difficulties and guarding their interests by refusing to turn "an internal war in Laos" into "a big war between two sides." After pursuing a moderate but steady course, they were now reaping the benefits. This positive outcome was the result of strategies that contained a prudent mix of political and military struggle. That had entailed "struggling for a Laos independent and neutral [and] creating a coalition government" that was the product of "negotiations" as well as "battle." Had Pathet Lao leaders failed to judge correctly the balance of forces in their country and to understand the advantages conveyed by balance on diplomatic struggle, "the Laotian revolution would not have won as it did." "If the struggle had been in excess of the situation, especially an excessive military struggle" without regard to the larger political context, Le Duan wrote with the situation in South Vietnam clearly in mind, "there would have been other reactions by the imperialists" and "all those things would not have brought today's victory." Revolutionary restraint, in short, had secured an acceptable agreement that the major powers were pledged to honor and which improved the long-term prospects for victory of the Pathet Lao.

Le Duan acknowledged that differences between Laos and South Vietnam made neutralization of the latter more difficult. Washington assigned much greater importance to South Vietnam than to Laos and was convinced that "any form of relaxation" of its hard-line policies below the seventeenth parallel would eventuate in a "win" for the communists and "complete defeat" for itself. An immediate task of the revolution was to change that perception. One reason for the difficulty was that Laos bordered on China and South Vietnam did not. Hanoi believed that fact had made Washington more flexible in dealing with Laos, more willing to accept neutrality, because the introduction of American forces there could easily lead to a "heated confrontation" between Americans and Chinese, and "this heat might produce results that the Americans cannot completely measure." American forces in South Vietnam were much less likely to produce such a concern. In addition, the situation in South Vietnam was more overtly directed by the DRVN, at least relative to the situation in Laos. The prospect of war with North Vietnam might be tolerable in Washington, but the prospect of war with China was not.

In his statement's most revealing section, Le Duan explained that "the revolutionary task of our country at present is to protect and secure peace in the North to build socialism and liberate the South in order to arrive at the peaceful unification of the Fatherland." This, he insisted, compelled the party to "have a correct approach to our activities in each region for the entire country generally." A war in the North "would create complex difficulties in the entire country," difficulties that might threaten the revolution itself. The party could "win" in the South as comrades won in Laos, Le Duan wrote, but only if "we know how to control the revolution." That meant the party must adjust its actions and goals to the realities created by the present balance of forces.

The purpose of neutrality was not to settle the fate of South Vietnam once and for all, Le Duan intimated; it was instead to bring about a gradual reduction and then complete withdrawal of American forces, and after that a diminishment of their assistance to the Saigon government. Neutrality was, in short, a "method" to dismantle the puppet regime and replace it with one that would be "*independent*"

(Le Duan's emphasis). At a minimum, Le Duan suggested, pursuing neutralization of the South would buy time for revolutionary forces there.

Le Duan's letter suggests that Hanoi now thought the Geneva Agreement on Laos not only workable but a promising model for a diplomatic settlement in South Vietnam. It suggests just as strongly that DRVN leaders would accept a coalition government in Saigon while the details of reunification were worked out. These, in Le Duan's words to COSVN, were the "moderate requirements" of the Vietnamese revolution at this juncture. Adroitly pursued, those requirements might produce in South Vietnam the kind of advance-through-compromise communists had just won in Laos and, incidentally, might avert further deterioration of the military situation in the South and war with the United States.

Southern revolutionaries would be understandably skeptical of this reasoning. To allay that skepticism, Le Duan tried to assure them that his and the party's proposal would appeal to war-weary southerners and thereby enhance the legitimacy of communism in the South. It was also, he said with equal assurance, compatible with the aims of the diplomatic struggle. Revolutionary struggle, he argued metaphorically, was like wielding a sword to fend off an enemy swordsman: it was much easier with a shield. The legitimacy provided by mass support for the struggle in the South would function as such a shield. That support was now lacking. "If one only uses the sword and does not have a shield," Le Duan concluded didactically, "surely he will find himself at the mercy of . . . the enemy."[123]

On 19 July, a day after Le Duan communicated these thoughts to COSVN, the NLF took the first step toward implementing them. Specifically, it proposed in a public statement to end the conflict in the South and resolve the political problem there by instituting a cease-fire, which would be followed by the withdrawal of American military personnel; forming a provisional government of national concord representing all parties, political groupings, and persuasions pending free elections under the terms of the 1954 Geneva accords; neutralizing South Vietnam from the rivalries of the Cold War; and guaranteeing that neutrality by international treaty as part of a neutral zone in Southeast Asia that included Cambodia and Laos.[124]

An Australian assessment of this proposal stands up quite well in hindsight. Hanoi and its allies in China and the Soviet Union "have recently stepped up efforts to gain international support for the convening of a Geneva-type conference on south Vietnam," the assessment began. Their aim was to "exploit the precedent of the Laotian settlement and the favorable atmosphere resulting from it to obtain international support for a similar type settlement in south Vietnam" and thus secure the withdrawal of American military personnel from South Vietnam, just as the earlier settlement had called for the withdrawal of foreign troops from Laos. Hanoi "might expect that the further deterioration of the situation in south Vietnam would increase international and domestic pressures on the United States

Government to accept a negotiated settlement," while helping the NLF become "a party at any international conference which might eventuate" from the effort to produce that settlement. "In taking up proposals for the neutralization of south Vietnam," DRVN leaders were "playing down their parallel objective of achieving reunification of the south with the north on their own terms." "They might well expect," the assessment surmised, "that if they could obtain the withdrawal of United States forces and the replacement of the Diem Government by a regime amenable to communist pressure, a unified communist Vietnam would be the almost certain outcome in the long run." But since Diem was "unlikely in any circumstances to agree to internal negotiations for the withdrawal of United States military aid and the neutralization of south Vietnam," Hanoi had nothing to lose and much to gain domestically and internationally by at least appearing to be open to negotiations on those issues.[125]

THE CHALLENGES OF NEUTRALIZATION

As they prepared to negotiate the future of the South, DRVN leaders considered recognizing the NLF as a provisional revolutionary government. The Front already had a national flag and a national anthem, and regularly addressed messages to sovereign states and the UN in the name of the South Vietnamese people.[126] But though North Vietnamese propaganda portrayed it as having the attributes of a shadow government, DRVN leaders had always balked at calling it or treating it as a provisional government.[127] The British Consulate thought that a decision to do so now or in the future hinged partly on the outcome of "political bargaining between the constituent parties in the Front and partly on the [outcome of the evolving] military situation" in the South. "If the Front were to look like [it was] winning without further assistance from outside, the D.R.V. would probably prefer to avoid setting up a Government until the communist party was in a position to take over according to the North Vietnamese model," the consulate noted. "If however the Viet Cong were to reach an impasse or even be pushed back by the Diem Government," creation of a provisional revolutionary government would become "essential" to "obtain larger scale aid from outside" and to "have a *locus standi* in the event of an international conference." In either case, the consulate concluded, the new provisional government would "call for international recognition and presumably receive it from the communist countries" and perhaps some nonaligned states. It might then ask for material and diplomatic support from friendly governments, including the DRVN, which might use the request to justify increased involvement in southern affairs.[128]

In the end Hanoi decided against the move. The NLF had no defined territorial base, and if such a base was proclaimed, it would surely be attacked and destroyed by Diem's forces. Furthermore, establishing a rebel government in the South would likely complicate relations with Moscow, which would have to decide whether to recognize the new entity. To do so would presumably commit Moscow to the struggle in the South to a degree it had never been willing to make. To refuse to do so would compromise the new government and jeopardize Soviet-DRVN relations.[129] But most importantly, Hanoi refused to recognize the NLF as a provisional government because that would have radically raised the stakes in the struggle below the seventeenth parallel. The international community might interpret the gesture as a violation of the Geneva accords, which would taint the image of the revolution abroad and undermine the diplomatic struggle. Also, Hanoi could not be sure that the new government would remain under its control.[130] Placing known communists or northerners at its helm was out of the question, for that would "shatter the deception of non-involvement by the D.R.V." "Relative nonentities," on the other hand, however reliable, would deprive the government of credibility. To have legitimacy, the new government would have to include independent nationalists and other noncommunists with their own political bases over whom Hanoi would have no influence.[131] Such individuals could very well hijack the foreign policy of the new government, with potentially disastrous implications for the reunification struggle and the revolution more broadly. In fact, even treating the NLF as a de facto government was problematic because it encouraged independent thinking on the part of its members and risked compromising Hanoi's already tenuous control of the liberation movement below the seventeenth parallel.[132]

In October 1962, the new British consul general, J. K. Blackwell, produced a particularly trenchant analysis of Hanoi's refusal to transform the NLF into a revolutionary government. On the basis of information he credited to undisclosed and presumably communist sources, Blackwell surmised that the "common policy" on Vietnamese reunification of the NLF and Hanoi "may only be a façade to cover up a serious disagreement of principle" between the two. In negotiating a common stance on this issue, the NLF had "tried to insist on their proposal that South Vietnam together with Cambodia and Laos should form a group of neutral Southeast Asian states whose independence and neutrality would be guaranteed by an International Conference." But that solution had not appealed to DRVN leaders, who feared it would "put off reunification of Vietnam indefinitely and make it much more difficult for them to subvert and take over South Vietnam." From this disagreement, Blackwell surmised that the NLF "is more independent" of Hanoi "than has so far been generally assumed." It was also "likely" that "such independent views (if indeed they do exist) will be firmly suppressed by the DRV Government."[133]

Blackwell may have been right about the existence of a rift between Hanoi and the NLF. To be sure, southern communist leaders had never had any qualms about manifesting their disagreement with Hanoi over certain issues. But in the end, they always fell into line. However, this was different. The NLF was led by communists, but its members were from all walks of South Vietnamese society. As a united front, it was more likely to deviate from the party line than were purely communist organs. During talks with Chinese officials in Beijing, for example, a visiting NLF delegation reiterated the importance of the proposal for creating an enduring "neutralized zone" in Southeast Asia consisting of Laos, Cambodia, and South Vietnam. Then, in a clear show of autonomy from and perhaps even defiance of Hanoi, the NLF delegation signed a joint statement with the Chinese Committee for Afro-Asian Solidarity that made no mention of Vietnamese reunification and stated instead that South Vietnam "must be prepared to form a neutral zone with Cambodia and Laos, in which their respective sovereignty is fully retained." This statement was the NLF delegation's own, having presumably never been approved by DRVN authorities. "There is little doubt," the British chargé in Beijing remarked of this defection from VWP orthodoxy, that DRVN leaders "look forward instead to the emergence of a united communist Vietnam" and not to a neutral zone that included the "sovereign" southern half of their nation.[134]

To jump-start negotiations on a neutral South Vietnam, Hanoi turned to France, applying "quite a lot" of pressure to get Paris to agree to mediate between the two Vietnams and between the DRVN and concerned western governments.[135] It nudged this initiative along by renewing a trade agreement with French authorities and making a series of other conciliatory gestures.[136] There may have been another motive in Hanoi's courtship of Paris: widening the gulf separating France from the RVN and its American allies. As previously noted, Paris was never keen on Diem. At the time, the French were in a row with Saigon over the anti-Diem activities of Vietnamese exiles in France.[137] Possibly, Hanoi thought that by throwing a "sop line" to the French, by suggesting that a "special position" could be reserved for them in a neutral South Vietnam, it could edge them away from "the firm Anglo-American policy on South Vietnam."[138] The British Embassy in Saigon concluded on the basis of these and other North Vietnamese overtures to Paris that Hanoi was "actively seeking" to detach the French from the United States and other western allies. "The Communists hope they can split the French from the Americans not only to weaken the present regime [in Saigon] but to secure active support for their 'international policy.'" Such "market research into the exploitable characteristics and weaknesses" of the West, the embassy thought, in veiled praise of Hanoi's diplomatic maneuverings, was "quite thorough."[139]

It is a telling testament to the subtlety of Hanoi's behavior in this course of events that it made no formal proposal in 1962 for an international conference on neutralizing the South. That reticence may have been an expression of its desire to wait on events there. Hanoi "may think that the Viet Cong can still win militarily or at least that the West will weary of the struggle and be prepared to compromise," the British Consulate calculated in September 1962, in which case it "will get better terms [at that time] than by holding a conference now." Possibly also, the consulate thought, Hanoi "may have come to the conclusion that America is willing to go to almost any lengths to prevent a communist victory in South Vietnam." If that was indeed the case, it "may therefore be waiting for the Americans to get themselves still more involved in the fighting which would strengthen [its] case, in any future conference, that the South Vietnamese question had degenerated into a war between the Americans (assisted by a few South Vietnamese stooges) and the Vietnamese people." Hanoi "may [thus] be waiting for the combination of war-weariness, neutralist propaganda and the ever latent xenophobia to take effect in South Vietnam" before publicly and officially requesting an international conference on neutralization of the South.[140]

According to this interpretation, Hanoi did not advance a formal proposal for such a conference in order not to paint itself into a corner. It did, however, continue to circumspectly signal a desire to negotiate the issue. During a meeting with the Indian commissioner on the ICSC, Ho Chi Minh spoke "in very moderate terms" of Diem and the regime in Saigon. Ho also endorsed an Indian proposal to negotiate the matter under the auspices of the ICSC as part of an effort to reunite divided families.[141] This diplomatic game served Vietnamese communist interests by signaling to both allies and enemies that Hanoi wanted no wider war and was prepared to use diplomacy to preclude that eventuality. That stance satisfied Hanoi's allies while increasing the pressure on its enemies to limit hostilities in the South, and furthered the prospects of a peaceful settlement.

TEMPORARY NEUTRALITY

All things considered, it appears that DRVN leaders indeed wanted some kind of diplomatic resolution of the crisis in the South, at least for a time. But that did not mean they were prepared to forgo the central goal of the revolution—national unification under their governance. It simply meant that they wanted to avert a wider war, for now. In fact, while Hanoi may have been ready to discuss neutrality and even agree to it, it never envisaged a neutral South to be permanent, or to become sovereign, as some NLF members had suggested earlier. A month after he had written his letter to COSVN in support of neutralization, Le Duan indicated that to him at least neutrality represented "a halfway house to a communist takeover," a way of getting rid of Diem and the Americans before pursuing revolutionary objectives by other means.[142] "The only solution" Vietnamese communists entertained, western diplomats surmised at the time, "is reunification of the two halves, which they have suggested might come about gradually after the South had got rid of President Ngo Dinh Diem and established a broadly based coalition government ready to negotiate with the North." Inferences that Hanoi would accept prolonged neutrality of the South and thus indefinite postponement of reunification were merely intended to manipulate world opinion, they thought.[143]

"The North Vietnamese approach is shrewd," French diplomats cynically observed. It aimed to "avoid all semblance of violating the Geneva accords" while seeking to bring to power in Saigon a new, ostensibly neutral government, which, by persuasion or by threat, would gradually acquiesce to Hanoi's tutelage. Reunification would thus be achieved duplicitously, but by "the free will of the people of the southern zone."[144] Nguyen Vu Tung concluded that Hanoi's support of neutralization aimed at "winning internal and external support" and "enlisting the sympathy of nationalist countries," both central aims of the diplomatic struggle.[145] According to a revealing Central Committee report, the party endorsed neutralization on the one hand to "win over" the "middle classes" below the seventeenth parallel and sympathetic people in socialist and neutral countries and, on the other, to "isolate to a high degree" the American imperialists.[146] Permanent or long-term neutrality for the South was never seriously entertained by the VWP, the same report intones.

Similarly, Hanoi never actually favored the idea that South Vietnam should join Cambodia and Laos in a neutral bloc in Southeast Asia, as "independent elements" in the NLF maintained. In fact, it rejected the idea because it "might result in South Vietnam becoming permanently part of a neutral '*cordon sanitaire*' between the communist and western blocs."[147] Also, if South Vietnam were integrated into a neutral Indochinese zone, the NLF might become even more independent and act contrary to guidelines set by the party leadership in Hanoi. Such concerns are further evidence that Hanoi and at least some members of the NLF did not always see eye to eye on major issues.[148] So apparent did this eventually become that historian Edwin Moïse later concluded that any agreement between Saigon and the NLF saying they would coexist below the seventeenth parallel with or without Hanoi's concurrence or acquiescence was "necessarily going to be a farce." "If the NLF had been a genuine united front in which communist and noncommunist forces shared power," Moïse continued, "it would have opened up a serious possibility that a neutral government in which communists and noncommunists shared power could be created by a peace settlement." However, Moïse concludes, "the united front was largely a sham: [its] noncommunist leaders ... were there more as window dressing than as genuine power sharers."[149]

ABANDONING NEUTRALIZATION

In the end, nothing came of the effort to solve the South Vietnam imbroglio through neutralization. Prospects for a diplomatic settlement, even a temporary or imperfect one, faded almost as rapidly as they materialized. Within days after members of the DRVN National Assembly declared that the NLF had embraced "peace negotiations" to "bring about gradual reunification," that "progress" was being made to "restore normal relations between the two zones," and that that progress constituted "an important step toward achieving the peaceful reunification of our country," the unraveling of the Geneva Agreement on Laos became obvious.[150] The coalition government in Vientiane proved to be so weak and ineffective that neither Hanoi nor Washington suspended its activities in the small country. Hanoi refused to pull the remainder of its forces from Laos and continued to use supply lines running through the country, while Washington sustained its military and other aid to Laotian clients, which expedited the resumption of political strife. Hanoi justified its violations of the Laotian accords by pointing to those of Washington. "It is clear," the DRVN Foreign Ministry noted in October, "that the United States and countries aligned with it still deliberately interfere in the internal affairs [and] the foreign policy of Laos, creating not insignificant difficulties for the coalition government."[151] As previously suggested, it is likely that DRVN leaders were initially willing to respect the spirit of the Laotian accords because they would benefit more than the Americans from mutual withdrawal. But it is equally likely that they never intended to duly follow the letter of the accords. The Pathet Lao was still too weak to survive on its own. Completely deprived of Vietnamese assistance, including the presence of North Vietnamese "volunteer" forces and advisers, it would have no way of protecting itself, to say nothing of consolidating its hold on those parts of the country it claimed to control. Moreover, "a truly neutral Laos would have been a disaster for the Vietnamese communists," as Edwin Moïse has noted, "because it would have meant closing down the Ho Chi Minh Trail."[152]

Whoever was to blame for it, the failure of the Laotian "experiment" in neutrality dampened enthusiasm in the VWP for any diplomatic engagement of Saigon and Washington.[153] Specifically, it discredited the idea of neutralizing the South and quickly prompted party militants to advocate for other approaches—namely, war—to achieve reunification. "With the outbreak of hostilities in Laos" that followed the collapse of the neutralization effort there, according to one contemporary assessment, "the vision of many Vietnamese, in both North and South, of a [South] Vietnam with a neutral coalition government on the Laotian model, with close economic and cultural links with North Vietnam, leading in course of time to reunification by mutual agreement, has been tarnished."[154] Earlier, in April 1962, Hanoi had warned that "if the American imperialists continue to destroy the [1954] Geneva accords and expand [their] colonial war in the South, continue to threaten the security of our North, then they will have to bear complete responsibility for the disastrous consequences they provoked."[155] The failure of the accords on Laos thus played into the hands of militants and other opponents of neutrality and diplomacy, legitimating their views while convincing many fence-sitters and even moderates in the party of the duplicity and intemperance of the Americans.

The outcome of the Cuban missile crisis of October 1962 further underscored the risks and limitations of diplomacy for those in the VWP. It also shamed Khrushchev and peaceful coexistence with him. "The Russian call for peaceful coexistence has much less appeal" among Vietnamese, foreign diplomats in the

DRVN capital reported shortly after the Cuban crisis.[156] This, of course, also increased the allure of militant views concerning national liberation.[157] In late October, prime minister Pham Van Dong, who usually sided with moderates on such issues, told a reporter from the French communist newspaper *L'Humanité* that his government "strongly supports national liberation movements in the world, against all forms of colonization." Observers at the time thought those comments "put the DRV firmly into the eastern wing of the socialist camp."[158]

The failure of the 1962 Geneva Agreement on Laos, acknowledged in the National Assembly in February 1963, and the outcome of the Cuban crisis, plus the concomitant collapse of the Sino-Soviet truce, may well have killed the last chance for a diplomatic compromise to avert precipitous expansion of the war in the South. For Le Duan, a committed militant who thought that some kind of settlement on the South could be reached that year, the collapse of the Laotian accords represented incontrovertible evidence of the deceitfulness of Washington and the reactionaries who were allied with it. It thus invalidated the little faith in negotiations he may have regained since the 1954 Geneva accords, while reinforcing his belief that only war could produce the liberation of the South. After the onset of war against the United States in 1965, Le Duan would obdurately refuse to even entertain the possibility of using negotiations to bring about the end of hostilities.

Tensions between moderates and militants in the VWP ran high in the aftermath of the events just described.[159] During a January 1963 visit to Hanoi by a Soviet delegation, Ho Chi Minh confided to his guests that the outcome of the Cuban affair had alienated many VWP members, who felt that Moscow had abandoned Havana as it had abandoned them.[160] Foreign observers noted a growing dissonance between Hanoi's adherence to Soviet theses and an official attitude favoring a diplomatic solution in the South on the one hand, and the "fundamental identity of views" on national liberation held by "the mass of the party membership" with those of Beijing on the other.[161]

While Hanoi remained "loth to sacrifice" economic progress above the seventeenth parallel for a wider war in the South that carried with it many risks, increasing numbers on both sides of the seventeenth parallel clamored for an escalation of the southern insurgency and for greater DRVN involvement.[162] "The policies of aggression and expansion of the war of the U.S.-Diem clique have made the situation in the South extremely dangerous," Nguyen Van Hien of the NLF told the DRVN National Assembly in late 1962. "The war in the South is widening each day and directly threatening the security of the DRVN, directly threatening peace in Indochina and [the rest of] Southeast Asia."[163] Perhaps sensing the inevitability of a wider war, the National Assembly drew a parallel between the present plight of the DRVN and the recent agony of North Korea: "The Vietnamese people have deep fondness and profound sympathy for the Korean people" because both their countries had been "divided and invaded by the Americans."[164]

By year's end, foreign observers were noting "ominous indications" that "both the guerrilla warfare in the South and the active participation of the North in it may intensify." In a joint statement, the DRVN and NLF insisted that "the 16 million North Vietnamese compatriots will support more actively the South Vietnamese compatriots' liberation struggle." The ICSC reported that during the last weeks of 1962 "a number of items" which it recognized as "conclusive evidence of subversion south of the seventeenth parallel by the Northern authorities"—namely, military hardware—had been transferred "quite openly" to the NLF and PLAF.[165] "For the past few weeks," French diplomats in Hanoi reported on the last day of the year, "the balance traditionally maintained by the DRV between China and the Soviet Union has been affected and the balance is now tilting, more obviously, in favor of the first."[166] Things were coming to a head in Hanoi and the rest of Vietnam.

6

Choosing War, 1963

Moscow's decisions to withdraw its missiles from Cuba—over Castro's strong objections—and to join Washington in banning aboveground nuclear testing a few months later roused opponents of peaceful coexistence and polarized the socialist camp in 1963. In China, these decisions contributed to a further radicalization of domestic and foreign policy. The same year, a Buddhist crisis punctuated by the self-immolation of monks and the assassinations of Diem and his brother Ngo Dinh Nhu in a military coup turned South Vietnam into a flashpoint of the global Cold War. In the immediate aftermath of Kennedy's assassination, his successor, Lyndon Johnson, announced that the United States would stay the course in South Vietnam. At the time of Kennedy's death, there were sixteen thousand U.S. military advisers there, and American determination to support Saigon became stronger than ever.

Events that year markedly impacted the VWP. They emboldened militants and amplified existing cleavages among leaders and rank-and-file members. The coup against Diem and Nhu was particularly consequential, occasioning as it did a special session of the Central Committee during which moderates and militants aired their differences and vigorously debated options in the South. By the time the session adjourned, the militants had won the debate and a decision had been made to dramatically escalate the armed struggle below the seventeenth parallel and provide comprehensive DRVN support for it. With their victory, militants led by Le Duan took over party decision-making, staging a coup of sorts of their own, and instituted a purge of those who disagreed with their views.

A PARTY DIVIDED

By 1963, the cumulative effects of the disappointments, frustrations, and stresses discussed in preceding chapters had combined to deepen and harden the division within the VWP into a schism. Party leaders continued to present "a façade of unanimity," but western diplomats in Hanoi detected clear signs of internal strains between "a pro-Soviet and a pro-Chinese faction."[1] Though neither faction was actually beholden to a foreign ideological ally, as previously explained, moderates and militants in the party were thus identified, respectively, by foreign observers at the time, as they have been by many analysts since. The main point of dispute is by now familiar: how to balance military and political struggle in the South, whether to follow Soviet or Chinese revolutionary prescriptions in dealing with the situation there.

By this time leading "pro-Soviet" moderates—"rightists" or "revisionists" in militant parlance—included Ho Chi Minh and defense minister General Vo Nguyen Giap, the two most prominent figures in the party, whose ideological stances still carried great weight, as well as deputy prime minister Le Thanh Nghi, vice president Ton Duc Thang, and foreign minister Ung Van Khiem. The most ardent "pro-Chinese" militants—"leftists"—remained first secretary Le Duan, GPD chairman General Nguyen Chi Thanh, chairman of the Party Organization Committee Le Duc Tho, and deputy prime minister Pham Hung, plus a growing retinue of prominent figures, including chairman of the State Planning Committee Nguyen Duy Trinh, chairman of the National Assembly's Standing Committee Truong Chinh, chairman of the Education and Propaganda Department and secretary of the Party Cultural and Ideological Committee To Huu, vice chairman of the Standing Committee of the National Assembly Hoang Van Hoan, chief of the PAVN General Staff Van Tien Dung, and minister of public security Tran Quoc Hoan.[2] Most of these men were also members of the Secretariat, which included none of the leading moderates. Le Duan, Le Duc Tho, and Pham Hung additionally served on the National Reunification Committee, a Politburo subcommittee in charge of dealing with southern affairs.[3]

Admittedly, signs of the intensity and divisiveness of the dispute within the party abounded by then.[4] In January, the Indian commissioner on the ICSC reported that "a heightened tension had recently manifested itself" in Hanoi "between partisans of Moscow and partisans of Peking." Ho Chi Minh seemed particularly "worried" about "the maneuvers of the Sinophile faction," the commissioner added.[5] In February, on the occasion of the eightieth anniversary of the death of Karl Marx, the Secretariat had the party press, Truth Publisher (Nha xuat ban Su that), circulate materials by and about Marx, encouraging cadres and members to "rediscover" his teachings on the value of socialist unity and the dangers of contentiousness.[6] A March editorial in *Nhan dan* called on Vietnamese and other communists to set aside their ideological differences and instead "exchange views and experiences in comradeship and in the spirit of proletarian internationalism" with a view to "strengthening unity and identity of mind among the Communist and Workers' Parties."⁷ At the Nguyen Ai Quoc School for training party cadres in Hanoi, the dispute was so intense that shouting matches and even fisticuffs became common between moderate and militant trainees, and the foreign minister had to intervene personally.⁸ "Is your squabbling necessary; does it serve the revolution?" he rhetorically asked students at the school. "Unite in the interests of the revolution," he urged.⁹

Conflicting constructions of "objective realities" fueled the intraparty dispute at all levels. Militant constructions were largely informed by revolutionary orthodoxies, as well as admiration for the Chinese revolutionary model. Moderate positions derived from what adherents considered the pragmatic needs of the struggle against the United States and the lessons to be learned from the Soviet revolutionary example. The gist of the militant critique was that moderates were forswearing the core precepts of Marxism-Leninism, that they were opportunists guided by strictly nationalist and sometimes even bourgeois interests.

The ideological content of the dispute within the party in 1963 is well documented in that year's issues of *Hoc tap* and other party publications, which became a forum for debating the merits of leftist and rightist ideas. Nguyen Chi Thanh, for example, wrote in *Hoc tap* that the roots of rightism lay in part in a psychological mindset "left by the former imperialist and feudalist regime." To Thanh, rightism was characterized by "admiration for and fear of the imperialists; a complex state of national inferiority; the cult of the imperialist culture and technology; respect for an order of precedence for high and low classes; a concern with rank, honor, and position; a paternalistic, bureaucratic, and [authoritarian] attitude; and predilection to favor males over females." Thus burdened, rightists failed to "understand the true nature of proletarian dictatorship."¹⁰ Revisionism, "a euphemism for Soviet heresy" cherished by moderates, was no better in the eyes of its critics.¹¹ Advocates of revisionism, which influenced the conduct of foreign relations, would suspend the international class struggle in favor of accommodation—peaceful coexistence—with imperialists, Le Duc Tho charged. Revisionism thus constituted, in Tho's words, "a platform from which imperialism may sow disunity in the socialist camp and the international communist movement and sabotage the revolutionary cause of the working class and oppressed peoples in the world."¹²

Revisionists, their detractors thought, wanted the working class to "abandon its mission of carrying out the world revolution," which would "make permanent" the supremacy of capitalism and imperialism. Such a stance was "completely contrary" to the spirit of "the era of transition from capitalism to socialism."¹³ To militants, revisionism and rightism were peas in the same pod. Rightism was a "hooked chain" that bound the "bourgeois thoughts" of gullible and unthinking party members to the bourgeois ideological system, thus providing, to mix metaphors, "fertile ground for revisionism." It was therefore imperative for loyal and committed revolutionaries to oppose rightism in order to "deprive revisionism of a terrain to penetrate the healthy body of our party."[14] As this suggests, militants saw themselves as selfless devotees of revolution, espousing as they did a view that placed their own cause at the center of world revolution.

According to militants, the obvious flaw in rightist, moderate thought was its disregard for the fate of southern compatriots. Preoccupied by their own lives and personal enjoyment, moderate elements in the party, according to their critics, paid too little heed to the welfare of their brethren who were being victimized by reactionaries and imperialists in the South. Peace in the North encouraged among people of moderate inclination "a desire to enjoy an easy and comfortable life" and "a fear of difficulties and hardships." These in turn caused susceptible "comrades" to "neglect in some measure the revolutionary ideal," to "relax their struggle spirit," to embrace one form or another of revisionism.[15] The "duty" of loyal northerners and especially of party members among them was to "collaborate with the southern compatriots in undertaking the vigorous struggle against the U.S. imperialists."[16] The parallel duty to build socialism in the North was no excuse for relaxing the struggle in the South. The northern situation required that "our cadres and party members [there] have an elevated sense of responsibility toward the struggle for national unification and the struggle against modern revisionism and rightist opportunism."[17] Vietnamese militants saw merit in what Mao called "continuous revolution," in keeping the party and the masses constantly mobilized, and therefore vigilant. Their vehement condemnations of rightist and revisionist thinking evinced intense frustration at their inability to get Ho and Giap in particular to support increased DRVN aid for the southern insurgency even at this late date.

STAYING THE COURSE

In mid-January the British Consulate estimated that "militarily a rough equilibrium has been reached in the South" and "neither side . . . seems capable of achieving a decisive victory without committing itself further than it deems safe." The consulate surmised that DRVN leaders "doubtless hesitate to commit themselves openly to active military support of the Vietcong as this might well result in North Vietnam becoming a battlefield between the Americans and the Chinese." They thus accepted the impasse in the South as a "fact of life."[18] "It would be excessive to speak of a serious loss of equilibrium" in the balance Hanoi sought to maintain between political and military struggle in the South, French diplomats noted.[19]

For Hanoi, to the consternation of militants, the southern revolution still had to be accomplished by southerners, "self-sufficiently," as decreed by the Third Party

Congress, and in ways that avoided adventurous and dangerous maneuvering.[20] In a *Nhan dan* editorial, foreign minister Ung Van Khiem insisted that the people and government of the DRVN still "approved and supported the policy of peace and peaceful coexistence between nations with different political regimes advocated by the USSR and other socialist countries."[21] The DRVN leadership's position on these issues was unequivocal; it even launched a propaganda and education campaign in February to ensure compliance with its judgment.[22] Ho Chi Minh remained especially concerned that a major war would needlessly sacrifice Vietnamese lives and threaten the revolution in the long run.[23] The "last thing" he and other moderates wanted at that point was for the insurgency in the South to "escalate into a Korea-type war between the Americans and the Chinese," foreign observers surmised.[24] Nearly a decade after the Geneva accords, Ho, Giap, and other moderates still fretted over the prospect of "open and official" DRVN intervention in the South.[25]

When the Central Committee met in early spring, it concerned itself mainly with assessing the progress of the five-year plan.[26] Reports were positive. In 1958, for example, only 4.74 percent of rural households belonged to a collective; by 1963, the figure was 87.7 percent. However, long-standing problems persisted: food shortages in the countryside, lack of support for government programs among ethnic minorities in highland regions, unsatisfactory industrial output, lack of advanced tools and technologies, and poor management of programs.[27] Agricultural production had failed to keep pace with the growing population, retarding development generally. Until these problems were remedied, the Politburo would not amend the party's strategy in the South.

Moscow's continued objection to a military solution in the South reinforced those convictions. The outcome of the Cuban missile crisis had scarred Khrushchev personally and his Politburo generally by demonstrating the pitfalls of brinksmanship. On thin ice politically because of that outcome, the Soviet leadership was in no mood to take a similar risk in Indochina.[28] As historian Ilya Gaiduk has noted, after the Cuban debacle Khrushchev was "much more reluctant to plunge into adventures that promised dubious dividends in the Cold War confrontation."[29] During a visit to Hanoi in January, Yuri Andropov, the head of the CPSU's Department for Liaison with Communist and Workers' Parties in Socialist Countries, privately pressed upon his hosts the imperative to act carefully and give the Americans no pretext for involving their own forces in the South.[30] "The road to socialism is the road of peace," Andropov told them. "The crisis in the Caribbean Sea region"—that is, the Cuban missile crisis—"was resolved by peaceful means." Hanoi had therefore to settle its differences with Saigon and the Americans in the same way, he insisted.[31]

Prime minister Pham Van Dong summarized the views that governed party and state policy at the time in a report to the National Assembly in April.[32] In doing so, he genuflected before the importance of assistance from socialist countries to the future of the Vietnamese revolution, but stressed the limited results of efforts so far to build socialism in the North and repeated the statistical analysis of those limitations. Concerning the situation in the South, Dong reiterated the usual list of ills resulting from American interference there, then made a surprisingly strong appeal for a diplomatic solution. Affirming Hanoi's commitment to peace and the 1954 Geneva accords, he suggested that a negotiated settlement was still possible, provided certain minimum conditions were met. "Reunification through a peaceful solution," Dong said, "means [it] must not [take place] by war, by violence, but by negotiations, an agreement, [and] mutual concessions without one side coercing or dominating the other." To achieve this, as soon as possible officials from the two regions should meet to discuss national reunification. "Our country is part of the world," Dong said in a reiteration of Hanoi's internationalist concerns. "The revolutionary cause of our people is closely linked to the revolutionary cause of the world's people. The process of the revolutionary struggle of our people is a microcosm of the process of revolution for the people of the world."

Dong's call for talks may have been sincere, but it was unlikely to deliver peace in the South. A month before he presented his report to the National Assembly, Dong had told the Polish commissioner on the ICSC that Hanoi remained open to a negotiated settlement provided certain conditions were met. But those conditions were prohibitive from Washington and Saigon's perspective, including as they did strict observance of the 1954 Geneva accords, which banned foreign troops and bases in Vietnam as well as military alliances with parties outside Vietnam. "Nothing is possible as long as the Americans have not disengaged from Vietnam," Dong bluntly told a French diplomat during a discussion in May on the likelihood of a negotiated solution for South Vietnam.[33] Dong's conditions included other terms that Washington and Saigon were likely to reject out of hand despite the reasonableness of the language in which he proposed them: formation of a "liberal and democratic régime" in Saigon and convening of an international conference of major powers who pledged to honor and enforce an agreement that enshrined these conditions.[34]

So the old party strategy endured. As it habitually did when facing an impasse in the South or pressure from militants to escalate armed struggle there, Hanoi intensified the diplomatic struggle. This time, it instructed DRVN and NLF representatives abroad to redouble their efforts to describe the agony of the southern people by generating and disseminating information to that effect.[35] According to a Hungarian diplomat, the "main activity" of the DRVN Embassy staff in Budapest became propaganda work, including "giving lectures" about war against imperialism while trying to "obtain as much economic aid as possible" for their country.[36] "The primary diplomatic strategy of our government," Ho noted in May, was to "acquire new friends every day."[37] "All their efforts, diplomatic and propaganda," were "directed towards getting the Americans out of South Vietnam" by mobilizing world opinion against them, a western diplomat said of Hanoi's diplomacy.[38] DRVN and NLF representatives overseas also emphasized increased American interference in southern affairs, involvement of U.S. personnel in military operations against the NLF, expansion of the strategic hamlet program, and use of toxic chemicals in rural areas. Hanoi—Ho, Giap, and their followers, to be precise—refused to give up hope that rallying world opinion against Washington might bring about national reunification without a major war.

THE RADICALIZATION OF MILITANTS

By spring 1963, militants were increasingly insistent that the party and the government more directly and aggressively support the southern insurgency by providing sophisticated weaponry to the PLAF, sanctioning all-out war, and deploying PAVN main-line forces to the South. Such insistence was beginning to have substantial results. In March the French Delegation noted of the DRVN that its "military involvement in the South is taking on such proportions that we can no longer consider it a 'technical assistance.'"[39] Hanoi had to "struggle protractedly and fiercely for national unification," militants were claiming, and to "trust the correct fighting methods adopted by the southern people," that is, armed struggle.[40] A *Nhan dan* editorial boldly noted in March that Chinese revolutionary theses "constitute a creative application of Marxism-Leninism," suggesting that Moscow was wrong to condemn them.[41] It was the shared sentiment of party militants that Hanoi, in the words of historian Jean Lacouture, was being "overcautious and far too slow in intervening" to protect the revolutionary movement below the seventeenth parallel.[42] The situation was now more pressing than ever because the pool of southern regroupees fit for deployment to the South to help the insurgency was nearly exhausted, and conditions were not improving sufficiently.[43]

Circumstances inside and outside Vietnam contributed to the radicalization of militants and the growing popularity of their views within the party during the first half of 1963.[44] The most specific of these circumstances was the outcome of a firefight at Ap Bac in January. During a one-day encounter between a small force of PLAF guerrillas and a much larger force of ARVN regulars with American advisers, the well-entrenched guerrillas held their ground and inflicted heavy casualties on ARVN forces, forcing their retreat.[45] For supporters of military struggle as the key to southern liberation, that episode was a watershed. "This victory put in evidence the fighting spirit and the extraordinary courage of the patriotic forces as well as their capacity [for military victory in] the American 'special war,'" a party history noted.[46] To militants, the outcome of the battle attested to the vulnerability of Saigon's armed forces. "This was the first time in the plains region," an official history of the PAVN relates, "that our liberation and guerrilla armed forces achieved victory in a large-scale, battalion-size battle with enemy forces nearly 10 times more numerous [and possessing] vastly superior equipment, weapons, [and] firepower." The engagement thus "proved" the ability of communist-led forces to "defeat" the Americans and their "puppets" in a major combat operation.[47] Specifically, Ap Bac demonstrated that "our full-time troops" could wage war successfully in the South "with appropriate force levels and adequately organized and equipped, with tactical and technical training, relying on a firm People's War battlefield posture and with the support of the political struggle forces of the masses."[48]

The results at Ap Bac, a party historian has concluded, were a turning point in the revolution because they "supplied evidence that the popular forces had found the way of coping with the most modern weapons and tactics" of the enemy.[49] By taking advantage of the élan created by the victory and the resulting disarray in the South Vietnamese army in the area of the engagement, militants reasoned, revolutionary forces could win a decisive military victory in the South before the United States had time to enlarge its military commitment to Saigon, provided of course that Hanoi offered its full support. Le Duan became convinced that the Americans had suffered a loss of confidence so great that they realized "they could not defeat us" under current conditions.[50] So inspiring was this single episode at Ap Bac that COSVN launched a mobilization campaign called "Emulate Ap Bac, Kill Pirates, Attack."[51] Interestingly, shortly thereafter revolutionary forces demonstrated an increasing ability to destroy strategic hamlets or entice peasants to abandon them.[52] These events plus unrest among the South's Buddhists prompted Saigon to proclaim a "national state of siege," which militants hoped Hanoi would capitalize upon.[53]

The radicalization of Chinese domestic and foreign policy that resumed after mid-1962 was a second factor behind the stiffening resolve of VWP militants.[54] According to historian Xiaoming Zhang, the creation in February 1962 of MACV had caused "deep concern" in Beijing, presaging as it might an extension to Vietnam of the conflict China had recently had with the United States in Korea and might soon have again over Taiwan.[55] By summer of that year, historian Lorenz Lüthi has noted, "the ideological radicalization of domestic politics had started" in China.[56] More importantly, PRC leaders now finally supported the liberation of southern Vietnam by military struggle, and even proclaimed it their "duty" to support the Vietnamese politically and materially "in order to promote an Asia-wide or even world-wide revolution."[57] This was music to the ears of Vietnamese militants and may well have convinced more fence-sitters and even some moderates of the appropriateness of war in the South. Consistent with its new position, the PRC significantly increased military aid to Vietnam starting that year.[58] Beijing's decision to finally unreservedly support violent struggle in Vietnam and its simultaneous renewed denunciations of peaceful coexistence intensified the revolutionary passion of Vietnamese militants and steeled their thinking on the direction liberation of the South should take and the central role the DRVN should play in it.[59] "Mao's aggressiveness, optimism, and commitment to Vietnam," one scholar has written of these developments, promised "a continuation of a familiar relationship." Here was, in effect, "the most prominent international instance of [Beijing's] newly radicalized commitment to continuing revolution."[60]

A visit to Hanoi by Chinese president Liu Shaoqi in May 1963 reinforced the perception among militants and possibly others that confrontationalism rather than caution was the better option for revolutionary success in Vietnam.[61] Tellingly, just days before Liu's visit, foreign minister Ung Van Khiem, a leading moderate and critic of Beijing, was replaced by Xuan Thuy, a friend of China and implacable enemy of the West in everything having to do with the Cold War.[62] Rejecting the possibility of a negotiated solution to the conflict below the seventeenth parallel, Liu told his hosts that "the Vietnamese people cannot sleep and eat at ease for a single day so long as the Southern part is not liberated from the cruel rule of the U.S.-Diem clique." Under NLF leadership and "with the support of their countrymen in the North," Liu continued, the people of the South "will finally succeed in driving out the U.S. aggressors and accomplish the sacred task of Vietnam's reunification after a protracted and arduous struggle." "In the matter of such an important battle of principles" as the conflict between socialism and capitalism, "we cannot be spectators or follow a half-way line," as Moscow was doing. Now was the time to struggle more fiercely, Liu claimed. The imperialist camp was rapidly disintegrating owing to "inherent contradictions," while socialism and "the national revolutionary movement" were "rising like the sun in the East."

Diplomacy or the desire for peace without victory, Liu continued in obvious criticism of Moscow, "must not be used to abolish the socialist countries' duty to support the revolutionary struggles of the oppressed nations and peoples" or "to supersede the revolutionary line of the proletariat of various countries and their parties." "In order to carry out peaceful coexistence," Liu added, "what is required is, first of all, to carry out resolute struggle against the imperialist policies of aggression and war and not to liquidate this struggle, and it is even more impermissible to liquidate the struggles of the oppressed nations and people." Even while building socialism at home, socialist countries "must resolutely support the revolutionary struggles of all oppressed nations and peoples." That was, Liu asserted, "their compelling international duty." Wherever there existed oppression by imperialism and its reactionary allies, including in southern Vietnam, the people must "rise up in revolution."[63]

According to one account, during one semipublic meeting Liu praised Stalin, an affront to Khrushchev so potentially serious that the Vietnamese press decided not to report it.[64] To be sure, the vehemence of Liu's rhetoric surprised his Vietnamese hosts, but his tone as well as the substance of what he said validated the views of many of them. During Liu's stay, the British consul complained, references to the relations between China and the DRVN as being as close as "lips and teeth" were repeated "ad nauseam." "Although in her official attitudes the D.R.V.

continues to keep the balance between the Russian and Chinese wings of the Communist movement," the consul continued, there was "little doubt" after Liu's visit that many in the upper echelon of the party had "much in common with the Chinese."[65] One study suggests that Liu's visit "marked the ascendency of the pro-Chinese cause in North Vietnam."[66] Another study notes that the diminished levels of Soviet assistance in its aftermath, as Chinese aid increased, encouraged many in the VWP to rank Moscow's commitment to world revolution "in the rear area of the conflict rather than at its center."[67] To French diplomats on site, the mere presence of Liu in Hanoi at that juncture "marked a worrisome turn in the foreign policy of North Vietnam," pushing as it did, according to the Canadians, "the DRVN towards the Peking position" on conflict with the West.[68]

To offset the visit's potentially harmful effects on Soviet-Vietnamese relations, Ho Chi Minh allegedly insisted on the inclusion in Vietnamese speeches of references to the need for unity in the communist camp as well as to Hanoi's "deep concern at the differences now existing in the international communist movement and the socialist camp."[69] At the ceremonies concluding Liu's visit, Ho repeated his litany that the CPSU and the CCP "are the two biggest parties and bear the greatest responsibility in the international communist movement," and that the unity of those parties "is the pillar of the unity of the socialist camp and the international communist movement."[70]

Contemporaneous international developments also encouraged the hardening of views in the VWP. To a man, militants considered the outcome of the Cuban missile crisis a demonstration of Khrushchev's cowardice and the bankruptcy of peaceful coexistence, though it was also a major setback for the capitalist camp, which had to accept the continued existence of the Castro regime. In addition, they saw the result of the Algerian war of independence as a stunning victory over imperialism. Historian Odd Arne Westad has suggested that the result of the Algerian conflict was a "key reason" for the radicalization of militants in Vietnam and for the growing importance of their views among DRVN leaders.[71] In conjunction with continuing decolonization in Asia and Africa and the emergence of new Marxist insurgent movements in Latin America, these developments convinced militants and others of the inherent weakness of imperialism and the growing strength of world revolutionary forces. In the wake of so many "progressive" developments, it was easy to read them collectively as portending the eventual demise of capitalism and the triumph of proletarian internationalism. The age of "transition from capitalism to socialism as the dominant system in the world" had begun; a new revolutionary tide was swelling across the globe, and Vietnamese communists had to help it along.[72]

The political situation in Laos further emboldened militants. The emergence there of increasingly powerful pro-American factions indicated that Washington was continuing its clandestine operations in flagrant violation of the previous year's accords (which Hanoi itself continued to violate, notably by reintroducing main-line troops plus assorted political and military specialists).[73] The neutralist government of Prince Souvanna Phouma teetered on the brink of collapse because of those violations, and "counterrevolutionary" elements seemed poised to seize the reins of power once it fell. "The situation in Laos has become very serious," Pham Van Dong had told the National Assembly earlier in 1963. The Americans had "strengthened their occupation forces in Thailand" in preparation for "increased intervention in Laos." They had also illegally repositioned reactionary forces in Laos "to create a chaotic situation." Washington hoped by these actions to "demonstrate that the policies of peaceful neutrality and rule" by a rickety coalition of three disparate factions "could not be maintained," and that the recent Geneva agreement on Laos "in the end had produced no results." It would then use those conclusions to "carry out its wicked designs."[74] In light of circumstances in Laos and elsewhere, militants surmised, the VWP had no choice but to revise its revolutionary strategy and escalate armed struggle in the South.

MISSED OPPORTUNITIES FOR PEACE?

Some authors have argued with varying degrees of persuasiveness that there was still hope for a negotiated solution after 1962, that Hanoi and Saigon were in fact moving toward a diplomatic settlement of their differences in or around the summer of 1963. The tenor of their argument suggests that leftist influence in Hanoi remained negligible at this point or at least too weak to preclude such an accommodation.[75] "The period from early 1962 to mid-1963 witnessed a more forthcoming North Vietnamese position on the subject of diplomacy than had been seen previously," historian Fredrik Logevall has written of this view, intimating "the possibility in the middle of 1963 for fashioning some kind of political solution to the Indochina conflict, whether by way of a bilateral North-South deal or a multipower conference."[76] In an influential book, Ellen Hammer similarly posited that "contacts between the two sides," possibly initiated in 1962 and facilitated by the Polish representative on the ICSC, Mieczyslaw Maneli, were "going well" in mid-1963, bringing Hanoi and Saigon close to an agreement. "The talks were not about a detailed agreement; it was too soon for that," she wrote. "They dealt with parallel actions each side might take, such as lessening guerilla activities and limiting military initiatives." "Northerners saw advantages in dealing with Ngo Dinh Diem at this stage," Hammer believed, because of food shortages in the North, the vulnerability of Hanoi to "unwelcome pressures" from the Chinese due to the Sino-Soviet split, and fear of American military intervention.[77]

It is indeed true that thanks to Polish as well as French intercession, Hanoi had established and was using a secret channel to communicate with Saigon by mid-1963.[78] French records confirm that secret "contacts" at a "high level" between

Saigon and Hanoi existed in May, and meetings between the two sides had taken place in the South Vietnamese capital. None other than Ngo Dinh Nhu, Diem's brother and chief adviser, represented the RVN in the meetings, and it was said that he actually "controls these relations" on the RVN side; his opposite on the DRVN side, however, remains unknown.[79] But Hanoi never intended to use these contacts to resolve political or military matters, or to negotiate the differences between northern and southern authorities diplomatically unless, of course, Saigon was ready to capitulate. It used them instead to address trade and cultural issues—namely, resumption of the exchange of goods and postal services between the two halves of the country, raised on at least two occasions previously, as well as the staging of soccer matches between teams from the two Vietnams.[80] The goods to be exchanged included coal, which the DRVN had in abundance, for rice, which it pressingly needed and which the agricultural South produced in surplus amounts.

Hanoi's diplomatic démarches thus aimed not to restore peace in Vietnam but to advance its political agenda while easing a pressing economic concern. They cannot be taken as preliminaries to serious probing for peace or as evidence that a substantive effort was made and missed by anyone in the spring and summer of 1963. As historian Margaret Gnoinska has demonstrated on the basis of Polish documentary evidence, Warsaw "did not launch any secret peace initiative in Vietnam" during 1963. Rather, Hanoi asked ICSC commissioner Maneli to convey to "those interested" in Saigon that it wanted to begin cultural exchanges and trade, namely, coal for rice, with the South before any diplomatic settlement could be considered, and Warsaw obliged. "The North Vietnamese did not ask Maneli to relay to the South Vietnamese any specific questions or suggestions of a political nature," Gnoinska notes, and she found no evidence that Hanoi "made serious attempts to sway the Saigon regime to its side through the Polish channel."[81]

As Hanoi explored the possibility of low-level commercial and cultural exchanges with the South, French president Charles de Gaulle issued a sudden call for neutralizing South Vietnam and creating an unaligned but inclusive coalition government there.[82] By one account the call was "virtually [for] a return to the main principles of the [1954] Geneva Conference," including "the need for unity, independence and good neighbourliness." It was also at least somewhat "anti-American" and "Delphic."[83] Though Hanoi refused to comment on the call, a North Vietnamese diplomat in Algiers confided to a French counterpart that some DRVN leaders found it "positive."[84] Unfortunately for them, nothing came of de Gaulle's proposal.[85]

Gareth Porter has noted that soon after de Gaulle made his call, individuals in Washington, Saigon, and Hanoi began talking up plans to neutralize South Vietnam and end hostilities. The plans, Porter believes, failed to materialize due to the machinations of hawks in the Kennedy administration.[86] By this time, we now know, no plan for neutralizing the South stood a real chance of adoption or of producing a workable peace if it were adopted. Through most of 1963 Hanoi was in the throes of a divisive debate over strategic policy, and by the time de Gaulle made his proposal, militants were winning that debate. As that occurred, calls for neutralization and peace were too little too late, coming as they did after the collapse of Laotian neutrality had shown the "worthlessness" of international agreements negotiated from a position of relative weakness and with no adequate mechanisms of enforcement.[87] According to historian Edward Miller, even if Hanoi had wanted to negotiate, peace would still not have materialized because Diem and Nhu thought they were winning the war against southern insurgents, and thus viewed peace talks merely as a "prelude to Hanoi's capitulation."[88]

THE PARTY BEGINS TO CRACK

In view of both the provocations and the opportunities it believed it faced, the militant faction in the VWP demonstrated patience and restraint. There is no evidence the faction tried to force events by openly attacking key moderate leaders in Hanoi, disheartened though it was by their obdurateness. The integrity of the party, like that of the socialist camp, was as sacrosanct to militants as it was to moderates. Although the Sino-Soviet dispute had long been a source of contention within the party, the leadership had always remained publicly united in responding to it. Throughout that ordeal, in the words of Douglas Pike, the VWP "demonstrated remarkable consistency in dealing with the dispute, by evaluating it and basing responses to each unfolding development" on its own revolutionary objectives.[89] A coup or some other premature bid for power by militants was an option, but it risked alienating fence-sitters and the party base, and could tarnish if not altogether discredit the leftist cause. Militants therefore bided their time, waiting for circumstances to change to their advantage even as they nudged those circumstances along.

By summer, party decision-makers were under pressure to accept Chinese revolutionary prescriptions not only from within but also from foreign allies. In June a delegation of visiting North Koreans made a "strenuous" effort to push Vietnamese leaders "from [their] perch on the fence definitively into the Peking camp" or at least to "produce some pro-Chinese statements." The leaders resisted the effort, fearing that they would be going too far by supporting a North Korean and Chinese line that was openly defiant of Moscow.[90] Shortly thereafter, the Chinese Embassy launched a "paper war" in Hanoi, distributing "tracts" in Vietnamese that were actually translations of items from Beijing's *People's Daily* denouncing peaceful coexistence and revisionism. The embassy circulated the tracts to those who visited its reading room and to the thirty thousand PRC nationals then residing in the capital.[91] To avoid complicating its relationship with Moscow, Hanoi politely asked the embassy to refrain from distributing such tracts, and the practice ceased without incident.

The ever observant British Consulate had come to believe by then that despite such initiatives the "natural sympathies" of most VWP members were now "largely with the Chinese," and wondered how much longer it would be before that became more manifest.[92] Not long, it turned out. That same month, the party organ *Hoc tap* began featuring a series of articles showcasing leftist thinking on various issues.[93] The first of the articles was a virulent condemnation of revisionism in the form of an attack on Yugoslavia but in language that only thinly veiled criticism of those in the party who supported peaceful coexistence and the strategic status quo below the seventeenth parallel, and through them the Soviet Union. "The main road, the main way for the proletariat to seize power," that article read, "is to use revolutionary violence to throw off the yoke of the bourgeoisie, smash the old State apparatus and set up the proletarian dictatorship."[94]

Two other equally revealing articles appeared in September. The first implicitly condemned the CPSU's embrace of peaceful coexistence and its criticism of China and others in the socialist camp who questioned that embrace. "Treating class brothers as enemies on account of ideological differences," it read, "trying in a thousand and one ways to create difficulties for the fraternal countries in the matter of their economic development and strengthening their ability to defend themselves, at the same time considering enemies as friends, doing a cosmetic job on them, even helping the bourgeois reactionaries of other countries in their expansionist moves, in attacking and provoking the fraternal countries, are the most important visible manifestations of the communists who have completely departed from Marxist-Leninist socialism."[95]

The second *Hoc tap* article, "Peace or Violence," was highly theoretical and underscored the importance some party members, namely militants, accorded to Marxist-Leninist determinism and the merits they placed in revolutionary violence. "Modern revisionist and rightist opportunists are distorting Marxist-Leninist theories on the historical role of violence and giving great publicity to pacifism," it noted. Such people "know nothing about the law of social evolution." Renouncing violent revolution or timidly pursuing military struggle reduced "proletarian revolution and proletarian dictatorship to empty words." Similarly, pursuing revolutionary goals by political rather than violent means "will leave the working class without adequate preparation for overcoming difficulties, for defeating the exploiting classes, and for establishing its dictatorship." Violence was the "midwife" of revolutionary change; victims of exploitation and domination "must resort to revolutionary violence to smash counterrevolutionary violence" and "win their own emancipation so that society may advance according to the law of historical development." The history of the Vietnamese revolution "proves that to overthrow the exploiters who use violence to dominate the people," there was no other path than "the path of violence," as Le Duan had advanced in 1956.[96] That article subsequently received "Chinese acclaim" for its "uncompromising denunciation of the *embourgeoisement* of certain sectors of communist ideology."[97]

There were other signs of the new preponderance of leftist sympathies in party ranks. Arguably the most notable was Hanoi's decision to join Beijing in condemning the Partial Nuclear Test Ban Treaty negotiated by Washington and Moscow in August on grounds that the treaty amounted to a surrender of socialist interests to capitalist imperial ambitions.[98] "The position of the Chinese government is absolutely correct and reasonable and completely reflects the desires and aspirations of peace-loving people worldwide," a *Hoc tap* item noted.[99] "Socialist countries other than the Soviet Union must not be denied the means of defense," a Vietnamese observer said of the treaty.[100] Since not all nuclear weapons were to be destroyed, a *Nhan dan* editorial boldly charged, a partial ban served only imperialist and Soviet interests.[101] The treaty "will hamper the fraternal socialist countries from helping one another so as to raise the defense capability of our camp to the level of the requirements of modern military science," another editorial noted.[102]

In this and other editorials and official commentaries, implicit denunciations of Moscow "went as far as possible."[103] "It was clear," read a western assessment, "that sooner or later [the DRVN] would have to stand up and be counted on one side or the other [of the Sino-Soviet dispute], and this time came when she had to decide whether or not to [endorse] the Nuclear Test Ban Treaty."[104] The French Delegation similarly surmised that the stance on the Partial Nuclear Test Ban Treaty "in fact constituted a declaration, the clearest so far, of alignment with Chinese theses."[105] Hanoi's position on the treaty reportedly made the Soviets "more discontented" with Hanoi than they had ever been, and they made "no secret of it."[106] The Soviet ambassador confirmed that when, clearly frustrated, he told a French diplomat that he put little stock in the declarations or actions of the DRVN because it was a "weak and small country."[107]

In an equally bold move reflecting the shifting political currents in the VWP, Hanoi at this time dispatched a large retinue of PAVN military advisers to the South to "militarize the looser, more self-contained guerrilla units" of the PLAF, convert those units "into more traditional armed forces," and prepare them for "more orthodox military assignments."[108] The advisers' dispatch did not go unnoticed by RVN authorities, who complained to the ICSC about Hanoi's growing involvement in the southern insurgency.[109] Indeed, that year 7,850 additional troops and political and military advisers infiltrated the South from the North, fewer than the year before but only because of the earlier exhaustion of the pool of southern regroupees.[110] For a Canadian observer, the continuing infiltration and other "provocations" were clear indications of the preponderance of militant influence in Hanoi.[111] By this time it allegedly took "the full weight" of Ho Chi Minh's authority to prevent the party from openly and fully committing the DRVN to war in the South.[112]

In October, on the anniversary of the 1938 Munich accords, *Nhan dan* ran a revealing editorial indicative of the militant mood now prevailing in Hanoi. According to the editorial, there were two ways of responding to aggressive imperialism. One consisted of "preserving the unity of the socialist camp," "rallying the peoples of the world behind a large united front and launching a powerful mass movement," and "attacking resolutely and continuously to keep in check warmongering imperialists." The other way, the "bad" way, entailed following the approach of politicians at Munich, allowing oneself to be duped by the professed goodwill of the enemy and making "concession after concession" to the enemy. "The lesson of Munich," the editorial concluded, "has demonstrated that the policy of defeatism is extremely dangerous since it creates, for the imperialists, favorable conditions for the pursuit of their aggressive designs."[113] To western analysts, the editorial was "a pretext to evoke the current international situation and vigorously condemn all policies of appeasement," "an apology for Chinese theses," and a "barely veiled critique" of Moscow's peaceful coexistence policy.[114] "The DRVN espousal of the Peking line continues, although it is by no means so extreme as to include direct criticism of the Moscow position," the Canadian representative inferred from the contents of that and other recent articles and editorials.[115]

THE COUP AGAINST DIEM

The climatic episode that would push Hanoi into a definitively militant strategy in the South came in the fall, when the political landscape there changed suddenly and radically. On 2 November 1963, Diem and his brother Nhu were killed in a coup by ARVN officers. General Duong Van Minh thereafter became head of the Saigon government. Publicly, DRVN leaders dismissed Diem's overthrow as a mere change of personnel, further proof of the bankruptcy of Washington's policies in the South. Privately, however, they were alarmed. Specifically, they feared that the new leadership might rally popular support for its policies, setting back the revolution in the South. "Signs of this fear are the constant warnings in the North Vietnamese press and on the South Vietnamese Liberation Radio to the people of South Vietnam not to be duped by the new Government's talk of 'democracy and freedom,'" western observers noted.[116]

DRVN leaders believed then and Vietnamese scholars believe now that Washington engineered the coup.[117] In *Hoc tap*, Ha Van Lau of the Foreign Ministry immediately postulated that the Kennedy administration, bent on precipitating a wider war, had sanctioned the coup because Diem had failed to "satisfy" Washington's requirements of "saving" the South and "crushing the Viet Cong rebellion."[118] By most Vietnamese accounts, the Kennedy administration engineered the overthrow to gain greater freedom of action in the South.[119] Diem had behaved too independently, according to these sources, and Washington replaced him with a more pliable leader.[120] Luu Doan Huynh, a late Vietnamese diplomat, noted that as early as 1962 Hanoi began noticing "increasing contradictions" between Diem's regime and Washington and felt some trepidation, not knowing what this might presage.[121] For many in Hanoi, the coup confirmed what they suspected all along: that the United States had from the beginning intended to assume the colonial mantle from the French in Indochina.

To many in the VWP, the coup was tantamount to revolution, marking as it did the transition from a bourgeois reactionary to a military counterrevolutionary regime in Saigon.[122] Reprehensible as the former had been, it was preferable to the latter because it had included civilian and nationalist elements. Leaders of the new regime were nothing but lackeys handpicked by Washington for their eagerness to benefit from America's neocolonial project. In the words of historian Le Cuong, the Kennedy administration had replaced a nepotistic regime with a "most submissive" one.[123] The French historian Philippe Franchini has drawn a parallel conclusion. "The arrival to power of a junta suggested the reinforcement of [Saigon's] ties to the United States," Franchini has written, the "expected effect" of which for Hanoi was "an increased American engagement that threatened to imperil the southern liberation movement."[124]

In the more direct language of a former Hanoi official, the coup "increased the danger of U.S. direct military intervention" in South Vietnam.[125] The new leadership in Saigon existed, according to another source, for the express purpose of creating political conditions that would enable the Americans to step up the hostilities in the South to their fullest extent.[126] In this reading, removing Diem eliminated the chief obstacle to Washington's goal of sending its own combat forces into Vietnam. "The fact that the Americans had put people in power in Saigon who represented no one but themselves was a political factor of tremendous importance for the party," one analyst noted.[127] British diplomats in Hanoi were quick to discern "the bitterness of the DRV's attitude towards the apparently more implacable military junta" that presided in Saigon thereafter.[128]

These concerns notwithstanding, some in the party believed the coup might be a blessing if it could be turned into "the first step towards the final disintegration of the American position" in the South.[129] To those who thought this way, Diem had been "one of the strongest individuals resisting the people and Communism," a leader who had done "everything that could be done in an attempt to crush the revolution," and he had had success. Insofar as these things were true, the coup "will prove contrary to the calculations of the U.S. imperialists" and "will not be the last misjudgment by Washington."[130] Western observers agreed that Diem had been surprisingly resourceful in creating a strong political base for himself in the South while resisting Washington's attempt to take control of the war effort there.[131]

The weight of these calculations is difficult to measure. There is no doubt that Diem had been a strong political leader who had some meaningful successes in resisting the communists. But his overthrow was "not an unmixed blessing" for Hanoi, as U.S. government analyst and historian George K. Tanham has noted, because it rid the South of "the greatest object of hate" among southerners and thus of "an important motivating element for some parts of the NLF." Indeed, Tanham contends, membership in the NLF "dropped" shortly after the coup as many southern rebels considered their struggle for peace and justice to be over.[132]

THE CENTRAL COMMITTEE'S NINTH PLENUM

The coup in Saigon led to a period of reassessment in Hanoi, and eventually to a coup of sorts there as well.[133] Immediately, it prompted an emergency session of the Central Committee to discuss, in the bland language of subsequent official accounts, "the international tasks of the party."[134] David Elliott has suggested that the session's purpose was to decide whether to negotiate with the new leadership in Saigon with a view to creating a coalition administration there.[135] Negotiations to that end would be consistent with earlier party initiatives and might allow southern revolutionary forces to consolidate their recent gains in the countryside. But any such agreement would likely mean an indefinite postponement of reunification, which militants could be expected to oppose, especially at this juncture.[136]

The plenum in fact addressed issues that went well beyond these concerns and produced irrevocable changes in the VWP's revolutionary strategy and the party itself. Discussion involved not only the situation internationally and in the South, but also the growing division within the party and relations with the Chinese and the Soviets. According to a foreign observer at the time, the timing of the plenum represented "the most solid confirmation of disputes within the party."[137] Indeed, it was in this uncertain, troubling context that Diem's overthrow and the resulting changes in the South brought the conflict between party moderates and militants to a head. Circumstances within the party leadership as well as below the seventeenth parallel and in the socialist camp generally had combined to force the party either to formally commit itself to the leftist stance on strategic as well as theoretical issues or to mute that and other criticism of peaceful coexistence and revisionism and resign itself to whatever happened below the seventeenth parallel.[138] Failure to make a clear choice on these alternatives, to resolve the militant-moderate conflict once and for all, would confuse the party faithful as well as southern revolutionaries and the Vietnamese people, and would cloud, if not compromise, relations with Moscow and Beijing. The plenum therefore became the setting in which the VWP would address and resolve that conflict.

The plenum opened on 22 November.[139] In early sessions, party notables reported on conditions in Vietnam and elsewhere to establish the correctness of their views and reinforce or sway the thinking of peers. The façade of party unity, the "infallibility" of Marxism-Leninism, as well as the conventions of Vietnamese propriety dictated that the reports and their presentation be tactful and formulaic. Vo Nguyen Giap, for example, discussed the ongoing modernization of the armed forces in language that stressed not only the progress being made but the continued need for caution in the South.

The deliberative discussions that followed were reportedly more contentious.[140] Since the sessions were private and records of them—if they exist—are still unreleased, information about those discussions is limited. It appears, however, that formulaic congeniality disappeared as soon as the occasion for it passed. In view of the stakes, participants had every reason to state their views frankly, or if not frankly then calculatingly according to their sense of the way the ideological wind was blowing. Deep and long-standing cleavages within the party were thus exposed, and for the moment the party seemed to tear itself asunder. Ho Chi Minh reportedly offered in advance to moderate these debates, but militants prevented that lest his stature bend the plenum to his will.[141] According to one of his biographers, Ho stormed out of the deliberations because of their contentiousness and excused himself from further participation.[142] A document in the Russian archives suggests that on 25 December, while the plenum was still in session, Ho went to the Soviet Embassy and told the ambassador he was retiring from politics, presumably because of the intractability of the debates in the plenum and the challenges to his authority.[143]

The least circuitous and most significant contribution to the debate was the formal address by first secretary Le Duan, who asserted himself and his thinking as never before during the proceedings.[144] Le Duan stated his hard-line views pointedly and with a view to rallying the committee behind them and securing endorsement for the strategic decisions those views dictated. Entitled "Some Questions concerning the International Tasks of Our Party," his speech was spirited and full of specifics couched in the orthodoxies of Marxism-Leninism. It conveyed militants' growing concern with what they saw as a world crisis and with the dangers and opportunities they believed that crisis presented to the larger cause of world revolution and the specific cause of the Vietnamese revolution.

Le Duan based his case concerning the need for the party to change course in the South less on the "objective" situation there than on a surprisingly positive analysis of the world situation. Formerly, when the Soviet Union was still weak, he said, "it was necessary at certain times to make concessions to the enemy in order to gain temporary relaxation and temporary peace, to gain time to consolidate and increase [the socialist camp's] strength so as to cope with new clashes with imperialism." Now, however, the tide had changed: "We are strong, while the enemy is weak." "The forces of revolution, socialism, and peace have greatly surpassed the forces of reaction and war of imperialism," he told the plenum. "Revolution is, therefore, not on the defensive, and the strategy of revolution should not be a defensive one." In Vietnam as elsewhere in the colonial and semicolonial world, the "strategy of revolution" must be "an offensive strategy to smash one by one the war policies of imperialism headed by the United States until its war plans are completely smashed." The time had come to "take the offensive against imperialist war policy and defeat it."

The words and their thrust were indirect, but they clearly conveyed his meaning: the Vietnamese were entitled to follow the revolutionary strategy dictated by their own circumstances. The purpose of the debate at the plenum was to define the interests of Vietnam as a member of the socialist camp facing a unique set of circumstances and to decide how best to act on those interests and address those circumstances. The first secretary left no doubt about where he stood on those issues. To liberate the South and reunify the country, the VWP could temporize no longer; it had to move to a strategy predicated on war below the seventeenth parallel.

In light of that necessity, Le Duan also boldly insisted that the party must combat the rightist opportunists and revisionists in its ranks. "The purposes of opposing modern revisionism," he explained, were "to strengthen the struggle against imperialism, to vigorously promote the revolutionary cause of the people of the world, to safeguard the international communist movement and the socialist camp, and also to defend our party and the revolutionary cause of our party and people." Le Duan's speech thus called for war not only against Saigon and the Americans in the South, but also against moderate tendencies within the VWP.

RESOLUTION 9

By the time the plenum ended, Le Duan and the party's militant wing had carried the day, and the balance of power within the VWP had shifted. The Central Committee's final resolution acknowledged the legitimacy of the concerns raised by Le Duan and other militants as well as the correctness of the policies they recommended and had, in fact, been pushing for all along. Considering his authority as head of the party and the validation of his views by recent events, it seems certain that the first secretary was instrumental in bending the plenum and the party in that direction. "This resolution was the outcome of the struggle inside our party which had begun with Khrushchov's [sic] public attack on China in 1960," Hoang Van Hoan observed later.[145]

"Resolution 9," as it came to be known (because this was the Central Committee's ninth plenum since the National Congress of 1960), consisted of two separate documents: a public communiqué released on 20 January 1964, which listed the domestic and international tasks of the party, and a "secret" assessment of the situation in the South and the requirements for military struggle there.[146] Both are remarkable for detailing the new revolutionary line and illuminating the nature and seriousness of the party's commitment to an essentially Maoist interpretation of Marxism-Leninism and world revolution.

Entitled "On the World Situation and the International Tasks of Our Party," the communiqué warned of the deceitfulness of Washington's ostensible "peace strategy" and of the pitfalls of negotiating with imperialists.[147] The Americans had relied on "modern revisionism" within the socialist bloc to "achieve 'peaceful evolution'" as a model for relations between the socialist and capitalist blocs, hoping thereby to "cause a number of socialist countries to degenerate ideologically and politically and gradually restore capitalism." Unfortunately, they were succeeding in that endeavor. Without pointing a finger at anyone, the document insisted that revisionists within the socialist bloc "have done their best to collaborate" with Washington's effort, and consequently they "dare not encourage and support the revolutionary wars aimed at weakening" imperialism and capitalism. "On the contrary," revisionists had "tried to hinder the world revolutionary movement," criticized true communists as "dogmatic" and "warlike," and discouraged wars of national liberation for fear they would lead to a world war.

Given Khrushchev's widely known fear of a Soviet-American conflagration and public denunciations of Chinese "dogmatism," these passages were a clear indictment of his views. Interestingly, until this time, party attacks on revisionism had always been directed at Yugoslavia. Now, however, the party was attacking other unnamed betrayers of Marxism-Leninism, who could only include Khrushchev. Revisionists "in a number of fraternal parties," the communiqué continued, now espoused the "views of the Tito revisionist clique," and like it were "undermining the international communist movement in the ideological field" even though, unlike Belgrade, they were not yet "lackeys of the imperialists." These were remarkably bold contentions, to say the least.

The second document, the "secret" one, was entitled "Strive to Struggle, Rush Forward to Win New Victories in the South." It specifically addressed the revolution in the South and insisted that pursuing peaceful coexistence there—offering to negotiate with "imperialists" and their "lackeys" and otherwise hoping for a diplomatic settlement of differences between the two sides—under current circumstances amounted to a demonstration of weakness so great as to be tantamount to capitulation. "The more we manifest our goodwill, the more exacting the imperialists will be," the document noted. "The more concessions we make, the more insatiable they will be" in their demands.

Under current conditions at home and abroad, the document asserted, war alone could enable Vietnam to achieve national liberation, reunification, and complete sovereignty. The party therefore had to escalate the insurgency below the seventeenth parallel dramatically and without delay to defeat the Americans and their local allies once and for all. The successes of the Russian, Chinese, and Cuban revolutions demonstrated that "seizing power through violent means is correct and necessary."

Unlike Resolution 15 of 1959, this document spelled out in explicit terms the guidelines for implementing the new strategy.[148] Since the enemy used military power "as a principal tool to maintain his domination," the people must "use revolutionary war to counter the enemy's anti-revolutionary war" and "liberate" themselves. "Only in this way can the revolution win a decisive victory." The prospect envisioned here included large-scale warfare for an unknown period of time: "This armed struggle must follow the rules of war" and involve "main forces." It must also "attain its highest mission, which is to destroy the enemy's forces," to destroy "the enemy's combat ability." This would obviously require major increases in northern assistance to the southern insurgency, which the Central Committee also sanctioned. "It is time for the North to increase aid to the South," to "bring into fuller play its role as the revolutionary base of the whole nation." A "maximum effort to defeat the enemy" meant fully committing the DRVN to military victory in the South, including deploying PAVN units to assist the PLAF, if necessary.

To achieve victory, the war effort would pursue two primary, "essential" objectives. The first and most critical was "gradual annihilation," leading to "complete disintegration" of ARVN forces. Communist-led troops "must adopt the tactic of annihilation attacks," whether "killing one soldier, capturing one weapon," or "destroying entire units of the enemy." Conducted efficiently, these efforts would bring victory in a "not very long period." The Central Committee was confident that revolutionary forces could win a decisive victory over ARVN forces before Washington introduced its own combat forces. American decision-makers "clearly understand that if they become bogged down in a large-scale protracted war, then they will fall into an extremely defensive position internationally." If Washington did commit troops before revolutionary forces achieved a decisive victory, the committee estimated that their number would not exceed one hundred thousand. In that case, "the revolution in South Viet-Nam will meet more difficulties, the struggle will be stronger and harder" and the "transitional period" longer, but victory would come all the same.

The second "essential" objective of the military struggle, according to the document, was to destroy Saigon's strategic hamlet program to ensure the revolutionary forces' access to the South's human and material resources. In place of the strategic hamlets they destroyed, revolutionary forces would organize "combat villages," previously mandated by the party. Paralleling this effort would be a comprehensive political struggle to create "an anti-American alliance" between the NLF and other groups with "anti-American tendencies," including ethnic minorities and religious sects. Indoctrination campaigns would convince people of their "sacred" duty to "stand up and save the country," and would make soldiers in Saigon's armed forces "realize that their own interests are identical to those of the people." One way to encourage the latter would be to show clemency to rank-and-file prisoners of war. Political struggle would henceforth "keep pace" with armed struggle, not the other way around.

As these efforts developed in the South, the VWP would intensify its diplomatic struggle to encourage sympathetic perceptions of the revolution internationally. "We must make every effort to motivate various peace organizations, labor unions, youths, women, lawyers, [and] other professional organizations of various peoples in the world" to "take stronger actions in asking the U.S. imperialists to end their aggressive war, withdraw their troops, military personnel, and weapons from South Vietnam, and let the South Vietnamese people settle their own problems." The diplomatic struggle would also continue its efforts to win "the sympathy and support of the people of the nationalist and imperialist countries," including the United States and France, thus "gaining the sympathy of antiwar groups in the United States and taking full advantage of the dissensions among the imperialists."

Finally, to achieve absolute unity of thought and purpose within the party, vital to triumphing expeditiously under the new strategy, the document sanctioned a purge of party members "afraid of sacrifices," who used socialist transformation in the North as an excuse to forgo liberation in the South or "failed to realize the relationship between the revolutionary tasks of our people in both zones." In other words, it called for the demotion, dismissal, or marginalization of known influential moderates. The document also called upon party leaders to "pursue the systematic education of cadres and party members in Marxism-Leninism," centralize their control over the southern insurgency, and disseminate Resolution 9 with explicit explanations of its meaning and instructions for its implementation.

To mollify communists at home and abroad who might question the soundness and legitimacy of the new course endorsed by the Central Committee, the resolution stressed that waging military struggle in the South was not contrary or even a threat to world peace. Vietnam's impending war of national liberation would actually constitute "an active contribution" to the goal of world peace, a noble effort to "thwart the U.S. imperialists' plot of turning South Viet-Nam into a military base to oppose the socialist camp, rekindle the Indochinese war, and expand the war in Southeast Asia." War was just or unjust; communists supported the former and opposed the latter. "Opposing war in general without distinction between just and unjust war is, in fact, opposing revolutionary wars too."

Resolution 9 portended a consequential realignment of the party's revolutionary strategy. It represented, in fact, the most significant party pronouncement on the situation in the South since the decision to accept the Geneva accords in 1954. It also set the DRVN on an irreversible collision course with the United States. The bold and ambitious program adopted by the Central Committee effectively gave DRVN decision-makers a blank check to wage war in the South. It sanctioned the first major revision of the party's strategy vis-à-vis the South since Resolution 15 of January 1959 and, in retrospect, expedited the onset of the Vietnam War.[149] In its tone and substance, Resolution 9 amounted to a declaration of war on the Saigon regime, and the United States by extension. With its adoption by the Central Committee, the earlier effort to separate the revolutionary processes in the North and South was abandoned. Henceforth, the DRVN would invest itself comprehensively in the liberation of the South by military struggle. The revolution would be, once again, a single national effort, with the party and the nation together "*building the North peacefully while carrying out war against the Americans in the South.*"[150] Military officials at once set about bringing the PAVN to "wartime strength" in preparation for sending to the South "complete units at their full authorized strength of personnel and equipment."[151] Meanwhile, the DRVN substantially increased its material assistance to the NLF, and to the PLAF in particular. "Immediately," as Ang Cheng Guan has written, "war preparations went into full swing in both North and South," and the level and intensity of violence below the seventeenth parallel soon increased markedly.[152] Thus, as historian Lien-Hang Nguyen has put it, "militant hawks achieved the categorical response in 1963 that they had wanted in 1959: mobilization of the entire country behind the war effort." Military strategists "abandoned the idea of winning the southern struggle through protracted warfare and instead ordered a major buildup of conventional military force to bring the war to a speedy end," she concluded.[153]

In the context of the time, adoption of the new strategy signaled Hanoi's acceptance of Chinese revolutionary theses and its unequivocal rejection of Soviet ones. It was to avoid the impression of partiality to China in the Sino-Soviet dispute that Hanoi limited the distribution of the full text of Resolution 9 and classified as "secret" the part addressing the revolution in the South. The North Vietnamese "could not afford to [further] alienate the Soviet Union altogether" by widely disseminating a text so at odds with Soviet views.[154] In substance if not in tone, Resolution 9 seemed to be pro-Chinese, but in fact it simply captured the aspiration of VWP militants, who espoused Chinese revolutionary prescriptions but never answered to Beijing nor openly supported Beijing in its dispute with Moscow.

Aware of the potentially ruinous implications for relations with Moscow of its decision to endorse Resolution 9, the Central Committee included in the "secret" document, which it understood Hanoi would eventually have to relay to Moscow, an insistent statement that the new revolutionary strategy was consistent with declarations on the responsibilities of national communist parties to the world revolution adopted in Moscow in 1957 and 1960. The document also emphasized that certain strategies of revolutionary struggle, including peaceful coexistence, which might be appropriate for members of the socialist camp such as the Soviet Union were not, just now, appropriate for Vietnam. Lastly, it stressed that the VWP attached great importance to its unity and friendship with the CPSU, that Moscow was then as always the head of the socialist camp, and that the Soviet Union remained Hanoi's model and inspiration for achieving socialist modernity in the DRVN.

THE PURGE OF MODERATES

Adoption of Resolution 9 precipitated an important reshuffling of the DRVN leadership, as leftist militants seized the opportunity to stage—and win—a power play, a coup of a different kind, against moderates in the VWP. Within days after the plenum, militants set out to denounce and remove from top and other echelons those suspected of opposing or even questioning the new orthodoxy, irretrievably changing the balance of power in Hanoi. Without unity "among all party members on the basis of unanimity with the party's line concerning the construction of socialism in North Vietnam and the struggle for national unification," Nguyen Chi Thanh commented, "our party surely cannot lead all our people successfully in carrying out the revolution."[155]

As head of the Party Organization Committee charged with keeping tabs on party members, Le Duc Tho—henceforth doubling as Le Duan's second-in-command, a role he had previously assumed in COSVN during the Indochina War—justified the denunciations of party members and meted out their punishments.[156] He insisted that dissidents be dismissed from leadership positions and otherwise ostracized to prevent them from using their offices and influence for "antiparty" purposes.[157] "Each comrade must be thoroughly imbued with the resolution of the ninth party Central Committee conference," Tho believed. The commitment of party leaders to the new revolutionary line, like that of cadres and members, had to be "unequivocal and definite"; otherwise "revisionism will develop and benefit class enemies." To preserve party integrity, "each comrade must be forced to submit to the party's iron discipline." "We are determined not to tolerate the practice of expressing views in an unorganized manner on the party's lines, policies, resolutions, and instructions," Tho insisted.

Tho identified the targets of this latest "rectification campaign," as the party called the effort to achieve conformity, as those who "separate themselves from the party," who "refused to express their views at party meetings" but "gathered in small groups" after meetings and "spoke in terms that counter party resolutions." Such behavior violated party discipline and undermined unity by creating dissension and schism, and it "must be stopped as soon as possible." "The struggle against rightist thought and revisionist influences," Tho claimed, "must spearhead the ideological struggle in our party at the present time."[158]

Though the evidence is not definitive, militants appear to have planned their "silent" coup against moderates before the plenum, using ruse and indirection to pinpoint those in the party's upper echelon who might criticize or reject the agenda

Le Duan intended to lay before the Central Committee. Acting on the first secretary's behalf a few days before the plenum, for example, party theoretician Truong Chinh, who was not only fully rehabilitated in 1963 but became a close collaborator of Le Duan, asked the head of the Institute of Philosophy, Hoang Minh Chinh, to prepare proposals for consideration at the upcoming meeting.[159] A decorated hero of the war with France, Chinh had studied in Moscow from 1957 to 1960, and in 1963 was a staunch proponent of peaceful coexistence and economic competition rather than armed struggle. Predictably, the proposals he prepared reflected these convictions and alerted militants to his likely response to Le Duan's agenda.

Those who supported Hoang Minh Chinh's proposals during the plenum became marked individuals. Besides Chinh himself, they included such men as former foreign minister Ung Van Khiem, deputy chairman of the National Commission for Science and Technology Bui Cong Trung, vice president of the Vietnamese-Soviet Friendship Association Duong Bach Mai, deputy minister of culture Le Liem, former personal secretary to Ho Chi Minh Vu Dinh Huynh, and PAVN colonel Le Vinh Quoc.[160] Quoc's opposition to violent struggle was notable for revealing a deep schism within the PAVN over military strategy in the South, including the deployment of PAVN units there. A number of PAVN officers were evidently "loathe" to intensify the armed struggle or dispatch their units to the South because they abided by Giap's position that modernization of the PAVN had to be completed before the party shifted gears in the South.[161] Besides, the goals of the southern military struggle identified in Resolution 9 were such, these officers understood, that their men, trained for conventional warfare to defend the North, would first have to be retrained in the guerilla tactics peculiar to a "people's war" to fight with maximum efficiency, which would take time.

The purge of "rightist deviationists" extended beyond the leaders already named and even beyond the party and the PAVN. Within weeks after the plenum, Tran Quoc Hoan's Ministry of Public Security was targeting civil servants, intellectuals, artists, and journalists suspected of sympathizing with Chinh's views, supporting the party's old line, or questioning the merits of dramatically escalating hostilities in the South. Tho's Organization Committee also ordered all members and cadres to attend "re-education" classes to "absorb" the substance and party interpretations of Resolution 9.[162] Soon, all party and state organs had proffered their commitment to revolutionary militancy, and a "repressive," antimoderate atmosphere prevailed in Hanoi.[163] Punishment for opponents or critics of the new orthodoxy ranged from demotion to dismissal from the party and the government, as well as other organizations, and from house arrest to death.[164] Several unrepentant moderates in the Central Committee, including some who held high posts in the government, were demoted.[165] DRVN nationals studying in countries whose governments supported peaceful coexistence, including the Soviet Union, were ordered home for re-education.[166] A number of ambassadors may also have been recalled to be re-educated and otherwise apprised of the party's new revolutionary line.[167] "In sum," as Lien-Hang Nguyen has concluded, all those "exposed to peaceful coexistence ideas were considered suspect and treated as such."[168]

The most famous victim of Tho and the militants was none other than Ho Chi Minh. By the time of the 1963 plenum, Ho's stubborn and ultimately misguided faith in peaceful struggle, in strategic moderation in the South—to say nothing of age and deteriorating health—had already cost him some of his power and influence in the party.[169] In the plenum's aftermath, he had little of either left. Since the signing of the 1954 Geneva accords, Ho had personified the moderate, conciliatory, risk-avoiding consensus within the VWP, the hope and purpose of which was to prevent another devastating war as long as conditions permitted.[170] Khrushchev's peaceful coexistence promised to meet that end, and Ho and many of his contemporaries had found it attractive. Le Duan and the party's militant wing thus had to neutralize Ho's influence. To justify sidelining him, they propagated among party members the "theory of two mistakes," according to which Ho had twice made "fatal mistakes" due to misguided optimism and fear of war: the first was agreeing in 1946 to let French forces return to Vietnam unopposed; the second was consenting to a cease-fire and to the country's partition in 1954.[171]

In view of Ho's unique reputation at home and abroad, however, the militants could not—even if that had been their desire—completely exclude him from political and diplomatic processes in which his sheer stature was useful to the revolution. Without Ho, the regime in Hanoi would "lose much of its attraction" domestically and internationally, as foreign observers noted.[172] Still the embodiment of the revolution in Vietnam and a symbol of revolutionary hope across the socialist world, the Third World, and beyond, Ho was a necessary asset, particularly for the diplomatic struggle. Despite their ideological differences, his personal relationship with Mao had been instrumental in securing Chinese support for the Vietnamese revolution.[173] Now, in his declining years—he died in 1969—the new militant regime in Hanoi used him in a largely ceremonial, but nonetheless crucial, role as goodwill ambassador and "symbolic head of state."[174] He became the venerable face of the revolution, a moderating voice to the rest of the world for a coterie of ideologues lacking his poise, appeal, and sagacity. After the plenum, the militants actually relied on Ho to mend relations with Moscow and smooth over problems rising from the Sino-Soviet split.[175] According William Duiker, Ho spent his time thereafter "fulfilling his growing image as the spiritual father of all Vietnamese people and the soul of the Vietnamese revolution."[176] He took on the persona of "Uncle Ho," cultivating—compelled under the circumstances to cultivate—an image as affable father of the nation and "demi-God" of the revolution.[177]

Ho's most prominent disciple and ideological ally, Vo Nguyen Giap, was also marginalized, though his postplenum role is more uncertain than Ho's. After Ho, Giap was the most recognizable face of the Vietnamese revolution. Like Ho, he was a personable man whose views carried weight inside and outside the party. Ho had led the political and diplomatic struggles for independence; Giap had won the military victories. Many at home and abroad knew him as the architect of the spectacular triumph over the French at Dien Bien Phu, after which his military genius captivated observers of Vietnamese affairs. To the troops he commanded and the revolutionaries he inspired, Giap was a hero. Though his innermost thoughts on the matter are poorly documented, he seems to have agreed with the decision to cease hostilities after Dien Bien Phu in the summer of 1954. Certainly he thereafter unflinchingly supported Ho and advocated revolutionary caution, for he too believed that resumption of warfare in the South before the socialist project in the North and modernization of the armed forces were completed would be risky and counterproductive. What is more, Giap respected Soviet strategic thinking. He was thus a big problem for the new leadership, in the party and in the armed forces, especially as his opinions were so widely respected.[178] It was therefore against great odds that militants were able to neutralize Giap's influence, though one report suggests that even before the 1963 plenum his star had begun to fade and he was "being squeezed out" by a more "pro-Peking group" of younger generals.[179]

Most party members appear to have gone along with the purges and the new orthodoxy because they recognized that the old guard had been variously naive, negligent, or incompetent. The centerpieces of their revolutionary strategy in the South—political struggle, respect for the Geneva accords, and since 1959, limited armed struggle—had by 1963 largely failed to deliver positive results. The "temporary" partition of the country was now a decade old and widely regarded as a fact in international politics. The repatriation of Viet Minh troops to the North and the moratorium on military struggle initially imposed on those who stayed had had disastrous, near-fatal implications for the southern communist movement. Perhaps the most obvious acknowledgment of these errors had been Hanoi's decision of 1959 to start redeploying to the South most troops it had ordered to regroup to the North in 1954–55. Yet even after its errors became obvious, the old guard's response had been reluctant, timid, and limited, no more than marginally effective at best and widely unpopular among southern revolutionaries and their sympathizers. It also helped the militants that this old guard made no serious attempt to resist or organize a countercoup. Ho, Giap, and most of their allies seem by the time of the Ninth Plenum to have resigned themselves to the notion that the time had come for a new strategy in the South and, with that, a new balance of power in Hanoi. That may have averted the kind of dislocations communist states sometimes experienced after restructuring their leadership.

The thoroughness with which the militants acted may suggest cynicism or paranoia on their part. But in the context of Cold War Vietnam, it is more likely that these mostly parochial men, schooled in the limiting dogmas of Marxism-

Leninism, believed that what they did was necessary and just. Growing tensions in the South and mounting difficulties in the North required concentration on vital issues; dissidence was intolerable. A leadership of "real" communists, of men who feared no sacrifice and no necessity, they thought, had better odds of guiding the revolution to victory than one dominated by half-hearted temporizers who would minimize the loss of lives and property and put the interests of individuals above those of the party, the state, and the revolution. The latest rectification campaign, the purge of moderates, demonstrated the determination of militants to achieve total unity of thought and purpose within leadership circles and throughout the rest of the party. Le Duan's regime wanted peers who agreed with it and underlings who obeyed unquestioningly and interpreted literally such slogans as "Independence or Death."

Within weeks of Resolution 9's adoption, militant thinking prevailed in the Politburo and the Central Committee. After Le Duan and Le Duc Tho, the most prominent members of the new ruling elite were Nguyen Chi Thanh and Pham Hung. These men would dominate party decision-making for years, with the exception of Thanh, who died in 1967.[180] Until his death, Thanh was a special beneficiary of the new regime. Since Le Duan and other militants understood that Giap's eclipse might elicit opposition in the PAVN, they ostentatiously praised Thanh, the only other full general in the North Vietnamese armed forces, citing the centrality of his role in the leadership. The praise seems to have appeased the armed forces and convinced military leaders and their men that the displacement of Giap was not a displacement of the PAVN or of its command structure in the ruling ranks of the party and the state.[181]

These multiple consequences of the Ninth Plenum produced irrevocable changes in the party and the government, as well as in the conduct of the Vietnamese revolution. Le Duan's rule—his supreme authority over party decision-making—would endure for twenty-three years, well past the period of this study and the triumphant events of 1975. Like Stalin and Mao before him, Le Duan centralized authority in a new executive structure in the party and government.[182] He incontestably became "first among equals" in Hanoi. Because he, unlike Ho, kept a low public profile—a calculated move since he had little charisma and projected arrogance, Le Duan acted as "the mastermind behind the scenes."[183] That in turn enabled him to conduct the revolution on his terms, which meant, among other things, total commitment to violent liberation of the South and implacable opposition to the American presence in Vietnam. For all these reasons, it seems incorrect to say, as one scholar has said, that the militant-moderate strategic debate within the VWP came to an end only with the decision to launch the Tet Offensive in 1968.[184] That debate ended when the Central Committee adopted Resolution 9 and Le Duan's command of and influence over the party became essentially absolute.

7

Waging War, 1964

Nineteen sixty-four was a good year for Beijing. In January it normalized relations with France, elevating the PRC's stature while sowing discord between Paris and Washington. In October, it detonated an atomic bomb, becoming only the fifth country to do so. With that step, Beijing gained not only international notoriety but also a guarantee against American military action in China. Days later, the Soviet Presidium ousted Mao's nemesis, Nikita Khrushchev, from power. Khrushchev's fall seemed to bode well for Sino-Soviet relations. As it turned out, Moscow's foreign policy remained essentially unchanged thereafter, and Beijing was soon accusing the new Soviet leadership of practicing "Khrushchevism without Khrushchev."

Despite chronic turmoil in Saigon, the Johnson administration remained committed to the preservation of a noncommunist South Vietnam, and to that end augmented its assistance to the RVN. The number of U.S. advisers below the seventeenth parallel soon reached 23,000. Following an attack on a U.S. airfield outside Saigon that left four American servicemen dead, the National Security Council recommended that the United States begin bombing targets in the DRVN. The Johnson administration drafted plans to that end but did not implement them, choosing instead to exercise prudence and wait on events in the South.

Within weeks after the VWP adopted Resolution 9, PLAF forces fully backed by the North initiated major combat operations with a view to annihilating ARVN forces. Though it had sanction to do so, the Politburo in Hanoi hesitated before committing PAVN units to the fight, hopeful that the PLAF would vanquish Saigon's armed forces before the United States deployed its own troops to help them, thereby avoiding potentially debilitating complications. In the aftermath of the

Tonkin Gulf incident, sensing that time was becoming of the essence, the Politburo fatefully decided to order the first PAVN units to enter the South to expedite the collapse of ARVN forces. By year's end, Washington still had not committed combat forces to the fight, but the Vietnam War had begun.

SEEKING DECISIVE VICTORY

Adoption of Resolution 9 augured the onset in South Vietnam of a risky strategy of offensive military struggle waged by main-line forces answering to the VWP against vital allies of the greatest military power in the world. In the rhetoric of the Cold War, the southern revolutionary effort would henceforth aim to "roll back," not just "contain," reactionary authority and imperialist outreach below the seventeenth parallel. For the first time, Hanoi had a strategy in which liberation of the South measured in terms of cost and commitment was at least as important as socialist transformation of the North. It is certainly no coincidence that this shift occurred as men with strong ties to the South consolidated their hold over party decision-making. It had taken a decade for this to happen, but the militants, who had never reconciled themselves to the moratorium on armed struggle in the South in 1954 and thereafter, finally had what they wanted.

David Elliott has described the evolution of Vietnamese strategy after 1954 as "a gradual process of accretion of new thinking and new strategic precepts, making it difficult to date the point at which a fully formulated version of an 'anti-American strategy' was in place." The pivotal point in that process, he suggests, "roughly coincided with the new Kennedy administration's more aggressive approach toward Vietnam."[1] That seems to date the change to 1961 or 1962. As it turns out, the formal articulation of the change—of Hanoi's anti-American strategy, which eventuated in the Vietnam War—was Resolution 9. The resulting grant of authority to the Politburo to wage war in the South, the legendary blank check, was Hanoi's equivalent of Washington's Tonkin Gulf Resolution, passed by the American Congress in August 1964 and addressed below. Just as the latter would give the Johnson administration authority to engage U.S. ground forces in Indochina, so Resolution 9 authorized Le Duan's regime to initiate "massed combat operations" below the seventeenth parallel. The Politburo thus had its sanction to go to war several months before the Johnson administration did.

Consistent with Resolution 9, communist-led forces in the South began "a new period of combat" in January 1964. Specifically, they dramatically increased the scale and frequency of military operations, effectively taking the conflict with Saigon and the Americans to an unprecedented level.[2] To the militants who now monopolized decision-making in Hanoi, that represented "the only correct road to liberation."[3] Meanwhile, the VWP Secretariat directed the PAVN General Staff to intensify the training and "readiness activities" of the armed forces in the North so that when the time came "we could send battalions and regiments with their full authorized strength in troops, weapons, and equipment to fight on the battlefields of South Vietnam."[4] Until then, native South Vietnamese in the PLAF, including many who had left in 1954–55 only to return a few years later, would bear the brunt of the fighting.

Within weeks "VC incidents" in the South were up 40 percent and more serious armed attacks up 75 percent. The PLAF initiated most major battles, forcing the ARVN into a defensive posture.[5] The strength and effectiveness of revolutionary forces increased progressively that year as Hanoi finally gave "full support" to the NLF and the PLAF.[6] American reconnaissance flights over Laos soon detected massive buildups of materiel presumably intended for the PLAF.[7] From these increases, Washington concluded that the DRVN was "forcing the military pace" in Laos and South Vietnam with one intention: to bring about "a showdown" below the seventeenth parallel.[8]

Vietnamese sources leave no doubt that that was indeed the case. In line with Resolution 9, "the most decisive requirement" of the revolution was by now "disintegration" of the ARVN, a revealing Central Committee report noted.[9] Military struggle was "the deciding factor" to meet that end and generate a "decisive victory" within "a relatively short period of time."[10] Possibly, that meant two years, the time the party thought it had before Washington would be able to deploy its own combat forces in sufficient numbers and with sufficient equipment to challenge revolutionary forces effectively.[11] The conflict in the South was no longer a "just struggle," the Central Committee surmised; it had become a "just war."[12]

Why did Hanoi think the NLF/PLAF could achieve "decisive victory" before Americanization of the war could be accomplished? Why was it so "optimistic" about its chances for promptly winning the military contest below the seventeenth parallel without even deploying PAVN units?[13] First and foremost, Hanoi believed that "objective" conditions in the South were conducive to a speedy victory. On 30 January a second coup in Saigon ousted Diem's assassins. In its aftermath, the situation in the RVN quickly "turned to disarray."[14] According to a SEATO Council report, the military situation became "extremely bad," and there were no signs of it improving anytime soon.[15] Deterioration of the military situation in the South was compounded by "the absence of a will to fight" on the part of some ARVN forces and the "tacit complicity with the NLF of a large portion of the rural population."[16] Politically and militarily, Canada's ICSC delegation agreed, the scene below the seventeenth parallel was "disturbing and unsettled." Unrest among Buddhists as well as Catholics suggested continuing and perhaps even mounting instability.[17] Making matters worse for Saigon and Washington was the fact that southern opinion was becoming increasingly "indifferent to the political games of power" in the RVN because "people are tired of war."[18] An American assessment deplored the resulting "gradual abrading of the popular will to resistance" against communist insurgents.[19] Canadian diplomats in the North Vietnamese capital reported that "general impression gathered from observers and foreign reps [in Hanoi] is that DRVN authorities are taking progressively more optimistic view of developments in RVN." "Opinions offered by local officials are that war is going extremely well and total collapse may be expected after one or two more 'coups.'"[20]

A second factor in Hanoi's miscalculation was suggested in a *Hoc tap* article in January: the leadership there believed that socialist solidarity and the prospect of Chinese and Soviet involvement in an Americanized war would produce caution, perhaps even indecision, in Washington, certainly for a time and possibly long enough to delay the introduction of U.S. ground forces until the PLAF had had time to crush ARVN forces. "As long as imperialism exists, the imperialists can wage wars of aggression against small and weak countries," the article stated. However, "the existence of the [big] socialist countries" and the recent momentum of world socialist and anti-imperialist movements confronted the Americans with a situation in which they had to be careful. In the foreseeable future at least, they were unlikely to dare committing their forces to any one of these multiple small wars that threatened to break out against them around the world. Should they do so, socialist and other anti-imperialist forces in Vietnam and elsewhere would surely prevail.[21]

Finally, as historian Gareth Porter has pointed out, DRVN leaders convinced themselves that in the near future Washington would refrain from committing its combat forces in the South because of "contradictions" at home and abroad. According to this reasoning, the intervention of American combat forces "would be opposed not only by the Vietnamese people, the socialist camp, and the [global] national liberation movement, but also by neutralist states, U.S. allies, and even the American people themselves." Furthermore, Porter advanced, the leaders may have believed, as the logic in *Hoc tap* suggested, that Washington "could not afford to concentrate too many of its resources in a single place at the expense of its commitments elsewhere in the world."[22] Imperial overreach, in other words, militated against massive American intervention in Vietnam. An official Vietnamese source validates Porter's assessment, contending that neither domestic nor international circumstances permitted Washington "immediately and all at once" to "commit the full force of U.S. military might to the Vietnam War."[23] If American policymakers did send U.S. combat forces to Vietnam, Hanoi estimated that intervention would be too limited to be determinative. More correctly, it calculated—albeit on the basis of quintessentially Marxist-Leninist considerations that did not accurately capture the Johnson administration's actual thinking in the issue—that Washington would not use nuclear weapons in Vietnam, whatever the circumstances, despite Moscow's fears on this point. "The imperialists wage wars to gain colonies, to turn them into dumping grounds for their goods, to force them to supply raw materials," to exploit their labor force, *Hoc tap* reminded readers.

Washington would never want to "seize a piece of land which has been contaminated by nuclear fallout," where "imperialists themselves dare not set foot."[24]

THE NEW REGIME ASSERTS ITSELF

The resulting changes in revolutionary strategy paralleled equally dramatic changes in party discourse. "Our southern compatriots can expect nothing from the 'sincere desire for peace' of the U.S. aggressors," *Hoc tap* told readers in early 1964, "and cannot wait 15 or 20 years—when the socialist camp triumphs over the imperialist camp in the economic competition—to solve the problem of unifying Vietnam." Instead, "they must rise up" violently, as the Chinese people had risen up under Mao in the 1940s.[25] In the words of historian K. C. Chen, *Hoc tap* here "reaffirm[ed]" the decisions of the Ninth Plenum, rebutting the argument that people in the South should "pin their hope" on a diplomatic solution. It also "denied the thesis that [southerners] should wait for twenty more years for the reunification of Vietnam through peaceful and economic competition." Instead, it upheld the imperative that Vietnamese revolutionaries should integrate political struggle with a more vigorous armed struggle.[26]

For the militants now calling the shots in Hanoi, war was "unavoidable" if the VWP was to resolve the contradictions dividing Vietnam from the United States and its allies. The struggle in the South was a zero-sum game; it could end only in "the disappearance of one [side] and the survival of the other." "As long as imperialism exists, there will be the possibility of war. As long as class and class struggle exist there will be the possibility of revolutionary war in a country. As long as the oppression of a people by another people exists there will be the possibility of a war of national liberation." It was therefore the "fundamental duty" of the Vietnamese, like other progressive peoples, to "step up revolutions for the liberation of peoples and the [world] socialist revolution." It was also their duty to prosecute these revolutions by "making them continually successful, driving imperialism back step by step, knocking out imperialism organ by organ, and advancing toward complete destruction of imperialism."[27]

Though more bellicose and dogmatic than its predecessor, the new regime was also cautious in its own way and calculating.[28] It undertook at once to supply the NLF and PLAF with more advisers and materiel, as just noted, but directed them to work incrementally, to consolidate and safeguard the progress they made. "Attacks in stages" to "secure victory in stages" sloganized the strategy; revolutionary forces would not "win everything immediately."[29] The regime justified this caution in two ways. The PLAF was just now unable to defeat an enemy bloated on increased American aid in a single "general attack."[30] Also, piecemeal progress in the South was less likely to hasten American intervention.[31] "We must find every means to limit the enemy to the kind of 'special war'" now raging, the Politburo advised. "If the U.S. increases its involvement but the puppet armed forces are primary," then the war in the South would remain "special"; however, "if the U.S. escalates to a point where U.S. forces are primary," then the war would become "limited." In the latter case, Washington was certain to introduce combat forces into the South and likely to use those forces to invade the North.[32] That could have ruinous consequences; the recent experience of North Korea certainly suggested that. But averting an American invasion was also necessary because Moscow insisted that it would not be drawn into a military confrontation with the United States over Vietnam. Le Duan and other VWP militants may have resented Moscow for its stubborn refusal to condone military struggle in Vietnam, but even they recognized that achieving southern liberation would prove much more difficult if not impossible without Soviet political and, most crucially, material support. An "era of prolonged revolutionary crisis" had begun.[33] If all went well, it would result in the destruction of Saigon's armed forces before Washington understood what was happening and Moscow had a chance to punish Hanoi for its defiance.

The most obvious sign of Hanoi's continued prudence was the delay in deploying PAVN units to the South.[34] Admittedly, committing combat-ready PAVN units would fortify the communist-led military effort, but the liabilities seemed for the time being to exceed the benefits. Dispatching PAVN units to the South would notably increase the possibility of not just direct U.S. involvement in the South but also American invasion of the DRVN. It would surely outrage Moscow, possibly even end Soviet aid. The PAVN, for its part, was technically ready to fight but could benefit from more training and better supplying. Finally, the international community would likely condemn infiltration of PAVN units into the South at that point as a flagrant violation of the Geneva accords. If the condemnations were sufficiently strong and widespread, they might belie the claim that the conflagration in the South was a southern affair and in so doing validate Washington's contention that it was in fact spawned and abetted by the North. Should that contention gain credence, it would tarnish the revolutionary effort, undercut the diplomatic struggle, and perhaps even provide a sound pretext for direct American intervention.

Foreign observers thought that another explanation for Hanoi's continued caution might have to do with the inability of the forces at its disposal to sustain, for the time being at least, a "two-front" war, in the North and the South. Extension of the war to the North, a likely outcome following the deployment of PAVN units to the South, would be especially problematic because local militias were unprepared to fight. "We notice a certain neglect in the training of paramilitary forces by North Vietnamese cadres," the French Delegation noted. Furthermore, according to this French assessment, the northern population "has a tendency to only concentrate its efforts on economic production," and thus had no desire or incentive to prepare for its own defense. The consensus among the people was that national defense should be the exclusive responsibility of PAVN forces. "Such an attitude," the assessment reckoned, "constitutes revisionism" in the language of DRVN authorities and might pose a significant problem in the event of American aggression against the North.[35] Even *Hoc tap* acknowledged northerners' "fairly widespread lack of interest" in the southern insurgency, as well as their tendency to blame poor conditions in the DRVN on the situation in the South."[36] Le Duan and his comrades thus "moved warily."[37]

Ideally for Hanoi, the PLAF would succeed in crushing the ARVN before the Americans committed their own troops. As long as that scenario remained plausible, as long as the apparent liabilities outweighed the potential benefits of direct northern military intervention in the South, Hanoi could—and would—resist deploying PAVN units to the area below the seventeenth parallel.

RESISTING ALIGNMENT WITH BEIJING

Resolution 9 and the concomitant silencing of opposition voices markedly impacted Hanoi's relations with the Soviet Union and the PRC. Knowing that Moscow would be none too pleased by the results of the VWP Central Committee's Ninth Plenum, Hanoi sent a delegation of high-ranking leaders, including Le Duan and Le Duc Tho, to Moscow to assure Soviet leaders that Resolution 9 constituted neither a challenge to peaceful coexistence nor a statement of intent to align with Beijing in the Sino-Soviet dispute, that it was simply a policy document dealing with conditions in and specific necessities for Vietnam. When the delegation asked for Soviet endorsement of Hanoi's new strategy and material support for its implementation, Khrushchev responded that the Soviet Union could not approve such a hazardous initiative and would provide no weaponry to help the NLF/PLAF or the DRVN meet their objectives militarily in the South.[38] That the VWP had failed to consult Moscow before shifting gears in the South, opting instead to present the Soviets with a fait accompli, clearly rankled Khrushchev.[39] "Something much less than complete identity of views was reached," one report of the meeting noted.[40] The Vietnamese received "no promise of Soviet aid"; in fact, they left Moscow "with nothing."[41]

During and after the delegation's visit, the Soviets remained adamant that Hanoi escalate the hostilities in the South no further, resolve its problems there diplomatically, and do nothing else that might devolve into a nuclear confrontation between themselves and the United States.[42] In retrospect, the visit itself proved more important than its results. The fact that Le Duan and Le Duc Tho, respectively the number one and two figures in the new DRVN regime, personally traveled to Moscow to confer with Khrushchev demonstrated their desire to maintain close ties to the Soviet Union.[43] The Canadian Embassy in Moscow inferred from the "amiable tone" of the concluding joint communiqué that the Vietnamese had succeeded, to a degree at least, in assuring the Soviets that they hoped to maintain adequate relations with Moscow even as they engaged in war in the South and the Sino-Soviet dispute continued.[44]

Mao, who had recently finally endorsed violent revolution in Vietnam, for his part was most gratified by news of the adoption of Resolution 9 and by what he thought were sure signs that the Vietnamese were aligning with Beijing in the Sino-Soviet dispute. At once he substantially increased Chinese assistance, both military and economic, to the DRVN.[45] The increase rested on not just ideological but also political calculations: the desire to "guarantee Hanoi's obligation to stand on China's side" in the Sino-Soviet split and to demonstrate that "the center of world revolution had shifted to Beijing."[46] In fact, for Beijing at this point, Hanoi may have been "less important as an ideological ally than as the best and closest living example of the ongoing processes of world revolution."[47] According to a cynical estimate, the PRC helped Vietnam at this point because it hoped thereby—naïvely in retrospect—to extend its hegemony over Indochina.[48] For its own aggrandizement, in this view, Beijing was prepared to support war in Vietnam "to the last Vietnamese."[49] More reassuringly, in June Chinese foreign minister Chen Yi promised Hanoi increased support in the event hostilities spread in the South, including troop support if the United States invaded the North: "The Chinese people will not sit idly," Chen pledged, "while the Geneva agreements are completely torn up and the flames of war spread" to North Vietnam.[50]

Whatever motivated these promises, Mao misread the meaning of Resolution 9. Despite what the substance and attendant consequences of the resolution suggested, Hanoi would not side openly with Beijing in the Sino-Soviet dispute. Completely at odds with the Soviets over southern strategy, Le Duan's regime nonetheless wanted no break with Moscow, as Tirana and Beijing had made, and insisted instead on continuing to cultivate the VWP's traditional relationship with the CPSU, as just noted.[51] The French general delegate thought militant leaders in Hanoi remained "honestly concerned" about the negative effects of the Sino-Soviet split on the socialist camp, and thus avoided polemics against Moscow even when adhering to Chinese revolutionary prescriptions.[52]

When Beijing proposed a meeting of Asian communist parties without Soviet participation and promised Hanoi a billion *yuan* in aid if it refused further assistance from Moscow, Hanoi demurred.[53] The reasons for the demurral were calculated, reflecting the operational realism of decision-makers who remained highly dogmatic on larger, strategic matters. Indeed, the means Le Duan and his entourage used to meet their desired ends often reflected pragmatism on their part, but those ends remained the product of rigid ideological convictions. In this instance, the Politburo understood that the international clout of the Soviet Union was greater than that of China, and Moscow's nuclear arsenal represented important insurance against an American invasion of North Vietnam.[54] Also, Soviet industrial technology remained necessary for socialist development in the North, to which they remained committed. Hanoi's problem continued to be, as economists Adam Fforde and Suzanne Paine have documented, that the DRVN had an "aggravated shortage economy," which had to import "almost all modern means of production," principally from the Soviet Union.[55] Lastly, the Soviet military arsenal far surpassed anything the Chinese had to offer and would be indispensable for protecting the DRVN in the event of war with the United States.[56] "Hanoi's own arms and ammunition production capability is limited," American intelligence estimates indicated in 1964. "It produces only small quantities of mortars, bazookas, grenades, and light arms." Its arms repair capabilities were similarly limited. "The most notable North Vietnamese inadequacies," this estimate added, "are concentrated in heavy ordnance equipment such as artillery and armor."[57]

Despite recent advances in all areas of Vietnamese deficiency, China remained incapable of supplying the machinery and expertise necessary to enable the DRVN to manufacture and stockpile the weaponry necessary to fight the Americans.[58] It produced little sophisticated military hardware of its own, which partially explained its staggering human losses in the Korea War. "If the DRV did get deeply committed to China in the Sino-Soviet dispute," a British assessment noted with these considerations in mind, "then Soviet reprisals, involving sharp declines in the level of Russian/E[ast] European trade, economic aid and military aid could be confidently predicted."[59] At that time, the Soviet Union and Eastern Europe accounted for a much larger share of DRVN foreign trade than China, 55 percent compared to 30 percent, according to an American estimate.[60] In practice, then, Hanoi had to stay "on good terms" with Moscow to continue receiving "desperately needed machinery and certain raw materials which the Chinese cannot furnish."[61] Though military aid from Moscow was just then less than that from Beijing, southern liberation, national reunification, and socialist transformation might be unachievable without Soviet support.[62]

Geography and history were also likely factors that encouraged Hanoi to keep its distance from Beijing. Vietnamese militants were enamored with China's revolutionary achievements, but they remained wary of Chinese interference in Vietnamese affairs and thus "justifiably apprehensive about future Chinese policy and actions" relating to Vietnam. "The Vietnamese for all their talk of the brotherhood of communists have not forgotten their 1,000 years of subjection to China," the British Consulate noted.[63] According to this reasoning, Hanoi preserved its alliance with Moscow because that allowed it to offset Chinese influence in Vietnam and the rest of Indochina.[64] Breaking with Moscow and complete unity of views with China, coupled with more or less absolute dependence on Chinese aid, could turn the DRVN into "little more than another Chinese province."[65] Le Duan and his regime would never submit to a revolutionary strategy dictated by either Beijing or Moscow.[66]

Finally, Hanoi rejected alignment with Beijing because it understood that to do so would not alter Soviet behavior but only widen the fissures in the socialist camp.[67] As Le Duc Tho noted, the VWP had no quarrel with the CPSU; rather, it thought individuals within it embraced erroneous views. "Our party," Tho wrote, "draws a political line between the Tito revisionist clique that betrays Marxism-Leninism and persons that [sic] commit mistakes in revising Marxism-Leninism in a number of brother parties."[68] Some sources suggest that a preliminary draft of Resolution 9 named Khrushchev as a revisionist, but, at Le Duan's urging, his name was dropped.[69] A document in the Vietnamese archives, the draft of a report Pham Van Dong presented, in revised form, to the National Assembly, seems to substantiate that suggestion. One section of the fifty-page report was "sanitized," redacted by censors. That section discusses the need for the party and government to "resolutely oppose [twenty to twenty-two characters here sanitized, enough for a reference to "Nikita Khrushchev and" in Vietnamese] modern revisionism in order to protect" the unity of the socialist movement.[70] A personal attack on Khrushchev would likely have led to an open break with Moscow, much as had happened to Albania after Hoxha publicly denounced the Soviet leader and pointedly aligned his country with China in the Sino-Soviet dispute. "In toeing the Chinese ideological line," Ottawa concluded, "Hanoi has meticulously avoided overt criticism of the Soviet Union and has refrained from indulging in Sino-Soviet polemics." Since the DRVN was "a small state without the complex international interests of either of its two giant allies, the North Vietnamese would clearly prefer to be left free to tackle their own internal problems and this can be the case only when a state of harmony exists within the communist camp."[71]

VOICING DISPLEASURE AT MOSCOW

Although Hanoi would not align with Beijing in the Sino-Soviet dispute, there were ample signs of its displeasure with Moscow. For example, the only foreign-language bookstore in the capital displayed Chinese and Albanian but not Russian works on ideology; the Russian works on display were technical manuals and novels.[72] Also, the DRVN now hosted larger numbers of Chinese than Soviet technical experts, including military advisers. On the basis of these and other indicators, the British Consulate surmised that "Chinese influence in all spheres" was fast becoming "much greater than that of the Russians" in the North.[73] Government officials soon regularly referred to Chinese as "comrades" and Soviets as "friends," even in conversations with Soviet diplomats.[74] These tendencies clearly disturbed Soviet diplomats, who concluded that Hanoi was now "mainly pro-Chinese."[75] Equally revealing were public references by Vietnamese to Soviet and other European communists in the capital as "Communist Americans" because of their "bourgeois" lifestyle. That perception stemmed largely from the fact that Eastern Europeans in Hanoi tended to live in large houses with servants and had access to automobiles. In these things, they contrasted with the PRC nationals, including diplomats, whom Beijing ordered to live under the same conditions as average Vietnamese, sharing the same standard of living without exception.[76]

The leadership in Hanoi also expressed its dissatisfaction with Moscow through veiled, deniable polemics. References to Tito and "Yugoslav revisionism" in *Hoc tap* and other publications were unmistakable stand-ins for Khrushchev and peaceful coexistence. Pointedly, party publications denounced revisionism in the same language the Chinese had used against the Soviets in 1960–61.[77] A dangerously bold denunciation of revisionism, and thus implicitly of Khrushchev, appeared in *Hoc tap* in January 1964. It included criticism of individual revisionists in the socialist camp, clearly implying that Khrushchev's turpitude was second only to Tito's. Revisionists, the article insisted, were damaging the cause of world revolution. They failed to acknowledge capitalism as the intrinsic cause of colonialism and imperialism, as well as the wars and oppressions those "isms" spawned. They thus failed to see that to drop the struggle against those "isms" for the chimera of peaceful coexistence was an act of "political naïveté." The idea that peace could be achieved without destroying capitalism and imperialism was "an illusion." There was no shortcut to a better world. To renounce the struggle against capitalism and imperialism was to act "without any class spirit," "to close one's eyes to objective realities," to "distort Marxism-Leninism." Such attitudes desecrated revolutionary ideology and amounted to counterrevolutionary malpractice. To pursue accommodation with the West was "by [its] nature, a plot to protect the capitalist system," a preliminary not to "the funeral of capitalism" but to "the funeral of socialism." Lenin had said it long ago: imperialism, "with all its capitalist strength and its perfectly organized military techniques, cannot, under any circumstances, live beside the Soviet Union."

If peaceful coexistence was counterrevolutionary, the article continued, the fear that escalating the war in the South might force Moscow into a nuclear confrontation was irrational. "In the recent Korean War between socialist Korea and imperialist United States, there was neither peaceful coexistence nor nuclear war," the article noted. Similarly, "between the Korean people and U.S. imperialists at present there is still neither peaceful coexistence nor nuclear war." More recently, the Cuban missile crisis had similarly demonstrated that nuclear war was a remote possibility. "In the past revolutionary struggle between the Cuban people and the U.S. imperialists, there was neither peaceful coexistence nor nuclear war"; there was instead a "state of 'cold war.'" As a result of its defiance, Cuba "earned the right to survive beside the imperialist United States" and "'coexist' with it" on Havana's terms.[78]

In June, *Hoc tap* published another scathing criticism of revisionism, arguably the harshest to date. This editorial was remarkable less for its substance than for its tone. Entitled "Preserving International Solidarity and Struggling against Divisive Maneuvers," it repeated the usual charges against revisionism, reviled the "treachery" of those who condoned it, and iterated the importance of adhering to the "just line" of Marxism-Leninism, which meant avoiding the trappings of peaceful coexistence. The ferocity of the attack was unprecedented. "If Hanoi is not yet at the point of delivering personal insults, its tone is nonetheless becoming increasingly polemical," the French general delegate wrote of the editorial. "Until now, when [Hanoi] wanted to criticize the Soviet line, it was the revisionism of Tito and his clique that was highlighted." That was no longer the case. "If the *Hoc tap* editorial does not go as far as naming the CPSU and its chief, its contents leave no doubt about the identity of the modern revisionists targeted by the criticism." If there were uncertainties before as to where the VWP stood on matters of East-West relations and the Sino-Soviet dispute over revolutionary strategy, the editorial dissipated them. "Through this editorial of polemical tone and of clearly directed criticisms," the French delegate opined, "the DRVN has taken a definitive step on the path of pure and simple alignment with Chinese positions."[79]

Why had Hanoi adopted so strident a tone? The French delegate believed the leadership felt it had to "strive for unity in order to allow the struggle against revisionism to achieve its objectives, that is the triumph of Marxism-Leninism, the squashing of revisionism, and the elimination of leaders guilty of [revisionism]." "The Chinese could not ask for more," he concluded.[80] Hanoi's exasperation with Moscow was confirmed when the former boldly rejected an invitation from the CPSU to participate in a conference of world communist parties to address the Sino-Soviet dispute and other problems.[81] Shortly thereafter, DRVN authorities prohibited the sale of *Pravda*, the CPSU organ available only at the foreign-language bookstore in Hanoi, to its own nationals so they would not find out how Soviet positions on current issues contrasted with those of Hanoi.[82] The new regime was clearly not shy about signaling its displeasure to Moscow.[83] What it was shy about, as noted earlier, was breaking its alliance with the Soviets. One scholar has attributed the boldness of the militants now in charge of DRVN decision-making to their confidence that "active elements" in the CPSU would sooner or later convince Khrushchev to revisit his stance on peaceful coexistence or would engineer his removal from power.[84]

In retrospect, one can say that DRVN leaders were as tactful as they had to be on matters concerning relations with allies and the Sino-Soviet dispute. They championed socialist solidarity because they needed the benefits it promised domestically, but also because they considered it imperative for the success of the world revolution, in which they firmly believed. In 1964, Hanoi was less pro-Chinese than anti-peaceful coexistence.[85] Its increasing dependence on China was "very largely unwilling," and its long-standing admiration of the Soviet Union never changed.[86] But by then, it had concluded that the CPSU's stance on capitalist-socialist relations threatened the future of the revolution in the South and around the world generally. That belief probably accounted for the panicky aspects of the views expressed in *Hoc tap* and the subtle and not-so-subtle belittlement of the Soviets. Insofar as this was indeed the case, the course pursued by Hanoi was contoured less by fear of offending Moscow than by genuine concern for the consequences of disarray in the socialist camp and of peaceful coexistence. The Soviets could do little to change this mindset. Moscow at that juncture—as at any other, for that matter—had "minimal influence" in Hanoi; it was, in fact, often a mere "spectator to events" in that country.[87]

SEEKING UNITY AND IDEOLOGICAL CONFORMITY AT HOME

As the purge of "deviationists" in the VWP and other circles continued, some critics of the new road to liberation in the South kept making trouble. "Many comrades do not yet understand clearly the theoretical and practical bases of strategic and tactical matters" or "the essence of the differences in the international communist movement," the Politburo noted. Also, a number of cadres and members remained "under the influence of revisionism," and therefore "do not yet fully grasp the basic requirements for victory and the central issues of the party line."[88] Le Duc Tho himself complained a little later that many "comrades" did not yet share the "viewpoints" of the Central Committee and continued to "express their own view."[89] To address this problem, the party stressed "the development of the spirit of revolutionary struggle and of workers' socialist consciousness" and redoubled its effort to combat rightism, revisionism, and individualism in party ranks.[90] In fact, the work of ideological indoctrination soon reached "exaggerated" levels.[91]

The seriousness of persisting problems was such that the VWP Secretariat convened a "special political conference" on 27–28 March to address them. The conference assembled 320 representatives of mass organizations, ethnic and religious minorities, and other groups.[92] The evident purpose was to "demonstrate the complete unity of all elements of North Vietnamese society" behind the party's decision to "upgrade the importance of supporting the war in the South."[93] According to another statement, the aim was to "bolster morale and to arouse enthusiasm for greater united effort to overcome chronic problems," including "the apparent lack of collective drive" and "popular apathy in the face of continued hardships" along the new road to southern liberation.[94] The conference may also have been prompted by concern that an American attack on the DRVN was imminent, suggested by the simultaneous decision to place air-defense units on wartime status.[95]

The conference showcased Ho Chi Minh and other luminaries who appealed for unity and ideological conformity, and called on the northern people to support Hanoi and its policies. The contents of Ho's address are suggestive of the party's problems.[96] Instead of summarizing and praising the new strategy in the South, Ho dwelled on the party's commitment to peaceful reunification of the country. Party and government leaders alike, Ho declared, supported the demands of the NLF that "an end be put to the U.S. imperialists' intervention in South Viet-Nam, that U.S. troops and arms be withdrawn, and that the people of South Viet-Nam be left to solve by themselves their internal affairs." Coming on the heels of Resolution 9, these formulations suggested that Ho dissented from the new strategic line more than he endorsed it.

But Ho did not stop here. "With regard to the peaceful reunification of Viet-Nam," he continued, "our government has repeatedly made clear its views and attitude" and "unreservedly" supported the "urgent demand of our people throughout the country" to "reunify the Fatherland by peaceful means." Pending national reunification, he said, DRVN authorities would "undertake not to spread propaganda to divide the people or in favor of war" and "not use military forces" against the South Vietnamese regime. Implicitly, Ho criticized the new militancy, which by one account was "remarkable against the backdrop of the official anti-revisionist stand of the December Central Committee plenum and the subsequent spate of documents attacking, indirectly but unmistakably, Soviet policy." Possibly, Ho attempted through his speech to use his popularity inside and outside the party to "reassert more moderate policy lines."[97] According to an American assessment, Ho's speech indicated that moderates might have been "fighting a rear guard action" against the militants now in charge of DRVN decision-making.[98]

Despite this slant, the Politburo did not censure Ho's speech. Perhaps the militants who now controlled that organ hoped that the speech's conciliatory tone would serve their purposes, including appeasement of those who continued to hope for a negotiated solution. Ho's tone and sedateness may have reassured critics that the new revolutionary line had important continuities with the old one. Certainly that would have reverberated to the advantage of the new regime, and thereby of national unity in a time of uncertainty and transition, and may also have alerted the North Vietnamese people to the challenges that lay ahead. Interestingly, none of the leading militants addressed the Secretariat's conference. "The most striking aspect of the conference," one assessment noted, was its failure to address Resolution 9 and the "attendant internal antirevisionist campaign."[99] That was no doubt by design. The purposes of the conference were surely best served among doubters by featuring speakers such as Ho and Giap, who were widely respected for their judiciousness.

In the ensuing days and weeks, the addresses of Ho and other moderates were widely publicized in the North. The final resolution of the conference, which concluded that "our entire party, entire people, entire armed forces have united and must unite even more," was similarly disseminated.[100] "The special political conference and the Central Committee's Resolution 9 are a bright torch for our people and a powerful source of encouragement for each [social] class to have fervent revolutionary momentum in the face of new important responsibilities," a member of the National Assembly observed.[101] An official assessment concluded that Ho's pleas for unity had the potential to "establish big results" provided "ideological propaganda and education" continued to emphasize "close unity of consciousness."[102] Hanoi indeed stressed Ho's themes that year, as well as hard work and sacrifice. "Each of us must work like two," Ho Chi Minh had insisted.[103] It did not hurt these efforts that the United States soon precipitated a series of incidents that authenticated the views of the leadership.

To muster support for the new revolutionary line in the armed forces, in May *Hoc tap* commemorated the tenth anniversary of Dien Bien Phu by highlighting the parallels between the party's triumphant strategy then and that adopted at the Ninth Plenum. "The lesson of Dien Bien Phu" was that strategies and tactics like those outlined in Resolution 9 explained the 1954 victory. Back then, the commitment to ideological conformity—the "education given us by the party"—and the "sweeping struggle" against "rightist [i.e., moderate] negative thinking" had led to the defeat of an enemy "many times stronger in weapons and equipment." The recent debate over strategy had echoed the deliberations that preceded the victory at Dien Bien Phu: whether merely to defend liberated areas or "assume an active, offensive posture." In the earlier instance, cadres cowed by fear had favored defense, which would surely have led to annihilation. "Thanks to the skillful strategic leadership of the party Central Committee," the revolution had instead followed an aggressive, bellicose course that led to the enemy's "destruction." A bold, forward strategy had saved the revolution in 1954; it would do the same now.[104]

Quelling popular dissent in the North was more problematic. Groups and individuals across the DRVN continued to engage in subversive activities, which the Politburo took seriously enough to counter.[105] Among them were "counterrevolutionaries," including spies and foreign agents, as well as corrupt civil servants and disloyal party members.[106] Of greatest concern to the authorities, however, were religious and ethnic minorities. Catholics remained an especially problematic group. Despite the party's every effort, relations with them remained strained. In early 1964, individual priests still engaged in seditious activities; entire parishes "had not yet participated directly in the struggle against imperialism"; and some party members and cadres still harbored prejudice against Catholics.[107] Hanoi also worried about the subversive potential of the Buddhist clergy, whose 1963 protests in the South had played a meaningful role in the demise of the Diem regime. Those protests, the Central Committee feared, might have radicalized their counterparts in the North.[108] Ethnic minorities also balked at following the new "mass line," while some communities and individuals in the general population manifested "subjective tendencies" and "impatience." That is, some displayed excessive eagerness to transform the North and liberate the South, while others were overcome by the "fear of difficulties" characteristic of "backward masses." Finally, party leaders and security forces were fearful of disaffection in highland minority regions and prioritized the indoctrination, mobilization, and "pacification" of people there.[109]

Out of Politburo concerns about these and related problems, in April 1964 there emerged an "emulation" campaign under the slogan "Each Person Works Like Two, Strives to Build and Protect the North, and Actively Supports the Southern Liberation Revolution." The aims of the campaign were to encourage unity by exhorting northerners to remind themselves of the sufferings of compatriots in the South, the need to sacrifice on the southerners' behalf, and the need to steel themselves for war in the North. The Americans were for all intents and purposes waging war in the South, DRVN leaders thought, and sabotaging the North. In light of the Central Committee's decision to dramatically escalate the insurgency in the South, Washington's next move would likely involve aerial and naval bombardments of the DRVN itself, the leaders portentously noted.[110]

HEIGHTENING CONCERNS ABOUT AMERICAN INTERVENTION

On 19 April, "reactionary" elements in the Laotian armed forces staged a coup in Vientiane. Though Prince Souvanna Phouma continued as prime minister there, the new coalition he presided over was henceforth dominated by right-wingers.[111] Hanoi immediately accused the United States of engineering the coup.[112] For DRVN leaders, this recalled Diem's overthrow by military counterrevolutionaries and reinforced militant convictions about the reach of American subversion in Indochina. Shortly thereafter, Laotian government forces with air support from the Americans and their Thai allies clashed with communist forces in various parts of Laos, heightening concerns in Hanoi about the situation across Indochina.[113] DRVN leaders suspected, with good cause, that the successive coups in Saigon and Vientiane foreshadowed an overthrow of the neutralist government of Norodom Sihanouk and its replacement with one controlled by factions beholden to the United States.[114]

On 6 July, Hanoi placed its navy on wartime status in response to increasingly intrusive patrols in the Tonkin Gulf by American warships, some of which it believed had violated DRVN territorial waters.[115] The warships, we now know, collected intelligence, intercepted North Vietnamese communications, and may have provided indirect support to South Vietnamese commando units engaged in subversion in the DRVN. By this time the latter program was spreading disinformation about widespread resistance to the DRVN government, flooding the country with counterfeit currency to create economic havoc, and encouraging dissidence among ethnic minorities.[116] These operations contributed to Hanoi's difficulties administering minority-dominated areas in the North.[117]

Concerns about American intentions in Vietnam and the rest of Indochina prompted Hanoi to place the rest of its armed forces on wartime alert.[118] By the end of July 1964, as an official history of the PAVN puts it, "all preparations for combat by our armed forces" had "essentially been completed."[119] By that time DRVN leaders were also bracing civilians for imminent war, directing them to dig trenches in Hanoi and elsewhere, and testing alarm sirens, all of which helped persuade "skeptics and those indifferent of the reality of the danger" that war was indeed in the offing.[120]

Rising tensions with the United States were not happenstance; they resulted largely from the Central Committee's decision to endorse a war to defeat Saigon and its backers in the South. This reality was not lost on DRVN leaders, who understood the implications of their decision so well that they anticipated Washington's next move with relative accuracy and prepared accordingly. Hanoi declared itself ready to "cope with any situation" and braced the North for war a full month before the first attack. A similar scenario played out below the seventeenth parallel, where Hanoi prepared revolutionary forces for possible combat against American forces. Just as the militant Vietnamese version of Marxism-Leninism had conditioned the decision to endorse war, so it now informed Hanoi's actions. The perception of Washington as capable of every transgression conditioned Le Duan and his close advisers to plan for the most unenviable contingencies, just as it convinced them that only war could "liberate" the South and that negotiations with the United States were pointless.[121] After Resolution 9, they never gave the people in either half of Vietnam false hopes that a wider war could be averted, even though that remained their own hope. As committed ideologues, they accepted "worst-case beliefs" about Washington.[122]

Concerned about the mounting tensions in Vietnam, Beijing dispatched Zhou Enlai to Hanoi to discuss and assess the situation. Beijing's policy was to help the Vietnamese materially and politically meet their current revolutionary objectives, while preparing the PRC to deal with American military intervention in Indochina. Zhou repeated Chen Yi's pledge that should Washington invade the DRVN, Beijing would send armed forces to North Vietnam to resist the invaders.[123] The apparent full commitment of Beijing to the liberation cause in Vietnam only reinforced the views of leftist ideologues in the VWP.

REJECTING NEGOTIATIONS

Confidence in their forces' ability to expeditiously decimate the ARVN, support for that endeavor from China, and their own assessment of other "objective realities" prompted DRVN leaders to reject secret peace overtures that Washington advanced through the Canadians that summer. In May, the Johnson administration asked Ottawa to open a channel with Hanoi via its ICSC commissioner. The aim was to inform Hanoi that Washington held it "directly responsible" for ongoing hostilities in the South, and although "US public and official patience with North Vietnamese aggression is growing extremely thin," the American president was "fundamentally a man of peace" still willing to consider a negotiated settlement of the crisis below the seventeenth parallel.[124] By official account, Washington was "requesting Canadian good offices to 'convey signals' to Hanoi both so that the North Vietnamese leaders would understand the seriousness of the United States determination and also in order to learn something of North Vietnam's intentions."[125]

During an 18 June meeting, the Canadian ICSC commissioner, Blair Seaborn, apprised Pham Van Dong of Hanoi's responsibility for the southern insurgency and Johnson's desire for peace, adding that "the greatest devastation would of course result for the DRVN" should the conflict in the South continue to escalate. Dong "understood [the] importance and context" of the message and the "seriousness with which [the] USA views the situation in Southeast Asia," Seaborn thought, but he rejected the American threat and expressed no desire to negotiate. Defiantly, in words that reflected the ruling clique's belief that diplomacy was futile under current conditions, Dong told Seaborn that "if war was pushed to [the] North, we are a socialist country, one of the socialist countries, you know, and the people will rise"; the Vietnamese would "struggle regardless of sacrifice."[126] After the meeting, Seaborn told Ottawa he saw "no signs of war weariness in Hanoi" and "no indications of weakening resolve among the DRVN leadership."[127] Dong's assertions "carried a good deal of conviction as if really believed," he added. On the basis of his exchanges with Dong and other ranking North Vietnamese, Seaborn concluded that "DRVN leaders are completely convinced that military action at any level is not going to bring success" for Washington and its allies in Saigon.[128] In other words, Hanoi saw no need to negotiate because it thought it could, and surely would, win the enhanced military effort it had just launched in the South.

At a second meeting with Dong in August, shortly after the Tonkin Gulf incident discussed below, Seaborn reiterated the American threat of escalation and Washington's appeal for negotiations. Dong became "very angry" upon hearing the threat, provocatively stating that the "more [the] USA spreads war, [the] greater will be its ultimate defeat."[129] After this meeting, Seaborn told Ottawa that Dong again "gave no indication of being worried by [the] firmness of [the] USA [message] I delivered." "I think he is genuinely convinced that things are bound to go his way in Indochina and that there is therefore no need to seek compromise."[130] Later that year, at Washington's urging, Seaborn tried to arrange a third meeting with Dong, but the prime minister refused even to see him.[131] While the previous regime in Hanoi had always been shy about the prospect of war with the United States, Le Duan's team was clearly less so.

Like de Gaulle's neutralization scheme of the year before, Washington's initiative through the Canadians, backed as it was by a blustering threat that ignored Hanoi's understanding of its situation and purposes, was too little too late. In fact, the chances for a diplomatic solution at that point were even slimmer than they had been the year before—that is, essentially nonexistent. Le Duan and his associates were firmly at the helm in Hanoi by now, and nothing short of American capitulation would constitute agreeable terms for a settlement. "What is the only solution?" a member of the DRVN National Assembly asked in reference to a diplomatic settlement during a July session. "It is that the Americans must respect and strictly adhere to the 1954 Geneva accords; it is that the American imperialists withdraw their forces from Vietnam at once," he answered—that they, in short, capitulate.[132] Indeed, at this point a settlement acceptable to Hanoi would have to include not only immediate, unilateral, and unconditional American disengagement from Indochina but also replacement of the regime in Saigon with a provisional coalition dominated by neutralists and communists, and prompt unification of Vietnam under its aegis. No one in Washington could conceive of such demands by so puny a state as the DRVN, and certainly not as preconditions for negotiations. The two sides thus literally talked past each other. The impasse would have to be resolved on battlefields in Vietnam and in arenas of international politics, and that was just fine for Le Duan's regime.

Some historians believe that even at this late date VWP leaders could have been coaxed into compromise—that Washington, not Hanoi, was the intransigent party. Short of capitulation, there is little Washington could now have offered that had any prospect of influencing Hanoi's behavior. Thus the most that can be said of the view that compromise was still possible is that Hanoi may have agreed to *talk* but not to *negotiate*.[133] Admittedly, the DRVN publicly and sometimes privately professed willingness to engage in "contacts" *(tiep xuc)*, in its terminology, with its enemies or third parties to discuss the situation in the South, but it never intended to negotiate earnestly. Instead, it sought to probe American and South Vietnamese intentions while improving its international image.

For example, earlier in the year the director of the External Affairs Bureau of the DRVN Foreign Ministry had asked for a meeting with the British consul. During the meeting, in circuitous language, the director indicated Hanoi's willingness to "carry on a dialogue" with London with a view to formal talks on the future of the South. "It is difficult to see at present what this could be," the consul wrote of the initiative, "but I think there are signs—and this approach to us may be one of them—that the D.R.V. Government is prepared to be more flexible in their approach to the South Vietnamese question if they saw any possibility of a solution which would remove from South Vietnam what they consider as American aggression there and a threat to North Vietnam."[134] In this instance, the contact served as a safety valve for Hanoi should problems in the South worsen, just as it created a more positive impression of the DRVN leadership in London.

The more the DRVN seemed committed to peaceful settlement in the South, the easier it was to win battles of public opinion at home and abroad and to secure political and material support from the Soviet Union. But Hanoi had no thought of entering into "peace negotiations" *(thuong luong hoa binh)*, that is, actually to work for a diplomatic solution. "At this stage," the Canadian Department of External Affairs surmised in July on the basis of the Seaborn-Dong talks, as well as public and private statements by DRVN leaders, there was "no indication" that a constructive dialogue between Hanoi and Washington was even possible.[135]

Hanoi refused to work toward a diplomatic solution at that point for two main reasons. First, it did not trust Washington's motives in asking for negotiations. American peace overtures were deceitful delaying tactics to gain time for the regime in Saigon, window dressing to dissimulate the Johnson administration's true intention of waging war in the South until the liberation movement was annihilated.[136] Second, an interlude of negotiations could only soften the now steely resolve of DRVN leaders and other militants in both halves of Vietnam who had long wanted to use force to bring about reunification. When a western diplomat asked in confidence in the summer of 1964 for his reaction to a recent suggestion by Norodom Sihanouk that there be a new Geneva Conference on Indochina, DRVN foreign minister Xuan Thuy replied bluntly that a Geneva agreement "solving" the Vietnamese crisis already existed; it was for the Americans and their Saigon allies to implement that agreement since they were the ones violating it.[137]

At that juncture Hanoi might have accepted a bilateral agreement with Saigon neutralizing the South on terms similar to those negotiated for Laos in 1962, but the neutrality would be brief, simply a means for Hanoi to achieve its goal furtively. "Bringing about neutrality," the party then calculated, "will have a very big impact on intermediary classes in the South, undermine capitalist classes, win over socialist and neutral countries, divide the imperialists and isolate to a large degree the American imperialists and their puppets." In other words, neutrality would serve revolutionary purposes, compelling Washington to withdraw its presence in the South and its aid to the Saigon regime, both necessary preconditions of a neutralization agreement. Neutrality would thus not be nonalignment. On the contrary, the only formula Hanoi would agree to "is to be guided by our party." Neutrality and the concomitant coalition government that would oversee it "can only occur once our forces in the South are very strong, in a vantage position totally to our advantage," which would enable Hanoi to steer the neutral government on a "correct" course.[138]

As this suggests, Hanoi's nonnegotiable objective was political amalgamation of the area below the seventeenth parallel into the polity created above that line in 1954, under exclusive control of the party. This is what Washington would have to agree to, even agree to facilitate, if it wanted a diplomatic settlement with Hanoi in 1964. That is what it means to say that DRVN leaders sought peace "on their terms."[139] They would agree to stopgap measures on the way to their objective, but only as ploys to expedite American disengagement and only when absolutely necessary. They had nothing to negotiate but the specifics of American disengagement and their takeover of the South. They had negotiated in 1954 in Geneva with humiliating and devastating results. To assume that Le Duan's regime would repeat that error in 1964 is therefore misguided. To that regime, peace meant independence, prompt national unification, triumphant socialism—in a word, victory.

To appreciate these realities, it is important to remind ourselves of the nature of the men who controlled decision-making in Hanoi in 1964. Le Duan, Le Duc Tho, Nguyen Chi Thanh, Pham Hung, and the regime's other leading figures were hardline, invested communists. Their worldview was rooted in battle-hardened experience and lifetimes of sacrifice for the revolution, in the South specifically. Like many who fought there during the Indochina War, they had felt betrayed by the decision to forgo total victory after Dien Bien Phu and negotiate instead. The Geneva fiasco, as they looked back on it, had been an exercise in compromise that reinforced their sense of betrayal. Repatriated to the North at different times before and after that fiasco, they witnessed the near annihilation of the southern revolutionary movement they had fought so hard for because of an old guard's faith in diplomacy, its renunciation of violence, and its fear of war with the United States.

These personal experiences steeled their thinking and sense of revolutionary purpose, and made any diplomatic arrangement that fell short of their terms unimaginable. There was no realistic chance that such men could have negotiated a settlement acceptable to Washington or Saigon under the circumstances that existed in 1964. William Turley was not entirely incorrect when he wrote that Hanoi may have been willing to negotiate "but not over what it maintained were basic national rights that had been guaranteed by the Geneva Agreements."[140] Nguyen Vu Tung said it better in his assessment of VWP diplomacy: "Opening contacts with the [enemy] during this time was not a priority for the DRV, due to both internal and external factors."[141]

Though Hanoi felt no compulsion to negotiate with Saigon, unless of course its maximalist demands were met, some members of the NLF may have secretly contacted RVN authorities to discuss reduction of the scale of hostilities and the possibility of solving their differences diplomatically. In June, the RVN minister of state confessed to the British ambassador in Saigon that "he was in touch with certain Viet Cong elements with the tacit consent of the [RVN] Prime Minister." The ambassador reported to London that he thought this initiative from Saigon constituted "positive evidence" of a disposition on Saigon's part to negotiate with the NLF and vice versa. It also confirmed a previous report that General Nguyen Khanh, the RVN prime minister after the 30 January coup, "was contemplating an eventual deal with the insurgents."[142] What sidetracked these contacts is unclear, though they obviously came to nothing. In reality, they would have solved nothing, since core NLF/PLAF leaders answered to Hanoi, and the latter wanted no part of an actual compromise agreement.

PURSUING SOCIALIST TRANSFORMATION IN THE NORTH

As the storm gathered in the South, the party continued the socialist transformation of the DRVN. As strongly as he felt about liberating the South, Le Duan never believed that it warranted abandoning the economic transformation of the North. Committed to the goals of communism generally, the first secretary considered both objectives imperative. Despite his sympathies for Chinese revolutionary theses, he respected Soviet successes in transforming the national economy, and in fact considered the Soviet Union a model for Vietnam.[143] He especially admired the policies and leadership style of Stalin, who completed the transformation of the Soviet Union in the face of overwhelming difficulties in the 1930s and despite the long and costly resistance against fascist aggression in World War II. In fact, Le Duan may have consciously sought to emulate the Soviet leader's approach in his own effort to build socialism in the DRVN while combatting American "fascists" in the South.[144] If the Soviets could contain and eventually vanquish a powerful invading force in the midst of their country's socialist transformation, why could the Vietnamese not do the same? Le Duan's speeches and writings often stressed the need to replicate in Vietnam the successes of the Soviet transformation under Stalin: industrialization, collectivization, socialism, and the defeat of fascism. The first secretary and other "extremists" had been "in the forefront in pushing the regime's program of economic self-reliance through the expansion of heavy industry," an American assessment noted. They had "criticized unnamed other members of the leadership for softness on economic policy," and proven intolerant of moderate tendencies generally.[145] "The most indispensable foundation for socialism is heavy industry," Le Duan often said, quoting Lenin. "Whoever forgets this is not a Communist."[146]

That Le Duan and his regime felt strongly that industrialization was necessary for reunification as well as for socialism needs emphasis. American meddling and the attendant spread of bourgeois ways and values below the seventeenth parallel were bound to complicate reunification. It might take years to re-educate people and reconstitute institutions in the South to the extent necessary to achieve national integration, even after the Americans were gone. Unless the North was economically developed and functionally socialist, the nation would have to depend on foreign aid during this transition. If the dependence was large and long enough, it would threaten the purity of the revolution by limiting the party's freedom of action. Since its inception, the DRVN had depended on economic and military assistance from its socialist allies, a dependence that had only accrued over time. Once unification was achieved, that would have to change. The Vietnamese revolution was for "national salvation" as well as socialism; its purposes would be lost if the nation remained dependent on foreign largess. As a communist vanguard, the VWP had to lessen the country's dependence on allies with a view to ultimately achieving autarky. Failure to do so would undermine the party's legitimacy and credibility, if not soon then later.[147] "Reliance on the strength of our own people," the Politburo declared in February 1964, was "fundamental" to the triumph of the revolution.[148] Hanoi accorded "fundamental importance" to economic self-sufficiency in 1964, given the uncertainty of foreign, specifically Soviet, assistance, western observers thought. An article in *Hoc tap* actually condemned unspecified forms of "premature" international economic cooperation and interdependence within the socialist camp as a "modern revisionist trend."[149]

The achievement of autarky demanded improvements in agricultural production and productivity. Early in 1964 the Politburo had declared agricultural output unsatisfactory. "Because [agricultural] production has not yet developed strongly, because mistakes have been made in managing the circulation, distribution, and consumption" of foodstuffs, the Politburo assessed, the rural economy was developing poorly. Despite progress in collectivization, problems remained in the countryside. Some communities still experienced periodic food shortages, while others met their own needs but failed to meet government quotas. Hoarding, waste, avarice, and corruption variously compounded these and other problems in rural areas.[150] These, too, threatened to compromise the struggle in the South.

THE GULF OF TONKIN INCIDENT AND 5 AUGUST ATTACK

Soon, economic difficulties seemed less worrying, though certainly still pressing. In late July DRVN authorities reported American attacks on the islands of Hon Ngu and Hon Me, situated approximately three and nine miles, respectively, off the Vietnamese coast.[151] On 2 August, American and North Vietnamese naval forces clashed in the Gulf of Tonkin. Two days later, the U.S. Navy reported attacks by North Vietnamese torpedo boats on two American destroyers in the same area.[152] This "Tonkin Gulf incident" prompted the Johnson administration to order reprisal air strikes against targets in the DRVN on 5 August, and the U.S. Congress to pass the Tonkin Gulf Resolution on 7 August.[153] The resolution authorized the Johnson administration to use all befitting means, including deployment of U.S. combat forces, to protect American interests in Indochina, much as Resolution 9 had given Le Duan's regime sanction to commit the DRVN and the PAVN to the liberation of the South. Hanoi denied involvement of its armed forces in any incident on 4 August, a denial whose sincerity may be inferred from a statement by the

Standing Committee of the National Assembly on 10 August praising the DRVN's air defense and naval units for their performance in the battles of 2 and 5 August 1964, with no mention of a battle or incident on 4 August.[154] A PAVN spokesman told the ICSC shortly thereafter that "in the night of August 4, 1964, the weather was very bad," and "at one point about 100 kilometers east of Quang Binh coast . . . there were many explosions, flares and noise of aircraft motors as if a [sic] fighting had actually taken place." Whatever had taken place that night, he said, had not involved PAVN forces.[155]

The air strikes on 5 August represented an extension of the southern crisis to the North, the first of its kind. Put another way, southerners were "at last able to bring the war home to the North, to begin to allow northerners to feel their vulnerability to U.S. military power—a feeling that had existed south of the 17th parallel for many years." That development facilitated the rebuilding of the "psychological bridge" between North and South that had been "damaged by the post-Geneva separation of the two Vietnams."[156] The strikes also made northerners "extremely angry," the British Consulate reported, and precipitated mass demonstrations "as near to spontaneous as such things ever are in communist countries."[157] In more ways than one, the bombing validated the calls for vigilance Hanoi had been issuing since late 1963, particularly those concerned with the imminence of American aggression against the North.

Only recently Hanoi had been worried about northerners' lack of support for war in the South and the lack of preparedness of northern militias. All that changed after 5 August. The attack helped authorities in the North meet one of the chief aims of the special political conference in March and other recent efforts: rallying the masses fully behind the leadership. DRVN authorities pounced on the opportunity to exploit "to the fullest, at the psychological level," the bombing and related developments, as they "exalted hatred for the Americans."[158] This not only bolstered popular support for the party and state, as well as for the causes of southern liberation and northern economic transformation, but it also cemented party cohesion and emboldened the armed forces. "The association between need for increased military vigilance and preparedness and the importance of increased production is being strongly emphasized and the civil population urged on to greater efforts and the overfulfillment of production norms," the Canadian representative in Hanoi wrote of these circumstances.[159] The events of early August "were certainly turned to the advantage of the North," the British Consulate surmised.[160] Within hours of the air strikes, new trenches and bomb shelters were being dug around the clock in the Hanoi area. This was accompanied by evacuation to the suburbs and countryside of unnecessary individuals, namely, the elderly, children, and women not gainfully employed.[161]

The 5 August attack also reverberated internationally, as Hanoi "squeezed" the "last bit of propaganda value" out of it overseas.[162] In a prescient assessment made shortly after the event, the British Consulate commented that DRVN leaders more than ever "believe themselves to be engaged in a Communist crusade of liberation directed primarily against the Americans, and will not be intimidated. Nor will they be deflected by bombing." American attacks against the DRVN and its supply lines in Laos increased their problems, the consulate noted, but would have no real effect on Hanoi. "Roads will be rebuilt, bridges replaced by simple bamboo structures, and supply dumps resupplied." It was a mistake, the consulate concluded, to think that DRVN leaders "would be forced to call a halt to their resupply operations in the South" or to order the PLAF to suspend its operations because of air strikes. American attacks and other threats to the DRVN "only strengthen their resolution."[163] In hindsight, those were prophetic words.

COMMITTING PAVN UNITS TO THE SOUTH

A few days after the bombing, the Central Committee met to assess its meaning and effects and to formulate suitable responses.[164] Given—as the bulk of the existing evidence suggests—that there was no attack by their torpedo boats on 4 August, party members in attendance had to understand the next day's air strikes as essentially unprovoked aggression. Those strikes thus legitimated the views of militant ideologues in the VWP: the imperatives of capitalism had driven the United States to create a pretext to employ force to thwart the Vietnamese revolution and defend its lackeys in Saigon. As Edwin Moïse has pointed out in his comprehensive study of the Tonkin Gulf incident, since there was no PAVN–U.S. Navy confrontation on the night of 4 August, "the logical conclusion" of DRVN leaders in the wake of the 5 August attack "would have been that it was pointless to avoid direct combat actions by North Vietnamese forces in an effort to avoid provoking the United States"; the United States was already provoked.[165]

Regardless of how one interprets Hanoi's reaction to the attack, in its aftermath the Central Committee recommended immediate deployment of PAVN units to the South. The wanton nature of the attack made the recommendation sensible, especially since war with American ground forces could still be avoided if communist forces won a quick, decisive victory in the South. While little is known of the Central Committee's discussion of these matters, it evidently thought it was best under the circumstances to deploy PAVN forces to the South sooner rather than later. The committee also recommended immediately sending an advance unit, the 808th battalion, for reconnaissance purposes.[166]

On the basis of the Central Committee's recommendation to escalate hostilities, as well as its own interpretation of recent American undertakings, the Politburo decided, during a meeting on 25–29 September, to "*take advantage of this opportune time to try and defeat completely the puppet army before American forces intervened.*"[167] At this "opportune moment" in the revolution, the Politburo made the fateful choice of ordering PAVN main-line units to the South. If an official history can be believed, most members of the Politburo at this point were confident that PAVN involvement below the seventeenth parallel would expedite the triumph of the revolution there.[168] This decision effectively culminated the gradualist approach that had characterized the party's revolutionary strategy since 1954. Le Duan and other decision-makers thought the NLF and PLAF had done well since the beginning of the year, but not well enough that events could be left to develop at their own pace in light of recent American attacks on the North. The revolution was now in a race against the clock; it had to redouble the effort to annihilate ARVN forces and complete that task before Washington could get its own forces into Vietnam in sufficient numbers to fight effectively.

To those ends, the Politburo directed the Central Military Commission and the PAVN General Staff to prepare a new strategic plan and "supply concrete guidance" to southern guerrilla units for sustaining and expanding "massed combat operations" and expediting the "destruction and disintegration of the bulk of the Saigon puppet army."[169] That is, the commission needed to take into account that PAVN units would soon be joining the fight in the South and adjust military strategy and tactics accordingly. The British Consulate was not incorrect in surmising that "the American show of force" on 5 August, "far from intimidating the North Vietnamese, seemed to have aroused them to still greater efforts" and instilled in them "a mood of confidence, even of arrogance."[170]

In September, Hanoi deployed to the South a retinue of ranking party and PAVN officials, including Nguyen Chi Thanh, with orders to increase the military pressure on Saigon. Thanh was a central figure in the ruling elite, as already noted, and a proponent of reunification "at any price." His deployment attested to Hanoi's sense of urgency and the totality of its commitment to war in the South. Thanh replaced Nguyen Van Linh as head of COSVN, another symbolic move reflecting the determination of Le Duan's regime to exercise direct and absolute control over activities there, which were about to involve PAVN units.[171] "His command of COSVN," historian Lien-Hang Nguyen wrote of Thanh, "marked the beginning of the end of southern autonomy in the field of military matters."[172] The ranking cadres accompanying Thanh were experienced in building and deploying main-line units, exercising military leadership, and assuming combat command.[173] They set out at once to "strengthen leader cadres for the southern revolution" and reinforce the PLAF, whose numbers needed to grow and whose "scale of organization still had only reached the regimental level."[174]

The arrival of high-ranking officials from the DRVN, presaging as it did the infiltration of the first PAVN combat units, marked the onset of a "northernization" of sorts of the ongoing military struggle below the seventeenth parallel. The reasoning was simple: because the NLF/PLAF, abetted by the North since the start of the year, had so far failed to win a decisive victory, northern boys would be entrusted to do what southern boys had not been able to do for themselves, to borrow from Lyndon Johnson's idiolect.[175] By the end of September, specific PAVN units had orders to make final preparations for their journey south.[176] The first units—the 18th, 95th, and 101st regiments of the 325th division—began leaving for the South on 20 November, a little more than a hundred days after the Tonkin Gulf incident.[177] PAVN troops subsequently captured by ARVN forces and interviewed by the ICSC indicated that some outfits may have started marching south as early as October.[178]

Some scholars have interpreted this sequence of events as evidence that it was only after the Tonkin Gulf incident that Hanoi decided to commit the DRVN fully to southern liberation, intimating that the American 5 August attack rather than Resolution 9 precipitated the dramatic escalation of hostilities.[179] Thus Ang Cheng Guan has characterized the Tonkin Gulf incident as "an important turning point in the Vietnamese communists' struggle" since it "stiffened the attitude of the Vietnamese communists" and "convinced [them] on intervening directly in the war" below the seventeenth parallel.[180]

In fact, as explained earlier, Hanoi had dramatically escalated hostilities and the North's involvement since the start of the year, right after adoption of Resolution 9. To be sure, policymakers delayed dispatching PAVN units to the South, but that did not mean the decision was pending at the time of the Tonkin Gulf incident. In effect, what the incident, and the 5 August bombing in particular, did was to persuade the Politburo to advance the schedule of PAVN deployments it was already preparing but had hoped would not be warranted. The timing of the troop deployments was a tactical choice, not a strategic decision. The incidents of early August are important only to the extent that they influenced timing. Increased American bellicosity concentrated attention on the strategic goal of annihilating Saigon's armed forces. The response to the 5 August attack marked not a break with past policy but an acceleration of the course of action set in motion by Resolution 9.

Hanoi's behavior in this matter thus paralleled that of Washington after passage of the Tonkin Gulf Resolution. Like Johnson's White House, Le Duan's regime took several months before moving combat forces into the South after obtaining sanction—the proverbial blank check—to resort to war to meet its objectives there. Resolution 9 and the Tonkin Gulf Resolution authorized, among other things, the deployment of regular combat units to South Vietnam, but in both cases only when decision-makers thought it befitting to do so, as circumstances warranted. The Central Committee resolution represented "the formal authorization for increasing North Vietnam's military presence in the South in 1964 and the years that followed."[181] It was the task of Le Duan and others in the Politburo and the Central Military Commission to work out the details. It took them months, largely because they thought time was on their side and the PLAF might win the military contest below the seventeenth parallel without PAVN troop support. In addition,

DRVN leaders had been reluctant to send PAVN units into the South for fear the international community would condemn the action, as previously noted. But the attack of 5 August gave them a valid pretext to proceed with the troop deployments, thereby making the North's commitment to the South virtually total. The PLAF attack on the U.S. base at Pleiku of early 1965, addressed in the epilogue, would serve as the Johnson administration's own 5 August episode.

CHINESE SUPPORT

Shortly after the Tonkin Gulf incident, other developments improved the North's prospects for quick victory, or so Hanoi believed. As a gesture of solidarity and perhaps to deter further U.S. attacks on the North, Beijing gave the DRVN fifty-one MiG jet fighters, agreed to train Vietnamese pilots to fly them, and began constructing airfields in southern China as sanctuaries for the DRVN's new air force.[182] The PRC also sent to the DRVN large stocks of new weaponry, which were promptly relayed to the PLAF and markedly enhanced their combat effectiveness. By year's end, the PLAF possessed a respectable arsenal that included AK-47 rifles, 7.63mm machine guns, 82mm mortars, rocket-propelled grenade launchers (RPGs), recoilless rifles of various calibers, and other weapons.[183] The infiltration of almost eighteen thousand northern combat troops into the South before the end of the year, including the aforementioned full-strength PAVN battalions and regiments, was perhaps the greatest boon for the liberation effort in the South.[184]

While socialist solidarity encouraged Beijing to assist the Vietnamese, Chinese sources indicate that Mao believed Washington was planning another "war of aggression against China," and thought arming the PLAF and the PAVN might preclude that scenario or, if not, would help defend the PRC.[185] Whatever its motives, Beijing's assistance bolstered the DRVN's military capabilities, including its fledgling air-defense system, and with it confidence that Hanoi could prevail in the looming confrontation with the Americans.[186] "The [VWP], which during its 9th Plenum made the struggle against revisionism one of the essential conditions for the defense of the socialist camp, is more than ever loyal to that principle"; accordingly, its relations with the CCP were now "very close."[187]

Beijing's successful nuclear weapons test of 16 October was a considerable shot in the arm for Vietnamese proponents of all-out war in the South. That success meant that China would henceforth be an even more credible deterrent to American invasion of the North, thereby further bolstering the DRVN's national security and confidence. The event was hugely popular in the DRVN and substantially increased the esteem there for the PRC, which was already high.[188] In a congratulatory message to Beijing, Pham Van Dong exulted that this "success of the Chinese people" represented "an important contribution to strengthening the socialist camp," one the Vietnamese people and Hanoi "highly appreciate."[189] The success occasioned in the DRVN an unprecedented wave of enthusiasm. "Never, to my knowledge," French general delegate Jacques de Buzon noted, "had the attachment of the DRVN to the People's Republic been expressed so manifestly and on such a scale." "This extraordinary manifestation of fraternal solidarity with China, which Soviet diplomats and those from other people's democracies are witnessing, is taking full effect and conveying a clear meaning," he added.[190] Celebration of Beijing's achievement plus "the reserve observed toward the Soviet Union," another French report noted, "confirm that the hostility Hanoi has always manifested toward the Moscow [Partial Nuclear Test Ban] Treaty of August 1963 has not abated." They also confirmed that the unity of views between Hanoi and Beijing was, at that point, nearly absolute.[191] In fact, it may have been more "absolute" then than at any time before or after in the history of Sino-DRVN relations.

As Hanoi moved closer than ever to Beijing on matters relating to revolutionary struggle, the DRVN government made "great efforts" to change the attitudes of the Vietnamese people toward China. In new history books, for example, the millennium-long Chinese occupation of Vietnam was shown to have been due to "the greed of an imperialistic government" and not to the Chinese people themselves, who had always been "friends of the Vietnamese."[192] Also, the NLF's Liberation Radio appealed to the people of Chinese ancestry in South Vietnam to "stand up to struggle for their own salvation!"[193] In the interests of diplomatic struggle and political struggle in the South, Hanoi was careful not to suggest that it was following Chinese dictates unquestioningly, which they in fact never did. "To cultivate an image of defiant independence in the face of an immensely stronger opponent suits its propaganda objectives in the underdeveloped world and especially in South Vietnam," the Canadian representative noted. It also "avoids arousing latent domestic fears of a Chinese occupation and enables it to build up its military strength unnoticed by most of the world."[194]

KHRUSHCHEV'S OUSTER

Hanoi's improving prospects by the fall of 1964 were not fortuitous. They were instead the result of galvanizing the people behind their leaders following the American air attack of 5 August. A more concrete cause was the news out of Moscow in October: Nikita Khrushchev, the chastened champion of peaceful coexistence and longtime critic of revolutionary militancy in Vietnam, was out as head of the CPSU. His replacement until things shook themselves out in Moscow was a collective leadership that included first secretary Leonid Brezhnev, prime minister Alexei Kosygin, and president Nikolai Podgorny.[195] What the change meant for Hanoi was not immediately clear, but it could only be, it seemed, good news. After all, historian Ilya Gaiduk has written, Khrushchev "never attached due importance to the conflict in Indochina," "relegated the development of

Soviet-North Vietnamese relations to a low place on his foreign policy agenda," and never visited the DRVN.[196]

According to western observers, Khrushchev's "brutal eviction" gave "great hope" to DRVN leaders.[197] Only recently, Hanoi had been disappointed by the Soviets' "conspicuously offhand" reaction to the events of early August.[198] Now it was elated. "The Soviet people and the true communists in the Soviet Union resolutely protect Marxism-Leninism just like they protect the pupils of their eyes," *Hoc tap* said of Khrushchev's ouster.[199] As that statement suggests, Hanoi interpreted Khrushchev's removal to mean that the CPSU had recognized the untenability of peaceful coexistence as a strategy for world revolution and had taken the first step in replacing it with a more suitable one. Its first official message to Brezhnev and the new Soviet leadership reflected that interpretation; it was especially warm and differed in tone from previous messages to Moscow.[200] Some in Hanoi, however, were skeptical. A high-ranking official in the DRVN Foreign Ministry, for example, told the British consul soon after Khrushchev's ouster that he expected little change in Moscow's policy concerning Indochina because revisionist views had been so widespread within the CPSU.[201]

The skeptics were soon vindicated. The change of leadership in Moscow translated into no immediate change in Soviet strategic thinking on Indochina.[202] Moscow merely practiced "Khrushchevism without Khrushchev," as the Chinese put it.[203] In fact, the new CPSU leadership condemned the tone and substance of the *Hoc tap* article mentioned above, precipitating a flap in Soviet-DRVN relations. According to the Soviet Embassy in Hanoi, the article constituted "an open attack on the policy of the Soviet Union and, especially, the 20th and 22nd Party Congress[es]."[204] Indeed, Moscow's displeasure was such that DRVN authorities withdrew the article. According to an East German diplomat, shortly after publication of the *Hoc tap* piece, the Soviet ambassador visited prime minister Pham Van Dong to ask about the thinking behind the article. Dong allegedly evaded a clear response, but over the ensuing days "representatives of the editorial board of *Hoc tap* visited diplomatic missions, removed the copies [of the offending issue] already delivered, and replaced them with new ones, from which the article had been cut out." Later, Le Duan told the Soviet ambassador that publishing the article had been a mistake and apologized for it.[205]

The apology was no doubt sincere, but it did not mean that Le Duan's regime was reconsidering its stance on revisionism or revolutionary strategy. "If Hanoi is taking precautionary measures with Moscow," the French Delegation reported, "its political sympathies remain, at the core, unchanged."[206] That was also the view in Moscow, where officials expressed concern that Chinese influence in North Vietnam had become "almost exclusive."[207] According to the Canadian representative in Hanoi, there were no signs after Khrushchev's ouster that DRVN leaders considered retreating from their "pro-Chinese position" on domestic and international issues. Instead, Hanoi resumed its role of mediator in the Sino-Soviet dispute to put the dispute "in a context where it will represent [the] least danger to [the socialist] bloc and hence [to the] DRVN." To that end, Hanoi now agreed to participate in a special conference of world communist parties in Moscow to address the dispute, as long as its purpose was to "temper conflict in private rather than exacerbate it in public." Though reconciliation of Sino-Soviet differences might never be achieved, the Canadian representative thought, "agreement to conceal differences will tend to ensure DRVN maximum freedom of maneuver in pursuing [its] own domestic and foreign policies and give China less reason, excuse or opportunity to enforce rigid doctrinal allegiance and [a] paralyzing politico-economic alliance."[208]

Neither Khrushchev's removal nor the new military situation in Vietnam was enough to prompt Moscow to abandon its commitment to a diplomatic solution in the South.[209] In a letter to foreign minister Xuan Thuy in late December, his Soviet counterpart, Andrei Gromyko, insisted that Moscow "takes the view that in order to normalize and peacefully settle" the crisis in South Vietnam and the rest of Indochina, "the strict observance of the 1954 Geneva Agreements on Indochina and the 1962 Geneva Agreement on Laos" must be "ensured by all countries concerned," including the DRVN.[210] For the time being, Moscow would provide only "token" assistance to Hanoi.[211] DRVN leaders were no doubt disappointed with this rigidity, but they were also unmoved by it. Appeals to Geneva agreements no longer resonated in Hanoi.

THE VIETNAM WAR BEGINS

On 11 October, the VWP's Central Military Commission ordered the PLAF to prepare a major campaign in the South jointly with PAVN units to "annihilate a part of the enemy's main force units," destroy strategic hamlets, and expand liberated areas in the southwest along the Cambodian border, as well as in the Central Highlands. The campaign was to take place in two phases between December 1964 and March 1965. On the last day of October, zealous southern revolutionaries attacked an American airfield at Bien Hoa, just northeast of Saigon, killing four U.S. servicemen and wounding thirty. The American ambassador to the RVN, Maxwell Taylor, considered the attack "a deliberate act of escalation" as well as "a change of the ground rules under which [communist forces] have operated up to now."[212]

The rules indeed changed in late 1964. The campaign ordered by the Central Military Commission got underway in Interzone V on 6 December with a massive assault on ARVN forces at An Lao. According to an official history, the assault marked "the first time in [Interzone V] that we used the new tactic of coordinating main force units with local and guerilla forces" in a major battle.[213] The assault was a success, enabling Nguyen Chi Thanh and COSVN to throw caution to the wind, insisting in its aftermath that the strategy in the South was now "attack, attack, and only attack."[214] Canadian diplomats in Saigon spoke of a "time of 'general intensification'" of hostilities in Vietnam thereafter.[215] "Heartened by their successes, real or imaginary, strengthened by their friends' support, and comforted by their enemies' apparent discomfiture, the D.R.V. leadership could not but be encouraged to maintain its confident posture," the British Consulate concluded at year's end. "In their view the war will continue until it is 'won' or a negotiated settlement, on terms much more favorable than in 1954, is reached."[216]

As 1964 gave way to 1965, the DRVN was at war in and with the RVN, and making preparations for an American onslaught against the North. "The capital has become a city of war," a foreign diplomat reported following a visit to Hanoi in mid-December. "Anti-aircraft guns have been positioned on rooftops, and people are busy digging trenches in the streets."[217] Although Americans did not know it at the time, the Vietnam War had begun.

Epilogue

On 7 February 1965, elements of the PLAF attacked a U.S. Special Forces camp at Pleiku, in the Central Highlands, killing eight Americans and injuring more than one hundred others.[1] That was the last straw for Washington, its 5 August episode. The Johnson administration began sustained bombings of North Vietnam in early March and, days later, deployed combat troops to South Vietnam, at first to protect U.S. air bases, and eventually to "search [for] and destroy" enemy ground forces.[2]

The sudden Americanization of the war and the bombings of the North distressed DRVN leaders, who had hoped Washington would keep its own troops out of Vietnam awhile longer and not attack the North continuously. The party and the government, they reckoned, were not entirely ready for war with the United States on both sides of the seventeenth parallel. Among party cadres and rank-and-file members, "the influences of revisionism have not yet been successfully overcome, and there are still manifestations of individualism."[3] The leaders blamed this on the continued presence in party ranks of enemies who sought to "destroy" the VWP from within.[4]

DRVN leaders at once redoubled the effort to purge party ranks of subversive thoughts and individuals. It would take at least a year, they estimated, to cleanse the party and ensure that cadres and members thought and acted fittingly, or at least well enough to lead the masses effectively in this new period of struggle.[5] To the same end, they notably expanded party membership.[6] To guarantee success in the "American War," the spirit of the party needed to infuse the people of Vietnam. "Despite the intensification of the war in the South and the possibility of an extension of hostilities to the North," the Canadian representative in Hanoi had accurately reported in January, Hanoi "will continue to give priority to domestic consolidation," particularly in the ideological "sphere."[7]

Within days after the beginning of U.S. combat operations, Hanoi announced that the struggle for reunification had entered a new phase, that of "limited war," and launched what it called the "Anti-American Resistance for National Salvation." The central aims of the resistance were to mitigate the effects of bombings in the North and pursue the attrition of enemy ground forces in the South. In April, DRVN leaders sanctioned a mass mobilization effort to meet those ends, the "Three Readinesses" campaign, which urged men in the North to be ready to fight, join the armed forces, and perform whatever other task was required of them.[8] As part of this campaign, the authorities extended indefinitely the period of service of PAVN soldiers and recalled to service officers and men discharged earlier because of budget cuts. They also swelled the ranks of militia forces, from 1.4 million in 1964 to 2 million in mid-1965.[9] The guiding principle behind these measures was "Let the Entire People Fight the Enemy and Take Part in the National Defense."[10] Because the anti-American resistance was a "total" effort involving everyone, Hanoi also launched the "Three Responsibilities" campaign, which directed able-bodied women to work as substitutes for male combatants; urge civilian men to participate as necessary in active resistance against the American aggressors; and fight if called upon to do so by the authorities.[11]

At an emergency meeting convened in response to the initial deployment of U.S. troops in the South, the Central Committee addressed the prospect of an American invasion of the North, long a concern of the leadership. It concluded that the Americans were indeed likely to "extend their war of aggression" above the seventeenth parallel.[12] Despite this possibility and the concomitant intensification of the ground war in the South and the air war in the North, Le Duan's regime reaffirmed its commitment to core revolutionary objectives and prompt and decisive military victory. The regime also refused to abandon or even neglect the pursuit of socialism in the DRVN, insisting on its continued transformation into a "great rear base," even as it strengthened its defensive capabilities "on all fronts" and provided considerable assistance to "the front line in the South."[13] The *mot d'ordre* in the North thus became "Producing while Fighting," promoted by the authorities through a variety of new patriotic worker and peasant slogans, such as "Carry Out Production Work as Vigorously as Fighting," "Hold Firm Both Your Hammer and Your Rifle," "Work Twice as Hard to Make Up for the Lost Time," "Hold Both Our Plough and Our Rifle," and "Fight the Enemy Wherever He Comes and Resume Production after the Fight."[14]

Following the start of the war's Americanization, Beijing encouraged Hanoi to press the military struggle and refuse to negotiate.[15] Any willingness to talk to Washington after March 1965, the Chinese counseled, would manifest "weakness in the face of American imperialism."[16] Besides, the Johnson administration called for peace talks only to "deceive public opinion," Chinese foreign minister Chen Yi told his Vietnamese counterpart.[17] But Hanoi needed no such counsel; its mind was already made up on such issues. In the aftermath of the failures of the 1954 and 1962 Geneva accords, DRVN leaders, and Le Duan in particular, had developed a "Munich syndrome" of their own, an aversion to negotiations under circumstances in which they thought they looked weak or inferior to their enemy. David Marr has observed of this syndrome that "DRV leaders resolved never again to be put in a position where matters of vital Vietnamese national interest were subject to big power bargaining."[18] If they ever were to negotiate, it would only be from a position of absolute strength.

Moreover, at this juncture, Hanoi felt it had to appear confident in its ability to triumph, to remain defiant. Thus DRVN leaders spurned all American and third-party efforts to jump-start negotiations. They had to be careful in doing so, however. If the public perception became that Hanoi had spurned an equitable diplomatic solution in favor of imposing a draconian peace, the revolution and the anti-American resistance would lose vital support and sympathy from abroad. Such a loss would compromise the diplomatic struggle and enable the Johnson administration to carry on its "war of aggression" with impunity, without fear of the domestic and international consequences of escalation. Hanoi had thus to convince the rest of the world, including the American people, that it longed for peace, while making clear to "warmongers" in Washington that it had no intention of abdicating its revolutionary purposes.

The consonance of policy and purpose between Hanoi and Beijing vexed Moscow, which still felt that a war in Vietnam was detrimental to its interests and those of the socialist camp. Nonetheless, Soviet leaders agreed to assist the DRVN, at least in defending itself.[19] The reasons for this are obviously complex and involved the fact that to do otherwise would have compromised Moscow's stance as leader of the socialist camp and rearguard against naked capitalist imperialism.[20] Soviet aid to the DRVN was soon growing exponentially to include conventional heavy armaments, as well as surface-to-air missiles to help protect the North from American air attacks and Soviet personnel to install them. Yet at the same time, Moscow doggedly pressed Hanoi to negotiate with Washington and even tried to facilitate contacts between the two.[21] Unlike Hanoi, Soviet leaders "do not believe in our victory and this pushes them to search for a resolution of the Vietnamese question by way of negotiations," Le Duc Tho confided to a French journalist.[22] Pham Van Dong echoed that thought, telling a western diplomat that the Soviets and other East Europeans had hounded Hanoi to adopt more "moderate" attitudes toward negotiations ever since Washington had introduced combat forces in Vietnam.[23] DRVN leaders responded to such pressures as circumstances dictated. Fully aware of their dependence on aid from the Soviet Union and other eastern bloc countries, they tolerated the calls for negotiations and even pretended to act on them, but those calls actually fell on "totally deaf ears."[24]

As it privately dismissed the pleas and concerns of its European allies, Hanoi continued to publicly promote socialist solidarity between the Soviet Union and China to try and mend the Sino-Soviet rift.[25] This latter effort rested on the conviction that Washington took advantage of the dispute between Beijing and Moscow to "intensify to very high levels" its war in Vietnam.[26] To mitigate the deleterious effects of the dispute, Hanoi ordered its diplomats to make "absolutely" no derogatory comments about either China or the Soviet Union and instead emphasize the contributions of each to the Vietnamese revolution and socialist internationalism.[27] Hanoi also ordered party members and government officials to say nothing negative about the Soviets in private conversations with Chinese officials, and vice versa.

Far from deterring North Vietnamese decision-makers, the American military intervention solidified their resolve to fight resolutely, to pursue "victory at any price."[28]

· · ·

Hanoi's strategy and tactics during the "American War," which began in 1965 and ended in 1973 with the signing of the Paris agreement, were in many ways predictable. As they had been doing since before that war's onset, DRVN decision-makers relied on three separate yet interrelated modes of struggle—political, diplomatic, and military—to meet their aims. Military struggle was paramount to them for much of the war's duration, but even that decision, as demonstrated in this study, was made before, not after, the Americanization of hostilities in Vietnam.

The experiences of communist decision-makers—of Le Duan and members of his ruling clique—in the decade before 1965 were in that sense truly determinative, conditioning their thinking on everything ranging from how to wage war to when to sue for peace. Those experiences had been characterized by frustration and disappointment over the failed policies of the previous regime under Ho Chi Minh, which convinced the first secretary, Le Duc Tho, Nguyen Chi Thanh, Pham Hung, and other militants now at the helm of the party to spurn diplomatic compromise and pin their hopes on military struggle to meet their core goals. Specifically, the "lessons" they drew from that decade reinforced their faith in their revolutionary ideology and sense of purpose. These in turn informed their sense of the possibilities and challenges they faced during the American War. Fighting relentlessly, sacrificing selflessly, and winning totally became hallmarks of their worldview, which shaped both the course and the outcome of the Vietnam War.

In retrospect, there was little the United States could have done to change this mindset and thus alter either the course or the outcome of the war, short of resorting to disproportionate violence or surrendering—both of which it eventually did, in a sense. Le Duan and his like-minded peers had been calling for armed struggle in the South ever since the signing of the Geneva accords in 1954. These militants were not going to relinquish that aspiration once they finally controlled policy-making in Hanoi and could maneuver the situation to their apparent advantage. Persuaded that the socialist camp was behind them, that the masses in both halves of Vietnam were prepared to make the necessary sacrifices, that diplomacy would not resolve their dispute with Washington unless they negotiated from a position of strength, and most fundamentally, that history had vindicated their views and that their stance was therefore right, they conducted the anti-American struggle with unwavering determination. Revving up the pressure on the DRVN by gradual escalation—ever more U.S. troops in the South, ever more U.S. bombings of the North—was not going to disabuse them of their ideas and make them abandon their ambitions. They waged war against the United States with no discernible fear of consequences or concern for the suffering of their compatriots and the physical destruction of their country, because they believed history was on their side, and the triumph of the Vietnamese revolution would herald the triumph of the world revolution. The human and material cost of the war for the Vietnamese was indeed colossal, yet it was never high enough to compel decision-makers in Hanoi to renounce their core objectives or even amend them.

To counter those objectives, the United States sent more than half a million troops to fight communist-led forces in the South, killed hundreds of thousands of those forces (to say nothing of the collateral civilian casualties), sprayed the cancer-inducing defoliant Agent Orange across the southern countryside, destroyed Hue and other cities in order to "save" them during the Tet Offensive, and dropped more ordnance on Vietnam than it did on Germany and Japan in all of World War II. Unrepentant, the men in charge in Hanoi long refused to negotiate and then to negotiate earnestly, or to cease hostilities or otherwise assuage the agony of the Vietnamese masses. These too were conscious choices. A different leadership in Hanoi would surely have acted differently. However, in light of what is now known of intra-VWP affairs, it is unlikely that any different group of leaders, be they ever so "hawkish" or "dovish" on matters relating to the conduct of the war, could ever have seized power in the DRVN once the balance there had shifted in favor of Le Duan and his associates.

It was only in the aftermath of the dispiriting failure of the 1972 Spring Offensive—a desperate, no-holds-barred communist effort to achieve military victory in the South—that Hanoi demonstrated some tractability by finally agreeing to negotiate seriously. In October of that year, DRVN representatives at the Paris peace talks begun in 1968–69 submitted the first complete draft of a peace settlement, which, after some fine-tuning, the United States accepted. Unfortunately, the prospect of peace quickly dissipated as Saigon objected to several of the settlement's provisions and Washington decided to heed the concerns of its ally and seek further alterations to the document. By early December, after some more haggling, Washington and Hanoi were within one sentence of finalizing a new settlement acceptable to both sides, but the latter refused to make a final concession on language concerning the status of the demilitarized zone between the two Vietnams insisted upon by the Americans. Instead, it suspended the negotiations and temporized, hoping that antiwar sentiment in the United States, and in Congress specifically, would compel U.S. president Richard Nixon to withdraw the last U.S. troops from Vietnam and terminate American aid to Saigon with no condition other than the return of American prisoners of war.[29]

As had been the case in 1964 when the war began, in 1968 with the Tet Offensive, and in 1972 with the Spring Offensive, Le Duan and the Politburo again misjudged their chances for success while underestimating the swiftness and decisiveness of Washington's response to their actions. The Nixon administration answered this last suspension of negotiations with the massive "Christmas bombing" of Hanoi and Haiphong. This operation, code-named Linebacker II, dealt such a stunning blow, psychologically and physically, to the DRVN and its leadership that within days Hanoi conceded the contested language concerning the demilitarized zone. On 27 January 1973, the two sides signed the Paris agreement ostensibly ending their war.

Like the 1954 Geneva accords, the 1973 Paris agreement was, from the perspective of DRVN leaders at the time, a product of necessity mandated by the shortcomings of the military struggle. But, unlike their predecessors, who respected the accords they signed because they thought them workable, Le Duan and his regime honored the Paris agreement only as long and to the extent that it was expedient for them to do so. Thus they suspended hostilities and returned American and other prisoners, but otherwise acquiesced in the agreement only for the moment. That moment passed with the withdrawal of the last U.S. troops from Vietnam. At that point, Hanoi promptly began working on plans to take over the South militarily, assuming—correctly this time—that Washington would not come to the rescue of its embattled allies in Saigon once war resumed.

Within little more than two years after the signing of the Paris agreement— 30 April 1975 is the official date—the PLAF and the PAVN had defeated the ARVN, forced the abdication of the Saigon regime, and completed the "liberation" of the South. In July of the following year, Vietnam was formally reunified under the communist aegis, thereby fulfilling the central objective of the Vietnamese revolution. The road to that fulfillment had been long, turbulent, and more than ghastly at times, but Le Duan and other revolutionary leaders, at least, had occasion to celebrate.

NOTES

INTRODUCTION

1. A growing body of works on the Cold War stresses the agency of "small actors." See, among others, Piero Gleijeses, *Conflicting Missions: Havana, Washington, and Africa, 1959–1976* (Chapel Hill: University of North Carolina Press, 2003); and Matthew J. Connelly, *A Diplomatic Revolution: Algeria's Fight for Independence and the Origins of the Post–Cold War Era* (New York: Oxford University Press, 2002).

2. Patricia M. Pelley, *Postcolonial Vietnam: New Histories of the National Past* (Durham, N.C.: Duke University Press, 2002), 3.

3. The notion that for much of the period covered in this study there existed within the VWP two main, competing wings is admittedly simplistic. Presumably, there were several factions within the party, and no two members thought exactly alike on all issues. However, given the paucity of sources, both primary and secondary, on this matter, the moderate-militant binary is sensible as well as useful to contextualize the dilemmas confronting the party after 1954. Besides, it was essentially in such terms that close observers at the time characterized intra-VWP tensions and identified the ideological proclivities of core leaders. Hopefully, in the not-too-distant future Vietnamese authorities will start doing more to help us understand the history of their predecessors on their own terms. Also, I use the terms *moderate* and *militant* to identify the party's two rival wings because I find those more precise than *North-firster/South-firster* and other pairings used by scholars who have written on the topic. I owe a significant debt of gratitude to the Vietnam Studies Group and to Bill Turley, Hue-Tam Tai, Shawn McHale, Tuong Vu, and Balazs Szalontai in particular for their succor as I grappled with identifying the two factions.

4. According to Nigel Gould-Davies, "compromise, retreat, flexibility" and "avoidance of war," hallmarks of the moderate tendency in Vietnam, should not be interpreted to mean that its adherents were "realists," that is, practitioners of realpolitik. It was common for

devout communists during the Cold War, he suggests, to combine as Lenin did "an acutely realistic orientation to political action with an unswerving commitment to revolutionary goals." See Nigel Gould-Davies, "Rethinking the Role of Ideology in International Politics during the Cold War," *Journal of Cold War Studies* 1, no. 1 (Winter 1999): 100.

5. On Johnson's decision to commit U.S. ground forces to South Vietnam in 1965, see Fredrik Logevall, *Choosing War: The Lost Chance for Peace and the Escalation of War in Vietnam* (Berkeley: University of California Press, 2001).

6. "To say that Vietnamese communists thought of Marxism merely as a tool, that their revolution was not inspired by Moscow, that they were forced by circumstances against their will to align with the Soviet bloc, and that they were loyal to the Soviet Union only when there were contacts and aid," historian Tuong Vu writes, contradicts documentary evidence and "denigrates their revolutionary commitment and efforts." See Tuong Vu, "From Cheering to Volunteering: Vietnamese Communists and the Coming of the Cold War, 1940–1951," in Christopher Goscha and Christian Ostermann, eds., *Connecting Histories: The Cold War and Decolonization in Asia, 1945–1962* (Stanford, Calif.: Stanford University Press, 2009), 198.

7. Jeremi Suri, *Liberty's Surest Guardian: American Nation-Building from the Founders to Obama* (New York: Free Press, 2011), 211.

8. A new edition of the book was published in 1996. See William J. Duiker, *The Communist Road to Power in Vietnam*, 2nd ed. (Boulder, Colo.: Westview Press, 1996).

9. Carlyle A. Thayer, *War by Other Means: National Liberation and Revolution in Viet-Nam, 1954–60* (Cambridge, Mass.: Unwin Hyman, 1989).

10. Ang Cheng Guan, *The Vietnam War from the Other Side: The Vietnamese Communists' Perspective* (New York: RoutledgeCurzon, 2002); Ang Cheng Guan, *Vietnamese Communists' Relations with China and the Second Indochina Conflict, 1956–1962* (Jefferson, N.C.: McFarland, 1997).

11. Lien-Hang T. Nguyen, *Hanoi's War: An International History of the War for Peace in Vietnam* (Chapel Hill: University of North Carolina Press, 2012).

12. William S. Turley, *The Second Indochina War: A Concise Political and Military History*, 2nd ed. (Lanham, Md.: Rowman & Littlefield, 2009).

13. Ralph B. Smith, *An International History of the Vietnam War, Vol. 1: Revolution versus Containment, 1955–61* (London: Macmillan Press, 1983); Ralph B. Smith, *An International History of the Vietnam War, Vol. 2: The Struggle for Southeast Asia, 1961–65* (London: Macmillan Press, 1985); Ralph B. Smith, *An International History of the Vietnam War, Vol. 3: The Making of a Limited War, 1965–66* (London: Macmillan Press, 1991); Arthur J. Dommen, *The Indochinese Experience of the French and the Americans: Nationalism and Communism in Cambodia, Laos, and Vietnam* (Bloomington: Indiana University Press, 2001); Mari Olsen, *Soviet-Vietnam Relations and the Role of China, 1949–64* (New York: Routledge, 2006); Robert K. Brigham, *Guerrilla Diplomacy: The NLF's Foreign Relations and the Viet Nam War* (Ithaca, N.Y.: Cornell University Press, 1999); David W. P. Elliott, *The Vietnamese War: Revolution and Social Change in the Mekong Delta, 1930–1975*, concise ed. (Armonk, N.Y.: M. E. Sharpe, 2007); Chen Jian, *Mao's China and the Cold War* (Chapel Hill: University of North Carolina Press, 2001); Qiang Zhai, *China and the Vietnam Wars, 1950–1975* (Chapel Hill: University of North Carolina Press, 2000); Ilya V. Gaiduk, *Confronting Vietnam: Soviet Policy toward the Indochina Conflict, 1954–1963* (Washington, D.C.: Woodrow Wilson Center Press, 2003); Ilya V. Gaiduk, *The Soviet Union and the Vietnam War*

(Chicago: Ivan R. Dee, 1996); Donald S. Zagoria, *Vietnam Triangle: Moscow, Peking, Hanoi* (New York: Pegasus, 1967); W. R. Smyser, *The Independent Vietnamese: Vietnamese Communism between Russia and China, 1956–1969*, Southeast Asia Series no. 55 (Athens: Ohio University Center for International Studies, 1980).

14. On the origins of ideological decision-making in Vietnam, see Tuong Vu, "From Cheering to Volunteering," 172–204.

15. Le Duc Tho, "Let Us Strengthen the Ideological Struggle to Consolidate the Party," *Tuyen huan*, no. 4 (April 1964). Reproduced and translated in Folder 03, Box 25, Douglas Pike Collection: Unit 06—Democratic Republic of Vietnam, Vietnam Archive at Texas Tech University, 22.

16. Adam Fforde and Suzanne Paine, *The Limits of National Liberation: Problems of Economic Management in the Democratic Republic of Vietnam* (London: Croom Helm, 1987), 45; Mark L. Haas, *The Ideological Origins of Great Power Politics, 1789–1989* (Ithaca, N.Y.: Cornell University Press, 2005), 147.

1. CHOOSING PEACE, 1954–1956

1. *Viet Minh* is short for *Viet Nam Doc lap Dong minh hoi*, literally, Independence League of Vietnam.

2. France established the SOVN in Saigon in March 1949 with former emperor Bao Dai as chief of state and Tran Van Huu as president. A stereotypical puppet regime, the SOVN gained a veneer of legitimacy when the French National Assembly voted in April 1949 to repeal the *département* status of Cochinchina and grant autonomy to Vietnam (Tonkin, Annam, and Cochinchina) within the French Union (Union française). Under that arrangement, the SOVN government became ostensibly responsible for the domestic and some foreign affairs of Vietnam, and had its own army under its own flag.

3. On the circumstances that produced the Geneva accords, see Pierre Asselin, "The Democratic Republic of Vietnam and the 1954 Geneva Conference: A Revisionist Critique," *Cold War History* 11, no. 2 (May 2011): 155–95. The text of the "Agreement on the Cessation of Hostilities in Vietnam" is reproduced in United States Senate—Committee on Foreign Relations, *Background Information relating to Southeast Asia and Vietnam*, 90th Congress, 1st Session (Washington, D.C.: U.S. Government Printing Office, 1967), 50–62.

4. "Final Declaration of the Geneva Conference: On Restoring Peace in Indochina, 21 July 1954," in United States Department of State, *The Department of State Bulletin* 31, no. 788 (2 August 1954): 164–66. The Final Declaration listed all the participants in the conference but was unsigned. The participants included representatives from the United Kingdom and the Soviet Union, who cochaired the conference, plus the United States and the PRC, as well as the main parties immediately involved—that is, France, the SOVN, the pro-French governments of Laos and Cambodia, and the DRVN.

5. See "Statement by the Under Secretary of State at the Concluding Plenary Session of the Geneva Conference, 21 July 1954," in ibid. During the Geneva Conference, U.S. secretary of state John Foster Dulles reportedly told French prime minister Pierre Mendès France that his government could not be party to an agreement on Indochina endorsed by the "Red Chinese" because "we cannot give them [even] indirect recognition." See "Conversations Franco-Anglo-Américaines (compte rendu)" [Franco-Anglo-American Conversations

(summary)], 23 October 1954, Bôite 5, Dossier: Indochine [hereafter D:I], Archives de Pierre Mendès France à l'Institut Pierre Mendès France, Paris [hereafter AIPMF], 211–12.

6. "Chi thi cua Ban Bi thu, ngay 27 thang 7 nam 1954: Tuyen truyen ve nhung Hiep dinh cua Hoi nghi Gionevo—Tinh hinh va nhiem vu moi" [Secretariat Instruction, 27 July 1954: Information on the Agreements of the Geneve Conference—New Situation and Responsibilities], in Dang Cong san Viet Nam, *Van kien Dang—Toan tap,* Tap 15: 1954 [Party Documents—Complete Series, Vol. 15: 1954] (Hanoi: Nha xuat ban Chinh tri quoc gia, 2001) [hereafter *VKD:* 1954], 238–41.

7. Fredrik Logevall, *Embers of War: The Fall of an Empire and the Making of America's Vietnam* (New York: Random House, 2012), 619. I expound on the DRVN leadership's reasoning for accepting and abiding by the Geneva accords in 1954–55 in Pierre Asselin, "Choosing Peace: Hanoi and the Geneva Agreement on Vietnam, 1954–55," *Journal of Cold War Studies* 9, no. 2 (Spring 2007): 95–126.

8. According to Christian Lentz, VWP cadres "led everyday forms of state formation in wartime and in the early independent DRV." They were "trained individuals" who "worked alongside, and monitored the attitudes of, peasant bureaucrats performing everyday official tasks in line agencies, local government, or mass organizations." See Christian C. Lentz, "Mobilization and State Formation on a Frontier of Vietnam," *Journal of Peasant Studies* 38, no. 3 (July 2011): 569.

9. "Chi thi cua Ban Bi thu, ngay 30 thang 7 nam 1954: Ve viec chap hanh lenh dinh chien" [Secretariat Instruction, 30 July 1954: On the Matter of Implementing the Cease-fire], in *VKD:* 1954, 248–49.

10. "Chi thi cua Ban Bi thu, ngay 31 thang 8 nam 1954: Ve viec don tiep bo doi, thuong binh, mot so can bo va dong bao mien Nam ra Bac" [Secretariat Instruction, 31 August 1954: On the Matter of Repatriating to the North Southern Soldiers, the Wounded, Some Cadres, and Compatriots], in *VKD:* 1954, 259.

11. Entry for 14 December 1954 in "Diary of Sherwood Lett, Commissioner, Canadian Delegation to the ICSC, Hanoi, Vietnam," R219-121-3-# (ICSC files), Vol. 3068 [Part 1], Record Group [hereafter RG] 25, Library and Archives Canada, Ottawa [hereafter LAC], 109.

12. "Note du Général Ély: a/s de la mission de la Délégation française au Nord Vietnam dans le cadre général de la politique de la France en Indochine" [Note from General Ély: On the French Delegation's Mission in North Vietnam in the Context of France's Policy in Indochina], undated [November 1954], Bôite 7, D:I, AIPMF, 7.

13. Commissioner, Canadian Delegation to ICSC for Vietnam, Hanoi, to Secretary of State for External Affairs, Ottawa, 11 November 1954, R219-121-3-# (ICSC files), Vol. 3068 [Part 3], RG 25, LAC, 1.

14. Entry for 14 December 1954 in "Diary of Sherwood Lett, Commissioner, Canadian Delegation to the ICSC, Hanoi, Vietnam," 109.

15. See Christopher E. Goscha and Stein Tønnesson, "Le Duan and the Break with China: A 1979 Document Translated by Christopher E. Goscha, with an Introduction by Stein Tønnesson," *Cold War International History Project Bulletin,* no. 12/13 (Fall/Winter 2001): 277.

16. Céline Marangé, *Le communisme vietnamien, 1919–1991* [Vietnamese Communism, 1919–1991] (Paris: Presses de Sciences Po, 2012), 304.

17. On that role, see Pierre Asselin, "Le Duan, the American War, and the Creation of an Independent Vietnamese State," *Journal of American East-Asian Relations* 10, nos. 1–2

(Spring–Summer 2001): 1–27; and Lien-Hang T. Nguyen, *Hanoi's War: An International History of the War for Peace in Vietnam* (Chapel Hill: University of North Carolina Press, 2012).

18. Mark Bradley argues that incarceration in French colonial prisons radicalized many Vietnamese communists. See Mark Philip Bradley, *Imagining Vietnam and America: The Making of Postcolonial Vietnam, 1919–1950* (Chapel Hill: University of North Carolina Press, 2002), 40. See also Peter Zinoman, *The Colonial Bastille: A History of Imprisonment in Vietnam, 1862–1940* (Berkeley: University of California Press, 2001).

19. On Le Duan's formative years, see Bui Tin, *Following Ho Chi Minh: Memoirs of a North Vietnamese Colonel* (Honolulu: University of Hawaii Press, 1999), 33; Huynh Kim Khanh, *Vietnamese Communism, 1925–1945* (Ithaca, N.Y.: Cornell University Press, 1982), 101n19, 162; Tran Thanh, "Dong chi Le Duan, nha lanh dao kiet xuat cua Dang ta, nha ly luan Macxit-Leninnit sang tao, nguoi hoc tro xuat sac cua Chu tich Ho Chi Minh" [Comrade Le Duan, Illustrious Leader of Our Party, Innovative Marxist-Leninist Theoretician, Devoted Pupil of President Ho Chi Minh], in Vien nghien cuu Ho Chi Minh va cac lanh tu cua Dang, *Le Duan va cach mang Viet Nam* [Le Duan and the Vietnamese Revolution] (Hanoi: Nha xuat ban Chinh tri quoc gia, 1997), 9–12; "Tieu su dong chi Le Duan, Tong Bi thu Ban Chap hanh Truong uong Dang Cong san Viet Nam" [Biography of Comrade Le Duan, General Secretary of the Central Committee of the Vietnamese Communist Party], in Nguyen Khoa Diem, ed., *Le Duan: Mot nha lanh dao loi lac, mot tu duy sang tao lon cua cach mang Viet Nam* [Le Duan: An Outstanding Leader, an Innovative Thinker of the Vietnamese Revolution] (Hanoi: Nha xuat ban Chinh tri quoc gia, 2002), 9–11; and Lien-Hang T. Nguyen, *Hanoi's War*, 17–31.

20. "Tieu su dong chi Le Duan," 10.

21. Tran Van Dinh, ed., *This Nation and Socialism Are One: Selected Writings of Le Duan, First Secretary, Central Committee, Vietnamese Workers' Party* (Chicago: Vanguard Books, 1976), 250n14; J. J. Zasloff, *Political Motivation of the Vietnamese Communists: The Vietminh Regroupees* (Santa Monica, Calif.: RAND, 1968), v, 26; William J. Duiker, *The Communist Road to Power in Vietnam*, 2nd ed. (Boulder, Colo.: Westview Press, 1996), 183; Lien-Hang T. Nguyen, *Hanoi's War*, 31; Commissioner, Canadian Delegation to ICSC for Vietnam, Hanoi, to Secretary of State for External Affairs, Ottawa, 11 November 1954, 1.

22. "Le Duan, First Secretary of the Lao Dong Central Committee," 11 March 1973, 20-VIET N-6, Vol. 9167 [Part 1], RG 25, LAC, 1; "Factions within the North Vietnamese Regime: Their Bearing, If Any, on Policy Pursued towards South Vietnam," undated [1960], FO 371/160122, National Archives of the United Kingdom, Kew [hereafter NAUK], 3.

23. "Nghi Quyet cua Bo Chinh tri: Ve tinh hinh moi, nhiem vu moi va chinh sach moi cua Dang" [Politburo Resolution: On the New Situation, New Tasks, and New Policy of the Party], in *VKD*: 1954, 283–315.

24. Ban chi dao tong ket chien tranh truc thuoc Bo chinh tri, *Chien tranh cach mang Viet Nam, 1945–1975: Thang loi va bai hoc* [The Vietnamese Revolutionary War, 1945–1975: Victory and Lessons] (Hanoi: Nha xuat ban Chinh tri quoc gia, 2000), 88; and Trung tam Khoa hoc xa hoi va nhan van quoc gia—Vien su hoc, *Lich su Viet Nam, 1954–1965* [History of Vietnam, 1954–1965] (Hanoi: Nha xuat ban Khoa hoc xa hoi, 1995), 54–65, 179–80.

25. "Vietnam: Chronology," part of "Memorandum for the Minister," 9 March 1965, 21-13-VIET-ICSC [PT 1.1], Vol. 10122, RG 25, LAC, 3.

26. "Thong tri cua Ban Bi thu, ngay 22 thang 11 nam 1954: Ve may viec can lam de chinh don bien che trong quan doi" [Secretariat Circular, 22 November 1954: On the Tasks to Reorganize the Personnel in the Armed Forces], in *VKD:* 1954, 370–72.

27. Bui Tin, *From Enemy to Friend: A North Vietnamese Perspective on the War* (Annapolis: Naval Institute Press, 2002), 11.

28. "Conversations Franco-Anglo-Américaines (compte rendu)" [Franco-Anglo-American Coversations (summary)], 23 October 1954, Bôite 5, D:I, AIPMF, 211–12.

29. Douglas Pike, *PAVN: People's Army of Vietnam* (New York: Da Capo Press, 1991), 41. The Canadian delegation to the ICSC subsequently acknowledged that "it seems unlikely that it will be possible to show . . . that the PAVN [that is, the DRVN's regular armed forces] is directly responsible for subversive activities" in areas investigated by the commission. See Canadian Delegation to the ICSC in Vietnam, Hanoi, to Secretary of State, Department of External Affairs, Ottawa, 4 July 1955, R219-121-3-E (ICSC files), Vol. 3069 [Part 1], RG 25, LAC, 1.

30. "Notes of the Freedoms Committee Meeting (10 of 1965) held on Wednesday the 22nd September, 1965 in the Indian Delegation, ICSC in Vietnam, Saigon," 100-10-6 [Pt. 1], Vol. 32, RG 25, LAC, 2; "Report of Mobile Team 26 on Incident 26E under Article 38 of Geneva Agreement" (1955), 50052-A-12-40 [4E-FP (3.1)], Vol. 4667, RG 25, LAC, 2.

31. "Note du Ministère des Affaires Étrangères: a/s application des accords sur la cessation des hostilités" [Note from the Ministry of Foreign Affairs: On Implementation of the Cease-fire Accords], 19 October 1954, Bôite 6, D:I, AIPMF, 4.

32. According to a French estimate, more than a third of Viet Minh forces consisted of "irregulars" who under the terms of the Geneva accords had to disarm but not regroup north of the seventeenth parallel. See "Observations présentées par le Président Bidault au cours du débat général dans la scéance du 24 mai 1954" [Observations Presented by President Bidault during the General Debate at the 24 May 1954 Session], undated, #4, Cabinet du Ministre: P. Mendès France (1954–1955) [hereafter CM:PMF], Archives Diplomatiques de France, La Courneuve [hereafter ADF], 5.

33. Canadian Delegation to the ICSC in Vietnam, Hanoi, to Secretary of State, Department of External Affairs, Ottawa, 4 July 1955, 2. According to William Duiker, between 50,000 and 90,000 of an estimated 100,000 Viet Minh troops in the South in 1954 regrouped to the North, some with their families. See Duiker, *Communist Road to Power,* 183. William Turley claims it was 87,000 troops and 43,000 civilians. See William S. Turley, *The Second Indochina War: A Concise Political and Military History,* 2nd ed. (Lanham, Md.: Rowman & Littlefield, 2009), 25.

34. British Consulate General, Hanoi [hereafter BCGH] to Foreign Office, London [hereafter FO], 31 August 1956, FO 371/123395, NAUK, 1.

35. Quoted in Zasloff, *Political Motivation,* 59.

36. BCGH to FO, 31 August 1956, 1.

37. "Report of Mobile Team 55 concerning the Situation regarding Freedom of Movement in Thanh Hoa Province," 14 April 1955, 50052-A-12-40 [4E-FP (2.2)], Vol. 4667, RG 25, LAC, 5.

38. Appendix A, 14 April 1955, 50052-A-12-40 [4E-FP (2.2)], Vol. 4667, RG 25, LAC.

39. "Report on Freedom of Movement by Mobile Team 56 (Nghe An Province)" (1955), 50052-A-12-40 [4E-FP (3.2)], Vol. 4667, RG 25, LAC, 7.

40. Dang Cong san Viet Nam—Ban Chap hanh Dang bo thanh pho Ha Noi, *Lich su Dang bo thanh pho Ha Noi, 1954–1975* [History of the Hanoi City Party Committee, 1954–1975] (Hanoi: Nha xuat ban Ha Noi, 1995), 10. The "transfer" of Hanoi and the withdrawal of French forces from the city "unfolded in perfect order and without notable incidents." See French Delegation, Hanoi [hereafter FDH], to Ministry of Foreign Affairs, Paris [hereafter MFA], 11 October 1954, #157, Asie-Océanie [hereafter AO]: 1944–1955, ADF, 1; and "Entretien Guy La Chambre—Sainteny du 12 Octobre 1954 sur l'entrée du Viet Minh à Hanoi" [Guy La Chambre—Sainteny Meeting of 12 October 1954 on the Viet Minh's Entry into Hanoi], undated [October 1954], Bôite 7, D:I, AIPMF, 1.

41. "Chi thi cua Ban Bi thu, ngay 5 thang 9 nam 1954: Ve viec dau tranh chong Phap va bon Ngo Dinh Diem du do va bat ep mot so dong bao ta vao mien Nam [Secretariat Instruction, 5 September 1954: On the Matter of Struggling against the Enticement of and Pressures on Some of Our Compatriots in the South by the French and Ngo Ding Diem]," in *VKD*: 1954, 263–70.

42. "Situation en Indochine [Situation in Indochina]," 30 November 1954, #157, AO: 1944–1955, ADF, 5.

43. French General Commission, Saigon, to MFA, 12 January 1955, Bôite 6, D:I, AIPMF, 7.

44. BCGH to FO, 27 January 1955, FO 371/117099, NAUK, 1.

45. Peter Hansen, "*Bac Di Cu*: Catholic Refugees from the North of Vietnam and Their Role in the Southern Republic, 1954–1959," *Journal of Vietnamese Studies* 4, no. 3 (Fall 2009): 173–211; Tran Thi Lien, "Les catholiques vietnamiens dans la République du Viêtnam (1954–1963)" [Vietnamese Catholics in the Republic of Vietnam (1954–1963)], in Pierre Brocheux, ed., *Du conflict d'Indochine aux conflits indochinois* [From the Indochina Conflict to the Indochinese Conflicts] (Paris: Éditions Complexe, 2000), 53–80; Anthony James Joes, *The War for South Vietnam, 1954–1975* (Westport, Conn.: Praeger, 2001), 36.

46. Seth Jacobs, *America's Miracle Man in Vietnam: Ngo Dinh Diem, Religion, Race, and U.S. Intervention in Southeast Asia* (Durham, N.C.: Duke University Press, 2004), 131.

47. Canadian Delegation to the ICSC in Vietnam, Hanoi, to Secretary of State, Department of External Affairs, Ottawa, 4 July 1955, 6.

48. "Note de Mendès France à Guy La Chambre" [Note from Mendès France to Guy La Chambre], 4 January 1955, Bôite 5, D:I, AIPMF, 3.

49. Pierre Journoud, *De Gaulle et le Vietnam, 1945–1969: La réconciliation* [De Gaulle and Vietnam, 1945–1969: The Reconciliation] (Paris: Tallandier, 2011), 65.

50. "Note de Mendès France à Guy La Chambre," 4 January 1955, 3; "Conversations Franco-Anglo-Américaines (compte rendu)," 23 October 1954, 209.

51. On Hinh, see Arthur J. Dommen, *The Indochinese Experience of the French and the Americans: Nationalism and Communism in Cambodia, Laos, and Vietnam* (Bloomington: Indiana University Press, 2001), 271–72. Paris itself acknowledged that Hinh and other military commanders in the South "each played their own game and refused to recognize Diem's authority." See "Conversations Franco-Anglo-Américaines (compte rendu)," 23 October 1954, 208.

52. "Dien cua Ban Bi thu, ngay 6 thang 10 nam 1954: Ve nhan dinh tinh hinh va chu truong cong tac moi" [Secretariat Cable, 6 October 1954: On Evaluation of the Situation and Policies Relating to New Responsibilities], in *VKD*: 1954, 328–29; Trung tam Khoa hoc xa

hoi va nhan van quoc gia—Vien su hoc, *Lich su Viet Nam*, 179; Dang Cong san Viet Nam, *Nhung su kien lich su Dang, Tap III* [Party Historical Events, Volume 3] (Hanoi: Nha xuat ban Thong tin ly luan, 1985), 12–13.

53. Logevall, *Embers of War*, 626.
54. "Vietnam: Chronology," 2.
55. "Note du Ministère des Affaires Étrangères: a/s application des accords sur la cessation des hostilités," 7; "Dien cua Ban Bi thu, ngay 6 thang 10 nam 1954," 327–28.
56. "Vietnam: Annual Review for 1955," 23 January 1956, FO 371/123388, NAUK, 2.
57. Vien Lich su Dang—Hoi dong bien soan lich su Nam Trung bo khang chien, *Nam Trung bo khang chien, 1945–1975* [The Resistance in Southern Trung Bo, 1945–1975] (Hanoi: Tong cong ty phat hanh sach Lien ket xuat ban, 1992), 235–36.
58. Vo Chi Cong, *Tren nhung chang duong cach mang* [On the Revolutionary Paths] (Hanoi: Nha xuat ban Chinh tri quoc gia, 2001), 148–52.
59. "Quyet nghi cua Lien Khu uy IV, ngay 26 thang 9 nam 1954: Ve cong tac o Thua Thien va Quang Tri (Thi hanh Chi thi cua Bo Chinh tri ve tinh hinh moi va nhiem vu cong tac moi cua mien Nam)" [Resolution of the Interzone IV Executive Committee, 26 September 1954: On the Tasks in Thua Thien and Quang Tri (Implementing the Politburo Instruction on the New Situation and New Tasks and Responsibilities of the South)], in *VKD*: 1954, 560–62; Vien Lich su Dang—Hoi dong bien soan lich su Nam Trung bo khang chien, *Nam Trung bo khang chien*, 227–29.
60. "Nghi quyet Hoi nghi Lien Khu uy V, tu ngay 18 den 21 thang 10 nam 1954 [Resolution of the Interzone V Executive Committee Conference, 18–21 October 1954]," in *VKD*: 1954, 577–607.
61. Vo Chi Cong, *Tren nhung chang duong*, 163–65.
62. "Chi thi cua Ban Chap hanh Trung uong, ngay 17 thang 12 nam 1954: Tuyen truyen van dong day manh dau tranh chong de quoc My can thiep vao Dong Duong va pha hoai Hiep dinh dinh chien" [Central Committee Instruction, 17 December 1954: Propaganda Activity to Strengthen the Struggle against American Intervention in Indochina and Sabotaging of the Cease-fire Agreement], in *VKD*: 1954, 409–19.
63. "Tinh hinh hien tai va nhiem vu truoc mat: Bao cao cua dong chi Truong Chinh o Hoi nghi Trung uong lan thu bay mo rong (tu 3 den 12-3-1955)" [Current Situation and Responsibilities before Us: Report of Comrade Truong Chinh at the Seventh Enlarged Plenum (3–12 March 1955)], in Dang Cong san Viet Nam, *Van kien Dang—Toan tap*, Tap 16: 1955 [Party Documents—Complete Series, Vol. 16: 1955] (Hanoi: Nha xuat ban Chinh tri quoc gia, 2002) [hereafter *VKD*: 1955], 116.
64. On the challenges of the party in southern Vietnam during the Indochina War, see Christopher E. Goscha, *Vietnam: Un état né de la guerre, 1945–1954* [Vietnam: A State Born from War] (Paris: Armand Colin, 2011).
65. "Tinh hinh hien tai va nhiem vu truoc mat," 129, 135.
66. BCGH to FO, 19 January 1955, FO 371/117099, NAUK, 3.
67. "Loi khai mac cua Ho Chu tich, ngay 3 thang 3 nam 1955, tai Hoi nghi lan thu bay mo rong Ban Chap hanh Trung uong Dang Lao dong Viet Nam (khoa II)" [Opening Address of President Ho, 3 March 1955, at the Seventh Enlarged Plenum of the Second Central Committee of the Vietnamese Workers' Party], in *VKD*: 1955, 93.
68. Logevall, *Embers of War*, 620.

69. BCGH to FO, 4 April 1955, FO 371/117100, NAUK, 2; Logevall, *Embers of War*, 631–32.

70. Benedict J. Tria Kerkvliet, *The Power of Everyday Politics: How Vietnamese Peasants Transformed National Policy* (Ithaca, N.Y.: Cornell University Press, 2005), 38.

71. BCGH to FO, 15 February 1955, FO 371/1171099, NAUK, 1.

72. BCGH to FO, 3 May 1955, FO 371/117100, NAUK, 2; FDH to MFA, 28 April 1955, #167, AO: 1944–1955, ADF, 1.

73. BCGH to FO, 1 July 1955, FO 371/117100, NAUK, 1.

74. Quoted in BCGH to FO, 24 June 1955, FO 371/117222, NAUK, 1.

75. French General Commission, Saigon to MFA, 22 January 1955, Bôite 7, D:I, AIPMF, 5.

76. C. Cheysson letter, 9 January 1955, Bôite 6, D:I, AIPMF, 2.

77. "Bao cao cua dong chi Truong Chinh tai Hoi nghi Trung uong lan thu tam, hop tu ngay 13 den 20-8-1955, doan ket nhan dan toan quoc dau tranh de thuc hien thong nhat Viet Nam tren co so doc lap va dan chu" [Report of Comrade Truong Chinh at the Eighth Central Committee Plenum, 13–20 August 1955, on Uniting the People of the Entire Country to Struggle for Achieving Vietnamese Unification Independently and Democratically], in *VKD: 1955*, 485.

78. "Chi thi cua Trung uong, so 14-CT/TW, ngay 16 thang 4 nam 1955, ve van de tiep tuc pha am muu gay phi cua de quoc" [Resolution of the Center, no. 14-CT/TW, 16 April 1955, on the Issue of Continuing to Defeat the Provocations of the Imperialists], in *VKD: 1955*, 260.

79. "Nghi quyet cua Hoi nghi Trung uong lan thu bay mo rong, hop tu ngay 3 den ngay 12-3-1955" [Resolution of the Seventh Enlarged Central Committee Plenum, Meeting 3–12 March 1955], in *VKD: 1955*, 207.

80. Ho Chi Minh, *Toan Tap*, Tap VI [Collected Works, Vol. 6] (Hanoi: Nha xuat ban Su that, 1986), 589; Ang Cheng Guan, *Vietnamese Communists' Relations with China and the Second Indochina Conflict, 1956–1962* (Jefferson, N.C.: McFarland, 1997), 13.

81. "Ket luan cuoc thao luan o Hoi nghi trung uong lan thu bay (Hop tu ngay 3 den ngay 12-3-1955)" [Closing Remarks at the Seventh Central Committee Plenum (Meeting 3–12 March 1955)], in *VKD: 1955*, 177.

82. *American Imperialism's Intervention in Vietnam* (Hanoi: Foreign Languages Publishing House, 1955), 17–18.

83. "President Eisenhower to the President of the Council of Ministers of Vietnam (Ngo Dinh Diem)," undated [transmitted 24 October 1954], in United States Department of State, *Foreign Relations of the United States, 1952–1954: Volume 13, Indochina (in two parts), Part 2* (Washington, D.C.: U.S. Government Printing Office, 1982), 2167.

84. Logevall, *Embers of War*, 630. For a more comprehensive analysis of Washington's involvement in Vietnamese affairs after the Geneva accords, see Kathryn C. Statler, *Replacing France: The Origins of American Intervention in Vietnam* (Lexington: University Press of Kentucky, 2007); and Edward Miller, *Misalliance: Ngo Dinh Diem, the United States, and the Fate of South Vietnam* (Cambridge, Mass.: Harvard University Press, 2013), chapter 3. On France's diminishing role in Vietnam after 1954, see Pierre Grosser, "La France et l'Indochine (1953-1956): Une 'carte de visite' en 'peau de chagrin,'" PhD diss., Institut d'Études Politiques de Paris, 2002.

85. "Ket luan cuoc thao luan o Hoi nghi trung uong lan thu bay," 177.
86. Quoted in BCGH to FO, 27 May 1955, FO 371/117100, NAUK, 1.
87. On this concept, see Thomas J. Christensen, *Useful Adversaries: Grand Strategy, Domestic Mobilization, and Sino-American Conflict, 1947–1958* (Princeton, N.J.: Princeton University Press, 1996). The quoted passage is from page 6.
88. "Nghi quyet cua Ban Bi thu, so 03-NQ/TW, ngay 29 thang 1 nam 1955: 'Thanh lap Tieu ban dan toc'" [Secretariat Resolution, no. 03-NQ/TW, 29 January 1955: "Establishing a National Sub-Committee"], in *VKD*: 1955, 37; "Dien cua Ban Bi thu, ngay 9 thang 2 nam 1955, gui Xu uy Nam Bo va Lien khu uy V, ve chong am muu dich du do va cuong ep giao dan di cu vao Nam" [Secretariat Cable, 9 February 1955, Sent to the Nam Bo Executive Committee and Interzone V Executive Committee, on Opposing the Enemy's Plan to Entice and Pressure Catholics Who Migrate to the South], in *VKD*: 1955, 54.
89. "Chi thi cua Ban Bi thu, so 06-CT/TW, ngay 10 thang 2 nam 1955, ve viec chong hoi nghi khoi xam luoc Dong Nam A o Bang Coc" [Secretariat Instruction, no. 06-CT/TW, 10 February 1955, on the Matter of Opposing the Bangkok Conference of the Southeast Asia Aggression Bloc], in *VKD*: 1955, 61.
90. "Chi thi cua Bo Chinh tri, so 26-CT/TW, ngay 15 thang 6 nam 1955, tinh hinh hon loan o mien Nam va nhiem vu cong tac cu cua chung ta o mien Nam Viet Nam" [Politburo Resolution, no. 26-CT/TW, 15 June 1955, on the Troubling Situation in the South and Our Actual Tasks and Responsibilities in Southern Vietnam], in *VKD*: 1955, 361–62, 387.
91. "Chi thi cua Bo Chinh tri, so 07-CT/TW, ngay 16 thang 2 nam 1955, day manh dau tranh pha am muu cua dich trong viec du do va cuong ep giao dan di cu vao Nam" [Politburo Instruction, no. 07-CT/TW, 16 February 1955, on Strengthening the Struggle to Destroy the Enemy's Plan to Entice and Pressure Catholics Who Migrate to the South], in *VKD*: 1955, 71.
92. Pham Van Dong quoted in *American Imperialism's Intervention in Vietnam*, 14.
93. BCGH to FO, 1 October 1955, FO 371/117101, NAUK, 2.
94. BCGH to FO, 12 November 1955, FO 371/117101, NAUK, 2; "Vietnam: Annual Review for 1955," 10; Dommen, *Indochinese Experience of the French and the Americans*, 343. According to the British consul, it was "symptomatic of the different treatment which we are enjoying here that my staff and I were invited [by DRVN authorities] to join the newly formed 'International Club,' ostensibly planned as a meeting place for '*diplomates et assimilés*' and [DRVN] officials" (BCGH to FO, 12 November 1955, 2).
95. French General Delegation, Hanoi [hereafter FGDH], to MFA, 18 June 1956, #71, AO: Vietnam Nord [hereafter VN], ADF, 8.
96. Logevall, *Embers of War*, 620.
97. Quoted in "Rapport du Président Indien de la Commission de Contrôle en Indochine sur les entretiens avec Ho Chi Minh" [Report on Meetings with Ho Chi Minh by the Indian Commissioner on the ICSC], 27 October, Bôite 6, D:I, AIPMF, 1–2.
98. BCGH to FO, 14 June 1955, FO 371/117100, NAUK, 1.
99. BCGH to FO, 3 May 1955, 1.
100. BCGH to FO, 27 August 1955, FO 371/117101, NAUK, 1.
101. "Vietnam: Annual Review for 1955," 1, 3.
102. Jessica M. Chapman, *Cauldron of Resistance: Ngo Dinh Diem, the United States, and 1950s Southern Vietnam* (Ithaca, N.Y.: Cornell University Press, 2013), 114. See also Jessica

M. Chapman, "The Sect Crisis of 1955 and the American Commitment to Ngo Dinh Diem," *Journal of Vietnamese Studies* 5, no. 1 (Winter 2010): 37–85.

103. "Note: a/s des responsabilités dans l'origine du conflit vietnamien" [Note: On the Issue of Responsibility in the Origins of the Vietnamese Conflict], 8 March 1965, #147, AO: Vietnam Conflit, ADF, 1.

104. Quoted in BCGH to FO, 27 May 1955, FO 371/117100, NAUK, 1.

105. "Dien cua Ban Bi thu, ngay 15 thang 5 nam 1955" [Secretariat Cable, 15 May 1955], in *VKD: 1955*, 299.

106. On the "downgrading" of COSVN, see Edwin E. Moïse, *Historical Dictionary of the Vietnam War* (Lanham, Md.: Scarecrow Press, 2001), 408.

107. Philippe Franchini, *Les guerres d'Indochine, Vol. 2: De la bataille de Dien Bien Phu à la chute de Saïgon* [The Indochina Wars, Vol. 2: From the Battle of Dien Bien Phu to the Fall of Saigon] (Paris: Éditions Pygmalion/Gérard Watelet, 1988), 182; Duiker, *Communist Road to Power*, 184, 186.

108. BCGH to FO, 4 April 1955, FO 371/117100, NAUK, 1.

109. BCGH to FO, 6 June 1955, FO 371/117100, NAUK, 1 (emphasis in original).

110. Reported in BCGH to FO, 3 January 1955, FO 371/1171099, NAUK, 1.

111. BCGH to FO, 5 August 1955, FO 371/117100, NAUK, 1.

112. BCGH to FO, 14 June 1955, 1–2.

113. Canadian Delegation to the ICSC in Vietnam, Hanoi, to Secretary of State, Department of External Affairs, Ottawa, 4 July 1955, 7.

114. Quoted in Commonwealth Secretariat, "Vietnam: Background Paper," September 1967, R219-121-3-E [Part 3], Vol. 9523, RG 25, LAC, 14. See also "Vietnam: Chronology," 2. The position of Diem's regime regarding the 1956 elections was articulated in Republic of Vietnam, *The Problem of Reunification in Vietnam* (Saigon: Ministry of Information, 1958). Diem would, in fact, declare 20 July 1954, the day of the signing of the Geneva agreements, a "day of shame" *(jour de la honte)*. Quoted in Tranh-Minh Tiet, *Les relations Americano-Vietnamiennes de Kennedy à Nixon: Tome I—Kennedy-Ngo Dinh Diem* [US-Vietnamese Relations from Kennedy to Nixon: Volume 1—Kennedy-Ngo Dinh Diem] (Paris: Nouvelles Éditions Latines, 1971), 35.

115. Vien nghien cuu chu nghia Mac-Lenin va tu tuong Ho Chi Minh, *Lich su Dang Cong san Viet Nam, Tap 2: 1954–1975* [History of the Communist Party of Vietnam, Volume 2: 1954–1975] (Hanoi: Nha xuat ban Chinh tri quoc gia, 1995), 35.

116. Quoted in Chapman, *Cauldron of Resistance*, 119.

117. "Vietnam: Annual Review for 1955," 4.

118. Mark Moyar, *Triumph Forsaken: The Vietnam War, 1954–1965* (New York: Cambridge University Press, 2006), 58.

119. David W. P. Elliott, *The Vietnamese War: Revolution and Social Change in the Mekong Delta, 1930–1975*, concise ed. (Armonk, N.Y.: M. E. Sharpe, 2007), 97.

120. Philippe Devillers, "Le passage du relais au Viet-nam, juin 1954–avril 1956" [The Passing of the Torch in Vietnam, June 1954–April 1956], in Charles-Robert Ageron and Philippe Devillers, eds., *Les guerres d'Indochine de 1945 à 1975* [The Indochina Wars from 1945 to 1975] (Paris: Institut d'Histoire du Temps Présent, 1996), 138.

121. The plan is summarized in BCGH to FO, 8 September 1955, FO 371/117101, NAUK, 1.

122. Trung tam khoa hoc xa hoi va nhan van quoc gia—Vien su hoc, *Lich su Viet Nam*, 12. The VFF became a northern umbrella organization closely linked to the VWP. Incorporating movements, organizations, and individuals representing various social classes, ethnic groups, and religions, it relied on mass participation and mobilization to promote national unity in the face of external aggression and internal subversion, and supervised the activities of state agencies and employees. See Nguyen Van Binh, ed., *Mat tran To quoc Viet Nam: Nhung chang duong lich su (1930–2010)* [The Vietnam Fatherland Front: Historical Phases, 1930–2010] (Hanoi: Nha xuat ban Lao dong, 2009), 242–53. According to the French General Delegation in Hanoi, the VFF was "a mass organization" consisting of representatives from "all organizations" and "all different social classes" in the DRVN. Its charge was facilitating implementation in the DRVN of "the policy line defined by the Government under the tutelage of the [VWP]." The VWP issued directives; the VFF mobilized the masses behind them. See FGDH to MFA, 9 April 1959, #17, AO: VN, ADF, 2.

123. "Vietnam: Annual Review for 1955," 1.

124. On the referendum, see Jessica M. Chapman, "Staging Democracy: South Vietnam's 1955 Referendum to Depose Bao Dai," *Diplomatic History* 30, no. 4 (September 2006): 671–703.

125. Seth Jacobs, *Cold War Mandarin: Ngo Dinh Diem and the Origins of America's War in Vietnam* (Lanham, Md.: Rowman & Littlefield, 2006), 85.

126. A positive assessment of the referendum is offered in Dommen, *Indochinese Experience of the French and the Americans*, 298.

127. Pham Van Dong letter to the two cochairmen of the Geneva Conference on Indochina, 14 February 1956, FO 371/123446, NAUK, 2.

128. "Vietnam: Annual Review for 1955," 6.

129. Logevall, *Embers of War*, 649. In March 1946, Ho agreed on behalf of the DRVN to the return of the French in Vietnam for a period of five years in exchange for recognition by Paris of the "Republic of Vietnam" as a "free state" within the Indochinese Federation and the French Union. Many Vietnamese considered these "6 March Accords" tantamount to "abandonment of national independence." See Marangé, *Le communisme vietnamien*, 164–65.

130. Vien nghien cuu chu nghia Mac-Lenin, *Lich su Dang Cong san Viet Nam*, 35.

131. Cao Van Luong et al., *Lich su Viet Nam* [Vietnamese History] (Hanoi: Nha xuat ban Khoa hoc xa hoi, 1995), 68.

132. "Dien cua Trung uong, ngay 8 thang 3 nam 1956: Gui Xu uy Nam Bo va Lien khu uy mien Nam Trung Bo" [Cable from the Center, 8 March 1956: Sent to the Nam Bo Executive Committee and the Interzone Committee of Southern Trung Bo], in Dang Cong san Viet Nam, *Van kien Dang—Toan tap*, Tap 17: 1956 [Party Documents—Complete Series, Vol. 17: 1956] (Hanoi: Nha xuat ban Chinh tri quoc gia, 2002) [hereafter *VKD*: 1956], 77–78.

133. "Vietnam: Annual Review for 1955," 4.

134. BCGH to FO, 14 May 1956, FO 371/123394, NAUK, 2.

135. "Thuyet trinh cua Tieu ban nghien cuu du luat Nghia vu quan su" [Presentation by the Sub-Committee for Research on the Military Service Law], 15 April 1960, Ho so 64: Ho so ky hop thuc 12 QH khoa I, tu ngay 11–15.4.1960. Tap 3: Phien hop ngay 15.4.1960: Chuyet trinh, tham luan Nghi quyet ve ke hoach va ngan sach Nha nuoc nam 1960, Luat Nghia vu

Quan su, that bai cua che do Diem, Phong Quoc hoi, Vietnam National Archives Center 3, Hanoi, 2; "Summary of Events in North Vietnam (DRV) for February 1959," 1.

136. "Fiche sur les forces militaires et paramilitaires de la RDVN" [File on Military and Paramilitary Forces of the DRVN], 13 February 1956, #19, AO: VN, ADF, 2.

137. FGDH to MFA, 22 June 1956, #19, AO: VN, ADF, 1–2.

138. By the end of 1956, the PAVN reportedly included 250,000 men in regular units and 50,000 in regional units, as well as an additional 200,000 serving in paramilitary and militia units ("Fiche sur les forces militaires et paramilitaires de la RDVN," 1–2).

139. Vien nghien cuu chu nghia Mac-Lenin, *Lich su Dang Cong san Viet Nam*, 56.

140. "Chi thi cua Ban Bi thu, so 08/CT-TW, ngay 4 thang 2 nam 1956: Ve lanh dao cong tac thuong nghiep trong nam 1956" [Secretariat Instruction, no. 08/CT-TW, 4 February 1956: On Leading Commercial Activity in the Year 1956], in *VKD*: 1956, 43.

141. Ang Cheng Guan, *Vietnamese Communists' Relations with China*, 22.

142. BCGH to FO, 14 May 1956, 2.

143. Pham Van Dong letter to the two cochairmen of the Geneva Conference on Indochina, 14 February 1956, 3.

144. "Chi thi cua Ban Bi thu, so 09/CT-TW, ngay 17 thang 2 nam 1956: Ve chu truong doi hop lai Hoi nghi Gionevo de ban bien phap thi hanh Hiep nghi Gionevo 1954" [Secretariat Instruction, no. 09/CT-TW, 17 February 1956: On the Policy of Reconvening the Geneva Conference to Discuss Methods of Implementing the 1954 Geneva Agreement], in *VKD*: 1956, 60.

145. FGDH to MFA, 1 March 1956, #71, AO: VN, ADF, 1–2.

146. BCGH to FO, 14 May 1956, 2.

147. Galia Golan, *Soviet Policies in the Middle East: From World War II to Gorbachev* (New York: Cambridge University Press, 1990), 47.

148. "General Policy of the Soviet Union in Vietnam" (undated), 20-USSR-1-3-VIET N, Vol. 10853 [Part 1], LAC, 1.

149. Duiker, *Communist Road to Power*, 187; Ilya V. Gaiduk, *Confronting Vietnam: Soviet Policy toward the Indochina Conflict, 1954–1963* (Washington, D.C.: Woodrow Wilson Center Press, 2003), 92.

150. FGDH to MFA, 22 July 1956, #71, AO: VN, ADF, 2.

151. "Nghi quyet cua Hoi nghi Ban chap hanh Trung uong Dang Lao dong Viet Nam lan thu chin mo rong, hop tu ngay 19 den 24 thang 4 nam 1956" [Resolution of the Ninth Enlarged Plenum of the Central Committee of the Vietnamese Workers' Party, Meeting 19–24 April 1956], in *VKD*: 1956, 167–72.

152. Mari Olsen, *Soviet-Vietnam Relations and the Role of China, 1949–64* (New York: Routledge, 2006), 59, 61, 68.

153. "Loi be mac cua Chu tich Ho Chi Minh tai Hoi nghi Ban chap hanh Truong uong Dang Lao dong Viet Nam lan thu chin mo rong, hop tu ngay 19 den ngay 24 thang 4 nam 1956" [Closing Address of President Ho Chi Minh at the Ninth Enlarged Plenum of the Central Committee of the Vietnamese Workers' Party, Meeting 19–24 April 1956], in *VKD*: 1956, 174.

154. Franchini, *Guerres d'Indochine*, 182–83; Ang Cheng Guan, *Vietnamese Communists' Relations with China*, 26; and "Bao cao cua Bo Chinh tri tai Hoi nghi lan thu chin Ban Chap hanh Trung uong, hop tu ngay 19 den 24 thang 4 nam 1956: Ve viec quan triet nguyen tac

lanh dao tap the, de cao vai tro cua Dang" [Politburo Report at the Ninth Enlarged Plenum of the Central Committee of the Vietnamese Workers' Party, Meeting 19–24 April 1956: On the Issue of Grasping Thoroughly the Principle of Concrete Leadership, to Increase the Role of the Party], in *VKD:* 1956, 157–66.

155. "Bao cao cua Bo Chinh tri tai Hoi nghi lan thu chin Ban Chap hanh Trung uong," 157–66.

156. BCGH to FO, 11 May 1956, FO 371/123393, NAUK, 2; FGDH to MFA, 20 November 1956, #37, AO: VN, ADF, 2; FGDH to MFA, "Visite de M. Tcheou En Lai à Hanoi" [Visit by Mr. Zhou Enlai to Hanoi], 23 November 1956, #37, AO: VN, ADF, 3. For both ideological and pragmatic reasons, Hanoi supported Soviet intervention in Hungary to suppress the uprising there. "We must resolutely fight the maneuvers of imperialists seeking to overthrow socialist states," it publicly affirmed. "It is necessary to keep supporting the revolutionary movement of Hungarian workers and peasants." Quoted in FGDH to MFA, 22 November 1956, #37, AO: VN, ADF, 1.

157. Quoted in FGDH to MFA, 7 July 1956, #31, AO: VN, ADF, 1.

158. BCGH to FO, 11 May 1956, 2.

159. "Extent of Opposition to the Regime in North Vietnam," 5 June 1956, FO 371/123394, NAUK, 1.

160. Quoted in Joes, *War for South Vietnam,* 42.

161. Soviet Peace Committee, *U.S. Aggression in Vietnam: Crime against Peace and Humanity* (Moscow: Novosti Press Agency Publishing House, 1965).

162. Logevall, *Embers of War,* 652.

163. Bui Diem, *In the Jaws of History* (Bloomington: Indiana University Press, 1999), 88–89.

164. On the consolidation of Diem's power, see Dommen, *Indochinese Experience of the French and the Americans,* 280–305. Interestingly, Dommen believes that had national elections taken place in July 1956, "there is little doubt that [Ho Chi Minh] would have lost in a free and fair contest with Diem" (ibid., 342). See also Chapman, *Cauldron of Resistance*; and Miller, *Misalliance.*

165. "Vietnam: Annual Review for 1955," 2.

166. Laure Cournil and Pierre Journoud, "Une décolonization manquée: L'armée nationale du Vietnam, de la tutelle française à la tutelle américaine (1949–1965)" [A Failed Decolonization: The Vietnamese National Army from French Tutelage to American Tutelage, 1949–1965], *Outre-Mers* 99, nos. 370–71 (2011): 73; "Annual Review of Events in Vietnam for 1956," 22 January 1957, FO 371/129701, NAUK, 1–2, 6; Commonwealth Secretariat, "Vietnam: Background Paper," 11.

167. FGDH to MFA, 4 September 1956, #71, AO: VN, ADF, 2–3, 5.

168. FGDH to MFA, 3 November 1956, #16, AO: VN, ADF, 3, 5.

169. "Memorandum," 10 November 1956, FO 371/123396, NAUK, 1.

170. "Annual Review of Events in Vietnam for 1956," 4. Classification was conditioned by property size and wealth, as well as "whether [households] had hired people or used tenants, and whether they had lent money for profit" (Kerkvliet, *Power of Everyday Politics,* 45).

171. "Memorandum," 10 November 1956, 7.

172. Franchini, *Guerres d'Indochine,* 181. During the land reform campaign, Hanoi regularly deployed units of southern regroupees to enforce policies and quell upheavals, since

they had no ties to the northern population and were therefore more loyal to DRVN authorities (Zasloff, *Political Motivation,* 44–45).

173. On the shortcomings of the land reform campaign generally, see Edwin E. Moïse, *Land Reform in China and North Vietnam* (Chapel Hill: University of North Carolina Press, 1983).

174. For an excellent treatment of the plenum, see Marangé, *Le communisme vietnamien,* 273–77. See also Ang Cheng Guan, *Vietnamese Communists' Relations with China,* 35–36.

175. "Memorandum," 10 November 1956, 1.

176. "Annual Review of Events in Vietnam for 1956," 4; Duiker, *Communist Road to Power,* 189.

177. Marangé, *Le communisme vietnamien,* 264; FGDH to MFA, 29 October 1956, #16, AO: VN, ADF, 1; "Memorandum," 10 November 1956, 3, 5.

178. BCGH to FO, 31 October 1956, FO 371/123395, NAUK, 1.

179. BCGH to FO, 14 May 1956, 2.

180. Quoted in FGDH to MFA, 29 October 1956, #16, AO: VN, ADF, 2, 5, 10 (appendix 3). According to French diplomats, the Central Committee never actually met in September–October; the decision to sack Truong Chinh and his associates was made during a meeting of 760 party cadres held in Hanoi on 21 October ("Memorandum," 10 November 1956, 7).

181. Ang Cheng Guan, *Vietnamese Communists' Relations with China,* 37.

182. On Tho and his relationship to Le Duan, see Lien-Hang T. Nguyen, *Hanoi's War,* 17–31.

183. FGDH to MFA, 10 October 1956, #71, AO: VN, ADF, 1.

184. BCGH to FO, 26 October 1956, FO 371/123395, NAUK, 2.

185. Peter Zinoman, "Nhan Van-Giai Pham and Vietnamese 'Reform Communism' in the 1950s: A Revisionist Interpretation," *Journal of Cold War Studies* 13, no. 1 (2011): 98.

186. Lien-Hang T. Nguyen, *Hanoi's War,* 37. On the periodicals episode generally, see Zinoman, "Nhan Van-Giai Pham," 60–100.

187. "Note pour Monsieur le President du Conseil: République Democratique du Vietnam" [Note for Mr. the Prime Minister: Democratic Republic of Vietnam], 7 June 1958, #35, AO: VN, ADF, 1.

188. Dennis J. Duncanson, *Government and Revolution in Vietnam* (London: Oxford University Press, 1968), 179.

189. Ang Cheng Guan, *Vietnamese Communists' Relations with China,* 21.

190. Kevin Ruane, *War and Revolution in Vietnam, 1930–1975* (London: UCL Press, 1998), 41.

191. Franchini, *Guerres d'Indochine,* 189–90.

192. Ang Cheng Guan, *The Vietnamese War from the Other Side: The Vietnamese Communists' Perspective* (New York: RoutledgeCurzon, 2002), 15–16; Turley, *Second Indochina War,* 36.

193. Le Kinh Lich, ed., *The 30-Year War, 1945–1975,* Vol. 2: *1954–1975* (Hanoi: The Gioi Publishers, 2002), 31.

194. Lien-Hang T. Nguyen, *Hanoi's War,* 18, 32.

195. Turley, *Second Indochina War,* 35.

196. The missive appears in United States Department of State, *Working Paper on North Viet-Nam's Role in the War in South Viet-Nam* (Washington, D.C.: U.S. Government Printing Office, 1968), Appendix Item No. 204. I used a translation of the document by Robert Brigham.

197. Vien nghien cuu chu nghia Mac-Lenin, *Lich su Dang Cong san Viet Nam*, 52; Le Mau Han, *Dang Cong san Viet Nam: Cac Dai hoi va Hoi nghi Trung uong* [The Vietnamese Communist Party: Congresses and Central Committee Plenums] (Hanoi: Nha xuat ban Chinh tri quoc gia, 1995), 73–74; Duiker, *Communist Road to Power*, 189.

198. Logevall, *Embers of War*, 688.

199. Jeffrey Race, *War Comes to Long An: Revolutionary Conflict in a Vietnamese Province* (Berkeley: University of California Press, 1972), 82–83; Bernard B. Fall, "South Vietnam's Internal Problems," *Pacific Affairs* 31, no. 3 (September 1958): 257; Carlyle A. Thayer, *War by Other Means: National Liberation and Revolution in Viet-Nam, 1954–60* (Cambridge, Mass.: Unwin Hyman, 1989), 142–51; Nguyen Dinh Uoc, "Nha chien luoc loi lac" [An Outstanding Strategist], in Vien nghien cuu Ho Chi Minh va cac lanh tu cua Dang, *Le Duan va cach mang Viet Nam* [Le Duan and the Vietnamese Revolution] (Hanoi: Nha xuat ban Chinh tri quoc gia, 1997), 99.

200. Ang Cheng Guan, *Vietnamese Communists' Relations with China*, 47; and Ang Cheng Guan, *Vietnamese War from the Other Side*, 19–20.

2. CHANGING COURSE, 1957–1959

1. "The Question of the Admission of Vietnam to the United Nations," 30 April 1957, R219-121-3-E [Part 2], Vol. 3069, Record Group [hereafter RG] 25, Library and Archives Canada, Ottawa [hereafter LAC], 5.

2. "Évolution de la RDVN en 1957" [Development of the DRVN in 1957], 20 January 1957, #31, Asie-Océanie [hereafter AO]: Vietnam Nord [hereafter VN], Archives Diplomatiques de France, La Courneuve [hereafter ADF], 12.

3. "The Situation and Likely Developments over the Next Eighteen Months in North and South Vietnam, Laos, and Cambodia," 15 July 1957, R219-121-3-E [Part 2], Vol. 3069, RG 25, LAC, 5.

4. "Vietnam: Annual Report for 1957," 10 January 1958, FO 371/136114, National Archives of the United Kingdom, Kew [hereafter NAUK], 1–2.

5. "Economic Conditions in North Vietnam," in report entitled "The Situation in Vietnam," 30 September 1957, R219-121-3-E [Part 2], Vol. 3069, RG 25, LAC, 2.

6. Edwin E. Moïse, *Land Reform in China and North Vietnam* (Chapel Hill: University of North Carolina Press, 1983), 261–62; Benedict J. Tria Kerkvliet, *The Power of Everyday Politics: How Vietnamese Peasants Transformed National Policy* (Ithaca, N.Y.: Cornell University Press, 2005), 46.

7. "Vietnam: Annual Report for 1957," 1.

8. "The Year 1957," undated, FO 371/136118, NAUK, 14.

9. Christian C. Lentz, "Mobilization and State Formation on a Frontier of Vietnam," *Journal of Peasant Studies* 38, no. 3 (July 2011): 574.

10. Seth Jacobs, *America's Miracle Man in Vietnam: Ngo Dinh Diem, Religion, Race, and U.S. Intervention in Southeast Asia* (Durham, N.C.: Duke University Press, 2004), 254–62.

11. Fredrik Logevall, *Embers of War: The Fall of an Empire and the Making of America's Vietnam* (New York: Random House, 2012), 678.

12. Robert K. Brigham, *Guerrilla Diplomacy: The NLF's Foreign Relations and the Viet Nam War* (Ithaca, N.Y.: Cornell University Press, 1999), 9. See also William S. Turley, *The Second Indochina War: A Concise Political and Military History*, 2nd ed. (Lanham, Md.: Rowman & Littlefield, 2009), 38; and Marilyn B. Young, *The Vietnam Wars 1945–1990* (New York: HarperCollins, 1991), 60–69. Tran Van Giau confirms that this period was the "darkest hour" of the revolutionary movement in the South. See William J. Duiker, *Ho Chi Minh: A Life* (New York: Theia, 2000), 661n71.

13. "The Situation and Likely Developments over the Next Eighteen Months in North and South Vietnam, Laos, and Cambodia," 1; "Vietnam: Annual Report for 1957," 5, 7, 8; "The Question of the Admission of Vietnam to the United Nations," 9.

14. "Vietnam: Annual Report for 1957," 4; Ang Cheng Guan, *The Vietnamese War from the Other Side: The Vietnamese Communists' Perspective* (New York: RoutledgeCurzon, 2002), 20.

15. Carlyle A. Thayer, *War by Other Means: National Liberation and Revolution in Viet-Nam, 1954–60* (Cambridge, Mass.: Unwin Hyman, 1989), 111; Ang Cheng Guan, *Vietnamese War from the Other Side*, 21.

16. Vien nghien cuu chu nghia Mac-Lenin va tu tuong Ho Chi Minh, *Lich su Dang Cong san Viet Nam, Tap 2: 1954–1975* [History of the Communist Party of Vietnam, Volume 2: 1954–1975] (Hanoi: Nha xuat ban Chinh tri quoc gia, 1995), 94, 96.

17. Lien-Hang T. Nguyen, *Hanoi's War: An International History of the War for Peace in Vietnam* (Chapel Hill: University of North Carolina Press, 2012), 32.

18. Commonwealth Secretariat, "Vietnam: Background Paper," September 1967, R219-121-3-E [Part 3], Vol. 9523, RG 25, LAC, 17.

19. Ang Cheng Guan, *Vietnamese War from the Other Side*, 24; Ilya V. Gaiduk, *Confronting Vietnam: Soviet Policy toward the Indochina Conflict, 1954–1963* (Washington, D.C.: Woodrow Wilson Center Press, 2003), 101.

20. British Consulate General, Hanoi [hereafter BCGH], to Foreign Office, London [hereafter FO], 3 March 1958, FO 371/136118, NAUK, 2.

21. "Summary of Events in North Vietnam (DRV) during July 1958," undated [August 1958?], FO 371/136119, NAUK, 2.

22. Pham Van Dong letter to Ngo Dinh Diem, 7 March 1958, #312, AO: Vietnam Conflit, ADF, 3.

23. French Embassy, Saigon, to Ministry of Foreign Affairs, Paris [hereafter MFA], 30 April 1958, #312, AO: VN, ADF, 3.

24. Trung tam Khoa hoc xa hoi va nhan van quoc gia—Vien su hoc, *Lich su Viet Nam, 1954–1965* [History of Vietnam, 1954–1965] (Hanoi: Nha xuat ban Khoa hoc xa hoi, 1995), 13; BCGH to FO, 2 May 1958, FO 371/136118, NAUK, 3.

25. Vien nghien cuu chu nghia Mac-Lenin, *Lich su Dang Cong san Viet Nam*, 79.

26. "Bao cao ve nhiem vu ke hoach ba nam (1958–1960) phat trien va cai tao kinh te quoc dan" [Report on the Responsibilities of the Three-Year Plan (1958–1969) of Development and Improvement of the People's Economy], in Dang Cong san Viet Nam, *Van kien Dang—Toan tap*, Tap 19: 1958 [Party Documents—Complete Series, Vol. 19: 1958] (Hanoi: Nha xuat ban Chinh tri quoc gia, 2002) [hereafter *VKD*: 1958], 451–524.

27. Céline Marangé, *Le communisme vietnamien, 1919–1991* [Vietnamese Communism, 1919–1991] (Paris: Presses de Sciences Po, 2012), 284.

28. Quoted in "Minutes," 20 August 1958, FO 371/136119, NAUK, 2.

29. "Bao cao ve nhiem vu ke hoach ba nam (1958–1960)," 451–524.

30. Tran Van Dinh, ed., *This Nation and Socialism Are One: Selected Writings of Le Duan, First Secretary, Central Committee, Vietnamese Workers' Party* (Chicago: Vanguard Books, 1976), 10.

31. Duiker, *Ho Chi Minh*, 506.

32. Trinh's remarks are reported in BCGH to Southeast Asia Division, London [hereafter SEAD], 21 December 1958, FO 371/144390, NAUK, 1.

33. Chen Jian, *Mao's China and the Cold War* (Chapel Hill: University of North Carolina Press, 2001), 75.

34. British Embassy, Saigon [hereafter BES], to FO, "Review of Events in North Vietnam (the D.R.V.) during 1961," 31 January 1962, FO 371/166697, NAUK, 5.

35. "The VWP and the International Communist Movement," Folder 08, Box 02, Douglas Pike Collection [hereafter DPC]: Unit 13—The Early History of Vietnam, Vietnam Archive at Texas Tech University [hereafter VATTU], 14–15.

36. Ibid.

37. French General Delegation, Hanoi [hereafter FGDH], to MFA, 28 April 1960, #31, AO: VN, ADF, 7.

38. Nguyen Dang Vinh, Dang Viet Thuy, and Le Ngoc Tu, eds., *Viet Nam: 30 nam chien tranh gia phong va bao ve To quoc, 1945–1975—Bien nien su kien* [Vietnam: 30 Years of War for Liberation and Protection of the Fatherland, 1945–1975—Annals of Events] (Hanoi: Nha xuat ban Quan doi nhan dan, 2005), 243.

39. Le Mau Han, *Dang Cong san Viet Nam: Cac Dai hoi va Hoi nghi Trung uong* [The Vietnamese Communist Party: Congresses and Plenums] (Hanoi: Nha xuat ban Chinh tri quoc gia, 1995), 65. On the situation facing the southern revolution at that juncture, see "Nghi quyet Hoi nghi Xu uy Nam Bo lan thu tu, thang 11–1959" [Resolution of the Fourth Plenum of the Nam Bo Executive Committee, November 1959], in Dang Cong san Viet Nam, *Van kien Dang—Toan tap*, Tap 20: 1959 [Party Documents—Complete Series, Vol. 20: 1959] (Hanoi: Nha xuat ban Chinh tri quoc gia, 2002) [hereafter *VKD: 1959*], 977–80; and Brigham, *Guerrilla Diplomacy*, 9–10.

40. Vo Chi Cong, *Tren nhung chang duong cach mang* [On the Revolutionary Paths] (Hanoi: Nha xuat ban Chinh tri quoc gia, 2001), 148–52.

41. "Bao cao cua Bo Chinh tri tai Hoi nghi Ban chap hanh Trung uong lan thu 15 (mo rong), hop tu ngay 12 den 22-1-1959: Ve tinh hinh mien Nam" [Report of the Politburo at the Fifteenth Plenum (expanded) of the Central Committee, Meeting from 12 to 22 January 1959: On the Southern Situation], in *VKD: 1959*, 1–56.

42. "Nghi quyet Hoi nghi Trung uong lan thu 15 (mo rong): Ve tang cuong doan ket, kien quyet dau tranh giu vung hoa binh, thuc hien thong nhat nuoc nha" [Resolution of the Fifteenth Plenum (expanded): On Increasing Unity and Determination to Struggle to Preserve Peace and Achieve Unification of the State], in *VKD: 1959*, 57–92.

43. Kenneth Lieberthal, *Governing China: From Revolution through Reform* (New York: W. W. Norton, 2004), 75.

44. "Nghi quyet Hoi nghi Trung uong lan thu 15," 75.
45. "Bao cao cua Bo Chinh tri tai Hoi nghi Ban chap hang Trung uong lan thu 15 (mo rong)," 37–41.
46. "Nghi quyet Hoi nghi Trung uong lan thu 15," 81.
47. "Summary of Events in North Vietnam (DRV) for April 1959," May 1959, FO 371/144390, NAUK, 2.
48. "History of the NLF, 1954–63" [CRIMP Document], undated, Folder 03, Box 01, DPC: Unit 05—National Liberation Front, VATTU, 5.
49. Quoted in Le Hong Linh, *Cuoc dong khoi ky dieu o mien Nam Viet Nam 1959–1960* [Wonderful Uprising in Southern Vietnam, 1959–1960] (Da Nang: Nha xuat ban Da Nang, 2006), 259.
50. Quoted in ibid.; *Theo mien Dong Nam Bo khang chien, Tap 3* [Following the Resistance in Eastern Nam Bo, Volume 3] (Hanoi: Nha xuat ban Quan doi nhan dan, 1993), 69.
51. Nguyen Thi Dinh, *No Other Road to Take: Memoirs of Mrs. Nguyen Thi Dinh*, Cornell Southeast Asia Program Data Paper 102 (Ithaca, N.Y.: Cornell Southeast Asia Program, 1976), 61.
52. "Nghi quyet Hoi nghi Trung uong lan thu 15," 64.
53. Ibid.; Vien nghien cuu chu nghia Mac-Lenin, *Lich su Dang Cong san Viet Nam*, 101.
54. Nguyen Manh Hung, "The Vietnam War in Retrospect: Its Nature and Some Lessons," in Lawrence E. Grinter and Peter M. Dunn, eds., *The American War in Vietnam: Lessons, Legacies, and Implications for Future Conflicts* (New York: Greenwood Press, 1987), 15–25.
55. Philippe Devillers, "La lutte pour la réunification du Viêt Nam entre 1954 et 1961" [The Struggle for Reunification in Vietnam between 1954 and 1961], in Jean Chesneaux, Georges Boudarel, and Daniel Hémery, eds., *Tradition et révolution au Viêt Nam* [Tradition and Revolution in Vietnam] (Paris: Éditions Anthropos, 1971), 350.
56. Nguyen Thi Dinh, *No Other Road to Take*, 62–63.
57. George McT. Kahin and John Lewis, *The United States in Vietnam* (New York: Dial Press, 1969), 120.
58. Sophie Quinn-Judge, "The Ideological Debate in the DRV and the Significance of the Anti-Party Affair, 1967–68," *Cold War History* 5, no. 4 (November–December 2005): 487.
59. "Nghi quyet Hoi nghi Trung uong lan thu 15," 64.
60. Vien nghien cuu chu nghia Mac-Lenin va tu tuong Ho Chi Minh, *Lich su Dang Cong san Viet Nam*, 101.
61. "Factions within the North Vietnamese Regime: Their Bearing, If Any, on Policy Pursued towards South Vietnam," undated [1960], FO 371/160122, NAUK, 1.
62. On the specifics of the incident, see Ang Cheng Guan, "The Huong Lap and Phu Loi Incidents, and the Decision to Resume Armed Struggle in South Vietnam," *War and Society* 15, no. 1 (May 1997): 3–22.
63. "Summary of Events in North Vietnam (DRV) for January 1959," undated [February 1959], FO 371/144390, NAUK, 1.
64. Marangé, *Le communisme vietnamien*, 286.
65. "History of the NLF, 1954–63," 5.

66. "Chi thi cua Bo Chinh tri, thang 3-1959: Ve nhiem vu xay dung can cu cach mang Tay Nguyen" [Politburo Instruction, March 1959: On the Task of Building the Tay Nguyen Revolutionary Base], in *VKD: 1959*, 245-59.

67. The response of DRVN authorities to the second Taiwan Strait crisis is detailed in "Review of Events in North Vietnam (DRV) during September 1958," 7 October 1958, FO 371/136119, NAUK, 3. On 4 September 1958, during the crisis, Beijing issued a declaration on China's territorial sea, stating that its "breadth . . . shall be twelve nautical miles," eventually the international standard. The declaration made repeated references to Taiwan and mentioned the Jinmen (Quemoy) and Mazu (Matsu) Islands, as it was intended to reinforce Beijing's claim over these territories, "still occupied by the United States armed forces" ("Declaration on China's Territorial Sea," 4 September 1958, reproduced in United States Department of State, *Limits in the Seas: Straight Baselines—People's Republic of China*, no. 43 [1 July 1972], 2-3). Ten days later, DRVN prime minister Pham Van Dong sent his PRC counterpart, Zhou Enlai, a note stating that his government "recognizes [ton trong]" Beijing's declaration. In light of the ongoing crisis, the DRVN's concerns about the separatist regime in Saigon abetted by Washington, and Hanoi's reliance on Beijing for economic and other aid, the note was an exercise in diplomatic propriety more than anything else. In subsequent years, however, it would haunt Vietnamese communist authorities. As Beijing and Hanoi, among other governments, began to tussle over control of two archipelagos in the South China or Eastern Sea, the Spartlys (Nansha) and the Paracels (Hsisha/Xisha), which had also been mentioned in the Chinese declaration of 4 September 1958, Chinese authorities used Dong's 1958 note as evidence that Hanoi had renounced its sovereignty over those islands. On this, see also the comments by historian Balazs Szalontai at www.bbc.co.uk/vietnamese/vietnam/story/2008/01/080124_vietnamchinaphamvandong.shtml.

68. Hoang Trang, *Toan dan doan ket chong My, cuu nuoc duoi ngon co tu tuong Ho Chi Minh, 1954-1975* [The Entire People Unites against the United States for National Salvation under the Banner of Ho Chi Minh Thought] (Hanoi: Nha xuat ban Chinh tri quoc gia, 2005), 90.

69. Jean Lacouture, "Viet Cong," undated, Folder 14, Box 04, DPC: Unit 02—Military Operations, VATTU, 3.

70. Ang Cheng Guan, "Southeast Asian Perceptions of the Domino Theory," in Christopher E. Goscha and Christian Ostermann, eds., *Connecting Histories: The Cold War and Decolonization in Asia, 1945-1962* (Stanford, Calif.: Stanford University Press, 2009), 311-12.

71. "History of the NLF, 1954-63," 9.

72. Le Hong Linh, *Cuoc dong khoi*, 269.

73. "Chi thi cua Ban Bi thu gui X.U.N.B., ngay 7-5-1959" [Secretariat Instruction to the Nam Bo Executive Committee, 7 May 1959], in *VKD: 1959*, 515.

74. Thayer, *War by Other Means*, 185.

75. "Nghi quyet Hoi nghi Trung uong lan thu 15," 84.

76. David W. P. Elliott, *The Vietnamese War: Revolution and Social Change in the Mekong Delta, 1930-1975*, concise ed. (Armonk, N.Y.: M. E. Sharpe, 2007), 166.

77. Thayer, *War by Other Means*, 185.

78. William R. Andrews, *The Village War: Vietnamese Communist Revolutionary Activity in Dinh Truong Province, 1960-64* (Columbia: University of Missouri Press, 1973), 33.

79. Vien nghien cuu chu nghia Mac-Lenin va tu tuong Ho Chi Minh, *Lich su Dang Cong san Viet Nam,* 104.

80. "History of the NLF, 1954–63," 6.

81. Bui Kim Dinh, "Tim hieu nguyen nhan cuoc dung dau lich su o Viet Nam (1954–1975)" [Understanding the Cause of Historical Encounters in Vietnam, 1954–1975], *Tap chi Lich su Dang* [Journal of Party History], no. 186 (May 2006): 68.

82. Tai Sung An, "Hanoi's 15th Plenum Resolution—May 1959," Folder 010, Box 30, DPC: Unit 05—National Liberation Front, VATTU, 277 (emphasis in original).

83. Quoted in French Legation, Hungary, to MFA, 1 April 1959, #31, AO: VN, ADF, 4.

84. Tran Quoc Tu, "Peace and Revolution," *Hoc tap* (January 1964). Reproduced and translated in Folder 03, Box 25, DPC: Unit 06—Democratic Republic of Vietnam, VATTU, 11.

85. BCGH to SEAD, 30 April 1959, FO 371/144390, NAUK, 1.

86. "Summary of Events in North Vietnam (DRV) for May 1959," undated [June 1959], FO 371/144390, NAUK, 1.

87. "Summary of Events in the Democratic Republic of Vietnam for March 1959," April 1959, FO 371/144390, NAUK, 1; and "Summary of Events in North Vietnam (DRV) for April 1959," May 1959, FO 371/144390, NAUK, 1. By one account, within a year of the promulgation of currency reform in February 1959, "those few bourgeois who in 1958 still lived in relative comfort" were now "reduced to the common level." "It is remarkable how uniform is the apparent level of existence" in parts of the DRVN, the account concluded (BCGH to FO, 11 April 1960, FO 371/152746, NAUK, 1).

88. William S. Turley, "Civil-Military Relations in North Vietnam," *Asian Survey* 9, no. 12 (December 1969): 885–86.

89. "Summary of Events in North Vietnam (DRV) for February 1959," undated [March 1959], FO 371/144390, NAUK, 1; Turley, "Civil-Military Relations," 886.

90. "Chi thi cua Ban Bi thu, so 146-CT/TW, ngay 4-7-1959: Ve ke hoach chinh huan can bo, dang vien" [Secretariat Instruction, no. 146-CT/TW, 4 July 1959: On the Plan to Re-educate Cadres, Party Members], in *VKD:* 1959, 573–85.

91. Vien nghien cuu chu nghia Mac-Lenin va tu tuong Ho Chi Minh, *Lich su Dang Cong san Viet Nam,* 98n1.

92. Nguyen Dinh Binh, ed., *Ngoai giao Viet Nam, 1945–2000* [Vietnamese Diplomacy, 1945–2000] (Hanoi: Nha xuat ban Chinh tri quoc gia, 2005), 170–71.

93. "Chi thi cua Ban Bi thu, so 146-CT/TW," 573–85.

94. Douglas Pike, "Basic Causes of the Vietnam War," Folder 010, Box 30, DPC: Unit 05—National Liberation Front, VATTU, 9.

95. BES to BCGH, 21 October 1960, FO 371/152747, NAUK, 1.

96. FGDH to MFA, 22 October 1959, #17, AO: VN, ADF, 2.

97. Tai Sung An, "Hanoi's 15th Plenum Resolution," 283.

98. Economic Attaché, FGDH to Ministry of Finance and Economic Affairs, Paris, 16 March 1959, #35, AO: VN, ADF, 5; "Vietnam—Annual Report for 1959" (BES to FO), 27 January 1960, FO 371/152737, NAUK, 12.

99. Marangé, *Le communisme vietnamien,* 286.

100. Nguyen Vu Tung, "The 1961–1962 Geneva Conference: Neutralization of Laos and Policy Implications for Vietnam," paper presented at "Indochina between the Two

Geneva Accords (1954–1962): The Failure of Peace?," Université du Québec à Montréal, Canada, 6–7 October 2006, 2–3. The paper was published as Nguyen Vu Tung, "The 1961–1962 Geneva Conference: Neutralization of Laos and Policy Implications for Vietnam," in Christopher E. Goscha and Karine Laplante, eds., L'échec de la paix en Indochine / The Failure of Peace in Indochina (1954–1962) (Paris: Les Indes savantes, 2010), 255–68.

101. Hoc vien Chinh tri quoc gia Ho Chi Minh—Khoa lich su Dang, Lich su Dang Cong san Viet Nam, Tap 1 [History of the Communist Party of Vietnam, Volume 1] (Hanoi: Nha xuat ban Chinh tri quoc gia, 1997), 153; and Bo Quoc phong—Vien lich su Quan su Viet Nam, Lich su khang chien chong My cuu nuoc, 1954–1975, Tap 2 [History of the Anti-American Resistance for National Salvation 1954–1975, Vol. 2] (Hanoi: Nha xuat ban Chinh tri quoc gia, 1996), 224–36.

102. Bui Kim Dinh, "Tim hieu nguyen nhan," 68.

103. King C. Chen, "Hanoi's Three Decisions and the Escalation of the Vietnam War," Political Science Quarterly 90, no. 2 (Summer 1975): 257.

104. "Danh sac can bo di B trong nam 1961" [List of Cadres Who Went South in 1961], undated, Ho so 876, Danh sac can bo di B trong nam 1961, Phong Uy ban Thong nhat Nha nuoc, Vietnam National Archives Center 3, Hanoi [hereafter VNAC3].

105. Canadian Delegation [ICSC], Saigon, to Under Secretary of State for External Affairs, Ottawa, 19 January 1966, 20-22-VIET S-1, Vol. 9387 [Part 3], RG 25, LAC, 1.

106. "Danh sac can bo di B trong nam 1961."

107. On the sea infiltration route, see Christopher E. Goscha, "The Maritime Nature of the Wars for Vietnam, 1945–75: A Geo-Historical Reflection," War and Society 24, no. 2 (November 2005): 53–92.

108. Thayer, War by Other Means, 185.

109. Turley, Second Indochina War, 39, 80.

110. Lien-Hang T. Nguyen, "Between the Storms: An International History of the Second Indochina War, 1968–1973" (PhD diss., Yale University, 2008), 13, 31.

111. Turley, Second Indochina War, 41.

112. Logevall, Embers of War, 690.

113. Elliott, Vietnamese War, 119.

114. Lien-Hang T. Nguyen, Hanoi's War, 59.

115. Zhihua Shen and Danhui Li, After Leaning to One Side: China and Its Allies in the Cold War (Washington, D.C.: Woodrow Wilson Center Press, 2011), 24–26.

116. The quoted passage is from Lien-Hang T. Nguyen, Hanoi's War, 59.

117. Logevall, Embers of War, 691.

118. Ang Cheng Guan, "Southeast Asian Perceptions of the Domino Theory," 312.

119. "Bao cao tai Hoi nghi Ban chap hanh Trung uong lan thu 16 (mo rong), hop ngay 16 den 30–4 va ngay 1 den ngay 10-6-1959: Kien quyet dua nong thon mien Bac nuoc ta qua con duong hop tac hoa nong nghiep tien len chu nghia xa hoi" [Report to the Sixteenth Plenum (expanded) of the Central Committee, Meeting 16–30 April and 1–10 June [sic] 1959: Resolutely Guiding the Peasants in the North of Our Country on the Path to Agricultural Collectivization to Advance Socialism], in VKD: 1959, 290, 295, 356.

120. "Nghi quyet cua Hoi nghi trung uong lan thu 16 (mo rong), thang 4, nam 1959: Ve van de hop tac hoa nong nghiep" [Resolution of the Sixteenth Plenum (expanded) of the

Central Committee, April 1959: On the Issue of Agricultural Collectivization], in *VKD: 1959*, 394.

121. BCGH to SEAD, 26 June 1959, FO 371/144390, NAUK, 1–2.
122. "Vietnam—Annual Report for 1959," 13.
123. BCGH to SEAD, 3 September 1959, FO 371/144390, NAUK, 1.
124. "Vietnam—Annual Report for 1959," 11, 16.
125. BCGH to SEAD, 25 July 1959, FO 371/144390, NAUK, 1.
126. BCGH to SEAD, 21 July 1959, FO 371/144390, NAUK, 1.
127. Quoted in ibid., 2.
128. "Bao cao cua Lien khu uy V, thang 11–1959: Ve tinh hinh Lien khu V" [Report by Interzone V, November 1959: On the Situation in Interzone V], in *VKD: 1959*, 1022.
129. Nguyen Thi Dinh, *No Other Road to Take*, 62.
130. Bo Quoc phong—Vien Lich su quan su Viet Nam, *Lich su quan su Viet Nam, Tap 11*, 101.
131. Bernard Fall, *Vietnam Witness* (New York: Praeger, 1966), 239.
132. Douglas Pike, *Viet Cong: The Organization and Techniques of the National Liberation Front of South Vietnam* (Cambridge: Massachusetts Institute of Technology Press, 1966), 102.
133. Quoted in Andrews, *Village War*, 55–56.
134. FGDH to MFA, 14 January 1960, #33, AO: VN, ADF, 2.
135. Gabriel Kolko, *Anatomy of a War: Vietnam, the United States, and the Modern Historical Experience* (New York: Pantheon Books, 1985), 97, 103. See also Kahin and Lewis, *United States in Vietnam*, 120; and David Hunt, *Vietnam's Southern Revolution: From Insurrection to Total War* (Amherst: University of Massachusetts Press, 2008), 56.
136. Bo Quoc phong—Vien Lich su quan su Viet Nam, *Lich su quan su Viet Nam, Tap 11: Cuoc khang chien chong My, cuu nuoc, 1954–1975* [Military History of Vietnam, Volume 11: The Anti-American Resistance for National Salvation] (Hanoi: Nha xuat ban Chinh tri quoc gia, 2005), 100; and Diep Dinh Hoa, "Khoi nghia Vinh Thanh (6-2-1959)" [The Vinh Thanh Uprising, 6 February 1962], *Nghien cuu Lich su* [Historical Studies], no. 326 (January 2003): 35–48.
137. Le Hong Linh, *Cuoc dong khoi*, 259–60.
138. Elliott, *Vietnamese War*, 118–19.
139. "History of the NLF, 1954–63," 15.
140. Jeffrey Race, *War Comes to Long An: Revolutionary Conflict in a Vietnamese Province* (Berkeley: University of California Press, 1972), 114.
141. "History of the NLF, 1954–63," 14, 21.
142. "Problems—Deviant Ideas and Mistaken Notions Which Must Be Promptly Corrected and Resolved," *Hoc tap* (August 1960). Reproduced and translated in Folder 16, Box 04, United States Department of State Collection, VATTU, 5.
143. Turley, *Second Indochina War*, 43.
144. Portions of the text of Law 10/59 and an official interpretation of its application are reproduced in Marvin E. Gettleman et al., eds., *Vietnam and America: A Documented History* (New York: Grove Press, 1995), 156–60.
145. "Vietnam—Annual Report for 1959," 2.
146. Vien nghien cuu chu nghia Mac-Lenin va tu tuong Ho Chi Minh, *Lich su Dang Cong san Viet Nam*, 98.

147. "De cuong bai noi chuyen ve cuoc dong khoi nam 1960 cua tinh uy Ben-tre" [Outline of Speech on the 1960 General Uprising by the Ben Tre Provincial Committee], undated, Ho so 233: De cuong bai noi chuyen ve cuoc dong khoi nam 1960 cua tinh uy Ben-tre, Phong Uy ban dieu tra toi ac cua de quoc My o Viet Nam, VNAC3, 4, 6.

148. The resolution is reproduced as "Nghi quyet Hoi nghi Xu uy Nam Bo lan thu tu, thang 11–1959" [Resolution of the Fourth Plenum of the Nam Bo Executive Committee], in *VKD: 1959*, 977–1006.

3. TREADING CAUTIOUSLY, 1960

1. Vien nghien cuu chu nghia Mac-Lenin va tu tuong Ho Chi Minh, *Lich su Dang Cong san Viet Nam, Tap 2: 1954–1975* [History of the Communist Party of Vietnam, Volume 2: 1954–1975] (Hanoi: Nha xuat ban Chinh tri quoc gia, 1995), 106.

2. "De cuong bai noi chuyen ve cuoc dong khoi nam 1960 cua tinh uy Ben-tre" [Outline of Speech on the 1960 Uprising by the Ben Tre Provincial Comittee], undated [March 1976?], Ho so 233: De cuong bai noi chuyen ve cuoc dong khoi nam 1960 cua tinh uy Ben-tre, Phong Uy ban dieu tra toi ac cua de quoc My o Viet Nam, Vietnam National Archives Center 3, Hanoi [hereafter VNAC3], 4, 6. A recent and insightful account of the important role of women in the uprising is *Ben Tre Dong khoi va Doi quan toc dai* [The Ben Tre Uprising and the Long-Haired Army] (Hanoi: Nha xuat ban Phu nu, 2009).

3. Nguyen Thi Dinh, *No Other Road to Take: Memoirs of Mrs. Nguyen Thi Dinh*, Cornell Southeast Asia Program Data Paper 102 (Ithaca, N.Y.: Cornell Southeast Asia Program, 1976), 62–63.

4. *An Outline History of the Vietnam Workers' Party, 1930–1975*, 2nd ed. (Hanoi: Foreign Languages Publishing House, 1978), 101.

5. Vo Thi Hoa, "Dang bo Tay Ninh van dong dong bao theo dao Cao Dai tham gia khang chien chong My, cuu nuoc" [The Tay Ninh Party Committee's Activities regarding the Participation of Cao Dai Compatriots in the Anti-American Resistance for National Salvation], *Tap chi Lich su Dang* [Journal of Party History], no. 185 (April 2006): 57–58.

6. "History of the NLF, 1954–63" [CRIMP Document], undated, Folder 03, Box 01, Douglas Pike Collection [hereafter DPC]: Unit 05—National Liberation Front, Vietnam Archive at Texas Tech University [hereafter VATTU], 14.

7. Fredrik Logevall, *Embers of War: The Fall of an Empire and the Making of America's Vietnam* (New York: Random House, 2012), 698.

8. Vien nghien cuu chu nghia Mac-Lenin va tu tuong Ho Chi Minh, *Lich su Dang Cong san Viet Nam*, 110.

9. Han Van Tam, "Nghi thuat gianh thang loi tung buoc ket hop voi nhung thang loi quyet dinh trong khang chien chong My, cuu nuoc" [The Art of Gaining Gradual Victory in Combination with Decisive Victory in the Anti-American Resistance for National Salvation], *Tap chi Lich su quan su* [Journal of Military History], no. 171 (March 2006): 9.

10. On that program, see Edward Miller, *Misalliance: Ngo Dinh Diem, the United States, and the Fate of South Vietnam* (Cambridge, Mass.: Harvard University Press, 2013), 177–84.

11. "Dien van be mac cua Ton Duc Thang, Truong ban Thuong truc Quoc hoi" [Closing Address by Ton Duc Thang, Chair of the Standing Committee of the National Assembly],

15 April 1960, Ho so 64: Ho so ky hop thuc 12 QH khoa I, tu ngay 11–15.4.1960. Tap 3: Phien hop ngay 15.4.1960: Chuyet trinh, tham luan Nghi quyet ve ke hoach va ngan sach Nha nuoc nam 1960, Luat Nghia vu Quan su, that bai cua che do Diem, Phong Quoc hoi, VNAC3, 2.

12. "Thuyet trinh cua Tieu ban nghien cuu du luat Nghia vu quan su" [Presentation by the Sub-Committee for Research on the Military Service Law], 15 April 1960, Ho so 64: Ho so ky hop thuc 12 QH khoa I, tu ngay 11–15.4.1960. Tap 3: Phien hop ngay 15.4.1960: Chuyet trinh, tham luan Nghi quyet ve ke hoach va ngan sach Nha nuoc nam 1960, Luat Nghia vu Quan su, that bai cua che do Diem, Phong Quoc hoi, VNAC3, 2.

13. "Dien van be mac cua Ton Duc Thang, Truong ban Thuong truc Quoc hoi," 2.

14. "Dien mat cua Trung uong Dang, so 160, ngay 28, thang 4, nam 1960: Gui xu uy Nam Bo" [Secret Party Center Cable, no. 160, 28 April 1960: Sent to Nam Bo Executive Committee], in Dang Cong san Viet Nam, *Van kien Dang—Toan tap,* Tap 21: 1960 [Party Documents—Complete Series, Vol. 21: 1960] (Hanoi: Nha xuat ban Chinh tri quoc gia, 2002) [hereafter *VKD:* 1960], 289, 293.

15. Philippe Devillers, "La lutte pour la réunification du Viêt Nam entre 1954 et 1961," in Jean Chesneaux, Georges Boudarel, and Daniel Hémery, eds., *Tradition et révolution au Viêt Nam* [Tradition and Revolution in Vietnam] (Paris: Éditions Anthropos, 1971), 346.

16. "Tham luan: Hoan toan dong y voi du an ke hoach Nha nuoc nam 1960 va y rieng ve tinh hinh mien Nam, Pham Van Bach, Ben tre ve" [Address: Complete Agreement with Draft State Plan for 1960 and Personal Opinions about the Situation in the South, Pham Van Bach, Ben Tre], 15 April 1960, Ho so 64: Ho so ky hop thuc 12 QH khoa I, tu ngay 11–15.4.1960. Tap 3: Phien hop ngay 15.4.1960: Chuyet trinh, tham luan Nghi quyet ve ke hoach va ngan sach Nha nuoc nam 1960, Luat Nghia vu Quan su, that bai cua che do Diem, Phong Quoc hoi, VNAC3, 2.

17. "Nghi quyet Hoi nghi Lien khu uy V (mo rong), ngay 4-5-1960" [Resolution of the Plenum (expanded) of the Interzone V Executive Committee, 4 May 1960], in *VKD:* 1960, 1095–1127.

18. Khuat Bien Hoa, *Dai tuong Le Duc Anh* [General Le Duc Anh] (Hanoi: Nha xuat ban Quan doi nhan dan, 2005), 61–62. Still, the southern fighters considered the weapons they had to be "priceless."

19. "Nghi quyet Hoi nghi Xu uy Nam Bo lan thu V, thang 7 nam 1960" [Resolution of the Fifth Plenum of the Nam Bo Executive Committee, July 1960], in *VKD:* 1960, 1059–94.

20. French General Delegation, Hanoi [hereafter FGDH], to Ministry of Foreign Affairs, Paris [hereafter MFA], 2 May 1960, #44, Asie-Océanie [hereafter AO]: Vietnam Conflict [hereafter VC], Archives Diplomatiques de France, La Courneuve [hereafter ADF], 2, 4.

21. From a Sino-Vietnamese communiqué quoted in FGDH to MFA, 16 May 1960, #37, AO: Vietnam Nord [hereafter VN], ADF, 8.

22. From Pham Van Dong's comments to a French diplomat quoted in ibid., 9. The DRVN government expressed its belief that the Paris summit would enhance the prospects for a permanent détente between the capitalist and socialist camps on the occasion of May Day 1960. See FGDH to MFA, 5 May 1960, #17, AO: VN, ADF, 2. According to a French assessment, through the first part of the year Hanoi "refrained from questioning the good faith and will of President Eisenhower to achieve a peaceful coexistence between East and West." The summit's failure, however, "had a profound echo in the country." Most notably, it provoked "violent attacks" on the United States in the local press as it "proved" to DRVN

authorities that "the Americans are preparing a war of aggression in Asia" (FGDH to MFA, 23 May 1960, #31, AO: VN, ADF, 2, 7).

23. FGDH to MFA, 16 July 1960, #33, AO: VN, ADF, 7.

24. FGDH to MFA, 12 September 1960, #37, AO: VN, ADF, 1.

25. British Consulate General, Hanoi [hereafter BCGH], to Southeast Asia Department, London [hereafter SEAD], 31 October 1960, FO 371/152747, National Archives of the United Kingdom, Kew [hereafter NAUK], 3.

26. The editorial is reproduced in FGDH to MFA, 26 November 1960, #16, AO: VN, ADF.

27. BCGH to Foreign Office, London [hereafter FO], 11 April 1960, FO 371/152746, NAUK, 2.

28. On the origins and development of the dispute, see Odd Arne Westad, ed., *Brothers in Arms: The Rise and Fall of the Sino-Soviet Alliance, 1945–1963* (Washington, D.C.: Woodrow Wilson Center Press, 1998); Sergei Radchenko, *Two Suns in the Heavens: The Sino-Soviet Struggle for Supremacy, 1962–1967* (Stanford, Calif.: Stanford University Press, 2009); and Lorenz Lüthi, *The Sino-Soviet Split, 1956–1966* (Princeton, N.J.: Princeton University Press, 2008).

29. FGDH to MFA, 28 April 1960, 12–13, 15–16.

30. Quoted in FGDH to MFA, 25 July 1960, #35, AO: VN, ADF, 1.

31. FGDH to MFA, 16 July 1960, 2; FGDH to MFA, 16 August 1960, #37, AO: VN, ADF, 2; FGDH to MFA, 12 September 1960, #37, AO: VN, ADF, 2–3; FGDH to MFA, 2 November 1960, #35, AO: VN, ADF, 1.

32. FGDH to MFA, 16 July 1960, 7–8, 22–23.

33. BCGH to FO, 4 August 1960, FO 371/152746, NAUK, 4; "Factions within the North Vietnamese Regime: Their Bearing, If Any, on Policy Pursued toward South Vietnam," undated [1960], FO 371/160122, NAUK, 1–2; British Embassy, Bangkok to FO, 29 August 1960, FO 371/152747, NAUK, 1.

34. FGDH to MFA, 18 July 1960, #44, AO: VC, ADF, 1–2.

35. French Embassy, Ottawa to MFA, 17 September 1960, #44, AO: VC, ADF, 1.

36. Quoted in Ilya Gaiduk, "Containing the Warriors: Soviet Policy toward the Indochina Conflict, 1960–65," in Lloyd C. Gardner and Ted Gittinger, eds., *International Perspectives on Vietnam* (College Station: Texas A&M University Press, 2000), 63.

37. Quoted in Ilya V. Gaiduk, *Confronting Vietnam: Soviet Policy toward the Indochina Conflict, 1954–1963* (Washington, D.C.: Woodrow Wilson Center Press, 2003), 112.

38. Gaiduk, "Containing the Warriors," 63.

39. Quoted in Gaiduk, *Confronting Vietnam*, 105.

40. Beijing pressed for economic development in the DRVN also in hope that the Vietnamese would achieve autarky. Its promotion of autarky in Vietnam and elsewhere was an explicit rejection of the CPSU policy of socialist economic interdependence characterized by "economic specialization, long-term plan co-ordination and division of labor" within the socialist bloc. This divergence of views fueled the Sino-Soviet dispute. See Donald S. Zagoria, "Khrushchev's Attack on Albania and Sino-Soviet Relations," *China Quarterly*, no. 8 (October–December 1961): 11.

41. Qiang Zhai, *China and the Vietnam Wars, 1950–1975* (Chapel Hill: University of North Carolina Press, 2000), 82–83.

42. Khuat Bien Hoa, *Dai tuong Le Duc Anh*, 60.
43. Qiang Zhai, *China and the Vietnam Wars*, 84–85.
44. FGDH to MFA, 6 October 1960, #37, AO: VN, ADF, 2–3.
45. Jay Tao, "Mao's World Outlook: Vietnam and the Revolution in China," *Asian Survey* 8, no. 5 (May 1968): 417.
46. Aleksandr Fursenko and Timothy Naftali, *Khrushchev's Cold War: The Inside Story of an American Adversary* (New York: W. W. Norton, 2006), 328; Robert Service, *Comrades! A History of World Communism* (Cambridge, Mass.: Harvard University Press, 2007), 320. Most of the articles in the Chinese press actually criticized Tito and Yugoslavia but were clearly intended as denunciations of Khrushchev's and the CPSU's "deviations." See Zhihua Shen and Danhui Li, *After Leaning to One Side: China and Its Allies in the Cold War* (Washington, D.C.: Woodrow Wilson Center Press, 2011), 164–65.
47. Chen Jian, "A Crucial Step toward the Breakdown of the Sino-Soviet Alliance: The Withdrawal of Soviet Experts from China in July 1960," *Cold War International History Project Bulletin*, nos. 8–9 (Winter 1996–97): 246, 249–50; Xiaoming Zhang, "Communist Powers Divided: China, the Soviet Union, and the Vietnam War," in Gardner and Gittinger, eds., *International Perspectives on Vietnam*, 82.
48. FGDH to MFA, 28 April 1960, 11.
49. BCGH to BES, 13 December 1960, FO 371/152747, NAUK, 1.
50. "Resolution of the Third National Congress of the Viet Nam Workers' Party on the Tasks and Line of the Party in the New Stage," in *Third National Congress of the Viet Nam Workers' Party: Documents, Volume 1* (Hanoi: Foreign Languages Publishing House, undated), 235.
51. "Loi phat bieu cua Ho Chu tich" [Speech by President Ho], 15 April 1961, Ho so 64: Ho so ky hop thuc 12 QH khoa I, tu ngay 11–15.4.1960. Tap 3: Phien hop ngay 15.4.1960: Chuyet trinh, tham luan Nghi quyet ve ke hoach va ngan sach Nha nuoc nam 1960, Luat Nghia vu Quan su, that bai cua che do Diem, Phong Quoc hoi, VNAC3, 2.
52. "Chi thi cua Ban Bi thu, so 26-CT/TW, ngay 15 thang 9 nam 1961: Ve viec tich cuc cong tac giup do cach mang mien Nam" [Secretariat Instruction, no. 26-CT/TW, 15 September 1961: On the Effort to Actively Help the Southern Revolution], in Dang Cong san Viet Nam, *Van kien Dang—Toan tap*, Tap 22: 1961 [Party Documents—Collected Works, Vol. 22: 1961] (Hanoi: Nha xuat ban Chinh tri quoc gia, 2002), 472–74.
53. Balazs Szalontai, *Kim Il Sung in the Khrushchev Era: Soviet-DPRK Relations and the Roots of North Korean Despotism, 1953–1964* (Stanford, Calif.: Stanford University Press, 2005), 163.
54. P. J. Honey, "The Position of the DRV Leadership and the Succession to Ho Chi Minh," *China Quarterly*, no. 9 (January–March 1962): 28.
55. "Bai noi cua dong chi Ho Chi Minh thay mat Doan dai bieu Dang Lao dong Viet Nam trong cuoc Hoi nghi dai bieu cac Dang Cong san va Dang Cong nhan hop o Matxcova (11–1960)" [Speech by Comrade Ho Chi Minh on Behalf of the Delegation of the Vietnamese Workers' Party at the Meeting of Communist and Workers' Parties in Moscow, November 1960], in *VKD: 1960*, 1035–46.
56. William E. Griffith, "The November 1960 Moscow Meeting: A Preliminary Assessment," *China Quarterly*, no. 11 (July–September 1962): 55. The pro-Soviet bias was also

apparent in a 7 December *Nhan dan* editorial on the Moscow Conference reproduced in FGDH to MFA, 8 December 1960, #16, AO:VN, ADF.

57. Honey, "Position of the DRV Leadership," 28.

58. The comments by the Yugoslav diplomat are reported in British Embassy, Paris, to FO, 15 February 1962, FO 371/160125, NAUK, 1.

59. Quoted in Vladislav M. Zubok, *A Failed Empire: The Soviet Union in the Cold War from Stalin to Gorbachev* (Chapel Hill: University of North Carolina Press, 2008), 138–39; Mark Atwood Lawrence, *The Vietnam War: A Concise International History* (New York: Oxford University Press, 2008), 68.

60. Nguyen Dy Nien, *Ho Chi Minh Thought: On Diplomacy* (Hanoi: The Gioi Publishers, 2004), 125–26 (emphasis in original).

61. "The VWP and the International Communist Movement" Folder 08, Box 02, DPC: Unit 13—The Early History of Vietnam, VATTU," 15.

62. Nguyen Dinh Binh, ed., *Ngoai giao Viet Nam, 1945–2000* [Vietnamese Diplomacy, 1945–2000] (Hanoi: Nha xuat ban Chinh tri quoc gia, 2005), 175.

63. George McT. Kahin and Robert Scalapino, "Excerpts from National Teach-in on Vietnam Policy" in Marcus G. Raskin and Bernard B. Fall, eds., *The Viet-Nam Reader: Articles and Documents on American Foreign Policy and the Viet-Nam Crisis* (New York: Random House, 1965), 294.

64. British Embassy, Paris, to FO, 15 February 1962, FO 371/160125, NAUK, 1.

65. William J. Duiker, *The Communist Road to Power in Vietnam*, 2nd ed. (Boulder, Colo.: Westview Press, 1996), 193; FGDH to MFA, 22 September 1960, #33, AO:VN, ADF, 1–3.

66. "Nhiem vu va phuong huong cua ke hoach 5 nam lan thu nhat phat trien kinh te quoc dan (1961–1965): Bao cao bo sung tai Dai hoi dai bieu toan quoc lan thu III do dong chi Nguyen Duy Trinh trinh bay, ngay 7-9-1960" [Tasks and Direction of the First Five-Year Plan to Develop the National Economy (1961–1965): Report Presented by Comrade Nguyen Duy Trinh at the Third National Congress, 7 September 1960], in *VKD: 1960*, 835–36; BCGH to FO, 26 September 1960, FO 371/152747, NAUK, 3.

67. The ambassador's comments are reported in BCGH to British Embassy, Saigon [hereafter BES], 9 April 1960, FO 371/152746, NAUK, 1.

68. FGDH to MFA, 8 October 1960, #33, AO:VN, ADF, 4.

69. BCGH to BES, 9 April 1960, 1.

70. British Embassy, Bangkok, to FO, 31 August 1960, FO 371/152747, NAUK, 1.

71. FGDH to MFA, 8 October 1960, 3–4.

72. Ho Chi Minh, *Tuyen tap* [Collected Works] (Hanoi: Nha xuat ban Su that, 1960), 772.

73. "Political Report of the 2nd Central Committee to the Congress," in Communist Party of Vietnam, *75 Years of the Communist Party of Vietnam (1930–2005): A Selection of Documents from Nine Party Congresses* (Hanoi: The Gioi Publishers, 2005), 212.

74. Hoang Anh, "Relationship between Accumulation and Consumption, and Diligent and Economical Building of the Country," in *Third National Congress of the Viet Nam Workers' Party: Documents, Volume 3* (Hanoi: Foreign Languages Publishing House, undated), 226; "Nhiem vu va phuong huong cua ke hoach 5 nam lan thu nhat," 818.

75. "Nhiem vu va phuong huong cua ke hoach 5 nam lan thu nhat," 831.

76. Ho Chi Minh is quoted in Truong Chinh, *Écrits, 1946–1975* [Selected Writings, 1946–1975] (Hanoi: Éditions en langues étrangères, 1977), 634.

77. Eero Palmujoki, *Vietnam and the World: Marxist-Leninist Doctrine and the Changes in International Relations, 1975–93* (New York: St. Martin's Press, 1997), 31.

78. Qiang Zhai, *China and the Vietnam Wars*, 74.

79. Excerpts from Giap's speech are quoted in BCGH to SEAD, 26 September 1960, FO 371/152747, NAUK, 3.

80. See Szalontai, *Kim Il Sung in the Khrushchev Era*.

81. BCGH to SEAD, 31 October 1960, and FGDH to MFA, 7 November 1960, #16, AO:VN, ADF.

82. Reproduced in FGDH to MFA, 19 December 1960, #16, AO:VN, ADF.

83. A summary of the statute is in BCGH to SEAD, 31 October 1960. For the statute itself, see "Dieu le Dang (do Dai hoi dai bieu toan quoc clan thu III cua Dang thong qua)" [Party Statute (Ratified by the Party's Third National Congress)], FO 371/152747, NAUK; and FGDH to MFA, 7 November 1960, #16, AO:VN, ADF.

84. Lien-Hang T. Nguyen, *Hanoi's War: An International History of the War for Peace in Vietnam* (Chapel Hill: University of North Carolina Press, 2012), 53–56. An organ of the PAVN's GPD, the *Bao ve* ("protection") was officially mandated to "guarantee the total loyalty of every military officer and unit toward the party" and to "investigate and deal with those who deviate from its policies." In reality, it also monitored individuals outside the armed forces, including other branches of the party and the DRVN government. In that sense it served not only the GPD but the VWP Organization Committee and the Ministry of the Interior. See Bui Tin, *Following Ho Chi Minh: Memoirs of a North Vietnamese Colonel* (Honolulu: University of Hawaii Press, 1999), 54–55.

85. Quoted in Céline Marangé, *Le communisme vietnamien, 1919–1991* [Vietnamese Communism, 1919–1991] (Paris: Presses de Sciences Po, 2012), 280. Lavrentiy Beria was Stalin's infamous secret police chief.

86. Hoang Anh, "Relationship between Accumulation and Consumption," 225.

87. BCGH to FO, 26 September 1960, 3.

88. *Third National Congress of the Viet Nam Workers' Party: Documents, Volume 1*, 222.

89. Nguyen Chi Thanh, "We Must Study, Support and Develop What Is New," *Hoc tap* (June 1961). Reproduced and translated in Folder 12, Box 10, DPC: Unit 08—Biography, VATTU, 4–5.

90. A comprehensive assessment of that aspect of the congress plus excerpts from certain speeches at the congress are in BCGH to FO, 24 September 1960, FO 371/152747, NAUK. On the Soviet accusations against Beijing, see French Consulate General, Hong Kong, to MFA, 10 October 1960, #16, AO:VN, ADF, 3.

91. Quoted in FGDH to MFA, 12 September 1960, #16, AO:VN, ADF, 1–3.

92. Le Mau Han, *Dang Cong san Viet Nam: Cac Dai hoi va Hoi nghi Trung uong* [The Communist Party of Vietnam: Congresses and Plenums] (Hanoi: Nha xuat ban Chinh tri quoc gia, 1995), 93.

93. Duiker, *Communist Road to Power*, 194.

94. FGDH to MFA, 9 September 1959, #19, AO:VN, ADF, 1–2; Duiker, *Communist Road to Power*, 194.

95. Quoted in William S. Turley, *The Second Indochina War: A Concise Political and Military History*, 2nd ed. (Lanham, Md.: Rowman & Littlefield, 2009), 45. On the formation of the NLF and the PLAF, see Robert K. Brigham, *Guerrilla Diplomacy: The NLF's Foreign Relations and the Vietnam War* (Ithaca, N.Y.: Cornell University Press, 1999), 11–18; and Tran Cong Tuong and Pham Thanh Vinh, *The N.L.F.: Symbol of Independence, Democracy and Peace in South Vietnam* (Hanoi: Foreign Languages Publishing House, 1967). Though Hanoi proclaimed its formation in 1960, the NLF did not hold its first formal congress until 1 January 1962.

96. Committee for Cultural Relations with Foreign Countries, "The Valiant Struggle for Liberation of the South Vietnamese People" (Hanoi, October 1965), 2.

97. George A. Carver, "The Real Revolution in South Vietnam," *Foreign Affairs*, no. 43 (April 1965): 406.

98. Republic of Vietnam, *Vietnam Report: Why Bomb North Viet Nam?* (Saigon: Ministry of Information, undated), 2. The South Vietnamese government issued this pamphlet in 1965 or 1966.

99. "Manifesto of the South Viet Nam National Front for Liberation," in *Manifesto of the South Viet Nam National Front for Liberation* (undated, no publisher), 6.

100. "Program of the South Viet Nam National Front for Liberation" in ibid., 10–15.

101. On the NLF generally, see Truong Nhu Tang, *A Viet Cong Memoir* (New York: Vintage Books, 1985); Douglas Pike, *Viet Cong: The Organization and Techniques of the National Liberation Front of South Vietnam* (Cambridge: Massachusetts Institute of Technology Press, 1966); Brigham, *Guerrilla Diplomacy*; and Tran Van Tra, *Nhung chang duong lich su cua B2 thanh dong, Tap I: Hoa binh hay chien tranh* [History of the B2 Theater, Volume 1: Peace or War] (Hanoi: Nha xuat ban Quan doi nhan dan, 1992), 231–42, which describes Hanoi's position regarding the NLF.

102. Tran Minh Truong, *Hoat dong ngoai giao cua Chu tich Ho Chi Minh tu 1954 den 1969* [Diplomatic Activities of President Ho Chi Minh from 1954 to 1969] (Hanoi: Nha xuat ban Cong an nhan dan, 2005), 45–46.

103. Nguyen Dy Nien, *Ho Chi Minh Thought*, 139. On "people's diplomacy," see Harish C. Metha, "'People's Diplomacy': The Diplomatic Front of North Vietnam during the War against the United States, 1965–1972" (PhD diss., McMaster University, 2009).

4. BUYING TIME, 1961

1. "Chi thi cua Bo Chinh tri, ngay 24 thang 1 nam 1961: Ve phuong huong va nhiem vu cong tac truoc mat cua cach mang mien Nam" [Politburo Instruction, 24 January 1961: On the Direction and Tasks Facing the Southern Revolution], in Dang Cong san Viet Nam, *Van kien Dang—Toan tap*, Tap 22: 1961 [Party Documents—Complete Series, Vol. 22: 1961] (Hanoi: Nha xuat ban Chinh tri quoc gia, 2002) [hereafter *VKD*: 1961], 153–55.

2. Ibid., 155.

3. "Du thao de cuong gio thieu ve tinh hinh ve duong loi cach mang mien Nam" [Draft of Presentation on the Situation and Revolutionary Line in the South], undated [1962], Ho so 252: Du thao de cuong ve tinh hinh va duong loi cach mang Mien nam 1962, Phong Uy ban Thong nhat Chinh phu, Vietnam National Archives Center 3, Hanoi [hereafter VNAC3], 10; "Chi thi cua Bo Chinh tri, ngay 24 thang 1 nam 1961," 158, 163.

4. William J. Duiker, *The Communist Road to Power in Vietnam*, 2nd ed. (Boulder, Colo.: Westview Press, 1996), 219.

5. William S. Turley, *The Second Indochina War: A Concise Political and Military History*, 2nd ed. (Lanham, Md.: Rowman & Littlefield, 2009), 44.

6. Le Duan, "Gui anh Muoi Cuc va cac dong chi Nam Bo, ngay 7 thang 2 nam 1961" [Sent to Brother Muoi Cuc and the Nam Bo Comrades, 7 February 1961], in *Thu vao Nam* [Letters to the South] (Hanoi: Nha xuat ban Quan doi nhan dan, 2005), 7–15.

7. Turley, *Second Indochina War*, 45; Bo Quoc phong—Vien Lich su quan su Viet Nam, *Lich su quan su Viet Nam, Tap 11: Cuoc khang chien chong My, cuu nuoc, 1954–1975* [Military History of Vietnam, Volume 11: The Anti-American Resistance for National Salvation] (Hanoi: Nha xuat ban Chinh tri quoc gia, 2005), 141.

8. Canadian Delegation [ICSC], Saigon, to Under Secretary of State for External Affairs, Ottawa, 19 January 1966, 20-22-VIET S-1, Vol. 9387 [Part 3], Record Group [hereafter RG] 25, Library and Archives Canada, Ottawa [hereafter LAC], 1. Hanoi infiltrated 6,300 personnel in 1961, and 12,850 the following year.

9. For an outline of the origins and functions of the organization, see Le Xuan An, "Chien khu D, Chien khu Duong Minh Chau—An toan khu cua Trung uong Cuc mien Nam trong khang chien chong My, cuu nuoc" [Resistance Zone D, the Duong Ming Chau Resistance Zone: Secure Zone of the Central Office for South Vietnam in the Anti-American Resistance for National Salvation], *Tap chi Lich su Dang* [Journal of Party History], no. 186 (January 2006): 47–49, 60.

10. David W. P. Elliott, *The Vietnamese War: Revolution and Social Change in the Mekong Delta, 1930–1975*, concise ed. (Armonk, N.Y.: M. E. Sharpe, 2007), 158; Turley, *Second Indochina War*, 47.

11. "Intelligence Summary on Lao Dong Central Committee Membership of the Central Office for South Vietnam," Folder 25, Box 01, United States Department of State Collection, Vietnam Archive at Texas Tech University [hereafter VATTU], 1. According to Edwin Moïse, "When the decision to establish the [COSVN] was first made, the intention may have been to give it authority over the Communist war effort in South Vietnam as a whole." "But if so," Moïse noted, "this idea was abandoned almost immediately," as "it was instead given authority over what became known as the B2 Front, roughly the southern half of South Vietnam." See Edwin E. Moïse, *Historical Dictionary of the Vietnam War* (Lanham, Md.: Scarecrow Press, 2001), 409.

12. Elliott, *Vietnamese War*, 158–59.

13. "Dien mat cua Trung uong gui XU Nam Bo, LKU V, so 28/DM, ngay 14 thang 3 nam 1961: Ve to chuc va nhiem vu cua Trung uong Cuc mien Nam" [Secret Cable from the Center Sent to the Executive Committees of Nam Bo, Interzone V, no. 28/DM, 14 March 1961: On the Organization and Tasks of the Central Office for Southern Vietnam], in *VKD: 1961*, 263–65.

14. "Intelligence Report on Command Relationships between the Lao Dong Party and the Central Office for South Vietnam," 1964, Folder 25, Box 01, United States Department of State Collection, VATTU.

15. "Intelligence Summary on Lao Dong Central Committee Membership," 1.

16. Elliott, *Vietnamese War*, 137, 161. According to Elliott, political indoctrination courses could last anywhere from one week to one year (ibid., 139). By official account, there

were approximately 35,000 party members below the seventeenth parallel in 1961 (ibid., 152).

17. "Danh sac can bo di B trong nam 1961" [List of Cadres Who Went South in 1961], undated, Ho so 876: Danh sac can bo di B trong nam 1961, Phong Uy ban Thong nhat Nha nuoc, VNAC3.

18. Douglas Pike, *Viet Cong: The Organization and Techniques of the National Liberation Front of South Vietnam* (Cambridge: Massachusetts Institute of Technology Press, 1966), 73.

19. "Chi thi cua Trung uong Cuc mien Nam, so 4, ngay 27 thang 11 nam 1961: Ve van de doi ten Dang cho Dang bo mien Nam" [Central Office for Southern Vietnam Instruction, no. 4, 27 November 1961: On the Problem of Changing the Name of the Southern Party Committee], in *VKD*: 1961, 653–54.

20. French Embassy, Saigon, to Ministry of Foreign Affairs, Paris [hereafter MFA], 27 January 1962, #1, Asie-Océanie [hereafter AO]: Vietnam Conflict [hereafter VC], Archives Diplomatiques de France, La Courneuve [hereafter ADF], 2–4.

21. "Intelligence Summary on Lao Dong Central Committee Membership," 3.

22. Pike, *Viet Cong*, 73.

23. "Du thao de cuong gio thieu ve tinh hinh ve duong loi cach mang mien Nam," 10.

24. Nguyen Vu Tung, "Coping with the United States: Hanoi's Search for an Effective Strategy," in Peter Lowe, ed., *The Vietnam War* (London: MacMillan Press, 1998), 42.

25. British Embassy, Saigon [hereafter BES], to Foreign Office, London [hereafter FO], "Review of Events in North Vietnam (the D.R.V.) during 1961," 31 January 1962, FO 371/166697, National Archives of the United Kingdom, Kew [hereafter NAUK], 5.

26. Nguyen Chi Thanh, "We Must Study, Support and Develop What Is New," *Hoc tap* (June 1961). Reproduced and translated in Folder 12, Box 10, Douglas Pike Collection [hereafter DPC]: Unit 08—Biography, VATTU, 4–5.

27. "Bao cao tai Hoi nghi Ban Chap hanh Trung uong lan thu tam, ngay 26 thang 3 nam 1963" [Report at the Eighth Plenum of the Central Committee, 26 March 1963], in Dang Cong san Viet Nam, *Van kien Dang—Toan tap*, Tap 24: 1963 [Party Documents—Complete Series, Vol. 24: 1963] (Hanoi: Nha xuat ban Chinh tri quoc gia, 2003), 256.

28. Adam Fforde and Suzanne Paine, *The Limits of National Liberation* (London: Croom Helm, 1987), 39.

29. Dong's remarks are reported in British Consulate General, Hanoi [hereafter BCGH], to Southeast Asia Department, London [hereafter SEAD], 19 July 1961, FO 371/160122, NAUK, 1.

30. Balazs Szalontai, *Kim Il Sung in the Khrushchev Era: Soviet–DPRK Relations and the Roots of North Korean Despotism, 1953–1964* (Stanford, Calif.: Stanford University Press, 2005), 155.

31. "Review of Events in North Vietnam (the D.R.V.) during 1961," 1.

32. French General Delegation, Hanoi [hereafter FGDH], to MFA, May 1961, #31, AO: Vietnam Nord [hereafter VN], ADF, 2.

33. FGDH to MFA, 1 September 1961, #71, AO: VN, ADF, 1.

34. Ibid.

35. FGDH to MFA, 1 October 1961, #72, AO: VN, ADF, 21.

36. Céline Marangé, *Le communisme vietnamien, 1919–1991* [Vietnamese Communism, 1919–1991] (Paris: Presses de Sciences Po, 2012), 283.

37. FGDH to MFA, 1 June 1961, #71, AO: VN, ADF, 1, 3, 12.
38. FGDH to MFA, 1 August 1961, #71, AO: VN, ADF, 3.
39. For more on U.S.-RVN clandestine operations in the DRVN, see Thomas L. Ahern, Jr., *The Way We Do Things: Black Entry Operations into North Vietnam,* Center for the Study of Intelligence (May 2005), available through the website of the National Security Archive.
40. FGDH to MFA, 1 August 1961, 1, 10, 21.
41. FGDH to MFA, 25 July 1961, #44, AO: VN, ADF, 1.
42. FGDH to MFA, July 1961 [day illegible], #19, AO: VN, ADF, 1.
43. FGDH to MFA, 1 August 1961, 1, 10, 21.
44. FGDH to MFA, 16 August 1961, #19, AO: VN, ADF, 1; FGDH to MFA, 1 September 1961, 10.
45. FGDH to MFA, 1 September 1961, 1.
46. FGDH to MFA, 1 October 1961, 22.
47. Ibid., 1, 10, 21; FGDH to MFA, 1 September 1961, 1, 9, 11.
48. FGDH to MFA, 1 October 1961, 4; FGDH to MFA, 1 November 1961, #72, AO: VN, ADF, C.3; FGDH to MFA, 1 December 1961, #72, AO: VN, ADF, 3; FGDH to MFA, 1 January 1962, #72, AO: VN, ADF, C.4.
49. FGDH to MFA, 1 December 1961, #72, AO: VN, ADF, A.6.
50. FGDH to MFA, 1 October 1961, 3; FGDH to MFA, 1 November 1961, A.11.
51. "Calendar of Events in North Vietnam during 1961," undated, FO 371/166697, NAUK.
52. "Bai noi cua Chi tich Ho Chi Minh tai Hoi nghi lan thu nam Ban Chap hanh Trung uong Dang (khoa III)" [Speech by President Ho Chi Minh at the Fifth Plenum of the Party Central Committee (Third Session)], in *VKD:* 1961, 410.
53. "Calendar of Events in North Vietnam during 1961."
54. "Review of Events in North Vietnam (the D.R.V.) during 1961," 1.
55. "Bao cao cua Bo truong Bo Ngoai giao Ung Van Khiem ve ket qua cua Hoi nghi Gione-vo ve Lao (tay ky hop thu 5 cua QH khoa 2, ngay 23 thang 10 nam 1962)" [Report of Foreign Minister Ung Van Khiem on the Results of the Geneva Conference on Laos (at the Fifth Meeting of the Second Session of the National Assembly, 23 October 1962)], 23 October 1962, Ho so 740: Ho so ky hop thu nam cua QH khoa II tu ngay 22.27.10.1962. Tap 2: Phien hop ngay 23.10.1962: Bao cao to trinh, Nghi quyet cua QH UBTVQH, PTT ve cong tac cua UBTVQH, ve tong quyet toan ngan sach Nha nuoc, ket qua Hoi nghi Gionevo ve Lao, ve to chuc HDND va UBHC cac cap, Phong Quoc hoi, VNAC3, 8.
56. "'Bao cao ve tinh hinh mien Nam va tinh hinh dau tranh thong nhat nuoc nha cua ta' cua Uy ban Thong nhat" ["Report on the Situation in Southern Vietnam and the Situation of the Struggle for Reunification of Our Country" by the Committee for Reunification], 24 October 1961, Ho so 728: Ho so ky hop thu ba cua QH khoa II tu ngay 23–27.10.1961. Tap 2: Phien hop ngay 24.10.1961: Bao cao, to trinh cua UBTVQH, Bo Ngoai giao, Uy ban Thong nhat, Bo Tai chinh, Phu Thu tuong ve cong tac cua UBTVQH, tinh hinh the gio va cong tac ngoai giao, mien Nam ve thong nhat nuoc nha, Phong Quoc hoi, VNAC3, 1.
57. FGDH to MFA, 20 March 1961, #44, AO: VC, ADF, 2.
58. French Embassy, Saigon, to MFA, "Note d'information: République Démocratique du Viêtnam" [Information Note: Democratic Republic of Vietnam], 11 May 1961, #31, AO: VN, ADF, no page number (file page number 156).

59. "Bao cao cua Uy ban Thuong vu QH do Pho chu tich UBTVQH, Nguyen Xien" [Report by the Standing Committee of the National Assembly by the Vice-President of the Standing Committee of the National Assembly, Nguyen Xien], 24 October 1961, Ho so 728: Ho so ky hop thu ba cua QH khoa II tu ngay 23–27.10.1961. Tap 2: Phien hop ngay 24.10.1961: Bao cao, to trinh cua UBTVQH, Bo Ngoai giao, Uy ban Thong nhat, Bo Tai chinh, Phu Thu tuong ve cong tac cua UBTVQH, tinh hinh the gio va cong tac ngoai giao, mien Nam ve thong nhat nuoc nha, Phong Quoc hoi, VNAC3, 4.

60. "Tham luan ve cong tac ngoai giao cua CP cua Ong Phan-van-Su, dai bieu Vinh-long" [Address on the Diplomatic Work of the Government by Mr. Phan Van Su, Representative from Vinh Long], 26 October 1961, Ho so 729: Ho so ky hop thu ba cua QH khoa III tu ngay 23–27.10.1961. Tap 3: Phien hop ngay 26.10.1961: Thuyet trinh ve tong quyet toan ngan sach Nha nuoc nam 1960, tham luan ve tang cuong phap che, tinh hinh mien Nam va dau tranh chong My, thong nhat dat nuoc, cong tac ngoai giao, Phong Quoc hoi, VNAC3, 2.

61. Foreign Ministry cable to Prime Minister, 4 December 1961, Ho so 7727: Bao cao cua PTT ve viec cong nhan va dat quan he ngoai giao voi cac nuoc nam 1960–61, Phong Phu Thu tuong, VNAC3, 1; Minister for Foreign Trade cable to Prime Minister, 2 March 1961, Ho so 7795: Cong van cua PTT, BBNG, Uy ban doan ket nhan dan A phi cua Viet Nam v/v giup do nhan dan An-gie-ri 200 tan bot mi nam 1961, Phong Phu Thu tuong, VNAC3, 1.

62. "'Bao cao tinh hinh the gio va cong tac ngoai giao' doc truoc ky hop thu ba cua Quoc hoi khoa hai (ngay 24 thang 10.1961)—Bo Truong Bo Ngoai giao Ung Van Khiem" ["Report on the World Situation and Diplomatic Tasks" Read before the Third Meeting of the Second Session of the National Assembly (24 October 1961—Foreign Minister Ung Van Khiem)], 24 October 1961, Ho so 728: Ho so ky hop thu ba cua QH khoa II tu ngay 23–27.10.1961. Tap 2: Phien hop ngay 24.10.1961: Bao cao, to trinh cua UBTVQH, Bo Ngoai giao, Uy ban Thong nhat, Bo Tai chinh, Phu Thu tuong ve cong tac cua UBTVQH, tinh hinh the gio va cong tac ngoai giao, mien Nam ve thong nhat nuoc nha, Phong Quoc hoi, VNAC3, 11.

63. Vien nghien cuu chu nghia Mac-Lenin va tu tuong Ho Chi Minh, *Lich su Dang Cong san Viet Nam, Tap 2: 1954–1975* [History of the Communist Party of Vietnam, Volume 2: 1954–1975] (Hanoi: Nha xuat ban Chinh tri quoc gia, 1995), 161.

64. "Thong tri cua Ban Bi thu, so 45-TT/TW, ngay 31 thang 10 nam 1961: Ve mo mot cuoc dau tranh rong rai va manh ma chong am muu can thiep moi cua de quoc My o mien Nam Viet Nam" [Secretariat Circular, no. 45-TT/TW, 31 October 1961: On Opening a Wide and Strong Struggle against the New Aggression Scheme of the American Imperialists in Southern Vietnam], in *VKD*: 1961, 484–89.

65. FO to BES, 12 January 1962, FO 371/166725, NAUK, 1.

66. "Tham luan cua ong Dang-thai-Mai, dai bieu Nghe-an" [Address by Mr. Dang Thai Mai, Representative from Nghe An], 26 October 1961, Ho so 729: Ho so ky hop thu ba cua QH khoa III tu ngay 23–27.10.1961. Tap 3: Phien hop ngay 26.10.1961: Thuyet trinh ve tong quyet toan ngan sach Nha nuoc nam 1960, tham luan ve tang cuong phap che, tinh hinh mien Nam va dau tranh chong My, thong nhat dat nuoc, cong tac ngoai giao, Phong Quoc hoi, VNAC3, 4.

67. Seventy-two percent of the ICSC's rulings were in Hanoi's favor between August 1954 and January 1959. See Ramesh Thakur, "India's Vietnam Policy, 1946–1979," *Asian Survey* 19, no. 10 (October 1979): 961.

68. "Review of Events in North Vietnam (the D.R.V.) during 1961," 3.
69. Thakur, "India's Vietnam Policy," 963.
70. FGDH to MFA, 1 July 1961, #71, AO: VN, ADF, 2.
71. Quoted in Thakur, "India's Vietnam Policy," 963. See also Mieczyslaw Maneli, *War of the Vanquished* (New York: Harper & Row, 1971), 77–78.
72. Douglas A. Ross, "Middlepowers as Extra-Regional Balancer Powers: Canada, India, and Indochina, 1954–62," *Pacific Affairs* 55, no. 2 (Summer 1982): 197, 204–5. Ross concludes that the behavior of the ICSC "did serve to inhibit the North Vietnamese leadership. At the very least, it made the option of indirect attack on the south far more attractive than invasion." "It is very possible that the 'indirect' attack on the Saigon government," he continues, "which received Hanoi's blessing sometime in 1959, might very well have begun in earnest two to three years sooner," in which case American intervention "might ... have been required in 1958–59, not in 1963–64" (ibid., 207, 208).
73. "Thong tri cua Ban Bi thu, so 45-TT/TW," 485.
74. "Chi thi cua Ban Bi thu, so 21-CT/TW, ngay 4 thang 7 nam 1961: Ve mo dot dau tranh chinh tri rong lon nhan dip 20-7-1961" [Secretariat Instruction, no. 21-CT/TW, 4 July 1961: On Opening a Wider Political Struggle on the Occasion of 20 July 1961], in *VKD: 1961*, 365–66.
75. "Review of Events in North Vietnam (the D.R.V.) during 1961," 3–4.
76. Bo Ngoai giao, *Chan dung nam co Bo truong Ngoai giao* [Portraits of Five Foreign Ministers] (Hanoi: Nha xuat ban Chinh tri quoc gia, 2005), 592–93.
77. "Review of Events in North Vietnam (the D.R.V.) during 1961," 2. By one account, during his trip Dong also asked his hosts that all debt owed by the DRVN to its allies as of 1 January 1961 be "liquidated," that is, forgiven. See FGDH to MFA, 14 August 1961, #31, AO: VN, ADF, 1.
78. "'Bao cao tinh hinh the gio va cong tac ngoai giao' doc truoc ky hop thu ba cua Quoc hoi khoa hai (ngay 24 thang 10.1961)—Bo Truong Bo Ngoai giao Ung Van Khiem," 4.
79. "Nghi quyet ve tinh hinh the gioi va cong tac ngoai giao cua CP" [Government Resolution on the World Situation and Diplomatic Work], Ho so 730: Ho so ky hop thu ba cua QH khoa II tu ngay 23–27.10.1961. Tap 4: Phien hop ngay 27.10.1961: Nghi quyet ve tong quyet toan ngan sach Nha nuoc nam 1960, sap nhap Dong Trieu vao Hong Quang, ve tinh hinh the gioi va cong tac ngoai giao cua CP, Phong Quoc hoi, VNAC3, 2.
80. Quoted in FGDH to MFA, "Visite de M. Bernard Fall au Président Pham Van Dong" [Visit of Mr. Bernard Fall with President Pham Van Dong], 16 July 1962, #31, AO: VN, ADF, 7.
81. "Nghi quyet Hoi nghi Trung uong lan thu 15 (mo rong): Ve tang cuong doan ket, kien quyet dau tranh giu vung hoa binh, thuc hien thong nhat nuoc nha" [Resolution of the Fifteenth Plenum (expanded): On Increasing Unity and Determination to Struggle to Preserve Peace and Achieve Unification of the State], in Dang Cong san Viet Nam, *Van kien Dang—Toan tap*, Tap 20: 1959 [Party Documents—Collected Works, Vol. 20: 1959] (Hanoi: Nha xuat ban Chinh tri quoc gia, 2002), 67. During a visit to Hanoi in September 1960, a representative of the Moroccan Communist Party declared that Vietnamese political and military successes had encouraged Moroccans to strive for independence, and currently, "the light of your example" guided "our valiant Algerian brothers." Quoted in FGDH to MFA, 12 September 1960 (I), #16, AO: VN, ADF, 2.

82. "Tham luan ve cong tac ngoai giao cua CP cua Ong Phan-van-Su, dai bieu Vinh-long," 3.

83. Luu Van Loi, *Fifty Years of Vietnamese Diplomacy, 1945-1995*, Vol. 1: *1945-1975* (Hanoi: The Gioi Publishers, 2000), 139; "Thong cao cua UB thuong vu QH" [Declaration by the National Assembly Standing Committee], 29 July 1961, Ho so 791: Ho so phien hop thu 22 cua UBTVQH khoa II ngay 29.7.1961 quy dinh thoi gian bau cu HDND xa, thi tran o KTT Thai Meo, xet de nghi khen truong, ve thai do cua UBTVQH voi viec xam luoc Tuy-ni-di cua Phap va bao cao Hoi nghi Gio-ne-vo giai quyet van da Lao, Phong Quoc hoi, VNAC3, 1.

84. French Embassy, Saigon, to MFA, 20 September 1960, #31, AO: VN, ADF, 1.

85. "Tham luan ve phong trao cong tac ngoai giao cua CP cua Ong Phan-van-Su, dai bieu Vinh-long" [Address on the Diplomatic Work of the Government by Mr. Phan Van Su, Representative from Vinh Long], 26 October 1961, Ho so 729: Ho so ky hop thu ba cua QH khoa III tu ngay 23-27.10.1961. Tap 3: Phien hop ngay 26.10.1961: Thuyet trinh ve tong quyet toan ngan sach Nha nuoc nam 1960, tham luan ve tang cuong phap che, tinh hinh mien Nam va dau tranh chong My, thong nhat dat nuoc, cong tac ngoai giao, Phong Quoc hoi, VNAC3, 2.

86. "Nghi quyet Hoi nghi Trung uong lan thu 15," 58, 62; Truong Chinh, *Écrits, 1946-1975* [Selected Writings, 1946-1975] (Hanoi: Éditions en langues étrangères, 1977), 6.

87. Quoted in FGDH to MFA, 12 September 1960 (II), #16, AO: VN, ADF, 2.

88. Bui Kim Dinh, "Tim hieu nguyen nhan cuoc dung dau lich su o Viet Nam (1954-1975)" [Understanding the Cause of Historical Encounters in Vietnam, 1954-1975], *Tap chi Lich su Dang* [Journal of Party History], no. 186 (May 2006): 68.

89. "Tham luan cua ong Dang-thai-Mai," 1-2.

90. FGDH to MFA, 20 February 1961, #31, AO: VN, ADF, 1.

91. "Review of Events in North Vietnam (the D.R.V.) during 1961," 3.

92. The French position is related in British Embassy, Paris, to FO, 21 December 1961, FO 371/160125, NAUK, 1; and FGDH to MFA, 1 December 1961, #72, AO: VN, ADF, 1.

93. Quoted in BCGH to BES, 23 April 1962, FO 371/166712, NAUK, 2.

94. Ibid.

95. "Review of Events in North Vietnam (the D.R.V.) during 1961," 1.

96. French Embassy, Moscow, to MFA, 28 June 1961, #35, AO: VN, ADF, 2.

97. FGDH to MFA, 1 March 1961, #31, AO: VN, ADF, 1.

98. FGDH to MFA, 8 March 1961, #19, AO: VN, ADF, 1-2.

99. French Embassy, Moscow, to MFA, 27 June 1961, #35, AO: VN, ADF, 2; BCGH to BES, 23 April 1962, 1; Szalontai, *Kim Il Sung in the Khrushchev Era*, 164.

100. FGDH to MFA, 12 June 1961, #35, AO: VN, ADF, 2.

101. Szalontai, *Kim Il Sung in the Khrushchev Era*, 178.

102. "Review of Events in North Vietnam (the D.R.V.) during 1961," 3-4.

103. Aleksandr Fursenko and Timothy Naftali, *Khrushchev's Cold War: The Inside Story of an American Adversary* (New York: Norton, 2006), 336; Mark Atwood Lawrence, *The Vietnam War: A Concise International History* (New York: Oxford University Press, 2008), 68.

104. Qiang Zhai, *China and the Vietnam Wars, 1950-1975* (Chapel Hill: University of North Carolina Press, 2000), 83-85.

105. Khuat Bien Hoa, *Dai tuong Le Duc Anh* [General Le Duc Anh] (Hanoi: Nha xuat ban Quan doi nhan dan, 2005), 60.

106. Jay Tao, "Mao's World Outlook: Vietnam and the Revolution in China," *Asian Survey* 8, no. 5 (May 1968): 417.

107. Donald S. Zagoria, "Khrushchev's Attack on Albania and Sino-Soviet Relations," *China Quarterly*, no. 8 (October–December 1961): 3

108. Lorenz Lüthi, *The Sino-Soviet Split, 1956–1966* (Princeton, N.J.: Princeton University Press, 2008), 197.

109. Sergei Radchenko, *Two Suns in the Heavens: The Sino-Soviet Struggle for Supremacy, 1962–1967* (Stanford, Calif.: Stanford University Press, 2009), 24; Zagoria, "Khrushchev's Attack on Albania," 1–19. Unable to reach consensus with Khrushchev on Albania and other issues, Zhou Enlai left the conference on 23 November, a week before it closed.

110. "Calendar of Events in North Vietnam during 1961."

111. Ang Cheng Guan, *Vietnamese Communists' Relations with China and the Second Indochina Conflict, 1956–1962* (Jefferson, N.C.: McFarland, 1997), 206.

112. Szalontai, *Kim Il Sung in the Khrushchev Era*, 187.

113. "Calendar of Events in North Vietnam during 1961."

114. Ang Cheng Guan, *Vietnamese Communists' Relations with China*, 214.

115. Xiaoming Zhang, "Communist Powers Divided: China, the Soviet Union, and the Vietnam War," in Lloyd C. Gardner and Ted Gittinger, eds., *International Perspectives on Vietnam* (College Station: Texas A&M University Press, 2000), 83.

116. BCGH to SEAD, 1 January 1962, FO 371/166712, NAUK, 2.

117. "Du thao de cuong gio thieu ve tinh hinh ve duong loi cach mang mien Nam," 11.

118. Philip E. Catton, *Diem's Final Failure: Prelude to America's War in Vietnam* (Lawrence: University Press of Kansas, 2002), 74.

119. Seth Jacobs, *Cold War Mandarin: Ngo Dinh Diem and the Origins of America's War in Vietnam, 1950–1963* (Lanham, Md.: Rowman & Littlefield, 2006), 122.

120. "Du thao de cuong gio thieu ve tinh hinh ve duong loi cach mang mien Nam," 11.

121. Bo Quoc phong—Vien Lich su quan su Viet Nam, *Lich su quan su Viet Nam, Tap 11*, 142.

122. "History of the NLF, 1954–63" [CRIMP Document], undated, Folder 03, Box 01, DPC: Unit 05—National Liberation Front, VATTU, 6–7.

123. "Chi thi cua Ban Bi thu, so 19-CT/TW, ngay 11 thang 5 nam 1961: Ve phat dong dau tranh chong am muu de quoc My dinh dua quan vao mien Nam Viet Nam" [Secretariat Instruction, no. 19-CT/TW, 11 April 1961: On the Mobilization Struggle against the American Imperialists' Plan to Introduce Troops into Southern Vietnam], in *VKD: 1961*, 323–24.

124. "'Bao cao ve tinh hinh mien Nam va tinh hinh dau tranh thong nhat nuoc nha cua ta' cua Uy ban Thong nhat," 3.

125. "Vietnam: Chronology," part of "Memorandum for the Minister," 9 March 1965, 21-13-VIET-ICSC [Pt. 1.1], Vol. 10122, RG 25, LAC, 3.

126. "'Bao cao ve tinh hinh mien Nam va tinh hinh dau tranh thong nhat nuoc nha cua ta' cua Uy ban Thong nhat," 1.

127. Mark Moyar, *Triumph Forsaken: The Vietnam War, 1954–1965* (New York: Cambridge University Press, 2006), 124.

128. Catton, *Diem's Final Failure*, 87–88, 90.

129. Ibid., 93, 97, 133.
130. Moyar, *Triumph Forsaken*, 156–60.
131. Catton, *Diem's Final Failure*, 120, 141, 187–88.
132. John B. O'Donnell, "The Strategic Hamlet Program in Kien Hoa Province, South Vietnam: A Case Study of Counter-Insurgency," 11 May 1965, Folder 13, Box 06, John Donnell Collection, VATTU, 48–49, 57, 59.
133. Catton, *Diem's Final Failure*, 137.
134. Quoted in Elliott, *Vietnamese War*, 175.
135. Ibid., 164.
136. Catton, *Diem's Final Failure*, 138.
137. The latter referred to joint South Vietnamese-American covert activities against or within the DRVN.
138. PLAF strength stood at approximately 17,000 troops at the time (Turley, *Second Indochina War*, 63).
139. "Nghi quyet Hoi nghi R lan thu I (mo rong)" [Resolution of the First Plenum (expanded) of R (i.e., COSVN)], in *VKD*: 1961, 656–730. For an English translation of the document, see "Draft of COSVN Resolution 1," October 1961, Folder 02, Box 12, DPC: Unit 06—Democratic Republic of Vietnam, VATTU.
140. In short, southern leaders wanted to "increasingly attack the enemy and expand our movement, rapidly develop and strengthen our forces in every respect, completely change the balance of forces between us and the enemy, actively pave the way for a general uprising and be ready to seize every opportunity to achieve big successes."
141. Gareth Porter, "Hanoi's Strategic Perspective and the Sino-Soviet Conflict," *Pacific Affairs* 57, no. 1 (Spring 1984): 12.
142. "It will only be by means of revolutionary overthrow of the ruling bourgeoisie that peace can be attained" in the world, Beijing maintained publicly at this time, and "this is an unprecedentedly favorable new epoch for proletarian revolution in the countries of the world and for the national revolution in the colonies and semi-colonies." Quoted in Thomas Perry Thornton, "Peking, Moscow, and the Underdeveloped Areas," *World Politics* 13, no. 4 (July 1961): 492.
143. "Thong tri cua Ban Bi thu, so 45-TT/TW," 485.
144. Duiker, *Communist Road to Power*, 220–21.
145. "'Bao cao tinh hinh the gio va cong tac ngoai giao' doc truoc ky hop thu ba cua Quoc hoi khoa hai (ngay 24 thang 10.1961)—Bo Truong Bo Ngoai giao Ung Van Khiem," 4.
146. "Thu cua QH gui dong bao mien Nam" [National Assembly Letter to Southern Compatriots], Ho so 730: Ho so ky hop thu ba cua QH khoa II tu ngay 23–27.10.1961. Tap 4: Phien hop ngay 27.10.1961: Nghi quyet ve tong quyet toan ngan sach Nha nuoc nam 1960, sap nhap Dong Trieu vao Hong Quang, ve tinh hinh the gioi va cong tac ngoai giao cua CP, Phong Quoc hoi, VNAC3, 2.
147. Turley, *Second Indochina War*, 48.
148. "Note d'information: Position de certaines personnalités de la R.D.V.N. à l'égard de l'opposition vietnamienne non communiste, et de la réunification du Vietnam" [Information Note: Stance of Certain DRVN Figures on Noncommunist Vietnamese Opposition, and Vietnamese Reunification], 3 June 1961, #1, AO: VN, ADF, 1–2.

149. Le Quang Dao, "Let Us Step Up Army Building and Consolidation of National Defense," *Hoc tap*, no. 12 (December 1961). Reproduced and translated in Folder 10, Box 13, DPC: Unit 06—Democratic Republic of Vietnam, VATTU, 34–36, 38.

150. FGDH to MFA, 1 January 1962, #72, AO: VN, ADF, 4.

151. BCGH to FO, "Visit of Chinese Military Delegation to North Vietnam," 3 January 1962, FO 371/166713, NAUK, 1.

152. "'Bao cao tinh hinh the gio va cong tac ngoai giao' doc truoc ky hop thu ba cua Quoc hoi khoa hai (ngay 24 thang 10.1961)—Bo Truong Bo Ngoai giao Ung Van Khiem," 9.

153. "'Bao cao ve tinh hinh mien Nam va tinh hinh dau tranh thong nhat nuoc nha cua ta' cua Uy ban Thong nhat," 1.

154. British Embassy, Peking, to FO, 1 January 1962, FO 371/166713, NAUK, 1.

155. "Visit of Chinese Military Delegation to North Vietnam," 3.

156. Bui Tin, *Following Ho Chi Minh: Memoirs of a North Vietnamese Colonel* (Honolulu: University of Hawaii Press, 1999), 45. The Chinese military delegation, Bui Tin writes, traveled to Hanoi "to suggest that our southern compatriots should only attack at section or company level, never at battalion strength."

157. Qiang Zhai, *China and the Vietnam Wars*, 113.

158. Ye's comments are reported in "Visit of Chinese Military Delegation to North Vietnam," 3.

159. Giap's comments are quoted in ibid., 2–3.

160. "Canadian Report on Visit of Chinese Military Mission to DRV," 2 February 1962, FO 371/166713, NAUK, 2.

161. Ang Cheng Guan, *Vietnamese Communists' Relations with China*, 213.

162. "Visit of Chinese Military Delegation to North Vietnam," 3.

163. "Tham luan ve k.h. xam luoc moi cua de quoc My vao mien Nam Viet Nam cua ong Nguyen-van-Huong, dai bieu Long Xuyen" [Address on the New Aggression of the American Imperialists in Southern Vietnam of Mr. Nguyen Van Huong, Representative of Long Xuyen], Ho so 729: Ho so ky hop thu ba cua QH khoa II tu ngay 23–27.10.1961. Tap 3: Phien hop ngay 26.10.1961: thuyet trinh ve tong quyet toan ngan sach Nha nuoc nam 1960, tham luan ve tang cuong phap che, tinh hinh mien Nam va dau tranh chong My, thong nhat dat nuoc, cong tac ngoai giao, Phong Quoc hoi, VNAC3, 2–3.

164. Ibid., 6–7.

165. Ibid., 9–10.

166. "Tham luan cua o. Tran-tong, dai bieu tinh Quang nam doc tai QH, khoa II, ky hop thu III ve tinh hinh mien Nam" [Address by Mr. Trang Tong, Representative of Quang Nam Province before the National Assembly, Second Session, Third Meeting on the Situation in the South], Ho so 729: Ho so ky hop thu ba cua QH khoa II tu ngay 23–27.10.1961. Tap 3: Phien hop ngay 26.10.1961: thuyet trinh ve tong quyet toan ngan sach Nha nuoc nam 1960, tham luan ve tang cuong phap che, tinh hinh mien Nam va dau tranh chong My, thong nhat dat nuoc, cong tac ngoai giao, Phong Quoc hoi, VNAC3, 5.

5. EXPLORING NEUTRALIZATION, 1962

1. "Tuyen bo cua QH nuoc VNDCCH huong ung loi kieu goi cua Xo Viet toi cao Lien Xo ve viec giam bot quan so" [Statement by the DRVN National Assembly in Support of the

Declaration by the Supreme Soviet on the Reduction of Military Forces], 23 January 1960, Ho so 636: Ho so ve viec QH Viet Nam ve cac nuoc huong ung, ung ho loi kieu goi cua Xo viet toi cao Lien Xo ve dau tranh lam diu tinh hinh the gio, giai tru quan bi va hop tac hoa binh tu 1957–1960, Phong Quoc hoi, Vietnam National Archives Center 3, Hanoi [hereafter VNAC3], 2; Qiang Zhai, *China and the Vietnam Wars, 1950–1975* (Chapel Hill: University of North Carolina Press, 2000), 93.

2. Ban chi dao Nghien cuu ly luan va thuc tien Trung uong Dang nhan dan cach mang Lao, *Lich su Dang nhan dan cach mang Lao* [History of the People's Revolutionary Party of Laos] (Hanoi: Nha xuat ban Chinh tri quoc gia, 2005), 111. Most, including Souphanouvong, escaped from prison in May 1960 (ibid., 114).

3. British Embassy, Saigon [hereafter BES], to Foreign Office, London [hereafter FO], "Vietnam—Annual Report for 1959," 27 January 1960, FO 371/152737, National Archives of the United Kingdom, Kew [hereafter NAUK], 12; "Loi tuyen bo cua cu Ton Duc Thang, Chu tich Uy ban TW MTTQVN voi Thong tan xa Lien Xo" [Statement by Ton Duc Thang, President of the Central Committee of the Vietnam Fatherland Front for the Soviet News Agency], October 1959, Ho so 636: Ho so ve viec QH Viet Nam ve cac nuoc huong ung, ung ho loi kieu goi cua Xo viet toi cao Lien Xo ve dau tranh lam diu tinh hinh the gio, giai tru quan bi va hop tac hoa binh tu 1957–1960, Phong Quoc hoi, VNAC3, 1.

4. William J. Duiker, *The Communist Road to Power in Vietnam*, 2nd ed. (Boulder, Colo.: Westview Press, 1996), 201.

5. "'Bao cao tinh hinh the gio va cong tac ngoai giao' doc truoc ky hop thu ba cua Quoc hoi khoa hai (ngay 24 thang 10.1961)—Bo Truong Bo Ngoai giao Ung Van Khiem" ["Report on the World Situation and Diplomatic Tasks" Read before the Third Meeting of the Second Session of the National Assembly (24 October 1961—Foreign Minister Ung Van Khiem], 24 October 1961, Ho so 728: Ho so ky hop thu ba cua QH khoa II tu ngay 23–27.10.1961. Tap 2: Phien hop ngay 24.10.1961: Bao cao, to trinh cua UBTVQH, Bo Ngoai giao, Uy ban Thong nhat, Bo Tai chinh, Phu Thu tuong ve cong tac cua UBTVQH, tinh hinh the gio va cong tac ngoai giao, mien Nam ve thong nhat nuoc nha, Phong Quoc hoi, VNAC3, 12–13.

6. Roger M. Smith, "Cambodia's Neutrality and the Laotian Crisis," *Asian Survey* 1, no. 5 (July 1961): 19–20; Ang Cheng Guan, *The Vietnamese War from the Other Side: The Vietnamese Communists' Perspective* (New York: RoutledgeCurzon, 2002), 62–63.

7. Christopher E. Goscha, "The Revolutionary Laos of the Democratic Republic of Vietnam: The Making of a Transnational 'Pathet Lao Solution' (1954–1956)," in Christopher E. Goscha and Karine Laplante, eds., *L'Échec de la paix en Indochine / The Failure of Peace in Indochina (1954–1962)* (Paris: Les Indes savantes, 2010), 64.

8. "Summary of Vietnamese Aid to the Lao Revolution (1945–1975)," Science Section of the General Department of Rear Services, People's Army of Vietnam, 6 (document in Christopher Goscha's possession). See also Ang Cheng Guan, *Vietnamese Communists' Relations with China and the Second Indochina Conflict, 1956–1962* (Jefferson, N.C.: McFarland, 1997), 175–76.

9. Ban chi dao Nghien cuu ly luan va thuc tien Trung uong Dang nhan dan cach mang Lao, *Lich su Dang nhan dan cach mang Lao*, 119; French General Delegation, Hanoi [hereafter FGDH], to Ministry of Foreign Affairs, Paris [hereafter MFA], 24 July 1961, #44, Asie-Océanie [hereafter AO]: Vietnam Conflit [hereafter VC], Archives Diplomatiques de France, La Courneuve [hereafter ADF], 1.

10. FGDH to MFA, 1 June 1961, #71, AO: Vietnam Nord [hereafter VN], ADF, 1, 4.

11. For the best treatment of this topic, see Goscha, "Revolutionary Laos of the Democratic Republic of Vietnam," 61–84.

12. "Tieu ban nghien cuu cong tac Lao: De an cong tac kinh te tai chinh giup chinh phu Lao" [Laotian Affairs Research Sub-Committee: Program for Economic and Financial Assistance to the Government of Laos], 31 September 1961, Ho so 7809: De an, bao cao cua Ban Liep te T-W, Bo Quoc phong va tieu ban nghien cuu cong tac Lao ve tinh hinh vien tro cho Lao nam 1961, Phong Phu Thu tuong, VNAC3, 7.

13. Hoang Van Hoan, *A Drop in the Ocean: Hoang Van Hoan's Revolutionary Reminiscences* (Beijing: Foreign Languages Press, 1988), 382. According to another source, the "Lao Operations Committee" was called CP 31 ("Summary of Vietnamese Aid to the Lao Revolution (1945–1975)," 6.

14. "De an: Vien tro cho Vuong quoc va Pathet Lao nam 1961 cua Ban tiep te TW" [Program: Supplies for the Kingdom and Pathet Lao for 1961 by the Central Supply Committee], 8 August 1961, Ho so 7809: De an, bao cao cua Ban Liep te T-W, Bo Quoc phong va tieu ban nghien cuu cong tac Lao ve tinh hinh vien tro cho Lao nam 1961, Phong Phu Thu tuong, VNAC3, 1; "Dien van cua Bo truong Bo ngoai giao" [Message from the Foreign Minister], 30 November 1961, Ho so 7809: De an, bao cao cua Ban Liep te T-W, Bo Quoc phong va tieu ban nghien cuu cong tac Lao ve tinh hinh vien tro cho Lao nam 1961, Phong Phu Thu tuong, VNAC3, 1.

15. "Tieu ban nghien cuu cong tac Lao: De an cong tac kinh te tai chinh giup chinh phu Lao," 2.

16. "Dien van cua Bo truong Bo ngoai giao," 1.

17. "Cong cuoc hau can—Bao cao cong tac vien tro cho Lao nam 1961" [The Great Logistical Undertaking: Report on the Supply Work for Laos in 1961], 20 February 1962, Ho so 7809: De an, bao cao cua Ban Liep te T-W, Bo Quoc phong va tieu ban nghien cuu cong tac Lao ve tinh hinh vien tro cho Lao nam 1961, Phong Phu Thu tuong, VNAC3, 1, 15.

18. "Tong ket so vu khi dan duoc cua Trieu tien vien tro Pathet Lao trong nam 1961—Viet Nam da chuyen giao tu thang 1/1962 den thang 9/1962" [Summary of the Amount of Weapons (and) Ammunition Supplied by Korea to the Pathet Lao in 1961—Delivered by Vietnam between January and September 1962], 25 October 1962, Ho so 7809: De an, bao cao cua Ban Liep te T-W, Bo Quoc phong va tieu ban nghien cuu cong tac Lao ve tinh hinh vien tro cho Lao nam 1961, Phong Phu Thu tuong, VNAC3, 1. North Korea was the only member of the socialist camp to offer aid exclusively to the Pathet Lao.

19. "De an: Vien tro cho Vuong quoc va Pathet Lao nam 1961," 2–5.

20. Quoted in Aleksandr Fursenko and Timothy Naftali, *Khrushchev's Cold War: The Inside Story of an American Adversary* (New York: W. W. Norton, 2006), 327.

21. "Cong cuoc hau can—Bao cao cong tac vien tro cho Lao nam 1961," 1.

22. FGDH to MFA, 24 July 1961, 2.

23. Fursenko and Naftali, *Khrushchev's Cold War*, 334.

24. "Tieu ban nghien cuu cong tac Lao: De an cong tac kinh te tai chinh giup chinh phu Lao," 1, 3; FGDH to MFA, 22 December 1960, #35, AO: VN, ADF, 1.

25. "De an: Vien tro cho Vuong quoc va Pathet Lao nam 1961," 1, 6.

26. Thomas Perry Thornton, "Peking, Moscow, and the Underdeveloped Areas," *World Politics* 13, no. 4 (July 1961): 501–2.

27. Ilya V. Gaiduk, *Confronting Vietnam: Soviet Policy toward the Indochina Conflict, 1954–1963* (Washington, D.C.: Woodrow Wilson Center Press, 2003), 152–53.

28. Mari Olsen, *Soviet-Vietnam Relations and the Role of China, 1949–64: Changing Alliances* (New York: Routledge, 2006), 109–10.

29. Vladislav M. Zubok and Constantine Pleshakov, *Inside the Kremlin's Cold War: From Stalin to Khrushchev* (Cambridge, Mass.: Harvard University Press, 1997), 258. See also Marek Thee, *Notes of a Witness: Laos and the Second Indochina War* (New York: Random House, 1973), 201, 205.

30. British Consulate General, Hanoi [hereafter BCGH], to Southeast Asia Department, London [hereafter SEAD], 1 January 1962, FO 371/166712, NAUK, 1–2.

31. "Tieu ban nghien cuu cong tac Lao: De an cong tac kinh te tai chinh giup chinh phu Lao," 1.

32. "De an: Vien tro cho Vuong quoc va Pathet Lao nam 1961," 1.

33. "Tham luan ve tinh hinh Lao cua ong Nguyen Van Chi, dai bieu Khanh-hoap" [Address on the Situation in Laos by Mr. Nguyen Van Chi, representative of Khanh Hoap], 26 October 1961, Ho so 729: Ho so ky hop thu ba cua QH khoa III tu ngay 23–27.10.1961. Tap 3: Phien hop ngay 26.10.1961: Thuyet trinh ve tong quyet toan ngan sach Nha nuoc nam 1960, tham luan ve tang cuong phap che, tinh hinh mien Nam va dau tranh chong My, thong nhat dat nuoc, cong tac ngoai giao, Phong Quoc Hoi, VNAC3, 3.

34. Nguyen Dinh Binh, ed., *Ngoai giao Viet Nam, 1945–2000* [Vietnamese Diplomacy, 1945–2000] (Hanoi: Nha xuat ban Chinh tri quoc gia, 2005), 193; BCGH to SEAD, 1 January 1962, 1–2. The British Consulate concurred with that assessment, noting that Laotian neutrality would "give the D.R.V. security from its landward side, and rid them [sic] of the fear of a U.S. military base being established there" (ibid., 1).

35. William S. Turley, *The Second Indochina War: A Concise Political and Military History*, 2nd ed. (Lanham, Md.: Rowman & Littlefield, 2009), 67.

36. BCGH to SEAD, 1 January 1962, 2.

37. "DRV attitude to the neutralization of Laos and Viet Nam," 9 February 1962, FO 371/166712, NAUK, 1.

38. On the negotiations, see Arthur J. Dommen, *The Indochinese Experience of the French and the Americans: Nationalism and Communism in Cambodia, Laos, and Vietnam* (Bloomington: Indiana University Press, 2001), 443–54. The agreement actually consisted of three documents: the *Declaration on the Neutrality of Laos*, signed by all parties in attendance except the Laotian factions; a *Protocol to the Declaration*, listing the obligations of the signatories regarding withdrawal from Laos of foreign military personnel and the introduction of new forces; a *Statement of Neutrality of the Government of Laos*, signed by the new coalition government's foreign minister. Interestingly, the Laotian factions signed no formal agreement between themselves. According to Ilya Gaiduk, the outcome of the battle of Nam Tha expedited finalization of the agreement. See Gaiduk, *Confronting Vietnam*, 177.

39. Hugh Toye, *Laos: Buffer State or Battleground?* (London: Oxford University Press, 1968), 172.

40. "Bao cao cua Bo truong Bo Ngoai giao Ung Van Khiem ve ket qua cua Hoi nghi Gio-ne-vo ve Lao (tay ky hop thu 5 cua QH khoa 2, ngay 23 thang 10 nam 1962)" [Report of Foreign Minister Ung Van Khiem on the Results of the Geneva Conference on Laos (at the Fifth Meeting of the Second Session of the National Assembly, 23 October 1962)],

23 October 1962, Ho so 740: Ho so ky hop thu nam cua QH khoa II tu ngay 22.27.10.1962. Tap 2: Phien hop ngay 23.10.1962: Bao cao to trinh, Nghi quyet cua QH UBTVQH, PTT ve cong tac cua UBTVQH, ve tong quyet toan ngan sach Nha nuoc, ket qua Hoi nghi Gionevo ve Lao, ve to chuc HDND va UBHC cac cap, Phong Quoc hoi, VNAC3, 1–2.

41. Nguyen Vu Tung, "The 1961–1962 Geneva Conference: Neutralization of Laos and Policy Implications for Vietnam," in Goscha and Laplante, eds., *Failure of Peace in Indochina*," 255.

42. "Review of Events in North Vietnam (the D.R.V.) during 1962," FO 371/170088, NAUK, 3.

43. "Summary of Vietnamese Aid to the Lao Revolution (1945–1975)," 6.

44. "History of the Vietnamese Volunteer Groups and Vietnamese Military Specialists in Laos, 1945–1975: Group 100—Military Advisor; Group 959—Military Specialists" (document in Christopher Goscha's possession).

45. "Thu cua dong chi Le Duan, Bi thu thu nhat Dang Lao dong Viet Nam giu Trung uong Cuc mien Nam, ngay 18 thang 7 nam 1962: Ve cach mang mien Nam" [Letter from Comrade Le Duan, First Secretary of the Vietnamese Workers' Party, Sent to the Central Office for Southern Vietnam, 18 July 1962: On the Southern Revolution], in Dang Cong san Viet Nam, *Van kien Dang—Toan tap*, Tap 23: 1962 [Party Documents—Complete Series, Vol. 23: 1962] (Hanoi: Nha xuat ban Chinh tri quoc gia, 2002) [hereafter *VKD*: 1962], 707.

46. Party leaders, a former VWP cadre asserted, "always considered Indochina as one geographical entity and a single battlefield." See Bui Tin, *From Enemy to Friend: A North Vietnamese Perspective on the War* (Annapolis, Md.: Naval Institute Press, 2002), 11.

47. Nguyen Dinh Binh, ed., *Ngoai giao Viet Nam,* 192.

48. "Bao cao cua Bo truong Bo Ngoai giao Ung Van Khiem ve ket qua cua Hoi nghi Gio-ne-vo ve Lao," 3–4.

49. Quoted in FGDH to MFA, 1 August 1962, #73, AO: VN, ADF, 1.

50. Ken Post, *Revolution, Socialism and Nationalism in Viet Nam*, Vol. 3: *Socialism in Half a Country* (Belmont, Calif.: Wadsworth, 1989), 145.

51. Nguyen Vu Tung, "The 1961–1962 Geneva Conference," 263.

52. "Manifesto of the South Viet Nam National Front for Liberation" and "Program of the South Viet Nam National Front for Liberation," in *Manifesto of the South Viet Nam National Front for Liberation* (undated, no publisher); Robert K. Brigham, *Guerrilla Diplomacy: The NLF's Foreign Relations and the Viet Nam War* (Ithaca, N.Y.: Cornell University Press, 1999), 21–22.

53. Canberra to All Posts: "South Vietnam's Communist Proposals for an International Conference," 3 August 1962, FO 371/166763, NAUK, 2.

54. Ibid.; "Thong tri cua Ban Bi thu, so 45-TT/TW, ngay 31 thang 10 nam 1961: Ve mo mot cuoc dau tranh rong rai va manh me chong am muu can thiep moi cua de quoc My o mien Nam Viet Nam" [Secretariat Circular, no. 45-TT/TW, 31 October 1961: On Opening a Wide and Strong Struggle against the New Plan of Intervention of the American Imperialists in Southern Vietnam], in Dang Cong san Viet Nam, *Van kien Dang—Toan tap,* Tap 22: 1961 [Party Documents—Collected Works, Vol. 22: 1961] (Hanoi: Nha xuat ban Chinh tri quoc gia, 2002), 485.

55. Quoted in MFA, "Note pour le Cabinet du Ministre" [Note for the Council of Ministers], 15 December 1961, #33, AO: VN, ADF, 2.

56. The comments by Indian commissioner M. Parthasarathi are reported in BES to SEAD, 3 January 1962, FO 371/166725, NAUK, 1.

57. FO to BES, 12 January 1962, FO 371/166725, NAUK, 1.

58. Quoted in FO Minutes on "Demands for an International Conference on Vietnam, 1960–September 1963," 20 September 1963, FO 371/170153, NAUK, 1.

59. FGDH to MFA, 6 March 1962, #36, AO: VN, ADF, 1.

60. "Demands for an International Conference on Vietnam, 1960–September 1963," 2; FGDH to MFA, 1 May 1962, #73, AO: VN, ADF, 3.

61. BCGH to SEAD, 9 June 1962, FO 371/166763, NAUK, 1.

62. "Vietnam," 5 July 1962, FO 371/166763, NAUK, 1

63. "Trich tuyen bo cua UB TWMTDTGPMN, 20.7.1962" [Excerpt from the Declaration of the Central Committee of the National Liberation Front for South Vietnam, 20 July 1962], Ho so 231: Trich tuyen bo cua UBTWMTDTGPMN VN va MTTQVN tu 1955 den 1962, Phong Uy ban dieu tra toi ac cua de quoc My o Viet Nam, VNAC3, 3.

64. FGDH to MFA, 1 August 1962, B3.

65. Nguyen Vu Tung, "The 1961–1962 Geneva Conference," 259.

66. "Nghi quyet cua Bo Chinh tri, hop ngay 26–27, thang 2, nam 1962: Ve cong tac cach mang mien Nam" [Politburo Resolution, Meeting on 26–27 February 1962: On the Southern Revolution], in *VKD: 1962*, 163.

67. Brigham, *Guerrilla Diplomacy*, 21.

68. Quoted in David W. P. Elliott, *The Vietnamese War: Revolution and Social Change in the Mekong Delta, 1930–1975*, concise ed. (Armonk, N.Y.: M. E. Sharpe, 2007), 176.

69. Quoted in Duiker, *Communist Road to Power*, 220–21.

70. The number of American military personnel in South Vietnam, which stood at 3,205 at the end of 1961, jumped to approximately 9,000 by the end of 1962. See Seth Jacobs, *Cold War Mandarin: Ngo Dinh Diem and the Origins of America's War in Vietnam, 1950–1963* (Lanham, Md.: Rowman & Littlefield, 2006), 127; Mark Moyar, *Triumph Forsaken: The Vietnam War, 1954–1965* (New York: Cambridge University Press, 2006), 155.

71. Elliott, *Vietnamese War*, 175; BES to SEAD, 3 January 1962, 1.

72. Jacobs, *Cold War Mandarin*, 128.

73. "Hanh dong quan su phieu luu cua de quoc My mo rong chien tranh xam luoc o mien Nam Viet Nam duong bi dong bao mien Nam va toan dan kien quyet chong lai va ngay cang bi du luan hoa binh va dan chu tren the gioi kich liet len an: Bao cao truoc Quoc hoi khoa II ky hop thu 4 (thang 4 nam 1962) do Chu nhiem UBTN Nguyen van Vinh trinh bay" [The Adventurous Military Activities of the American Imperialists to Expand the War of Aggression in Southern Vietnam Are Resisted by the Determination of the Southern Compatriots and the Entire People and the Ever-Increasing Public Opinion Supportive of Peace and Democracy in the World: Report Presented before the Second Session, Fourth Meeting, of the National Assembly (April 1962) by the Chair of the Committee on National Reunification, Nguyen Van Vinh], 4 April 1962, Ho so 733: Ho so ky hop thu tu cua QH khoa II tu ngay 17–26.4.1962. Tap 2: Phien hop ngay 18.4.1962: Bao cao ve cong tac cua UBTVQH, ve bau cu bo sung DBQH, ve thuc hien ke hoach Nha nuoc nam 1962, thuc hien ngan sach Nha nuoc nam 1962, cong tac toa an va kiem sat nhan dan, Phong Quoc hoi, VNAC3, 2–3.

74. BES to SEAD, 13 March 1962, FO 371/166713, NAUK, 1.

75. FO to British Embassy, Washington, 23 March 1962, FO 371/166713, NAUK, 1.

76. Edward Miller, "Undoing the 'Limited Partnership': The Neutralization of Laos and the Origins of the Crisis of 1963 in South Vietnam," paper presented at the international workshop entitled "The Failure of Peace? Indochina between the Two Geneva Accords, 1954–1962," Université du Québec à Montréal, 6–7 October 2006, 9; Edward Miller, *Misalliance: Ngo Dinh Diem, the United States, and the Fate of South Vietnam* (Cambridge, Mass.: Harvard University Press, 2013), 247.

77. Moyar, *Triumph Forsaken*, 153. During the first half of 1962, South Vietnamese armed forces "went on the offensive and dislodged Communist forces from their most exposed positions" (Turley, *Second Indochina War*, 69).

78. Pham Huy Duong and Pham Ba Toan, *Ba muoi nam chien tranh giai phong: Nhung tran danh di vao lich su* [Thirty Years of Liberation War: Historical Battles] (Hanoi: Nha xuat ban Cong an nhan dan, 2005), 272.

79. Quoted in Elliott, *Vietnamese War*, 178. See also Philip E. Catton, *Diem's Final Failure: Prelude to America's War in Vietnam* (Lawrence: University Press of Kansas, 2002), 187–90.

80. Elliott, *Vietnamese War*, 175.

81. "Vietnam," 5 July 1962, 1.

82. Miller, "Undoing the 'Limited Partnership,'" 9.

83. Turley, *Second Indochina War*, 71.

84. FGDH to MFA, 1 November 1962, #73, AO: VN, ADF, 4.

85. FGDH to MFA, 1 November 1962, #1, AO: VC, ADF, 2–3.

86. "Review of Events in North Vietnam (the D.R.V.) during 1962," 1–2.

87. FGDH to MFA, 1 March 1962, #72, AO: VN, ADF, 4.

88. "Review of Events in North Vietnam (the D.R.V.) during 1962," 2.

89. British Embassy, Paris, to FO, 15 February 1962, FO 371/160125, NAUK, 1.

90. "Bao cao cua Bo truong Bo Ngoai giao Ung Van Khiem ve ket qua cua Hoi nghi Gio-ne-vo ve Lao," 4.

91. British Embassy, Paris, to FO, 15 February 1962, 2.

92. FGDH to MFA, 3 March 1962, #36, AO: VN, ADF, 8.

93. BCGH to SEAD, 16 February 1962, FO 371/166716, NAUK, 2.

94. The comments are reported in British Embassy, Paris, to FO, 15 February 1962, 1; BCGH to SEAD, 16 February 1962, 2.

95. These comments by a Yugoslav diplomat are reported in British Embassy, Paris, to FO, 15 February 1962, 1.

96. BCGH to SEAD, 16 February 1962, 2.

97. "Review of Events in North Vietnam (the D.R.V.) during 1962," 1.

98. Reported in BES to SEAD, 3 January 1962, 1.

99. FGDH to MFA, 3 March 1962, #36, AO: VN, ADF, 8.

100. "Canadian Report on Visit of Chinese Military Mission to DRV," 2 February 1962, FO 371/166713, NAUK, 3.

101. Céline Marangé, *Le communisme vietnamien, 1919–1991* [Vietnamese Communism, 1919–1991] (Paris: Presses de Sciences Po, 2012), 301.

102. Lorenz Lüthi, *The Sino-Soviet Split, 1956–1966* (Princeton, N.J.: Princeton University Press, 2008), 194–218.

103. "Bao cao cua Bo truong Bo Ngoai giao Ung Van Khiem ve ket qua cua Hoi nghi Gio-ne-vo ve Lao," 4.

104. BES to FO, "Review of Events in North Vietnam (the D.R.V.) during 1961," 31 January 1962, FO 371/166697, NAUK, 3–4.

105. The French position is related in British Embassy, Paris, to FO, 21 December 1961, FO 371/160125, NAUK, 1.

106. Quoted in BCGH to SEAD, 16 February 1962, 2.

107. "Bao cao cong tac Toa an nhan dan toi cao" [Report on the Work of the Supreme People's Tribunal], Ho so 733: Ho so ky hop thu tu cua QH khoa II tu ngay 17–26.4.1962. Tap 2: Phien hop ngay 18.4.1962: Bao cao ve cong tac cua UBTVQH, ve bau cu bo sung DBQH, ve thuc hien ke hoach Nha nuoc nam 1962, thuc hien ngan sach Nha nuoc nam 1962, cong tac toa an va kiem sat nhan dan, Phong Quoc hoi, VNAC3, 4.

108. "Bao cao cua dong chi Vien, truong Vien kiem sat nhan dan toi cao truoc QH khoa II ky hop thu tu cong tac Toa an nhan dan toi cao" [Report by Comrade Vien, Head of the People's Court of Investigation, before the Fourth Meeting, Second Session of the National Assembly], Ho so 733: Ho so ky hop thu tu cua QH khoa II tu ngay 17–26.4.1962. Tap 2: Phien hop ngay 18.4.1962: Bao cao ve cong tac cua UBTVQH, ve bau cu bo sung DBQH, ve thuc hien ke hoach Nha nuoc nam 1962, thuc hien ngan sach Nha nuoc nam 1962, cong tac toa an va kiem sat nhan dan, Phong Quoc hoi, VNAC3, 10–11.

109. International Commission for Supervision and Control in Vietnam, "Special Report to the Co-Chairmen of the Geneva Conference on Indo-China," 2 June 1962, R219-121-3-E (ICSC files), Vol. 9522 [Part 1], Record Group 25, Library and Archives Canada, Ottawa, 7.

110. Douglas A. Ross, "Middlepowers as Extra-Regional Balancer Powers: Canada, India, and Indochina, 1954–62," *Pacific Affairs* 55, no. 2 (Summer 1982): 205.

111. "Note: a/s des responsabilités dans l'origine du conflit vietnamien" [Note: On the Issue of Responsibility in the Origins of the Vietnamese Conflict], 8 March 1965, #147, AO: VC, ADF, 1.

112. "Review of Events in North Vietnam (the D.R.V.) during 1962," 3; "Déclaration du Government de la République Démocratique du Vietnam sur le rapport spécial adressé aux Co-Presidents de la Conference de Genève de 1954 par les délégués indien et canadien à la Commission International de Contrôle au Vietnam" [Statement by the Democratic Republic of Vietnam Government on the Special Report by the Indian and Canadian Delegates to the International Control Commission in Vietnam Addressed to the Cochairs of the 1954 Geneva Conference], 4 June 1962, #45, AO: VN, ADF, 1.

113. Brigham, *Guerrilla Diplomacy*, 21.

114. "Dien van be mac cua Truong Chinh" [Closing Address by Truong Chinh], 27 October 1962, Ho so 742: Ho so ky hop thu nam cua QH khoa II tu ngay 22–27.10.1962. Tap 4: Phieu hop ngay 27.10.1962: Tham luan cua DBQH ve to chuc HDND va UBHC cac cap, ve tinh hinh mien Nam va thong nhat nuoc, Phong Quoc hoi, VNAC3, 4–5.

115. "Bao cao cua Bo truong Bo Ngoai giao Ung Van Khiem ve ket qua cua Hoi nghi Gio-ne-vo ve Lao," 9.

116. "Review of Events in North Vietnam (the D.R.V.) during 1962," 1–2.

117. FGDH to MFA, 1 August 1962, B3.

118. FGDH to MFA, 1 March 1962, 3.

119. Quoted in FGDH to MFA, "Visite de M. Bernard Fall au Président Pham Van Dong" [Visit by Mr. Bernard Fall to President Pham Van Dong], 16 July 1962, #31, AO: VN, ADF, 3.

120. Duiker, *Communist Road to Power*, 222–23.

121. Bernard B. Fall, ed., *Ho Chi Minh: On Revolution—Selected Writings, 1920–66* (London: Pall Mall, 1967), 352–58; Ang Cheng Guan, *Vietnamese War from the Other Side*, 64.

122. "Thu cua dong chi Le Duan, Bi thu thu nhat Dang Lao dong Viet Nam giu Trung uong Cuc mien Nam, ngay 18 thang 7 nam 1962," 705–25.

123. Foreign diplomats concurred with that assessment. Successful negotiations leading to the creation of a neutralist regime in the South willing to "co-exist and co-operate with the North" and allow for "many humanitarian measures," such as interchange of families, resumption of postal service, and restoration of trade, would not only "meet with deep popular approval" but also enhance the image and prestige of the DRVN and its communist leadership among southerners ("Review of Events in North Vietnam (the D.R.V.) during 1962," 2; BCGH to SEAD, 1 January 1962, 3).

124. "South Vietnam: Communist Proposals for an International Conference" (Australian Government Report), 3 August 1962, FO 371/166763, NAUK, 1.

125. Canberra to All Posts: "South Vietnam's Communist Proposals for an International Conference," 1–3.

126. BCGH to SEAD, 23 July 1962, FO 371/166725, NAUK, 1; BCGH to SEAD, 28 February 1962, FO 371/166725, NAUK, 1.

127. BES, "Notes on History, Organisation and Policy to Date of the Front for the National Liberation of South Vietnam," 5 September 1962, FO 371/166725, NAUK, 1.

128. BCGH to BES, 3 September 1962, FO 371/166725, NAUK, 1.

129. British Embassy, Paris to FO, 15 February 1962, 2.

130. BCGH to BES, 3 September 1962, 1.

131. FO to BES, 16 March 1962, FO 371/166725, NAUK, 1.

132. BES, "Notes on History, Organisation and Policy to Date of the Front for the National Liberation of South Vietnam," 1.

133. BCGH to SEAD, 31 October 1962, FO 371/166725, NAUK, 2.

134. Office of the British Chargé d'Affaires, Beijing, to SEAD, 25 September 1962, FO 371/166713, NAUK, 1.

135. BCGH to SEAD, 12 March 1962, FO 371/166725, NAUK, 1.

136. FO to British Embassy, Paris, 14 May 1962, FO 371/166725, NAUK, 1.

137. BES, "Notes on History, Organisation and Policy to Date of the Front for the National Liberation of South Vietnam," 3.

138. FO to British Embassy, Paris, 14 May 1962, 1.

139. P. H. Roberts (BES), "The Front for the National Liberation of South Vietnam," August 1962, FO 371/166725, NAUK, 8–9.

140. BCGH to SEAD, 21 September 1962, FO 371/166737, NAUK, 1.

141. Mr. Goburdhan's visit with Ho is summarized in BES to BCGH, 26 September 1962, FO 371/166725, NAUK, 1.

142. BCGH to SEAD, 6 August 1962, FO 371/166710, NAUK, 1.

143. Ibid.; BCGH to SEAD, 1 January 1962, 2.

144. FGDH to MFA, 1 February 1962, #72, AO: VN, ADF, 2–3.

145. Nguyen Vu Tung, "The 1961–1962 Geneva Conference," 258.

146. "Du thao de cuong gioi thieu ve tinh hinh ve duong loi cach mang mien Nam" [Introductory Draft Report on the Situation and Path of the Southern Revolution], undated, Ho so 252: Du thao de cuong ve tinh hinh va duong loi cach mang mien Nam 1962, Phong Uy ban Thong nhat Nha nuoc, VNAC3, 26.

147. BCGH to SEAD, 21 August 1962, FO 371/166725, NAUK, 1; BCGH to SEAD, 4 December 1962, FO 371/166725, NAUK, 1–2.

148. "Review of Events in North Vietnam (the D.R.V.) during 1962," 2.

149. Edwin E. Moïse, "The Mirage of Negotiations," in Lloyd C. Gardner and Ted Gittinger, eds., *The Search for Peace in Vietnam, 1964–1968* (College Station: Texas A&M University Press, 2004), 81.

150. "Tham luan van de dau tranh thong nhat To quoc, Nghiem-xuan-Yem, dai bieu Dang Dan chu Viet Nam" [Address on the Issue of the Fatherland Reunification Struggle, Nghiem Xuan Yem, Representative of the Democratic Party of Vietnam], 3; and "Tham luan ve van de dau tranh thong nhat cua dai bieu Dang Xa hoi Viet Nam, Hoang Minh Giam" [Address on the Issue of the Reunification Struggle by the Representative of the Vietnamese Socialist Party, Hoang Minh Giam], 6. Both in Ho so 742: Ho so ky hop thu nam cua QH khoa II tu ngay 22–27.10.1962. Tap 4: Phieu hop ngay 27.10.1962: Tham luan cua DBQH ve to chuc HDND va UBHC cac cap, ve tinh hinh mien Nam va thong nhat nuoc, Phong Quoc hoi, VNAC3.

151. "Bao cao cua Bo truong Bo Ngoai giao Ung Van Khiem ve ket qua cua Hoi nghi Gio-ne-vo ve Lao," 5.

152. Moïse, "Mirage of Negotiations," 81.

153. Author conversation with a retired DRVN diplomat who prefers to remain anonymous, Hanoi, Vietnam, July 2006.

154. "Notes on North Vietnam by J. K. Blackwell, H.M. Consul General, Hanoi," 22 April 1963, FO 371/170098, NAUK, 3.

155. "Hanh dong quan su phieu luu cau de quoc My mo rong chien tranh xam luoc o mien Nam Viet Nam," 13.

156. BCGH to SEAD, 3 November 1962, FO 371/166712, NAUK, 1.

157. Sergei Radchenko, *Two Suns in the Heavens: The Sino-Soviet Struggle for Supremacy, 1962–1967* (Stanford, Calif.: Stanford University Press, 2009), 44.

158. Dong's remarks and the western response to them appear in BCGH to SEAD, 3 November 1962, 1.

159. "Tham luan ve tinh hinh Lao, dai bieu Pham-ngoc-Que, Phu-yen" [Address on the Situation in Laos by Representative Pham Ngoc Que of Phu Yen], Ho so 749, Ho so ky hop thu sau cua QH khoa II tu ngay 28.4.1963—08.5.1963. Tap 7: Phien hop ngay 08.5.1963: Tham luan cua DBQH ve dau tranh thong nhat dat nuoc o mien Nam, ve tinh hinh Tay Nguyen, ve tang cuong quan ly kinh te tai chinh, Nghi quyet va bao cao cua CP, Phong Quoc hoi, VNAC3, 4.

160. Balazs Szalontai, *Kim Il Sung in the Khrushchev Era: Soviet–DPRK Relations and the Roots of North Korean Despotism, 1953–1964* (Stanford, Calif.: Stanford University Press, 2005), 192.

161. BCGH to SEAD, 3 November 1962, 1.

162. BCGH to SEAD, 9 December 1962, FO 371/166712, NAUK, 1.

163. "Loi chao mung Quoc hoi VNDCCH cua g.s. Nguyen Van Hien, truong dai bieu MTDTGPMNVN, 23.10.1962 [Welcome Address before the DRVN National Assembly by Professor Nguyen Van Hien, Head Representative of the NLF, 23 October 1962], Ho so 740: Ho so ky hop thu nam cua QH khoa II tu ngay 22.27.10.1962. Tap 2: Phien hop ngay 23.10.1962: Bao cao to trinh, Nghi quyet cua QH UBTVQH, PTT ve cong tac cua UBTVQH, ve tong quyet toan ngan sach Nha nuoc, ket qua Hoi nghi Gionevo ve Lao, ve to chuc HDND va UBHC cac cap, Phong Quoc hoi, VNAC3, 4.

164. "Tuyen bo cua QH nuoc VNDCCH ung ho chu truong cua Hoi nghi nhan dan toi cao nuoc chu nghia dan chu cong hoa Trieu-tien doi de quoc My rut khoi Nam Trieu-tien nham hoa binh thong nhat nuoc Trieu-tien, 27.10.1962 [Declaration by the DRVN National Assembly Supporting the Supreme People's Assembly of the Democratic People's Republic of Korea Demanding the Withdrawal of American Imperialists from South Korea to Bring About the Peaceful Reunification of Korea, 27 October 1962], Ho so 742: Ho so ky hop thu nam cua QH khoa II tu ngay 22-27.10.1962. Tap 4: Phien hop ngay 27.10.1962: Tham luan cua DBQH ve to chuc HDND va UBHC cac cap, ve tinh hinh mien Nam va thong nhat nuoc, Phong Quoc hoi, VNAC3.

165. "Report of Visit to North Vietnam by a Delegation of the South Vietnam Liberation National Front (from Canadian Element of the I.C.C.)," 5 November 1962, FO 371/170115, NAUK, 4–5.

166. FGDH to MFA, 1 January 1963, #74, AO: VN, ADF, 2.

6. CHOOSING WAR, 1963

1. "The Current Position of North Vietnam in the Sino-Soviet Dispute," 26 February 1963, FO 371/170103, National Archives of the United Kingdom, Kew [hereafter NAUK], 1.

2. Jean Lacouture, *Ho Chi Minh: A Political Biography* (New York: Random House, 1968), 248. The DRVN had four deputy prime ministers at the time.

3. Lien-Hang T. Nguyen, *Hanoi's War: An International History of the War for Peace in Vietnam* (Chapel Hill: University of North Carolina Press, 2012), 53.

4. A party resolution dated 11 February 1963 on the "tasks and direction of the effort to organize and build the party" did not even allude to the existence of tensions within the VWP. See "Nghi quyet cua Ban Bi thu, so 69-NQ/TW, ngay 11 thang 2 nam 1963: Ve nhiem vu va phuong huong cong tac to chuc, xay dung Dang nam 1963" [Secretariat Resolution, no. 69-NQ/TW, 11 February 1963: On the Tasks and Direction of the Effort to Organize, Build the Party in 1963], in Dang Cong san Viet Nam, *Van kien Dang—Toan tap,* Tap 24: 1963 [Party Documents—Complete Series, Vol. 24: 1963] (Hanoi: Nha xuat ban Chinh tri quoc gia, 2003) [hereafter *VKD*: 1963], 82–92.

5. The comments are reported in French General Delegation, Hanoi [hereafter FGDH], to Ministry of Foreign Affairs, Paris [hereafter MFA], 17 January 1963, #36, Asie-Océanie [hereafter AO]: Vietnam Nord [hereafter VN], Archives Diplomatiques de France, La Courneuve [hereafter ADF], 1.

6. "Thong tri cua Ban Bi thu, so 112-TT/TW, ngay 28 thang 2 nam 1963: Ve ky niem 80 nam ngay mat cua Cac Mac" [Secretariat Circular, no. 112-TT/TW, 28 February 1963: On the Eightieth Anniversary of the Death of Karl Marx], in *VKD*: 1963, 178.

7. Quoted in FGDH to MFA, 18 March 1963, #17, AO: VN, ADF, 2.

8. The Nguyen Ai Quoc schools were a "comprehensive system of theoretical schools of the party from the central level to the provinces and districts." Their mission was "training or giving complementary theoretical courses" to "responsible cadres in various localities." After 1957, the Nguyen Ai Quoc School (Section I) in Hanoi trained "high- and middle-ranking cadres and political lecturers for the various branches" of the party. It also ran "special courses for elaborate study of problems of Marxism-Leninism applied to the practice of the Vietnamese revolution" organized by the party itself. See Ho Hai, "The Nguyen Ai Quoc Schools," *Vietnam*, no. 148 (1970): 9.

9. "Nguyen Dinh Phuong, "Mot vai ky niem ve Bo truong Xuan Thuy" [Some Memories of Foreign Minister Xuan Thuy], in Bo Ngoai giao, *Chan dung nam co Bo truong Ngoai giao* [Portraits of Five Foreign Ministers] (Hanoi: Nha xuat ban Chinh tro quoc gia, 2005), 323–24.

10. Nguyen Chi Thanh, "Let Us Improve Our Proletarian Stand and Ideology, and Unite and Struggle for New Successes," *Hoc tap*, no. 10 (October 1963). Reproduced and translated in Folder 02, Box 25, Douglas Pike Collection [hereafter DPC]: Unit 06—Democratic Republic of Vietnam, Vietnam Archive at Texas Tech University [hereafter VATTU], 19.

11. "North Vietnam Today," November 1965, 20-VIET-N-1-4, Vol. 9001, Record Group [hereafter RG] 25, Library and Archives Canada, Ottawa [hereafter LAC], 2.

12. Le Duc Tho, "Let Us Strengthen the Ideological Struggle to Consolidate the Party," *Tuyen huan*, no. 4 (April 1964). Reproduced and translated in Folder 03, Box 25, DPC: Unit 06—Democratic Republic of Vietnam, VATTU, 13.

13. Tran Quoc Tu, "Peace and Revolution," *Hoc tap*, no. 1 (January 1964). Reproduced and translated in Folder 03, Box 25, DPC: Unit 06—Democratic Republic of Vietnam, VATTU, 15.

14. Le Duc Tho, "Let Us Strengthen the Ideological Struggle to Consolidate the Party," 16. See also "Nghi quyet cua Bo Chinh tri, so 95-NQ/TW, ngay 4 thang 2 nam 1964: Ve nhiem vu cong tac tu tuong trong nam 1964" [Politburo Resolution, no. 95-NQ/TW, 4 February 1964: On the Tasks of Ideological Work in 1964], in Dang Cong san Viet Nam, *Van kien Dang—Toan Tap*, Tap 25: 1964 [Party Documents—Complete Series, Vol. 25: 1964] (Hanoi: Nha xuat ban Chinh tri quoc gia, 2003) [hereafter referred to as *VKD*: 1964], 59.

15. Nguyen Chi Thanh, "Let Us Improve Our Proletarian Stand and Ideology," 20. See also "Chi thi cua Bo Chinh tri, so 74-CT/TW, ngay 27 thang 1 nam 1964: Ve viec to chuc hoc tap Nghi quyet Hoi nghi lan thu chin cua Trung uong ve van de quoc te" [Politburo Instruction, no. 74-CT/TW, 27 January 1964: On the Effort to Organize the Ninth Plenum of the Central Committee on International Problems], in *VKD*: 1964, 59.

16. Nguyen Chi Thanh, "Let Us Improve Our Proletarian Stand and Ideology," 6.

17. Ibid., 10.

18. British Consulate General, Hanoi [hereafter BCGH], to Southeast Asia Department, London [hereafter SEAD], 14 January 1963, FO 371/170103, NAUK, 1.

19. FGDH to MFA, 1 January 1963, #74, AO: VN, ADF, 4.

20. "Dien cua Ban Bi thu giu Trung uong Cuc mien Nam, ngay 24 thang 1 nam 1963: Khen ngoi va dong vien toan the Dang bo va dong bao mien Nam" [Secretariat Cable to the Central Office for Southern Vietnam, 24 January 1963: Praising and Encouraging the Entire Party Branch and Compatriots in the South], in *VKD*: 1963, 69.

21. The editorial is translated and reproduced in FGDH to MFA, 31 January 1963, #36, AO: VN, ADF, 2.

22. "Chi thi cua Ban Bi thu, so 60-CT/TW, ngay 25 thang 2 nam 1963: Ve nhiem vu cong tac tuyen giao trong nam 1963" [Secretariat Instruction, no. 60-CT/TW, 25 February 1963: On the Responsibilities for Carrying Out Propaganda and Education Work], in *VKD*: 1963, 157–70.

23. Pierre Brocheux, *Ho Chi Minh* (Paris: Presses de Sciences Po, 2000), 184; "Nghi quyet cua Trung uong Cuc mien Nam, thang 7 nam 1963: Ve cong tac chong, pha khu, ap chien chien luoc, gom dan" [Central Office for Southern Vietnam Resolution, July 1963: On the Effort to Oppose and Destroy Strategic Hamlets That Imprison People], in *VKD*: 1963, 878.

24. "Notes on North Vietnam" by J. K. Blackwell, H. M. Consul General, Hanoi, 22 April 1963, FO 371/170098, NAUK, 3.

25. BCGH to British Embassy, Moscow, 7 March 1963, FO 371/170108, NAUK, 2.

26. "Phuong huong, nhiem vu ke hoach phat trien kinh te va van hoa 5 nam lan thu nhat (1961–1965): Bao cao tai Hoi nghi lan thu tam cua Ban Chap hanh Trung uong Dang, ngay 27 thang 3 nam 1963" [Direction, Responsibilities of the First Five-Year Plan for Economic and Cultural Development (1961–1965): Report before the Eighth Plenum of the Central Committee, 27 March 1963], in *VKD*: 1963, 287–442.

27. FGDH to MFA, 8 August 1963, #75, AO: VN, ADF, D1.

28. Roger E. Kanet, "The Soviet Union and the Third World from Khrushchev to Gorbachev: The Place of the Third World in Evolving Soviet Global Strategy," in Roger E. Kanet, ed., *The Soviet Union, Eastern Europe and the Third World* (New York: Cambridge University Press, 1987), 7.

29. Ilya Gaiduk, "Containing the Warriors: Soviet Policy toward the Indochina Conflict, 1960–65," in Lloyd C. Gardner and Ted Gittinger, eds., *International Perspectives on Vietnam* (College Station: Texas A&M University Press, 2000), 75.

30. FGDH to MFA, 14 January 1963, #36, AO: VN, ADF, 3; and FGDH to MFA, 21 January 1963, #36, AO: VN, ADF, 1–2.

31. "Dien van cua d/c I.V. An-do-ro-pop, 16.1.63" [Address by Comrade I. V. Andropov, 16 January 1963], Ho so 1046: Ho so ve doan dai bieu Xo viet toi cao Lien Xo do ong Andropop lam truong doan sang tham Viet Nam tu ngay 12–20.01.1963. Tap 2: Dien van, dien tu va cac loi phat bieu trong thoi gian doan o Viet Nam, Phong Quoc hoi, Vietnam National Archives Center 3, Hanoi [hereafter VNAC3], 4.

32. "Bao cao cua Chinh phu do TT Pham Van Dong trinh bay, 29.4.1963" [Government Report by Prime Minister Pham Van Dong, 29 April 1963], Ho so 744: Ho so ky hop thu sau cua QH khoa II tu ngay 28.4.1963—08.5.1963. Tap 2: Phien hop ngay 29.4.1963: Bao cao cua UBTVQH va CP va cong tac cua UBTVQH, ve tinh hinh mien Bac, mien Nam va quoc te, ve du an phat trien kinh te quoc dan 5 nam lan thu 1 (1961–1965) va ke hoach nam 1963, Phong Quoc hoi, VNAC3. On Dong's support for moderate policies, see "Factions within the North Vietnamese Regime: Their Bearing, If Any, on Policy Pursued towards South Vietnam," undated [1960], FO 371/160122, NAUK, 4.

33. Quoted in "Note: Conversation avec M. de La Boissière," 25 September 1963, 2.

34. British Embassy, Paris, to SEAD, 27 March 1963, FO 371/170103, NAUK, 1.

35. "Chi thi cua Ban Bi thu, so 63-CT/TW, ngay 5 thang 6 nam 1963: Ve viec to chuc mot tuan le dau tranh vao dip 20 thang 7 nam 1963" [Secretariat Instruction, no. 63-CT/TW, 5 June 1963: On the Effort to Organize One Week of Celebration on the Occasion of 20 July 1963], in *VKD*: 1963, 585–90; and Nguyen Dinh Liem, ed., *Quan he Viet Nam—Trung quoc:*

Nhung su kien 1961–1970 [Vietnam-China Relations: Developments, 1961–1970] (Hanoi: Nha xuat ban Khoa hoc xa hoi, 2006), 243.

36. Janos Radvanyi, *Delusion and Reality: Gambits, Hoaxes, and Diplomatic One-Upmanship in Vietnam* (South Bend, Ind.: Gateway, 1978), 13.

37. "Loi phat bieu cua Ho Chu tich trong phien hop be mac ngay 8 thang 5 nam 1963" [Presentation by President Ho at the Closing Session, 8 May 1963], Ho so 749: Ho so ky hop thu sau cua QH khoa II tu ngay 28.4.1963—08.5.1963. Tap 7: Phien hop ngay 08.5.1963: Tham luan cua DBQH ve dau tranh thong nhat dat nuoc o mien Nam, ve tinh hinh Tay Nguyen, ve tang cuong quan ly kinh te tai chinh, Nghi quyet va bao cao cua CP, Phong Quoc hoi, VNAC3, 4.

38. "Notes on North Vietnam," 2.

39. FGDH to MFA, 1 March 1963, #74, AO: VN, ADF, B3.

40. Nguyen Chi Thanh, "Let Us Improve Our Proletarian Stand and Ideology," 12.

41. FGDH to MFA, 1 April 1963, #74, AO: VN, ADF, 6. The 13 March editorial is translated and reproduced in FGDH to MFA, 21 March 1963, #17, AO: VN, ADF.

42. Lacouture, *Ho Chi Minh*, 220.

43. By a somewhat later official account, Hanoi had by the end of 1963 dispatched to the South approximately 40,000 cadres and troops consisting primarily of southern regroupees. Those forces constituted half of PLAF regulars and 80 percent of cadres and technical personnel in southern revolutionary organs. See Military Institute of Vietnam, *Victory in Vietnam: The Official History of the People's Army of Vietnam, 1954–1975*, trans. Merle L. Pribbenow (Lawrence: University Press of Kansas, 2002), 115.

44. "The D.R.V. and the Sino-Soviet Dispute," 1.

45. David M. Toczek, *The Battle of Ap Bac, Vietnam* (Annapolis, Md.: Naval Institute Press, 2001), 65–108; Mark Moyar, *Triumph Forsaken: The Vietnam War, 1954–1965* (New York: Cambridge University Press, 2006), 186–205.

46. *Brève Histoire du Parti des Travailleurs du Viet Nam, 1930–1970* [Brief History of the Vietnamese Workers' Party] (Hanoi: Éditions en langues étrangères, 1970), 110.

47. Bo Quoc phong—Vien Lich su quan su Viet Nam, *Lich su quan su Viet Nam, Tap 11: Cuoc khang chien chong My, cuu nuoc, 1954–1975* [Military History of Vietnam, Volume 11: The Anti-American Resistance for National Salvation] (Hanoi: Nha xuat ban Chinh tri quoc gia, 2005), 148.

48. Military Institute of Vietnam, *Victory in Vietnam*, 120.

49. Nguyen Khac Vien, "The Impotence of American Technique in the Face of the People's War," *Vietnamese Studies* 5, no. 12 (1966): 119.

50. Bo Quoc phong—Vien Lich su quan su Viet Nam, *Lich su quan su Viet Nam, Tap 11*, 148; from a February 1965 letter reproduced in Le Duan, *Thu vao Nam* [Letters to the South] (Hanoi: Nha xuat ban Su that, 1985), 69.

51. "Nghi quyet Hoi nghi TWC lan thu hai, so 2/NQ, thang 3 nam 1964" [Resolution of the Second Plenum of the Central Office for Southern Vietnam, no. 2/NQ, March 1964], in *VKD*: 1964, 701–2.

52. "Tham luan ve phong trao day tranh pha 'ap chien luoc' cua dong bao mien Nam d/b Gia-dinh Tran van Nguyen tring bay" [Address on the Movement to Destroy "Strategic Hamlets" of the Southern Compatriots by the Representative from Gia Dinh, Tran Van Nguyen], Ho so 749: Ho so ky hop thu sau cua QH khoa II tu ngay 28.4.1963—08.5.1963. Tap 7: Phien hop ngay 08.5.1963: Tham luan cua DBQH ve dau tranh thong nhat dat nuoc o

mien Nam, ve tinh hinh Tay Nguyen, ve tang cuong quan ly kinh te tai chinh, Nghi quyet va bao cao cua CP, Phong Quoc hoi, VNAC3, 6–7.

53. "Report of the Activities of the International Commission in Vietnam, August 1963," 21-13-VIET-ICSC-8 [FP.1], Vol. 10125, RG 25; LAC, 1. On the 1963 Buddhist crisis, see Howard Jones, *Death of a Generation: How the Assassinations of Diem and JFK Prolonged the Vietnam War* (New York: Oxford University Press, 2003); Edward Miller, *Misalliance: Ngo Dinh Diem, the United States, and the Fate of South Vietnam* (Cambridge, Mass.: Harvard University Press, 2013), chapters 8–9.

54. On Sino-Vietnamese relations to that point, see Ang Cheng Guan, *Vietnamese Communists' Relations with China and the Second Indochina Conflict, 1956–1962* (Jefferson, N.C.: McFarland, 1997).

55. Xiaoming Zhang, "The Vietnam War, 1964–1969: A Chinese Perspective," *Journal of Military History* 60, no. 4 (October 1996): 734–35, 746.

56. Lorenz Lüthi, "The Vietnam War and China's Third-Line Defense Planning before the Cultural Revolution, 1964–1966," *Journal of Cold War Studies* 10, no. 1 (Winter 2008): 48. On the further radicalization of Chinese foreign policy at this time, see also Chen Jian, *Mao's China and the Cold War* (Chapel Hill: University of North Carolina Press, 2001), 210–11.

57. Xiaoming Zhang, "Vietnam War," 734–35, 746. See also Qiang Zhai, *China and the Vietnam Wars, 1950–1975* (Chapel Hill: University of North Carolina Press, 2000), 117–18.

58. Lüthi, "The Vietnam War and China's Third-Line Defense," 48.

59. On Chinese perceptions of the Soviet Union and its relationship to the United States at the time, see Chun-tu Hsueh and Robert C. North, "China and the Superpowers: Perception and Policy," in Chun-tu Hsueh, ed., *China's Foreign Relations: New Perspectives* (New York: Praeger, 1982), 20. For a more recent perspective and an assessment of new Chinese sources on the topic, see Michael H. Hunt and Odd Arne Westad, "The Chinese Communist Party and International Affairs: A Field Report on New Historical Sources and Old Research Problems," *China Quarterly*, no. 122 (June 1990): 258–72. While the Chinese would denounce Khrushchev openly and by name, the VWP never did so. See King C. Chen, ed., *China and the Three Worlds: A Foreign Policy Reader* (White Plains, N.Y.: M. E. Sharpe, 1979), 20.

60. Brantly Womack, *China and Vietnam: The Politics of Asymmetry* (New York: Cambridge University Press, 2006), 173.

61. Min Chen, *The Strategic Triangle and Regional Conflict: Lessons from the Indochina Wars* (Boulder, Colo.: Lynne Rienner, 1992), 22.

62. Balazs Szalontai, *Kim Il Sung in the Khrushchev Era—DPRK Relations and the Roots of North Korean Despotism, 1953–1964* (Stanford, Calif.: Stanford University Press, 2005), 187–88. Khiem stepped down as foreign minister, according to one version of events, because he was behind a pro-Soviet communiqué issued at the conclusion of a visit to Hanoi by Czechoslovak president Antonin Novotny in January (Martin Grossheim, "'Revisionism' in the Democratic Republic of Vietnam," *Cold War History* 5, no. 4 [November–December 2005]: 453). According to British diplomats, Xuan Thuy was "much less approachable than his predecessor" and insisted on speaking Vietnamese or Chinese but not French with western diplomats despite a thorough grasp of the latter (BCGH to SEAD, 18 August 1964, FO 371/175486, NAUK, 1). The substitution of foreign

ministers became a good indicator during this period of the attitude of VWP leaders toward the situation in the South and, by extension, the Sino-Soviet dispute. Ung Van Khiem personified the prevailing consensus within the VWP leadership until spring 1963, as he was very much pro-Soviet and distrustful of Beijing and the revolutionary line it peddled. Xuan Thuy, his ideological nemesis, replaced him just as the VWP's position on the southern revolution hardened and Hanoi moved closer to Beijing. Thuy himself was replaced by the more "middle-of-the-road" Nguyen Duy Trinh in April 1965, days after Moscow pledged substantial political and material, including military, support for the DRVN, and just before the commencement of war with the United States mandated rapprochement with Moscow.

63. Excerpts from Liu's speeches are quoted in BCGH to SEAD, 20 May 1963, FO 371/170105, NAUK, 2.

64. FGDH to MFA, 18 May 1963, #38, AO: VN, ADF, 9.

65. BCGH to SEAD, 20 May 1963, 1, 4.

66. William E. Griffith, *The Sino-Soviet Rift* (Cambridge: Massachusetts Institute of Technology Press, 1964), 192–93.

67. Hoang Van Chi, *From Colonialism to Communism: A Case History of North Vietnam* (New York: Pall Mall Press, 1964), 71.

68. FGDH to MFA, 1 June 1963, #74, AO: VN, ADF, 2; "Monthly Review of Events in North Vietnam, June–July 1963," 20-VIET N-2-1, Vol. 10067 [Part 1], RG 25, LAC, 1.

69. BCGH to SEAD, 20 May 1963, FO 371/170105, NAUK, 1, 4.

70. Ho's comments are reported in "'The World Situation and Our Party's International Mission': As Seen from Hanoi, 1960–1964," September 1971, Document no. 98, Vietnam Documents and Research Notes, Box 2, Folder 03, Viet-Nam Documents and Research Notes Collection, VATTU, 55–67.

71. Odd Arne Westad, *The Global Cold War: Third World Interventions and the Making of Our Times* (New York: Cambridge University Press, 2005), 135–36.

72. Gareth Porter, "Hanoi's Strategic Perspective and the Sino-Vietnamese Conflict," *Pacific Affairs* 57, no. 1 (Spring 1984): 8.

73. By December 1963, North Vietnamese personnel in Laos included 11,600 main-line, "volunteer" troops, 337 military specialists, 364 political specialists, and 100 other specialists and technicians ("Summary of Vietnamese Aid to the Lao Revolution [1945–1975]," Science Section of the General Department of Rear Services, People's Army of Vietnam, 7 [document in Christopher Goscha's possession]).

74. "Bao cao cua Chinh phu do TT Pham Van Dong trinh bay, 29.4.1963," 105.

75. Francis X. Winters, *The Year of the Hare: America in Vietnam, January 25, 1963–February 15, 1964* (Athens: University of Georgia Press, 1997); Fredrik Logevall, *Choosing War: The Lost Chance for Peace and the Escalation of War in Vietnam* (Berkeley: University of California Press, 2001), 6–12; Mieczyslaw Maneli, *War of the Vanquished* (New York: Harper and Row, 1971), 121–29, 187–91, 198–208; Donald S. Zagoria, *Vietnam Triangle: Moscow, Peking, Hanoi* (New York: Pegasus, 1967), 108; and Arthur J. Dommen, *The Indochinese Experience of the French and the Americans: Nationalism and Communism in Cambodia, Laos, and Vietnam* (Bloomington: Indiana University Press, 2001), 530–35.

76. Logevall, *Choosing War*, 12.

77. Ellen J. Hammer, *A Death in November: America in Vietnam, 1963* (New York: Oxford University Press, 1987), 223–24.

78. According to historian Pierre Journoud, Roger Lalouette, the French ambassador in Saigon, was responsible for the "origination" of this "point of contact *[prise de contact]*" between Hanoi and Saigon in 1963. Earlier that year, Lalouette had shared with Maneli the details of a three-phase plan he had devised. The plan called for the opening of a dialogue between Hanoi and Saigon, followed by coordination of economic and cultural exchanges, and culminating in the beginning of negotiations on substantive political issues. "Seduced by the qualities of the French diplomat as much as by the audacity of his plan," Journoud writes, "Maneli decided to transmit the message to Hanoi." See Pierre Journoud, *De Gaulle et le Vietnam, 1945–1969: La réconciliation* [De Gaulle and Vietnam, 1945–1969: The Reconciliation] (Paris: Éditions Tallandier, 2011), 113.

79. "Note: Conversation avec M. de La Boissière" [Note: Conversation with M. de La Boissière], 25 September 1963, #38, AO: VN, ADF, 2–3. Possibly, Nhu's interlocutor was DRVN minister of health Dr. Pham Ngoc Thach. According to French records, "One day [Thach] had drunk a fair amount during a reception" in Hanoi and "he intimated to the director of the French school [there] that he 'travel[s] regularly to South Vietnam,'" presumably to negotiate with authorities there.

80. Saigon's position on the talks differed. In October 1963, a State Department official confided in a Canadian counterpart that "Nhu seemed to have [the] feeling that he might be able to do a deal with North Vietnam, perhaps in [the] next few months, whereby he could obtain [a] ceasefire in [the] South in return for a) withdrawal of USA military personnel, and b) permission for North-South trade to remedy [the] North's difficult economic position." But Nhu and his brother had no intention of surrendering to Hanoi. "Nhu was apparently confident," the American official added, "that after the ceasefire he would be quite capable of worsting the communists ideologically in the South with his own peasant programme and his own type of corporate state." See Washington to Ottawa, 4 October 1963, 20-VIET S-1-4, Vol. 9001 [Part 1], RG 25, LAC, 2–4.

81. Margaret K. Gnoinska, "Poland and Vietnam, 1963: New Evidence on Secret Communist Diplomacy and the 'Maneli Affair,'" Cold War International History Project Working Paper no. 45, Woodrow Wilson Center, Washington, D.C., 2005, 1–6.

82. On de Gaulle's call for neutralization, see Journoud, *De Gaulle et le Vietnam*, 117–31; Marianna P. Sullivan, *France's Vietnam Policy: A Study in Franco-American Relations* (Westport, Conn.: Greenwood Press, 1978), 62–83; and Charles G. Cogan, "'How Fuzzy Can One Be?': The American Reaction to De Gaulle's Proposal for the Neutralization of (South) Vietnam," in Lloyd C. Gardner and Ted Gittinger, eds., *The Search for Peace in Vietnam, 1964–1968* (College Station: Texas A&M University Press, 2004), 144–61.

83. British Embassy, Paris, to Foreign Office, London [hereafter FO], 30 August 1963 [shared with Ottawa], 20-VIET-S-1-4, Vol. 9001, RG 25, LAC; and "Report of Activities of the International Commission in Vietnam, September 1963, 21-13-VIET-ICSC-8, Vol. 10125 [FP 1], RG 25, LAC, 1.

84. Quoted in "Notes: Réactions dans le monde à la déclaration du Général de Gaulle" [Notes: World Reaction to the Statement by General de Gaulle], 18 September 1963, #162, AO: Vietnam Conflit, ADF, 2.

85. Gareth Porter, "Coercive Diplomacy in Vietnam: The Tonkin Gulf Crisis Reconsidered," in Jayne Werner and David Hunt, eds., *The American War in Vietnam* (Ithaca, N.Y.: Cornell Southeast Asia Program, 1993), 18–20.

86. Gareth Porter, *Perils of Dominance: Imbalance of Power and the Road to War in Vietnam* (Berkeley: University of California Press, 2005), 108–26.

87. Dommen, *Indochinese Experience of the French and the Americans*, 495.

88. Miller, *Misalliance*, 304.

89. Douglas Pike, "The Impact of the Sino-Soviet Dispute on Southeast Asia," in Herbert J. Ellison, ed., *The Sino-Soviet Conflict: A Global Perspective* (Seattle: University of Washington Press, 1982), 189.

90. "Monthly Review of Events in North Vietnam, June–July 1963," 1–2; "Comments on 'Report on the Visit of Liu Shao Chi and Chen Yi to Hanoi,'" by P. Roberts, 28 June 1963, FO 371/170105, NAUK, 3.

91. BCGH to SEAD, 2 September 1963, FO 371/170098, NAUK, 2–3.

92. BCGH to SEAD, 1 June 1963, FO 371/170098, NAUK, 1; "Summary of Events in North Vietnam, July 1963," undated, FO 371/170098, NAUK, 2.

93. John Donnell and Melvin Gurtov, *North Vietnam: Left of Moscow, Right of Peking* (Santa Monica, Calif.: RAND, 1968), 33. One of the most revealing articles was Nguyen Chi Thanh's "Ai se thang ai o mien Nam Viet Nam?" [Who Will Defeat Whom in Vietnam?], *Hoc tap*, no. 7 (July 1963): 18–21, translated as "Qui vaincra au Sud Vietnam?" *Études Vietnamiennes*, no. 1 (1964): 13–22.

94. "The Renegade Tito Again Spits Out the Poison of Revisionism," *Hoc tap*, no. 7 (July 1963): 16; quoted in Ken Post, *Revolution, Socialism and Nationalism in Viet Nam, Volume 3: Socialism in Half a Country* (Belmont, Calif.: Wadsworth, 1989), 162.

95. "Raise High the Banner of the Prohibition of Nuclear Weapons and Direct the Spearhead of the Struggle against U.S. Imperialism," *Hoc tap*, no. 9 (September 1963): 15; quoted in Post, *Revolution, Socialism and Nationalism*, 163.

96. Hong Chuong, "Peace or Violence," *Hoc tap*, no. 9 (September 1963). Reproduced and translated in Folder 01, Box 03, DPC: Unit 01—Assessment and Strategy, VATTU, 1–17.

97. "Monthly Review of Events in North Vietnam, September–October 1963"; 20-VIET N-2-1; Vol. 10067 [Part 1]; RG 25; LAC, 3 (emphasis in original).

98. Qiang Zhai, *China and the Vietnam Wars*, 124; Joachim Glaubitz, "Relations between Communist China and North Vietnam," in Robert A. Rupen and Robert Farrell, eds., *Vietnam and the Sino-Soviet Dispute* (New York: Praeger, 1967), 63.

99. The article is translated and reproduced in FGDH to MFA, 30 September 1963, #36, AO: VN, ADF. The quote is from page 4 of the reproduction.

100. Qiang Zhai, *China and the Vietnam Wars*, 124.

101. *Nhan dan*, 4 August 1963, 8.

102. Quoted in Post, *Revolution, Socialism and Nationalism*, 163.

103. FGDH to MFA, 12 August 1963, #36, AO: VN, ADF, 2.

104. BCGH to SEAD, 19 November 1963, FO 371/170099, NAUK, 2.

105. FGDH to MFA, 9 October 1963, #75, AO: VN, ADF, B3.

106. BCGH to SEAD, 2 September 1963, FO 371/170098, NAUK, 2.

107. FGDH to MFA, 30 September 1963, 4.

108. Douglas Pike, *Viet Cong: The Organization and Techniques of the National Liberation Front of South Vietnam* (Cambridge: Massachusetts Institute of Technology Press, 1966), 102.

109. Mission in Charge of Relations with the ICSC, Saigon, to Secretariat General of the ICSC, Saigon, 10 December 1963, 21-13-VIET-ICSC-8, Vol. 10125 [FP 1], RG 25, LAC, 1.

110. Canadian Delegation [ICSC], Saigon, to Under Secretary of State for External Affairs, Ottawa, 19 January 1966, 20-22-VIET S-1, Vol. 9387 [Part 3], RG 25, LAC, 1.

111. FO to Canada House, London, 23 October 1963, FO 371/170103, NAUK, 1.

112. Ton That Thien, *The Foreign Politics of the Communist Party of Vietnam: A Study in Communist Tactics* (New York: Crane Russak, 1989), 128.

113. Quoted in FGDH to MFA, 9 October 1963, #36, AO: VN, ADF, 2.

114. Ibid.

115. "Monthly Review of Events in North Vietnam for November 1963," 20-VIET N-2-1, Vol. 10067 [Part 1], RG 25, LAC, 1.

116. BCGH to SEAD, 19 November 1963, FO 371/170099, NAUK, 4.

117. According to Le Cuong, Washington "secretly" decided to "change horses mid-stream" immediately following the battle of Ap Bac. See Le Cuong, "Phong trao Phat giao mien Nam Viet Nam nam 1963 voi cuoc dao chinh lat do che do Ngo Dinh Diem (01–11–1963)" [The 1963 Buddhist Movement in Southern Vietnam and the Overthrow of Ngo Dinh Diem], paper presented at the Second International Conference on Vietnamese Studies, Ho Chi Minh City, Vietnam, 14–16 July 2004, 4.

118. Ibid.; Ha Van Lau, "Kennodi phai Mac Namara va Taylo sang Viet Nam de lam gi?" [Kennedy Sent MacNamara and Taylor to Vietnam to What End?], *Hoc tap*, no. 11 (November 1963): 60.

119. "Du thao de cuong gio thieu ve tinh hinh va duong loi cach mang mien Nam, so 226 T/TM" [Draft Program Introducing the Situation and Direction of the Southern Revolution, no. 226T/TM], undated (1962), Ho so 252: Du thao de cuong ve tinh hinh va duong loi cach mang Mien Nam, 1962-, Phong Uy ban Thong nhat Chinh phu, VNAC3, 16; Bo Quoc phong—Vien Lich su quan su Viet Nam, *Lich su quan su Viet Nam, Tap 11*, 149. A history of the period by an American scholar suggests that the Vietnamese were not completely wrong in assuming the United States was primarily responsible. According to Mark Moyar, "ultimate responsibility" for Diem's fate "belonged to [U.S. ambassador to RVN] Henry Cabot Lodge, to the President who appointed and refused to fire Lodge, and to the individuals who were giving Lodge information and advice on the political situation" in South Vietnam (Moyar, *Triumph Forsaken*, 273).

120. "Diem was a 'modern nationalist,'" one source contends, and "it was his determination to push ahead with his own nation-building agenda that was a major source of the tensions in U.S.-Vietnamese relations." See Phillip E. Catton, *Diem's Final Failure: Prelude to America's War in Vietnam* (Lawrence: University Press of Kansas, 2002), 2; and Miller, *Misalliance*, chapter 9.

121. Robert S. McNamara, James Blight, and Robert Brigham, *Argument without End: In Search of Answers to the Vietnam Tragedy* (New York: Public Affairs, 1999), 200.

122. A 1967 Hanoi publication referred to "a military dictatorship" replacing the "nepotic [sic] and feudal" regime of Ngo Dinh Diem. See Tran Cong Tuong and Pham Thanh Vinh, *The N.L.F.: Symbol of Independence, Democracy and Peace in South Vietnam* (Hanoi: Foreign Languages Publishing House, 1967), 15.

123. Le Cuong, "Phong trao Phat giao mien Nam," 5.

124. Philippe Franchini, *Les guerres d'Indochine, Vol. 2: De la bataille de Dien Bien Phu à la chute de Saïgon* [The Indochina Wars, Vol. 2: From the Battle of Dien Bien Phu to the Fall of Saigon] (Paris: Éditions Pygmalion / Gérard Watelet, 1988), 266.

125. Quoted in McNamara, Blight, and Brigham, *Argument without End*, 201. According to Nguyen Vu Tung, "This situation . . . increased the danger of a U.S. direct military intervention" (Nguyen Vu Tung, "The 1961–1962 Geneva Conference: Neutralization of Laos and Policy Implications for Vietnam," in Christopher E. Goscha and Karine Laplante, eds., *L'échec de la paix en Indochine / The Failure of Peace in Indochina [1954–1962]* [Paris: Les Indes savantes, 2010], 251).

126. Bo Quoc phong—Vien Lich su quan su Viet Nam, *Lich su quan su Viet Nam, Tap 11*, 150.

127. Dommen, *Indochinese Experience of the French and the Americans*, 572.

128. BCGH to SEAD, 11 January 1964 [shared with Ottawa], 3.

129. BCGH to SEAD, 19 November 1963, FO 371/170099, NAUK, 4.

130. Moyar, *Triumph Forsaken*, 286; "Political Bureau Resolution," November 1963, Folder 02, Box 1, DPC: Unit 06—Democratic Republic of Vietnam, VATTU.

131. Jeffrey Race, "The Origins of the Second Indochina War," *Asian Survey*, no. 5 (May 1970): 360–63.

132. George K. Tanham, *Communist Revolutionary Warfare: From the Vietminh to the Viet Cong* (Westport, Conn.: Praeger Security International, 2006), 70, 72. See also Fredrik Logevall, *Embers of War: The Fall of an Empire and the Making of America's Vietnam* (New York: Random House, 2012), 683.

133. Report of Activities of the International Commission in Vietnam, December 1963, 21-13-VIET-ICSC-8, Vol. 10125 [FP 1], RG 25, LAC, 1.

134. Pham Huy Duong and Pham Ba Toan, *Ba muoi nam chien tranh giai phong: Nhung tran danh di vao lich su* [Thirty Years of Liberation War: Historical Battles] (Hanoi: Nha xuat ban Cong an nhan dan, 2005), 328.

135. David W.P. Elliott, *The Vietnamese War: Revolution and Social Change in the Mekong Delta, 1930–1975*, concise ed. (Armonk, N.Y.: M. E. Sharpe, 2007), 430. See also the comments by Nguyen Khac Huynh, a senior researcher at the Institute of International Relations in Hanoi, in McNamara, Blight, and Brigham, *Argument without End*, 92.

136. King C. Chen, "Hanoi's Three Decisions and the Escalation of the Vietnam War," *Political Science Quarterly* 90, no. 2 (Summer 1975): 251.

137. Quoted in Grossheim, "'Revisionism' in the Democratic Republic of Vietnam," 457.

138. McNamara, Blight, and Brigham, *Argument without End*, 201.

139. Lien-Hang T. Nguyen and Martin Grossheim offered that date, though it remains unknown precisely when the meeting opened or concluded. See Lien-Hang T. Nguyen, "The War Politburo: North Vietnam's Diplomatic and Political Road to the Tet Offensive," *Journal of Vietnamese Studies* 1, nos. 1–2 (February/August 2006): 16; and Grossheim, "'Revisionism' in the Democratic Republic of Vietnam," 457. The fact that after more than forty years Hanoi has never disclosed the dates of the plenum, either when it convened or when it adjourned, suggests that much more than meets the eye was at stake then. While some foreign scholars claim that the plenum may have extended into the new year (Ang Cheng Guan, "The Vietnam War, 1962–64: The Vietnamese Communist Perspective,"

Journal of Contemporary History 35, no. 4 [October 2000]: 616), a reproduction of the final resolution of the plenum released recently by the VWP is dated December 1963. See "Nghi quyet cua Hoi nghi lan thu chin Ban Chap hanh Trung uong Dang Lao dong Viet Nam: Ve tinh hinh the gio va nhiem vu quoc te cua Dang ta, thang 12 nam 1963" [Resolution of the Ninth Plenum of the Central Committee of the Vietnamese Workers' Party: On the World Situation and the International Tasks of Our Party, December 1963], in *VKD*: 1963, 716.

140. William S. Turley, *The Second Indochina War: A Concise Political and Military History*, 2nd ed. (Lanham, Md.: Rowman & Littlefield, 2009), 82; Dommen, *Indochinese Experience of the French and the Americans*, 573.

141. William J. Duiker, *Ho Chi Minh: A Life* (New York: Theia, 2000), 537; Grossheim, "'Revisionism' in the Democratic Republic of Vietnam," 458; and Brocheux, *Ho Chi Minh*, 246.

142. Duiker, *Ho Chi Minh*, 537.

143. Mari Olsen, *Soviet-Vietnam Relations and the Role of China, 1949-64: Changing Alliances* (New York: Routledge, 2006), 129-30.

144. The full text of the speech is reproduced in Le Duan, *Some Questions concerning the International Tasks of Our Party: Speech at the Ninth Plenum of the Third Central Committee of the Viet Nam Workers' Party* (Beijing: Foreign Languages Press, 1964).

145. Hoang Van Hoan, *A Drop in the Ocean: Hoang Van Hoan's Revolutionary Reminiscences* (Beijing: Foreign Languages Press, 1988), 318.

146. Lien-Hang T. Nguyen, *Hanoi's War*, 66.

147. "Nghi quyet cua Hoi nghi lan thu chin Ban Chap hanh Trung uong Dang Lao dong Viet Nam: Ve tinh hinh the gio va nhiem vu quoc te cua Dang ta, thang 12 nam 1963," 716-800.

148. "Nghi quyet cua Hoi nghi lan thu chin Ban Chap hanh Trung uong Dang Lao dong Viet Nam: Ra suc phan dau, tien len gianh nhung thang loi moi o mien Nam, thang 12 nam 1963" [Resolution of the Ninth Plenum of the Central Committee of the Vietnamese Workers' Party: Strive to Struggle, Rush Forward to Win New Victories in the South, December 1963], in *VKD*: 1963, 811-62.

149. "Hoi nghi Ban Chap hanh Trung uong Dang lan thu chin (Thang 12—1963)" [Ninth Plenum of the Central Committee, December 1963], in Nguyen Trong Phuc, ed., *Tim hieu lich su Dang Cong san Viet Nam: Qua cac Dai hoi va Hoi nghi Trung uong, 1930-2002* [Understanding the History of the Vietnamese Communist Party: Congresses and Central Committee Plenums, 1930-2002] (Hanoi: Nha xuat ban Lao dong, 2003), 530-38.

150. "Nghi quyet cua Hoi nghi lan thu chin Ban Chap hanh Trung uong Dang Lao dong Viet Nam: Ra suc phan dau, tien len gianh nhung thang loi moi o mien Nam, thang 12 nam 1963," 860 (emphasis in original).

151. Military Institute of Vietnam, *Victory in Vietnam*, 125-26.

152. Ang Cheng Guan, *The Vietnam War from the Other Side: The Vietnamese Communists' Perspective* (New York: RoutledgeCurzon, 2002), 75. According to historian Georges Boudarel, the plenum marked the decision to fully commit the North to the violent liberation of the South, to "intervene militarily . . . in support of the National Liberation Front." See Georges Boudarel, *Cent fleurs éclosent dans la nuit du Viêt Nam* [One hundred Flowers Blooming in the Night of Vietnam] (Paris: Jacques Bertoin, 1991), 258.

153. Lien-Hang T. Nguyen, "Between the Storms: An International History of the Second Indochina War, 1968-1973" (PhD diss., Yale University, 2008), 31.

154. Sophie Quinn-Judge, "The Ideological Debate in the DRV and the Significance of the Anti-Party Affair, 1967–68," *Cold War History* 5, no. 4 (November–December 2005): 483.

155. Nguyen Chi Thanh, "Let Us Improve Our Proletarian Stand and Ideology," 5.

156. Duiker, *Ho Chi Minh*, 505; Bui Tin, *Following Ho Chi Minh: Memoirs of a North Vietnamese Colonel* (Honolulu: University of Hawaii Press, 1999), 32. For a more comprehensive yet partisan assessment of Le Duc Tho, see *Nho ve Anh Le Duc Tho* [Remembering Le Duc Tho] (Hanoi: Nha xuat ban Chinh tri quoc gia, 2001).

157. The VWP announced the launching of the "rectification campaign" in *Nhan dan* on 3 and 4 February 1964.

158. Le Duc Tho, "Let Us Strengthen the Ideological Struggle to Consolidate the Party," 19, 23.

159. Bui Tin, *Following Ho Chi Minh*, 46, 53, 55–56. Hoang Minh Chinh later admitted that Truong Chinh in fact "coaxed and cajoled" him into preparing the materials in question (Lien-Hang T. Nguyen, "War Politburo," 45n68).

160. Grossheim, "'Revisionism' in the Democratic Republic of Vietnam," 454–58; Franchini, *Guerres d'Indochine*, 271; Bui Tin, *Following Ho Chi Minh*, 54–55. Other notable individuals affected by these events included *Quan doi Nhan dan* editor Hoang The Dung, head of military operations Do Duc Kien, director of military intelligence Nguyen Minh Nghia, secretary to the defense minister Le Minh Nghia, and *Su that* publishing house deputy head Nguyen Kien Giang.

161. Turley, *Second Indochina War*, 82–83. Shortly after the plenum, Quoc requested and was granted a transfer to the Soviet Union and served in the armed forces there until his retirement.

162. Grossheim, "'Revisionism' in the Democratic Republic of Vietnam," 459–60.

163. Lien-Hang T. Nguyen, "War Politburo," 45n66. See also Judy Stowe, "Révisionnisme au Vietnam" in *Communisme*, nos. 65–66 (2001): 233–49. Some dissidence, of course, remained. In fact, the VWP would conduct a second round of purges in 1967, just before launching the Tet Offensive, during which several of the individuals who had been ostracized and demoted immediately after the Ninth Plenum were arrested and committed to lengthy prison terms. On that episode see Lien-Hang T. Nguyen, "War Politburo," 45; and Quinn-Judge, "Ideological Debate," 479–500.

164. The death of Duong Bach Mai shortly after the plenum (April 1964) led to speculations that foul play was involved. The East German Foreign Ministry in fact considered Mai a casualty of the leftists' power play whose "elimination" was "deliberate" (Grossheim, "'Revisionism' in the Democratic Republic of Vietnam," 460).

165. Turley, *Second Indochina War*, 82.

166. BCGH to SEAD, 29 September 1964, FO 371/175486, NAUK, 1; Grossheim, "'Revisionism' in the Democratic Republic of Vietnam," 464–66.

167. BCGH to SEAD, 1 August 1964, FO 371/175481, NAUK, 1.

168. Lien-Hang T. Nguyen, "War Politburo," 18.

169. Brocheux, *Ho Chi Minh*, 204.

170. Ibid., 184; Vu Thu Hien, *Dem giua ban ngay: Hoi ky chinh tri cua mot nguoi khong lam chinh tri* [Day Turns into Night: Political Memoirs of a Non-Politician] (Stanton, Calif.: Van Nghe, 1997), 230; Turley, *Second Indochina War*, 81.

171. Grossheim, "'Revisionism' in the Democratic Republic of Vietnam," 454–55.

172. BCGH to SEAD, 4 January 1963, FO 371/170097, NAUK, 1.
173. William J. Duiker, *The Communist Road to Power in Vietnam*, 2nd ed. (Boulder, Colo.: Westview Press, 1996), 412n13.
174. Phnom Penh to Ottawa, 9 September 1967, 20-VIET N-6, Vol. 9167 [Part 1], RG 25, LAC, 1.
175. Ho went on to "play a crucial diplomatic role that helped North Vietnam to manage a policy of equilibrium between China and the Soviet Union," historian Lien-Hang T. Nguyen has written. See Lien-Hang T. Nguyen, "Cold War Contradictions: Toward an International History of the Second Indochina War, 1969–1973," in Mark Philip Bradley and Marilyn B. Young, eds., *Making Sense of the Vietnam Wars: Local, National, and Transnational Perspectives* (New York: Oxford University Press, 2008), 230; and Ang Cheng Guan, *Vietnam War from the Other Side*, 142. Ho's particularly good relationship with Mao Zedong was—in conjunction with other factors—instrumental in securing Chinese support for the Vietnamese struggle in the South, first against the French and then against the Americans. Ho, David Marr writes, "was eminently qualified simultaneously to charm the Chinese and to assert party independence." See David G. Marr, "Sino-Vietnamese Relations," *Australian Journal of Chinese Affairs*, no. 6 (July 1981): 53.
176. Duiker, *Ho Chi Minh*, 508.
177. Saigon (from Hanoi) to Ottawa, 22 June 1964, 29-39-1-2-A, Vol. 3092 [Part 1], RG 25, LAC, 2.
178. According to historian Martin Grossheim, Giap was placed under house arrest as early as mid-1963 (Grossheim, "'Revisionism' in the Democratic Republic of Vietnam," 454).
179. BCGH to British Embassy, Saigon, 8 November 1963, FO 371/170099, NAUK, 1.
180. Turley, *Second Indochina War*, 103. Historian Christopher Goscha characterized Le Duan and Le Duc Tho as the two most powerful party leaders during the Vietnam War. See Christopher E. Goscha, *Historical Dictionary of the Indochina War (1945–1954): An International and Interdisciplinary Approach* (Copenhagen: Nordic Institute of Asian Studies Press, 2011), 261.
181. Turley, *Second Indochina War*, 103.
182. On the consolidation of Le Duan's authority at this time, see Lien-Hang T. Nguyen, "Between the Storms," 23–36. By Le Duc Tho's own admission, a number of party members believed that the new circumstances and new leaders' "prejudices" restricted their "freedom of thought" (Le Duc Tho, "Let Us Strengthen the Ideological Struggle to Consolidate the Party," 20).
183. "Le Duan, First Secretary of the Lao Dong Central Committee," 11 March 1973, 20-VIET N-6, Vol. 9167 [Part 1], RG 25, LAC, 1.
184. "The launching of the Tet Offensive," Nguyen writes, "signified the end of a bitter, decade-long debate" over strategy within the VWP (Lien-Hang T. Nguyen, "War Politburo," 6).

7. WAGING WAR, 1964

1. David W. P. Elliott, "Hanoi's Strategy in the Second Indochina War," in Jayne S. Werner and Luu Doan Huynh, eds., *The Vietnam War: Vietnamese and American Perspectives* (New York: M. E. Sharpe, 1993), 69.

2. Military Institute of Vietnam, *Victory in Vietnam: The Official History of the People's Army of Vietnam, 1954–1975*, trans. Merle L. Pribbenow (Lawrence: University Press of Kansas, 2002), 122.

3. Quoted in King C. Chen, "Hanoi's Three Decisions and the Escalation of the Vietnam War," *Political Science Quarterly* 90, no. 2 (Summer 1975): 253–54.

4. Military Institute of Vietnam, *Victory in Vietnam*, 126.

5. Saigon to Ottawa, 18 April 1964, 20-22-VIET S-1, 9385 [Part 1], Record Group [hereafter RG] 25, Library and Archives Canada, Ottawa [hereafter LAC], 1–2.

6. British Embassy, Saigon [hereafter BES], to Foreign Office, London [hereafter FO], 1 January 1965, FO 371/180511, National Archives of the United Kingdom, Kew [hereafter NAUK], 1; "North Viet-Nam: Annual Review for 1964," 13 February 1965, FO 371/180511, NAUK, 4.

7. "Record of Conversation: Visit of Messrs Sullivan and Cooper to the Department," 3 June 1964, 29-39-1-2-A, Vol. 3092 [Part 1], RG 25, LAC, 2.

8. "Summary Record of Conversation between the Minister and Mr. Sullivan, May 29, 1964," 3 June 1964, 29-39-1-2-A, Vol. 3092 [Part 1], RG 25, LAC, 1; and "Record of Conversation: Visit of Messrs Sullivan and Cooper to the Department," 3 June 1964, 2.

9. "Du thao de cuong gio thieu ve tinh hinh va duong loi cach mang mien Nam, so 226 T/TM" [Draft Program Introducing the Situation and Direction of the Southern Revolution, no. 226 T/TM], undated (1964), Ho so 252: Du thao de cuong ve tinh hinh va duong loi cach mang Mien Nam, 1962–, Phong Uy ban Thong nhat Chinh phu, Vietnamese National Archives Center 3, Hanoi [hereafter VNAC3], 36, 49–50.

10. Military Institute of Vietnam, *Victory in Vietnam*, 124–25.

11. William J. Duiker, *The Communist Road to Power in Vietnam*, 2nd ed. (Boulder, Colo.: Westview Press, 1996), 250. That estimate is reasonable, though Vietnamese sources mention no specific deadline. An official party history states that the deadline was "a few years" *(mot vai nam)*. See Vien nghien cuu chu nghia Mac-Lenin va tu tuong Ho Chi Minh, *Lich su Dang Cong san Viet Nam, Tap 2: 1954–1975* [History of the Communist Party of Vietnam, Volume 2: 1954–1975] (Hanoi: Nha xuat ban Chinh tri quoc gia, 1995), 267.

12. "Du thao de cuong gio thieu ve tinh hinh ve duong loi cach mang mien Nam," 44.

13. "Report of International Commission Activities, February 1964," 21-13-VIET-ICSC-8, Vol. 10125 [FP 2.2], RG 25, LAC, 1.

14. "Note: La situation politique au Sud-Vietnam et la politique américaine" [Note: The Political Situation in South Vietnam and American Policy], 26 February 1964, #313, Asie-Océanie [hereafter AO]: Vietnam Conflit [hereafter VC], Archives Diplomatiques de France, La Courneuve [hereafter ADF], 1.

15. Office of the High Commissioner for Canada, Wellington, New Zealand, to the Under-Secretary of State for External Affairs, Ottawa, Canada, "SEATO Council Meeting, Manila, 13–15 April 1964: Recent Developments Affecting the Situation in the Treaty Area," 14 April 1964, 20-22-VIET S-1 [Part 1], Vol. 9385, RG 25, LAC, 3.

16. French Embassy, Saigon, to MFA, 23 February 1964, #131, AO: VC, ADF, 1.

17. "Report on the Activities of the International Commission in Vietnam for the Month of May, 1964," 21-13-VIET-ICSC-6 [FP.1], Vol. 10125, RG 25, LAC, 2.

18. "Note: Situation au Vietnam," 4 February 1964, #313, AO: VC, ADF, 2.

19. "Report from the Executive Director–Comptroller of Central Intelligence (Kirkpatrick) and the Station Chief in Saigon (de Silva) to the Director of Central Intelligence

(McCone)," 10 February 1964, in United States Department of State, *Foreign Relations of the United States, 1964-1968*, Vol. 1: *Vietnam, 1964* (Washington, D.C.: U.S. Government Printing Office, 1992) [hereafter *FRUS: I, VN, 1964*], 65.

20. Canadian Embassy, Saigon (from Hanoi), to Ottawa, undated (1964), 20-Viet-N-1-4, Vol. 9001, RG 25, LAC, 3.

21. Tran Quoc Tu, "Peace and Revolution," *Hoc tap*, no. 1 (January 1964). Reproduced and translated in Folder 03,Box 25, Douglas Pike Collection [hereafter DPC]: Unit 06—Democratic Republic of Vietnam, Vietnam Archive at Texas Tech University [hereafter VATTU], 8a.

22. Gareth Porter, "Hanoi's Strategic Perspective and the Sino-Vietnamese Conflict," *Pacific Affairs* 57, no. 1 (Spring 1984): 13.

23. Military Institute of Vietnam, *Victory in Vietnam*, 137. The use of the term *Vietnam War (chien tranh Viet Nam)* in this context, in this source and others, indicates that to Vietnamese military historians a state of actual war existed in Vietnam by 1964, before the introduction of U.S. combat forces.

24. Tran Quoc Tu, "Peace and Revolution," 24.

25. "Balance of Forces and the Strategy of Offense," *Hoc tap*, no. 1 (January 1964). Reproduced and translated in Folder 03, Box 25, DPC: Unit 06—Democratic Republic of Vietnam, VATTU, 20.

26. King C. Chen, "Hanoi vs. Peking: Policies and Relations—A Survey," *Asian Survey* 12, no. 9 (September 1972): 808.

27. Tran Quoc Tu, "Peace and Revolution," 8, 9, 27.

28. Ang Cheng Guan, "The Vietnam War, 1962-64: The Vietnamese Communist Perspective," *Journal of Contemporary History* 35, no. 4 (October 2000): 618.

29. "Du thao de cuong gio thieu ve tinh hinh ve duong loi cach mang mien Nam," 34.

30. Ibid., 56.

31. According to William Duiker, Hanoi remained reluctant to go all out and deploy PAVN units "out of fear that such actions could trigger an escalation of the U.S. role in the war" on the one hand, and because it had promised Moscow and Beijing that "even if the United States should intervene directly in the South, the DRVN would restrain Washington from extending the war to North Vietnam" on the other. See William Duiker, "Waging Revolutionary War: The Evolution of Hanoi's Strategy in the South, 1959-1965," in Werner and Huynh, eds., *Vietnam War*, 31.

32. "Chi thi cua Bo Chinh tri, so 81-CT/TW, ngay 7 thang 8 nam 1964: Ve tang cuong san sang chien dau chong moi am muu cua dich khieu khich va pha hoai mien Bac" [Politburo Instruction, no. 81-CT/TW, 7 August 1964: On Increasing Preparation to Struggle against the Enemy's Plan to Sabotage and Destroy the North], in Dang Cong san Viet Nam, *Van kien Dang—Toan Tap*, Tap 25: 1964 [Party Documents—Complete Series, Vol. 25: 1964] (Hanoi: Nha xuat ban Chinh tri quoc gia, 2003) [hereafter *VKD: 1964*], 189.

33. "Du thao de cuong gio thieu ve tinh hinh ve duong loi cach mang mien Nam, 33."

34. According to western estimates, by 1964 the PAVN disposed of sixteen regular divisions (280,000 men), several militias (180,000 men), and a public security/border force (20,000 men). In addition to these effectives, Hanoi could "immediately mobilize" a reserve militia force numbering an additional 400,000 ("Note: a/s de l'Armée Nord-Vietnamienne" [Note: On the North Vietnamese Army], 23 May 1964, #19, AO: Vietnam Nord [hereafter VN], ADF, 1.

35. FGDH to MFA, 2 June 1964, #76, AO: VN, ADF, C3.
36. Department of State—Bureau of Intelligence and Research, "Hanoi Foresees Victory in South Vietnam—But Only after Long Guerrilla War," 15 February 1964, 20-22-VIET S-1 [Part 1], Vol. 9385, RG 25, LAC, 5.
37. Fredrik Logevall, *Embers of War: The Fall of an Empire and the Making of America's Vietnam* (New York: Random House, 2012), 711.
38. Balazs Szalontai, *Kim Il Sung in the Khrushchev Era: Soviet–DPRK Relations and the Roots of North Korean Despotism, 1953–1964* (Stanford, Calif.: Stanford University Press, 2005), 203.
39. Ilya V. Gaiduk, *Confronting Vietnam: Soviet Policy toward the Indochina Conflict, 1954–1963* (Washington, D.C.: Woodrow Wilson Center Press, 2003), 204.
40. Moscow to Ottawa, 14 February 1964, 20-VIET N-1-3, Vol. 8892 [Part 1], RG 25, LAC, 1.
41. French Embassy, Washington, to MFA, 17 February 1964, #313, AO: VC, ADF, 1; Mari Olsen, *Soviet–Vietnam Relations and the Role of China, 1949–64: Changing Alliances* (New York: Routledge, 2006), 131. For a detailed account of the meeting, see Ilya V. Gaiduk, *The Soviet Union and the Vietnam War* (Chicago: Ivan R. Dee, 1996), 6–10.
42. Olsen, *Soviet–Vietnam Relations*, 127; Kurt L. London, "Vietnam: A Sino-Soviet Dilemma," *Russian Review* 26, no. 1 (January 1967): 29. "The interest of the Soviet Union, both as a nation state and as a bastion of world communism," London noted, required "a long period of peace during which the much heralded 'transition to communism' can be effected."
43. French Embassy, Moscow, to MFA, 15 February 1964, #36, AO: VN, ADF, 2.
44. Moscow to Ottawa, 20 February 1964, 20-VIET N-1-3, Vol. 8892 [Part 1], RG 25, LAC, 2.
45. Chen Jian, "China's Involvement in the Vietnam War, 1964–1969," *China Quarterly*, no. 142 (June 1995): 384. Unlike Soviet aid during this period, Chinese aid was "less oriented toward key projects and was more multi-dimensional and flexible," which no doubt facilitated Vietnamese endeavors in the South following the adoption of military struggle. See Brantly Womack, *China and Vietnam: The Politics of Asymmetry* (New York: Cambridge University Press, 2006), 170–71.
46. Chen Jian, "China's Involvement in the Vietnam War," 383.
47. Womack, *China and Vietnam*, 173.
48. Joachim Glaubitz, "Relations between Communist China and North Vietnam," in Robert Rupen and Robert Farrell, eds., *Vietnam and the Sino-Soviet Dispute* (New York: Praeger, 1967), 66.
49. London, "Vietnam," 30.
50. Quoted in "China and North Viet-Nam," undated, FO 371/175487, NAUK, 1.
51. William J. Duiker, *Ho Chi Minh: A Life* (New York: Theia, 2000), 537.
52. The delegate's comments are reported in Saigon to Ottawa, 22 June 1964, 29-39-1-2-A, Vol. 3092 [Part 1], RG 25, LAC, 1.
53. *La vérité sur les relations vietnamo-chinoises durant les trente dernières années* [The Truth about Sino-Vietnamese Relations in the Past Thirty Years] (Hanoi: Ministère des Affaires étrangères, 1979), 47–48; Nguyen Khac Vien, *Vietnam: A Long History* (Hanoi: Foreign Languages Publishing House, 1987), 327.

54. "'Bao cao tinh hinh the gio va cong tac ngoai giao' doc truoc ky hop thu ba cua Quoc hoi khoa hai (ngay 24 thang 10.1961)—Bo Truong Bo Ngoai giao Ung Van Khiem" ["Report on the World Situation and Diplomatic Tasks" Read before the Third Meeting of the Second Session the National Assembly (24 October 1961—Foreign Minister Ung Van Khiem)], 24 October 1961, Ho so 728: Ho so ky hop thu ba cua QH khoa II tu ngay 23–27.10.1961. Tap 2: Phien hop ngay 24.10.1961: Bao cao, to trinh cua UBTVQH, Bo Ngoai giao, Uy ban Thong nhat, Bo Tai chinh, Phu Thu tuong ve cong tac cua UBTVQH, tinh hinh the gio va cong tac ngoai giao, mien Nam ve thong nhat nuoc nha, Phong Quoc hoi, VNAC3, 2; Qiang Zhai, "An Uneasy Relationship: China and the DRV during the Vietnam War," in Lloyd C. Gardner and Ted Gittinger, eds., *International Perspectives on Vietnam* (College Station: Texas A&M University Press, 2000), 137.

55. Adam Fforde and Suzanne Paine, *The Limits of National Liberation: Problems of Economic Management in the Democratic Republic of Vietnam* (London: Croom Helm, 1987), 29.

56. Olsen, *Soviet-Vietnam Relations*, 133–34. According to Ilya Gaiduk, "The Soviet Union followed a cautious policy of offering propaganda support and various, but modest, forms of economic and military assistance." See Ilya V. Gaiduk, "Soviet Policy toward US Participation in the Vietnam War," *History* 81, no. 261 (January 1996): 43–44.

57. The estimates are quoted in Washington to Ottawa, 23 June 1964, 29-39-1-2-A, Vol. 3092 [Part 1], RG 25, LAC, 4.

58. P.J. Honey, "The Position of the DRV Leadership and the Succession to Ho Chi Minh," *China Quarterly*, no. 9 (January–March 1962): 25.

59. Minutes on "Outlook for North Vietnam: Chinese Support for North Vietnam," 22 April 1964, FO 371/175487, NAUK, 2.

60. The estimate is referenced in ibid.

61. British Consulate General, Hanoi [hereafter BCGH], to BES, 9 December 1963, FO 371/170099, NAUK, 1.

62. Olsen, *Soviet-Vietnam Relations*, 115. On the extent and limits of Soviet power and influence in Indochina and elsewhere during this period, see Roger E. Kanet, "The Soviet Union and the Third World from Khrushchev to Gorbachev: The Place of the Third World in Evolving Soviet Global Strategy," in Roger E. Kanet, ed., *The Soviet Union, Eastern Europe and the Third World* (New York: Cambridge University Press, 1987), 4–9. Under Khrushchev, Kanet writes, the Soviet Union "was unable to provide the type of effective support that would permit it to stabilize throughout the Third World regimes which it viewed as friendly and generally supportive of Soviet interests" (ibid., 6).

63. BCGH to Southeast Asia Department, London [hereafter SEAD], 19 November 1963, FO 371/170099, NAUK, 2.

64. Reported in Saigon to Ottawa, 22 June 1964, 1–2.

65. Honey, "Position of the DRV Leadership and the Succession to Ho Chi Minh," 25, 35.

66. "Le Duan, First Secretary of the Lao Dong Central Committee," 11 March 1973, 20-VIET N-6, Vol. 9167 [Part 1], RG 25, LAC, 1.

67. Ang Cheng Guan, "Vietnam War, 1962–64," 615; Nguyen Khac Vien, *Vietnam*, 310; Womack, *China and Vietnam*, 172.

68. Le Duc Tho, "Let Us Strengthen the Ideological Struggle to Consolidate the Party," *Tuyen huan* (April 1964). Reproduced and translated in Folder 03, Box 25, DPC: Unit 06—Democratic Republic of Vietnam, VATTU, 18.

69. Hoang Van Hoan, *A Drop in the Ocean: Hoang Van Hoan's Revolutionary Reminiscences* (Beijing: Foreing Languages Press, 1988), 317.

70. "Bao cao cua Chinh Phu do Thu tuong Pham Van Dong trinh bay" [Government Report by Prime Minister Pham Van Dong], June 1964, Ho so 1158: Ho so ky hop thu nhat QH khoa III tu ngay 26.6.—03.07.1964. Tap 3: Phien hop ngay 27.6.1964: Bao cao cua UBT-VQH, CP ve tinh hinh bau cu DBQH, phong trao thi dua yeu nuoc, tinh hinh mien Nam, Phong Quoc hoi, VNAC3, 25. According to Melvin Gurtov, the VWP aimed to avoid "a full-fledged ideological or political commitment to either power" by keeping both powers "at bay with piecemeal gestures of approbation." See Melvin Gurtov, *Hanoi on War and Peace* (Santa Monica, Calif.: RAND, 1967), 181.

71. "North Vietnam Today," November 1965, 20-VIET-N-1-4, Vol. 9001, RG 25, LAC, 2–3.

72. "North Viet-Nam: Annual Review for 1964," 4.

73. BCGH to SEAD, 22 February 1964, FO 371/175487, NAUK, 1; French Embassy, Delhi, to MFA, 19 February 1964, #313, AO: VC, ADF, 1.

74. Ilya Gaiduk, "Containing the Warriors: Soviet Policy toward the Indochina Conflict, 1960–65," in Gardner and Gittinger, eds., *International Perspectives*, 72–73.

75. Olsen, *Soviet-Vietnam Relations*, 125.

76. BCGH to SEAD, 22 February 1964, 1–2.

77. See the remarks of Chinese leaders quoted in William E. Griffith, "The November 1960 Moscow Meeting: A Preliminary Reconstruction," *China Quarterly*, no. 11 (July–September 1962): 38–57.

78. Tran Quoc Tu, "Peace and Revolution, 15–18.

79. The editorial is summarized and discussed in FGDH to MFA, 20 June 1964, #17, AO: VN, ADF; and FGDH to MFA, 1 July 1964, #76, AO: VN, ADF, B2.

80. FGDH to MFA, 1 July 1964, B2.

81. FGDH to MFA, 20 October 1964, #36, AO: VN, ADF, 3.

82. FGDH to MFA, 5 October 1964, #76, AO: VN, ADF, B3.

83. French Embassy, Washington, to MFA, 17 February 1964, 1.

84. See Porter, "Hanoi's Strategic Perspective," 16–17.

85. According to the British Consulate, Hanoi favored China "chiefly because the Chinese are more ready to support 'national wars of liberation,' i.e., in this case the reunification of Vietnam under the North Vietnamese Government"; it was at odds with Moscow, whose "main interest" in Asia was "containing China and avoiding trouble in South East Asia." See BCGH to SEAD, 26 August 1964, FO 371/175486, NAUK, 1.

86. BCGH to SEAD, 9 September 1964, FO 371/175481, NAUK, 4.

87. Gaiduk, "Soviet Policy toward US Participation," 46. "North Vietnamese leaders were very independent in their policy towards the war," Gaiduk added, "and often presented their Soviet and Chinese counterparts with *faits accomplis*" (ibid., 42).

88. "Chi thi cua Bo Chinh tri, so 74-CT/TW, ngay 27 thang 1 nam 1964: Ve viec to chuc hoc tap Nghi quyet Hoi nghi lan thu chin cua Trung uong ve van de quoc te" [Politburo Instruction, no. 74-CT/TW, 27 January 1964: On the Effort to Organize the Study of the Resolution on International Problems of the Ninth Plenum of the Central Committee], in *VKD: 1964*, 43–44, 58.

89. Le Duc Tho, "Let Us Strengthen the Ideological Struggle to Consolidate the Party," 22.

90. FGDH to MFA, 7 January 1964, #75, AO: VN, ADF, A5; FGDH to MFA, 7 April 1964, #76, AO: VN, ADF, A4.

91. FGDH to MFA, 7 January 1964, A5. In addition to forty-eight hours of work each week, each cadre and party member was expected to attend thirty hours of "study sessions" each month and four monthly meetings of indefinite duration (ibid., A6).

92. Quoted in "Hanoi Conference Urges More Work, Ignores Ideology," 14 April 1964. This U.S. State Department document is located in 20-VIET N-1-3 [Part 1], Vol. 8892, RG 25, LAC, 1.

93. Thomas Latimer, "Hanoi's Leaders and the Policies of War," Folder 18, Box 01, John Donnell Collection, VATTU, 21.

94. "Hanoi Conference Urges More Work, Ignores Ideology," 1.

95. Military Institute of Vietnam, *Victory in Vietnam*, 128.

96. The text of the report by Ho Chi Minh is reproduced as "Bao cao Chu tich Ho Chi Minh tai Hoi nghi chinh tri dac biet, ngay 27–28 thang 3 nam 1964" [Report by President Ho Chi Minh at the Special Political Conference, 27–28 March 1964], in *VKD*: 1964, 90–108. See also Ho Chi Minh, *Toan tap*, Tap 11 [Collected Works, Vol. 11] (Hanoi: Nha xuat ban Chinh tri quoc gia, 2000), 220–35.

97. "Hanoi Conference Urges More Work, Ignores Ideology," 3, 5.

98. "Record of Conversation: Visit of Messrs Sullivan and Cooper to the Department," 3 June 1964, 3.

99. "Hanoi Conference Urges More Work, Ignores Ideology," 4.

100. The final resolution is quoted in "Nghi quyet ve ket qua cau Hoi nghi chinh tri dac biet," 4.4.1964 [Resolution on the Result of the Special Political Conference, 4 April 1964], Ho so 760: Ho so ky hop thu tam cua QH khoa II tu ngay 29.3–04.4.1964. Tap 5: Phien hop ngay 04.04.1964: Tham luan cua DBQH ve thuc hien ke hoach nam nam, ve cuoc dau tranh cua dong bao mien Nam, ve ket qua Hoi nghi Chinh tri dac biet, ve phat trien cong nghiep dia phuong, dao tao can bo KHKT, Phong Quoc hoi, VNAC3, 2; Bo Quoc phong—Vien Lich su quan su Viet Nam, *Lich su quan su Viet Nam, Tap 11: Cuoc khang chien chong My, cuu nuoc, 1954–1975* [Military History of Vietnam, Volume 11: The Anti-American Resistance for National Salvation] (Hanoi: Nha xuat ban Chinh tri quoc gia, 2005), 154.

101. "Tham luan ve phong trao dau tranh cua nhan dan mien Nam cua Tran-huu-Tuoc, dai bieu Thanh-hoa [Address on the Struggle Movement of the Southern People by Tran Huu Tuoc, Representative of Thanh Hoa], 4 April 1964, Ho so 760: Ho so ky hop thu tam cua QH khoa II tu ngay 29.3–04.4.1964. Tap 5: Phien hop ngay 04.04.1964: Tham luan cua DBQH ve thuc hien ke hoach nam nam, ve cuoc dau tranh cua dong bao mien Nam, ve ket qua Hoi nghi Chinh tri dac biet, ve phat trien cong nghiep dia phuong, dao tao can bo KHKT, Phong Quoc hoi, VNAC3, 1.

102. "Nghi quyet va ket qua cua Hoi nghi chinh tri dac biet, 4.4.1964," 2.

103. Quoted in "Tham luan thang loi Hoi ngi chinh tri dac biet cua Tran-van-De, dai bieu Ha-tinh" [Address on the Victory of the Special Political Conference by Tran Van De, Representative of Ha Tinh], 4 April 1964, Ho so 760: Ho so ky hop thu tam cua QH khoa II tu ngay 29.3–04.4.1964. Tap 5: Phien hop ngay 04.04.1964: Tham luan cua DBQH ve thuc hien ke hoach nam nam, ve cuoc dau tranh cua dong bao mien Nam, ve ket qua Hoi nghi Chinh tri dac biet, ve phat trien cong nghiep dia phuong, dao tao can bo KHKT, Phong Quoc hoi, VNAC3, 3.

104. Hoang Van Thai, "The Lesson of Dien Bien Phu," *Hoc tap*, no. 5 (May 1964). Reproduced and translated in Folder 03, Box 05, DPC: Unit 08—Biography, VATTU, 14–22.

105. "Chi thi cua Bo Chinh tri, so 81-CT/TW, ngay 7 thang 8 nam 1964," 189.

106. "Chi thi cua Bo Chinh tri, so 74-CT/TW, ngay 27 thang 1 nam 1964," 59.

107. "Chi thi cua Bo Chinh tri, so 81-CT/TW, ngay 7 thang 8 nam 1964," 187.

108. "Dang Lao dong Viet Nam—BCHTW—Bao cao tong ket tinh hinh dich va cong tac danh dich trong 2 nam 1962–1963 va phuong huong day manh cong tac dau tranh chong phan cach mang trong thoi gian toi (Tong ket viec thuc hien nghi quyet 39 cua BCT ve viec tang cuong dau tranh chong phan cach mang), 26.6.1964" [Vietnam Workers' Party—Central Committee—Summary of Enemy's Situation and the Effort to Fight the Enemy in 1962–1963 and the Direction of the Effort to Step Up the Struggle against Counterrevolutionaries in that Period (Summary of the Implementation of Central Committee Resolution 39 on the Effort to Intensify the Struggle against Counterrevolution), 26 June 1964], Ho so 262: Bao cao cua BCH TW Dang tong ket tinh hinh va cong tac danh dich trong 2 nam 1962–1963 va phuong huong day manh cong tac dau tranh chong phan cach mang trong thoi gian toi, Phong Uy ban Thong nhat Chinh phu, VNAC3, 7–8.

109. "Chi thi cua Ban Bi thu, so 73-CT/TW, ngay 24 thang 1 nam 1964: Ve tang cuong lanh dao cong tac tuyen giao doi voi cac dan toc thieu so o mien nui" [Secretariat Instruction, no. 73-CT/TW, 24 January 1964: On Increasing the Leadership in the Effort to Educate Minority Peoples in the Highlands], in *VKD*: 1964, 30.

110. The full text of the instruction is reproduced as "Chi thi cua Ban Bi thu, so 77-CT/TW, ngay 18 thang 4 nam 1964: Ve viec phat dong cao trao thi dua 'Moi nguoi lam viec bang hai, ra suc xay dung va bao ve mien Bac, tich cuc ung ho cach mang giai phong mien Nam'" [Secretariat Instruction, no. 77-CT/TW, 18 April 1964: On the Mobilization for the Emulation Movement "Each Person Works Like Two, Building and Protecting the North, Supporting the Southern Liberation Revolution"], in *VKD*: 1964, 116–26. The VWP elaborated on the meaning of the instruction in articles it published in *Nhan dan* on 9 and 11 April 1964 (see ibid., 117).

111. "Report on the Activities of the International Commission in Vietnam for the Month of May, 1964," 1.

112. *Nhan dan*, 21 April 1964; *12 années d'intervention et d'agression des impérialistes américains au Laos* [12 Years of American Intervention and Aggression in Laos] (n.p.: Éditions du Neo Lao Haksat, 1966), 52, 54. See also D. Gareth Porter, "After Geneva: Subverting Laotian Neutrality," in Nina S. Adams and Alfred W. McCoy, eds., *Laos: War and Revolution* (New York: Harper & Row, 1970), 179–212; Sandra C. Taylor, "Laos: The Escalation of a Secret War," in Jane Errington and B. J. C. McKercher, eds., *The Vietnam War as History* (New York: Praeger, 1990), 73–90.

113. Wallace J. Thies, *When Governments Collide: Coercion and Diplomacy in the Vietnam Conflict, 1964–1968* (Berkeley: University of California Press, 1980), 43.

114. Ton That Thien, *The Foreign Policy of the Communist Party of Vietnam: A Study of Communist Tactics* (New York: Crane Russak, 1989), 143–44.

115. Bo Quoc phong—Vien Lich su quan su Viet Nam, *Lich su quan su Viet Nam*, Tap 11, 172.

116. On these operations, see Richard H. Shultz, Jr., *The Secret War against Hanoi: Kennedy's and Johnson's Use of Spies, Saboteurs, and Covert Warriors in North Vietnam* (New York: HarperCollins, 1999).

117. "Chi thi cua Ban Bi thu, so 73-CT/TW, ngay 24 thang 1 nam 1964," 31.
118. "Chi thi cua Ban Bi thu, so 75-CT/TW, ngay 3 thang 3 nam 1964: Ve cong tac phong khong nhan dan" [Secretariat Instruction, no. 75-CT/TW, 3 March 1964: On the People's Air Defense], in *VKD: 1964*, 71.
119. Military Institute of Vietnam, *Victory in Vietnam*, 131.
120. FGDH to MFA, 1 July 1964, C1.
121. "Chi thi cua Bo Chinh tri, so 81-CT/TW, ngay 7 thang 8 nam 1964," 185, 188.
122. Mark L. Haas, *The Ideological Origins of Great Power Politics, 1789–1989* (Ithaca, N.Y.: Cornell University Press, 2005), 150.
123. Zhou's comments are quoted in Qiang Zhai, "An Uneasy Relationship," 110.
124. "Outline of Subjects for Mr. Seaborn," undated [May 1964], 29-39-1-2-A, Vol. 3092 [Part 1], RG 25, LAC, 1, 3–4.
125. "Record of Conversation: Visit of Messrs Sullivan and Cooper to the Department," 3 June 1964, 2.
126. Saigon (from Hanoi) to Ottawa, 20 June 1964, 29-39-1-2-A, Vol. 3092 [Part 1], RG 25, LAC, 2, 6.
127. Andrew Preston, "Mission Impossible: Canadian Secret Diplomacy and the Quest for Peace in Vietnam," in Lloyd C. Gardner and Ted Gittinger, eds., *The Search for Peace in Vietnam, 1964–1968* (College Station: Texas A&M University Press, 2004), 125.
128. Saigon (from Hanoi) to Ottawa, 22 June 1964, 29-39-1-2-A, Vol. 3092 [Part 1], RG 25, LAC, 3.
129. Saigon (from Hanoi) to Ottawa, 15 August 1964, 29-39-1-2-A, Vol. 3092 [Part 1], RG 25, LAC, 1, 3.
130. Saigon (from Hanoi) to Ottawa, 17 August 1964, 29-39-1-2-A, Vol. 3092 [Part 1], RG 25, LAC, 3.
131. Saigon (from Hanoi) to Ottawa, 18 December 1964, 29-39-1-2-A, Vol. 3092 [Part 1], RG 25, LAC, 1.
132. "Tham luan ve dau tranh thong nhat cua Bo-xuan-Tuan (?), dai bieu Hung-yen" [Address on the Reunification Struggle by Bo Xuan Tuan (?), Representative of Hung Yen], 3 July 1964, Ho so 1162: Ho so ky hop thu nhat QH khoa III tu ngay 25.06–03.07.1964. Tap 7: Phien hop ngay 03.07.1964 ve tham luan cua DBQH ve dau tranh thong nhat dat nuoc, phong trao thi dua, tang cuong luc luong quoc phong, Phong Quoc hoi, VNAC3, 3.
133. Gareth Porter, "Coercive Diplomacy in Vietnam: The Tonkin Gulf Crisis Reconsidered," in Jayne Werner and David Hunt, eds., *The American War in Vietnam* (Ithaca, N.Y.: Cornell Southeast Asia Program, 1993), 13–14. In fact, that matched their behavior precisely once talks actually began in 1968, before secret negotiations with the Nixon administration began. On this, see Pierre Journoud, "Des artisans de paix dans le secret de la diplomacie: Vers un règlement pacifique de la guerre au Vietnam, 1967–1973" [Peace Artisans in the Secret of Diplomacy: Toward a Peaceful Settlement of the War in Vietnam, 1967–1973], unpublished paper in author's possession. See note 29 in particular.
134. BCGH to SEAD, 19 March 1964, FO 371/175505, NAUK, 1–2.
135. Ottawa to Saigon, 7 July 1964, 29-39-1-2-A, Vol. 3092 [Part 1], RG 25, LAC, 1.
136. "Chi thi cua Bo Chinh tri, so 81-CT/TW, ngay 7 thang 8 nam 1964," 185.
137. BCGH to SEAD, 18 August 1964, FO 371/175486, NAUK, 1.

138. "Du thao de cuong gio thieu ve tinh hinh ve duong loi cach mang mien Nam," 26–27.

139. Ralph B. Smith, *Viet-Nam and the West* (London: Heinemann, 1968), 13.

140. William S. Turley, *The Second Indochina War: A Concise Political and Military History*, 2nd ed. (Lanham, Md.: Rowman & Littlefield, 2009), 88.

141. Nguyen Vu Tung, "The 1961–1962 Geneva Conference: Neutralization of Laos and Policy Implications for Vietnam," in Christopher E. Goscha and Karine Laplante, eds., *L'échec de la paix en Indochine / The Failure of Peace in Indochina (1954–1962)* (Paris: Les Indes savantes, 2010), 266.

142. BES to FO, 23 June 1964, FO 371/175505, NAUK, 1.

143. "Nam vung quy luat kinh te va thuc te trong nuoc de lam tot cong tac xay dung va quan ly nen kinh te xa hoi chu nghia (Bai noi cua dong chi Le Duan, Bi thu thu nhat Ban Chap hanh Trung uong Dang tai Hoi nghi Trung uong lan thu 10, ngay 26 thang 12 nam 1964)" [Understanding Economic Law and Reality in the Country to Execute Well the Building and Administration of the Socialist Economy (Speech by Comrade Le Duan, First Secretary of the Central Committee at the Tenth Plenum of the Central Committee, 26 December 1964)], in *VKD*: 1964, 512.

144. See Le Duan's "Duong loi cach mang xa hoi chu nghia o mien Bac" [The Socialist Revolutionary Line in the North], in *Cach mang xa hoi chu nghia o Viet-Nam, Tap I* [The Socialist Revolution in Vietnam, Volume 1] (Hanoi: Nha xuat ban Su that, 1976), 11–49.

145. The assessment is quoted in Washington to Ottawa, 23 June 1964, 29-39-1-2-A, Vol. 3092 [Part 1], RG 25, LAC, 5.

146. Le Duan, "Duoi la co ve vang cua Dang, vi doc lap tu do, vi chu nghia xa hoi, tien len gianh nhung thang loi moi (2–1970)" [Under the Bright Banner of the Party, for Independence and Freedom, for Socialism, to Bring About New Victories (February 1970)], in *Cach mang xa hoi chu nghia o Viet-Nam*, Vol. 2, 17.

147. See Huynh Kim Khanh, *Vietnamese Communism, 1925–1945* (Ithaca, N.Y.: Cornell University Press, 1982). Khanh stresses that the self-reliance of Vietnamese communists was one of their greatest strengths and assets.

148. "Chi thi cua Bo Chinh tri, so 74-CT/TW, ngay 27 thang 1 nam 1964," 57.

149. "Survey of Developments in North Vietnam during 1964—Economic Affairs," (1965), 20-VIET-N-1-4, Vol. 9001, RG 25, LAC, 1.

150. "Nghi quyet cua Bo Chinh tri, so 92-NQ/TW, ngay 17 thang 1 nam 1964: Ve tang cuong quan ly phan phoi luong thuc, quan ly thi truong luong thuc va dieu chinh gia mua luong thuc" [Politburo Resolution, no. 92-NQ/TW, 17 January 1964: On Improving the Administration of Foodstuff Allocation, the Administration of Foodstuff Markets, and Adjusting the Price of Foodstuffs], in *VKD*: 1964, 12, 13, 15. A "number" of party members and government functionaries "engaged in acts of corruption," a party report noted. While corruption itself was not a major hindrance to the fulfillment of revolutionary tasks, its implications for the relationship between the authorities and the people were troubling. Less widespread but also problematic were the loose morals of party and government personnel, especially their practice of "adultery." Left unchecked, such "evils" would "damage the prestige" of the party and government. See "Chi thi cua Bo Chinh tri, so 74-CT/TW, ngay 27 thang 1 nam 1964," 59.

151. "Final Minutes (Verbatim Record) of the 668th Meeting of the International Commission for Supervision and Control in Vietnam," 13 August 1964, 21-13-VIET-ICSC-8 [FP. 1], Vol. 10125, RG 25, LAC, 2; Washington to Ottawa, 8 August 1964, 29-39-1-2-A, Vol. 3092 [Part 1], RG 25, LAC, 1. The United States at the time recognized DRVN territorial water to extend three, not twelve, nautical miles from its coast.

152. For an authoritative account of those events, see Edwin E. Moïse, *Tonkin Gulf and the Escalation of the Vietnam War* (Chapel Hill: University of North Carolina Press, 1996).

153. Lloyd C. Gardner, *Pay Any Price: Lyndon Johnson and the Wars for Vietnam* (Chicago: Ivan R. Dee, 1995), 134.

154. *Nhan dan*, 20 September 1964; "Thong cao cua UBTVQH, 10.8.1964" [Communiqué by the Standing Committee of the National Assembly, 10 August 1964], Ho so 1235: Ho so phien hop thu 3 cua UBTVQH khoa III ngay 10.8.1964 ve su kien vinh Bac Bo ngay 5.8.1964 va bo nhiem dai su, Phong Quoc hoi, VNAC3, 1. Edwin Moïse concluded that the North Vietnamese conducted no attacks against Americans vessels on 4 August (Moïse, *Tonkin Gulf*).

155. "Final Minutes (Verbatim Record) of the 668th Meeting of the International Commission for Supervision and Control in Vietnam," 3.

156. Robert S. McNamara, James Blight, and Robert Brigham, *Argument without End: In Search of Answers to the Vietnam Tragedy* (New York: Public Affairs, 1999), 186.

157. BCGH to SEAD, 2 September 1964, FO 371/175481, NAUK, 2.

158. FGDH to MFA, 1 September 1964, #76, AO: VN, ADF, A6.

159. "Memorandum for the Commissioner [Saigon] from the Permanent Representative, Hanoi," 24 August 1964, 20-VIET-N-1-4, Vol. 9001, RG 25, LAC, 1.

160. "North Viet-Nam: Annual Review for 1964," 1.

161. "Memorandum for the Commissioner [Saigon] from the Permanent Representative, Hanoi," 17 August 1964, 20-VIET-N-1-4, Vol. 9001, RG 25, LAC, 1.

162. Saigon (from Hanoi) to Ottawa, 17 August 1964, 2.

163. "North Viet-Nam: Annual Review for 1964," 4.

164. Duiker, *Communist Road to Power*, 249–50.

165. Moïse, *Tonkin Gulf*, 252.

166. Turley, *Second Indochina War*, 84.

167. Bo Quoc phong—Vien Lich su quan su Viet Nam, *Lich su quan su Viet Nam, Tap 11*, 155; Vien nghien cuu chu nghia Mac-Lenin va tu tuong Ho Chi Minh, *Lich su Dang Cong san Viet Nam*, 267 (emphasis in original).

168. Vien nghien cuu chu nghia Mac-Lenin va tu tuong Ho Chi Minh, *Lich su Dang Cong san Viet Nam*, 267.

169. Bo Quoc phong—Vien Lich su quan su Viet Nam, *Lich su quan su Viet Nam, Tap 11*, 155.

170. BCGH to SEAD, 2 September 1964, FO 371/175481, NAUK, 1.

171. Turley, *Second Indochina War*, 103–4.

172. Lien-Hang T. Nguyen, "Between the Storms: An International History of the Second Indochina War, 1968–1973" (PhD diss., Yale University, 2008), 35.

173. Bo Quoc phong—Vien Lich su quan su Viet Nam, *Lich su quan su Viet Nam, Tap 11*, 156.

174. Military Institute of Vietnam, *Victory in Vietnam*, 128.

175. "But we are not about to send American boys nine or ten thousand miles away from home to do what Asian boys ought to be doing for themselves," Johnson remarked in a speech in Akron, Ohio, in October 1964.

176. From the testimony of a PAVN prisoner of war reproduced in Canadian Delegation, ICSC, Saigon, to Under Secretary of State for External Affairs, Ottawa, "Report on Interrogation of Prisoners of PAVN 325th Division," Enclosure 2, Appendix C, 21-13-VIET-ICSC-4, Vol. 10124, RG 25, LAC, 13.

177. McNamara, Blight, and Brigham, *Argument without End*, 185–86; Military Institute of Vietnam, *Victory in Vietnam*, 126; Mark Moyar, *Triumph Forsaken: The Vietnam War, 1954–1965* (New York: Cambridge University Press, 2006), 332–33; *50 nam Quan doi nhan dan Viet Nam* [50 Years of the People's Army of Vietnam] (Hanoi: Nha xuat ban Quan doi nhan dan, 1995), 199; and Vien nghien cuu chu nghia Mac-Lenin va tu tuong Ho Chi Minh, *Lich su Dang Cong san Viet Nam*, 268. I am grateful to Bill Turley, Mark Moyar, and Ang Cheng Guan for personally helping me in elucidating this matter.

178. "Report on Interrogation of Prisoners of PAVN 325th Division," Enclosure 2, Appendix C, 15.

179. See, for instance, Porter, "Coercive Diplomacy," 49.

180. Ang Cheng Guan, *The Vietnam War from the Other Side: The Vietnamese Communists' Perspective* (New York: RoutledgeCurzon, 2002), 80–81.

181. Tai Sung An, "Hanoi's 15th Plenum Resolution—May 1959," Folder 010, Box 30, DPC: Unit 05—National Liberation Front, VATTU, 282n226. An official history of the PAVN confirms that assessment, stating that Resolution 9 "laid out correct, timely policies and directions" for "sending main force troops to the South." See Military Institute of Vietnam, *Victory in Vietnam*, 72. The same conclusion is presented in Ralph. B. Smith, *An International History of the Vietnam War*, Vol. 2: *The Struggle for Southeast Asia, 1961–65* (New York: St. Martin's Press, 1986), 346–49; and Gunter Lewy, *America in Vietnam* (Oxford: Oxford University Press, 1978), 39.

182. Qiang Zhai, "Uneasy Relationship," 110–11.

183. Turley, *Second Indochina War*, 104.

184. Bo Quoc phong—Vien Lich su quan su Viet Nam, *Hau phuong chien tranh nhan dan Viet Nam, 1945–1975* [The Rear Base of the Vietnamese People's War] (Hanoi: Nha xuat ban Quan doi nhan dan, 1997), 174; Military Institute of Vietnam, *Victory in Vietnam*, 127. According to the latter, only approximately nine thousand cadres and PAVN troops infiltrated the South in 1964.

185. Xiaoming Zhang, "The Vietnam War, 1964–1969: A Chinese Perspective," *Journal of Military History* 60, no. 4 (October 1996): 741–42.

186. "North Viet-Nam: Annual Review for 1964," 4.

187. FGDH to MFA, 5 October 1964, B1, B3–B4.

188. BCGH to SEAD, 17 October 1964, FO 371/175486, NAUK, 1.

189. "Traduction de la lettre du 21 Octobre adressée par M. Pham van Dong, Premier Ministre du Gouvernment de la RDVN, à M. Chou En-lai" [Translation of a Letter Dated 21 October from Mr. Pham Van Dong, Prime Minister of the DRVN Government, to Mr. Zhou Enlai], 23 October 1964, #38, AO: VN, ADF, 1.

190. FGDH to MFA, 21 October 1964, #38, AO: VN, ADF, 1, 5–6.

191. FGDH to MFA, 26 October 1964, #38, AO: VN, ADF, 2–3.
192. BCGH to SEAD, 29 September 1964, FO 371/175486, NAUK, 1.
193. BES to SEAD, 15 October 1964, FO 371/175487, NAUK, 1.
194. "Memorandum for the Commissioner [Saigon] from the Permanent Representative, Hanoi," 8 September 1964, 5.
195. On the CPSU Central Committee's 15 October decision to relieve Khrushchev of his duties as head of the party and the government, see William Taubman, *Khrushchev: The Man and His Era* (New York: W. W. Norton, 2003), 3–17.
196. Gaiduk, *Confronting Vietnam*, 210.
197. FGDH to MFA, 9 November 1964, #36, AO: VN, ADF, 10.
198. "Relations between the Soviet Union and North Vietnam," 17 February 1966, 20-USSR-1-3-VIET N [Part 1], Vol. 10853, RG 25, LAC, 2; Gaiduk, *Confronting Vietnam*, 206.
199. Porter, "Hanoi's Strategic Perspective," 16–17.
200. FGDH to MFA, 9 November 1964, #76, AO: VN, ADF, B4.
201. BCGH to SEAD, 17 October 1964, FO 371/175486, NAUK, 1.
202. Lorenz Lüthi, "Twenty-Four Soviet Bloc Documents on Vietnam and the Sino-Soviet Split, 1964–1966," *Cold War International History Project Bulletin*, no. 16 (2008) [hereafter *CWIHPB* 16]: 368.
203. Nicholas Khoo, *Collateral Damage: Sino-Soviet Rivalry and the Termination of the Sino-Vietnamese Alliance* (New York: Columbia University Press, 2011), 20–21.
204. "Remarks by the GDR Embassy in Hanoi on the Article in *Hoc tap* No. 11/1964, 12 November 1964 [Excerpts]," in *CWIHPB* 16, 372.
205. Ibid. That episode is also related in FGDH to MFA, 9 November.
206. FGDH to MFA, 8 December 1964, #76, AO: VN, ADF, B4.
207. "Note: Position soviétique sur les affaires du Sud-Est asiatique" [Note: Soviet Position on Southeast Asian Affairs], 9 December 1964, #313, AO: VN, ADF, 2.
208. Saigon (from Hanoi) for Ottawa, 21 November 1964, 20-VIET N-1-3 [Part 1], Vol. 8892, RG 25, LAC, 1, 2, 4.
209. Gaiduk, "Soviet Policy towards US Participation," 49.
210. "Letter from A. A. Gromyko, Minister for Foreign Affairs of the USSR, to Xuan Thuy, Minister for Foreign Affairs of the DRV," 30 December 1964, reproduced in L. V. Kotov and R. S. Yegorov, *Militant Solidarity, Fraternal Assistance* (Moscow: Progress Publishers, 1970), 31–33.
211. Gaiduk, "Containing the Warriors," 74; French Embassy, Moscow, to MFA, 27 November 1964, #313, AO: VN, ADF, 1–2.
212. "Telegram from the Embassy in Vietnam to the Department of State," 1 November 1964, in *FRUS: I, VN, 1964*, 873.
213. Vien nghien cuu chu nghia Mac-Lenin va tu tuong Ho Chi Minh, *Lich su Dang Cong san Viet Nam*, 268–69.
214. Quoted in King C. Chen, "Hanoi vs. Peking," 812.
215. Quoted in Washington, DC, to Ottawa, 19 December 1964, 20-22-VIET S-1, 9387 [Part 2], RG 25, LAC, 6.
216. "North Viet-Nam: Annual Review for 1964," 2.
217. The comments by the Cambodian foreign minister are reported in French Mission at the United Nations to MFA, 19 December 1964, #313, AO: VC, ADF, 1.

EPILOGUE

1. Marilyn B. Young, *The Vietnam Wars, 1945—1990* (New York: HarperCollins, 1991), 135. Possibly, a local commander planned and ordered the attack on Pleiku without sanction from Hanoi. See Robert S. McNamara, James Blight, and Robert Brigham, *Argument without End: In Search of Answers to the Vietnam Tragedy* (New York: Public Affairs, 1999), 173.

2. Fredrik Logevall, *Choosing War: The Lost Chance for Peace and the Escalation of War in Vietnam* (Berkeley: University of California Press, 2001), 344, 363; and Arthur J. Dommen, *The Indochinese Experience of the French and the Americans: Nationalism and Communism in Cambodia, Laos, and Vietnam* (Bloomington: Indiana University Press, 2001), 636.

3. "Chi thi cua Bo Chinh tri, so 88-CT/TW, ngay 2 thang 1 nam 1965: Ve cuoc van dong chinh huan mua xuan nam 1965" [Politburo Instruction, no. 88-CT/TW, 2 January 1965: On Re-education Activities during Spring 1965], in Dang Cong san Viet Nam, *Van kien Dang—Toan tap*, Tap 26: 1965 [Party Documents—Complete Series, Vol. 26: 1965] (Hanoi: Nha xuat ban Chinh tri quoc gia, 2003) [hereafter *VKD: 1965*], 3.

4. "Chi thi cua Ban Bi thu, so 90-CT/TW, ngay 1 thang 3 nam 1965: Ve viec mo cuoc van dong nang cao tinh than canh giac cach mang, y thuc to chuc ky luat, lam tot cong tac tham tra chinh tri va cai tien cong tac quan ly doi ngu can bo, dang vien de bao ve dang (goi tat la cuoc van dong bao ve dang)" [Secretariat Instruction, no. 90-CT/TW, 1 March 1965: On the Matter of Beginning Activities to Elevate Revolutionary Vigilance, Promoting Organizational Discipline, Performing Well the Task of Political Investigation and Improvement of the Administration of Cadres and Party Members to Protect the Party (All Known as Activities to Protect the Party)], in ibid., 44.

5. Ibid., 47.

6. "Chi thi cua Ban Bi thu, so 95-CT/TW, ngay 8 thang 4 nam 1965: Ve viec dieu dong can bo phuc vu cho yeu cau xay dung quan doi trong tinh hinh va nhiem vu moi" [Secretariat Instruction, no. 95-CT/TW, 8 April 1965: On the Matter of Appointing Cadres to Serve the Requirement of Building the Armed Forces in the New Situation and Responsibilities], in ibid., 137–39.

7. "Memorandum for Commissioner, Saigon, from the Permanent Representative, Hanoi," 15 January 1965, 20-VIET N-1-4, Vol. 9001 [Part 1], RG 25, LAC, 1.

8. Hy Van Luong, *Revolution in the Village: Tradition and Transformation in North Vietnam, 1925–1988* (Honolulu: University of Hawaii Press, 1992), 202.

9. Military Institute of Vietnam, *Victory in Vietnam: The Official History of the People's Army of Vietnam, 1954–1975*, trans. Merle L. Pribbenow (Lawrence: University Press of Kansas, 2002), 164.

10. Quoted in *History of the Communist Party of Vietnam* (Hanoi: Foreign Languages Publishing House, 1986), 195.

11. Nguyen Thi Thap, *Lich su phong trao phu nu Viet nam* [History of the Vietnamese Women's Movement] (Hanoi: Nha xuat ban Phu nu, 1981), 109; "Chi thi cua Ban Bi thu, so 99-CT/TW, ngay 8 thang 6 nam 1965: Ve phuong huong, nhiem vu cua cong tac van dong phu nu truoc tinh hinh moi" [Politburo Instruction, no. 99-CT/TW, 8 June 1965: On the Direction, Responsibilities, and Work to Mobilize Women in the New Era], in *VKD: 1965*, 198–203. Hanoi's immediate response to the Americanization of hostilities in 1965 is discussed in greater detail in Pierre Asselin, "Hanoi and Americanization of the War in

Vietnam: New Evidence from Vietnam," *Pacific Historical Review* 75, no. 3 (August 2005): 427–431.

12. "Nghi quyet Hoi nghi trung uong lan thu 11 (dac biet), ngay 25, 26, 27 thang 3 nam 1965: Ve tinh hinh va nhiem vu cap bach truoc mat" [Resolution of the Special Eleventh Plenum of the Central Committee, 25–27 March 1965: On the New Situation and Pressing Responsibilities Ahead], in *VKD:* 1965, 105.

13. Ibid, 108; "De cuong bao cao tai Hoi nghi Ban chap hanh Trung uong lan thu 11 (dac biet), hop tu ngay 25 den ngay 27 thang 3 nam 1965: Kip thoi chuyen huong viec xay dung va phat trien kinh te quoc dan phuc vu dac luc nhiem vu cach mang ca nuoc trong tinh hinh moi" [Draft Report at the Special Eleventh Plenum of the Central Committee, 25–27 March 1965: Promptly Adjusting the Work to Build and Develop the People's Economy to Efficiently Serve the Revolutionary Responsibilities of the Entire Country in the New Era], in *VKD:* 1965, 58, 65; "Thong bao cua Ban Bi thu, so 56-TB/TW, ngay 1 thang 4 nam 1965: Nhung quy dinh cua Bo Chinh tri ve viec to chuc lanh dao cong tac tiep tuc cai tao xa hoi chu nghia doi voi cong thuong nghiep tu ban tu doanh, thu cong nghiep va thuong nghiep nho" [Secretariat Circular, no. 56-TB/TW, 1 April 1965: The Stipulations of the Politburo on the Matter of Organizing the Leadership of the Effort to Continue Building Socialism with Regard to Private Capitalist Trade, Handicraft, and Small Business], in *VKD:* 1965, 119–25.

14. "Chi thi cua Ban Bi thu, so 94-CT/TW, ngay 2 thang 4 nam 1965: Ve cong tac tu tuong trong tinh hinh truoc mat" [Secretariat Instruction, no. 94-CT/TW, 2 April 1965: On Ideological Work in the Situation Ahead], in ibid., 127; "Government Report Submitted by Prime Minister Pham Van Dong, April 1965," reproduced in *Against U.S. Aggression: Main Documents of the National Assembly of the Democratic Republic of Vietnam, 3rd Legislature—2nd Session, April 1965* (Hanoi: Foreign Languages Publishing House, 1966), 40.

15. "Zhou Enlai and Pakistani president Ayub Khan, Karachi, 2 April 1965," in Odd Arne Westad, Chen Jian, Stein Tønnesson, Nguyen Vu Tung, and James G. Hershberg, eds., "77 Conversations between Chinese and Foreign Leaders on the Wars in Indochina, 1964–1977," Cold War International History Project Working Paper no. 22, Woodrow Wilson Center, Washington, D.C., 1998 [hereafter "77 Conversations"], 77. According to Lorenz Lüthi, Beijing strenuously objected to Moscow's February 1965 proposal to reconvene the Geneva Conference. "China's antagonistic attitude toward negotiations," he writes, "was rooted in Mao's view of the country's place in the world and, ultimately, its domestic politics." See Lorenz Lüthi, *The Sino-Soviet Split, 1956–1966* (Princeton, N.J.: Princeton University Press, 2008), 316, 336. According to French documents, Beijing was amenable to the idea of convening an international conference to resolve the Vietnamese crisis until the commencement of American combat operations; thereafter, its stance hardened and it considered holding such a conference "impossible." See Direction des Affaires Politiques Asie-Océanie —Ministère des Affaires Étrangères [hereafter DAPAO], "Chronologie des principales interventions française à propos du Vietnam depuis Juillet 1962" [Chronology of Main French Interventions about Vietnam since July 1962], 6 April 1965, #162, Asie-Océanie [hereafter AO]: Vietnam Conflit [hereafter VC], Archives Diplomatiques de France, La Courneuve [hereafter ADF], 5. A portion of the discussion that follows is drawn from Pierre Asselin, "'We Don't Want A Munich': Hanoi's Diplomatic Struggle during the American War, 1965–1968," *Diplomatic History* 36, no. 3 (June 2012): 547–82.

16. "Oral Statement of the PRC Government, Transmitted by PRC Vice Foreign Minister Liu Xiao to the Chargé d'Affaires of the USSR in the PRC, Cde. F. V. Mochulskii, on 27 February 1965," in Lorenz Lüthi, "Twenty-Four Soviet Bloc Documents on Vietnam and the Sino-Soviet Split, 1964–1966," *Cold War International History Project Bulletin*, no. 16 (2008) [hereafter *CWIHPB* 16]: 376.

17. "Chen Yi and Nguyen Duy Trinh, Beijing, 17 December 1965," in Westad et al., eds., "77 Conversations," 89. American proposals for peace talks were to Beijing "a mere ploy to eliminate revolutionary forces in Vietnam," historian Niu Jun has written. See Niu Jun, "The Background to the Shift in Chinese Policy toward the United States in the Late 1960s," in Priscilla Roberts, ed., *Behind the Bamboo Curtain: China, Vietnam, and the World beyond Asia* (Washington, D.C.: Woodrow Wilson Center Press, 2006), 339. Beijing also condemned Moscow's "mistaken policy of Soviet-American cooperation for the solution of international problems" and of the "Vietnam question" specifically ("Oral Statement by the Head of the Department for the USSR and for the Countries of Eastern Europe of MFA PRC, Yu Zhan, Transmitted to the Embassy on 8 June 1965," in *CWIHPB* 16, 380). As Lorenz Lüthi has noted, at the onset of the American War, "Beijing pursued a hard line," "rejecting any negotiated settlement" and "advocating people's war as the only method to fight" (Lüthi, *Sino-Soviet Split*, 338).

18. David G. Marr, "Sino-Vietnamese Relations," *Australian Journal of Chinese Affairs*, no. 6 (July 1981): 53. See also Pierre Journoud, "La France, cinquième partie aux négociations?," in Pierre Journoud and Cécile Ménétrey-Monchau, eds., *Vietnam, 1968–1976: La sortie de guerre/Exiting a War* (Brussels: Peter Lang, 2011).

19. Ilya V. Gaiduk, *The Soviet Union and the Vietnam War* (Chicago: Ivan R. Dee, 1996), 46.

20. British Embassy, Saigon, to Southeast Asia Department, London [hereafter SEAD], 21 October 1965, FO 371/ 180536, National Archives of the United Kingdom, Kew [hereafter NAUK], 2.

21. Ang Cheng Guan, *The Vietnam War from the Other Side: The Vietnamese Communists' Perspective* (New York: RoutledgeCurzon, 2002), 107; Gaiduk, *Soviet Union and the Vietnam War*, 47–53, 79–80; Robert K. Brigham, *Guerrilla Diplomacy: The NLF's Foreign Relations and the Viet Nam War* (Ithaca, N.Y.: Cornell University Press, 1999), 60. Moscow hoped the war in Vietnam would end sooner rather than later because the "danger center for a new war is not Vietnam," Leonid Brezhnev told the French foreign minister in November. "It is in the heart of Europe, in Germany" (French Embassy, Moscow, to Ministry of Foreign Affairs, Paris [hereafter MFA], 4 November 1965, #162, AO: VC, ADF, 3).

22. Quoted in Ilya Gaiduk, "Peacemaking or Troubleshooting? The Soviet Role in Peace Initiatives during the Vietnam War," in Lloyd C. Gardner and Ted Gittinger, eds., *The Search for Peace in Vietnam, 1964–1968* (College Station: Texas A&M University Press, 2004), 264.

23. Reported in British Consulate General, Hanoi [hereafter BCGH], to Foreign Office, London [hereafter FO], 12 November 1965, FO 371/ 180526, NAUK, 1.

24. BCGH to SEAD, 18 November 1965, FO 371/180528, NAUK, 2.

25. Nguyen Dinh Binh, ed., *Ngoai giao Viet Nam, 1945–2000* [Vietnamese Diplomacy, 1945–2000] (Hanoi: Nha xuat ban Chinh tri quoc gia, 2005), 211; Luu Van Loi, *Ngoai giao Viet Nam, 1945–1995* [Vietnamese Diplomacy, 1945–1995] (Hanoi: Nha xuat ban Cong an nhan dan, 2004), 346.

26. Ban chi dao tong ket chien tranh truc thuoc Bo Chinh tri, *Chien tranh cach mang Viet Nam, 1945–1975: Thang loi va bai hoc* [Vietnam's Revolutionary War, 1945–1975: Victory and Lessons] (Hanoi: Nha xuat ban Chinh tri quoc gia, 2000), 155; Tran Quang Co, "Duong loi quoc te dung dan va sang tao cua Dang trong thoi ky chong My, cuu nuoc" [The Correct and Creative International Line of Our Party in the Anti-American, National Salvation Era], in Bo Ngoai giao, *Mat tran ngoai giao voi cuoc dam phan Paris* [The Diplomatic Front and the Paris Negotiations] (Hanoi: Nha xuat ban Chinh tri quoc gia, 2004), 68–69; Hoc vien quan he quoc te, *Ngoai giao Viet Nam hien dai: Vi su nghiep gianh doc lap, tu do, 1945–1975* [Contemporary Vietnamese Diplomacy: For the Cause of Securing Independence and Freedom] (Hanoi: Nha xuat ban Chinh tri quoc gia, 2001), 239; Nguyen Dinh Binh, ed., *Ngoai giao Viet Nam*, 202. "Our foremost international activity was strengthening strategic alliances," a study by the Institute of International Relations in Hanoi reports (Hoc vien quan he quoc te, *Ngoai giao Viet Nam hien dai*, 221).

27. Nguyen Dinh Binh, ed., *Ngoai giao Viet Nam*, 210–12.

28. Quoted in Maurice Vaïsse, "De Gaulle and the Vietnam War," in Gardner and Gittinger, eds., *The Search for Peace in Vietnam*, 163. The solidification of Vietnamese resolve following the start of U.S. combat operations in North and South Vietnam is underscored in British Embassy, Moscow, to FO, 7 April 1965, FO 371/180524, NAUK, 1; DAPAO, "Note," 25 August 1965, #162, AO: VC, ADF, 1; and French General Delegation, Hanoi, to MFA, 12 April 1966, #83, AO: VC, ADF, 4.

29. Pierre Asselin, "Revisionism Triumphant: Hanoi's Diplomatic Strategy in the Nixon Era," *Journal of Cold War Studies* 13, no. 4 (Fall 2011): 129–34. On the Paris negotiations more generally, see Pierre Asselin, *A Bitter Peace: Washington, Hanoi, and the Making of the Paris Agreement* (Chapel Hill: University of North Carolina Press, 2002); and Lien-Hang T. Nguyen, *Hanoi's War: An International History of the War for Peace in Vietnam* (Chapel Hill: University of North Carolina Press, 2012).

BIBLIOGRAPHY

PRIMARY SOURCES
Document Collections and Repositories

Canada
Library and Archives Canada

France
Archives de Pierre Mendès France à l'Institut Pierre Mendès France, Paris
Archives Diplomatiques de France, La Courneuve

United Kingdom
National Archives of the United Kingdom, Kew

United States
Vietnam Center and Archive at Texas Tech University, Lubbock

Vietnam
National Archives Center 3, Hanoi
National Library Document Collection, Hanoi
Revolution Museum Photograph Collection, Hanoi

Government/Party Documents and Documentary Histories

Against U.S. Aggression: Main Documents of the National Assembly of the Democratic Republic of Vietnam, 3rd Legislature—2nd Session, April 1965. Hanoi: Foreign Languages Publishing House, 1966.

American Imperialism's Intervention in Vietnam. Hanoi: Foreign Languages Publishing House, 1955.
Chen, King C., ed. *China and the Three Worlds: A Foreign Policy Reader*. White Plains, N.Y.: M. E. Sharpe, 1979.
Communist Party of Vietnam. *75 Years of the Communist Party of Vietnam (1930–2005): A Selection of Documents from Nine Party Congresses*. Hanoi: The Gio Publishers, 2005.
Dang Cong san Viet Nam. *Nhung su kien lich su Dang, Tap III* [Party Historical Events, Volume 3]. Hanoi: Nha xuat ban Thong tin ly luan, 1985.
———. *Van kien Dang—Toan tap* [Party Documents—Complete Series]. 54 vols. Hanoi: Nha xuat ban Chinh tri quoc gia, 1998–2008.
Fall, Bernard B., ed. *Ho Chi Minh: On Revolution—Selected Writings, 1920–66*. London: Pall Mall, 1967.
Gettleman, Marvin E., et al., eds. *Vietnam and America: A Documented History*. New York: Grove Press, 1995.
Ho Chi Minh. *Toan Tap, Tap VI* [Collected Works, Volume 6]. Hanoi: Nha xuat ban Su that, 1986.
———. *Toan tap, Tap 11* [Collected Works, Volume 11]. Hanoi: Nha xuat ban Chinh tri quoc gia, 2000.
———. *Tuyen tap* [Collected Works]. Hanoi: Nha xuat ban Su that, 1960.
Kotov, L. V., and R. S. Yegorov. *Militant Solidarity, Fraternal Assistance*. Moscow: Progress Publishers, 1970.
La vérité sur les relations vietnamo-chinoises durant les trente dernières années [The Truth about Sino-Vietnamese Relations in the Last Thirty Years]. Hanoi: Ministère des Affaires étrangères, 1979.
Le Duan. *Cach mang xa hoi chu nghia o Viet-Nam* [The Socialist Revolution in Vietnam]. 2 vols. Hanoi: Nha xuat ban Su that, 1976.
———. *Some Questions concerning the International Tasks of Our Party: Speech at the Ninth Plenum of the Third Central Committee of the Viet Nam Workers' Party*. Beijing: Foreign Languages Press, 1964.
———. *Thu vao Nam* [Letters to the South]. Hanoi: Nha xuat ban Su that, 1985.
———. *Thu vao Nam* [Letters to the South]. Hanoi: Nha xuat ban Quan doi nhan dan, 2005.
Manifesto of the South Viet Nam National Front for Liberation. No publisher, undated.
Nguyen Chi Thanh. "Qui vaincra au Sud Vietnam?" *Études Vietnamiennes*, no. 1 (1964): 13–22.
Republic of Vietnam. *The Problem of Reunification in Vietnam*. Saigon: Ministry of Information, 1958.
———. *Vietnam Report: Why Bomb North Viet Nam?* Saigon: Ministry of Information, undated.
Soviet Peace Committee. *U.S. Aggression in Vietnam: Crime against Peace and Humanity*. Moscow: Novosti Press Agency Publishing House, 1965.
Third National Congress of the Viet Nam Workers' Party: Documents. 3 vols. Hanoi: Foreign Languages Publishing House, undated.
Tran Van Dinh, ed. *This Nation and Socialism Are One: Selected Writings of Le Duan, First Secretary, Central Committee, Vietnamese Workers' Party*. Chicago: Vanguard Books, 1976.
Truong Chinh. *Écrits, 1946–1975* [Selected Writings, 1946–1975]. Hanoi: Éditions en langues étrangères, 1977.

United States Department of State. *The Department of State Bulletin* 31, no. 788 (2 August 1954).
———. *Foreign Relations of the United States.* Washington, D.C.: U.S. Government Printing Office, 1862– .
———. *Limits in the Seas: Straight Baselines—People's Republic of China.* International Boundary Study, series A, no. 43. Washington, D.C.: U.S. Government Printing Office, 1972.
———. *Working Paper on North Viet-Nam's Role in the War in South Viet-Nam.* Washington, D.C.: U.S. Government Printing Office, 1968.
United States Senate—Committee on Foreign Relations. *Background Information Relating to Southeast Asia and Vietnam,* 90th Congress, 1st Session. Washington, D.C.: U.S. Government Printing Office, 1967.
Westad, Odd Arne, Chen Jian, Stein Tønnesson, Nguyen Vu Tung, and James G. Hershberg, eds. "77 Conversations between Chinese and Foreign Leaders on the Wars in Indochina, 1964–1977." Cold War International History Project Working Paper no. 22, Woodrow Wilson Center, Washington, D.C., 1998.

Memoirs

Bui Diem. *In the Jaws of History.* Bloomington: Indiana University Press, 1999.
Bui Tin. *Following Ho Chi Minh: Memoirs of a North Vietnamese Colonel.* Honolulu: University of Hawaii Press, 1999.
Hoang Van Hoan. *A Drop in the Ocean: Hoang Van Hoan's Revolutionary Reminiscences.* Beijing: Foreign Languages Press, 1988.
Maneli, Mieczyslaw. *War of the Vanquished.* New York: Harper & Row, 1971.
Nguyen Thi Dinh. *No Other Road to Take: Memoirs of Mrs. Nguyen Thi Dinh.* Cornell Southeast Asia Program Data Paper 102. Ithaca, N.Y.: Cornell Southeast Asia Program, 1976.
Radvanyi, Janos. *Delusion and Reality: Gambits, Hoaxes, and Diplomatic One-Upmanship in Vietnam.* South Bend, Ind.: Gateway, 1978.
Thee, Marek. *Notes of a Witness: Laos and the Second Indochina War.* New York: Random House, 1973.
Truong Nhu Tang. *A Viet Cong Memoir.* New York: Vintage Books, 1985.
Vo Chi Cong. *Tren nhung chang duong cach mang* [On the Revolutionary Paths]. Hanoi: Nha xuat ban Chinh tri quoc gia, 2001.
Vu Thu Hien. *Dem giua ban ngay: Hoi ky chinh tri cua mot nguoi khong lam chinh tri* [Day Turns into Night: Political Memoirs of a Non-Politician]. Stanton, Calif.: Van Nghe, 1997.

SECONDARY SOURCES

Books, Monographs, and Articles

Sources in Vietnamese

50 nam Quan doi nhan dan Viet Nam [50 Years of the People's Army of Vietnam]. Hanoi: Nha xuat ban Quan doi nhan dan, 1995.
Ban chi dao Nghien cuu ly luan va thuc tien Trung uong Dang nhan dan cach mang Lao. *Lich su Dang nhan dan cach mang Lao* [History of the People's Revolutionary Party of Laos]. Hanoi: Nha xuat ban Chinh tri quoc gia, 2005.

Ban chi dao tong ket chien tranh truc thuoc Bo Chinh tri. *Chien tranh cach mang Viet Nam, 1945–1975: Thang loi va bai hoc* [Vietnam's Revolutionary War, 1945–1975: Victory and Lessons]. Hanoi: Nha xuat ban Chinh tri quoc gia, 2000.
Ben Tre Dong khoi va Doi quan toc dai [The Ben Tre Uprising and the Long-Haired Army]. Hanoi: Nha xuat ban Phu nu, 2009.
Bo Ngoai giao. *Chan dung nam co Bo truong Ngoai giao* [Portraits of Five Foreign Ministers]. Hanoi: Nha xuat ban Chinh tri quoc gia, 2005.
———. *Mat tran ngoai giao voi cuoc dam phan Paris* [The Diplomatic Front and the Paris Negotiations]. Hanoi: Nha xuat ban Chinh tri quoc gia, 2004.
Bo Quoc phong—Vien lich su Quan su Viet Nam. *Hau phuong chien tranh nhan dan Viet Nam, 1945–1975* [The Rear Base of the Vietnamese People's War]. Hanoi: Nha xuat ban Quan doi nhan dan, 1997.
———. *Lich su khang chien chong My cuu nuoc, 1954–1975*, Tap 2 [History of the Anti-American Resistance for National Salvation, 1954–1975, Vol. 2]. Hanoi: Nha xuat ban Chinh tri quoc gia, 1996.
———. *Lich su quan su Viet Nam, Tap 11: Cuoc khang chien chong My, cuu nuoc, 1954–1975* [Military History of Vietnam, Volume 11: The Anti-American Resistance for National Salvation]. Hanoi: Nha xuat ban Chinh tri quoc gia, 2005.
Bui Kim Dinh. "Tim hieu nguyen nhan cuoc dung dau lich su o Viet Nam (1954–1975)" [Understanding the Cause of Historical Encounters in Vietnam, 1954–1975]. *Tap chi Lich su Dang* [Journal of Party History], no. 186 (May 2006): 65–69.
Cao Van Luong, et al. *Lich su Viet Nam* [Vietnamese History]. Hanoi: Nha xuat ban Khoa hoc xa hoi, 1995.
Diep Dinh Hoa. "Khoi nghia Vinh Thanh (6-2-1959)" [The Vinh Thanh Uprising, 6 February 1962]. *Nghien cuu Lich su* [Historical Studies], no. 326 (January 2003): 35–48.
Han Van Tam. "Nghi thuat gianh thang loi tung buoc ket hop voi nhung thang loi quyet dinh trong khang chien chong My, cuu nuoc" [The Art of Gaining Gradual Victory in Combination with Decisive Victory in the Anti-American Resistance for National Salvation]. *Tap chi Lich su quan su* [Journal of Military History], no. 171 (March 2006): 9.
Hoang Trang. *Toan dan doan ket chong My, cuu nuoc duoi ngon co tu tuong Ho Chi Minh, 1954–1975* [The Entire People Unites against the United States for National Salvation under the Banner of Ho Chi Minh Thought]. Hanoi: Nha xuat ban Chinh tri quoc gia, 2005.
Hoc vien Chinh tri quoc gia Ho Chi Minh—Khoa lich su Dang. *Lich su Dang Cong san Viet Nam, Tap 1* [History of the Communist Party of Vietnam, Volume 1]. Hanoi: Nha xuat ban Chinh tri quoc gia, 1997.
Hoc vien quan he quoc te. *Ngoai giao Viet Nam hien dai: Vi su nghiep gianh doc lap, tu do, 1945–1975* [Contemporary Vietnamese Diplomacy: For the Cause of Securing Independence and Freedom]. Hanoi: Nha xuat ban Chinh tri quoc gia, 2001.
Khuat Bien Hoa. *Dai tuong Le Duc Anh* [General Le Duc Anh]. Hanoi: Nha xuat ban Quan doi nhan dan, 2005.
Le Hong Linh. *Cuoc dong khoi ky dieu o mien Nam Viet Nam 1959–1960* [Wonderful Uprising in Southern Vietnam, 1959–1960]. Da Nang: Nha xuat ban Da Nang, 2006.
Le Mau Han. *Dang Cong san Viet Nam: Cac Dai hoi va Hoi nghi Trung uong* [The Vietnamese Communist Party: Congresses and Central Committee Plenums]. Hanoi: Nha xuat ban Chinh tri quoc gia, 1995.

Le Xuan An. "Chien khu D, Chien khu Duong Minh Chau—An toan khu cua Trung uong Cuc mien Nam trong khang chien chong My, cuu nuoc" [Resistance Zone D, the Duong Ming Chau Resistance Zone: Secure Zone of the Central Office for South Vietnam in the Anti-American Resistance for National Salvation]. *Tap chi Lich su Dang* [Journal of Party History], no. 186 (January 2006): 47–49, 60.

Luu Van Loi. *Ngoai giao Viet Nam, 1945-1995* [Vietnamese Diplomacy, 1945-1995]. Hanoi: Nha xuat ban Cong an nhan dan, 2004.

Nguyen Dang Vinh, Dang Viet Thuy, and Le Ngoc Tu, eds. *Viet Nam: 30 nam chien tranh gia phong va bao ve To quoc, 1945-1975—Bien nien su kien* [Vietnam: 30 Years of War for Liberation and Protection of the Fatherland, 1945-1975—Annals of Events]. Hanoi: Nha xuat ban Quan doi nhan dan, 2005.

Nguyen Dinh Binh, ed. *Ngoai giao Viet Nam, 1945-2000* [Vietnamese Diplomacy, 1945-2000]. Hanoi: Nha xuat ban Chinh tri quoc gia, 2005.

Nguyen Dinh Liem, ed. *Quan he Viet Nam—Trung quoc: Nhung su kien 1961-1970* [Vietnam-China Relations: Developments, 1961-1970]. Hanoi: Nha xuat ban Khoa hoc xa hoi, 2006.

Nguyen Dinh Phuong. "Mot vai ky niem ve Bo truong Xuan Thuy" [Some Memories of Foreign Minister Xuan Thuy]. In Bo Ngoai giao, *Chan dung nam co Bo truong Ngoai giao,* 321–25.

Nguyen Dinh Uoc. "Nha chien luoc loi lac" [An Outstanding Strategist]. In Vien nghien cuu Ho Chi Minh va cac lanh tu cua Dang, *Le Duan va cach mang Viet Nam,* 97–105.

Nguyen Khoa Diem, ed. *Le Duan: Mot nha lanh dao loi lac, mot tu duy sang tao lon cua cach mang Viet Nam* [Le Duan: An Outstanding Leader, an Innovative Thinker of the Vietnamese Revolution]. Hanoi: Nha xuat ban Chinh tri quoc gia, 2002.

Nguyen Thi Thap. *Lich su phong trao phu nu Viet nam* [History of the Vietnamese Women's Movement]. Hanoi: Nha xuat ban Phu nu, 1981.

Nguyen Trong Phuc, ed. *Tim hieu lich su Dang Cong san Viet Nam: Qua cac Dai hoi va Hoi nghi Trung uong, 1930-2002* [Understanding the History of the Vietnamese Communist Party: Congresses and Central Committee Plenums, 1930-2002]. Hanoi: Nha xuat ban Lao dong, 2003.

Nguyen Van Binh, ed. *Mat tran To quoc Viet Nam: Nhung chang duong lich su (1930-2010)* [The Vietnam Fatherland Front: Historical Phases, 1930-2010]. Hanoi: Nha xuat ban Lao dong, 2009.

Nho ve Anh Le Duc Tho [Remembering Le Duc Tho]. Hanoi: Nha xuat ban Chinh tri quoc gia, 2001.

Pham Huy Duong and Pham Ba Toan. *Ba muoi nam chien tranh giai phong: Nhung tran danh di vao lich su* [Thirty Years of Liberation War: Historical Battles]. Hanoi: Nha xuat ban Cong an nhan dan, 2005.

Theo mien Dong Nam Bo khang chien, Tap 3 [Following the Resistance in Eastern Nam Bo, Volume 3]. Hanoi: Nha xuat ban Quan doi nhan dan, 1993.

"Tieu su dong chi Le Duan, Tong Bi thu Ban Chap hanh Truong uong Dang Cong san Viet Nam" [Biography of Comrade Le Duan, General Secretary of the Central Committee of the Vietnamese Communist Party]. In Nguyen Khoa Diem, ed., *Le Duan,* 9–11.

Tran Minh Truong. *Hoat dong ngoai giao cua Chu tich Ho Chi Minh tu 1954 den 1969* [Diplomatic Activities of President Ho Chi Minh from 1954 to 1969]. Hanoi: Nha xuat ban Cong an nhan dan, 2005.

Tran Quang Co. "Duong loi quoc te dung dan va sang tao cua Dang trong thoi ky chong My, cuu nuoc" [The Correct and Creative International Line of Our Party in the Anti-American, National Salvation Era]. In Bo Ngoai giao, *Mat tran ngoai giao voi cuoc dam phan Paris*, 57–76.

Tran Thanh. "Dong chi Le Duan, nha lanh dao kiet xuat cua Dang ta, nha ly luan Macxit-Leninnit sang tao, nguoi hoc tro xuat sac cua Chu tich Ho Chi Minh" [Comrade Le Duan, Illustrious Leader of Our Party, Innovative Marxist-Leninist Theoretician, Devoted Pupil of President Ho Chi Minh]. In Vien nghien cuu Ho Chi Minh va cac lanh tu cua Dang, *Le Duan va cach mang Viet Nam*, 9–12.

Tran Van Tra. *Nhung chang duong lich su cua B2 thanh dong, Tap I: Hoa binh hay chien tranh* [History of the B2 Theater. Vol. 1, Peace or War]. Hanoi: Nha xuat ban Quan doi nhan dan, 1992.

Trung tam Khoa hoc xa hoi va nhan van quoc gia—Vien su hoc. *Lich su Viet Nam, 1954–1965* [History of Vietnam, 1954–1965]. Hanoi: Nha xuat ban Khoa hoc xa hoi, 1995.

Vien Lich su Dang—Hoi dong bien soan lich su Nam Trung bo khang chien. *Nam Trung bo khang chien, 1945–1975* [The Resistance in Southern Trung Bo, 1945–1975]. Hanoi: Tong cong ty phat hanh sach Lien ket xuat ban, 1992.

Vien nghien cuu chu nghia Mac-Lenin va tu tuong Ho Chi Minh. *Lich su Dang Cong san Viet Nam, Tap 2: 1954–1975* [History of the Communist Party of Vietnam, Volume 2: 1954–1975]. Hanoi: Nha xuat ban Chinh tri quoc gia, 1995.

Vien nghien cuu Ho Chi Minh va cac lanh tu cua Dang. *Le Duan va cach mang Viet Nam* [Le Duan and the Vietnamese Revolution]. Hanoi: Nha xuat ban Chinh tri quoc gia, 1997.

Vo Thi Hoa. "Dang bo Tay Ninh van dong dong bao theo dao Cao Dai tham gia khang chien chong My, cuu nuoc" [The Tay Ninh Party Committee's Activities regarding the Participation of Cao Dai Compatriots in the Anti-American Resistance for National Salvation]. *Tap chi Lich su Dang* [Journal of Party History], no. 185 (April 2006): 57–58.

Sources in English and French

12 années d'intervention et d'agression des impérialistes américains au Laos [12 Years of U.S. Imperialist Intervention and Aggression in Laos]. N.p.: Éditions du Neo Lao Haksat, 1966.

Adams, Nina S., and Alfred W. McCoy, eds. *Laos: War and Revolution*. New York: Harper & Row, 1970.

Ageron, Charles-Robert, and Philippe Devillers, eds. *Les guerres d'Indochine de 1945 à 1975* [The Indochina Wars from 1945 to 1975]. Paris: Institut d'Histoire du Temps Présent, 1996.

Anderson, David. *The Vietnam War*. New York: Palgrave MacMillan, 2005.

Andrews, William R. *The Village War: Vietnamese Communist Revolutionary Activity in Dinh Truong Province, 1960–64*. Columbia: University of Missouri Press, 1973.

Ang Cheng Guan. "The Huong Lap and Phu Loi Incidents, and the Decision to Resume Armed Struggle in South Vietnam." *War and Society* 15, no. 1 (May 1997): 3–22.

———. "Southeast Asian Perceptions of the Domino Theory." In Goscha and Ostermann, eds., *Connecting Histories*, 301–31.

———. *Vietnamese Communists' Relations with China and the Second Indochina Conflict, 1956–1962*. Jefferson, N.C.: McFarland, 1997.

———. "The Vietnam War, 1962–64: The Vietnamese Communist Perspective." *Journal of Contemporary History* 35, no. 4 (October 2000): 601–18.

———. *The Vietnam War from the Other Side: The Vietnamese Communists' Perspective*. New York: RoutledgeCurzon, 2002.

Asselin, Pierre. *A Bitter Peace: Washington, Hanoi, and the Making of the Paris Agreement*. Chapel Hill: University of North Carolina Press, 2002.

———. "Choosing Peace: Hanoi and the Geneva Agreement on Vietnam, 1954–55." *Journal of Cold War Studies* 9, no. 2 (Spring 2007): 95–126.

———. "The Democratic Republic of Vietnam and the 1954 Geneva Conference: A Revisionist Critique." *Cold War History* 11, no. 2 (May 2011): 155–95.

———. "Hanoi and Americanization of the War in Vietnam: New Evidence from Vietnam." *Pacific Historical Review* 75, no. 3 (August 2005): 427–39.

———. "Le Duan, the American War, and the Creation of an Independent Vietnamese State." *Journal of American East-Asian Relations* 10, nos. 1–2 (Spring–Summer 2001): 1–27.

———. "Revisionism Triumphant: Hanoi's Diplomatic Strategy in the Nixon Era." *Journal of Cold War Studies* 13, no. 4 (Fall 2011): 101–37.

———. "Using the *Van Kien Dang* Series to Understand Vietnamese Revolutionary Strategy during the Vietnam War." *Journal of Vietnamese Studies* 5, no. 2 (Summer 2010): 219–24.

———. "The Vietnam War from the Other Side." In Mitchell Lerner, ed., *A Companion to Lyndon B. Johnson* (Oxford: Blackwell, 2012), 367–84.

———. "'We Don't Want A Munich': Hanoi's Diplomatic Struggle during the American War, 1965–1968." *Diplomatic History* 36, no. 3 (June 2012): 547–82.

Boudarel, Georges. *Cent fleurs éclosent dans la nuit du Viêt Nam* [One Hundred Flowers Blooming in the Night of Vietnam]. Paris: Jacques Bertoin, 1991.

———. "Essai sur la pensée militaire vietnamienne" [Essay on Vietnamese Military Thought]. In Chesneaux, Boudarel, and Hémery, eds., *Tradition et Révolution au Viêt Nam*, 460–95.

Bradley, Mark Philip. *Imagining Vietnam and America: The Making of Postcolonial Vietnam, 1919–1950*. Chapel Hill: University of North Carolina Press, 2002.

Bradley, Marc Philip, and Marilyn B. Young, eds. *Making Sense of the Vietnam Wars: Local, National, and Transnational Perspectives*. New York: Oxford University Press, 2008.

Brève Histoire du Parti des Travailleurs du Viet Nam, 1930–1970 [Brief History of the Vietnamese Workers' Party]. Hanoi: Éditions en langues étrangères, 1970.

Brigham, Robert K. *Guerrilla Diplomacy: The NLF's Foreign Relations and the Viet Nam War*. Ithaca, N.Y.: Cornell University Press, 1999.

———. "Vietnam at the Center: Patterns of Diplomacy and Resistance." In Gardner and Gittinger, eds., *International Perspectives on Vietnam*, 98–107.

Brocheux, Pierre, ed. *Du conflict d'Indochine aux conflits indochinois* [From the Indochina Conflict to the Indochinese Conflicts]. Paris: Éditions Complexe, 2000.

———. *Ho Chi Minh*. Paris: Presses de Sciences Po, 2000.

Bui Tin. *From Enemy to Friend: A North Vietnamese Perspective on the War*. Annapolis, Md.: Naval Institute Press, 2002.

Buttinger, Joseph. *Vietnam: A Political History*. New York: Praeger, 1968.

Carver, George A. "The Real Revolution in South Vietnam." *Foreign Affairs*, no. 43 (April 1965): 387–408.

Catton, Philip E. *Diem's Final Failure: Prelude to America's War in Vietnam*. Lawrence: University Press of Kansas, 2002.

Chapman, Jessica M. *Cauldron of Resistance: Ngo Dinh Diem, the United States, and 1950s Southern Vietnam*. Ithaca, N.Y.: Cornell University Press, 2013.

———. "The Sect Crisis of 1955 and the American Commitment to Ngo Dinh Diem." *Journal of Vietnamese Studies* 5, no. 1 (Winter 2010): 37–85.

———. "Staging Democracy: South Vietnam's 1955 Referendum to Depose Bao Dai." *Diplomatic History* 30, no. 4 (September 2006): 671–703.

Chen Jian. "China's Involvement in the Vietnam War, 1964–1969." *China Quarterly*, no. 142 (June 1995): 356–87.

———. "A Crucial Step toward the Breakdown of the Sino-Soviet Alliance: The Withdrawal of Soviet Experts from China in July 1960." *Cold War International History Project Bulletin*, nos. 8–9 (Winter 1996–97): 246, 249–50.

———. *Mao's China and the Cold War*. Chapel Hill: University of North Carolina Press, 2001.

Chen, King C. "Hanoi's Three Decisions and the Escalation of the Vietnam War." *Political Science Quarterly* 90, no. 2 (Summer 1975): 239–59.

———. "Hanoi vs. Peking: Policies and Relations—A Survey." *Asian Survey* 12, no. 9 (September 1972): 806–17.

Chen, Min. *The Strategic Triangle and Regional Conflict: Lessons from the Indochina Wars*. Boulder, Colo.: Lynne Rienner, 1992.

Chesneaux, Jean, Georges Boudarel, and Daniel Hémery, eds. *Tradition et révolution au Viêt Nam* [Tradition and Revolution in Vietnam]. Paris: Éditions Anthropos, 1971.

Christensen, Thomas J. *Useful Adversaries: Grand Strategy, Domestic Mobilization, and Sino-American Conflict, 1947–1958*. Princeton, N.J.: Princeton University Press, 1996.

Chun-tu Hsueh, ed. *China's Foreign Relations: New Perspectives*. New York: Praeger, 1982.

Chun-tu Hsueh and Robert C. North. "China and the Superpowers: Perception and Policy." In Chun-tu Hsueh, ed., *China's Foreign Relations*, 13–43.

Cogan, Charles G. "'How Fuzzy Can One Be?': The American Reaction to De Gaulle's Proposal for the Neutralization of (South) Vietnam." In Gardner and Gittinger, eds., *Search for Peace in Vietnam*, 144–61.

Connelly, Matthew J. *A Diplomatic Revolution: Algeria's Fight for Independence and the Origins of the Post-Cold War Era*. New York: Oxford University Press, 2002.

Cournil, Laure, and Pierre Journoud. "Une décolonization manquée: L'armée nationale du Vietnam, de la tutelle française à la tutelle américaine (1949–1965)" [A Failed Decolonization: The Vietnamese National Army from French Tutelage to American Tutelage, 1949–1965]. *Outre-Mers* 99, nos. 370–71 (2011): 67–81.

Currey, Cecil. *Victory at Any Cost: The Genius of Vietnam's Gen. Vo Nguyen Giap*. Washington, D.C.: Brassey's, 1997.

Davidson, Philip B. *Vietnam at War: The History, 1946–1975*. Novato, Calif.: Presidio Press, 1988.

Devillers, Philippe. "La lutte pour la réunification du Viêt Nam entre 1954 et 1961" [The Struggle for Reunification in Vietnam between 1954 and 1961]. In Chesneaux, Boudarel, and Hémery, eds., *Tradition et révolution au Viêt Nam*, 329–55.

———. "Le passage du relais au Viet-nam, juin 1954-avril 1956" [The Passing of the Torch in Vietnam, June 1954–April 1956]. In Ageron and Devillers, eds., *Guerres d'Indochine*, 126–42.

Dommen, Arthur J. *The Indochinese Experience of the French and the Americans: Nationalism and Communism in Cambodia, Laos, and Vietnam*. Bloomington: Indiana University Press, 2001.

Donnell, John, and Melvin Gurtov. *North Vietnam: Left of Moscow, Right of Peking*. Santa Monica, Calif.: RAND, 1968.

Duiker, William J. *The Communist Road to Power in Vietnam*. 2nd ed. Boulder, Colo.: Westview Press, 1996.

———. *Ho Chi Minh: A Life*. New York: Theia, 2000.

———. *U.S. Containment Policy and the Conflict in Indochina*. Stanford, Calif.: Stanford University Press, 1994.

———. "Waging Revolutionary War: The Evolution of Hanoi's Strategy in the South, 1959–1965." In Werner and Huynh, eds., *Vietnam War*, 24–36.

Duncanson, Dennis J. *Government and Revolution in Vietnam*. London: Oxford University Press, 1968.

Elliott, David W. P. "Hanoi's Strategy in the Second Indochina War." In Werner and Huynh, eds., *Vietnam War*, 66–94.

———. *The Vietnamese War: Revolution and Social Change in the Mekong Delta, 1930–1975*. Concise ed. Armonk, N.Y.: M. E. Sharpe, 2007.

Ellison, Herbert J., ed. *The Sino-Soviet Conflict: A Global Perspective*. Seattle: University of Washington Press, 1982.

Errington, Jane, and B. J. C. McKercher, eds. *The Vietnam War as History*. New York: Praeger, 1990.

Fall, Bernard B. "South Vietnam's Internal Problems." *Pacific Affairs* 31, no. 3 (September 1958): 241–60.

———. *The Two Vietnams: A Political and Military Analysis*. London: Pall Mall, 1966.

———. *Vietnam Witness*. New York: Praeger, 1966.

Fforde, Adam, and Suzanne Paine. *The Limits of National Liberation: Problems of Economic Management in the Democratic Republic of Vietnam*. London: Croom Helm, 1987.

Fitzgerald, Frances. *Fire in the Lake: The Vietnamese and the Americans in Vietnam*. New York: Vintage Books, 1973.

Franchini, Philippe. *Les guerres d'Indochine*. Vol. 2, *De la bataille de Dien Bien Phu à la chute de Saïgon* [The Indochina Wars. Vol. 2, From the Battle of Dien Bien Phu to the Fall of Saigon]. Paris: Éditions Pygmalion / Gérard Watelet, 1988.

Fursenko, Aleksandr, and Timothy Naftali. *Khrushchev's Cold War: The Inside Story of an American Adversary*. New York: W. W. Norton, 2006.

Gaiduk, Ilya V. *Confronting Vietnam: Soviet Policy toward the Indochina Conflict, 1954–1963*. Washington, D.C.: Woodrow Wilson Center Press, 2003.

———. "Containing the Warriors: Soviet Policy toward the Indochina Conflict, 1960–65." In Gardner and Gittinger, eds., *International Perspectives on Vietnam*, 58–76.

———. "Peacemaking or Troubleshooting? The Soviet Role in Peace Initiatives during the Vietnam War." In Gardner and Gittinger, eds., *Search for Peace in Vietnam*, 264.

———. "Soviet Policy toward U.S. Participation in the Vietnam War." *History* 81, no. 261 (January 1996): 40–54.

———. *The Soviet Union and the Vietnam War*. Chicago: Ivan R. Dee, 1996.

Gardner, Lloyd C. *Pay Any Price: Lyndon Johnson and the Wars for Vietnam*. Chicago: Ivan R. Dee, 1995.

Gardner, Lloyd C., and Ted Gittinger, eds. *International Perspectives on Vietnam*. College Station: Texas A&M University Press, 2000.

———. *The Search for Peace in Vietnam, 1964–1968*. College Station: Texas A&M University Press, 2004.

Giebel, Christoph. *Imagined Ancestries of Vietnamese Communism: Ton Duc Thang and the Politics of History and Memory*. Seattle: University of Washington Press, 2010.

Gilbert, Marc Jason. "Persuading the Enemy: Vietnamese Appeal to Non-White Forces of Occupation, 1945–1975." In Wilcox, ed., *Vietnam and the West*, 107–42.

Glaubitz, Joachim. "Relations between Communist China and North Vietnam." In Rupen and Farrell, eds., *Vietnam and the Sino-Soviet Dispute*, 56–69.

Gleijeses, Piero. *Conflicting Missions: Havana, Washington, and Africa, 1959–1976*. Chapel Hill: University of North Carolina Press, 2003.

Gnoinska, Margaret K. "Poland and Vietnam, 1963: New Evidence on Secret Communist Diplomacy and the 'Maneli Affair.'" Cold War International History Project Working Paper no. 45, Woodrow Wilson Center, Washington, D.C., 2005.

Golan, Galia. *Soviet Policies in the Middle East: From World War II to Gorbachev*. New York: Cambridge University Press, 1990.

Goscha, Christopher E. *Historical Dictionary of the Indochina War (1945–1954): An International and Interdisciplinary Approach*. Copenhagen: Nordic Institute of Asian Studies Press, 2011.

———. "The Maritime Nature of the Wars for Vietnam, 1945–75: A Geo-Historical Reflection." *War and Society* 24, no. 2 (November 2005): 53–92.

———. "The Revolutionary Laos of the Democratic Republic of Vietnam: The Making of a Transnational 'Pathet Lao Solution' (1954–1956)." In Goscha and Laplante, eds., *Failure of Peace in Indochina*, 61–84.

———. *Vietnam: Un état né de la guerre, 1945–1954* [Vietnam: A State Born from War]. Paris: Armand Colin, 2011.

Goscha, Christopher E., and Christian Ostermann, eds. *Connecting Histories: The Cold War and Decolonization in Asia, 1945–1962*. Stanford, Calif.: Stanford University Press, 2009.

Goscha, Christopher E., and Karine Laplante, eds. *L'échec de la paix en Indochine / The Failure of Peace in Indochina (1954–1962)*. Paris: Les Indes savantes, 2010.

Goscha, Christopher E., and Stein Tønnesson. "Le Duan and the Break with China: A 1979 Document Translated by Christopher E. Goscha, with an Introduction by Stein Tønnesson." *Cold War International History Project Bulletin*, nos. 12/13 (Fall/Winter 2001): 275–84.

Gould-Davies, Nigel. "Rethinking the Role of Ideology in International Politics during the Cold War." *Journal of Cold War Studies* 1, no. 1 (Winter 1999): 90–109.

Griffith, William E. "The November 1960 Moscow Meeting: A Preliminary Assessment." *China Quarterly*, no. 11 (July–September 1962): 38–57.

———. *The Sino-Soviet Rift*. Cambridge: Massachusetts Institute of Technology Press, 1964.
Grinter, Lawrence E., and Peter M. Dunn, eds. *The American War in Vietnam: Lessons, Legacies, and Implications for Future Conflicts*. New York: Greenwood Press, 1987.
Grossheim, Martin. "'Revisionism' in the Democratic Republic of Vietnam." *Cold War History* 5, no. 4 (November–December 2005): 451–77.
Gurtov, Melvin. *Hanoi on War and Peace*. Santa Monica, Calif.: RAND, 1967.
Haas, Mark L. *The Ideological Origins of Great Power Politics, 1789–1989*. Ithaca, N.Y.: Cornell University Press, 2005.
Hammer, Ellen J. *A Death in November: America in Vietnam, 1963*. New York: Oxford University Press, 1987.
Hansen, Peter. "*Bac Di Cu*: Catholic Refugees from the North of Vietnam and Their Role in the Southern Republic, 1954–1959." *Journal of Vietnamese Studies* 4, no. 3 (Fall 2009): 173–211.
Herring, George. *America's Longest War: The United States and Vietnam, 1950–1975*. 4th ed. New York: McGraw Hill, 2002.
Hess, Gary. *Vietnam and the United States: Origins and Legacy of War*. Boston: Twayne Publishers, 1990.
History of the Communist Party of Vietnam. Hanoi: Foreign Languages Publishing House, 1986.
Hoang Van Chi. *From Colonialism to Communism: A Case History of North Vietnam*. New York: Pall Mall Press, 1964.
Ho Hai. "The Nguyen Ai Quoc Schools." *Vietnam*, no. 148 (1970): 9–11.
Holcombe, Alec. "The Complete Collection of Party Documents: Listening to the Party's Official Internal Voice." *Journal of Vietnamese Studies* 5, no. 2 (Summer 2010): 225–42.
Honey, P. J. *Communism in North Vietnam: Its Role in the Sino-Soviet Dispute*. Westport, Conn.: Greenwood Press, 1973.
———. "The Position of the DRV Leadership and the Succession to Ho Chi Minh." *China Quarterly*, no. 9 (January–March 1962): 24–36.
Hunt, David. *Vietnam's Southern Revolution: From Insurrection to Total War*. Amherst: University of Massachusetts Press, 2008.
Hunt, Michael H., and Odd Arne Westad. "The Chinese Communist Party and International Affairs: A Field Report on New Historical Sources and Old Research Problems." *China Quarterly*, no. 122 (June 1990): 258–72.
Huynh Kim Khanh. *Vietnamese Communism, 1925–1945*. Ithaca, N.Y.: Cornell University Press, 1982.
Hy Van Luong. *Revolution in the Village: Tradition and Transformation in North Vietnam, 1925–1988*. Honolulu: University of Hawaii Press, 1992.
Jacobs, Seth. *America's Miracle Man in Vietnam: Ngo Dinh Diem, Religion, Race, and U.S. Intervention in Southeast Asia*. Durham, N.C.: Duke University Press, 2004.
———. *Cold War Mandarin: Ngo Dinh Diem and the Origins of America's War in Vietnam, 1950–1963*. Lanham, Md.: Rowman & Littlefield, 2006.
Jamieson, Neil. *Inventing Vietnam: The United States and State Building, 1954–1968*. Berkeley: University of California Press, 2008.
Joes, Anthony James. *The War for South Vietnam, 1954–1975*. Westport, Conn.: Praeger, 2001.
Jones, Howard. *Death of a Generation: How the Assassinations of Diem and JFK Prolonged the Vietnam War*. New York: Oxford University Press, 2003.

Journoud, Pierre. *De Gaulle et le Vietnam, 1945–1969: La réconciliation* [De Gaulle and Vietnam, 1945–1969: The Reconciliation]. Paris: Tallandier, 2011.
———. "La France, cinquième partie aux négociations?" [France, Fifth Party in the Negotiations?]. In Journoud and Menétrey-Monchau, eds., *Vietnam, 1968–1976*, 187–205.
Journoud, Pierre, and Cécile Menétrey-Monchau, eds. *Vietnam, 1968–1976: La sortie de guerre / Exiting a War.* Brussels: Peter Lang, 2011.
Kahin, George McT., and John Lewis. *The United States in Vietnam.* New York: Dial Press, 1969.
Kahin, George McT., and Robert Scalapino. "Excerpts from National Teach-in on Vietnam Policy." In Raskin and Fall, eds., *Viet-Nam Reader,* 289–306.
Kanet, Roger E. "The Soviet Union and the Third World from Khrushchev to Gorbachev: The Place of the Third World in Evolving Soviet Global Strategy." In Kanet, ed., *Soviet Union,* 3–22.
———, ed. *The Soviet Union, Eastern Europe and the Third World.* New York: Cambridge University Press, 1987.
Kerkvliet, Benedict J. Tria. *The Power of Everyday Politics: How Vietnamese Peasants Transformed National Policy.* Ithaca, N.Y.: Cornell University Press, 2005.
Khoo, Nicholas. *Collateral Damage: Sino-Soviet Rivalry and the Termination of the Sino-Vietnamese Alliance.* New York: Columbia University Press, 2011.
Kolko, Gabriel. *Anatomy of a War: Vietnam, the United States, and the Modern Historical Experience.* New York: Pantheon Books, 1985.
Lacouture, Jean. *Ho Chi Minh: A Political Biography.* New York: Random House, 1968.
Lawrence, Mark Atwood. *The Vietnam War: A Concise International History.* New York: Oxford University Press, 2008.
Le Kinh Lich, ed. *The 30-Year War, 1945–1975.* Vol. 2, *1954–1975.* Hanoi: The Gioi Publishers, 2002.
Lentz, Christian C. "Mobilization and State Formation on a Frontier of Vietnam." *Journal of Peasant Studies* 38, no. 3 (July 2011): 559–586.
Lewy, Gunter. *America in Vietnam.* New York: Oxford University Press, 1978.
Lieberthal, Kenneth. *Governing China: From Revolution through Reform.* New York: W. W. Norton, 2004.
Logevall, Fredrik. *Choosing War: The Lost Chance for Peace and the Escalation of War in Vietnam.* Berkeley: University of California Press, 2001.
———. "De Gaulle, Neutralization, and American Involvement in Vietnam, 1963–1964." *Pacific Historical Review* 61, no. 1 (February 1992): 69–102.
———. *Embers of War: The Fall of an Empire and the Making of America's Vietnam.* New York: Random House, 2012.
London, Kurt L. "Vietnam: A Sino-Soviet Dilemma." *Russian Review* 26, no. 1 (January 1967): 26–37.
Lowe, Peter, ed. *The Vietnam War.* London: MacMillan Press, 1998.
Lüthi, Lorenz, *The Sino-Soviet Split, 1956–1966.* Princeton, N.J.: Princeton University Press, 2008.
———. "Twenty-Four Soviet Bloc Documents on Vietnam and the Sino-Soviet Split, 1964–1966." *Cold War International History Project Bulletin,* no. 16 (2008): 367-98.
———. "The Vietnam War and China's Third-Line Defense Planning before the Cultural Revolution, 1964–1966." *Journal of Cold War Studies* 10, no. 1 (Winter 2008): 26–51.

Luu Van Loi. *Fifty Years of Vietnamese Diplomacy, 1945–1995, Volume 1: 1945–1975.* Hanoi: The Gioi Publishers, 2000.
MacLean, Ken. "Manifest Socialism: The Labor of Representation in the Democratic Republic of Vietnam, 1956–1959." *Journal of Vietnamese Studies* 2, no. 1 (February 2007): 27–79.
Marangé, Céline. *Le communisme vietnamien, 1919–1991* [Vietnamese Communism, 1919–1991]. Paris: Presses de Sciences Po, 2012.
Marr, David G. "Sino-Vietnamese Relations." *Australian Journal of Chinese Affairs*, no. 6 (July 1981): 45–64.
McNamara, Robert S., James Blight, and Robert Brigham. *Argument without End: In Search of Answers to the Vietnam Tragedy.* New York: Public Affairs, 1999.
Military Institute of Vietnam. *Victory in Vietnam: The Official History of the People's Army of Vietnam, 1954–1975.* Translated by Merle L. Pribbenow. Lawrence: University Press of Kansas, 2002.
Miller, Edward. *Misalliance: Ngo Dinh Diem, the United States, and the Fate of South Vietnam.* Cambridge, Mass.: Harvard University Press, 2013.
Miller, Edward, and Tuong Vu. "The Vietnam War as a Vietnamese War: Agency and Society in the Study of the Second Indochina War." *Journal of Vietnamese Studies* 4, no. 3 (Fall 2009): 1–16.
Moïse, Edwin E. *Historical Dictionary of the Vietnam War.* Lanham, Md.: Scarecrow Press, 2001.
———. *Land Reform in China and North Vietnam.* Chapel Hill: University of North Carolina Press, 1983.
———. "The Mirage of Negotiations." In Gardner and Gittinger, eds., *Search for Peace in Vietnam*, 73–82.
———. *Tonkin Gulf and the Escalation of the Vietnam War.* Chapel Hill: University of North Carolina Press, 1996.
Moyar, Mark. *Triumph Forsaken: The Vietnam War, 1954–1965.* New York: Cambridge University Press, 2006.
Nguyen, Lien-Hang T. "Cold War Contradictions: Toward an International History of the Second Indochina War, 1969–1973." In Bradley and Young, eds., *Making Sense of the Vietnam Wars*, 219–49.
———. *Hanoi's War: An International History of the War for Peace in Vietnam.* Chapel Hill: University of North Carolina Press, 2012.
———. "The War Politburo: North Vietnam's Diplomatic and Political Road to the Tet Offensive." *Journal of Vietnamese Studies* 1, nos. 1–2 (February/August 2006): 4–55.
Nguyen Dy Nien. *Ho Chi Minh Thought: On Diplomacy.* Hanoi: The Gioi Publishers, 2004.
Nguyen Khac Vien. "The Impotence of American Technique in the Face of the People's War." *Vietnamese Studies* 5, no. 12 (1966): 100–144.
———. *Vietnam: A Long History.* Hanoi: Foreign Languages Publishing House, 1987.
Nguyen Manh Hung. "The Vietnam War in Retrospect: Its Nature and Some Lessons." In Grinter and Dunn, eds., *American War in Vietnam*, 15–25.
Nguyen Vu Tung. "The 1961–1962 Geneva Conference: Neutralization of Laos and Policy Implications for Vietnam." In Goscha and Laplante, eds., *Failure of Peace in Indochina*, 255–68.

———. "Coping with the United States: Hanoi's Search for an Effective Strategy." In Lowe, ed., *Vietnam War*, 30–61.
Ninh, Kim N. B. *A World Transformed: The Politics of Culture in Revolutionary Vietnam, 1945–1965*. Ann Arbor: University of Michigan Press, 2002.
Niu Jun. "The Background to the Shift in Chinese Policy toward the United States in the Late 1960s." In Roberts, ed., *Behind the Bamboo Curtain*, 319–48.
Olsen, Mari. *Soviet-Vietnam Relations and the Role of China, 1949–64: Changing Alliances*. New York: Routledge, 2006.
An Outline History of the Vietnam Workers' Party, 1930–1975. 2nd ed. Hanoi: Foreign Languages Publishing House, 1978.
Palmujoki, Eero. *Vietnam and the World: Marxist-Leninist Doctrine and the Changes in International Relations, 1975–93*. New York: St. Martin's Press, 1997.
Pelley, Patricia M. *Postcolonial Vietnam: New Histories of the National Past*. Durham, N.C.: Duke University Press, 2002.
Perry Thornton, Thomas. "Peking, Moscow, and the Underdeveloped Areas." *World Politics* 13, no. 4 (July 1961): 491–504.
Pike, Douglas. "The Impact of the Sino-Soviet Dispute on Southeast Asia." In Ellison, ed., *Sino-Soviet Conflict*, 185–205.
———. *PAVN: People's Army of Vietnam*. New York: Da Capo Press, 1991.
———. *Viet Cong: The Organization and Techniques of the National Liberation Front of South Vietnam*. Cambridge: Massachusetts Institute of Technology Press, 1966.
Porter, Gareth. "After Geneva: Subverting Laotian Neutrality." In Adams and McCoy, eds., *Laos: War and Revolution*, 179–212.
———. "Coercive Diplomacy in Vietnam: The Tonkin Gulf Crisis Reconsidered." In Werner and Hunt, eds., *American War in Vietnam*, 9–22.
———. "Hanoi's Strategic Perspective and the Sino-Soviet Conflict." *Pacific Affairs* 57, no. 1 (Spring 1984): 7–25.
———. *Perils of Dominance: Imbalance of Power and the Road to War in Vietnam*. Berkeley: University of California Press, 2005.
Post, Ken. *Revolution, Socialism and Nationalism in Viet Nam*. Vol. 3, *Socialism in Half a Country*. Belmont, Calif.: Wadsworth, 1989.
Prados, John. *Vietnam: The History of an Unwinnable War, 1945–1975*. Lawrence: University Press of Kansas, 2009.
Preston, Andrew. "Mission Impossible: Canadian Secret Diplomacy and the Quest for Peace in Vietnam." In Gardner and Gittinger, eds., *Search for Peace in Vietnam*, 117–43.
Qiang Zhai. *China and the Vietnam Wars, 1950–1975*. Chapel Hill: University of North Carolina Press, 2000.
———. "An Uneasy Relationship: China and the DRV during the Vietnam War." In Gardner and Gittinger, eds., *International Perspectives on Vietnam*, 108–39.
Quinn-Judge, Sophie. "The Ideological Debate in the DRV and the Significance of the Anti-Party Affair, 1967–68." *Cold War History* 5, no. 4 (November–December 2005): 479–500.
———. "Through a Glass Darkly: Reading the History of the Vietnamese Communist Party, 1945–1975." In Bradley and Young, eds., *Making Sense of the Vietnam Wars*, 111–34.

Race, Jeffrey. "The Origins of the Second Indochina War." *Asian Survey*, no. 5 (May 1970): 359–82.

———. *War Comes to Long An: Revolutionary Conflict in a Vietnamese Province.* Berkeley: University of California Press, 1972.

Radchenko, Sergei. *Two Suns in the Heavens: The Sino-Soviet Struggle for Supremacy, 1962–1967.* Stanford, Calif.: Stanford University Press, 2009.

Raskin, Marcus G., and Bernard B. Fall, eds. *The Viet-Nam Reader: Articles and Documents on American Foreign Policy and the Viet-Nam Crisis.* New York: Random House, 1965.

Roberts, Priscilla, ed. *Behind the Bamboo Curtain: China, Vietnam, and the World beyond Asia.* Washington, D.C.: Woodrow Wilson Center Press, 2006.

Ross, Douglas A. "Middlepowers as Extra-Regional Balancer Powers: Canada, India, and Indochina, 1954–62." *Pacific Affairs* 55, no. 2 (Summer 1982): 185–209.

Ruane, Kevin. *War and Revolution in Vietnam, 1930–1975.* London: UCL Press, 1998.

Rupen, Robert A., and Robert Farrell, eds. *Vietnam and the Sino-Soviet Dispute.* New York: Praeger, 1967.

Schurmann, H. F. "The Third International Sovietological Conference." *China Quarterly*, no. 4 (October–December 1960): 102–13.

Service, Robert. *Comrades! A History of World Communism.* Cambridge, Mass.: Harvard University Press, 2007.

Shultz, Richard H., Jr. *The Secret War against Hanoi: Kennedy's and Johnson's Use of Spies, Saboteurs, and Covert Warriors in North Vietnam.* New York: HarperCollins, 1999.

Smith, Ralph B. *An International History of the Vietnam War.* Vol. 1, *Revolution versus Containment, 1955–61.* London: Macmillan Press, 1983.

———. *An International History of the Vietnam War.* Vol. 2, *The Struggle for Southeast Asia, 1961–65.* New York: St. Martin's Press, 1986.

———. *An International History of the Vietnam War.* Vol. 3, *The Making of a Limited War, 1965–66.* London: Macmillan Press, 1991.

———. *Viet-Nam and the West.* London: Heinemann, 1968.

Smith, Roger M. "Cambodia's Neutrality and the Laotian Crisis." *Asian Survey* 1, no. 5 (July 1961): 17–24.

Smyser, W. R. *The Independent Vietnamese: Vietnamese Communism between Russia and China, 1956–1969.* Southeast Asia Series no. 55. Athens: Ohio University Center for International Studies, 1980.

Statler, Kathryn C. *Replacing France: The Origins of American Intervention in Vietnam.* Lexington: University Press of Kentucky, 2007.

Stowe, Judy. "Révisionnisme au Vietnam." *Communisme*, nos. 65–66 (2001): 233–49.

Sullivan, Marianna P. *France's Vietnam Policy: A Study in Franco-American Relations.* Westport, Conn.: Greenwood Press, 1978.

Suri, Jeremi. *Liberty's Surest Guardian: American Nation-Building from the Founders to Obama.* New York: Free Press, 2011.

Szalontai, Balazs. *Kim Il Sung in the Khrushchev Era: Soviet–DPRK Relations and the Roots of North Korean Despotism, 1953–1964.* Stanford, Calif.: Stanford University Press, 2005.

———. "Political and Economic Crisis in North Vietnam, 1955–1956." *Cold War History* 5, no. 4 (November–December 2005): 395–426.

Tai, Hue-Tam Ho. *Vietnamese Radicalism and the Origins of the Vietnamese Revolution.* Cambridge, Mass.: Harvard University Press, 1992.

Tanham, George K. *Communist Revolutionary Warfare: From the Vietminh to the Viet Cong.* Westport, Conn.: Praeger Security International, 2006.

Tao, Jay. "Mao's World Outlook: Vietnam and the Revolution in China." *Asian Survey* 8, no. 5 (May 1968): 416–32.

Taubman, William. *Khrushchev: The Man and His Era.* New York: W. W. Norton, 2003.

Taylor, Sandra C. "Laos: The Escalation of a Secret War." In Errington and McKercher, eds., *Vietnam War,* 73–90.

Thakur, Ramesh. "India's Vietnam Policy, 1946–1979." *Asian Survey* 19, no. 10 (October 1979): 957–76.

Thayer, Carlyle A. *War by Other Means: National Liberation and Revolution in Viet-Nam, 1954–60.* Cambridge, Mass.: Unwin Hyman, 1989.

Thies, Wallace J. *When Governments Collide: Coercion and Diplomacy in the Vietnam Conflict, 1964–1968.* Berkeley: University of California Press, 1980.

Toczek, David M. *The Battle of Ap Bac, Vietnam.* Annapolis, Md.: Naval Institute Press, 2001.

Ton That Thien. *The Foreign Policy of the Communist Party of Vietnam: A Study of Communist Tactics.* New York: Crane Russak, 1989.

Toye, Hugh. *Laos: Buffer State or Battleground?* London: Oxford University Press, 1968.

Tran Cong Tuong and Pham Thanh Vinh. *The N.L.F.: Symbol of Independence, Democracy and Peace in South Vietnam.* Hanoi: Foreign Languages Publishing House, 1967.

Tranh-Minh Tiet. *Les relations Americano-Vietnamiennes de Kennedy à Nixon: Tome I— Kennedy-Ngo Dinh Diem* [US-Vietnamese Relations from Kennedy to Nixon: Volume 1—Kennedy-Ngo Dinh Diem]. Paris: Nouvelles Éditions Latines, 1971.

Tran Thi Lien. "Les catholiques vietnamiens dans la République du Viêtnam (1954–1963) [Vietnamese Catholics in the Republic of Vietnam (1954–1963)]." In Brocheux, ed., *Du conflict d'Indochine aux conflits indochinois,* 53–80.

Turley, William S. "Civil-Military Relations in North Vietnam." *Asian Survey* 9, no. 12 (December 1969): 879–99.

———. *The Second Indochina War: A Concise Political and Military History.* 2nd ed. Lanham, Md.: Rowman & Littlefield, 2009.

Vaïsse, Maurice. "De Gaulle and the Vietnam War." In Gardner and Gittinger, eds., *Search for Peace in Vietnam,* 162–65.

Vu, Tuong. "From Cheering to Volunteering: Vietnamese Communists and the Coming of the Cold War, 1940–1951." In Goscha and Ostermann, eds., *Connecting Histories,* 172–206.

Werner, Jayne S., and David Hunt, eds. *The American War in Vietnam.* Ithaca, N.Y.: Cornell Southeast Asia Program, 1993.

Werner, Jayne S., and Luu Doan Huynh, eds. *The Vietnam War: Vietnamese and American Perspectives.* Armonk, N.Y.: M. E. Sharpe, 1993.

Westad, Odd Arne, ed. *Brothers in Arms: The Rise and Fall of the Sino-Soviet Alliance, 1945–1963.* Washington, D.C.: Woodrow Wilson Center Press, 1998.

———. *The Global Cold War: Third World Interventions and the Making of Our Times.* New York: Cambridge University Press, 2005.

Wiest, Andrew. *Vietnam's Forgotten Army: Heroism and Betrayal in the ARVN.* New York: New York University Press, 2008.

Wilcox, Wynn, ed. *Vietnam and the West: New Approaches*. Ithaca, N.Y.: Cornell University Press, 2010.
Winters, Francis X. *The Year of the Hare: America in Vietnam, January 25, 1963–February 15, 1964*. Athens: University of Georgia Press, 1997.
Womack, Brantly. *China and Vietnam: The Politics of Asymmetry*. New York: Cambridge University Press, 2006.
Xiaoming Zhang. "Communist Powers Divided: China, the Soviet Union, and the Vietnam War." In Gardner and Gittinger, eds., *International Perspectives on Vietnam*, 77–97.
———. "The Vietnam War, 1964–1969: A Chinese Perspective." *Journal of Military History* 60, no. 4 (October 1996): 731–62.
Young, Marilyn B. *The Vietnam Wars, 1945–1990*. New York: HarperCollins, 1991.
Zagoria, Donald S. "Khrushchev's Attack on Albania and Sino-Soviet Relations." *China Quarterly*, no. 8 (October–December 1961): 1–19.
———. *Vietnam Triangle: Moscow, Peking, Hanoi*. New York: Pegasus, 1967.
Zasloff, J. J. *Political Motivation of the Vietnamese Communists: The Vietminh Regroupees*. Santa Monica, Calif.: RAND, 1968.
Zhihua Shen and Danhui Li. *After Leaning to One Side: China and Its Allies in the Cold War*. Washington, D.C.: Woodrow Wilson Center Press, 2011.
Zinoman, Peter. *The Colonial Bastille: A History of Imprisonment in Vietnam, 1862–1940*. Berkeley: University of California Press, 2001.
———. "NhanVan-Giai Pham and Vietnamese 'Reform Communism' in the 1950s: A Revisionist Interpretation." *Journal of Cold War Studies* 13, no. 1 (2011): 60–100.
Zubok, Vladislav M. *A Failed Empire: The Soviet Union in the Cold War from Stalin to Gorbachev*. Chapel Hill: University of North Carolina Press, 2008.
Zubok, Vladislav M., and Constantine Pleshakov. *Inside the Kremlin's Cold War: From Stalin to Khrushchev*. Cambridge, Mass.: Harvard University Press, 1997.

Dissertations and Unpublished Papers

Grosser, Pierre. "La France et l'Indochine (1953–1956): Une 'carte de visite' en 'peau de chagrin.'" [France and Indochina, 1953–1956: A "Visiting Card" Reduced to a "Shagreen"]. PhD diss., Institut d'Études Politiques de Paris, 2002.
Journoud, Pierre. "Des artisans de paix dans le secret de la diplomacie: Vers un règlement pacifique de la guerre au Vietnam, 1967–1973" [Peace Artisans in the Secret of Diplomacy: Toward a Peaceful Settlement of the War in Vietnam, 1967–1973].
Le Cuong. "Phong trao Phat giao mien Nam Viet Nam nam 1963 voi cuoc dao chinh lat do che do Ngo Dinh Diem (01-11-1963)" [The 1963 Buddhist Movement in Southern Vietnam and the Overthrow of Ngo Dinh Diem (1 November 1963)]. Paper presented at the Second International Conference on Vietnamese Studies, Ho Chi Minh City, Vietnam, 14–16 July 2004.
Masur, Matthew. "Hearts and Minds: Cultural Nation-Building in South Vietnam, 1954–1963." PhD diss., Ohio State University, 2004.
Mehta, Harish C. "'People's Diplomacy': The Diplomatic Front of North Vietnam during the War against the United States, 1965–1972." PhD diss., McMaster University, 2009.
Miller, Edward. "Undoing the 'Limited Partnership': The Neutralization of Laos and the Origins of the Crisis of 1963 in South Vietnam." Paper presented at an international

workshop entitled "The Failure of Peace? Indochina between the Two Geneva Accords, 1954–1962," Université du Québec à Montréal, 6–7 October 2006.

Nguyen, Lien-Hang T. "Between the Storms: An International History of the Second Indochina War, 1968–1973." PhD diss., Yale University, 2008.

Stewart, Geoffrey. "Revolution, Modernization, and Nation-Building in Diem's Vietnam: Civic Action, 1955–1963." PhD diss., University of Western Ontario, 2010.

INDEX

Agent Orange, 210
"Agroville" program. *See* Rural Community Development Program
Albania, 86, 91, 108, 115, 116, 118, 130, 181, 183. *See also* Hoxha, Enver
Algeria, 104; war of independence, 11, 100, 105, 118, 154
Algiers, 156
American National Exhibition (Moscow, 1959), 49
"American War." *See* Vietnam War
Andropov, Yuri, 149
Ang Cheng Guan, 5, 43, 59, 66, 115, 169, 200
An Lao, 204
"Anti-American Resistance for National Salvation," 1, 208; aims of, 207
Army of the Republic of Vietnam (ARVN), 52, 55, 58, 69–70, 73, 74, 109, 129, 200; at battle of Ap Bac, 151–52; as communist target, 59, 166, 174–75, 177, 180, 190, 199, 204; and Diem overthrow, 160; defeat of, 211
August Revolution (1945), 12
Australia, 136–37

Bac Ky Committee for Education and Training (ICP), 16
Bac Lieu Province, 73
Ba Cut, 29

Ba Dinh Square, 12
Bandung Conference, 27–28, 133
Bao Dai, 12; as head of SOVN, 13, 32. *See also* State of Vietnam
Bao ve (PAVN security forces), 85, 241n84
Battle of Ap Bac (1963), 151–52, 269n117
Battle of Dien Bien Phu (1954), 11, 13, 14, 87, 105, 114, 130, 172, 194
Bay of Pigs invasion (1961), 100
Ben Tre Town/Province, 56, 62, 70, 73, 74, 75, 110
Beria, Lavrentiy, 85
Berlin, 75, 116; crisis of 1958, 49, 58; crisis of 1961, 91, 100
Berlin Wall, 91
Binh Tri Thien Province, 16
Binh van (propaganda work among enemy soldiers), 60
Binh Xuyen, 28, 29, 30
Blackwell, J. K., 138
Boun Oum, 119
Brazil, 116
Brezhnev, Leonid, 202, 203, 288n21. *See also* Communist Party of the Soviet Union; Soviet Union
Brigham, Robert, 128, 132–133
Budapest, 150
Bui Chu, 20
Bui Cong Trung, 170
Burma, 47, 123

309

Cambodia, 12, 17, 64, 204; communists in, 125; as neutral state, 123, 127, 130, 139, 141; U.S. interference in, 119. *See also* Sihanouk, Norodom

Canada: as ICSC member, 14–15, 102, 103, 159, 160, 176, 177, 197, 202, 218n29; mediation efforts (1964), 190–92. *See also* International Commission for Supervision and Control in Vietnam

Can Tho Province, 62, 73

Cao Dai, 21, 28, 29, 30, 54, 73

Castro, Fidel, 91, 145, 154. *See also* Cuba

Catton, Philip, 110

Central Highlands (Vietnam), 22, 58, 59, 60, 62, 68, 69, 73, 92, 94, 110, 204, 206

Central Military Commission (VWP), 124, 125, 199, 200, 204. *See also* People's Army of Vietnam; Vietnamese Workers' Party

Central Office (Directorate) for Southern Vietnam (COSVN), 15, 16, 29, 95–97, 110–13, 128, 129, 134, 136, 169, 204, 243n11; and strategic hamlet program, 110. *See also* Le Duan; Nam Bo Executive Committee; Nguyen Chi Thanh; Nguyen Van Linh

Chapman, Jessica, 28

Chau Doc Province, 73

Chen, K. C., 178

Chen Jian, 49

Chen Yi, 181, 190, 208

Cheysson, Claude, 24

Chiang Kai-shek. *See* Jiang Jieshi

China, 40, 94, 135; revolution of 1949, 165, 178; and Vietnam, 182. *See also* Chinese Communist Party; People's Republic of China

Chinese Communist Party (CCP), 15, 44, 72, 80, 94, 154, 201; Eighth National Congress (1956), 38; and Hundred Flowers movement (1956), 40. *See also* China; Mao Zedong; People's Republic of China

Chinh quyen van (propaganda work among civil servants in enemy regime), 76

Cholon, 69

"Christmas bombing" (1972). *See* Linebacker II

Cochinchina, 17

Cold War, 1, 5, 11, 26, 34, 44, 58, 63, 79, 91, 100, 101, 104, 118, 124, 149, 153; and Laos, 119; and Vietnam, 1, 2, 4, 12, 25, 27, 104, 145, 172

Committee for Afro-Asian Solidarity (PRC), 139

Communist Party of the Soviet Union (CPSU), 47, 80, 154, 168, 181, 183, 185, 202–203; support for national liberation, 81, 107; Twentieth Congress (1956), 34, 36; Twenty-Second Congress (1961), 108. *See also* Khrushchev, Nikita; Soviet Union

Con Dao (Poulo Condore) Island, 16

Congo (Leopoldville), 91, 100. *See also* Lumumba, Patrice

Congress (U.S.), 175, 196, 211

Council of Ministers (DRVN), 37, 67

Cuba, 100–101, 116, 130; missile crisis (1962), 118, 142–43, 145, 149, 154, 184; revolution of 1959, 91, 94, 100, 165. *See also* Castro, Fidel

Cultural and Ideological Committee (VWP), 146

Czechoslovakia, 104, 121

Dalai Lama, 49

Dao (ethnic minority), 46

De Buzon, Jacques, 202

Decolonization, 100, 104–5, 154

De Gaulle, Charles: call for neutralization of South Vietnam of 1963, 156, 191

Democratic People's Republic of Korea (North Korea), 65, 86, 104, 107, 121, 143, 179, 184; relations with DRVN, 157. *See also* Kim Il-sung

Democratic Republic of Vietnam (DRVN, North Vietnam), 1, 144, 186; acceptance of/respect for 1954 Geneva accords on Indochina, 1, 4, 12, 13–14, 22–23, 24, 27, 28, 102, 127, 141; agricultural collectivization/cooperatives in, 48, 66, 79, 83, 100, 149; anti-Diem initiatives, 21, 29; assistance to southern insurgents, 64–66, 75, 85–86, 120, 122, 124, 132, 144, 148, 159, 168, 176, 178, 198, 201; commitment to peaceful/political struggle in South Vietnam, 14, 15, 17, 21, 22–23, 26, 28, 29–30, 32–34, 39, 47, 60, 65, 78, 97, 101, 128, 167; commitment to victory in "American War," 207, 209–211, 289n28; and Catholics, 14, 19–20, 77, 83; compulsory military service/military mobilization in, 47, 62, 100, 190, 207; democratization and liberalization in, 37–40, 100; dependence on/solicitation of foreign aid, 4, 33, 50, 80, 81, 98–99, 100, 102, 104, 107, 131–32, 150, 181–82, 186, 195–96, 208, 247n77; deployment of PAVN units to South Vietnam, 7, 174–75, 176, 179, 180, 198–201, 284n181; deployment of southern regroupees to South Vietnam, 64–66, 95, 113, 159, 172, 264n43; deployment of support personnel to South Vietnam, 64, 96, 159; destruction in, 14, 48; diplomatic struggle/manipulation of world opinion, 18, 26–28, 34, 45–46, 63, 89, 101–2, 103–4, 117, 132, 140–41, 150–51, 167, 172, 179, 193, 208, 259n123; dissidence in, 38, 40, 46, 83, 98–100, 132, 189; economic hardship in, 24, 46, 66–67, 83, 97–99, 113, 149, 196; economic development of, 3, 5, 12, 17, 23–24, 33, 38–39, 48, 53, 61, 72, 97, 143; effects of U.S. bombings in, 197–98, 199, 200–201, 202, 207; evacuations of cities, 197; fear of U.S. intervention in Vietnam, 1, 3, 13, 14, 24–26, 44, 64, 91–92, 100–101, 113–14, 121, 123, 131, 134, 140, 149, 160, 178, 186, 194, 207, 275n31; food rationing in, 24, 83, 98; formation/expansion of militias, 24, 207; and Geneva accords/Conference on Laos (1961–62), 122–25; and ICSC, 102–4, 132–33; and Khrushchev's ouster, 203–4; land reform program (1953–56), 20, 24, 38–39, 46, 226n170; Liu Shaoqi visit (1963), 153–54; negotiations with France, 13, 224n129; negotiations with U.S., 142, 150, 190–95, 207–8, 210–11; and peaceful coexistence, 35, 86, 106, 125, 126, 130, 142–43, 149, 160, 162, 171, 184, 186, 203–4; as police state, 77, 85; recognition by PRC, 12; recognition by Soviet Union, 12; relations with Cambodia, 17, 119; relations with France, 18, 29, 34, 126–27, 139; relations with India, 103, 127, 133; relations with Laos, 17–18, 119, 120–22, 125, 142, 189; relations with PRC, 1, 28, 34, 50–51, 63, 79, 89, 99, 100, 104, 114–16, 131, 133, 144, 157–58, 181–83, 278n85; relations with Soviet Union, 1, 28, 34, 35, 36, 45, 50–51, 63, 89, 100, 104, 107, 130, 131–32, 138, 143, 159, 168–69, 171, 179, 180–82, 183–86, 203–4, 278n85; relations with SOVN/RVN, 14, 29–30, 31, 47–48, 78, 127, 142, 150, 155–57, 162, 192–95; repression in, 40–41, 77, 99–100; "resistance centers" in, 99–100; and reunification elections of 1956, 3, 6, 12, 14, 20, 28, 30, 37, 39, 130; RVN commando infiltrations into, 99–100, 111, 189; secret contact with UK (1964), 192; and Sino-Soviet dispute, 3, 4, 45, 50–51, 77, 78–82, 86, 104, 106–8, 112, 115, 118, 131, 181, 182, 183, 204, 208; and socialist unity/proletarian internationalism, 4, 5, 36, 80–81, 82, 86, 101–2, 104, 108, 118, 177, 185–86, 208; "Three Readinesses" campaign, 207; "Three Responsibilities" campaign, 207; and UN membership, 45, 78; women in, 207; and world revolution, 35, 50, 57, 81, 82, 104, 106, 150, 154, 210. *See also* Five-year plan; Ho Chi Minh; Le Duan; "North-first" policy; People's Army of Vietnam; "People's diplomacy"; Pham Van Dong; Three-year plan; Viet Minh; Vietnamese Workers' Party

"Denounce the Communists" *(To Cong)* campaign (SOVN), 30–31, 33. *See also* Ngo Dinh Diem
Department for Liaison with Communist and Workers' Parties in Socialist Countries (CPSU), 149
Department of External Affairs (Canada), 193
Détente (Soviet Union–U.S.), 34–35, 44, 49, 63, 72, 76, 79, 118. *See also* Partial Nuclear Test Ban Treaty; Peaceful coexistence; Soviet Union; U-2 incident; United States
Devillers, Philippe, 56
Dong Anh, 98
Duiker, William, 4–5, 87, 112, 134, 171
Duong Bach Mai, 170
Duong Van Minh, 160

East Germany. *See* German Democratic Republic
Egypt, 104. *See also* United Arab Republic
Eisenhower, Dwight, 25, 44, 72; presidential administration, 11, 24, 37, 49, 74. *See also* United States
Elliott, David, 31, 60, 68, 69, 110, 129, 162, 175

Fall, Bernard, 134
Federal Republic of Germany (West Germany), 25
Federation of Trade Unions (DRVN), 15
Five-year plan (DRVN, 1961–65), 83–87, 107, 134, 149. *See also* Democratic Republic of Vietnam; "North-first" policy
Foreign Office (UK), 102, 127, 129
"Former Resistance Fighters of the Nam Bo Region," 75
Four-Power Paris Summit. *See* Paris Summit
France, 75, 113, 131, 155, 167; end of colonial rule in Vietnam, 12; High Command (Vietnam), 37; *mission civilisatrice* in Indochina, 12; occupation of Indochina (1945–46), 12; recognition of Algerian independence, 118; recognition of PRC, 174; relations with DRVN, 46; relation with U.S., 20–21; and SOVN, 12, 13, 25. *See also* Geneva accords on Vietnam/Indochina; Indochina War
Franchini, Philippe, 161

Gaiduk, Ilya, 122, 149, 202
General Political Department (GPD, PAVN), 15, 146
General Staff (PAVN), 79, 146, 175, 199
Geneva, 127

312   INDEX

Geneva accords on Laos (1962), 118, 124–25, 126, 127, 134–35, 204, 208, 254n38; collapse of, 6, 118, 142, 143, 154–55. *See also* Geneva Conference on Laos; Laos; Pathet Lao

Geneva accords on Vietnam/Indochina (1954), 2, 11, 12, 17, 27, 66, 95, 102–3, 109, 112, 114, 115, 120, 125, 140, 142, 149, 150, 167, 171, 179, 193, 204, 208, 209, 211; collapse of, 36–37, 132; "Final Declaration of the Geneva Conference," 13, 27, 215n4; provisions of, 13; reunification elections of 1956, 12, 13, 28, 36; signing of, 1, 13; and voluntary migration of civilians, 13, 19–20. *See also* Geneva Conference on Indochina; International Commission for Supervision and Control

Geneva Conference on Indochina (1954), 14, 34, 126, 127, 156. *See also* Geneva accords on Vietnam/Indochina

Geneva Conference on Laos (1961–62), 122–25, 126, 130, 131; origins of, 119–20, 122. *See also* Geneva accords on Laos; Laos; Pathet Lao

German Democratic Republic (East Germany), 121

Germany, 25, 44, 116, 210, 288n21

Gnoinska, Margaret, 156

Goa, 103

Golan, Galia, 34

Goscha, Christopher, 120

Government Workers' Trade Union (DRVN), 57

Great Britain. *See* United Kingdom

"Great Leap Forward" (PRC), 48, 49, 107

Gromyko, Andrei, 204

Guatemala, 11

Guinea. *See* Republic of Guinea

Guzmán, Jacobo Árbenz, 11

Hainan Island, 49

Haiphong, 16, 98; U.S. bombing of, 211

Hai Xo, 51

Hammer, Ellen, 155

Hanoi, 3, 19, 36, 98, 157, 185, 219n40; U.S. bombing of, 211; preparations for war, 190, 197, 205

Hau Kien Village, 16

Ha Van Lau, 160

Hmong (ethnic minority), 46, 99

Hoa Binh, 99

Hoa Hao, 21, 28, 29, 30, 54

Hoang Minh Chinh, 170

Hoang Quoc Viet, 15, 39

Hoang Van Hoan, 40, 87, 120, 146, 164

Hoang Van Thai, 106

Ho Chi Minh, 16, 25, 32, 37, 39, 58, 62, 78, 80, 84, 87, 89, 108, 130, 131, 134, 143, 146, 170, 173, 209; acting general secretary of VWP, 40; as "Asian Tito," 82; declaration of Vietnamese independence, 12; and diplomatic struggle, 27, 28, 150–51, 172, 273n175; mediation of Sino-Soviet and other communist disputes, 80–81, 82, 108, 154, 163, 171; moderate tendencies of, 40, 41, 50, 53, 61, 106, 126, 146, 148, 149, 151, 159–60, 171, 187; and peaceful coexistence, 35; personality cult of, 35–36, 171; "rectification" address of 1956, 38; "rectification" address of 1961, 100; sidelining from VWP leadership, 82, 163, 171; and "special political conference" of 1964, 186–88; support for 1954 Geneva accords, 5–6, 15, 23, 36, 171; visit to Burma (1958), 47. *See also* Democratic Republic of Vietnam; Vietnamese Workers' Party

Ho Chi Minh Trail, 64, 108, 120, 124, 142

Hoc tap (journal, DRVN), 46, 61, 69, 97, 113, 159, 160, 177, 178, 180, 184–86, 196; on Khrushchev's ouster, 203; and VWP strategic debate of 1963, 147–48

Hon Me Island, 196

Hon Ngu Island, 196

Houa Phanh (Sam Neua) Province, 123

Ho Viet Thang, 39

Hoxha, Enver, 108, 183. *See also* Albania

Hue, 210

Hungary, 104; revolution of 1956, 40, 226n156

India, 34, 46, 49, 133; as ICSC member, 102–3, 146. *See also* International Commission for Supervision and Control in Vietnam; Nehru, Jawaharlal

Indochina, 1, 12, 17, 22, 26, 104, 122, 125, 127, 143, 192, 202, 203, 255n46

Indochina War, 1, 11, 13, 15, 16, 23, 45, 55, 75, 76, 95, 105, 111, 112, 120, 169, 170, 194; internationalization of, 12–13; onset of, 12. *See also* Democratic Republic of Vietnam; France; Geneva accords on Vietnam/Indochina; Viet Minh; Vietnamese Workers' Party

Indochinese Communist Party (ICP), 16

Indonesia, 104

Institute of International Relations (Hanoi), 89

Institute of Philosophy (Hanoi), 170

International Commission for Supervision and Control in Vietnam (ICSC), 14, 24, 27, 30, 102–4, 109, 114, 116, 144, 146, 150, 154, 155–56, 159, 176, 197, 200, 247n72; and regroupment

of military forces in Vietnam, 18–19; report of June 1962, 132–33; and voluntary migration of civilians in Vietnam, 19–20. *See also* Canada; Geneva accords on Vietnam/Indochina; India; Poland
International Conference on the Settlement of the Laotian Question (1961–62). *See* Geneva Conference on Laos
Interzone V, 204; Executive Committee of, 22, 47, 75, 89
Iran, 11

Jacobs, Seth, 20
Japan, 210; occupation of Indochina in World War II, 12
Jiang Jieshi (Chiang Kai-shek), 11, 49. *See also* Republic of China
Jinmen (Quemoy) Islands, 58, 232n67
Johnson, Lyndon, 109, 145, 200; presidential administration, 3, 174, 175, 193, 196, 200–201, 206, 207, 208; secret peace offer to Hanoi (1964), 190–92. *See also* United States

Kennedy, John F., 37, 113, 114, 116; assassination of, 145; presidential administration, 91, 93, 100–101, 128, 132, 156, 160–61, 175. *See also* United States
Khrushchev, Nikita, 36, 81, 107, 153, 154, 164, 180, 183, 184; attack on Albania, 91, 108, 118, 130, 142; and Berlin, 58, 91; and Cuban missile crisis, 149; denunciation of Stalin, 34; and Laos, 121; ouster from power, 174, 202–4; and peaceful coexistence, 34, 35, 42, 44, 63, 72, 79, 171, 185; visit to U.S., 49. *See also* Communist Party of the Soviet Union; Soviet Union
Khu Mu (ethnic minority), 46
Kien Hoa Province, 110
Kien Phong Province, 69
Kim Il-sung, 65. *See also* Democratic People's Republic of Korea
Kinmen Islands. *See* Jinmen Islands
Kong Le, 119
Kosygin, Alexei, 202
Korea, 25, 65, 152
Korean War, 11, 13, 107, 115, 121, 149, 182, 184

Lacouture, Jean, 151
Lai Chau, 99
Land Reform Committee (DRVN), 39
Lao Cai, 99
Laos, 12, 17, 64, 94, 130, 135, 139, 140; civil war in, 100, 119–22, 154–55, 189; neutralization of, 118, 126, 134–35; U.S. interference in, 101, 116. *See also* Geneva accords on Laos; Geneva Conference on Laos; Pathet Lao; Souvanna Phouma
Law 10/59 (RVN), 70, 103. *See also* Ngo Dinh Diem
Le Cuong, 161
Le Duan (Le Van Nhuan), 7, 16–17, 21, 40, 57, 87, 93–94, 108, 170, 171, 179, 203; as acting general secretary of the VWP, 47, 77, 95; advocacy of war in South Vietnam, 41–43, 164; appointment as VWP first secretary, 86–87; attack on moderates in the VWP, 164; and battle of Ap Bac, 152; commitment to socialist transformation in DRVN, 195–96, 207; control of VWP decision-making, 145, 173; "Directions of the Southern Revolution" (1956), 41–43, 51, 159; emulation of Stalin, 173, 195; and Fifteenth Plenum of the VWP Central Committee, 51; fourteen-point "action plan," 41; and Geneva accords on Laos (1962), 125, 143; as head of COSVN, 15–16; as head of Nam Bo Executive Committee, 17, 29; letter to COSVN of July 1962, 134–37, 140; militant views of, 32, 42–43, 50, 142, 146, 173; and NLF, 88; and neutralization of South Vietnam, 128, 134–37, 140; opposition to 1954 Geneva accords and to negotiations, 6, 15–17, 23, 143, 192, 194, 208, 209–10; regime of, 175, 181, 182, 191–92, 194, 199, 200, 203, 207, 211; "Some Questions concerning the International Tasks of Our Party (address at Ninth Plenum of VWP Central Committee, 1963), 163–64; visit to Moscow (1964), 180–81. *See also* Central Office (Directorate) for Southern Vietnam; Democratic Republic of Vietnam; Nam Bo Executive Committee; Vietnamese Workers' Party
Le Duc Tho, 40, 57, 84, 87, 146, 173, 183, 208, 209; and Le Duan, 16, 169; as head of VWP Organization Committee, 40, 169, 170–71; opposition to 1954 Geneva accords, 16, 194; visit to Moscow (1964), 180–81; and VWP strategic debate of 1963, 147–48. *See also* Organization Committee; Vietnamese Workers' Party
Le Liem, 170
Lenin, Vladimir, 48, 195, 214n4
Le Quang Dao, 113
Le Thanh Nghi, 40, 87, 146
Le Van Luong, 15, 39. *See also* Organization Committee
Le Van Nhuan. *See* Le Duan

Le Vinh Quoc, 170, 272n161
L'Humanité (newspaper, France), 143
Liberation Army of South Vietnam, 95. See also People's Liberation Armed Forces
Liberation Radio (NLF), 160, 202
"Limited war," 100, 179, 207
Linebacker II, 211
Liu Shaoqi: visit to Hanoi (1963), 153–54
Logevall, Fredrik, 24, 25, 32, 46, 155
Long An Province, 69
Lumumba, Patrice, 100. See also Congo (Leopoldville)
Lüthi, Lorenz, 152
Luu Doan Huynh, 161

Mali, 103
Maneli, Mieczyslaw, 155–56, 267n78. See also International Commission for Supervision and Control in Vietnam; Poland
Manila Pact, 11. See also Southeast Asia Treaty Organization
Mao Zedong, 15, 65, 173, 174, 178; and "continuous revolution," 44, 49, 148, 152–53; opposition to peaceful coexistence/Khrushchev, 44, 72; and Vietnam, 108, 181, 201, 287n15. See also Chinese Communist Party; People's Republic of China
Marangé, Céline, 99
Marr, David, 208
Marx, Karl, 146
McCarthy, Joseph, 11
Mekong Delta, 60, 69, 92, 108
Mekong River, 123
Mikoyan, Anastas, 35
Military Assistance Advisory Group (MAAG, U.S.), 25, 127
Military Assistance Command, Vietnam (MACV, U.S.), 127, 129, 152
Miller, Edward, 129, 157
Ministry of Foreign Affairs (DRVN), 26, 30, 89, 99, 101, 102, 142, 160, 192, 203
Ministry of Public Security (DRVN), 85, 170
Moïse, Edwin, 141, 142, 198
Mongolia, 104, 121
Morocco, 103, 247n81
Mosaddegh, Mohammad, 11
Moscow, 91
Moscow Conference: of 1957, 47, 63, 168; of 1960, 80, 81, 168
Moyar, Mark, 31, 109, 129
Munich accords (1938), 160, 208
My Tho Province, 73

Nam Bo Executive Committee (Xu uy Nam Bo), 17, 29, 56, 70, 72, 75, 76, 89, 95. See also Central Office (Directorate) for Southern Vietnam; Le Duan
Nam Lua, 28
Nasser, Gamal Abdel, 11. See also Egypt; United Arab Republic
National Assembly (DRVN), 25, 36, 37, 48, 49, 62, 70, 74, 80, 98, 101, 105, 106, 113, 116, 123, 124, 125, 143, 149–50, 154, 183, 192; and diplomatic solution for South Vietnam, 127; and failure of Geneva accords on Laos (1962), 142; on neutralization of South Vietnam, 141–42; Standing Committee of, 74, 146, 197; and Tonkin Gulf incident, 197
National Commission for Science and Technology (DRVN), 170
National Front for the Liberation of South Vietnam (NLF, Viet Cong), 73, 92, 96, 97, 104, 108–110, 111, 116, 117, 124, 133, 137, 141, 143, 144, 148, 150, 153, 166, 168, 176, 187, 242n95; challenges, 129, 162, 199; contacts with RVN government, 194–95; and diplomatic struggle/manipulation of world opinion, 150–51; manifesto/program, 88; and neutralization of South Vietnam, 126–28, 136, 139, 140; origins of, 54–55, 87–90; and VWP, 137–39, 141. See also Nguyen Van Hien; People's Liberation Armed Forces
Nationalist China. See Republic of China
Nationaliste (newspaper, Cambodia), 127
National Reunification Committee (VWP), 146
National Security Council (U.S.), 174
Nehru, Jawaharlal, 133. See also India; Nonaligned movement/states
"New democracy," 84
Nghe An Province, 19, 38
Ngo Dinh Diem, 17, 21, 25, 109, 134, 140, 155, 157, 176; anti-communism of, 21; ascent to SOVN premiership, 14, 21; assassination/overthrow of, 145, 160–62, 176, 189, 269n119; Catholics and, 20; creation of RVN, 31–32; consolidation/expansion of power, 6, 28, 31, 32, 37, 44, 46, 51–52, 72, 109–110, 161–62; domestic challenges to authority, 21, 28; and France, 20–21; refusal to honor 1954 Geneva accords, 12, 14, 30, 31, 37; repression of dissidents/communists by, 12, 30–31, 33, 42, 62–63, 69–70, 103, 116–17; regime of, 11, 20, 74. See also Republic of Vietnam; Rural Community Development ("Agroville") Program; State of Vietnam; Strategic hamlet program

Ngo Dinh Nhu, 109, 156, 157, 267n80; assassination of, 145, 160
Nguyen, Lien-Hang, 5, 41, 47, 85, 168, 171, 199
Nguyen Ai Quoc School (Hanoi), 147, 262n8
Nguyen Chi Thanh, 21, 57, 87, 97, 146, 173, 209; as head of COSVN, 199, 204; opposition to 1954 Geneva accords, 15–16, 194; promotion to full general, 87; and VWP strategic debate of 1963, 147–48, 169. *See also* Central Office (Directorate) for Southern Vietnam; People's Army of Vietnam; Vietnamese Workers' Party
Nguyen Duy Trinh, 40, 48–49, 87, 146, 266n62
Nguyen Dynasty, 12
Nguyen Khanh, 194. *See also* Republic of Vietnam
Nguyen Thi Dinh, 56
Nguyen Van Hien, 104, 143. *See also* National Front for the Liberation of South Vietnam
Nguyen Van Hinh, 21, 219n51
Nguyen Van Linh, 95, 199. *See also* Central Office (Directorate) for Southern Vietnam
Nguyen Vu Tung, 64, 97, 125, 126, 127, 141, 194
Nhan dan (newspaper, DRVN), 24, 28, 67, 77, 146, 149, 151, 160
Nhan van (periodical, DRVN), 40
Niger, 103
Nixon, Richard, 44, 49; as U.S. president, 211. *See also* United States
Nonaligned movement/states, 4, 27, 34, 45, 119, 133. *See also* India; Nehru, Jawaharlal
North Atlantic Treaty Organization (NATO), 25
"North-first" policy (DRVN), 6, 14, 35, 38, 48, 51, 73, 85, 92, 112. *See also* Democratic Republic of Vietnam
North Korea. *See* Democratic People's Republic of Korea
North Vietnam. *See* Democratic Republic of Vietnam

October (Russian) Revolution (1917), 50, 165
Olsen, Mari, 122
Organization Committee (VWP), 15, 39, 84, 146, 169, 170. *See also* Le Duc Tho; Le Van Luong; Vietnamese Workers' Party

Paris peace agreement (1973), 209, 211
Paris peace talks (1968–73), 210–11
Paris Summit (1960), 75, 76, 237n22
Park Chung-hee, 101. *See also* Republic of Korea
Partial Nuclear Test Ban Treaty (1963), 145, 159, 202. *See also* Détente

Party Committee of South Vietnam (PCSVN), 96. *See also* People's Revolutionary Party; Vietnamese Workers' Party
Pathet Lao, 119, 120, 121, 122, 123, 134–35, 142. *See also* Geneva accords on Laos; Geneva Conference on Laos; Laos; Souphanouvong
Peaceful coexistence. *See* Democratic Republic of Vietnam; Détente; Ho Chi Minh; Khrushchev, Nikita; Soviet Union
Pelley, Patricia, 2
People's Army of Vietnam (PAVN), 15, 19, 63, 64, 65, 85, 87, 132, 151, 168, 170, 173, 180, 190, 211, 218n29; advisers in United Arab Republic, 105; amalgamation of southern regroupees into, 19; convoys attacked in DRVN, 99; demobilization of personnel, 33, 74, 83, 207; deployment of units to South Vietnam, 7, 95, 151, 166, 174–75, 176, 179, 196, 198, 199–201, 284n181; five-year-plan of modernization, 3, 33, 62, 113; ideological training in, 100; in Laos, 120, 142, 266n73; mutiny in, 99; and PLAF, 87–88, 95, 159, 204; repression of dissidence in DRVN by, 38, 98–100; state of, 33, 225n138, 275n34; tensions within, 19, 99; and Tonkin Gulf incident, 197. *See also* Central Military Commission; General Staff; Viet Minh; "Volunteer troops"
People's Daily (newspaper, PRC), 157
"People's diplomacy" (DRVN), 89. *See also* Democratic Republic of Vietnam
People's Liberation Armed Forces (PLAF), 87–88, 95, 108, 109, 124, 144, 151, 168, 177, 180, 195, 198, 199, 201, 211, 250n138, 264n43; attack on U.S. airfield at Bien Hoa (1964), 204; attack on U.S. base at Pleiku (1965), 201, 206, 286n1; and battle of Ap Bac, 151–52; in major combat operations, 174, 175, 204–5; and PAVN, 159, 166, 204; setbacks suffered by, 129. *See also* Liberation Army of South Vietnam; National Front for the Liberation of South Vietnam
People's Republic of China, 11, 19, 39, 104, 107; assistance to DRVN, 12, 33–34, 152, 154, 181–82, 183, 184, 201–2, 276n45; commitment to violent revolution/national liberation, 3, 79, 152, 153–54, 181, 190, 207–8, 250n142, 287n15; denunciations of Khrushchev/peaceful coexistence, 44, 79, 157–58, 239n46; deployment of troops to Vietnam, 181, 190; ideological radicalization in, 145, 152–53; and Indochina War, 12; normalization of relations with France, 174; proposal for conference on

People's Republic of China (*continued*)
South Vietnam, 127; recognition of DRVN, 12; relations with DRVN, 79, 107–8, 152, 207–8; relations with India, 34, 49, 102–3, 133; relations with Laos, 121, 122; relations with Soviet Union, 12, 44, 72, 79, 91, 107–8, 118, 131, 174; successful testing of atomic bomb, 174, 201–2; support for 1954 Geneva accords/opposition to violent revolution in Vietnam, 15, 33, 79, 107–8, 115, 130, 131; support for Viet Minh, 12; and UN, 79. *See also* China; Chinese Communist Party; Mao Zedong; Sino-Indian War; Sino-Soviet dispute; Zhou Enlai

People's Revolutionary Party (PRP), 96–97. *See also* Party Committee of South Vietnam; Vietnamese Workers' Party

"People's war," 60, 61, 170, 288n17

Pham Hung, 16, 40, 87, 146, 173, 194, 209

Pham Van Dong, 27, 29, 30, 32, 78, 86, 87, 98, 104, 105, 131, 132, 134, 143, 149–50, 154, 183, 201, 203, 208, 247n77; letter to Ngo Dinh Diem of 1958, 48; note on China's territorial sea of 1958, 58, 232n67; secret talks with Blair Seaborn (1964), 191–92; support for 1954 Geneva accords, 15. *See also* Democratic Republic of Vietnam

Phan Van Dang, 51

Phat Diem, 20

Phnom Penh, 42

Phong Saly Province, 123

Phoui Sananikone, 119

Phoumi Novasan, 119

Phu Loi massacre, 57

Pike, Douglas, 63, 157

Plain of Jars, 119

Podgorny, Nikolai, 202

Poland, 104, 121; as ICSC member, 102, 150, 155. *See also* International Commission for Supervision and Control in Vietnam

Porter, Gareth, 112, 156, 177

Portugal, 103

Post, Ken, 126

Poulo Condore Island. *See* Con Dao Island

Pravda (newspaper, Soviet Union), 185

Project Beefup (U.S.), 128. *See also* United States

Qiang Zhai, 79, 115

Quang Binh, 197

Quang Ngai Province, 68

Quang Tri Province, 16

Quemoy Islands. *See* Jinmen Islands

Quynh Luu uprising (1956), 38

Rach Gia Province, 73

Republican Youth Movement (RVN), 109, 116

Republic of China (Nationalist China), 129, 152. *See also* Jiang Jieshi

Republic of Guinea (Guinea), 103

Republic of Korea (South Korea), 76, 116. *See also* Park Chung-hee; Rhee, Syngman

Republic of Vietnam (RVN, South Vietnam), 37, 72, 103, 205; abdication of regime (1975), 211; Buddhist crisis of 1963, 145, 176; coups in, 145, 176, 194, 269n122; creation of, 32; negotiations with NLF/DRVN, 194–95; objection to draft Paris agreement (1972), 210; relations with Republic of China, 129. *See also* Duong Van Minh; Ngo Dinh Diem; Nguyen Khanh

Resolution 9 (VWP, 1963), 3, 164–69, 170, 173, 174, 175, 176, 180, 181, 183, 187, 190, 196, 200, 284n181; "On the World Situation and the International Tasks of Our Party" (public communiqué), 164–65; "Strive to Struggle, Rush Forward to Win New Victories in the South" ("secret" section), 164–68. *See also* Vietnamese Workers' Party

Resolution 15 (VWP, 1959), 6, 45, 53–71, 72, 76, 78, 88, 89, 166, 168; guidelines, 59–61, 74; Politburo reservations about, 59–64; as product of southern pressures, 55–56; response of southern revolutionaries to, 67–69. *See also* Vietnamese Workers' Party

Revisionism (in Marxism-Leninism), 147–48, 184–85. *See also* Khrushchev, Nikita; Soviet Union; Vietnamese Workers' Party

Revolutionary Youth League, 16

Rhee, Syngman, 76. *See also* Republic of Korea

Romanian Communist Party, 79

Ross, Douglas, 103, 132

Rostow, Walt, 114

Royal Lao Army, 119

Rural Community Development ("Agroville") Program (RVN), 74, 109. *See also* Ngo Dinh Diem; Republic of Vietnam

Russian Revolution (1917). *See* October Revolution

Saigon, 18, 57, 69, 73, 139, 156, 174, 204

Sam Neua Province. *See* Houa Phanh Province

Sapa, 99

Seaborn, Blair: secret talks with Pham Van Dong (1964), 191–92. *See also* International Commission for Supervision and Control in Vietnam; Canada

Sihanouk, Norodom (Prince), 119, 128, 189, 193; proposal for conference on Lao, 119–20, 122; proposal for conference on South Vietnam, 127. *See also* Cambodia
Sino-Indian War (1962), 102–3, 118. *See also* People's Republic of China
Sino-Soviet dispute, 1, 3, 4, 72, 79–82, 86, 118, 181, 185; origins of, 44, 47, 49, 122. *See also* Communist Party of the Soviet Union; Democratic Republic of Vietnam; Ho Chi Minh; Khrushchev, Nikita; Mao Zedong; People's Republic of China; Soviet Union; Vietnamese Workers' Party
Soc Trang Province, 62
Son La, 99
Song Hao, 106
Souphanouvong (Prince), 119, 252n2. *See also* Pathet Lao
Southeast Asia, 27, 115, 124, 139, 140, 143; communism in, 11
Southeast Asia Treaty Organization (SEATO), 11, 25, 115; Council of, 176. *See also* Manila Pact
Southern Committee of the Patriotic Front, 29
South Korea. *See* Republic of Korea
South Vietnam, 135, 139, 140, 200, 204. *See also* Republic of Vietnam; State of Vietnam
Souvanna Phouma (Prince), 119, 120, 121, 123, 127, 155, 189; rump state under, 120–21. *See also* Laos
Soviet Union, 94, 104, 170; as cochair of 1954 Geneva Conference, 34; fear of war with U.S., 34–35, 78–79, 149; and peaceful coexistence, 3, 34–36, 42, 49, 63, 72, 79, 130, 145; recognition of DRVN, 12; relations with/assistance to DRVN, 78, 106, 108, 116, 122, 131, 149, 154, 159, 180, 186, 202–3, 208, 277n56, 278n87; relations with India, 118; relations with Laos, 121, 122; relations with PRC, 12, 44, 72, 79–80; relations with U.S., 12, 37, 91, 118; support for 1954 Geneva accords/diplomatic solution in Vietnam, 15, 33, 78, 127, 204, 208, 276n42, 288n21. *See also* Brezhnev, Leonid; Communist Party of the Soviet Union; Democratic Republic of Vietnam; Détente; Khrushchev, Nikita; Sino-Soviet dispute; Stalin, Joseph
Special Forces (U.S.), 206
"Special war," 178–79
Spring Offensive (1972), 210, 211
Sputnik, 49
Stalin, Joseph, 11, 15, 34, 35, 36, 153, 173, 195. *See also* Soviet Union

State of Vietnam (SOVN), 14, 25; abolition of, 32; creation of, 13, 215n2. *See also* Bao Dai; Ngo Dinh Diem
State Planning Commission (DRVN), 48, 146
Strategic hamlet program, 109–10, 129, 166–67. *See also* Ngo Dinh Diem; Republic of Vietnam
Suri, Jeremy, 4
Syria, 104. *See also* United Arab Republic

Taiwan Strait: crisis of 1954–55, 11; crisis of 1958, 49, 58
Tanham, George K., 162
Taylor, Maxwell, 114, 204
Taylor-Rostow mission (1961), 114
Tay Ninh Province, 73
Test Ban Treaty (1963). *See* Partial Nuclear Test Ban Treaty
Tet Offensive (1968), 210, 211, 272n163, 273n184
Thailand, 123, 155, 189
Thai-Meo Autonomous Zone (DRVN), 46, 99
Tham hoa (periodical, DRVN), 40
Thanh Hoa, 19
Thayer, Carl, 5, 60
Third World, 4, 45, 76, 79, 81, 100–101, 104–5, 118, 277n62
Three-year plan (DRVN, 1958–60), 48–49, 57, 66, 71. *See also* Democratic Republic of Vietnam; "North-first" policy
Thu Dau, 56
Tinh Gia District, 20
Tito, 82, 183, 184. *See also* Yugoslavia
Titov, Herman, 131–32
To Huu, 40, 146
Ton Duc Thang, 25, 74, 146
Tonkin Gulf, 189, 196
Tonkin Gulf incident, 7, 175, 191, 196–97, 198, 200, 201, 283n154
Tonkin Gulf Resolution (U.S.), 175, 196, 200
Tønnesson, Stein, 16
Tra Bong, 68, 69
Tran Duc Thao, 40
Tran Luong, 51, 95
Tran Minh Truong, 89
Tran Quoc Hoan, 85, 87, 146, 170
Tran Van Tra, 95
Tra Vinh Province, 73
Truong Chinh, 24, 58, 66, 87, 105, 146, 170; demotion as VWP general secretary (1956), 39, 227n180; and land reform in DRVN, 15; support for 1954 Geneva accords, 15, 23

Truth Publisher (Nha xuat ban Su that), 146, 272n160
Tunisia, 103
Turkey, 91, 113
Turley, William, 5, 65, 69, 93, 194

U-2 incident (1960), 72, 76. See also Détente
Ung Van Khiem, 101, 103–4, 106, 113, 124–25, 126, 131, 133, 146, 149, 153, 170, 265n62
Union of Chinese Residents (Hanoi), 77
United Arab Republic, 103–4, 105. See also Egypt; Syria
United Kingdom (Great Britain), 46, 75; as co-chair of 1954 Geneva Conference, 34, 127
United Nations (UN), 45, 78, 79, 137; Charter of, 113, 117
United States, 75, 94, 167; assistance to France, 13; assistance to SOVN/RVN, 11–12, 20, 25, 28, 44, 46, 52, 72, 74, 91, 109, 114, 116, 118, 128–29, 145, 174; bombing of DRVN, 196, 198, 206, 210–11; and Cambodia, 119; closure of consulate in Hanoi, 26; deployment of ground forces to Vietnam, 3, 175, 206, 208, 210; fear of communism in Southeast Asia, 13; and Laos, 119, 142, 176, 189; and "loss" of China (1949), 12; negotiations with DRVN, 191–92, 210–11; refusal to endorse 1954 Geneva accords, 13, 35–36, 37, 215n5; relations with Soviet Union, 11, 44, 72, 91, 118; training of SOVN/RVN forces/advisory presence in South Vietnam, 12, 25, 74, 103, 132, 145, 174; withdrawal of combat forces from Vietnam (1973), 211. See also Détente; Eisenhower, Dwight; Johnson, Lyndon; Kennedy, John F.; Nixon, Richard; Project Beefup; Tonkin Gulf Resolution
"Useful adversary," 26

Van Tien Dung, 87, 146
Vienna, 91
Viet Cong. See National Front for the Liberation of South Vietnam
Viet Minh, 12, 13, 17, 42, 54, 76, 88, 215n1, 218n32; refusal of troops to regroup to North Vietnam, 18; regroupment of troops to North Vietnam, 6, 12, 15, 16, 18–19, 21, 22, 65, 172, 218n33. See also Democratic Republic of Vietnam; Geneva accords on Vietnam/Indochina; Indochina War; People's Army of Vietnam
Vietnam, 12, 153, 177, 206; reunification of, 211; war in, 13, 205

Vietnamese-Soviet Friendship Association (DRVN), 170
Vietnamese Workers' Party (VWP), 2, 96; challenges in South Vietnam, 51–53, 96; and creation of provisional revolutionary government in South Vietnam, 137–38; and Diem overthrow, 145, 160–62; effects of Sino-Soviet dispute in, 50–51, 86; Fifteenth Plenum of the Central Committee (1959), 51–53; internationalism of, 104–6; and Marxism-Leninism, 4, 9, 24, 39, 55, 84, 104, 163, 164, 172–73, 177, 184–85, 190, 214n6; militant tendencies/militants in, 3, 7, 16–17, 23, 32, 47, 50–51, 55, 57, 60, 72, 76, 78, 86, 107, 112, 142–43, 145, 146, 147–48, 151–55, 157, 179, 190, 203–4, 209–10, 213n3; moderate tendencies/moderates in, 3, 7, 15, 32, 50–51, 76, 86, 87, 97, 106, 126, 146, 147, 213n3, 213n4; "Munich syndrome" of, 208; and neutralization of Laos, 118, 122–25; and neutralization of South Vietnam, 118, 125–44, 156–57, 193–94, 259n123; Ninth Plenum of the Central Committee (1963), 3, 145, 161–64, 172, 173, 178, 201, 270n139, 271n152, 272n163; and NLF, 137–39, 141; and Paris peace agreement (1973), 211; Politburo resolution on peaceful struggle in South Vietnam of September 1954, 5–6, 12, 17–18, 53, 95; power structure of, 9–10; purge/re-education of members, 7, 39–40, 67, 77, 145, 149, 169–73, 180, 186, 272n163; shifting balance of power within, 7, 164, 169–73, 210; "sinization" of, 77; and socialist modernity, 100, 107, 169; southern opposition/resistance to policies of, 21–23, 41–43, 88–89, 90, 94, 116–17, 138–39; southern pressures on top leadership, 55–56, 145, 250n140; "special political conference" of 1964, 186–88; Statute of 1960, 85; strategic debate of 1963, 7, 145, 157, 173; support for armed struggle in South Vietnam (1956), 6, 43; tensions/dissidence within, 1–2, 15–17, 23, 24, 32, 39–40, 45, 46, 57, 67, 71, 72, 76–78, 82–83, 112–13, 118, 131–32, 143–44, 145, 146–48, 157–60, 163–64, 186–89, 206–7, 213n3, 273n182; Tenth Plenum of the Central Committee (1956), 38–41; Third National Congress (1960), 72, 83–87, 116, 148–49, 164; underestimation of U.S. determination, 211; "unity of thought" within, 16, 112, 167, 169, 186; weakness in North Vietnam, 84–85, 282n150; weakness in South Vietnam, 22–23, 31, 33, 41, 46, 55, 62–63, 69, 70, 74, 76, 92–93, 94; worldview,

26, 178, 209. *See also* Democratic Republic of Vietnam; Ho Chi Minh; Le Duan; Organization Committee; Resolution 9; Resolution 15; Revisionism
Vietnam Fatherland Front (VFF), 31, 33, 105, 224n122
Vietnam War, 1, 3, 6, 18, 168, 175, 177, 205, 209, 275n23; as subject of study, 4
Viet Tri, 98, 99
Vinh, 98
Vinh Thanh, 68
Vo Chi Cong, 21, 51, 95
"Volunteer troops" (PAVN), 64, 65, 66, 120, 125, 142, 266n73. *See also* People's Army of Vietnam
Vo Nguyen Giap, 39, 78, 84, 87, 115, 187; bypassed as VWP first secretary, 86–87; and Dien Bien Phu victory, 14, 87; moderate tendencies of, 40, 41, 50, 53, 61, 106, 126, 146, 148, 149, 151; and modernization of PAVN, 15, 33, 163, 170, 172; sidelining from VWP leadership, 171–72, 173, 273n178; support for 1954 Geneva accords, 14, 15, 37, 172. *See also* People's Army of Vietnam; Vietnamese Workers' Party
Vo Van Kiet, 95
Vu Dinh Huynh, 170

Warsaw Pact, 25
Westad, Odd Arne, 154
West Germany. *See* Federal Republic of Germany
World Peace Council, 34
World War II, 12, 195, 210

Xiaoming Zhang, 152
Xieng Khouang Province, 122, 123
Xuan Thuy, 153, 193, 204, 265n62
Xuyen Moc District, 18

Ye Jiangying, 114–16, 251n156
Yugoslavia, 82, 118, 184. *See also* Tito

Zhou Enlai, 79, 81, 190, 249n109. *See also* People's Republic of China
Zinoman, Peter, 40

www.ingramcontent.com/pod-product-compliance
Lightning Source LLC
Chambersburg PA
CBHW021335230426
43666CB00006B/303